For the Soul of
Mankind

For the Soul of Mankind

THE UNITED STATES,
THE SOVIET UNION, AND
THE COLD WAR

Melvyn P. Leffler

HILL AND WANG
A division of Farrar, Straus and Giroux
New York

Hill and Wang
A division of Farrar, Straus and Giroux
18 West 18th Street, New York 10011

Printed in the United States of America
Published in 2007 by Hill and Wang

The Library of Congress has cataloged the hardcover edition as follows:
Leffler, Melvyn P., 1945–
    For the soul of mankind : the United States, the Soviet Union, and the
Cold War / Melvyn P. Leffler.— 1st ed.
        p. cm.
    Includes bibliographical references and index.
    ISBN-13: 978-0-8090-9717-3 (hardcover : alk. paper)
    ISBN-10: 0-8090-9717-6 (hardcover : alk. paper)
    1. United States—Foreign relations—Soviet Union.   2. Soviet Union—
Foreign relations—United States.   3. Cold War.   4. World politics—
1945–1989.   I. Title.

E183.8.S65L44 2007
327.7304709'045—dc22

                                                                    2006102333

Paperback ISBN-13: 978-0-374-53142-3
Paperback ISBN-10: 0-374-53142-0

Designed by Maggie Goodman

www.fsgbooks.com

13 15 17 19 20 18 16 14 12

For P.J.K.L.

CONTENTS

ILLUSTRATIONS

MAPS

ACKNOWLEDGMENTS

I have been working on this book since the middle 1990s, and many people and institutions have contributed to it. At the outset, I needed released time from my university obligations to do the research, and a joint fellowship from the National Archives and the University of Maryland allowed me to examine the official U.S. records housed at Archives II. That same year, 1995–96, I received a travel grant from the John F. Kennedy Library that enabled me to investigate key documents there. Soon thereafter, the Norwegian Nobel Institute invited me to Oslo for a month, and there I had time to think about the larger contours of this project and to begin writing essays that helped me to understand the issues I needed to explore in greater depth. Geir Lundestad, the director of the Norwegian Nobel Institute, and his staff were marvelous hosts, and the seminars they organized and the conversation they inspired made my days in Oslo among the most enjoyable and meaningful of my career.

When I became dean of the College and Graduate School of Arts and Sciences at the University of Virginia in 1997, I put this project on a back burner for four years. I resigned from that position in 2001 and applied for a fellowship at the Woodrow Wilson International Center for Scholars. I arrived there during the first week of September 2001 and witnessed the harrowing events of 9/11 on a television screen at the Ronald Reagan Building and International Trade Center, where the Wilson Center is located. Despite the turbulence and distractions of life in Washington in the aftermath of 9/11, I benefited enormously from the resources, support, and collegiality of the staff and scholars at the Wilson Center. I owe special thanks to Sam Wells,

Rob Littwak, and Christian Ostermann for making my fellowship year such a meaningful experience and for providing me with the opportunity to return to serious scholarship after four years as a university administrator. The following year, 2002–2003, I had the privilege to be the Harmsworth Professor at the University of Oxford, where, among other duties, I attended lectures and seminars and learned a great deal from some of the world's most eminent scholars of Russian and Soviet politics and some of the most influential writers of international history and relations. When I returned from Oxford, I knew the time had come to turn the years of research and thinking about this book into a manuscript. Fortunately, I received fellowship support from the United States Institute of Peace and the John W. Kluge Center of the Library of Congress, where I was selected as the Henry Kissinger Fellow. I am greatly indebted to those institutions for allowing me to have the time to write in an uninterrupted way among scholars and practitioners with widely disparate specialties but who were interested in my scholarship, and who forced me to think about the contemporary salience of my topic. Ginny Bouvier at the USIP took a particular interest in my work, and offered wonderful assistance and insightful comments on my chapters. The University of Virginia generously allowed me to take advantage of these many fellowship opportunities. I am grateful to Chuck McCurdy and to Ed Ayers for their support.

Many friends and colleagues made this book possible. Mark Kramer and Norman Naimark read the penultimate draft of this manuscript. Their attention to detail and their knowledge of the history of Soviet foreign policy saved me from committing numerous errors, and their capacity to conceptualize and analyze forced me to think more deeply about matters large and small. I am extremely grateful to them for the time they invested in my manuscript. I also called upon some of my oldest professional friends—Frank Costigliola, Robert McMahon, and David Painter—to review all or part of my manuscript. As they have done many times in the past, they read my chapters with care, pointed out issues I needed to address yet again, and sent me to new articles and books that I needed to consider. At the University of Virginia I am fortunate to have colleagues who were determined to help a former dean return to serious scholarship. Peter Onuf is a special friend with a special talent. He listened to my arguments, reconceptualized my ideas in fresh and innovative ways, and made them seem more interesting than I had ever imagined. Lunches with Peter were always seminars on my topic, with him probing, extrapolating, and summarizing. He made me appreciate what I was trying to do, and he inspired me to take risks. When Peter was not around, Brian Balogh often took his place, nurturing and supporting me, and always affirming that the book would get done. Beyond my home institution, my friend John Arthur never ceased asking me about my ideas and never ceased demanding that I clarify my thinking. Among the most thoughtful people I have ever known, John, a philosopher, taught me how to explore a question from a multitude of perspectives. His wisdom has enhanced my scholarship and sharpened my analytic capabilities. Two scholars who have helped me to expand my intellectual horizons are Odd Arne Westad and Chen Jian. Brilliant historians with unmatched knowledge of Soviet and Chinese source materials, and with an intellectual disposition different from my own, they have taught me a great deal about the role of ideology in the Cold War and the dynamics of great power rivalries in East Asia and the third world. I have also benefited from the insights offered by Vojtech Mastny, who graciously read two of the chapters of this book and offered sage advice. Just as I was finishing the manuscript, Vlad Zubok sent me extremely helpful comments on the Brezhnev and Gorbachev chapters. Over the years, I have learned a great deal about Soviet foreign policy from Vlad, and his wisdom informs many of the pages of this book.

When I conceived this project, I wanted to give the Soviet side of the Cold War the same attention as I gave to the American perspective. Yet I knew I was handicapped by inadequate knowledge of Russian and other languages. I have worked assiduously to compensate for this handicap, assuredly never overcoming it but benefiting enormously from the assistance of others. Since the early 1990s, the Cold War International History Project and the National Security Archive have been gathering documents from the "other side" of the Cold War, translating many of them, and disseminating them to interested scholars. Their "oral history" conferences have brought scholars and practitioners together and have served as incentives for governments to declassify documents that otherwise might have remained secret for decades. While I was a fellow at the Woodrow Wilson International Center in 2001–2002, Christian Ostermann acquainted me with the resources collected over many years by the Cold War International History Project, and Tom Blanton encouraged me to use the treasure trove of documents he and his associates had been collecting at the National Security Archive. This book simply would have been impossible without Christian's and Tom's help. Tom's loyal associates—Malcolm Byrne, Bill Burr, and Svetlana Savranskaya—assisted me at many key moments and directed me to the pertinent Russian, Chinese, Polish, East German, Czech, Hungarian, and American documents they had been gathering. To employ these documents to the fullest, I have relied on many translators. Pierre Du Quesnoy and Alexander Alexandrovich Melnikov began translating Russian documents for me in 2001–2002. During my fellowship year at the U.S. Institute of Peace, Isaiah Gruber and Anton Fedyashin, graduate students at Georgetown University, resumed the translating task with enthusiasm. Not only did they work with Svetlana at the National Security Archive to locate many of the most useful materials, but Isaiah also went to Harvard, where, with the guidance of Mark Kramer, he examined the microfiche collections of Russian archival materials now available there. At my own institution, Tim Naftali generously made available to me his translated set of the Malin notes of the presidium meetings during the Khrushchev years. These materials are no substitute for systematic research in the archives of Russia, China, and other countries, but thanks to the translations of these friends and assistants I have tried to illuminate the thinking in Moscow with almost the same fullness with which I have sought to analyze decision making in Washington.

Many friends have been generous in sharing documents with me, and alerting me to materials I needed to consult. Years ago Kai Bird lent me his photocopies from the W. Averell Harriman Papers. After perusing them, I made it my business to go to the Library of Congress to look at that collection, a collection that had not been accessible when I did my book on the national security policies of the Truman administration. Kai also gave me some key memos from his research on McGeorge and William Bundy, which helped me to place the Vietnam War in the larger context of the Cold War. No one has been more helpful in guiding me to documents than Bill Burr, whose knowledge of U.S. sources for the middle and late stages of the Cold War is unmatched. Nancy Mitchell informed me about the best materials at the Carter Library, and when I overlooked some key documents, she generously shared her copies with me. This book is very much enriched by the generosity of these friends and scholars.

Many students, past and present, have contributed to this book in significant ways. Years ago, when I was writing about the national security policy of the Truman administration, James Lewis, Laura Belmonte, Nick Cullather, and Andy Morris did research for me on the impact of public opinion on U.S. decision making during the early Cold War. Although I have drawn upon their research in previous books, I also have used their research findings to flesh out my thinking in the first chapter of this volume. Erin Mahan and Taylor Fain also tried to help me to take the pulse of public opinion in the United States during select periods of the Eisenhower, Kennedy, and Carter administrations. Their research informs the appropriate chapters of this volume. Gregory Pope, a very talented undergraduate student at Georgetown who wanted to gain research experience, also read through some of the key periodicals, such as *Time*, *Newsweek*, and the *Congressional Quarterly* during the Kennedy, Johnson, and Carter years. His short papers and photocopied packages of documents substantially enhanced my understanding of public opinion. Seth Center, Josh Botts, and Rob Rakove, current graduate students at the University of Virginia, generously shared their knowledge and research materials on the Kennedy, Johnson, Nixon, and Carter years, and Seth provided indispensable help putting together the bibliography and helping to select maps and photographs. Sarah Tuke, a hard-working undergraduate student, wrote a terrific research paper on U.S. decision making during the Vietnam War in the mid-1960s, and she gave me many of the materials she located in her own research, especially those from the Declassified Documents Reference Service. One of the joys of teaching is to see the maturation of students, and to profit from their wisdom. I have been fortunate indeed!

As this book neared completion, I had the benefit of the editorial assistance of Elisabeth Sifton. More than a decade ago, she helped me conceptualize the parameters of this book, and she never allowed me to forget about it during my deanship and afterward. Demanding and helpful, Elisabeth forced me to think about almost every sentence of this manuscript. Her questions impelled me to clarify and amplify. At a very tough time in her own life, she took untold hours to read and suggest improvements in the text. I am very much in her debt.

However much assistance an author receives from colleagues, friends, and graduate students, books like this don't get finished without the love and encouragement of family. Phyllis's critical eye and analytic mind helped sharpen the arguments and tighten the narrative of this book. She and our children, Sarah and Elliot, may have grown tired of the Cold War, but their patience, good humor, and incisive questioning made it possible for me to do much more than complete this book. To them I owe my appreciation of the goodness of life and the possibilities of the human experience.

For the Soul of
Mankind

INTRODUCTION

"The Cold War was a struggle for the very soul of mankind," former president George H. W. Bush wrote a few years ago. "It was a struggle for a way of life."[1]

A decade ago, when I began work on this book, I would not have thought that I would come to view the Cold War in this manner. In 1989 and 1990, when I was finishing a book on the Truman administration's national security policies, I had been stunned by contemporary developments. Free governments arose in Eastern Europe. The Berlin wall came down. Germany was unified. Soviet-American competition in the third world abated. The Cold War ended. I had never imagined that these events would occur in my lifetime. Less than a decade before, the Cold War seemed to be entering a deep freeze. After the Soviet invasion of Afghanistan, in December 1979, relations between the United States and the Soviet Union appeared more ominously hostile than at any time since the Cuban Missile Crisis of 1962. Responsible officials talked and wrote about waging and winning nuclear wars. People in

Moscow and Washington read articles about surprise attacks. Ideological foes inspired by malicious intentions were alleged to be on the prowl, seeking to take advantage of propitious moments to gain a preponderance of power. If officials were not vigilant—the same language was used in Moscow as well as in Washington—the adversary would employ its military power for blackmail. Concessions would lead to worse concessions. Allies would lose faith, clients would feel betrayed, the world balance of power would be upset, and vital security interests would be impaired. Leaders in Moscow and Washington never tired of telling their people that their way of life was at stake. The Cold War, it seemed, would last indefinitely or end in catastrophe.

Consequently, most of us were astonished by the turn of events when, in the half dozen years between 1985 and 1991, power in the international system was reconfigured and an ideological struggle that had engulfed the globe for almost a half century was ended.

How did this happen? Powerful men, Ronald Reagan and Mikhail Gorbachev, had dramatically altered the course of history. But if they were able to do this so decisively, I began to wonder whether other leaders might have done likewise. Why, after all, did the Cold War last as long as it did? Might there have been other moments, other opportunities when the conflict could have been resolved? If men so different ideologically as Reagan and Gorbachev could muster the will and the ability to change the Soviet-American relationship, might their predecessors have done so? Had they ever thought of doing so? If so, why did they fail, and Reagan and Gorbachev succeed?

Tantalizing documents and memoirs from Moscow, Budapest, Berlin, Warsaw, Prague, and Beijing began to appear. As I read many of the new books and articles based on these newly released archival materials, and as I began examining the documents themselves, I was struck with a surprising and repeated fact, often submerged beneath the more dramatic details about espionage, subversion, nuclear blackmail, and proxy wars: leaders in Moscow *and* Washington often realized that their competition was counterproductive. They often understood the liabilities of the Cold War dynamic. They knew that the global rivalry diverted resources from domestic priorities, and that the arms race made little sense. They realized that the Cold War involved them in civil wars and regional conflicts in Asia and Africa that bore little relation to the vital interests of their own nations. They recognized that local crises in faraway places might engage them in escalatory measures that could get out of control and lead to a nuclear exchange.

On the one hand, these new documents suggested that the Cold War leaders were wiser or at least more knowledgeable than I had imagined. They understood the risks they were taking and calculated the tradeoffs they were making. Although this was interesting, it was also troubling. Why did they continue a rivalry that courted disaster for all humankind? Why did they continue a rivalry that diverted resources from priorities their own people clearly favored? Why were they not content to demonstrate the superiority of their way of life without arms races and proxy wars? If they grasped, even occasionally, that they had much to gain from avoiding a cold war, or modulating it, or disengaging from it, why did they not do so? And why did things change in the mid-1980s?

Many explanations have been given for the behavior of the two superpowers during the Cold War. These explanations often focus on great men, some of whom were outrageously evil, such as Joseph Stalin, some of whom spoke nobly about freedom and diversity, such as John F. Kennedy, and all of whom are fascinating to us—for the power they wielded and for their potential to do good or bad in the world.

Other explanations focus on the configuration of power in the international system. All governments respond to dynamics in the international environment that are beyond their control, the argument goes. They seek to fill power vacuums or, alternatively, strive to survive in a dangerous world where threats abound and where the naïve are punished if they are lucky and perish if they are not.

But governments do not simply respond to changes in the international environment. Governments are run by men and women with ideas and historical memories. Their beliefs and memories influence their understanding of what is going on in the world, shape their perception of threat and opportunity, and inspire dreams and visions about what might be accomplished at home and abroad.

Yet these men and women cannot always do what they aspire to do, because they are buffeted by domestic interest groups, public opinion, and powerful bureaucracies. Democratic statesmen are sensitive to domestic constituencies and to legislative-executive relationships, and they are sometimes beholden to economic interest groups whose views they may not share. Leaders in authoritarian, even totalitarian, countries must also contend with bureaucracies that have divergent aims and concerns. No leader, anywhere, acts in a domestic vacuum in which policy can be made with indifference to internal constituents, bureaucracies, and interest groups.

Leaders also have their constituents abroad, formal allies and sometimes informal clients, governments with their own interests that they pursue vigorously, sometimes with cunning and guile and sometimes with a dazzling candor and boldness. These clients and allies are never as weak as they may seem, and great powers aiming for hegemony cannot disregard them.

In seeking to understand why the Cold War lasted as long as it did, I have pondered the role of human agency. I have looked at the so-called realist theories that focus on power and survival and that dwell on the distribution of power in the international system. I have examined the influence of ideas, ideologies, and historical memories and pondered how officials construct their own realities. I have weighed the impact of domestic opinion, interest groups, and bureaucracies, including the military-industrial complexes. I have tried to analyze the role of allies and clients. My desire was to follow the trail of the evidence, keeping in mind the many persuasive interpretations of great-power behavior during the Cold War. Yes, of course, this is a naïve statement. Its intent is to suggest that I was not consciously wed to a particular theory, and that I had an open mind about the interpretative power of different lines of inquiry. I wanted to think about all of them and weigh them against the evidence.

The documentation intrigued me. The records newly opened in Moscow and other communist countries after 1989, which most scholars never imagined seeing during the Cold War, are fascinating. Of course, they are incomplete, but they are suggestive. Access to Russian materials has waxed and waned over the last fifteen years. I have relied heavily on documents translated by the Cold War International History Project, the National Security Archive, and the Miller Center of the University of Virginia. For American records, I have spent lots of time at the presidential libraries and the National Archives. Normally, U.S. national security documents less than twenty-five years old would not be available in any significant numbers, but many of the most important ones can now be seen in the collections of the Cold War International History Project and the National Security Archive. These organizations and their institutional affiliates in the United States and around the globe have held "oral history" conferences with leading Cold War decision makers. For these meetings, they secured the declassification of treasure troves of documents, which I have employed systematically. In the latter parts of this book, I use these records to examine the erosion of détente in the 1970s and the end of the Cold War in the 1980s. There are fascinating transcripts of the meetings of Leonid Brezhnev with presidents Gerald Ford and Jimmy Carter and even more illuminating transcripts of the discussions between Gorbachev and Reagan. If I can convey a sense of the richness of these materials, I will have accomplished a good deal.

This book is not, however, a narrative history of the Cold War. Rather, it is an examination of five "moments" during it, that is, short intervals of time when officials in Moscow and Washington thought about avoiding or modulating the extreme tension and hostility between the United States and the Soviet Union. By exploring their motives and analyzing why they made the choices they did, I hope to illuminate the underlying dynamics of the Cold War overall.

The "moments" I have chosen for illustrative purposes are fascinating episodes in the Cold War. All through its history, U.S. and Soviet leaders struggled with crosscutting pressures. Postwar ferment in Europe, decolonization and revolutionary nationalism in Asia and Africa, and the revival of German (and Japanese) power were systemic conditions that captured the attention and circumscribed the choices of policy makers in Moscow and Washington. But the options they thought they had available were also strongly influenced by their ideological mind-sets and historical memories. Ideas, ideologies, beliefs, and experience shaped their perceptions of threat and opportunity arising from circumstances often beyond the control of even the most powerful men on earth.

My focus is on leaders, since I am interested in human agency as well as contingency in history. I look at Stalin and Truman; Malenkov and Eisenhower; Khrushchev, Kennedy, and Johnson; Brezhnev and Carter; and Gorbachev, Reagan, and Bush—at times when they believed they had choices to make. What did they want to do? What were their goals? Their motives? To what extent were they trapped by circumstance, pressured by allies or clients, buffeted by domestic constituencies, or imprisoned by ideas and historical memories? These men grappled with decisions that were of enormous consequence for their people and for human society worldwide. I want to convey a sense of the pressures they faced, the options they pondered, and the choices they made. Their often agonizing decisions were far less predetermined than one might think.

These decision makers could not control the fundamental dynamics. World War II had wrought destruction beyond human comprehension, unleashed unexpected political and social developments, bequeathed unanticipated configurations of power in the international arena, and catalyzed an unwanted atomic arms race. For three decades thereafter, peoples in Asia and Africa clamored for their independence, yearned for rapid modernization, and embraced revolutionary nationalist discourses that neither their former colonial masters nor Moscow or Washington could easily control. And once postwar reconstruction began, the questions of German and Japanese revival hovered over the capitals of the world. For decision makers in Moscow and Washington, as in all European capitals, no question was more important than the future of Germany. Would Germany stay divided? Would Germany be democratic? Would Germany be peaceful?

The meanings attributed to developments in the international arena were influenced by ideological axioms and historical experience. Marxism-Leninism and democratic capitalism shaped the visions of policymakers. Leaders in Moscow sincerely believed their government possessed the formula for the good life, and so did American leaders. In fact, the new archival materials reveal that public discourse did not depart a great deal from private conversations. Not only did Soviet and U.S. officials believe that their nations embodied a superior way of life, but their beliefs and memories affected their construction of "reality"—their perception of threats and opportunities in a turbulent world. Leaders had trouble liberating themselves from these ideas and memories even when they saw reason to do so.

This book, then, is about men and their ideas and their fears and their hopes. It is about ideology and memory. It is about structure and agency. It argues that officials in Washington and Moscow intermittently grasped the consequences of the Cold War, glimpsed the possibilities of détente, and yearned for peace, but they could not escape their fears or relinquish their dreams. Around the globe peoples were struggling to define their future and disputing the benefits of alternative ways of life, so the Cold War was indeed a struggle for the soul of mankind. Nobody can understand the Cold War without recognizing the disillusionment Europeans felt after decades of war, depression, and genocide; without realizing the fears that the possibility of German recovery inspired; without grasping the aspirations of Asian, African, and Latin American peoples for autonomy, modernization, and material advancement.

With so much turbulence, so much fear, and so much possibility, Soviet and U.S. statesmen were affected as much by their ideas and memory, by the pressures of allies and clients, and by the demands of constituents and the impulses of military and civilian bureaucrats as by rational calculations of national interests. They thought they were struggling for the soul of mankind. Yet in their quest for salvation and vindication, they made decisions that even by their own calculations perpetuated an often self-defeating conflict.

This is a history of lost opportunities, then, and it shows that opportunities are lost when leaders who wield great power are engulfed by circumstance and entrapped by ideology and memory. We can empathize with their fears and hopes and we can condemn their brutality and foolishness. But most of all, we should try to understand their behavior and to appreciate the courage, imagination, and determination of Gorbachev and Reagan (and Bush) to escape from a dynamic that had imprisoned their predecessors. It was not inevitable for the Cold War to end as it did.

THE ORIGINS OF
THE COLD WAR, 1945–48

Stalin and Truman

Stalin the Revolutionary

In 1909, Koba walked behind his wife's coffin, holding his infant son. She "softened my heart," he confided to an old friend. "Now she is dead, and with her passing goes my last drop of feeling for mankind." Placing his hand on his chest, Koba lamented, "Here, in here, everything is empty, unutterably empty."[1]

In his youthful adolescence Iosif Vissarionovich Dzhugashvili, later to take the name Stalin, had loved the name Koba. In Georgian folklore, Koba had been a romantic revolutionary, a Robin Hood character seeking to kill the tsar. Betrayed by one of his accomplices, Koba killed the betrayer. A few years after his wife's funeral, Iosif gradually changed his name from Koba to Stalin, meaning "man of steel." From romantic hero to man of steel; such was the evolution of Stalin's self-image.[2]

In 1909, Stalin was thirty-one years old. He was a relatively unknown, dedicated communist revolutionary, in and out of Russian prisons, in and out of labor camps, continually escaping from the police and from internal exile. He had no close friends, no intimate ties with other people, except perhaps his mother and his wife. As a child growing up in Georgia he had been repeatedly beaten and then abandoned by his father. His mother had nurtured him. With the help of others, she had sent the young Stalin to the Gori Church School and to the Tiflis Theological Seminary. He was a devout, intelligent, and ambitious student. His years of education there, the only formal education he ever had, left a significant imprint. Stalin learned to think in absolutes—in dogma, in ritual, and in struggle.[3] Yet he despised religion. "Endless prayers and enforced religious training," his daughter, Svetlana, later wrote, brought "extreme skepticism of everything heavenly, of everything sublime."[4]

The ideology of Marxism-Leninism became Stalin's religious doctrine; his ritualistic practice, the making of revolution. As a teenager in the seminary, he mastered Russian and began secretly reading radical and Marxist literature. In 1899, when he was twenty-one, he left the seminary, aligned himself with small groups of Georgian Marxists, and started agitating among the tiny working class in Tiflis and Baku. Stalin never had any real job. His job was revolution.[5]

What motivated Stalin's decision to become a revolutionary? Little is known, and even his most authoritative biographers have little to say on this subject. A few years after the Bolshevik revolution and long before he reached the pinnacle of power, he answered the question this way: "It is difficult to describe the process. First one becomes convinced that existing conditions are wrong and unjust. Then one resolves to do the best one can to remedy them."[6]

But, in fact, Stalin wrote and said rather little about injustice. "He had a cold heart," said Sergo Beria, son of one of Stalin's secret police chiefs, a man also with a very cold heart. Stalin's mind, wrote one of his most able Russian biographers, "lacked a single noble feature, a trace of humanitarianism, to say nothing of love of mankind."[7] Svetlana poignantly noted that her father joined the revolutionary movement "not as an idealistic dreamer of a beautiful future, like my mother's family . . . ; not as an enthusiastic writer like Gorky, who described in romantic hyperboles the coming Revolution. . . . He chose the way of a revolutionary because in him burned the cold flame of protest against society, in which he himself was at the bottom of the ladder and was supposed to remain there all his life. He wanted infinitely more, and there was no other road open to him but that of revolution."[8]

As a young revolutionary, Stalin mastered the basic texts of Marx and Lenin. He was an active propagandist and writer. But in these years he never wrote anything substantial, except on the treatment of non-Russian nationality groups within a revolutionary multinational state. In prison camps and in exile, Stalin often preferred the company of criminals and robbers to that of fellow revolutionaries. Although he had a good memory and an incisive mind, he chose to scheme, manipulate, organize, and act.[9]

Among his revolutionary brethren, he developed a reputation for his strong will and self-discipline. When the tsar was overthrown in February 1917, Lenin believed he could rely upon Stalin to get things done. In April, Lenin spoke in favor of Stalin's election to the Central Committee of the Communist Party.[10]

After the Bolsheviks seized power in November, Stalin assumed important military responsibilities. The new government faced multiple enemies from within and without. Great Britain, France, Poland, Japan, and the United States sent troops and provided assistance to numerous anti-Bolshevik factions operating on various fronts. Stalin became a virtual warlord. He requisitioned and distributed food supplies, organized the local branches of the Cheka, the new secret police, and took charge of regional military activities. He was ruthless and relentless, cunning and cruel. Like other communist commissars, he executed enemies, incompetents, and traitors within his own ranks. Hating to take orders from anyone, he wrangled with Leon Trotsky, the overall commander of the Red armies, throughout the civil war. But Stalin deferred to Lenin, whose leadership was unchallenged.[11]

In April 1922, after the Bolsheviks defeated their internal enemies, thwarted the allied intervention, and consolidated power, Stalin was made general secretary of the Communist Party's Central Committee. Biographers agree that Stalin used this key position, however gradually, to gain a monopoly of power. Lenin saw this happening. As he lay dying in 1923, he agonized over the leadership of the party, for he saw that the struggle between Trotsky and Stalin might tear it apart and destroy the revolution. He had no solution. But he warned, "Having become General Secretary, Comrade Stalin has concentrated unlimited power in his hands, and I am not sure that he will use that power with sufficient care." Stalin was, he wrote, "too rude." His job should be given to someone else who might be "more patient, more loyal, more respectful and attentive to the comrades, less capricious and so on."[12]

Stalin was not removed. He maneuvered deftly and capitalized on the rift between Trotsky and other Bolsheviks such as Grigori Zinoviev and Lev Kamenev. Stalin initially did not stake out clear positions on how to manage the economy, deal with the peasantry, or rapidly modernize the economy. In 1924, he wrote the most important theoretical tract of his career, "The Foundations of Leninism," but none of his comrades looked to him for theoretical solutions to basic issues. While leftists and rightists in the party argued fiercely over the role of the market, the organization of agriculture, and the pace of industrialization, Stalin shifted his alignments to defeat the Trotskyites and outwit the leftists. He then adopted the latter's program to vanquish Nikolai Bukharin, who was inclined to work with the kulaks, or wealthy peasants, and who envisioned a more peaceful and evolutionary transition to socialism. By 1930, Stalin was the fiercest proponent of rapid industrialization and collectivization.[13]

What is striking about Stalin and his gradual rise to unquestioned domination in the party and in the Soviet Union is his tactical ambiguity, pragmatic zealotry, and opportunism. "What stands out," writes one of his preeminent biographers, "is his slowness to adapt to crises and changes. His instinct at every key moment was to temporize, think things over, and only then adjust to the new situation."[14] In difficult political situations, a key aide wrote, "he frequently had no idea what to do or how to behave, but was able to disguise his hesitation, often acting after the event rather than providing leadership."[15]

One should not be too surprised by these tactical shifts. Stalin was fond of quoting Lenin: "A Marxist must take cognizance of real life," of concrete realities. Marxist-Leninist theory was a science that "does not and cannot stand still." Its "propositions and conclusions are bound to change in the course of time, are bound to be replaced by new conclusions and propositions corresponding to the new historical conditions."[16] Stalin's thinking was always fluid, shifting, tactical, and expedient. But theory and ideology were important to him, notwithstanding the simplicity and flexibility of his ideas. Marxism was the scientific study of history. Society was governed by certain laws. Communism represented the future. Change was inevitable. Struggle was essential. Power had to be seized and maintained.

There could be no revolutionary movement, he believed, without revolutionary theory. Theory and ideology provided a framework for comprehending the world and for interpreting the unfolding of events, a guide for understanding threats and grasping opportunities, a lens through which to see the changing correlation of forces among classes, a means for understanding the actions and machinations of imperial powers.[17]

Stalin believed that the "fundamental question of every revolution is the question of power."[18] The party had to preserve its power in the Soviet Union. Since the conditions for socialism did not yet exist, the party had to use the state to build socialism, for that alone justified its power.[19] "The construction of Socialism in the Soviet Union," Stalin wrote, "would be a momentous turning point in the history of mankind, a victory for the working class and peasantry of the U.S.S.R., marking a new epoch in the history of the world."[20]

But socialism, as he saw it, was endangered from within and without. Ideology and experience confirmed this view. Bourgeois ideas lingered in the minds of men and women even after the revolution and had to be eradicated. The proletarian state, Stalin said, must use force, unrestricted by law, to suppress the bourgeoisie. But it would take time, an entire historical epoch. In the meantime, the party had to stand at the head of the working class and serve as its general staff. It had to have "unity of will, complete and absolute unity of action."[21]

Unity at home was imperative, because even graver dangers lurked in the international arena. Imperial nations aimed to crush the revolution. Already by the mid-1920s, Stalin came to believe that Bolsheviks could not wait for revolution to succeed abroad. They had to "consolidate the dictatorship of the proletariat in one country, using it as a base for defeat of imperialism in all countries."[22] For Stalin, capitalist encirclement was an ongoing, mortal danger. Soviet Russia was weak. Indeed, the whole "history of Russia [was] one unbroken record of the beatings she suffered for falling behind, for her backwardness. She was beaten by the Mongol Khans. She was beaten by the Turkish beys. She was beaten by the Swedish feudal lords. She was beaten by the Polish and Lithuanian gentry. She was beaten by the British and French capitalists. She was beaten by the Japanese barons. All beat her for her backwardness."[23]

The immediate task was to strengthen Soviet Russia. Rapid industrialization was urgent. "The industrialization of the country would ensure its economic independence, strengthen its power of defense and create the conditions for the victory of Socialism in the U.S.S.R." In the late 1920s, Stalin claimed that his domestic foes, such as Bukharin, would unwittingly destroy the revolution. Their policies would preserve Soviet Russia as an agrarian nation, producing foodstuffs, exporting raw materials, and importing machinery. Such plans were tantamount to the "economic enslavement of the U.S.S.R. by the industrially developed foreign countries, a plan for the perpetuation of the industrial backwardness of the U.S.S.R. for the benefit of the imperialist sharks of the capitalist countries."[24]

Stalin could not tolerate such an approach. The first task of planning, he later explained, was "to ensure the independence of the socialist economy from the capitalist encirclement. This is absolutely the most important task. It is a type of battle with world capitalism."[25] In 1931, he exhorted industrial managers: "The tempo must not be reduced! . . . To slacken the tempo would mean falling behind. And those who fall behind get beaten. But we do not want to be beaten. No, we refuse to be beaten."[26] To be beaten would mean the defeat of the inevitable march of history.

To avoid defeat and achieve rapid industrialization, Stalin had to eradicate his enemies. He had, most of all, to crush the kulaks, who the party claimed were withholding food from the cities and thwarting his industrialization program. After Stalin ordered the collectivization of agriculture in 1928–29, he forced fifteen million people into collective farms; those who protested were arrested, shipped off to labor camps, or killed. Then he demanded even larger grain deliveries to the state. When famine erupted in 1932–34, he cared not a whit. Millions perished from starvation. He demanded silence..Merely to speak of the famine could mean death.[27]

With his second wife, Nadezhda Alliluyeva, Stalin was callous and domineering. Depressed, jealous, and suffering from migraine headaches, she committed suicide in 1932. Stalin, mortified, grieved as few had ever seen him grieve. "I can't go on living like this," he lamented. He threatened to resign, and ruminated about killing himself. But he lived and ruled. In fact, he grew more distant, more suspicious, and more paranoid. Ice, writes the historian Robert Service, "entered his soul."[28]

Between 1932 and 1938 Stalin extinguished every trace of opposition within the Politburo, the Kremlin's ruling body, although very little existed.

His lust for power was absolute. No longer did it suffice to defeat his foes; Stalin now had to have them executed. They might recant; they might admit they were enemies of the revolution, but they had to die. Tortured, they might acknowledge, falsely, that they conspired against Stalin, or the state, or socialism, but they had to die. They might acknowledge that they had schemed with enemies abroad, but they had to die. His old comrades from the revolution—Zinoviev, Kamenev, Bukharin—were shot. His former allies in the Politburo were shot. His military chieftains were shot. Friends and relatives were shot. The executioners were then shot. During 1937 and 1938, Stalin signed 383 lists, directly sending 40,000 human beings to their deaths. He also catalyzed a reign of terror by subordinate cadres everywhere. Overall, almost a million people died in the purges of 1937–38; millions more were sent to camps in Siberia and the Arctic, to the Gulag, where they died from work, starvation, disease, and despair.[29]

Top party officials shared Stalin's fears. They were acutely aware that their policies were failing. Millions of peasants and urban proprietors were angry and confused; millions of others had been killed or died of starvation. "Nobody really understood how the economy was working or should work, not even its new directors."[30] The party elite in Moscow put the blame on regional leaders; regional leaders accused their local enemies; rank-and-file communists wreaked revenge on local leaders they despised. In 1937–38 the result was mass terror and mass murder, some of it carefully orchestrated from above, some of it unleashed from below. But what united the perpetrators was their insecurity, their fear for the safety of the regime, and their concern for their careers, which they had linked to the success of socialism. In their worldview, "the future of humanity depended on socialism. Socialism in turn depended on the survival of the Soviet revolutionary experiment, which depended on keeping the Bolshevik regime united, tightly disciplined, and in control of a society that frequently exhibited hostility to that regime."[31]

Hence, party leaders united around Stalin, the man of steel, who could keep everything in check and preserve the revolution. He, in turn, was certain that his followers needed a tsar, a tsar with a vision of the future that transcended the petty everyday needs of humankind. Even his victims who knew him best did not contest his right to crush the foes of revolution. Facing death, Bukharin wrote a letter to his old comrade, Koba, pleading for his life but also acknowledging, with evident sincerity, that he "knew all too well that *great* plans, *great* ideas, and *great* interests take precedence over every-thing, and I know that it would be petty for me to place the question of my own person *on a par* with the *universal-historical* tasks, resting, first and fore-most, on your shoulders."[32]

On Stalin's mind was betrayal in time of war. Stalin and his allies worried that internal dissidents, disillusioned workers, disaffected peasants, and ag-grieved minorities might align with a foreign invader. The purges and mass deportations focused on national and social groups that might form a "fifth column" in time of war.[33] Many years later, V. M. Molotov, then premier, ad-mitted that many victims of the purges were not, in fact, spies. But they could not be trusted.[34]

In Moscow, the revival of German power under Hitler generated great anxiety. Stalin expected conflict, and Marxist-Leninist ideology predicted war, but whether it would be a war among the Kremlin's capitalist and fascist adversaries (which might ensnare the Soviet Union) or a direct assault on So-viet Russia was not clear. Ideology offered competing strategic visions and uncertain solutions. Stalin's foreign minister in the 1930s, Maxim Litvinov, advocated formation of popular fronts with bourgeois parties and bourgeois governments willing to collaborate with the Kremlin. Stalin himself em-braced this option for a few years, but not with a great deal of conviction. His ardor for it withered as Nazi Germany swallowed Austria in 1938 and the prospective Western allies practiced appeasement at the Munich Conference and relinquished slices of Czechoslovakia. Worried about Japanese aggres-sion as well, and seeing no indication that Britain was serious about military coordination in opposition to Hitler, Stalin switched directions, made Molo-tov his foreign minister, and opted for the infamous Non-Aggression Pact with Germany, signed in August 1939. Stalin "saw two great benefits in the new arrangement: the USSR would avoid immediate involvement in the pan-European war and at the same time it could embark on a search for security through spheres of influence in eastern Europe."[35]

Stalin used the alliance with Nazi Germany to act opportunistically. He invaded eastern Poland, annexed the Baltic states of Estonia, Latvia, and Lithuania, and fought Finland to achieve greater defense in depth. He had long believed that "to destroy the danger of foreign capitalist intervention, the capitalist encirclement would have to be destroyed."[36]

The fate of the peoples living in these countries was sorrowful. Stalinism now replicated itself in eastern Poland and the Baltic. Land was expropriated, property nationalized, local officials and businesspeople shot or imprisoned. Two million Poles were deported to some of the bleakest parts of Siberia. About twenty thousand Polish officers were rounded up on Stalin's personal orders and systematically shot in the tranquil forest around Katyn and in other areas. No potential Polish resistance to Soviet control would be tolerated.[37]

Stalin knew he would have to fight a war with Germany, although he tried to delay it as long as possible. He dramatically accelerated his rearmament efforts and staked out an ambitious claim for a sphere of influence in southeastern Europe, Iran, and Turkey. His new vision of security encompassed the Balkans, the Turkish Straits, and the Persian Gulf. But he was not prepared to launch a preemptive attack or a war of aggression, as some writers have suggested.[38]

Stalin wanted to buy time, capitalizing as much as he could on what he regarded as the intracapitalist conflict in the West, the war long contemplated by Leninist theory. Meanwhile, he sought to appease Hitler, knowing that it was just a matter of time until war erupted. Having decimated his officer corps in the purges, Stalin knew his new commanders required time to train their troops, to plan, and to configure their forces effectively. He worked assiduously to avoid provocations that might justify a German attack. In the spring of 1941, he disregarded warning after warning that an invasion was imminent. When a German soldier deserted on the eve of battle and warned the Soviet Union that the attack would occur the next day, Stalin ordered that he be shot. Until the very end, Stalin calculated that Hitler would not attack until he had defeated his capitalist-imperialist rivals, or with the forces he then had available, or so late in the spring, when only a few months remained for an offensive campaign before winter arrived.[39]

On 22 June 1941, 146 German divisions attacked the Soviet Union across a very broad front. Hitler's aim was to make Stalin's socialist commonwealth a slave state, yet Stalin failed utterly to comprehend this.[40] Ideology distorted his view of his adversaries. Now, however, "revolutionary patriotism," meaning the preservation of the Soviet state, was his main foreign policy goal.[41]

Stalin in World War II

Little more than a year after the German invasion, on 14 August 1942, *Pravda* printed a typical article, "Death to the Baby-Killers," and the next day the article reappeared in many local newspapers throughout the Soviet Union. The history of war, the article began, had never known such cruel acts as those being perpetrated by Hitler's fascist scoundrels and two-legged beasts. Everywhere in the lands they occupied, vile oppressors raped women, tormented old men, tortured POWs, and abused innocent children. Read these lines, comrades, the story went on; read this letter to a Red Army soldier from his sisters in the Smolensk region.

Vera and Zina wrote to their brother, Kolya, that it was hard to describe what they were enduring. Hitler's butchers had seized Valya Ivanova, secretary of the local soviet, wanting her to reveal the names of local partisans. They tied her hands, brought in her children, and cut off their right ears. Then they pitted out the right eye of her son and chopped off five fingers of her daughter's hand. Watching the torture of her children, Valya died of a heart attack. The Nazi cannibals then marched to the neighboring village, seized more children and the elderly, forced them into a shed, and set it ablaze.

The article ended with a long exhortation. We must endure; we must fight on; we must exterminate the German fascists. Kill the Germans; kill the child-devouring beasts. Either we defeat the German hordes, or they annihilate us and our children. Soviet soldiers, not a step backward! Save us, warriors of the Red Army, defenders of the Don and Kuban rivers. Save us! The blood of our children demands revenge; death to the baby-killers![42]

Suffering. Grief. Death. They were everywhere. On the battlefields and in German concentration camps, the Nazis killed nine million Soviet soldiers. Beyond the battlefields, the Nazis murdered, crushed, tormented, and enslaved. For them, as one of their own generals unabashedly stated, it "was an ideological war of extermination."[43]

In the Soviet lands they occupied, the Germans destroyed more than 1,700 towns and 70,000 villages, leaving more than 25 million people homeless. In these occupied areas, they murdered 7 million civilians and allowed 4 million additional people to die of hunger, disease, and indifference. The Germans captured and deported as slave labor another 5 million adults.

Ruins of Murmansk, 1942. The Nazi occupation caused intense hardship.

Overall, wartime deaths on the Soviet side amounted to 9 million soldiers and 26–27 million human beings in toto (these included several million killed on Stalin's orders). But such cold figures hardly begin to describe the personal tragedy that afflicted and beleaguered almost every human being in the Soviet Union. Even with the new documents, diaries, memoirs, and oral accounts, we can still scarcely imagine the sorrow and challenges of those years. "Virtually every individual had been involved in the war effort and was traumatized by the war experience."[44]

But along with the grief came a burning desire for revenge, vicious revenge. "If you haven't killed a German in the course of a day, your day has been wasted," wrote Ilya Ehrenburg, one of the most famous Soviet wartime correspondents and postwar writers. "If you have killed one German, kill another: nothing gives us so much joy as German corpses. Your mother says to you: kill the German! Your children beg of you: kill the German! Your country groans and whispers: kill the German! Don't miss him! Don't let him escape! Kill!"[45]

Mass murder was nothing new to Stalin. But now his socialist experiment was imperiled, his personal power threatened, his country's very existence at risk. He had misjudged his enemy. He was humiliated and infuriated. Hearing reports of the relentless advance of Hitler's armies during the first days of the attack, he muttered, "Lenin founded our state, and we've fucked it up."[46] During those terrible days in late June 1941, Stalin labored to organize the battlefront and sustain the homefront, but the news was devastating.[47] Hundreds of Soviet divisions were annihilated. Nazi troops headed toward Leningrad, Moscow, Kiev, and Odessa. Their method of waging war immediately became clear: prisoners of war, Jews, and civilian members of the Communist Party were slaughtered.

On 27 June, "Stalin abruptly stopped ruling." Sulking, he retreated alone to his dacha at Kuntsevo. When members of the Politburo came to the dacha on 30 June, Stalin appeared thin, haggard, and indecisive. Half expecting they were coming to arrest him, he queried, "Why have you come?" In fact, they had come to urge him to take command of the armed forces and to rally the people. They knew nobody but Stalin had the capacity to salvage the socialist experiment, now on the verge of extinction.[48]

On 3 July, Stalin addressed the nation. Invoking patriotism rather than communism, he told his listeners, whom he called "friends" and "brothers and sisters," that the country had been attacked without provocation. The homeland was endangered. Patriotism demanded sacrifice. The enemy was

Russians viewing German helmets, 1945. In places such as Leningrad, heroism and revenge characterized the Soviet victory.

fierce but could be defeated. It would not be an ordinary war; it would be a total war. The next day *Pravda* called it a "Fatherland war."[49]

But words could not stop the Nazi armies. They pushed forward on three fronts, besieging Leningrad and advancing hundreds of miles toward Moscow. There was chaos at the battlefronts and panic behind them. Stalin ordered the capital evacuated. Women and children fled the city. Looters took over. Stalin told his dead wife's sisters, "Things are very bad! Get yourself evacuated. One can't stay in Moscow." To them, Stalin seemed confused, even crushed.[50] During these first six months of war, 2.6 million Red Army soldiers were killed in action, almost 3.5 million were taken prisoner, and 500,000 were shot.[51]

And the civilian suffering never ceased. In Minsk, the Nazis imposed a regime of "permanent terror." Spontaneous acts of murder were the norm. Around Leningrad, the Nazis stopped the inflow of food and fuel. In that beleaguered city, thousands began to die every day from starvation. In the countryside, the Nazis systematically slaughtered Jews and partisans.[52]

But Stalin did mobilize his iron will. He was, after all, the man of steel. He did not leave Moscow, and he personally assumed overall command of the war effort. For those weaker than he, he had no mercy. He ordered that soldiers not retreat; should they do so, they were to be shot. He ordered that soldiers not surrender; should they do so, they would never be forgiven. If officers allowed themselves to be captured, their wives would be arrested. When Stalin's own son, that infant whom he carried in his arms on the day of his first wife's burial, and whom he immediately abandoned to the care of others, was captured by the Germans, Stalin refused to make a prisoner exchange. His son's wife was arrested and sent to a labor camp for two years.[53]

Stalin purged and shot the officers whom he regarded as responsible for the Soviet tragedy. He arrested and deported millions of ethnic Germans, Tatars, and other minorities whose loyalty he suspected. Though he placed the fate of the Red Army and the defense of Leningrad and Moscow in the hands of the young general Georgi Zhukov—a soldier of genius: tough, courageous, flexible, and demanding—he never fully trusted him and feared Zhukov's growing esteem. But Stalin was shrewd enough to realize that he had found a commander of determination and imagination. In December 1941, Zhukov organized a counteroffensive outside Moscow. He rallied his

men, brought in additional divisions from the Far East, and capitalized on
the frigid conditions and heavy snows that beleaguered the enemy. His soldiers fought fiercely and heroically, knowing the very existence of their country was at stake. And as soon as they advanced a few miles into the towns
occupied by the Germans, they witnessed the legacy of Nazi barbarity:
burned houses, starving children, raped women. Partisans were often found
hanging from trees, their mutilated bodies frozen and dangling in the wind.[54]

Stalin looked to the British to open a second front in western Europe to
divert Nazi forces and lift the pressure on Russian armies. At the same time,
he looked to the United States for vast supplies of munitions, trucks, and
food. In September 1941, Harry Hopkins, President Franklin D. Roosevelt's
personal emissary, visited Moscow and talked with Stalin. In December,
British foreign secretary Anthony Eden did the same. Many of their countrymen did not expect the Soviet Union to survive the Nazi onslaught. Most assumed that the Russians would capitulate as had the Poles and the Dutch, the
Czechs and the French. Stalin was a defiant supplicant. He desperately
needed Western help, but he also recognized that they desperately needed
him to continue fighting.

From the outset, Stalin made clear to the British and Americans that
notwithstanding his desire for material aid and a second front, in any postwar
settlement he intended to incorporate into the Soviet Union the parts of eastern Poland and the Baltic states that he had annexed in 1939 and 1940. With
the Germans marauding his country, seizing its assets, and threatening his
power, his concern with the security of his socialist state mounted. He was
determined to establish secure frontiers through territorial gains, but he also
aspired to an enduring alliance with his wartime allies. In June 1942, Stalin
ordered Foreign Minister Molotov to tell Roosevelt that he shared the American president's views: "It would be impossible to maintain peace in future
without creating a united military force by Britain, the USA and the USSR
capable of preventing aggression."[55]

But plans for a future peace gave way to the exigencies of war. Whether
Soviet peoples would fight was much in doubt. In Poland and the Baltic
states, as well as in Ukraine, the Crimea, and Soviet Russia, hundreds of
thousands, maybe a few million, Soviet citizens deserted or rebelled or col-
luded with the enemy. Still, the vast majority fought stoically, defiantly, heroically. Throughout, they were inspired by their passion to regain their land,

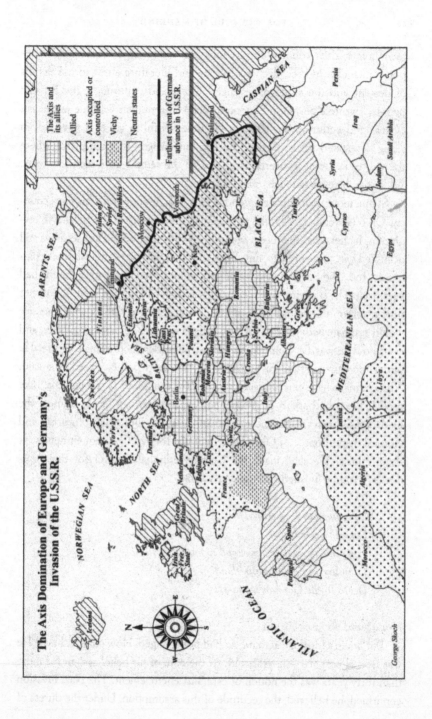

The Axis Domination of Europe and Germany's Invasion of the U.S.S.R.

The Axis and its allies

Allied

Axis occupied or controlled

Vichy

Neutral states

Farthest extent of German advance in U.S.S.R.

George Skoch

their homes, their country, and by their lust for revenge. Contemporary reports, memoirs and recollections, poetry and literature attest to the depths of despair and the allure of revenge. "Great and enduring is the Russian people," wrote Konstantin Simonov, another prominent wartime journalist. "Great and enduring but at the same time fearful in anger. I have driven along devastated roads, through burned-out villages, through places where the cup of suffering is overflowing, and all the same I have seen few tears. When one hates very much, one has few tears."[56]

Stalin, more than anyone, intended to wreak revenge and secure his country. On 6 November 1943, the twenty-sixth anniversary of the Bolshevik revolution, he heralded the recent victories on the battlefield. The Germans still occupied vast parts of his country, but they had failed to vanquish their communist foe. The Soviet state, Stalin said, would emerge stronger than it had ever been. The superiority of the socialist system had proven itself. But rather than dwell on the themes of socialism, Stalin intuitively knew what rhetoric would resonate with his countrymen. He never had been a good speaker, and even now he was far from eloquent. But he understood human nature. He understood the passion for revenge. "In the districts they seized," he said, "the Germans have exterminated hundreds of thousands of our citizens. Like the Medieval barbarians of Attila's hordes, the German fiends trample the fields, burn down villages and towns, and demolish industrial enterprises and cultural institutions. . . . Our people will not forgive the German fiends for these crimes. We shall make the German criminals answer for their misdeeds." And he finished with the peroration:

> Long live our Red Army!
> Long live our Navy!
> Long live our gallant men and women guerillas!
> Long live our great motherland!
> Death to the German invaders![57]

Not a word about socialism.

But Stalin's ideological mind-set had not changed. How could it have? He was now almost sixty-six years old. At the core of his belief system for more than forty years was the notion of capitalist encirclement. The Nazi invasion confirmed, he believed, the rectitude of this assumption. Under the duress of the Great Depression, fascism had become an extreme form of capitalism, and capitalist countries therefore had warred among themselves, just as Leninist theory postulated. But the fascists also sought to extinguish communism and destroy the Soviet Union, which is what had led to an alliance of convenience between the liberal capitalist democracies and the Soviet Union. Stalin did not trust Great Britain or the United States, but mutual dependence, inured hardship, and personal interaction generated his grudging respect and appreciation, especially for Roosevelt.[58] The anti-Hitler coalition, Stalin stated publicly, was "a firm association of peoples, and rests on a solid foundation."[59] The alliance, he repeated in May 1944, was not temporary, but "long-term." This was "his Bolshevik view" of the question.[60]

But would that alliance endure? For the rest of the war and into the immediate postwar years, Stalin wrestled with the dilemma of reconciling his concerns for security with his fears of capitalist encirclement, and the needs of the coalition with his obligations to the revolutionary project to which he had devoted his life. He formed numerous commissions to examine postwar Soviet foreign policy options. His subordinates pondered and wrangled, not knowing how the war would end, whether the United States would withdraw into its prewar isolation, or the extent to which class interests should or would reassert themselves. But, overall, security considerations trumped revolutionary ambitions. Still, ideology was operative: theory and experience suggested that capitalism would founder again, that Germany and Japan would revive, that the Soviet Union would remain endangered, and that intracapitalist wars would recur; hence the Kremlin conducted extensive espionage in the United States and Great Britain, even when the wartime coalition was at its height. But it was hard to sort out primary, secondary, and tertiary threats. Prudence and watchfulness would be essential. All Soviet leaders felt this way, even when they disagreed among themselves, which they most definitely did, on the definition of threat, the conception of strategy, and the role of ideology. But, overall, they were concerned far more with defense than with revolution. And hence they desired to sustain the allied coalition into the postwar years. It was to Soviet advantage to do so.[61]

Stalin often kept himself removed from these discussions among his subordinates, although he clearly authorized the commissions, requested the studies, and pondered their conclusions. After assessing the most recent documents and carefully appraising their different meanings, the Italian scholar

Silvio Pons has written, "the new expansionist tendency of the USSR continued to be conceived in a strategic context dominated by the priority of Soviet security."[62] In short, Stalin's overriding goal, more compelling than ever before, was to safeguard the Soviet homeland. World revolution was a dialectical process to which he swore ideological allegiance, but it had not been his primary goal in practice since the early 1920s. Revolution abroad was important to him insofar as it could help rid the Soviet Union of enemies on its borderlands: enemies like the Poles, whose weakness, vacillation, and hostility had, he believed, opened the path to Hitler's armies; enemies like the Czechs, who had capitulated to Hitler's demands; enemies like the Slovaks, Croats, Hungarians, Romanians, and even Bulgarians who, formally or informally, explicitly or implicitly, aligned themselves with Hitler's ambitions or abetted his agenda. "He is a revolutionary," Stalin long ago had stated, "who is prepared to defend, to protect the USSR without reservations, unconditionally. . . . He is an internationalist who is prepared to defend the USSR unreservedly, without hesitations, without conditions. . . . [M]oving forward the revolutionary movement is impossible without defending the USSR."[63]

Moscow remained the home of the Communist International, though Stalin formally dissolved the Comintern in 1943. From all over Europe and Asia, communists fled to Moscow to survive fascism, Nazism, and militarism. Otherwise, they joined resistance movements in their own countries, often forming the core of their forces and capturing admiration and support for their valiant struggle for freedom from fascism and militarism. Communism now stood for liberation and reform.[64] Stalin stood at the pinnacle of this worldwide movement, which heralded him as the stoic, determined, courageous leader who would not capitulate to the forces of darkness and evil. The war enshrouded him with the nobility and prestige that he could never gain in peacetime as the brutal leader of the dictatorship of the proletariat.

Stalin cared little for the revolutionary leaders he dealt with. Regardless of their ideological zeal, or sometimes because of it, he viewed them with the same suspicion that he viewed his former Soviet comrades and his current wartime partners. He believed, however, that as leader of the world's sole socialist country, the nation engaging most of the Nazi forces, he was needed by foreign comrades more than they were needed by him. So he used his authority to monitor or eliminate those who might defy him, and did so as deftly and brutally as he used his power to extinguish domestic opponents. He sought to use the world communist movement to enhance the security, power, and stature of the Soviet Union.[65]

There are many recollections, memoirs, minutes, and memoranda illuminating Stalin's consultations with communist leaders on strategy during and immediately after the war. Indisputably he was the director of the world communist movement. He was consulted and deferred to. He gave orders and sent agents abroad. But Stalin's exact plans were not clear; indeed he had no master plan, nor anything like it. Many foreign communists were puzzled or exasperated by the ambiguities emanating from Moscow, which sometimes confounded their own desires to be bolder. Stalin encouraged them not so much to seize power and bolshevize their societies as to establish broad popular coalitions with other democratic and socialist parties, a national front strategy. Radical measures, he told the French, the Italians, the Poles, and many others, must be avoided. Such measures would alienate potential supporters and jeopardize communists' "efforts to win over the majority of the people." The national front strategy, he said, required "concessions and compromises." Over the long run, he hoped communists would win power, but this goal was subordinate to preserving the alliance. Radicalism, he instructed the Polish communists, would mistakenly "make Poland a bone of contention" between the British, Russians, and Americans.[66]

The circumstances were propitious for socialist advances, but prudence was essential. "Bourgeois statesmen," Stalin told the head of a Yugoslav delegation in January 1945, "are very touchy and vindictive. You have to control your emotions; if you are guided by your emotions—you lose." When you are weak, he added, you need to be on the defensive; when strong, you should attack.[67]

For the time being, the communists definitely were not strong, but their opportunities were growing. They needed to be calculating, as Stalin thought he was. They needed to adapt strategies to meet existing circumstances. Repeatedly, he told communists in eastern and western Europe that the Russian model for seizing power and bolshevizing a country was not to be followed. Socialism could be achieved in other ways, under other "political systems— for example by a democracy, a parliamentary republic and even by a constitutional monarchy."[68] Extrapolating from a very detailed investigation of the Italian experience, a leading scholar writes, "Stalin's vagueness hardly demonstrates the development of a real strategy for Communist hegemony in Europe."[69]

Stalin did not encourage communist revolution because he was most preoccupied with enhancing the security, self-interest, and well-being of the Soviet Union. To do this, he wanted to preserve the allied coalition, for he believed it was in the interest of the Soviet Union to do so. There was a huge task of reconstruction ahead. The Americans might provide loans. At the very least, their cooperation, and British assent, would be needed to extract huge reparations from Germany—from the Ruhr and the Rhineland and from the eastern parts of the country that his armies would occupy. Most of all, British and American cooperation would be essential to control and monitor the revival of German and Japanese power. In June 1944, when Stalin met with members of the Polish Committee of National Liberation, the Lublin Poles, he told them that Poland "needs alliances with the Western states, with Great Britain, France, and friendly relations with America."[70]

Stalin's overriding concern as the war came to an end was to control against the revival of German power. In conversation after conversation, with communists and noncommunists, with east Europeans and west Europeans, with Americans and British, the specter of German power loomed large. Even "after the defeat of Germany the danger of war/invasion [sic] will continue to exist," he told Bulgarian and Yugoslav communists. "History teaches us," he said to the Lublin Poles, "that one must not wait long for recovery of the German power." "In 1871," Stalin remembered, "Germany attacked France. . . . Forty years later, in 1914, Germany attacked again. After the last World War, Germany restored its strength and began to wage war in 1939. Germany possesses an immense regenerative capability." If halfhearted measures were taken, Stalin believed, "we will have a new war in 15 years."[71]

No matter how total would be the impending German defeat, the Soviet Union could never feel secure. History, experience, and ideology shaped the Soviet view. The Germans, Stalin said, "do not believe in human feelings."[72] In March 1945, he said,

> We are now smashing the Germans, and many people now assume that the Germans will never be able to threaten us again. Well, that simply is not true. I HATE THE GERMANS. . . . It's

impossible to destroy the Germans for good, they will still be around. We are fighting the Germans and we will finish the job. But we must bear in mind that our allies will try to save the Germans and conspire with them. We will be merciless toward the Germans, but our allies will seek to treat them more leniently. This is why we, the Slavs, must be ready in case the Germans can get back on their feet and launch another attack against the Slavs.[73]

These views reflected the sentiments of all Russians living through the war, regardless of how they felt about their own communist regime. When Stalin refused to relinquish eastern Poland and Bessarabia after the war, when he rejected any consideration for the independence of the Baltic states, when he negotiated tenaciously at the Yalta Conference for a Polish government composed mainly of communists, when he sought to install and maintain friendly governments on the Soviet periphery, when he demanded the bulk of German reparation payments for the U.S.S.R., when he raised the question of having postwar bases in the Turkish Straits, when he delayed withdrawing Soviet troops from northern Iran, he was acting like a Russian tsar, seeking every opportunity to enhance the security and power of his country. Few Russians disputed the desirability of these goals, after the hardships and cruelties they had just suffered. "If ever a state had good reason to want to rule over Europe," comments the political scientist John Mearsheimer, "it was the Soviet Union in 1945. It had been invaded twice by Germany over a thirty-year period, and each time Germany made its victim pay an enormous blood price. No responsible Soviet leader would have passed up an opportunity to be Europe's hegemon in the wake of World War II."[74]

Stalin expected the Americans and the British to understand and to accommodate these security needs. In return, he was willing to acknowledge some of the compelling imperatives of his Western partners. He was willing to join the war against Japan and ensure its defeat, thereby helping Roosevelt minimize the loss of American lives while gaining strategic territory, ports, and railroads to serve the interests of the Soviet Union. Stalin was also willing to control the forces of revolution, so far as he could. In the civil war in China between the Nationalists and Communists, for example, he was willing to deal with the Nationalists and withhold recognition from the Communists. He was willing to tell communists in Greece, France, and Italy to desist from efforts to seize power even when conditions were arguably most propitious. Overall, he calibrated the forces of revolution spontaneously arising from the condition of depression, war, and liberation so as to serve the security requirements and national self-interest of Soviet Russia. "Stalin," writes Georgi Arbatov, a leading foreign-policy apparatchik in the Soviet regime, "manipulated internationalism to serve nationalism and imperial ambitions."[75]

Many of these points came up with T. V. Soong, the Chinese Nationalist emissary who met with Stalin just before and just after the Potsdam Conference in July 1945. The intent was to iron out the terms of the secret Yalta protocol about the Far East that Stalin and Roosevelt had negotiated. Soong wanted Stalin not only to repudiate the Chinese Communist Party but also to recognize China's sovereignty over Outer Mongolia and to admit partial Chinese control over the ports of Dairen, Port Arthur, and the major Manchurian railroads. The detailed, cryptic records we now have of these talks once again illuminate Stalin's overriding and persistent concern with security and frontiers. Japan, he warned, "will rise again like Germany." "We want an alliance with China to curb Japan." That nation, he elaborated several days later, "will not be ruined." After Versailles, "all thought Germany would not rise. 15–20 years, she recovered. Same would happen with Japan even if she is put on her knees."[76]

Though in comparison to the quest for security, the lure of revolution was secondary, the two were not always separable. In talks with Churchill in October 1944, Stalin had quickly assented to a percentage agreement that, in effect, gave the Soviet Union overwhelming influence in Bulgaria, Romania, and Hungary in exchange for abandoning the Greek communists to their fate at the hands of their domestic conservative opponents and Great Britain, which actively supported the latter. As his armies marched through eastern Europe, Stalin signed armistice agreements and set up governments that would be friendly to the Soviet Union and that would ensure the safety of Soviet military lines of communication. He argued with Roosevelt and Churchill at Yalta, insisting that the communist governing council he had set up in Lublin, Poland, constitute the majority in a Polish provisional government. Afterward, he acted ruthlessly to arrest, imprison, and kill selected Polish opponents. He unequivocally stated that the Soviet Union had to have a friendly Poland that would not be a corridor for future invaders of the Soviet Union.

In Bulgaria, Romania, and Hungary, which had been Germany's allies, he implemented a national front strategy, setting up broad coalition governments in which communists had important posts but were not yet dominant.[77] Under the terms of the armistice agreements that ended the war in eastern Europe, the Soviet Union had the right to form these provisional governments in behalf of the allied coalition, much as the British and Americans had done in 1943 in Italy. Soviet military commanders worked with local leaders to enhance communist strength and thwart noncommunist opponents. Stalin was willing to pay lip service to notions of free elections and self-determination, as he did at Yalta, but in practice he was determined to establish a sphere of influence that would safeguard the Soviet periphery for all time. "The Soviet dictator did not believe that a bourgeois government could be truly loyal and friendly to a socialist great power."[78]

In the spring of 1945, Stalin's armies launched their last offensive to reach Berlin and vanquish Nazi Germany. The fighting remained fierce. Casualties again were enormous. But the outcome was now inevitable, as British and American forces also attacked from the west. Hitler committed suicide. The Germans surrendered unconditionally. Soviet troops plundered and marauded. They raped, brutalized, and humiliated German women. Now was the time to even scores. Now was the time for Russian soldiers to restore their manhood, to overcome their sense of impotence arising from the Nazis' barbarous treatment of their wives, mothers, fathers, and children. Now was the time for the Germans to pay for their racial arrogance and ruthless exploitation. Within a few weeks, almost a hundred thousand Berlin women sought medical attention for rape. And the lamentations of German women, young and old, were poignant:

> *At home and still not at home,*
> *The Russians come every night*
> *Dear God I beg you*
> *Let me sleep and forget*
> *Forget . . .*
> *Shamed, humiliated, and besmirched*
> *I get up again with new wounds*

Forget . . .
Is a woman there only to be stepped on—enslaved?
Doesn't anyone ask about simple right?
Forget . . .
. . . .
I beg you God let me sleep and forget
And don't measure my life by what happens here.[79]

Stalin was measuring his life by what happened in Berlin. And he would neither forget nor forgive. This was his defining moment. Victor over the Germans. Savior of the revolution. Tsar of the Soviet peoples. Master of the
Kremlin. Arbiter of the fate of countries. Dictator of the proletariat.

At 2:00 a.m., on 9 May 1945, victory over Germany was announced on
Moscow radio. People, thinly dressed, poured out of their houses and along
the streets toward Red Square. "It was an extraordinary day, both in its joy
and in its sadness," recalled Ilya Ehrenburg. An elderly woman walked along
with a photograph, showing everyone her son who had died in battle. "She
wept and smiled." Young people rejoiced. Strangers embraced. The war and
the suffering had bred bonds and kindled hopes. "With everybody else,"
Ehrenburg continued, "I grieved, I despaired, I hated, I loved."[80]

All day long, throngs gathered in the streets. In front of the American embassy they shouted, "Hurrah for Roosevelt." The joy was "indescribable,"
wrote an American diplomat.[81] In the evening, two or three million people
gathered in Red Square to hear Stalin's words. He began not with "brothers
and sisters," as he had on 3 July 1941, but with "Men and Women compatri-
ots." "Its lack of warmth" impressed Ehrenburg, sensitive poet and writer.
But people did not care. Their country had triumphed. Stalin was their hero.
"Every word" he spoke "was convincing." The "salvoes of a thousand guns
sounded like an Amen."[82]

Stalin was at the pinnacle of his career. He reigned supreme in the Kremlin. His authority was unquestioned. So great was his power, so vast the
orchestrated tributes, that he disdained parades and dismissed public
adulation. He dressed modestly, acted modestly. He had aged under the
strain of war. He was sixty-seven now, short and increasingly stocky, with visibly thinning hair and a sallow, pockmarked face. He no longer was the militant, aggressive revolutionary; he had learned over time to listen, to withhold

his thoughts, to speak clearly and succinctly. With foreign leaders, such as Roosevelt and Churchill, he could be smiling, gracious, self-effacing; with subordinates, too, he could be convivial, warm, and generous. "Stalin," writes Sergo Beria, "was able to charm people. . . . He managed to give the people he was with the impression that Jupiter had come down from his Olympus for them. . . . He found subjects of conversation with everyone. . . . [H]e left each person he spoke to anxious to see him again, with a sense that there was now a bond that linked them forever."[83] Stalin spent more and more time at his dacha at Kuntsevo, worked late, slept late, and expected everyone to be available to him at all hours of the night. Often, he invited leading comrades in the Politburo for dinner. They ate lavishly; he did not. The alcohol flowed, but Stalin did not usually drink much. They talked politics, diplomacy, and affairs of state. They then gossiped, sang, watched films, and sometimes even danced. Stalin, the host, wanted joviality. He watched them carefully.[84]

Stalin's subordinates respected him and deferred, completely. He could be intimidating, humiliating, and murderous. The purges of high party comrades had ended during the war, but Stalin remained suspicious of everyone around him. They knew it and lived in dread. He monitored their lives. They dared not meet privately in large groups. They dared not travel together except with his permission. They dared not entertain Westerners. Lest this not suffice, to prevent cabals and preserve his ultimate right to decide affairs of state, he consciously set them against one another by establishing overlapping, competing jurisdictions. He created parallel instruments of governance in the party and government, each of which was monitored by multiple security services, which in return reported on one another.[85]

Stalin often remained inscrutable both to subordinates and to interlocutors. "He dominated his entourage by mystery," writes a recent biographer. "Everyone found it difficult to comprehend Stalin," writes another.[86] He could speak clearly, but what he was thinking was not clear. He could quote Lenin and Marx but in order to extrapolate different meanings, contrasting strategies, and divergent ends. Capitalists would founder, but the United States was strong. Capitalists would war against one another, but the Anglo-Americans were "closely connected." Crush the opposition (whoever they might be) but "make sure that the people are following you." Socialism is inevitable, but it might develop through the "parliamentary way."[87]

We can try to discern clear patterns in all of this, but that would be to misread Stalin. For him, there were certain constants, but never clear strategies. There would always be fear and suspicion, a lust for power and a craving for security. Ideology and experience dictated these constants. Lenin's texts were not necessary to clarify the truism that the world was a dangerous place—all Stalin had to do was look around him and see the legacy of war—but they explained why war had occurred. Capitalist dynamics generated conflict that could engulf and extinguish the socialist experiment. So might Germany and Japan when they recovered. So might domestic opponents. Threats abounded, and they were not phantom threats. As the historian Richard Overy has written:

> Soviet leaders were not living in a world of invented danger;
> they were fighting armed resistance on what was now Soviet
> soil, in areas where popular hostility to Soviet communism was
> widespread. Throughout the states liberated by the Red Army
> pro-Soviet forces were in the minority. The fragile control over
> these territories sharpened the conflict with the West, and pro-
> voked an almost constant state of alert against the threat of war
> and internal subversion. The hardening of Soviet attitudes to
> the West evident from 1946 onwards was a product of Soviet
> vulnerability as much as Soviet strength.[88]

Stalin pondered what to do. He did not want hostility with his erstwhile wartime partners. Sustaining the wartime coalition offered advantages: possible loans for reconstruction; possible reparations for rehabilitation; possible guarantees of security against a revival of German and Japanese power. While he disliked Churchill, he was upset by Roosevelt's death in April 1945. He had never let down his guard in dealing with them, knowing they were capitalist adversaries, but their interests and his had become intertwined and might remain so. On the morrow of victory, there was no anti-Americanism, nor would there be for many months.[89]

As Stalin headed off to the Potsdam Conference in mid-July 1945 to meet the new American president, Harry Truman, the future of international relations was still contingent. Truman thought he needed Stalin to help defeat Japan, and he needed Stalin to make a reality of Roosevelt's dream of a permanent peace based on the alliance forged in war. Stalin still believed he could get the Americans to accept his sphere of influence and abet his reconstruction. All three of the Allied powers thought they had a common interest in controlling the revival of German and Japanese power. Cooperation might be better than cold war.[90]

Truman

Harry S. Truman was born in 1884 in a simple house in rural Missouri. Until 1934, when he was unexpectedly elected to the U.S. Senate, his life was ordinary. While Stalin was agitating to overthrow the tsarist regime and escaping from labor camps in Russia, Truman farmed the land and dabbled in business; while Stalin plotted with Lenin and Trotsky in 1917 to seize power and create a Bolshevik government, Truman decided to support President Wilson's crusade to make the world safe for democracy and enlisted in the National Guard; while Stalin acted as a warlord in southern Russia and rallied support for the new communist regime, Truman ran a regimental canteen in Oklahoma and then commanded a battery of troops in France on the Western front; while Stalin assumed the post of general secretary of the Communist Party of the U.S.S.R., Truman floundered as a small businessman in postwar America; while Stalin outmaneuvered Trotsky and Bukharin and established himself as the most powerful man in the Kremlin, Truman served as an obscure local official in Thomas Pendergast's political machine in Jackson County, Missouri; while Stalin orchestrated the collectivization of agriculture and the destruction of the kulaks, Truman directed a newly created New Deal employment bureau in his home state; while Stalin murdered his former comrades and purged his top military commanders, Truman struggled to gain stature in Washington as the newly elected junior senator from the state of Missouri; while Stalin negotiated the alliance with Hitler and prepared for war, Truman worried about his reelection campaign; while Stalin oversaw the defense of Moscow and Leningrad, met with Churchill and Roosevelt, and organized the defeat of the Nazi war machine, Truman gained national visibility heading a Senate committee investigating the operations of the U.S. defense industry.

Because of the national visibility Truman achieved as a result of his work on this committee, and because he was acceptable to different factions of the

Democratic Party, Roosevelt chose him as his vice presidential running mate in 1944. The two men were strangers. Roosevelt never confided in Truman or trusted him with any significant responsibility. "He never did talk to me confidentially," Truman confessed, "about the war, or about foreign affairs or what he had in mind for the peace after the war."[91] On 12 April 1945, when Roosevelt died, Truman inherited the presidency of the most powerful and richest country in the history of the world. "Pray for me now," Truman whispered to friendly journalists.[92]

The new president was hardworking and ambitious, but he did not crave fame or power. Throughout his life, Truman earned less money than he would have liked, and this was a continuous source of disappointment. But "honor, ethics, and right living," he was fond of saying, were their "own reward." A modest yet proud man, full of folksy, plainspoken aphorisms, he wrote, "If I can't win straight, I'll continue to lose."[93]

During World War I, Truman had found that he was a natural leader. After he returned home from France and yet again floundered in business, he took considerable pride in his public service. As presiding administrative judge of Jackson County, he labored to provide better roads and commodious public buildings. He always wanted to do more than his meager jobs allowed. He sought higher public office, but the prospects were rarely auspicious. In 1932 and 1933 he failed to get the nomination for governor and for Congress. His political career seemed at an end. Despite his lifelong efforts always to maintain a positive disposition, he sounded distraught. "Tomorrow," he wrote in May 1933, "I'll be forty-nine," but "for all the good I have done the forty might as well be left off."[94]

In 1934, after several candidates turned down Boss Pendergast's overtures that they run for the U.S. Senate, Truman jumped at the opportunity. He was a determined campaigner, benefited from weak opponents, and capitalized on the Pendergast machine's ability to turn out the vote in Kansas City, where Truman himself was well known and respected for his record of service, especially as the federal reemployment director. When he got to Washington, he worked hard to earn the respect of his new colleagues and to cast aside his reputation as the "senator from Pendergast." He supported much of the legislation of the New Deal but was not regarded as a liberal reformer. When Pendergast was indicted for fraud and income-tax evasion in 1938, Truman was tarnished by his close association with the machine.

Roosevelt did not want him to run again. Truman thought of resigning, but then campaigned doggedly and eked out another improbable victory.[95]

Truman's foreign policy was fairly simple: he did not believe in isolation and he was against dictators. He favored low tariffs, open trade, and military preparedness. But these were not defining issues for him. In the 1930s he was not a crusader against totalitarianism. He spoke rarely about the menace of Nazism or communism. He once said that he hoped Hitler and Stalin would fight each other to extinction, but that was no more than a quip. Ever since his experience in World War I, he gave little thought to international affairs. He did not "give a whoop (to put it mildly) whether there is a League of Nations or whether Russia has a Red government or a purple one."[96]

Truman was simply pro-American. He loved his country, "God's country," as he was fond of calling it.[97] He admired the Constitution, "the greatest document of government ever put together."[98] He cherished American values: liberty, individual opportunity, and free enterprise. He championed the hardworking farmer and laborer and believed government should be used in thoughtful yet limited ways to help them. He opposed big corporations and military big shots. In early 1941, when internationalists were battling isolationists and seeking more support for the beleaguered French and British, Truman turned his attention to investigating the national defense program. He wanted to make sure that contracts were being fairly distributed, production was efficient, money was not being wasted, the fat cats were not getting all the best contracts, and his own Missouri constituents and manufacturers were being well served. Truman beautifully blended parochial nationalism with incipient internationalism. He became a strong proponent of the United Nations.

Even as he gained considerable notoriety as the chair of the Senate committee investigating the defense industry, his simple lifestyle and modest sense of self never changed. He disdained luxury and hated pretense. He woke early, worked hard, and often ate at the local Hot Shoppe.[99] He never ceased writing loving letters to his wife and daughter, who were often back in Independence, Missouri, while he was in Washington. He missed them, and he waited expectantly for their return letters. Yet he loved being a politician, close to the people, seemingly representing their views and getting the government to serve their needs. Once in the Senate, he did not strive for further high office; he did not seek the vice presidency or yearn to occupy the White

House. He had already accomplished more than he expected. He loved politics and liked the legislative infighting. He enjoyed a card game with friends and a glass (or two) of bourbon in the evening.

While Truman was serving his second term in the Senate and gaining the esteem of his colleagues and the attention of the public, the United States moved from depression to war. The Japanese attack on Pearl Harbor in December 1941 killed several thousand Americans, but the continental United States was unscathed by enemy attack. After Hitler declared war on America a few days later, the nation found itself fighting all three Axis powers—Germany, Japan, and Italy—yet fighting them far from America's shores. The American wartime experience was thus vastly different from that endured by any of the other major combatants. Young children and old men were not slaughtered by enemy occupation; sisters, daughters, and mothers were not raped. Homes were not bombed; villages and cities were not ruined.

Hard times ended. After a decade of depression, writes the historian Michael Adams, the "war inaugurated the greatest era of prosperity in human history." American gross national product increased 60 percent during the war; total earnings 50 percent. There was social unrest, labor agitation, racial conflict, and teenage vandalism, but life in America was unimaginably different from life in war-torn Europe and Asia. "Many Americans for the first time in history had more money than they knew what to do with." The numbers of middle-class Americans grew rapidly, as did home ownership. Despite rationing or perhaps because of it, people had more discretionary income than ever before. They bought washers and dryers, jewelry and cigarettes. Average department store purchases soared fivefold, from two to ten dollars, during the war. "Never in the history of human conflict," commented the economist John Kenneth Galbraith, "has there been so much talk of sacrifice and so little sacrifice." Teens, in particular, relished the opportunity to find jobs, make money, and spend it. They were beginning to shape a postwar consumer culture that would become the envy of the world, but nobody then was quite aware of its significance.[100]

Like most Americans during the war, Truman focused his attention on the spectacular rise in America's defense production, industrial capability, and strategic power. By the end of 1942, the United States was producing more arms than all the Axis states together. During 1943 it made almost three times as many armaments as did Soviet Russia. During the remainder of the conflict, the United States turned out two-thirds of all the Allied military equipment used in the war: 297,000 aircraft, 193,000 artillery pieces, 86,000 tanks, 2 million army trucks. By the end of the war, it had the capability to produce almost 100,000 planes and 30,000 tanks a year. In four years, overall industrial production doubled; the machine-tool industry trebled. In 1945, the United States had two-thirds of the world's gold reserves, three-fourths of its invested capital, half of its shipping vessels, and half of its manufacturing capacity. Its gross national product was three times that of the Soviet Union and more than five times that of Great Britain. It was also nearing completion of the atomic bomb, a technological and production feat of huge costs and proportions.[101]

Truman went to the Potsdam Conference knowing these facts. He was not eager to cross the ocean to meet his wartime allies, Churchill and Stalin. "How I hate this trip," he confided in his diary. "But I have to make it . . . and we must win."[102] The war in Europe was over, and it was critical to begin talking about postwar settlements for Germany and eastern Europe. It was even more critical to talk to Stalin about the war in the Pacific. Truman wanted Stalin to make good on his promise at Yalta to declare war on Japan within three months of Germany's defeat. If Russians attacked Japanese troops on the Chinese mainland, the Japanese emperor would have fewer troops to kill Americans when they invaded the home islands. This was of utmost importance to Truman, as his plans for the Potsdam Conference were made before the atomic bomb was secretly and successfully tested in New Mexico on 16 July.

Yet Truman was not comfortable fighting wars and planning peace. He knew little of these matters. He read report after report, memo after memo, but diplomacy baffled him. He was inexperienced, and he knew it. "I was so scared," he wrote Bess from Potsdam. "I didn't know whether things were going according to Hoyle or not."[103] His closest associates recognized that he was nervous, uneasy, and insecure. Sometimes he answered so quickly, almost before they finished their questions.[104] At such points, Truman thought he was demonstrating strength, but he was revealing weakness, at least to those who cared most about him.

Truman wanted to get along with Stalin. Some advisers, such as W. Averell Harriman, the American ambassador to the Soviet Union; Secretary of the Navy James V. Forrestal; and Admiral William Leahy, the wartime chief of staff, wanted him to take a tough stand against the Soviet Union. They told Truman that the Russians were looting eastern Germany and imposing communist regimes in eastern Europe. But Truman felt no passion about these matters, no deep empathy for peoples he neither knew nor understood. Stalin was a dictator, for sure, but one who, Truman felt, had the support of the Russian people. If not, they would not have fought so tenaciously; so let's get along, he jotted in his diary. Truman knew the Soviets were looting eastern Europe, but they had also been "thoroughly looted by the Germans over and over again and you can hardly blame them for their attitude." Truman knew the Soviets were seeking to set up police governments, but he felt that Stalin would eventually bow to American pressure on this issue. He had seen the Kremlin make concessions on the eve of Potsdam. "Yesterday was a hectic day," he wrote to his wife on 7 June 1945. "Had both good news and bad. Stalin agreed to our interpretation of the veto at San Francisco and a reconsideration of the Polish question, but we lost the election in Montana and the Republicans are jubilant over it."[105]

Equating the travail of the Polish people with the disappointment of Democrats in Montana, as he did, he was perfectly well disposed to deal with Stalin. "I want you to understand," he told his good friend Joseph Davies, the pro-Soviet former U.S. ambassador to the Kremlin, "that I am trying my best to save peace and to follow out Roosevelt's plan."[106] The plan was to sustain cooperation between the United States and the Soviet Union and to avoid a postwar rift. But Truman's gut instincts demanded that agreement be on American terms. He told Harriman, "We could not, of course, expect to get 100 percent of what we wanted but . . . on important matters . . . we should be able to get 85 percent."[107] Truman intended to protect American interests, even if he didn't have a precise definition of them. He had no particular sense of gratitude to the Russians for their war losses, no particular reverence for Churchill or the British for their heroism, no particular empathy for the plight of European peoples engulfed by the Depression and war. After several days of meetings at Potsdam with Stalin and Churchill, he wrote, rather proudly, to his wife:

> We had a tough meeting yesterday. I reared up on my hind legs and told 'em where to get off and they got off. I have to make it perfectly plain to them at least once a day that so far as this

president is concerned Santa Claus is dead and that my first interest is U.S.A., then I want the Jap War won and I want 'em both in it. Then I want peace—world peace and will do what can be done by us to get it. But certainly am not going to set up another [illegible] here in Europe, pay reparations, feed the world, and get nothing for it but a nose thumbing. They are beginning to awake to the fact that I mean business.[108]

Business meant getting along with the Russians and protecting U.S. interests. "I like Stalin," he wrote his wife. "He is straightforward. Knows what he wants and will compromise when he can't get it."[109] Differences over impor-

Allied leaders at the Potsdam Conference, 1945. Churchill, Truman, and Stalin still entertained hopes of postwar cooperation—even as they were intensely suspicious of one another's motives.

tant issues were to be expected. Truman felt no outrage about Stalin's record of repression. Not all the horror of Stalin's rule, of course, was then known, but the purges and killing of high party officials were a matter of public record, as was the ruthless suppression of kulaks and other opponents of the regime. Yet none of this mattered too much to the president. Even many years later, he acknowledged that at the time "I liked him a lot. . . . Stalin was a very gracious host, and at the table, he would grasp what was going on as quickly as anybody I ever came in contact with."[110] Those who believe the Cold War was inevitable because of Western horror at Stalin's cruelty are disregarding the contemporary record; those who believe that Truman immediately started the Cold War because of the advice and pressure of anti-Soviet advisers are mistaken. Stalin, Truman thought, was someone you could deal with. He would respect American power. Agreement was still possible.

Truman believed in American power and American righteousness. So did his newly appointed secretary of state, James F. Byrnes. Byrnes was a longtime Washington power broker, a former conservative senator from South Carolina, Supreme Court justice, and wartime overlord of the American economy. Truman liked Byrnes, who had befriended him as a new senator in the mid-1930s, and thought him shrewd, knowledgeable, and tough. He let Byrnes do most of the contentious bargaining at Potsdam on German reparations, Polish borders, and the composition of the new governments in Eastern Europe. Once Stalin agreed in the first days of the conference to attack Japan, Truman felt satisfied. "I've gotten what I came for," he confided to Bess on July 18. "Stalin goes to war August 15 with no strings on it. . . . I'll say that we'll end the war a year sooner now, and think of the kids who won't be killed. That's the important thing."[111]

To Truman and Byrnes, the atomic bomb meant more than the weapon that could defeat Japan and save American lives. It was a vast new instrument of American power. Truman went to Potsdam not knowing it would work; Admiral Leahy said it wouldn't; Byrnes thought it might "but he wasn't sure."[112] By all accounts, and there are many, news of the successful testing of the bomb enormously buoyed Truman's self-confidence. It "took a great load off my mind," he confided to Joe Davies.[113] The president did not order the atomic bomb dropped on Hiroshima to impress the Russians, as some historians claim; but nevertheless he believed that it would impress them and make them more manageable.

At Potsdam, Truman quietly took Stalin aside and elliptically mentioned that the United States had a powerful new weapon to use against Japan. Nothing more needed to be said. Nor did all the pressing issues have to be resolved at Potsdam. Truman was eager to go home. He grew impatient with the incessant haggling at the conference. Stalin, he thought, was stalling. He "doesn't know it," Truman again wrote his wife, "but I have an ace in the hole and another one showing—so unless he has threes or two pair (and I know he has not) we are sitting all right."[114] The "atomic bomb," Byrnes also was thinking, "had given us great power, and . . . in the last analysis, it would control."[115]

When Truman ordered that atomic bombs be dropped on Hiroshima and then Nagasaki, these were not tough decisions for him. They were necessary, in his mind, to save American lives. They vividly demonstrated American power; they confirmed that enemies of America would pay for their transgressions. The Japanese did pay, and then they capitulated, unconditionally, except for the preservation of the emperor. They had little choice, for Stalin's troops attacked at the same time, seized parts of Manchuria, invaded northern Korea, and set their sights on Hokkaido, Japan's northernmost home island.[116]

The war ended. The American people celebrated. Truman breathed a sigh of relief. He now eagerly delegated the responsibility for peacemaking to Secretary of State Byrnes, who he thought had performed ably at Potsdam. Truman wanted to turn his own attention to demobilization, reconversion, and the domestic issues he knew and understood. Byrnes for his part was eager to take command of the nation's foreign policy. He was sure of himself. The atomic bomb, he told his closest colleagues, was a great weapon that could be used to exact concessions from potential adversaries.[117] But experienced colleagues in the State and War departments had their doubts. They deeply resented Byrnes's attempts to monopolize American diplomacy. Many of them left office in September and October 1945, however, exhausted from years of wartime responsibility, and Byrnes was now in charge.

Byrnes was not as shrewd as he thought he was, nor was the Soviet Union easily threatened. At the first postwar meeting of foreign ministers in London in September, Byrnes thought he could outmaneuver Molotov and arrange for more representative governments in Romania and Bulgaria. But Molotov chafed at Byrnes's procedural moves and sneered at his not very subtle efforts 'to use America's atomic monopoly to leverage concessions. In fact, the Soviet foreign minister was willing to negotiate on some of these points—that is, until Stalin ordered him to stiffen his resolve. Let the conference end in deadlock, Stalin wired Molotov. Let Byrnes stew for a while. Stalin's adulatory comments about Byrnes in front of Truman at Potsdam had, typically, concealed the dictator's emerging contempt for a man who wielded power so flagrantly.[118]

Byrnes returned to Washington chastened. The Russians would not be intimidated, he realized. Perhaps, Byrnes now thought, the bomb could be used as a carrot rather than a stick. Perhaps the Soviets could be lured into a favorable agreement to regulate the future of atomic energy. Some of the Soviets' arguments, he believed, had merit. He had to concede a certain hypocrisy in the American insistence that the Soviets open up eastern Europe while the United States locked the Kremlin out of Japan. He could understand why the Soviets feared the revival of German power and why they wanted friendly governments on their periphery. It might make sense, he thought, to acquiesce to what was happening in Bulgaria and Romania, more or less, if in return the Kremlin promised to withdraw Soviet troops as soon as the peace treaties were negotiated. Moreover, a four-power treaty guaranteeing the demilitarization of Germany might hasten this process. In other words, Stalin's obsession with security might be assuaged by a demilitarization treaty while his domination of eastern Europe might be diluted by his agreement to withdraw Soviet troops from Hungary, Romania, and Bulgaria, as they just had been withdrawn from Czechoslovakia.[119]

To achieve an open sphere in eastern Europe, contain Soviet power, sustain the wartime alliance, and avoid hostile confrontations with Soviet Russia may have made sense, but Byrnes's swift tactical changes coupled with his arrogant behavior alienated cabinet colleagues, powerful senators, and key presidential aides. Truman grew frustrated with Byrnes, as he did with so many of his advisers in that autumn of 1945. The end of the war provided no respite for the inexperienced president. He was worried by labor strife and spiraling inflation. He was agitated by the biting criticism he was experiencing and by the souring of his party's prospects to win the 1946 midterm elections. "The Congress," he noted in his diary, "is balking; labor has gone crazy; management is not far from insane in selfishness." His cabinet had "Potomac fever."[120] Byrnes was conniving, striving for too much publicity,

Molotov and Stalin, 1945. After Potsdam, Stalin ordered
Molotov to take a tough stand in negotiating with
the Americans and British.

acting too independent, arousing too much controversy, trying to be too
clever, and alienating friends and foes alike.

Truman liked things in black and white. His closest advisers knew that he
did not like nuance or ambiguity.[121] In a major speech on Navy Day, 27 October, he set forth his views. The United States, he said, forswore the acquisi-
tion of any new territory. It championed democracy and self-determination.
It favored freedom of the seas, open trade, and global economic cooperation.
It supported the United Nations and Pan-Americanism. There would be no
return to isolationism. Never again, said Truman, would the United States be
caught by surprise. Never again would it relinquish its military superiority. It
would hold the atomic bomb as a "sacred trust" for all mankind. Its air and
naval forces would control the seas and dominate the skies. Aggression

would not be tolerated. America's interests would not be slighted nor would its ideals be compromised. The United States would not "compromise with evil."[122]

Although his writers designed the speech to force "our diplomatic appeasers to pay closer attention to the vital interests of America," there is no reason to think that Truman thought he was breaking new ground with this speech.[123] These ideals and interests were like apple pie and ice cream to Truman. The nation had to be strong and it had to be involved. Its interests and ideals had to be protected. This was, after all, God's country. The war had taught key lessons: no more surprise attacks, no more aggression. The United States had to be able to project its power far from American shores. The country needed bases around the globe. And no nation could be permitted to upset the balance of power in the Old World and gain control of the industrial infrastructure, raw materials, and skilled manpower of Europe and Asia. Germany and Japan had almost achieved this in the late 1930s and early 1940s, and American interests and ideals had been jeopardized. This could not be allowed to happen again.

The president jotted his thoughts on a piece of paper. Byrnes had to stop "babying" the Soviets. The Soviets had to get out of northern Iran, where they had been slow to withdraw their troops. They had to stop putting pressure on Turkey for bases in the Dardanelles. They had to install more democratic governments in Bulgaria and Romania. They had to agree to strong central governments in Korea and China. "Unless Russia is faced with an iron fist and strong language another war is in the making."[124]

Stalin and Truman

By the end of 1945 Stalin and Truman were eyeing each other warily. They were both angry with their foreign ministers for inclining toward compromise. They felt that their respective nations had the power and the right to forge a new international order that would enhance their security and their ideals. They were not inclined to tolerate opposition. But they also grasped that confrontation made little sense. They had more to gain from sustaining the alliance than from rupturing it, though cooperation was logical only if it served national interests. During 1946, they wavered between toughness and conciliation.

Stalin distrusted capitalists, and fear of encirclement by them was a constant in his thinking. Nonetheless, he had worked collaboratively with Roosevelt and Churchill during the war, thinking the conflict would end with Germany's dismemberment and a secure periphery. But then, suddenly, Roosevelt had died and Truman dropped two atomic bombs on Japan. Stalin was shaken by Roosevelt's passing. He was wary of Truman, but not disinclined to cooperate with him.[125] Yet Truman had great power and used it..

Stalin immediately interpreted Hiroshima as atomic blackmail against the U.S.S.R. "Hiroshima has shaken the whole world," he said. "The balance has been destroyed." He thought the Americans and the British were backtracking on the promise they had given at Yalta to allow the Russians to rule their sphere as they liked. "They want to force us to accept their plans on questions affecting Europe and the world. Well, that's not going to happen," Stalin told his closest confidants. Even before Truman told Byrnes to stop babying the Soviets, Stalin told Molotov that in dealing with the Americans and the British, "we cannot achieve anything serious if we begin to give in to intimidation or betray uncertainty. To get anything from this kind of partner, we must arm ourselves with the policy of tenacity and steadfastness."[126]

On 9 February 1946, Stalin gave a famous "election" address at the Bolshoi Theatre in Moscow, transmitted by radio to every part of the Soviet Union. Reviving the ideological language that was his lodestar, he said the war had not been an accident, nor was it the product of the mistakes of statesmen. "The war arose in reality as the inevitable result of the development of the world economic and political forces on the basis of monopoly capitalism." Perhaps peace could be preserved if capitalists redistributed markets and raw materials without conflict, "but this is impossible under the present capitalist development of the world economy."

The Soviet Union had become ensnared in this intracapitalist conflict, but World War II was "radically different" from World War I. The fascist states had extinguished "democratic liberties" in their own countries, established "cruel, terrorist regimes," and sought "world domination." "As far as our country is concerned," Stalin said, "the war was the most cruel and hard of all wars ever experienced in the history of our motherland." But it proved the superiority of the socialist system, the vitality of the multinational state, and the resiliency and heroism of the Red Army. The war also demonstrated the wisdom of collectivization and industrialization. "The party remembered

Territorial Changes After World War II

NORWEGIAN SEA

Finland
to U.S.S.R.

Leased to U.S.S.R. until 1955

Lake Ladoga

Norway

Sweden

N

BALTIC SEA
to U.S.S.R.

Leningrad

Estonia
to U.S.S.R.

Latvia
to U.S.S.R.

Lithuania
to U.S.S.R.

East Prus.

U.S.S.R.

Denmark

NORTH SEA

Netherlands

Germany

Berlin

Danzig
to Poland

to Poland

Warsaw

to U.S.S.R.

Belgium

Bonn

Lux.

Prague

Czechoslovakia

Poland

Norhern Bukovina

France

Switz.

Austria

Bratislava Bridgehead

Hungary

Subcarpathian Ruthenia

Romania

Bessarabia
to U.S.S.R.

Prut R.

to France

Trieste

Venezia-Giulia
to Yugoslavia

Belgrade

Bucharest

Dobruja
to Bulgaria

BLACK SEA

Italy

ADRIATIC SEA

Yugoslavia

Bulgaria

Sofia

Albania

Greece

Turkey

Allied Zones of Control

U.S. Zone

British Zone

Berlin

Soviet Zone

to Poland

Germany

Bonn

French Zone

United States Zone

U.S.

Sov.

Austria

French

Brit.

Malta (Br.)

MEDITERRANEAN SEA

Dodecanese Islands
to Greece from Italy

Egypt

Algeria

Libya

George Skoch

Lenin's word that without heavy industry it would be impossible to safeguard the independence of our country, that without it the Soviet system could perish." Hence the need "to organize a new mighty upsurge of the national economy," seeking the production of fifty million tons of pig iron annually, sixty million tons of steel, five hundred million tons of coal, and sixty million tons of oil. Alluding implicitly to the atomic bomb, Stalin said that science, too, had to be promoted "to surpass the achievements" of other countries. "Only under such conditions will our country be insured against any eventuality."[127]

Stalin's ideological preconceptions and personal paranoia made him suspect enemies everywhere. As the war drew to a close he confided: "The crisis of capitalism has manifested itself in the division of the capitalists into two factions—one fascist, the other democratic. . . . We are currently allied with one faction against the other, but in the future we will be against the first faction of capitalists, too."[128] Suspicious of the capitalists, fearful of Germany and Japan, and proud of Soviet achievements, he would be satisfied with nothing less than a friendly periphery. He wanted "to consolidate Soviet territorial gains, establish a Soviet sphere of influence in eastern Europe, and have a voice in the political fate of Germany and—if possible—of Japan."[129] He wanted security, and hoped to get it without rupturing the grand alliance.

This explains why he was so furious with Churchill's speech in Fulton, Missouri, in March 1946, when the former British prime minister declared that Stalin was building an iron curtain from the Baltic to the Balkans. "The following circumstances should not be forgotten," Stalin stated in a *Pravda* interview. "The Germans made their invasion of the USSR through Finland, Poland, Rumania, Bulgaria, and Hungary. The Germans were able to make their invasion through these countries because at the time, governments hostile to the Soviet Union existed in these countries." As a result millions of people in Russia died, many more than from the United States and the United Kingdom combined. Perhaps Churchill was inclined to forget these colossal sacrifices, but Stalin could not. "What can be surprising," Stalin fumed, "about the fact that the Soviet Union, anxious for its future safety, is trying to see to it that governments loyal in their attitude to the Soviet Union should exist in these countries?"[130]

Stalin thought the Americans and the British were maneuvering to squeeze the Soviet Union out of Germany, undermine its position of power in eastern Europe, and deny it the ten billion dollars in reparations it thought it had been promised at the Yalta Conference.[131] Soviet officials looked cynically upon the four-power German demilitarization treaty that Byrnes repeatedly proposed. Even Maxim Litvinov, the prewar foreign minister who was known for his pro-Western orientation, expressed dismay about U.S. motives. In July 1945, Litvinov had noted that the Ruhr and other industrial parts of western Germany, now in French, American, and British hands, produced 75 percent of Germany's coal and 70 percent of its steel and pig iron. The industry of the Ruhr, he warned, could be completely restored within one year and could support an army of several million soldiers. "If a serious conflict escalates between us and Western states, we will not be able to prevent the Western powers from turning the Ruhr region into a supply base either for Germans, whom they would enlist as Allies, or for their own armed forces." The Americans, Litvinov believed, were seeking to dupe the Russians by creating the impression that Soviet security could be guaranteed through this demilitarization treaty. In his view, which Stalin shared, Byrnes was trying to lay the groundwork for the most dangerous scenario imaginable, a premature termination of the occupation of Germany.[132]

It was not only that Stalin imagined threats; there *were* threats. Famine stalked his country. Unrest pulsated through the lands he annexed. Low-scale insurgencies and guerrilla war challenged his rule in the countries the Red Army occupied. Russian, Polish, and Ukrainian documents make it clear that Stalin and his internal security services "were profoundly concerned" with how Churchill's Fulton speech might buoy the morale of rebels and insurgents. Speculation about a third world war between the Anglo-Saxons and the Russians percolated through the resistance movements against Soviet power and inspired Ukrainian and other nationalists to imagine that in a new world conflict they might be liberated. "Throughout Soviet-occupied Eastern Europe, Churchill's Fulton speech was like a call to arms," or so it seemed inside the Kremlin and among Stalin's police chieftains.[133]

Ideology conditioned Stalin's thinking, but his suspicions were reinforced by experience and reality. In Romania, Poland, the Balkans, Ukraine, and Turkey, British and American officials conducted clandestine operations, albeit on a small scale, to nurture unrest and establish ties with opposition leaders. Of course, Stalin's brutal repression, his transfer of subject nationalities, and his wrangling for bits of Iranian and Turkish territory also fomented instability and encouraged the policies that exacerbated his suspicions.[134]

Yet Stalin was not embarked on a cold war. He was vacillating, saying contradictory things, pursuing divergent policies. Historians violently argue about Stalin's motivations and his goals precisely because his rhetoric and his actions were so inconsistent. In 1993, when Soviet documents from this period were first becoming available, the Norwegian historian Odd Arne Westad wrote, "Stalin's foreign policy is not as much inexplicable in its parts as incoherent in its whole." This description seems even truer now, in view of still more documents that have been brought to light.[135]

For although Stalin delayed the withdrawal of his troops from northern Iran, asked for new rights in the Turkish Straits, and installed progressively more communist governments in Poland, Romania, and Bulgaria, he also withdrew Soviet troops from Czechoslovakia and from the island of Bornholm in the Baltic; allowed free elections in the Soviet occupation zone in Austria and in parts of Hungary and Czechoslovakia; pulled Soviet troops out of Manchuria; and continued to discourage revolution or communist seizures of power in Greece, Italy, and France. In Germany, Stalin consolidated the Soviet hold over the Soviet occupation zone yet talked repeatedly, both privately and publicly, about honoring the Potsdam pledges to keep Germany unified and demilitarized. He told the German communists whom he had placed in power in Berlin to cease radical actions and plan for a unified Germany. He instructed them to join with Social Democrats in a new Socialist Unity Party (SED) and to position themselves to win elections in all four occupation zones. Yet the actions of Soviet armies in eastern Germany brutalized the people and eroded any popular support the communists might have garnered. Stalin, writes Norman Naimark, an eminent historian of Stalin's European policies, "had no firm plan for post-war Europe, not even what we would call today a 'road map.' . . . He was too tactically inclined for that" and too responsive to local circumstances and unforeseen developments.[136]

Stalin did not want a rift with the Western powers. Agreement with the United States, he told Polish communists in late 1945, was still possible.[137] Knowing that his election speech of 6 February 1946 had been interpreted in the West to mean that he was sundering the wartime alliance and resuming an ideological offensive, Stalin made repeated public and private efforts to clarify his views. After telling the new U.S. ambassador in Moscow, Walter Bedell Smith, that he believed the United States and Britain were united to thwart Soviet Russia, he insisted that he wanted to cooperate with them. "We should not be alarmed or apprehensive," said Stalin, "because of differences of opinion and arguments which occur in families and even between brothers because with patience and good will these differences would be reconciled." He said the same to Labour delegates and to journalists from Great Britain. There will be no war, he told Alexander Werth, the correspondent of Britain's *Sunday Times*. "I absolutely believe," he said, in the possibility of long-standing cooperation with his wartime allies. "Communism in one country is entirely possible, especially in such a country as the Soviet Union." If he had been seeking to orchestrate opinion against the Americans and British, it is hard to comprehend why he would have permitted such interviews to be printed in the Soviet press.[138] And in his last meeting in January 1946 with departing U.S. ambassador Averell Harriman, just two weeks before his Bolshoi speech, Stalin told him, "As to our foreign policy conceptions, the Soviet Union and the United States can find a common language." He then inquired whether it might still be feasible to get a large loan from the United States, as previously had been promised. He made clear that he would not make political concessions in return for the loan, but the money was still needed for postwar reconstruction. It would take six or seven years, he admitted, to restore the devastated districts of western Russia.[139]

But Stalin wanted Western cooperation also in order to control the possible revival of German and Japanese power. He was angered that the United States so blatantly monopolized the occupation of Japan, a nation that he deemed a perennial threat to Russia, and he could not accept American indifference to his strategic imperatives. He wanted to be treated as a partner, albeit a junior one.[140] In Germany, understanding that the Western allies would not agree to dismembering the country into separate zones and believing they were maneuvering to harness the Western zones' latent power to serve Western interests, Stalin shifted course. In mid-1945, he started to champion German unification and to favor German economic revival. His aim was a unified, demilitarized Germany in the Soviet sphere of influence, which he now believed would compete with Britain and America and constrain their domination of the international economy. Still, a unified, revived Germany might also maneuver out of control and join a Western capitalist alliance against Soviet Russia, or it might act independently, rearm, and aim for revenge and territorial revision. Conciliating the Germans, Stalin grasped, might make Germany less revanchist, but it would be risky. Hence cooperation with the Americans and the British was imperative, however suspicious he might be. At the very least, he knew that cooperation was indispensable if he was to get reparations from the western zones of Germany, which he desperately wanted for Russian reconstruction.[141]

A unified Germany, with all its attendant uncertainties, also made it more imperative to dominate the Soviet Union's Eastern European borderlands. Hence throughout 1946 and 1947, Stalin ordered Molotov to work with Byrnes and British foreign minister Ernest Bevin to complete peace treaties with the Eastern European nations that had fought with Germany during the war. Stalin wanted, writes one of Hungary's leading Cold War historians, to foster a communist "takeover in East Central Europe by peaceful means, while preserving Soviet-Western cooperation as well."[142]

Truman did not know how to deal with these twists and turns in Soviet policy, with the signs of truculence and the contrary evidence of self-restraint. In February 1946, his ablest diplomat in Moscow, George F. Kennan, sent a long telegram to Washington, saying that "at the bottom of the Kremlin's view of world affairs is a traditional and instinctive Russian sense of insecurity." The Soviets, Kennan concluded, did not believe in the possibility of any permanent reconciliation with the West.[143] But Ambassador Harriman left Moscow at about the same time with a typically ambivalent view of the Soviet dictator:

> It is hard for me to reconcile the courtesy and consideration that he showed me personally with the ghastly cruelty of his wholesale liquidations. Others, who did not know him personally, see only the tyrant in Stalin. I saw the other side as well—his high intelligence, that fantastic grasp of detail, his shrewdness and his surprising human sensitivity that he was capable of showing, at least in the war years. I found him better informed than Roosevelt, more realistic than Churchill, in some

ways the most effective of the war leaders. . . . I must confess
that for me Stalin remains the most inscrutable and contradictory character I have known—and leave the final word to the
judgment of history.[144]

President Truman did not have the luxury of waiting for the judgment of
history, of course. He had to make decisions in real time. He, too, wavered.
He was angry with Byrnes's temporizing. He was outraged by news of Soviet
wartime espionage against the Allies. He liked Churchill's tough words in his
Fulton address. He told the Soviets to get out of northern Iran. He instructed
the Joint Chiefs of Staff to draw up contingency war plans. He encouraged
Byrnes to unite the British and American zones in western Germany, to ameliorate conditions there, and to win the support of the German people. If the
Kremlin objected to Anglo-American moves, their views could be ignored.[145]

But Truman did not seek a showdown. He recognized the unrepresenta-
tive, Soviet-imposed governments in Romania and Bulgaria. In late 1945, he
asked General George C. Marshall, the renowned wartime army chief of
staff, to go to China to work out a settlement between the Communists and
Nationalists there. He encouraged Under Secretary of State Dean G. Acheson and his aides to work on a plan for the international control of atomic
energy. He continued to oversee the demobilization of U.S. forces. He
instructed Byrnes, much as Stalin instructed Molotov, to finish the peace
treaties regarding Eastern Europe, Italy, and Finland. He wanted General
Lucius D. Clay, the deputy military governor in Germany, to keep meeting
with his Soviet, British, and French counterparts on plans for the nation's
unification. Truman's closest aides, Clark Clifford and George Elsey, drew up
a long report in the summer of 1946 claiming that the Soviet Union was not
simply chiseling on its earlier agreements, as the president already believed,
but intent on world domination. When Secretary of Commerce Henry Wallace remonstrated against this view and spoke publicly in behalf of a more
conciliatory policy toward the Kremlin, Truman fired him. Yet at the same
time, the president locked the Clifford-Elsey report in a safe and bided his
time.

Truman was not eager to sunder the great wartime coalition he had inherited from Roosevelt. A breakdown would complicate his domestic priorities
and weaken his party. Strife with the Soviet Union, Truman knew, would re-

Left to right: Bevin, Molotov, and Byrnes, 1946. After the war ended, the three foreign ministers met often to see if they could resolve differences over Eastern Europe, Italy, and Germany.

quire foreign aid to beleaguered countries, more defense spending, fewer tax reductions, and spiraling inflation. Republicans were already lambasting him for rising prices, labor unrest, and high taxes. Notwithstanding the consensus among his foreign-policy advisers that the Soviet Union was a great threat, Truman did not quite know what to do. After his party suffered a humiliating defeat in the congressional elections of November 1946, he asked General Marshall to become his secretary of state, but gave him no marching orders, and the general himself was known for his prudence and restraint. Marshall did not want confrontation. He wanted to negotiate a German peace treaty with the Russians. Before he arrived in Moscow, however, worsening international conditions dashed any lingering hopes for a sustained détente.[146]

International Anarchy

Neither Truman nor Stalin wanted a cold war. Yet it came. Why?

The Cold War came because conditions in the international system created risks that Truman and Stalin could not accept and opportunities they could not resist. Neither the president of the most powerful country the world had ever known nor the cruelest dictator the world had ever witnessed was in control of events. And the beliefs and experiences of both men magnified their perception of threat and fear of betrayal. Each felt he had to act because danger loomed. Each felt he had to act because opportunity beckoned.

From the time World War II drew to a close, nothing frightened American policymakers more than the economic plight and social strife that the war had bequeathed. In April 1945, as the fighting in Europe was in its last stages, John J. McCloy, the influential assistant secretary of war, returned from a trip to Europe and presented an apocalyptic account of conditions. "There is a complete economic, social and political collapse going on in Central Europe, the extent of which is unparalleled in history." The situation in Germany, he told Secretary of War Henry L. Stimson, was "worse than anything probably that ever happened in the world." Writing in his diary, Stimson noted that he "had anticipated the chaos, but the details of it were appalling."[147]

A few months later, in July, Dean Acheson presented a similar view to the Senate Committee on Banking and Currency: "There is a situation in the world, very clearly illustrated in Europe, and also true in the Far East, which threatens the very foundations, the whole fabric of world organization which we have known in our lifetime and which our fathers and grandfathers knew." In liberated Europe, Acheson reported, railway and power systems had ceased to operate, "financial systems are destroyed. Ownership of property is in terrific confusion. Management of property is in confusion." Not since the eighth century, when the Muslims split the world in two, Acheson said, had conditions been so serious. Europe's industrial and social life had "come to a complete and utter standstill." The "whole fabric of social life," Acheson warned, "might go to pieces unless the most energetic steps are taken on all fronts."[148]

People suffered. People endured. People yearned for a better future. People discussed, disputed, and imagined alternative political and economic orders. Capitalism was blamed for the Depression, the war, and genocide. Describing conditions in Czechoslovakia, the historian Igor Lukes writes that after the war, "Many in Czechoslovakia had come to believe that capitalism . . . had become obsolete. Influential intellectuals saw the world emerging from the ashes of the war in black and white terms: here was Auschwitz and there was Stalingrad. The former was a by-product of a crisis in capitalist Europe of the 1930s; the latter stood for the superiority of socialism."[149] In November 1945, the British historian A.J.P. Taylor commented: "Nobody in Europe believes in the American way of life—that is, in private enterprise." People, he said, "want Socialism, but they also want the Rights of Man."[150]

This was not mere rhetoric. What concerned U.S. officials was what was happening on the streets and in the voting booths. Everywhere in Europe, communist and socialist support seemed to be mounting. In Belgium, the Communist Party grew from 9,000 in 1939 to 100,000 in November 1945; in Greece, from 17,000 in 1935 to 70,000 in 1945; in Italy, from 5,000 in 1943 to 1.7 million at the end of 1945; in Czechoslovakia, from 28,000 in May 1945 to 750,000 in September 1945. In France, Italy, and Finland, communists were already getting 20 percent of the total vote; in Belgium, Denmark, Norway, Holland, and Sweden, it was close to 10 percent. In Eastern European countries, 20 to 50 percent of the populace aligned with leftist parties.[151] Support for socialist parties made the left appear even more threatening to those in the center and on the right. In Great Britain, the Labour Party emerged triumphant in July 1945 and, to the astonishment of Americans, unseated Winston Churchill. Everywhere, people seemed to be clamoring for land reform, social welfare, and nationalization of industry. "They have suffered so much," said Acheson, "and they believe so deeply that governments can take some action which will alleviate their sufferings, that they will demand that the whole business of state control and state interference shall be pushed further and further."[152] To many Americans, private enterprise and free markets appeared endangered by a resurgent left.

Conditions in Asia, the Middle East, and Africa were no more reassuring. In Japan, fifteen million people were homeless and the economy near collapse. China was engulfed by political strife and civil war. In South Asia, the Congress Party under Mohandas K. Gandhi and Jawaharlal Nehru was continuing India's long struggle for independence. In Southeast Asia, revolutionary nationalist movements were blossoming. The communist leader Ho Chi Minh clamored for France's recognition of Vietnam's independence. Achmed Sukarno pleaded for Dutch recognition of Indonesia's sovereignty. Indeed, embedded in the entire international system was the problem of Europe's former colonies in Asia and Africa that now wanted independence; the solution to this problem would gradually reconfigure the international order, kindling in Moscow immense hopes for progress and change and generating in Washington immense fear and never-ending frustration.

U.S. officials hoped conditions would improve. In many places they did, but not enough to allay officials' apprehensions. In March 1946, Acheson told a congressional committee, "The commercial and financial situation of the world is worse than any of us thought a year ago it would be. Destruction is more complete, hunger more acute, exhaustion more widespread than anyone then realized. What might have been passed off as prophecies have become stark facts."[153] At cabinet meetings, Truman's advisers discussed food shortages and the social disorder and political upheaval they were engendering. "More people face starvation and even actual death," the president acknowledged, "than in any war year and perhaps more than in all the war years combined."[154]

What hovered over these deliberations were fears that Stalin would try to capitalize on these conditions. There would be "pestilence and famine in

The town of München-Gladbach, 1945. Wartime destruction in Germany was appalling, and the need for reconstruction urgent.

The ruined city of Caen, France, 1944. Rebuilding France and Western Europe, which would undercut the appeal of communism, was an urgent U.S. priority.

Central Europe next winter," Secretary of War Stimson had told President Truman on 16 May 1945. "This is likely to be followed by political revolution and Communistic infiltration." The next month, Undersecretary of State Joseph Grew gave the president a long report on the international communist movement. "Europe today," it concluded, was a breeding ground for "spontaneous class hatred to be channeled by a skillful agitator." Over the next two years, while Soviet and American officials wrangled over Eastern Europe, Iran, and Turkey, this perceived threat did not abate. The "greatest potential danger to U.S. security," the newly formed Central Intelligence Agency concluded in September 1947, "lies . . . in the possibility of the economic collapse of Western Europe and of the consequent accession to power of elements subservient to the Kremlin."[155]

Heavy snows and frigid temperatures during January and February 1947 transformed alarm to action. British officials confided that financial exigencies would force His Majesty's government to withdraw from the eastern Mediterranean, thereby exposing Greece and Turkey to additional risk. "The reins of world leadership," Assistant Secretary of State Will Clayton wrote, "are fast slipping from Britain's competent but now very weak hands. These reins will be picked up either by the United States or by Russia. If by Russia, there will almost certainly be war in the next decade or so with the odds against us."[156] Clayton feared that the Greek communists would gain power and align Greece with the Soviet Union. The success of the communists in Greece would have a bandwagon effect throughout Europe. President Truman put it this way:

> If we were to turn our back on the world, areas such as Greece, weakened and divided as a result of the war, would fall into the Soviet orbit without much effort on the part of the Russians. The success of Russia in such areas and our avowed lack of interest would lead to the growth of domestic Communist parties in such European countries as France and Italy, where they already were significant threats. Inaction . . . could result in handing to the Russians vast areas of the globe now denied to them.[157]

Truman took action. He delivered a special address to Congress on 12 March 1947, setting forth what became known as the Truman Doctrine. Thereafter, it "would be the policy of the United States to support free peoples who are resisting attempted subjugation by armed minorities or by outside pressures." He asked Congress to allocate four hundred million dollars in aid for Greece and Turkey. A "fateful hour" had arrived. Nations had to choose "between alternate ways of life. . . . If we falter in our leadership," Truman warned, "we may endanger the peace of the world."[158]

Three months later, after failing to make headway on a German settlement at a conference in Moscow, Secretary of State Marshall gave a commencement address at Harvard in which he proposed that the United States help to fund Europe's reconstruction should Europeans design a satisfactory plan for it. The Soviet Union was not acting aggressively, but it was consolidating its influence in Eastern Europe and maneuvering to capitalize on mounting unrest in Western Europe. "Europe is steadily deteriorating," said Assistant Secretary Clayton on 27 May. "Millions of people in the cities are slowly starving. . . . Without further and substantial aid from the United States, economic, social, and political disintegration will overwhelm Europe."

In the western zones of Germany, rations were cut to twelve hundred calories per day per person. Marshall and his assistants feared that without additional food deliveries they would lose "the great struggle . . . to prevent [Germany] going communistic."[159]

Truman understood that he needed to put events in a context that the American people could comprehend if they were to support the initiatives he was now contemplating. He explained that it was a struggle between alternative ways of life. It was not a military struggle but a political one, an ideological struggle, a spiritual struggle. Nations in much of the world, Truman stated in a speech at Baylor University just days before he announced the Truman Doctrine, were heading toward central planning. Free enterprise was challenged everywhere. And where free enterprise was endangered, so were other cherished freedoms, such as freedom of speech and of religion. In the president's view, all these freedoms were indivisible.[160] They were at risk because of the devastation wrought by the war, because of people's yearnings for a better future. They were at risk because strong communist parties were competing successfully for office, because armed minorities were willing to use force to seize power, and because the Kremlin hovered in the background willing to give succor to such efforts and eager to capitalize on them.

America's own future was at risk. "Our deepest concern with European recovery is that it is essential to the maintenance of the civilization in which the American way of life is rooted," Truman explained. "If Europe fails to recover, the people of these countries might be driven to the philosophy of despair [of totalitarianism]. Such a turn of events would constitute a shattering blow to peace and stability in the world. It might well compel us to modify our own economic system and to forgo, for the sake of our own security, the enjoyment of many of our freedoms and privileges."[161]

U.S. officials were motivated to act, then, not because Stalin was an evil dictator, killing millions of people in his own country and subjugating peoples on the periphery of the Soviet Union, but because of conditions in the international system, and out of fear that social turmoil and economic paralysis in Europe would play into communist hands, affording Stalin new opportunities to expand Soviet power. They also feared that floundering occupation policies in Germany and Japan might allow those countries to gravitate into a Soviet orbit and that decolonization in the third world would be exploited by the Kremlin. They had learned that once a totalitarian government possessed great power, it was likely to wage war, and even if it did not wage war, its control of huge resources and markets throughout Eurasia meant that it endangered America's free political economy. "If communism is allowed to absorb the free nations," Truman subsequently explained, "then we would be isolated from our sources of supply and detached from our friends. Then we would have to take defense measures which might really bankrupt our economy, and change our way of life so that we couldn't recognize it as American any longer."[162]

No country was more critical than Germany. The integration of Germany into the postwar international system was the overriding issue. "The only really dangerous thing in my mind," said George Kennan in 1946, "is the possibility that the technical skills of the Germans might be combined with the physical resources of Russia."[163] From the moment the war ended, top U.S. officials recognized that the revival of German coal production was essential for the economic revival of the rest of Europe, on which, in turn, social peace depended. During the Potsdam Conference, President Truman had ordered General Dwight D. Eisenhower, then commander of American troops in Europe, to make the production and export of twenty-five million tons of coal the number one priority of U.S. occupation policy in Germany (other than the health and safety of U.S. troops themselves). This priority had far-reaching implications. The successful large-scale mining of coal, acknowledged General Clay, meant "some restoration of the German economy, and some industrial activity to support coal mining."[164]

But the economy in the British, French, and American occupation zones floundered during 1946, causing immense consternation in Washington. When officials went to work designing the Marshall Plan, Kennan and his associates in the State Department maintained that reviving German production was the key to European recovery, yet they feared that a revived Germany might not be within their power to control. There was no certainty how it would behave once the occupation was over or how it would orient itself in the international system. When Marshall went to Moscow to discuss the future of Germany at the Big Four Council of Foreign Ministers in March 1947, he took John Foster Dulles, the prominent Republican foreign-policy spokesman, with him. Germany's economic potential, Dulles told Marshall, had to be integrated into western Europe without "giving economic mastery to the Germans." This was a daunting challenge, as Dulles recognized. Once they began recovering, he acknowledged, the Germans would "almost certainly be dominated by a spirit of revenge and ambition to recover a great power status." They might align with the Soviet Union or act independently. Either way, danger lurked.[165]

But it could not be avoided. Steps had to be taken to expedite coal production in the Ruhr. No reparations in the form of raw materials, machine tools, or anything else should be given to the U.S.S.R. German resources had to be harnessed for the recovery of western Europe. The Moscow conference partly foundered on this issue of reparations. Although Marshall hoped to sustain wartime cooperation, he told Stalin, he could not continue to haggle about the future of Germany. Action was imperative.[166] At a meeting on 3 July, Secretary of State Marshall, Secretary of War Robert Patterson, and Secretary of the Navy James Forrestal agreed: "Germany must cooperate fully in any effective European plan, and that the economic revival of Europe depends in considerable part on a recovery of German production—in coal, in food, steel, fertilizer, etc., and on efficient use of such European resources as the Rhine River."[167] A week later, General Clay was instructed to boost the level of industrial production in the western zones.

The American offensive—the Truman Doctrine, the Marshall Plan, and the rebuilding of western Germany—was a reaction to the anarchy in the international system, upon which the United States believed the Kremlin might capitalize. Fear drove policy. Truman and his advisers understood they were placing the reconstruction of western Europe and the cooptation of western Germany over their desire to sustain their wartime cooperation with the Soviet Union. They did not seek to provoke Stalin or to endanger Soviet security, but they believed they had to act as they did, even if it meant that the U.S.S.R. would feel provoked. Prudence demanded action.

Stalin was not surprised. The capitalists were acting as capitalists, seeking to form a bloc against Soviet Russia. Initially, he pondered Soviet participation in the Marshall Plan. He sent Molotov and a hundred technical advisers to a conference in Paris in July 1947 to discuss Marshall's overture for the European Recovery Program. But while Molotov negotiated, Stalin changed his mind. He saw encirclement. He believed, quite rightly, that the terms for participation included the opening of the east European nations where the Red Army was still enforcing Soviet control. The financial credits would prove illusory, he said, and would form a pretext to isolate the Soviet Union.

The Americans were trying to maneuver their way into Eastern Europe. They were seeking to harness German power against the Soviet Union. Stalin ordered the governments of Czechoslovakia and Poland, which were mightily enticed to participate, not to permit themselves to be lured by the American offer.[168]

But Stalin did much more than pressure his allies to rebuff American overtures. Seeing danger, he orchestrated a new round of purges in Eastern Europe, reshuffled the composition of governments, and planted his minions in power more firmly. Soviet delegates walked out of the Allied Control Council that was supposed to be governing Germany. The Kremlin tightened controls over access to Berlin, and suppressed opponents of the SED in the Soviet zone in eastern Germany. In Czechoslovakia, Stalin supported a communist seizure of power in February 1948; almost overnight a democratically elected government was transformed into a "People's Democracy." With other nations on the Soviet periphery, Stalin negotiated defense agreements. Inside his own country, he boosted military expenditures. "We do not wish for war," he said, "but we are not afraid of it."[169]

Stalin believed the capitalists had thrown down the gauntlet. Although he had been planning the move for quite some time, he convened a meeting in Poland in September 1947 and established the Communist Information Bureau (Cominform) to improve his control over and coordination among European communist parties. At this meeting, his representatives announced that the world was being divided into two camps. Peaceful coexistence was impossible. Western capitalist initiatives had to be thwarted. The Marshall Plan had to be defeated. Efforts to unite and reconstruct the western zones of Germany had to be challenged. If necessary, Stalin would blockade Berlin. The former capital of Nazi Germany, although officially administered by the four occupation powers and divided into four zones, lay inside Soviet-controlled east Germany and could be easily squeezed to counter Western initiatives. At a special session of the Politburo on 14 March 1948, Stalin explained his thinking: "The innumerable conferences taking place in recent years indicated clearly to us that we cannot come to an agreement with the camp opposing us just as water and fire are unable to come to terms. The present situation of a hostile yet peaceful world may still last for a long time but there will come a time when conflict, I repeat, will be inevitable."[170]

Ideology shaped Stalin's interpretation of the actions of America and

Britain, and provided a menu of possible responses. He could try to exploit divisions among the capitalist powers. He could try to mobilize the European proletariat to thwart the actions of their bourgeois governments. In fact, Stalin denounced French and Italian communists for their previous postwar collaboration with other political parties and now encouraged them to obstruct implementation of the Marshall Plan, but he also cautioned against adventurism, against acting too crudely, against provoking even more ominous reactions from the capitalist adversary.[171] Stalin told the Yugoslav communists that they should stop supporting the communists in Greece. That struggle should be postponed for a more propitious time, he insisted. "The entire question rests in the balance of forces. We must go into battle not when the enemy wants us to, but when it's in our interests."[172]

But if there were dangers in the international environment, communist ideology also postulated opportunities. Ever since the 1920s, Stalin had ruminated about a "coalition between the proletariat revolution in Europe and the colonial revolution in the East . . . against the world front of imperialism."[173] Now, in late 1947 and early 1948, Stalin returned to this theme with greater emphasis than ever before. He told a special session of the Politburo, on 14 March 1948, "we should energetically support the revolutionary struggle of the oppressed peoples of the dependent and colonial countries against the imperialism of America, England, and France." Many countries once controlled by European powers, Stalin explained, already "had entered the path of national liberation." Their struggles would help precipitate the crisis of capitalism long postulated by Marxist-Leninist theory. The Kremlin, he said, could do much to hasten the revolutionary process in Central and South America and, even more so, in Asia. We have already done a lot, he told his comrades, to "accelerate the emancipation of Asiatic peoples, although I think henceforth we should increase tenfold our work in this direction." China's liberation movement, Stalin maintained, would become a model for the future. Revolutionary nationalist turmoil in the third world provided boundless opportunities for the expansion of communist influence and the erosion of capitalist power.[174]

While Stalin acknowledged weakness in Europe and opportunity in Asia and Latin America, Truman and his advisers believed that they still had an opportunity to act from a position of strength in Europe. "In the necessary delicate apportioning of our resources," wrote Assistant Secretary of War

Howard C. Petersen in mid-1947, "the time element permits emphasis on strengthening the economic dikes against Soviet communism rather than upon preparing for a possible eventual, but not yet inevitable war."[175] If the passage of time was likely to mean the further accretion of state power, more experiments in central planning, and proliferating trade and exchange controls, it was urgent to act now while the correlation of forces was still in America's favor. If the food shortages, work stoppages, and political turmoil in the western zones of Germany portended uncertainty about the future of Germany, it was imperative to act now before the German communists and their Soviet backers outmaneuvered Western-oriented parties and politicians.

By the fall of 1947, U.S. officials no longer felt they had the time to try to work out cooperative agreements. They had to act quickly to mobilize West German resources for the economic reconstruction and financial stabilization of western Europe. At a London meeting of foreign ministers in December, Soviet officials continued to bargain meaningfully over the future of Germany even while the Kremlin fomented riots and demonstrations in France and Italy against the proposed Marshall Plan. Precisely because the international environment was so fraught with risk, and precisely because the communists in Italy had a real chance to win the elections scheduled for April 1948, Truman and Marshall pressed Congress to pass emergency relief legislation, and then they capitalized on the news of the communist coup in Prague to push for passage of the legislation supporting the Marshall Plan.

Even more important, they could no longer afford to haggle over the future of Germany. The Americans and British wanted to unify the British, French, and American zones in a federal republic, implement currency reform there, and boost industrial production, thereby integrating this new West Germany into a plan for European recovery. France equivocated and remonstrated, fearful that such Anglo-American initiatives might provoke Soviet aggression in the short run or create a German Frankenstein in the long run. "The thing that impressed me," said Will Clayton after talking to French officials in the fall of 1947, "was the intensity with which the French people . . . regarded the possibility of an attack by Germany again." Marshall tried to allay these worries, but he was insistent on moving ahead. "Maximum German contribution to European recovery," he wrote, "cannot be obtained without establishment of political organization of western Germany. . . . Failure to proceed would appear to Soviets as sign of weakness. . . . While appreciating French concern, US government does not believe that western nations can permit themselves to be deterred."[176]

In other words, the Soviet threats to blockade Berlin must not thwart the Western initiatives. Truman, Marshall, and their colleagues did not think the Soviet Union would go to war over Germany. George Kennan and Charles Bohlen, the nation's foremost experts on Soviet Russia, did not believe Stalin would attack. Indeed, the United States could try to build up West German power and leverage its way into the Soviet sphere precisely because it calculated that the Soviet Union was too weak to respond militarily. Stalin might threaten, might clamp down in his own sphere, and might try to blockade Berlin, but he was not ready for war. He could not ignore America's atomic monopoly. Stalin would defer to American power, Marshall calculated, even while he denounced it or denied it. The Soviet leader would bluster. He would repress. He would foment unrest. But these actions, Marshall told his cabinet colleagues, reflected Soviet "desperation," not strength. They are bluffing, said General Clay on 17 June 1948, "and their hand can and should be called now."[177]

Conditions in the international arena encouraged U.S. officials to go on the diplomatic offensive in 1947 and 1948. Digesting the lessons of recent history, U.S. officials believed they had to act before the skilled labor, resources, and industrial infrastructure of Europe fell into the grasp of a totalitarian adversary, which would put America's free political economy at risk. But if the existing correlation of forces enabled the United States to act swiftly in Western Europe and Japan, opportunities still abounded for the Kremlin to further its influence and its power in Eastern Europe, Asia, Africa, and Latin America.

Stalin never forswore his determination to safeguard Soviet security and to oversee the forces of worldwide revolution. So long as cooperation with the West promised the possibility of expediting reconstruction at home and controlling the revival of German and Japanese power abroad, he was prepared to cool the ardor of his revolutionary comrades and sometimes even betray them. But once Truman declared that he was waging a war against evil for the soul of mankind, Stalin saw that the international landscape was fraught not only with the dangers postulated by Marxist-Leninist ideology, but also with opportunities.

Indeed, danger and opportunity would define the Cold War. Embedded in the international system were social forces of order and disorder, vacuums of power, and wars of national liberation. Who would win the spiritual battle for the soul of mankind after depression, war, and genocide? Who would fill the vacuums of power in central Europe and northeast Asia after the defeat of Germany and Japan? How would wars of national liberation in Asia and Africa shape the international configuration of power after the demise of Europe's colonies? Stalin and Truman pondered these questions. They were wracked with fear and inspired by hope. Ideology and historical experience shaped the way they saw the dangers and the opportunities that lurked in the international system. But so did domestic politics.

Politics at Home

Truman was not eager to go on an offensive against the Soviet Union and international communism. By 1947–48, he knew that American public opinion had grown deeply suspicious of Russia, and that the Republican Party was eager to attack him for appeasing another totalitarian adversary. Yet he was far from certain that the public would support a vigorous foreign policy, which would be costly. In November 1946, voters had repudiated his party and put Republicans in control of both houses of Congress for the first time since the 1920s. But the election had been fought primarily on domestic issues. Many newly elected senators, such as Joseph McCarthy from Wisconsin and John Bricker from Ohio, were economic nationalists and political isolationists, more eager to attack the president for being soft on communists at home than to press him to do anything abroad.[178]

Truman's prestige was at rock bottom after the elections of November 1946, with only about 30 percent of Americans thinking he was doing a good job. Fed up with shortages and strikes, they were primarily concerned about the costs of housing and the price of meat. Businessmen wanted to crush unions; southern segregationists wanted to keep blacks in their place; America Firsters wanted to rid the country of domestic spies and communist traitors.

Truman acted in the international arena because he feared Stalin would exploit conditions to aggrandize Soviet power, not because he felt a groundswell of public opinion demanding new foreign-policy initiatives. The president and his advisers believed they were far ahead of the public in wanting to take action, and thought they had to "shock" or "electrify" the American people into support. In meetings with Democratic and Republican leaders of Congress, Secretary Marshall and Under Secretary Acheson realized they had to pose the threat in stark ideological terms if they were to garner congressional support for a policy of "containment." Truman's aides and State Department officials invested a huge amount of time in drafting the president's address to Congress asking for aid to Greece and Turkey. Truman insisted that the message be framed in simple language that the American people could understand. The looming contest was a struggle between good and evil, between freedom and slavery.[179] "I wanted no hedging in this speech," he recalled in his memoirs. "This was America's answer to the surge of expansion of communist tyranny. It had to be clear and free of hesitation and double talk."[180]

Domestic opinion was ripe. Support for Truman soared in the spring of 1947 as he took the offensive against the Soviet Union. Truman's intent was not to launch a crusade that would entrap him and his successors, but he did. His ideological language deeply resonated. Religious evangelicals and racial segregationists, right-wing extremists, and anti–New Dealers thrived on anticommunist rhetoric. Truman's creation of loyalty boards to screen the backgrounds of federal employees and his support of legislation to create the CIA and the National Security Council "neutered the Republican resurgence."[181]

But the president also became a prisoner of his own rhetoric.[182] Highlighting the communist menace abroad, how could he ignore it at home? In July 1946, 36 percent of Americans told pollsters that domestic communists should be either killed or imprisoned.[183] Truman's conservative foes exploited this public attitude and manipulated the president's language to suit their purposes. They wanted to expel communists from the government, crush "leftists," and repudiate the New Deal. Two weeks after the president delivered his Truman Doctrine message to Congress, J. Edgar Hoover, director of the Federal Bureau of Investigation, told the House Un-American Activities Committee that the administration was not doing enough to root out subversives. Public ire, he said, needed to be aroused. "Victory will be assured once communists are identified and exposed, because the public will take the first step of quarantining them so they can do no harm. Communism, in reality, is not a political party. It is a way of life—an evil and malignant way of life."[184]

The struggle to contain Soviet power became an ideological crusade. This was understandable. The American people had just vanquished one totalitarian foe; they now faced another. They knew Stalin's regime was ruthless and knew he was imposing "godless" communist governments on countries such as Poland and Romania, from which some Americans had themselves emigrated. They did not ask if Stalin was different from Hitler. They assumed the answer was clear. And they realized that Stalin had support in many lands beyond the Soviet periphery. Richard Nixon, a newly elected Republican congressman from California who had run a strong anticommunist campaign, visited Europe in early 1947. He saw that French and Italian communists were capitalizing politically on Europe's dire economic conditions. The threat was real, he believed, and immediate. "Communists throughout the world owe their loyalty not to the countries in which they live but to Russia," he said.[185]

Domestic political battles, therefore, reinforced the ideological and geostrategic convictions of U.S. officials. But Republicans and Democrats shared a common vocabulary: they believed they were in a battle to preserve the American way of life. "If Western Europe goes behind the Iron Curtain," declared Republican senator William Knowland, "the whole productive potential of that section of the world will fall into the Russian orbit . . . [and] the repercussions upon our own domestic economy would be . . . terrific." If the United States did not employ its vast power when it still had an opportunity to do so, George Kennan warned, it would face a Europe that "would be no less hostile" than the Europe of Hitler's dreams. Such a Europe would force the United States to change, requiring increases in defense spending, controls over the economy, more intense hunts for domestic subversives, and more infringements on personal freedoms. The United States, Truman predicted, might have to become a garrison state with "a system of centralized regimentation unlike anything we have ever known."[186]

Stalin's evolving policies were also a response to his domestic polity. Geopolitics, ideology, and personality shaped his attitudes, but his behavior cannot be fully understood except in the domestic context in which he operated. The Soviet people, Stalin knew, wanted a better way of life. They expected benefits, not more calls for sacrifice. Everybody, wrote the journalist Ilya Ehrenburg, "expected that once victory had been won, people would know real happiness." The war itself was already being "remembered as a time of freedom." It had catalyzed feelings of community and unleashed people's creativity and ingenuity, since they had been forced "time after time to make their own decisions, to take responsibility for themselves." It had been a period almost of spontaneous de-Stalinization. After victory, they expected better. We "believed that victory would bring justice," wrote Ehrenburg, "that human dignity would triumph."[187]

Stalin was not blind to the realities around him. His country was devastated, his people impoverished. His armies had conquered new lands, but ones inhabited by millions of discontented people. His soldiers returned with ideas and hopes that could not be trusted. The U.S.S.R. contained subject peoples and nationalities whose desire for autonomy had been intensified by resistance and war. The Soviet armed forces had performed heroically but now might capitalize on their popularity and challenge his power. Stalin had more stature than ever before, but he was personally insecure and fearful for his life. The nation had more power than ever before, but its long-term safety was far from assured. Communism had more resonance than ever before, but the system tottered within.

Rumblings of discontent abounded. Food was scarce, housing conditions abominable. In 1946, the Soviet grain harvest sank to 39.6 million tons compared with 95.5 million in 1940; in 1947, the nation had 14 million tons of flour compared with almost 29 million in 1940. And where food could be had, it was often inedible. "Workers and even low-level managers in rural areas endured a state of poverty which was almost beyond description." Parents could not feed or clothe their children. "Dreams of a calm, even if slow, advance forward were dashed forever."[188]

Demoralization prevailed everywhere, and Stalin's spies vigilantly reported news of spreading discontent. General V. N. Gordov, conqueror of Prague and Berlin, ruminated on conditions with F. T. Rybalchenko, his former chief of staff. "People are angry about their life and complain openly," Gordov said. "There is incredible famine." Rybalchenko retorted, "Policies are such [that] nobody wants to work. All collective farmers hate Stalin and wait for his end." The recorded conversation was sent to Stalin. Gordov and his wife were executed.[189]

There was seething discontent in the western borderlands of Soviet Russia and in the recently annexed territories. Suppressed nationality groups and ethnic minorities wanted a softening of the Soviet way of life and an opportunity for self-expression. During 1946, Ukrainian nationalist rebels continued to fight tenaciously. Stalin's secret police reported growing foreign espionage activity. Captured suspects said they were paid by Americans and British intelligence to gather information. Rebels spread rumors of an impending war between the United States and the U.S.S.R. that would lead to the liberation of Ukraine.[190]

Stalin's suspicions were stirred anew. He was determined to "deliver a blow" against any talk of "democracy," let alone subversion. He reorganized the internal Soviet police system throughout the western borderlands. He ordered Andrei Zhdanov to take charge of the propaganda administration in the party secretariat and to reimpose ideological purity on the nomenklatura and apparatchiks. He instructed Lavrenty Beria, the head of the secret police, to use slave labor to accelerate the Soviet atomic project. He reshuffled the top brass of the army and demoted Zhukov. The population of political prisoners held in a huge network of Soviet labor camps grew from 1,460,677 in 1945 to 2,199,535 in 1948; the numbers of ethnic minorities and repatriated soldiers forced to live in special settlements in forsaken places totaled almost 2.5 million at the end of 1946. Prisoners died each year by the tens of thousands: 81,917 in 1945; 30,715 in 1946; 66,830 in 1947; 50,659 in 1948.[191]

Stalin intimidated his subordinates one by one, not killing them but striking fear into their hearts, stripping away their independence, and reminding them that he was the source of their authority, even of their lives. Yet it was often difficult to discern what he wanted beyond a few key fundamentals: his unchallenged power, a single-party state guided by Marxist-Leninist ideology, and Soviet imperial control over the peoples of the U.S.S.R. and Eastern Europe. Over many economic matters Stalin allocated responsibility to his Council of Ministers. Defense and foreign-policy matters and ideological issues stayed within the province of the party's Politburo, which met informally and infrequently and which Stalin dominated. But the dictator's domination did not mean that his views were predetermined.[192]

Soviet records reveal that on many issues Stalin had no clear policy. On many matters he suspended action. Top officials discussed complex, often intersecting issues among themselves and with him—relations with the United States, the security of the Soviet Union, the future of Germany, the orientation of the communist parties abroad, the allocation of resources to industry and agriculture, the degree of national and cultural self-expression. But Stalin intervened only episodically and inconsistently.[193] Russocentrism, however, loomed larger and larger in his thinking. "The patriotic [Russian] component steadily increased its relative weight in comparison with the Marxist."[194]

But the mix remained inchoate. Stalin's ideology did not provide him with clear answers, nor did domestic politics shape his foreign policy. But at a time of international turmoil and internal ferment, the ideology, mixed with his personal paranoia, oriented his thinking and shaped his domestic crackdown. Nobody could be trusted, least of all capitalists. He was prepared to work with the United States, just as Truman wanted to get along with him, but on his own terms and to serve his own interests. Cooperation with the Western powers did not mean that he could allow Soviet security to be endangered or the communist experiment to be imperiled. Capitalists were stirring up discontent and brewing rebellion inside Eastern Europe and the western borderlands of the Soviet Union. They were thwarting his ambitions in Iran and Turkey. They were intent on rebuilding western Germany. They were dangerous scoundrels. The Marshall Plan confirmed his worst suspicions. It "tore the alliance apart," writes a recent biographer. Stalin regarded it as a device "to destroy Soviet military and political hegemony over Eastern Europe."[195]

Stalin now had no alternative but to confront his foreign adversaries. Ideology and history instructed that they could not be appeased. The loyalty and discipline of his subordinates were deemed imperative not only at home but throughout Eastern Europe. Dissidents were purged, obeisance demanded.

Allies and Clients

As the iron curtain descended across Europe, opportunity beckoned in Asia. Communists were waging a tenacious struggle to gain power in China, and revolutionary nationalist leaders such as Ho Chi Minh in Vietnam and Sukarno in Indonesia were battling the French and Dutch in behalf of their people's freedom.

After the war, Stalin initially did rather little to support prospective communist allies in Asia, Africa, or Latin America. His attitude toward Mao Zedong and the Chinese Communist Party's war against the Guomindang illustrated that his priority was Soviet Russia. Stalin claimed that conditions in China were not ripe for revolution, nor the material base and class structure conducive to success. In August 1945, he had signed an agreement with the Nationalists, since he wanted to secure Russia's periphery in northeast Asia, avoid a rift with the United States, and temper Washington's penchant to intervene in Asia on behalf of Jiang Jieshi. On key occasions, the Soviet army in Manchuria did provide arms and assistance to the Chinese communists, but Stalin urged Mao to compromise, share power, and reach a modus vivendi with the Guomindang. These actions disheartened Mao but did not alter his quest to gain power. As Stalin recounted to Bulgarian and Yugoslav communists in February 1948, the Chinese comrades agreed "in words," "but in practice kept accumulating forces."[196]

Stalin's priority was not revolution in Asia and the third world but the reconstruction of Soviet Russia and protection of its frontiers. Revolution, the ultimate goal, could be deferred, even subordinated, while the Kremlin assessed whether and for how long it could collaborate with its wartime allies in shaping the future of Germany and Japan, Russia's traditional enemies. Because of Stalin's desire to "take care of [his] relations with the United States," Mao had acknowledged in December 1945, Soviet forces had not done all they might have done to thwart the movement of Nationalist troops into key cities in Manchuria. Mao's revolution could wait, Stalin thought, until he assessed the Americans' willingness to share power in Japan. Revolution against France in Vietnam could also wait, Stalin calculated, until he could determine Ho's reliability and evaluate the evolution of French domestic politics.[197]

But once the Americans opted in the spring and summer of 1947 to focus on the reconstruction of Western Europe, and once French officials aligned their nation with the Americans and British in Germany and excised communists from the governing coalition in Paris, Stalin turned his attention to the vast opportunities that he thought he had to weaken the capitalists and encourage revolution in Asia. When the Truman administration reversed course in Japan in early 1948 and concentrated on rehabilitating Japan's economy rather than reforming its prewar institutions, Stalin, too, reversed course in China. He told Mao's emissaries that they now could count on him. "If socialism is victorious in China," Stalin said, "and [if] other countries follow the same road, we can consider the victory of socialism throughout the world to be guaranteed."[198]

World revolution remained a distant goal, however, not to be pursued at the expense of the interests and power of the Soviet Union. When he formed the Cominform in September 1947, Stalin's aim was to gain tighter control over his minions in Europe, not to encourage worldwide revolution. In fact, he chastised French and Italian communists for allowing themselves to be outmaneuvered and warned them not to engage in insurrectionary activity.[199] Ideology did not breed affinity for Stalin's communist comrades in foreign lands or make him more amenable to their wishes. His allies and clients learned to their dismay that they had to accommodate the twists and turns of his policies, even when they conflicted with their own interests and aspirations.[200]

Stalin despised signs of their independence and autonomy. He often was tentative and vague in communicating with communists in other nations, masking his own uncertainties. But when they acted on their own in ways he deemed harmful to Soviet interests, he could be brutally clear. He would not allow the national interests of other communist leaders to usurp his authority or interfere with his priorities. In August 1947, he was furious with Bulgarian and Yugoslav communist leaders for signing agreements without first consulting him. They were foolishly supporting the insurgency in Greece, in his view, and mistakenly seeking to intimidate Albania through the movement of Yugoslav troops. "These are leftist infatuations," he declared. Hereafter, Bulgaria and Yugoslavia must coordinate their foreign policies with the Kremlin. They must not do anything to provoke the capitalist adversary. "Right now a great electoral struggle is going on in America," Stalin lectured. "For us, it is of great importance to see what the future government there will be, because America is a powerful country, well armed. Its government is headed not by intellectuals but by moneybags who hate us terribly and look for any pretext to do us harm."[201]

Stalin, alone, would shape the foreign policies of his communist neighbors. Believing that Marshal Tito in Yugoslavia was defying his leadership, Stalin tried to destroy him. In June 1948, he orchestrated Yugoslavia's expulsion from the Cominform. And at the same time he took action that provoked the United States far more than anything Tito did: Soviet troops imposed a blockade on Berlin, stopping all railroad traffic between the isolated capital and the West.

Stalin wanted to prevent the formation of an independent West German republic that might become part of a Western bloc led by the United States.

If Great Britain, France, and the United States repudiated the agreements they had just signed regarding their zones in Germany, he said, he would lift the blockade. Otherwise, he would keep Berlin isolated from the rest of western Germany and seek to incorporate it into the Soviet zone.

Nothing he had done since the war had been quite so daring. If the Americans were to challenge the Soviet blockade, they might start a war in the heart of Europe. In fact, Stalin hoped that fear of such hostilities would induce France to force a reversal of the Anglo-American initiative.[202]

But Truman, Marshall, and their colleagues worked brilliantly to reassure their European allies. Believing that their own initiatives were critical to rebuilding Western Europe and restoring hope in democratic capitalism, they would not back off. Calculating that Stalin would not shoot down American planes and risk war, they decided to airlift supplies to Berlin. Understanding that they were asking their friends in Western Europe to take grave risks, Truman and Marshall acted to allay their fears: Marshall made it clear that U.S. troops would stay in Germany indefinitely, that Washington would provide military aid to France, and that emergency war planning would begin in earnest. More important, he and President Truman decided that the United States would join an alliance of likeminded democratic nations in the North Atlantic region, an alliance designed to deter Soviet aggression and provide reassurance against the Germans.

For some time British foreign secretary Ernest Bevin had been pressing the Americans to sign a North Atlantic treaty that would guarantee peace and security in the Old World. For 150 years, the United States had eschewed "entangling" alliances, and neither the public nor the Congress was demanding a rupture with this tradition. But Truman and Marshall knew they had to satisfy their European friends and guarantee their security. They knew they were asking the French and other Europeans to incur risks that their electorates might not support. The peoples of Europe, after all, yearned for peace and stability, not new crises and new confrontations. If American leaders were asking them to comply with American initiatives that might provoke a Soviet attack in the short run or spur German revanchism in the long run, the United States had to assume unprecedented risks and make unprecedented sacrifices.[203]

By responding to British overtures and French pleas, Truman and his advisers were demonstrating a capacity to empathize with allies in ways that

Stalin could never emulate. But Allied pressures did not motivate U.S. actions. Fear and opportunity lay behind American actions: fear that the Soviets might otherwise gain control of much of Eurasia without war unless the United States went on the offensive, and opportunity in knowing that the United States still had the power and wealth to defeat communism, contain Soviet power, and revive democratic capitalism. Once these beliefs prevailed in Washington policymaking circles, prospective allies were able to exert leverage in Europe and beyond.[204] Very soon thereafter, Truman and his advisers decided to support France in its war against communist-led insurgents in Indochina. The struggle for the soul of mankind was already assuming global dimensions.

Ideology, Personality, and the International System

Truman and Stalin became locked in a worldwide struggle, yet the shape of the struggle was not predetermined. Initially, both men saw reason to collaborate with their ideological adversaries. Both men grasped that national self-interest could be served through cooperative arrangements. As much as each leader preferred a world ordered along lines of either democratic capitalism or communism, neither initially believed that postwar reconversion, reconstruction, or security necessitated confrontation. Indeed, both men had reason to believe and did think that immediate goals could be served by containing competition and modulating conflict.

But the Cold War came, and it engulfed the world. Why?

Truman and Stalin could and did articulate the reasons for national self-restraint. They could and did warn friends and potential allies not to fuel the suspicions of sensitive and powerful adversaries. But they could not control their own fears and instincts, their passions and aspirations. The structure of the international system and their ideological mind-sets overcame their initial desire to sustain their nations' collaboration.

The condition of the international system engendered fears and opportunities. At the end of the war, international society was astir with demoralized peoples yearning for a better future after decades of depression, war, genocide, and forced migration. In the center of Europe and in northeast Asia the defeat of Germany and Japan left huge vacuums of power. In time—and not a very long time, contemporaries assumed—the occupations would end and the Germans and Japanese would reconstitute their governments and political economies. They would then decide how they would configure themselves in the international system, but their future trajectory was a huge, unsettling question mark. Elsewhere in the world—in Asia, Africa, and the Middle East—local leaders and indigenous elites felt emboldened to seek independence as they witnessed their colonial masters' strength erode. They were inspired by the rhetoric of freedom and the affirmations of the principle of national self-determination. They wanted to modernize their countries, overcome the humiliations of dependency, and extinguish the misery that came with poverty. Would they choose free enterprise and liberal democracy, or planned economies and the dictatorship of the proletariat?

Stalin and Truman had to make sense of these realities, to integrate them into belief systems that comported with their rational calculations of national self-interest, the exigencies of domestic politics, and the aspirations and sensibilities of potential friends and clients. They were agents of change and shapers of international history. But they were enveloped by structure and belief.

Stalin had an immense task of reconstruction ahead within the Soviet Union and confronted huge uncertainties abroad. Germany and Japan were defeated, but they would recover, as they had before, and they would have to be dealt with. Britain and America had been partners in the war, but they were also potential rivals and they could not be trusted. If there were challenges, there were also opportunities. Soviet armies were spread across Eastern Europe and parts of northeast Asia. Stalin had a unique opportunity to secure his borders and control Russia's periphery for the indefinite future. Free elections in many of the nations occupied by the Red Army would, he knew, bring in anti-Soviet governments. Why permit them? Yet free elections in Western Europe and self-determination in the colonial world offered considerable advantages.

Stalin had to balance incentives to cooperate and temptations to compete. More than anything else Stalin wanted to protect Soviet Russia against the revival of German and, secondarily, Japanese power, goals mandated by tradition and experience, by strategic necessity and national revenge. After World War II, no Russian or Soviet leader could forsake the opportunity to control the periphery and to shape developments in Germany and Japan. The international landscape was permissive. No nation existed that could contain Russian expansion; the vacuums could be filled to secure long-term ambitions.

Marxist-Leninist thinking lurked in Stalin's actions. Cooperation with capitalist countries might be possible, indeed desirable, at least in the short term, but it was not likely to endure. Capitalist wars might engulf the U.S.S.R., as had just occurred, or, more likely, capitalists might again seek to crush the Bolshevik experiment. Even while he confided to Polish communists that he was not ruling out agreement with the United States, Stalin believed, not without cause, that Washington was seeking to use its atomic monopoly "to intimidate us and force us to yield in contentious issues concerning Japan, the Balkans, and reparations." Likewise, he thought the United States was trying to maneuver its way into Eastern Europe and was hoping to divide Russia from its newfound allies in Poland, Romania, Bulgaria, and Yugoslavia. Beware of this, he told Polish leaders.[205]

Suspicion pulsated through all his transactions. Capitalists would trick, deceive, and try to crush communists. Don't accept the invitation to go to London, he warned his Polish comrades in 1945. "I assure you they are not inviting you for a good purpose. . . . There is a group of complete rascals and ruthless murderers in the Intelligence service who would fulfill any order given to them."[206] Marxist-Leninist thinking about the world inclined Stalin to exaggerate the dangers both of American atomic diplomacy and of Anglo-American espionage, which was occurring in the Soviet sphere of influence in Eastern Europe and even within Soviet Russia's western borderlands. Knowing the magnitude of discontent and the possibilities for widespread unrest, Stalin let his Bolshevik mentality and personal paranoia take over. He accepted the division of Europe into two camps as soon as he was convinced that the Americans were on the offensive, as they seemed to be when they announced the Truman Doctrine, articulated a program for European recovery, and orchestrated plans for the revival of the economies of Germany and Japan. Marxist-Leninist theory provided Stalin with no blueprint for a cold war, but it did give an explanation for the actions of capitalist adversaries and did outline a vision of endless possibilities for communist advancement in the third world.

Truman could not but fear, and he, too, had to act, although he did not seek a cold war. Stalin might not be seizing every opportunity to expand, as intelligence analysts repeatedly pointed out, and might be smart enough to back down when resisted, but he made enough aggressive moves to intensify Truman's anxieties. Just a few years before, other totalitarian foes had made menacing signs and then, unchecked, had declared war on the United States and dared to conquer much of the world. Why wait to take action, Truman thought, when America's wealth and power enabled it to act wisely and swiftly, if provocatively, to promote Europe's recovery, coopt western Germany and Japan, lift morale among dispirited peoples, and ignite hope in free-enterprise democracy?

Truman was a straightforward man and saw things in black and white. What he saw now was the incipient rise of another totalitarian power with an expansionist ideology. He was motivated not by Stalin's brutality—indeed he rarely talked about it—but by the challenge he saw to America's way of life. Our foreign policy, he said, "is the outward expression of the democratic faith we profess."[207]

Inaction or retreat meant that the American way of life would be endangered not simply abroad, but also at home. It meant that prospective allies would be abandoned and their resources and manpower relinquished to a potential adversary. Should this happen, Truman warned, "it would impose upon us a much higher level of mobilization than we have today. It would require a stringent and comprehensive system of allocation and rationing in order to husband our smaller resources. It would require us to become a garrison state, and to impose upon ourselves a system of centralized regimentation unlike anything we have ever known."[208] The president understood that the distribution of power in the international system had immense ramifications for democratic capitalism in the United States.

The structure of the international system intersected with the beliefs of human agents to produce the Cold War. Truman wanted to be sure that power centers such as Western Europe, West Germany, and Japan were kept out of Stalin's grasp. But these efforts had to be supplemented with additional initiatives. As Stalin turned eastward and southward in accord with Marxist-Leninist thinking about opportunities for communist advancement, Truman and his advisers realized that the sources of raw materials, investment earnings, and markets of the industrialized democracies in the third world had to be preserved. "Curiously enough," Kennan wrote to Secretary of State Marshall in December 1948, "the most crucial issue of the moment in our struggle with the Kremlin is probably the problem of Indonesia."[209]

A world in turmoil, where decolonization and revolutionary nationalism were embedded realities, meant that the Cold War could not be contained in Europe and northeast Asia. The lure of future victories in distant lands tempted Stalin; the fear of losses there agonized U.S. officials. In their very first national security strategy statement, approved by the president in December 1948, Truman's advisers explained their thinking: Soviet domination of Eurasia, they said, "whether achieved by armed aggression or by political and subversive means, would be strategically and politically unacceptable to the United States."[210]

Believing that "Communist ideology and Soviet behavior clearly demonstrate that the ultimate objective of the USSR is the domination of the world," Truman and his aides agreed that containment would not suffice. Their first objective, they said, was "to reduce the power and influence of the USSR to limits which no longer constitute a threat to the peace, national independence and stability of the world family of nations." Their second goal was "to bring about a basic change in the conduct of international relations by the government in power in Russia."[211]

In 1948, Stalin and Truman set forth the visions and the ambitions that would drive their nations for the next forty years. They could not do otherwise in an international order that engendered so much fear and so much opportunity.

II

THE CHANCE
FOR PEACE, 1953–54

Malenkov and Eisenhower

Stalin's Death

On 1 March 1953, at his dacha outside of Moscow, Stalin did not appear at his customary midday time. His servants and bodyguards grew worried as the hours passed and not a sound was heard. They did not dare enter his quarters without being summoned. At 6:30 p.m. a light went on in Stalin's room and they breathed a sigh of relief, but then nothing more was heard. The hours ticked away. Anxiety rose. At 11:00 p.m., after a nervous discussion, one of the guards gathered the day's mail and walked to a small dining area where Stalin often slept on a tiny cot. He found the aged dictator lying on the carpet in pajama pants and a white undershirt. His pants were wet with urine. He was barely conscious. When he saw the guard, Stalin weakly raised his hand but could not speak. "His eyes expressed horror and fear and were full of pleading." His servants lifted him onto a sofa. They were terrified.[1]

Too frightened to telephone for medical care because Stalin had recently charged his doctors with plotting to kill the Kremlin's top leaders, they tried to contact Lavrenti Beria, head of the secret police, and Georgi Malenkov,

Stalin's principal lieutenant. It was nighttime, and Beria could not be found. He was carousing somewhere in Moscow with his latest mistress. Malenkov would not do anything without Beria. So more time elapsed. Nobody would call the doctors unless Beria approved. Finally, Beria, plainly drunk, emerged, and he and Malenkov drove to the dacha together. Malenkov removed his new shoes so they would not squeak as the two men approached their now unconscious boss. Seeing him asleep and snoring on the sofa, Beria pretended that nothing was wrong. "What do you mean . . . starting a panic?" he shouted at a guard.[2]

As Stalin lay dying, still without medical care, Beria and Malenkov drove back to the Kremlin early in the morning of 2 March and met with Nikita Khrushchev, Moscow boss of the Communist Party, and Nikolai Bulganin, deputy chair of the Council of Ministers and former civilian head of the armed forces. We do not know what they said to one another, but they probably began to discuss the division of power in the absence of Stalin. Beria, Malenkov, and Khrushchev all had reason to believe that Stalin had been intending to dismiss them. Recently, he had talked many times about aging comrades not living up to his expectations. Beria felt certain that he would be not simply dismissed but killed. His exultation at the turn of events was clear to his comrades as they drove back to Stalin's dacha, arriving around 9:00 a.m.

Now they summoned doctors. The physicians were new—Stalin's usual doctors were in prison—and did not know anything about the health of their fallen leader; they trembled as they scrambled to assess his condition, then applied leeches behind his ears and cold compresses to his head. Of course, nothing much could be done, as Stalin had suffered a cerebral arterial hemorrhage. As they labored, Beria harangued them, saying they would be held accountable if their leader died. Stalin's daughter and son, Svetlana and Vasili, arrived, as did other leading members of Stalin's entourage.

As his lieutenants approached his bedside, Stalin opened his eyes and looked at them one by one. V. M. Molotov, former president and foreign minister, whose wife was then in jail, had tears streaming down his cheeks. So did many of the others. Kliment Voroshilov, one of Stalin's oldest associates, implored, "Comrade Stalin, we're here, your loyal friends and comrades. How do you feel, dear friend?" Stalin stirred, his face "contorted," but said nothing.[3]

Beria went back and forth from the dacha to the Kremlin. All his comrades sensed that he was taking charge. He was clever, determined, audacious, experienced, and defiant. He had run the secret police and the Gulag. After the war, he had managed the vast project to develop the atomic bomb. He was also brutal, signing the lists that sent men to their deaths, engaging in torture, seizing women off the streets and raping them. Beria knew that Stalin in recent months had wanted to blame him for the crimes of his regime. Thinking that Stalin might have left a last testament, as Lenin had done, Beria used one of his quick visits to the Kremlin to search Stalin's office and safe, probably taking incriminating documents with him. He then returned to the dacha. When Stalin opened his eyes again, Beria slipped to his knees and kissed his leader's hand, displaying loyalty and uttering praise. But when Stalin finally died at 9:50 a.m., on 5 March, with his housekeeper sobbing on his chest, Beria immediately looked at Malenkov and snapped, "Let's go."[4] Off to the Kremlin they drove, eager to finish preparations for the government's and the party's transition.

During their conversations at the dacha, Beria, Malenkov, Khrushchev, Bulganin, and several of Stalin's other top lieutenants agreed that Malenkov would become chair of the Council of Ministers. Beria, Molotov, Bulganin, and Lazar Kaganovich would be first deputies. Malenkov also would head the party, while Khrushchev would step down as Moscow party chief and focus on his work at the party's Central Committee. The Ministry of State Security would be integrated into the Ministry of Internal Affairs, with Beria at its head. Bulganin would become defense minister, Molotov foreign minister, and Anastas Mikoyan trade minister. The Presidium was shrunk, eliminating the newcomers whom Stalin had been promoting at the old oligarchs' expense. They assured one another that the new leadership would be collegial and collective. Yet they all knew that Beria was trying to take charge. Molotov sat at the key meeting "silent and aloof." Khrushchev muttered to his friend Bulganin that Beria would destroy them if they were not careful.[5]

Soviet citizens knew little of Stalin's condition until hours before he died. Then there was a massive public display of grief. People were shocked. They did not know what would happen next. "People roamed the streets," wrote Andrei Sakharov, the physicist who became father of the Soviet hydrogen bomb and one of the country's most famous and distinguished dissidents. They were "distraught and confused, with funeral music constantly sounding in the background."[6] Across the country, "the crowds began to gather in the squares. At first they were silent, listening to the radio news on crackling loudspeakers. Men and women wept, their shock giving way to bereavement and confusion. The crowds became hysterical. Mass demonstrations would continue until the day of the funeral, and in several cities . . . hundreds of people were crushed."[7]

People felt vulnerable. They were "worried about a general collapse, internecine strife, another wave of mass repressions, even civil war." They were not unaware of Stalin's crimes. They knew that life was bleak and the future would be harsh. But they believed Stalin had been leading them toward the construction of a new civilization based on social justice. "In the face of all I had seen," Sakharov wrote in his memoir, "I still believed that the Soviet state represented a breakthrough into the future, a prototype (though not as yet a fully realized one) for all other countries to imitate. That shows the hypnotic power of mass ideology."[8]

Soviet citizens had been convinced that the hardships they had endured through collectivization, the purges, and World War II were for a worthy cause. In the struggle for the soul of mankind, they represented the future, modernity. "Being modern was being on the road to communism, dealing with problems rationally and quantitatively, eschewing religious beliefs, extolling the constructions of dams, factories, and hydroelectric projects, measuring progress by material indicators, leaving ethnic and national identities behind, and treating history as just an interesting story."[9] Stalin had helped them to construct a new identity, a "new Soviet man," a new society based on the triumph of the proletariat, and a new international order dedicated to peace and the elimination of capitalist conflict and recurrent war. After all that had been endured, Sakharov continued, "the state, the nation, and the ideals of communism remained intact for me."[10]

Soviet citizens felt they had lost a great leader. In her scathing memoir of her father, Svetlana Alliluyeva nevertheless acknowledges that Stalin knew how "to appeal to the 'simple people' and their 'national ways,' loading his speeches with folksy sayings, wearing his trousers tucked inside his boots, the way Russian workers had done before the Revolution." For "the semi-literate, semi-blind peasants and workers, to whom his power offered a chance of becoming engineers, party bureaucrats, generals, state ministers, ambassadors (speaking only Russian), [for] those who had 'tended calves' in their youth, . . . [for] all these he became for a long time 'their very own.' "[11] They lamented his death, "the greatest of the great men of all times and nations. . . . Our party has been orphaned," grieved the workers of a Moscow rubber factory, "the Soviet people have been orphaned, the working people of the whole world have been orphaned."[12]

The new collective leadership felt unease. They had revered, feared, and hated Stalin, but they did not know how they would cope without him. "How are we going to live and work without Stalin?" Khrushchev wondered.[13] Before his death, Stalin had mocked them, saying, "You'll see, when I'm gone the imperialistic powers will wring your necks like chickens."[14] Malenkov, Beria, Khrushchev, and their colleagues knew they lacked legitimacy and recognized they had formidable adversaries abroad. They also realized that beneath the outpouring of sorrow among Soviet citizens, there was a simmering discontent, a yearning for the utopia that had been promised them and for which they had suffered so much—and if not a utopia, then at least a relaxation of the terror they felt and an improvement in the conditions of their daily lives.

Stalin's heirs agreed that Malenkov would be their official leader, the public face of their collective rule. But Beria was the dynamo behind Malenkov, though, being a Georgian and a police chief, he could not officially succeed Stalin. At a time when the national identity increasingly revolved around the sense of Russian greatness, it was impossible to contemplate another Georgian ruling the Soviet Union. Beria knew this, and he labored closely with Malenkov, with whom he had collaborated for many years. "My father proposed that Malenkov be Prime Minister," writes Beria's son, "because he thought he would be able to control him totally."[15] But in these first days and weeks after Stalin's death, Malenkov, Khrushchev, Beria, and Molotov appeared to agree on what needed to be done.[16]

They knew they had to calm the atmosphere and gain trust and legitimacy. They knew the U.S.S.R. was in terrible shape economically. They wanted to humanize communism, making it work for the people. Almost immediately they declared an amnesty that freed more than a million people from the prisons and labor camps of the Gulag. They renounced Stalin's old accusation of a doctors' plot, acknowledged it was a fabrication, and released the physicians from prison. They reduced the size of the security apparatus, prohibited the routine use of physical torture, and rationalized the economic functions of the forced labor camps. They decided to boost the production of consumer goods. They agreed that more power should be moved from the party apparatus to government institutions, which meant that the Politburo, still the supreme authority in the land, would have somewhat less influence and the Council of Ministers more.[17]

They grasped that to accomplish their domestic priorities they needed to relax tensions with the West. It was essential "to end the confrontation with the outside world," Beria said, in order to improve the standard of living of the Soviet people.[18] He was not alone in thinking this way. "We had doubts about Stalin's foreign policy," Khrushchev recollected. "He overemphasized the importance of military might for one thing, and consequently put too much faith in our armed forces. He lived in terror of an enemy attack."[19]

Yet Malenkov, Beria, and Khrushchev were true believers, imprisoned by their dependence on totalitarian methods and communist axioms, the most conspicuous of which was their fundamental conviction in the hostility of the capitalist West. They felt encircled, beleaguered. "The United States," Khrushchev said, conducted "an arrogant and aggressive policy towards us." The Americans never missed a chance to demonstrate their superiority, he thought. "Our country was literally a great big target range for American bombers operating from airfields in Norway, Germany, Italy, South Korea, and Japan."[20]

Yet the Kremlin's new masters sought to build a bridge. Beria, writes his son, "wanted to make clear to the Westerners that the USSR did not want confrontation and was abandoning its previous policy." Malenkov and Khrushchev shared the same intentions but, like Beria, feared the Americans would exploit their weakness, vulnerabilities, and divisions. They did not want to appear as supplicants. Why should they have, since they represented a superior civilization? But they knew they needed to relax tensions in order to focus on domestic priorities, redefine their goals, and buttress their values. Détente was essential to move their utopia forward. Coexistence and peace would be their mantras.[21]

All this was apparent at the funeral orations on 9 March. Malenkov, Beria, and Molotov spoke. The country had suffered "a most grievous, irreparable loss," Malenkov began. Stalin would never be forgotten. His name "justly takes its place beside the names of the greatest men in the history of mankind—Marx, Engels, and Lenin. . . . Comrade Stalin brought our country to a world historic victory of socialism, which ensured for the first time in many thousands of years of existence of human society the abolition of the exploitation of man by man." Stalin had understood that "the strength and might of our state are the most important conditions for the successful construction of Communism in our country. It is our sacred duty," Malenkov went on, "to continue to strengthen our great Socialist state."

Stalin's greatness, Malenkov also stressed, inhered in his construction of a multinational state. He overcame the economic and cultural backwardness of formerly oppressed peoples and brought them together "into one brotherly family . . . forging friendship among nations." Another sacred duty of Stalin's heirs, therefore, was to continue to breed friendship among the many peoples of the nation.

Malenkov then laid out the agenda for the future, underscoring continuities but intimating the possibility of new directions. The Communist Party remained the vanguard of the proletariat. It had to be strengthened and its unity preserved. The "unbreakable" bonds between party and people had to be fortified. All workers must remain vigilant in the "struggle against internal, inner, and the foreign enemies." The party, meanwhile, had to lead the country forward, ensuring that the "Socialist motherland" flourished. "We must develop by every means our Socialist industry, the bulwark of might and strength of our country. We must develop by every means our collective farm order. . . . We must strengthen the union of workers and collective-farm peasantry."

But then Malenkov hinted at something new: "In the internal sphere, our main task is ceaselessly to strive for further improvement in the material welfare of the workers, the collective farmers, the intelligentsia, and all the Soviet people. It is a law for our party and government to implement the duty of ceaselessly striving for the good of the people for the maximum satisfaction of its material and cultural needs."

Turning to foreign policy, Malenkov uttered the traditional platitudes, yet there, too, he hinted at a new direction. Fraternal ties had to be nurtured within the camp of peace, democracy, and socialism, he said, a camp that included the countries of Eastern Europe, the German Democratic Republic (East Germany), the Mongolian People's Republic, and "the great Chinese people." The Soviet Union had to support not only the "heroic Korean people" defending their homeland but also the Vietnamese people who were fighting for freedom and national independence. But, overall, the Soviet mission was to further the cause of peace, Malenkov emphasized. The U.S.S.R. would advance "a policy of international cooperation and development of business relations with all countries; a policy based on the Lenin-Stalin premise of the possibility of the prolonged coexistence and peaceful competition of two different systems, capitalist and Socialist. . . . We are true servants of the people, and the people want peace and hate war." The government wanted to prevent "the spilling of blood of millions of people and to ensure peaceful construction of a happy life. . . . The Communist Party and the Soviet Government insist that a policy of peace between nations is the only correct policy which corresponds with the interests of all nations."

Lest any listener forget that the mission of the Soviet Union was to configure a new way of life, Malenkov concluded with a peroration:

> Toilers of the Soviet Union . . . we have all that is necessary to build a Communist society. With firm faith in their limitless forces and possibilities, the Soviet people will proceed with the great cause of building Communism. There are no forces in the world which can stop the forward movement of Soviet society toward Communism.
>
> Farewell, our teacher and leader, our dear friend, our Comrade Stalin!
>
> Forward, along the road toward the complete victory of the great cause of Lenin and Stalin.[22]

Beria and Molotov reiterated Malenkov's key points, the commitment to peace and "a policy of international cooperation and development of business relations with all countries on the basis of reciprocity."[23]

Deeds followed words. Almost immediately, the Kremlin moved secretly to relax international tensions. Malenkov and the Council of Ministers sent instructions to China and North Korea to negotiate constructively in pursuit of an armistice agreement in Korea, where they had been locked in a dangerous, albeit limited, war for three years with American-led U.N. troops assisting South Korea.[24] Then, in a speech on 15 March at a meeting of the Supreme Soviet, Malenkov declared even more forcefully: "At the present time there is no disputed or unresolved question that cannot be settled

Funeral of Joseph Stalin, 1953. From left to right: Khrushchev, Beria, Malenkov, Bulganin, Voroshilov, Kaganovich. Stalin's anxious successors vowed to collaborate with one another and to seek peaceful coexistence with their foreign adversaries.

peacefully by mutual agreement of the interested countries. This applies to our relations with all states, including the United States of America."[25]

In the initial days after Stalin's death, the new leaders sought to present a united front. They distrusted Beria yet concurred with his wish to initiate domestic reforms, spur the production of consumer goods, and ease totalitarian controls. The challenge was to achieve these goals without having the regime unravel. "We were scared, really scared," Khrushchev remembered. "We were afraid the thaw might unleash a flood, which we wouldn't be able to control and which would drown us."[26] Malenkov was as fearful as Khrushchev. "To the best of my knowledge," wrote his son-in-law, "Malenkov had but one real interest in life and that was power." He did not want it to slip away.[27]

Malenkov was a shrewd and knowledgeable party man. Subsequently, after Khrushchev outmaneuvered him, Malenkov's historic role was discounted

and his talents trivialized. Beria called him a billy goat, Khrushchev said he was an "errand boy," and Molotov scorned his indifference to theoretical matters.[28] But Stalin had trusted him and promoted him to higher and higher party positions in the late 1920s and 1930s. Malenkov managed people skillfully and worked prodigiously hard. He could assimilate massive amounts of information and execute orders efficiently. He was not well educated, but he had studied the Marxist-Leninist liturgy and adroitly used ideology to support almost any position. Despite his sociable demeanor and unimpressive appearance—he was short and fat, "pear-shaped, with narrow shoulders and a big bottom"—he could be tough-minded and ruthless. In the late 1930s he had worked with Beria and the security apparatus to arrest alleged traitors. He was often present when prisoners were interrogated and tortured. "When Stalin orders him to get rid of a man, he does away with a thousand so as to be more sure," Beria told his son. Stalin knew he could rely on Malenkov's absolute loyalty and consummate efficiency. During the war, Stalin had appointed him to the State Defense Committee, which coordinated all civil and

Soviet premier Georgi Malenkov, 1953. He was a shrewd and
knowledgeable party man who sought to relax tensions without
relaxing Soviet vigilance and hopes for revolutionary gains.

military power. Malenkov administered the aircraft industry and in 1943 assumed responsibility for the economic reconstruction of areas recaptured from the Germans. After the war, he oversaw the shipment of German reparations and was a leader in both the party secretariat and the Council of Ministers. Although openly humiliated by Stalin and briefly demoted in 1946, Malenkov regained his ascendancy in the party and the government and formed skillful alliances with Beria and several other party oligarchs. Stalin assigned him the leading role in the 1952 party Congress. When Stalin died, Malenkov was the heir apparent.[29]

 As chairman of the Council of Ministers and leader of the Communist Party, Malenkov hoped to preserve harmony among the oligarchs while fashioning a more orderly government. Widely seen as a close colleague of Beria's, he was actually far more friendly with Khrushchev. Almost immediately after Stalin's death, Malenkov assented to relinquish key party duties to Khrushchev, whom he trusted and underestimated. Meanwhile, he spent many hours every day with Beria, making decisions and acting hastily to garner respect and legitimacy. He wanted to improve the quality of life in the Soviet Union and make the system work. To do this, he needed peace and a relaxation of international tensions.[30] He hoped the United States would give peace a chance.

Eisenhower's Response

Stalin's death posed a dilemma and an opportunity to the new administration in Washington. Little planning had been done in anticipation of the Soviet leader's passing, but Dwight David Eisenhower, the newly elected president of the United States, had given much thought to the problems of national security, as had his newly appointed secretary of state, John Foster Dulles. Indeed, few men since the Founding Fathers of the country had come to office with more experience or more knowledge of the problems of strategy, diplomacy, and war.

Eisenhower had won a smashing victory in the 1952 presidential election. He was one of the great heroes of World War II, the general who planned the Normandy invasion and defeated Hitler's armies on the Western front. Skilled in diplomacy, a master of human relations, he knew how to coax, cajole, compromise, and achieve fundamental goals. He was an able leader of men: determined, disciplined, organized, supportive, and self-confident. By nature an optimist, with a charming smile and a warm personality, the new president was also shrewd, smart, determined, and ambitious. Publicly, he often talked awkwardly and elliptically. Privately, he thought analytically and wrote lucidly. He could lose his temper, but he was usually discreet and tactful. He was adept at manipulating people, winning their trust and affection. He ceaselessly sent birthday cards to scores of friends and rarely lost an opportunity to offer praise or say something gracious.[31]

Eisenhower had grown up in Abilene, Kansas, at the turn of the century. Values and religion, history and ideas, were important to him. Abilene was small-town America, just one generation removed from its heyday as a cattle

town on the frontier. Life was quiet, uneventful, and hard. Ike's father
worked in a creamery owned by the River Brotherhood, a Mennonite religious sect. The Eisenhowers were not poor, but their surroundings were
modest. Ike was taught to be independent, hardworking, and frugal. He
could shape his own future if he got a good education and exploited the
opportunities that came his way. "Ambition without arrogance," he later recalled, "was quietly instilled in us."[32]

So was religion. Ike's parents believed in prayer and a merciful God. His
mother memorized large portions of the Bible. Ike's values were rooted in religion and democracy. Men and women were created in the image of God.
They had a duty to develop their intrinsic worthiness. In America, they were
free to do so. The United States encompassed a way of life based on human
freedom, individual self-worth, voluntary cooperation, and free enterprise. "I
believe fanatically in the American form of democracy," he wrote to his childhood friend Everett "Swede" Hazlett in 1947, "a system that recognizes and
protects the rights of the individual and that ascribes to the individual a dignity accruing to him because of his creation in the image of a supreme being
which rests upon the conviction that only through a system of free enterprise
can this type of democracy be preserved."[33]

Eisenhower had not expected to follow a military career. But a friend told
him about an opportunity to enter the U.S. Naval Academy at Annapolis.
Turned down because he was too old (twenty), he decided to apply to West
Point, which admitted applicants until they were twenty-two. He did well,
but not exceptionally, at the military academy and graduated in 1915. Despite
his desires, he was not sent overseas during World War I, but he performed
admirably in his wartime duties on the home front, mostly training officers
and organizing a tank battalion. During the 1920s and 1930s he slowly
climbed the military ladder and impressed many of his superior officers. He
performed brilliantly at the Command and General Staff College at Fort
Leavenworth and served ably under General Douglas MacArthur in the
Philippines in the late 1930s. When war erupted in September 1939, Eisenhower returned to the United States and rose rapidly as the U.S. Army
expanded. Immediately after the attack on Pearl Harbor, General George
Marshall, army chief of staff, asked Eisenhower to join his strategic planning
staff. Ike greatly impressed Marshall, who subsequently asked him to assume
command of the European Theater of Operations. Successively, Ike oversaw

the campaigns of Allied forces in North Africa, Italy, and Europe. By the end of the war, he was a celebrated military commander and one of the most famous people in the world. After victory, he served as army chief of staff, resigning in 1948 to assume the presidency of Columbia University. Responding to President Truman's personal request in late 1950, Eisenhower left Columbia and became supreme commander of NATO forces in Europe during the Korean War.[34]

When he ran successfully for the presidency in 1952, Eisenhower garnered the trust of the American people with his promise to extricate them from the hot war in Korea and to lead them in the Cold War against the forces of totalitarianism spearheaded by the Kremlin. Although Truman's policies of reconstructing Europe, integrating Western Germany, and joining NATO had thwarted the immediate Soviet threat in the Old World, communism was on the march in Asia. Mao Zedong and his comrades had seized power in China in October 1949 and were encouraging revolution throughout Asia, especially in Indochina. In June 1950, Kim Il Sung's communist government in North Korea had attacked South Korea, a move that Truman had countered by deploying U.S. troops to stop the aggression and getting U.N. backing. But when Americans went on the offensive, crossing the thirty-eighth parallel that marked the divide between North and South Korea, and tried to install U.S. power along China's borders, Mao intervened. Thereafter, the war in Korea stalemated, casualties mounted, and the American people grew disillusioned. Truman launched a mammoth rearmament program, developed the hydrogen bomb, and reconfirmed the nation's strategic goals in the most famous national security paper of the entire Cold War, NSC-68.[35]

While the country was mired in a protracted, limited war, on the home front, morale eroded. Senator Joseph McCarthy and his growing number of followers assailed the Truman administration and blamed its setbacks on communist infiltrators inside the American government. How else could one explain the successful testing of a Soviet atomic bomb in August 1949? How else could one explain the Chinese communist seizure of power in Beijing that same year? Traitors at home had to be imprisoned and communists abroad had to be vanquished, even if it meant using nuclear weapons. Lives and resources should not be squandered on a sideshow in Korea when the real menace resided in Beijing and Moscow. Eisenhower, Americans believed, was the man who could cope with the dilemmas of the Cold War and the nuclear age. Eisenhower, they believed, understood the meaning of the Cold War and could design a strategy to win it.[36]

In his inaugural address, Eisenhower explained his shared understanding of the Cold War:

> We sense with all our faculties that forces of good and evil are massed and armed and opposed as rarely before in history.
>
> In the presence of God, we are called as a people to give testimony in the sight of the world to our faith that the future shall belong to the free.
>
> Freedom is pitted against slavery; lightness against the dark.
>
> Conceiving the defense of freedom, like freedom itself, to be one and indivisible, we hold all continents and peoples in equal regard and honor. We reject any insinuation that one race or another, one people or another, is in any sense inferior or expendable.[37]

Ike believed that "the purpose of America [was] to defend a way of life rather than merely to defend property, territory, houses, or lives."[38] The "way of life" meant personal liberty, free enterprise, and equality of opportunity—all "a gift from the Almighty." Religious faith, he said, was "the essential foundation stone of free government."[39]

The Soviet Union challenged this American way of life. Statism and authoritarianism challenged democracy and freedom. This was an ideological conflict, not a military contest. In this struggle, Eisenhower believed, "The greatest weapon that freedom has against the Communist dictatorship is its ultimate appeal to the soul and spirit of man." Americans had to have faith that as they built the military strength of their country, "the virtues and appeal" of their system would "triumph over the desperate doctrines of Communism."[40]

Eisenhower selected a secretary of state who shared his views. John Foster Dulles was the son of a minister and the grandson and nephew of two secretaries of state. He had been educated at Princeton, studied in Europe, and earned his law degree at George Washington University. Through his father's and grandfather's contacts, he had joined one of New York's most prestigious law firms, Sullivan and Cromwell. He interrupted his law career to work for his uncle, Secretary of State Robert Lansing, served in the Wilson administration's Russian Bureau, and helped to orchestrate the initial American effort to defeat the Bolsheviks after the revolution of 1917. Before long, however, he turned his attention to the problem of German reparations, serving as legal adviser to the U.S. delegation to the Paris Peace Conference in 1919. Dulles struggled to limit French and British efforts to extract huge reparations from a defeated Germany. Their quest for vengeance, he believed, would ruin Wilson's peacemaking efforts. This view shaped his thinking for the rest of his life, even as he returned to Wall Street to make a fortune.[41]

Dulles is often caricatured as a moralist in international relations, but he was more complicated. His views were an amalgam of idealism and realism. He believed that Christians should translate their views into realities. But he possessed a realistic view of things, at the center of which was the corporate internationalist view that America's free enterprise system was inextricably connected with and dependent upon the world economy, a view that President Eisenhower also held. Like his new boss, Dulles also believed that the competition with the Kremlin was essentially ideological. And like Ike, Dulles was not an early cold warrior, but his fears and anxieties gradually mounted during the early postwar years.[42]

A Republican internationalist, Dulles had worked for Truman and Acheson to muster bipartisan support for their containment policies, but he grew disillusioned with them, partly out of political expediency and partly out of conviction. The Soviets, he believed, were a more formidable foe than the Democrats realized. The Kremlin shrewdly used the rhetoric of freedom, equality, fraternity, and peace to appeal to aggrieved workers in Europe and Japan. Just as worrisome, the communists used Marxist-Leninist slogans to castigate the West for its imperial exploitation of less-developed nations, portraying themselves as champions of freedom and progress. For people around the globe struggling for independence, the communists appeared dynamic, progressive visionaries, offering a future that was dramatically better than the present. The United States, Dulles worried, had lost its dynamism. "There has been a very definite shift in the balance of power in the world, and that shift has been in favor of Soviet communism." The policy of containment, he declared in 1952, was spiritually bankrupt. More inclined toward pessimism than Eisenhower, Dulles warned that the Cold War would be lost if the United States did not go on the offensive, if it did not seek to "roll back" communism.[43]

When Eisenhower and Dulles took office in January 1953, they wanted to make American foreign policy more vigorous and enhance national security at a lower cost. They believed that Truman and his advisers had been profligate. The real challenge, Ike maintained in one of his campaign speeches, "is to build the defense with wisdom and efficiency. We must achieve both security and solvency. In fact, the foundation of military strength is economic strength. A bankrupt America is more the Soviet goal than an America conquered on the field of battle." For the president, this was not mere rhetoric. He stressed these points time and again at meetings of the National Security Council. "I most firmly believe," Ike wrote his friend (and former ambassador to Great Britain) Lewis Douglas in May 1952, "that the financial solvency and economic soundness of the United States constitute together the first requisite to collective security in the free world. That comes before all else."[44]

Stalin's death provided a chance to recapture the offensive on the cheap.

Eisenhower and Dulles, 1956. They worked closely together to design strategies that would maintain NATO cohesion and thwart Soviet advances in the third world.

At a cabinet meeting on 6 March 1953, the president ridiculed the absence of plans. "We have no plan," he said. "We are not even sure what difference his death makes."[45] But there was considerable agreement among Eisenhower's psychological strategists and intelligence analysts that a great opportunity had arrived. "Our strategic guiding principle, as well as our secret goal," wrote William Morgan, acting head of the Psychological Strategy Board, "should be to do everything to encourage and promote chaos within the USSR."[46]

C. D. Jackson, the president's special assistant for Cold War operations, agreed with Morgan. Jackson was a personal friend of the president's as well as a wartime associate and former senior editor of *Life* magazine. He was eager to use psychological initiatives and covert actions to roll back Soviet power. He summoned outside experts such as political scientist Walt W. Rostow to help imagine what might be done. Stalin's death, Jackson and Rostow believed, had sent an emotional shock through the entire communist world. "Over the next days it constitutes a unique Soviet vulnerability." The United States could seize the overall initiative in the Cold War. The president, Jackson thought, should make a great speech, with diplomatic substance, outlining serious proposals consistent with U.S. national interests. He should call for a new meeting of foreign ministers to discuss key issues, including arms reductions, Germany, Austria, and Korea. "It is fundamental" that the initiative "strike the Russian peoples and the peoples of the Communist bloc, at a moment of emotional indecision and even bewilderment, with a new vision of possibilities."[47]

The State Department had its doubts. By aggressively heightening Cold War pressures, the United States might unintentionally help the Soviet Union's new regime to consolidate its position. "Significant opportunities to exploit Stalin's death by a speech are more likely to appear later on," said Under Secretary of State Walter Bedell Smith, a former general, CIA director, and one of Eisenhower's most trusted wartime aides. Moreover, Smith wrote, a meeting of the four foreign ministers might divide the United States, Britain, and France and set back ratification of the proposed European Defense Community (EDC). Creation of the EDC, as a framework for West German rearmament and the integration of West German forces into a Western European army linked to NATO, had been an overriding priority of the Truman administration, and Eisenhower and Dulles enthusiastically supported it. Nothing should be done, Smith argued, that might further delay French and West German ratification of the EDC.[48]

Jackson's idea for a presidential speech was discussed at a meeting of the National Security Council on 11 March. Jackson and Dulles presented their differing views. But the president was captivated by a proposal designed by the influential political journalist Samuel Lubell, who suggested that Eisenhower propose limits to be set on the amounts that governments could spend on armaments. The aim would be "to bring about the simultaneous demobilization of all the economies of the world, freeing immense resources, which are now being channeled into destructive purposes, into elevating living standards everywhere." The Russian people, Lubell thought, hungered for "better living conditions, for a little more goods in the department stores, for improved housing, for a little relaxation." Ike liked this line of thinking. Participants at the NSC meeting concluded: "Stalin's death presents an opportunity for the assertion of world leadership by President Eisenhower in the interests of security, peace, and a higher standard of living for all peoples." Jackson was instructed to take another crack at drafting a speech.[49]

Initially, U.S. intelligence analysts did not expect the new Kremlin leaders to shift course. Stalin's heirs, they thought, "would emphasize unremitting hostility to the West . . . , the enlargement of the Bloc economic base, and the increase of Bloc military power."[50] Consequently, the president and his advisers were surprised by Malenkov's statements, especially his speech to the Supreme Soviet on 15 March. Meanwhile, Ike fretted that Jackson, Dulles, and Emmet John Hughes, his speechwriter, were having so much difficulty drafting a speech for him. The president, not a little exasperated, wanted the United States to gain the international high ground, to be the champion of world peace. In a frank conversation with Hughes, Ike said he did not want to offer another indictment of the Soviet Union; that would be "asinine." He wanted to say something concrete. The armaments race made no sense. "Where will it lead us? At worst, to atomic warfare. At best, to robbing every people and nation on earth of the fruits of their own toil. . . . The past speaks for itself," Eisenhower continued, "I am interested in the future. Both their government and ours have new men in them. The slate is clean. Now let us begin talking to each other. And let us say what we have got to say so that every person on earth can understand it."[51]

Eisenhower told Hughes that the administration needed to design concrete proposals. If we "don't really have anything to offer, I'm not going to make a speech about it." Let's assume, Ike said, "that Malenkov was a reasonable man with whom we had some serious differences to iron out—we may know he isn't—but let's start with that assumption and talk accordingly." Hughes gently reminded the president that Dulles had serious reservations, and was not interested in exploring new ideas, regarding Korea, for example. Dulles did not expect a settlement of the war, said Hughes, "until we have shown—before all Asia—our clear superiority by giving the Chinese one hell of a licking." Ike snapped: "If Mr. Dulles and all his sophisticated advisers really mean that they can *not* talk peace seriously, then I am in the wrong pew. . . . Now either we cut out all this fooling around and make a serious bid for peace—or we forget the whole thing. . . . After all—I'm responsible for this country's goddam foreign policy. It's my job."[52]

In wanting to assume that there was a serious chance for peace, the president was not alone. The confluence of new leaders in Moscow and Washington could not but ignite discussion of new possibilities. In preparing for Dulles's testimony to Congress, State's policy planners noted that this may be a "pivotal point in history:—accession to leadership within same three months of new chiefs at Moscow and Washington, the two principal power sources in a bi-polar world."[53]

There were unmistakable signs of shifts in Soviet policy, irrefutable indications that Malenkov was probing for diplomatic openings. But Eisenhower's advisers could not agree on what to do or what type of speech should be given. In frustration, Jackson wrote the president on 2 April that for a month

we have given a virtual monopoly to the Soviets over the minds of people all over the world—and in that month, they have moved with vigor and disarming plausibility. . . . They have hammered home the idea that they alone are responsible for peace. They have proposed a Four Power conference on German unification. They have succeeded in cooing so convincingly that shooting down American and British planes is considered an almost minor incident in Europe and the United States.[54]

Officials at all levels of the Eisenhower administration speculated about the magnitude and meaning of the change. "Since the death of Stalin," wrote Carlton Savage of the State Department Policy Planning Staff (PPS), "there have been more Soviet gestures toward the West than at any other similar period."[55] Louis Halle, Savage's colleague on the PPS, wrote:

> No one knows the relative positions, today, of Malenkov, Beria, Molotov, and Bulganin. A struggle for power could manifest itself in the successive temporary ascendancy of rival groups and individuals, none being able to make their ascendancy permanent. Under such circumstances one would expect, in the course of time, a transformation of the Soviet system and Soviet policy until, when stability had at last been achieved, the Soviet state was something quite different from what it had been.[56]

Intelligence analysts worked assiduously to learn more about Malenkov. They had pitifully little information, and what they uncovered was not auspicious. Their information, said the CIA, led to the conclusion "that Malenkov, like Beria and probably Khrushchev (whose biography would be of equal interest), has been during all his adult life engaged in suppressive and terroristic activities against the peoples of the USSR. When enough information is collected it will probably show that he has been an accomplice in heinous crimes against humanity."[57]

Yet Malenkov was doing surprising things. Allen Dulles, director of the CIA and Foster's brother, told the NSC on 8 April that "there were quite shattering departures . . . from the policies of the Stalin regime. The Soviet peace offensive had come much earlier and was being pursued much more systematically than the CIA had expected." Dulles thought the Kremlin's aim was to "lessen the danger of global war." Soviet leaders, he had previously noted, "really BELIEVE this business of their being encircled—it's not true but I think they think it is. And they see no way out, and maybe would welcome one." The Soviets, he thought, did want to derail the EDC and did seek to retard the rearmament program in the United States. While these external policy changes could be seen purely as a change in tactics, not policies, Dulles was more puzzled by the meaning and significance of "the relaxation of domestic pressures." Some Soviet actions, he told the NSC, like the renunciation of the doctors' plot, were "astonishing." Dulles concluded that the succession crisis was not yet over, that "there was obviously deep tension and discontent in the Soviet Union," that the new regime needed a "breathing spell," and that there was "no ground for the belief that there would be any change in the basic hostility of the Soviet Union to the free world."[58]

But Eisenhower took issue with these conclusions. He agreed that "there was no ground to anticipate a basic change in Soviet policy toward the Western powers," but he also said

> there was also no ground for believing that no basic changes in Soviet policy were in the offing. It seemed to the President quite possible that the Soviet leaders may have decided that the time had come when a larger share of the wealth and resources of the Soviet Union must be diverted to civilian use and enjoyment, with the object of raising standards of living for the Soviet people. It was obvious to him, said the President, that discontent was rife in the Soviet Union, and it therefore behooved us to study the problem constantly in an effort to determine whether the Soviets were really changing their outlook, and accordingly whether some kind of modus vivendi might not at long last prove possible.[59]

The question was whether there was a chance for peace, and, if so, how to grasp it. The Soviet ambassador, Georgi Zarubin, invited Charles Bohlen for a talk just before Bohlen left Washington to take charge of the U.S. embassy in Moscow. Zarubin greeted Bohlen warmly, saying it was the obligation of ambassadors to improve bilateral relations. He alluded to positive steps that Moscow was taking in the armistice negotiations in Korea and hoped that progress in Korea could lead in other positive directions.[60]

Yet Ike's advisers remained deeply divided. Jackson simply wanted to exploit the opportunity of Stalin's death to capitalize on Soviet vulnerabilities. Dulles was willing to assent to a presidential speech but did not want Western priorities like the EDC to be compromised or jeopardized. Ike was determined to move ahead. "Damn it," he said to C. D. Jackson when his friend claimed that Kremlin leaders would never be mollified in their global ambitions by talk of schools and hospitals:

I don't know that you're right. I still remember that 4 hour session I had with Stalin. Why damn near all he talked about was "We have to get along with the US because we can't afford not to"—and he talked about all the things they needed, the homes, the food, the technical help. He talked to me about 7 people living in a single room in Moscow just as anxiously as you or I'd talk about an American slum problem. Hell, these boys HAVE to think in material terms—that's all they believe in.[61]

Ike's advisers knew there was deep public support for a peace initiative in the United States.[62] Amid the red scare and the McCarthy onslaught, there was a paradoxical yearning to explore the possibility of new directions. By no means a majority, but nevertheless a good many influential American journalists and newspapers believed that Malenkov might be seeking to change direction and engage the United States in constructive talks. A Gallup poll revealed that 78 percent of Americans supported a meeting between Ike and Malenkov to discuss contentious issues.[63]

No doubt, opinion was swayed by knowledge that Winston Churchill, once again the prime minister of England, was vigorously pushing for a summit meeting with the Russians. In a series of private letters to the president, "my dear Ike," as well as in public speeches, Churchill emphasized the opportunities that had emerged after Stalin's death. "Great hope has arisen in the world," he wrote. We must be cautious, he advised, not to derail the "natural growth of events."[64]

The question was whether the desire for peace could be effectively harnessed. In fact, the deeper question was whether the American administration, even Ike himself, really wanted to relax tensions or to win victories. There were clearly conflicting sensibilities and aspirations, not easily resolvable. Emmet Hughes pointedly asked Dulles whether his intent was to stir revolution and win the Cold War or to nurture East-West negotiations and relax tensions. One could not do both at the same time, Hughes emphasized. But Ike was trying to do just that, to square an impossible circle.[65]

On 16 April, Eisenhower finally delivered his speech to the American Society of Newspaper Editors. He began, "In this spring of 1953 the free world weighs one question above all others: the chance for a just peace for all peoples." At the end of World War II, Ike recalled, Russian soldiers and those of the Western Allies had met in the center of Europe. They were triumphant, joyous. All peoples yearned for peace. But their hopes had been dashed. The "common purpose lasted a minute and perished." The United States chose one direction and the Soviet Union, another. The path chosen by Americans was shaped by a belief in the self-determination of free peoples, their quest for justice and peace, a commitment to international cooperation, and an aversion to armaments. The Kremlin had a different vision, said the president, a vision of security preserved through force, armies, terror, and subversion. "The goal was power superiority at all cost. Security was to be sought by denying it to all others."

Soviet actions prompting Western reactions had led to a spiraling cold war and an arms race. Neither the Soviet Union nor its adversaries benefited. And if the trend continued, the scenarios were bleak. "The worst is atomic war." The best would be "a life of perpetual fear and tension." An arms race would drain the wealth of all peoples and prevent both the Soviet and American systems from achieving "true abundance and happiness for the peoples of this earth. . . . Every gun that is made, every warship launched, every rocket fired signifies, in the final sense, a theft from those who hunger and are not fed, those who are cold and are not clothed. . . . This is not a way of life, in any true sense. Under the cloud of threatening war, it is humanity hanging from a cross of iron."

And then the president beckoned for a better future. "This is one of those times in the affairs of nations when the gravest choices must be made, if there is to be a turning toward a just and lasting peace. . . . The whole world knows that an era ended with the death of Joseph Stalin. . . . Now a new leadership has assumed power in the Soviet Union. Its links to the past, however strong, cannot bind it completely. Its future is, in great part, its own to make." But a new era could evolve only if the Soviet Union demonstrated real deeds in the cause of peace, not rhetoric but concrete actions in Korea, Germany, Austria, and Indochina. If progress on these matters bred trust, "we could proceed concurrently with the next great work—the reduction of the burden of armaments now weighing upon the world." On this issue, the president talked concretely. We could agree, he said, on the limitation of the size of military forces, either by absolute numbers or by agreed international ratios; we could agree to limits on the production of certain strategic materials allocated to military purposes; we could agree to international control of atomic energy to promote its use for peaceful purposes and "to ensure the prohibition of atomic weapons"; we could agree to limits on other weapons of mass destruction. To enforce the agreements, Eisenhower said it was important to configure "a practical system of inspection under the United Nations."

If the United States, the Soviet Union, and their allies succeeded in seizing the opportunity, a new world order could be constructed. Peace could be fortified, said the president, "not by weapons of war but by wheat and by cotton, by milk and by wool, by meat and by timber and by rice. These are words that translate into every language on earth. These are needs that challenge this world in arms." The United States wanted to take the lead, as it had with the Marshall Plan, the president maintained. A substantial portion of the savings achieved by disarmament could be used to fund reconstruction in the underdeveloped areas of the world, "to stimulate profitable and fair world trade, to assist all peoples to know the blessings of productive freedom."

Progress waited upon only one question, Eisenhower declared: "What is the Soviet Union ready to do?" Would the Kremlin use its influence on its allies to bring about a truce in Korea and a genuine peace in Indochina and Asia? Would it allow self-determination in Eastern Europe? Would it agree to arms limits, safeguards, and "stringent U.N. control and inspection?"

Let us seize the chance for peace, Eisenhower concluded. Otherwise, "the judgment of future ages would be harsh and just." He spoke, he said, "without ulterior purpose or political passion, from our calm conviction that the hunger for peace is in the hearts of all peoples—those of Russia and of China no less than our own country." God "created men to enjoy, not destroy, the fruits of the earth and of their own toil. They aspire to this: the lifting, from the backs and from the hearts of men, of their burden of arms and of fears, so that they may find before them a golden age of freedom and of peace."[66]

The speech resonated broadly and engendered a profoundly favorable response.[67] But two days later, Secretary of State Dulles went before the same Society of Newspaper Editors and conveyed a different message in a different tone. The United States was acting from strength, he insisted. Since Eisenhower assumed the presidency, he had brought vigor and imagination to U.S. foreign policy. The Soviet leaders were engaged in a "peace defensive," not a "peace offensive." They were signaling changes in direction but could not be trusted. Their intentions remained inscrutable, and hence it was prudent for the United States to continue to insist on concrete demonstrations of their good intentions. "President Eisenhower's address is a fact which will inevitably influence the course of history," but how that course would go, Dulles would not predict. "That must always remain obscure so long as vast power is possessed by men who accept no guidance from the moral law."[68]

Several days later, Kremlin leaders responded in sober, thoughtful, modulated tones. First, they published Eisenhower's address in full, including the president's accusations that Stalin bore responsibility for the division of Europe, the onset of the arms race, and the Cold War. Then they published a long and respectful, albeit critical, rejoinder in *Pravda*. Eisenhower had asked for Soviet deeds, this editorial said, but had failed to outline what actions he would take in Korea, Germany, and Asia to effectuate the peace so dear to his heart. Likewise, Eisenhower blamed the Kremlin for the postwar trajectory of international relations but failed to acknowledge how Washington's own actions had disrupted the great wartime coalition. Worse yet, Dulles's address seemed belligerent and insulting, and had wrongly stated that Soviet leaders were responding to U.S. strength. The government of the Soviet Union had to protect its homeland and its friends, but it sought to negotiate all outstanding differences. The Kremlin invited the United States to communicate what it would do in behalf of the peace it sought. So far, Washington's intentions appeared conflicted and inscrutable. In the past, it had tried to dominate the world arena and endanger the interests of the Soviet Union. It was not clear what Eisenhower and Dulles intended for the future. But the Kremlin was determined to be constructive. "There are no grounds for doubting its readiness to assume a proportionate share in settling controversial international issues." The Kremlin was ready "for a serious, businesslike discussion of problems by direct negotiations and, when necessary, within the framework of the U.N."[69]

George Kennan and Charles Bohlen, the United States' two most eminent Kremlinologists, were impressed by this Soviet response. Kennan thought that "the present Soviet leaders are definitely interested in pursuing with us the effort to solve some of the present international difficulties," though it was not likely that they would negotiate publicly. "They are extremely sensitive lest people take their willingness to negotiate as a sign of weakness." In this respect, Secretary Dulles's comments were not helpful. But the new Kremlin leaders were saying, in their own peculiar way, "Put out your feelers: we will respond." For the Russians, Kennan reminded everyone, Germany "looms . . . as the most important of all U.S.-Soviet differences. . . . They are very conscious of the weakness of their position in eastern Germany. . . . They feel that if anyone is going to defend their interest in the solution of the German problem, it has to be they themselves."[70]

Writing from Moscow, Bohlen agreed that the editorial was important, thoughtful, and carefully conceived, yet conflicted. "The article is cautious and wary even to point of indecision and may reflect either the uncertainty of the present leadership or a compromise of differing views with it." For the moment, the best course was to use the themes expressed in the president's speech to keep the Soviets "off-balance" and to encourage them to reveal their intentions.[71]

At a meeting of the National Security Council on 28 April, the president and his advisers discussed what to do next. C. D. Jackson stressed that Washington, having seized the initiative, must keep it. Americans needed to work on plans for Austria and Germany. They had to show even greater strength in Korea. They must decide how to deal with China should an armistice agreement be concluded in Korea. Dulles was chagrined that so many of America's allies wanted to recognize the government of the People's Republic of China. When he emphasized that the United States had to display strength, the president concurred, saying also that we "must do our best to anticipate absolutely everything that the Russians were likely to do in the next weeks and months."[72]

But Dulles continued to be pessimistic. At a small meeting with the president on 8 May, he confided that

> practically everywhere one looks—Africa, Middle East (except British at Suez), India, South East Asia (except for U.S. at Korea and Japan), there is no strong holding point and danger everywhere of Communist penetration. South America is vulnerable. West Germany might take the Communist bait and block EDC, thus risking a NATO collapse. In the world chess game, the Reds have the better position.

Although new factors could alter current trajectories, "the existing threat posed by the Soviets to the Western world is the most terrible and fundamental in the latter's 1000 years of domination. The threat differs in quality from the threat of a Napoleon or a Hitler. It is like the invasion by Islam in the 10th century. Now the clear issue is: can western civilization survive?"

Dulles emphasized that the "present course we are following is a fatal one for us and the free world. It is just defensive: we are always worrying about what the Soviets will take next. Unless we change this policy, or get some break, we will lose bit by bit the free world, and break ourselves financially. . . . It is necessary to take a new different line." He spelled out briefly several possibilities. The administration could warn the Soviets that if one additional country were subverted, Washington would see it as a casus belli; or it could draw the line through a whole area, like Asia, and tell the Chinese that if another country fell to communism, the United States would take measures of its own choosing. The first option, in Dulles's view, risked global war; the second might not. A third possibility would be to go on the offensive and try to win back one or more areas—for example, all of Korea, or Hainan, or Albania. A fourth was to foment subversion within the Soviet empire, especially in Eastern Europe. The goal: "disturb the Kremlin; make it think more of holding what it has, less of gaining additional territory and peoples; turn the Soviet bloc into a loose alliance, without aggressive capacities, far different from Stalin's monolith."

Eisenhower listened intently. We needed, he said, to study alternative options and convince ourselves and our friends of the wisdom of whatever course we adopted. He did not pretend to know what should be done, but he stressed the importance of allies and frowned on the idea of "drawing a line." He noted that Dulles seemed to omit another option: "that we should depend less on material strength and think more of improving standards of living . . . as the way to gain true indigenous strength. We want people to see freedom and communism in their true light. . . . [I]t will take time, but it must be done or we will lose in the end." Dulles interjected: talk of liberty did not stop people from becoming communist. The president dismissed this view. "It's men's minds and hearts that must be won."[73]

Yet both men recognized that the dynamics of the international system made it difficult to win those hearts and minds. The future of Germany was still unknown, particularly so long as the EDC was not ratified in either West

Germany or France. There was "no hope" for Europe, Dulles said, "without integration," yet integration was imperiled by domestic political exigencies, especially in France.[74] If West Germany were not soon tied to the West, one of his experts wrote, "Germans may be tempted to adopt a more independent policy, which might be accompanied by a rapid growth of extreme nationalism, or an increase in Soviet-Communist influence, depending on the circumstances."[75] Germany could still escape the lure of the West. Instead of serving as a magnet to draw the Kremlin's East European satellites westward, Germany might slip into the Soviet orbit or spin out of control.[76]

Failure to integrate West Germany could set back West European recovery. And, in turn, economic stagnation could reignite the threat of communist political victories in France, Italy, Greece, and even Franco's Spain. "Lethargy and inaction in Europe," Eisenhower constantly worried, might "allow that Continent to fall into Soviet hands."[77]

More worrisome still was the unrest and uncertainty in Southeast Asia, the Middle East, Africa, and Latin America. At NSC meetings, there was constant talk of Indochina, Iran, Egypt, and Korea. "Bitterness" pervaded the Arab world, Dulles wrote Eisenhower, after visiting several countries in mid-May, where "the United States suffered from being linked with British and French imperialism."[78] Reflecting on the overall situation as the president's special assistant for Cold War affairs, C. D. Jackson lamented that the "world picture" was "deteriorating at an extraordinary rate." Every "ounce of skill and determination" had to be mustered, he wrote, "to bring the French to the realization that they must produce a global political plan . . . for the freedom of all these peoples."[79]

Conscious of America's vulnerability, Eisenhower reiterated that his commitment to his peace initiative was contingent on demonstrations of Soviet goodwill. He wrote Jiang Jieshi, now heading the Nationalist government on the island of Taiwan, on 5 May:

> We cannot assume that the threat posed by aggressive Communism has passed, or that it is passing. To the contrary, it appears that the recent Soviet posture is evidence of a change merely in tactics, of indeterminate degree and duration, dictated largely by necessity. I shall certainly consider it to be no more than this, until the Soviet Union demonstrates, by action rather than

words, that it has abandoned its plan of world conquest, and
that it is willing to join with the rest of the world in building a
world community in which all can enjoy the fruits of their labor
in peace and security.[80]

Yet the chance for peace could not be ignored. The reputation of "the
free world" would be tarnished, Ike also wrote Jiang, if its leaders disregarded "seemingly friendly moves on the part of the Communist bloc."
Moreover, such moves offered an opportunity to reduce defense costs. If
there was a chance for peace, Ike could ease the budget crisis in his own
country and translate savings into tax reductions for the American people.
He was under tremendous pressure from leaders of his own party, who
ridiculed him for not doing more to cut spending. Senator Robert Taft told
the president at a legislative leadership meeting that he "could not possibly
express the deepness of his disappointment" about the budgetary situation.[81]

The president firmly believed that security depended on solvency as well
as preparedness. Immediately upon assuming office, he had reconfigured the
National Security Council in order to include the secretary of the treasury,
George Humphrey, and the director of the budget, William Dodge, in its
meetings. Eisenhower regularly attended these sessions, participated vigorously in the discussions, and invested tremendous importance in them.
During the entire spring of 1953, the NSC grappled with the problem
of reconciling defense requirements with fiscal imperatives. The president
would not compromise national security, but he also feared that if the United
States had "to live in a permanent state of mobilization our whole democratic
way of life would be destroyed in the process."[82]

Suspicious though he was of the new men in the Kremlin, Ike could not
abandon his hope that after Stalin there was a chance for peace. A relaxation
of tensions might enable dollars to be saved at home and converted to investment and production, catalyze a program "of world betterment," and nurture "cooperation of all people, without recrimination or vindictiveness."[83]
Yet when Ike launched a systematic study of the options that Dulles had presented on 8 May, none of them envisioned the chance for peace. The president was torn between conflicting impulses. And since he said he would be
swayed by Soviet deeds, much depended on the attitudes and actions of the
new leaders in the Kremlin.

Turmoil in the Kremlin

Stalin's heirs were active and anxious, suspicious and collegial. They knew the Americans wanted to take advantage of their vulnerability and inexperience during the transition. To muster domestic support, they focused special attention on releasing prisoners and increasing the production of consumer goods. Yet they never ceased to warn of the likelihood of domestic subversion by foreign capitalists seeking to overthrow their state, which represented the future of humankind.[84]

While there was considerable substantive agreement among them about the need for reform, they distrusted one another, especially Beria. They distrusted his dynamism, his initiative, his power, and believed he was styling himself as a great reformer in order to muster public support and take over the regime.[85] They knew intimately his record of brutality and murder. They also knew that he was putting together dossiers on them and on their own former crimes. "Think yourself happy that these documents are in my hands," Beria supposedly said to Malenkov, "but behave reasonably in future."[86] "I understood that Beria was playing a double-game with me," Khrushchev recalled, "reassuring me while awaiting the moment to make short work of me as soon as he could."[87]

Meanwhile, they focused attention on Eastern Europe and especially on East Germany, where there was turmoil and disarray. They knew that Stalin had imposed far too much of an economic and military burden on the satellites. Reforms were imperative, and if the material conditions of life were not improved and repression softened, upheaval was likely. They summoned the East European leaders to Moscow, scheduling separate meetings with them.[88]

The remarkable records of these sessions reveal that Malenkov, Beria, and their comrades were intent on significant liberalization. In mid-June 1953, for example, the entire collective leadership of the Kremlin—Malenkov, Beria, Khrushchev, Molotov, Anastas Mikoyan, and Bulganin—met with the Hungarian party and state leader Matyas Rakosi and his entourage from Budapest.

Malenkov began with economic conditions. "We view Hungary's situation with a critical attitude. . . . Our impression is that the Hungarian comrades underestimate the problems. . . . The facts that we are familiar with indicate that the situation in the field of agriculture is not good. . . . There are problems in the area of trade as well. They provide few commodities for the population." Then he turned to the political oppression, which for years had been very severe in Hungary. "Persecutions were initiated against 250,000 people in the second half of 1952" alone. Seventy-five percent of these were stopped, "yet, the number is still rather high. . . . All these provoked dissatisfaction among the population."

When Beria took over, he lambasted Rakosi for both the economic failures and the political repression. Poor investments, he said, caused hardship in the countryside and diverted capital from light industry, "the industry that serves the population." And how could it be that in a country of 9.5 million people, "persecutions were initiated against 1,500,000 people?" The American and British imperialists, Beria warned, would capitalize on the discontent of the common people. "They have one goal: to overthrow the existing authorities and to restore the power of the capitalists." Arresting and beating people were countereffective; Rakosi would be feared but not respected. The loyalty and affection of the people had to be won. Then Bulganin moved in: Hungarian communists had abused their power and worsened the population's standard of living. "This is not the road to socialism but the road to a catastrophe," he said. "Today the Red Army is still in Hungary," Beria concluded, "but it will not be there forever. Therefore, we must prepare and become stronger so that nobody can do any harm to us."

"Why do we bring these things up so harshly?" Malenkov asked, drawing the session to a conclusion. "We, as Communists, are all responsible for the state of things in Hungary. The Soviet Union is also responsible for what kind of rule exists in Hungary. . . . We admit to the extreme military demands, but the [Hungarian] comrades executed these demands even beyond what we expected. Why should an army be maintained with such a size that it bankrupts the state?"

When Rakosi tried to defend himself, however meekly and politely, Beria responded: "We like you and respect you, that's why we criticize you." There was no excuse, repeated Malenkov and Beria, for the size and cost of the Hungarian army. The Hungarians carried Soviet wishes to an extreme. "Comrade Stalin gave incorrect instructions," Beria asserted. "If the great Stalin made mistakes," he said, "Comrade Rakosi can admit that he made mistakes too. . . . People must not be beaten." The government's policy toward the middle peasantry, he peremptorily added, "must be changed."[89]

A catastrophe, such as Bulganin warned, did occur—but not in Hungary. On 17 June, workers in East Berlin went on strike. Aggrieved laborers protested against the East German regime's demanding work rules, low wages, and tight regimentation of the economy. People were fed up with Walter Ulbricht, the leader of the East German communists, and with his government's attempt to "build socialism rapidly" in the German Democratic Republic. Hundreds of workers stormed a government building, and about twenty-five thousand demonstrated in the streets. Strikes and riots spread quickly throughout East Germany. By the late afternoon, Soviet commanders called out their troops and declared martial law. Russian soldiers and tanks fired on the protesters, dispersed the crowds, arrested hundreds of people, and executed several of them.[90]

The new leaders in the Kremlin had foreseen the possibility of such an uprising and had been seeking to avert it. Malenkov, Molotov, and Beria realized that Ulbricht's efforts were a disaster. The seething hostility of the people to his regime was perfectly apparent to Soviet occupation officials as well as to Beria's secret police. Moreover, during the previous two years almost five hundred thousand East Germans had fled to the West. In May, Soviet officials had agreed on a "new course" for East Germany that would relax the work rules, halt the formation of agricultural cooperatives, stop the squeeze on small private enterprise, and increase the production of consumer goods. Summoning Ulbricht and his colleagues to Moscow on 2 June, Kremlin leaders had warned that if conditions were not ameliorated, "a catastrophe will happen."[91]

But what Stalin's successors had in mind for Germany over the long run is not clear. The reforms they insisted on were intended to allay unrest among East Germans and gain more support among West Germans. And Soviet officials, just like policymakers in Washington, knew they had to champion German unification if they were to have credibility in either part of Germany. So the Soviet reform program aimed "for the construction of a single democratic peace-loving independent Germany."[92] But whether Molotov, Malenkov, and Khrushchev intended to negotiate seriously for a unified Germany is unclear. At the very least, they tried to blame Washington for splitting Germany, which they hoped would undermine the willingness of West Germans to join an integrated defense community in Western Europe.

Beria may well have wanted to explore a real settlement of the German question, given his wish to reduce Moscow's burdens and relax East-West tensions. One of his subordinates recollects that he "ordered me to prepare top-secret intelligence probes to test the feasibility of unifying Germany. He told me that the best way to strengthen our world position would be to create a neutral, unified Germany run by a coalition government. Germany would be the balancing factor between America and Soviet interests in Western Europe." Beria allegedly did not "want a permanently unstable socialist Germany whose survival relied on the support of the Soviet Union."[93] At a meeting of the Politburo, he incensed Molotov and offended Malenkov when he exclaimed, "The GDR? What does it amount to, this GDR? It is not even a real state. It's only kept in being by Soviet troops." The Kremlin needed a peaceful Germany, Beria said, "and it makes no difference whether or not it is socialist."[94] Beria's son also says that his father wanted to unify Germany, thinking that a "reunified Germany would be grateful to the Soviet Union and would agree to help it economically. We could even put up with a bourgeois Germany."[95]

Whether Beria would have acquiesced in the creation of a unified, independent, bourgeois Germany, or simply wanted a unified Germany in the Soviet orbit, as did most of his colleagues in the Kremlin, remains uncertain. But what is not uncertain is that at the same time that Soviet troops were putting down the uprising in East Germany and Kremlin leaders were pondering a long-term policy, Khrushchev and Malenkov, with Khrushchev in the lead, decided to get rid of Beria. They especially feared the reforms he was undertaking in the security apparatus, the Ministry of Internal Affairs (MVD). Secretly, Khrushchev and Malenkov approached each member of the leadership and garnered a consensus that Beria should be dismissed from his key posts. Even more stealthily, they got the army to side with them and arranged for Beria to be arrested.

Totally unsuspecting of the plot against him, Beria arrived at a meeting of the Presidium on 26 June. He was shocked when Malenkov opened the meeting saying it would focus on Beria's activities. He was guilty, Malenkov charged, of seeking "to place the MVD organs above the party and the state." He had abused power and sought to foment dissent among the collective leadership. Malenkov proposed that Beria be dismissed from his key positions. All the members attending supported this proposal. Malenkov then pressed a button. As planned, Marshal Zhukov and several uniformed officers entered the chamber and surrounded Beria. Malenkov then asked for calm and declared that Beria "is so cunning and so dangerous that only the devil knows what he might do now. I therefore propose that we arrest him immediately." All agreed, although few had expected matters would go this far.[96]

Within a week the plotters convened a meeting of the Central Committee to consider the charges against Beria. Malenkov, opening the session, assailed Beria's criminal activities, his efforts to divide the collective leadership, and his schemes to usurp power. Beria wanted to undermine the collective farms and jeopardize the food supply, he claimed. Overall, he "lost the face of a Communist," became a "bourgeois regenerate," and operated as "an agent of international imperialism."[97]

No issue consumed more attention at this Central Committee meeting than Beria's position on the German question. Beria, said Khrushchev, "most clearly showed himself to be an instigator, an agent of the imperialists, during the discussion of the German question, when he raised the question of rejecting socialist construction in the GDR and making concessions to the West." All the leaders, said Khrushchev, had acknowledged mistakes in their policies toward the GDR. All had agreed that the "construction of socialism" had moved too swiftly, alienating the Germans themselves. Yet they had all insisted, except Beria, that socialism in the GDR could not be forsaken, since to do so would jeopardize the security of the Soviet Union and the future of communism. "Can a democratic bourgeois Germany truly be neutral?" Khrushchev railed. "Is this possible?" Germany loomed as the great threat, ready to wreak revenge if Soviet leaders were not vigilant. "I gave [Beria] examples," said Bulganin, "on the neutrality of Germany in its time. . . . I pointed out that . . . Germany was disarmed, and then what happened? Germany rearmed and attacked the Soviet Union."[98]

Nobody voiced his concerns more clearly than Molotov. "None of us could forget," he said, "that Germany should be held responsible for unleashing the First World War, and that bourgeois Germany is responsible for unleashing the Second World War." For Marxists, he continued, the idea that a bourgeois Germany could be peaceful was impossible to contemplate. How could a bourgeois Germany not have aggressive and imperialistic aspirations? How could it not have ties to other imperialist countries? We must not repudiate "everything that had been won by the blood of our soldiers, the blood of our people, in a difficult struggle against Hitlerism. . . . Under the correct political course, the German Democratic Republic will become an ever more reliable friend of the Soviet Union, and will become a serious obstacle to the realization of imperialist plans in Europe."[99]

The invective against Beria illuminated how past experience, ideology, and the distribution of power in the international system militated against an agreement on the unification of Germany. "Comrades," Malenkov bellowed at the closing session of the plenary meeting on 7 July, "we must not for a minute forget the international situation, the existence of the Capitalist countries around us." The imperialists "cannot be reconciled to the fact that more and more countries and peoples are leaving their sphere of influence." Hence the Kremlin could not relax its guard. It would have to reaffirm its backing for Ulbricht and rekindle its support for socialism in the GDR. It would have to recalibrate its reform efforts throughout Eastern Europe, making certain they did not spark unrest. Revolutionary vigilance would have to be enhanced. "We must remember and never forget the Capitalist countries around us, who are sending and who will be sending into our midst their agents to undermine us."[100]

Beria pleaded for forgiveness. "Dear Georgi," he wrote to Malenkov, "I am seeking for your understanding, since you know me better than others." Yes, he acknowledged, his behavior at Presidium meetings had been insolent. His rudeness toward Comrades Khrushchev and Bulganin was inadmissible. "I am guilty [on this matter] without question and have to be denounced thoroughly." But, he beseeched,

> dear comrades, you should understand that I am a faithful sol-
> dier of our Motherland, a loyal son of the party of Lenin and
> Stalin and your loyal friend and comrade. Send me wherever
> you wish, to any kind of work. . . . See me out, I will be able
> to work ten more years and I will work with all my soul and
> with complete energy. I am saying this from the bottom of my
> heart.[101]

Several months later, Beria was formally tried. The sentence was pre-arranged. He had no counsel, no right to appeal. He had betrayed the motherland and sought to restore the bourgeoisie. Immediately, the guards tied his hands, ripped off his prison shirt, and gagged him with a towel. Standing in an undershirt, still struggling to plead his innocence, he was shot in the head at point-blank range by a three-star general.[102]

Arresting and executing Beria did not mean that the Kremlin leadership rejected his ideas. Neither security nor ideology would allow them to betray socialism in East Germany. But they realized that the Soviet Union's domestic priorities still demanded a relaxation of international tensions. As Malenkov closed the Central Committee plenum, he repeated that many tasks lay ahead if they were to fulfill their historic mission to build communism. They had to strengthen the party's contacts with the masses, he said, respond more sensitively to the demands of the workers, "show daily concern for the improvement of the material situation of the Soviet people, remembering that concern for the interests of the Soviet people is the Party's most important obligation."[103]

On 8 August, Malenkov gave a speech to the Supreme Soviet outlining the trajectory of Soviet domestic and foreign policy. He framed it in the ideological maxims of Marxism-Leninism. "The Communist party and the Soviet government know where and how to lead the people, because they are guided by the scientific theory of social development—Marxism-Leninism—the banner of which has been raised so high by our great father and teacher, Lenin, and the continuer of his cause, Stalin." In the past, the party had had to invest great effort in the development of heavy industry, fuel, power, and machine tools. Otherwise, the motherland would have been attacked, the revolution doomed, and capitalist encirclement triumphant. But now it was imperative to shift course. "The task consists of making a drastic change in the production of consumer goods and to ensure a speedier development of the light and food industries." The state had failed to spur the production of potatoes, vegetables, milk, and meat, Malenkov admitted. Housing was shoddy. School construction was inadequate. Hospitals were too few. Many enterprises were run incompetently and inefficiently. These shortcomings needed to be acknowledged, as well as the fact that the system had enormous potential. "The source of our strength is the mighty activity and initiative of workers, collective farmers, and intelligentsia. We have enormous possibilities for the implementation of our main task—the maximum satisfaction of the steadily growing material and cultural demands of the people."

Malenkov emphasized that international issues could not be ignored in

Lavrenti Beria, 1946. Stalin's brutal police chief
inspired fear, yet apparently he wanted to negotiate
a deal with the West over Germany. His comrades
arrested and killed him after Stalin's death.

examining domestic problems. The Soviet Union and its democratic allies
were a force for peace, he reiterated. The Kremlin had no territorial claims.
The new leaders had taken steps to ease tensions with its neighbors—Iran,
Afghanistan, Turkey, and Finland. They restored diplomatic relations with
Israel. Most important, they labored behind the scenes to orchestrate the
armistice in Korea, signed on 27 July. And they wanted to do more, he said.
They wanted to settle the German question. They were prepared to meet
with the foreign ministers of the other great powers. There were "no objective grounds for a collision" between the United States and the Soviet Union.
"We firmly believe that at the present moment there is no disputable or outstanding issue that could not be settled in a peaceful way on the basis of mutual agreement between the countries concerned. . . . We stood and stand for
a peaceful co-existence of two systems."

However, Malenkov made it clear that the Soviet Union would not be intimidated. Some Americans stressed their determination to negotiate from strength, yet the United States had wanted to preserve an atomic monopoly and couldn't. Now Malenkov proudly announced that the Soviet Union had its own hydrogen bomb. "As you see, convincing facts are shattering the wagging of tongues about the weakness of the Soviet Union." The language of force would not work against the Kremlin. Compromise and conciliation were essential. President Eisenhower said there was a chance for peace. There *was* a chance, Malenkov emphasized, but it demanded deeds from the United States as well as the Soviet Union. "It would be a crime before mankind if the certain relaxation which has appeared in the international atmosphere should be replaced by a new intensification of the tension." The United States would have to acclimate itself to a new world order in which eight hundred million people—one-third of humankind—had embraced socialism. Those people "cannot be compelled to abandon their historic achievements won with their blood and sweat."

In other words, there still was a chance for peace notwithstanding the crackdown in East Germany, the arrest of Beria, and the allegations that the Americans had been responsible for the ferment behind the iron curtain. Malenkov and his colleagues well understood that the achievement of their domestic priorities and the security of their state depended on a relaxation of the arms race, the settlement of the German question, and a more quiescent international atmosphere. They would try to give peace a chance. But the world needed to know that "Our cause is invincible. We shall proceed confidently forward, along the path of building Communist society in our country."[104]

A Chance for Peace?

The uprising in East Germany and the arrest of Beria tempted Eisenhower and Dulles to go on the offensive and practice Dulles's strategy of "rollback." At National Security Council meetings in late June and July, they and their colleagues ruminated on the significance of the recent events. Dulles thought the Russians had been caught "completely off guard." Since he considered their position in Germany untenable, he wanted to convene a four-power conference on the future of Germany. Dulles's brother reported that "the ousting of Beria [was] a tremendous shock to the Russian people." Jackson agreed: it was a "great opportunity for nurturing passive resistance throughout the bloc." Now was the time, he thought, to breed confusion and capitalize on the disarray in the Kremlin, and he submitted a detailed plan of psychological initiatives and covert actions to exploit the unrest in satellite states.[105] He thought the United States should try to undermine the puppet regimes the Kremlin had installed, but without fomenting mass rebellion. It should convince the free world, particularly Western Europe, that "love of liberty and hatred of alien oppression are stronger behind the Iron Curtain than it has been dared to believe and that resistance to totalitarianism is less hopeless than has been imagined."[106]

Eisenhower and Dulles carefully calibrated the U.S. response, however. They decided to work with Konrad Adenauer's government in West Germany to distribute food packages to East Berliners and East Germans. By mid-August, 865,000 East Germans had flocked to centers in West Berlin to pick up food, and by early October more than 5.5 million packages had been distributed. The East German and Soviet governments, embarrassed and infuriated, did all they could to stop the food program, confiscating identification cards and cracking down on organizers of the excursion trips to West Berlin. But the Kremlin also lightened its demands on the East German economy, canceled reparation obligations, and agreed to join a four-power foreign ministers' conference on the future of Germany.[107]

For U.S. policymakers, these events in East Germany were both tantalizing and sobering. American diplomats in Eastern Europe warned that "stirring up resistance elements or incitements to revolt might have the long-range effect of retarding a Soviet military withdrawal." Psychological warfare operations, they reminded their superiors in Washington, "should never be allowed to run ahead of our political and military policies." Moreover, the British and French feared that the food program and the psychological offensive might provoke a crisis, perhaps even triggering a Soviet move against West Berlin. U.S. officials knew their actions toward East Germany and in Eastern Europe had to be integrated into an overall assessment of how to deal with post-Stalinist Russia. But they were uncertain what should be done.[108]

Since early May, when Dulles had confided his anxieties to the president, Eisenhower had been orchestrating the most systematic review of national security policy since the onset of the Cold War. Under the direction of his assistant for national security affairs, Robert Cutler, three task forces were assembled to outline alternative courses of action. After weeks of careful preparation, the teams presented their ideas at an all-day meeting at the White House on 16 July attended by the president and his most important advisers.

Task Force A, under George Kennan, postulated that time was not running against the free world. It presented a program to augment and sustain U.S. military capabilities over the long run. Looking back to the containment policies that Kennan had designed in 1947 and 1948, Task Force A sought to increase the cohesion of the free world while fomenting subversion within the Soviet bloc. It aimed "to weaken Soviet power and bring about its withdrawal within traditional Russian boundaries," without risking global war.

Task Force B, under Major General James McCormack, outlined how the United States might draw a line around the existing Soviet bloc. Should the Kremlin or its partners try to advance beyond that line, they would risk global war: if communists seized power on "our side of the line," the United States would reserve the right and develop the means to take whatever actions were necessary to restore conditions compatible with U.S. national security interests. But Task Force B did not like the idea of peripheral wars, considering them uneconomical.

Task Force C, under Admiral Richard L. Conolly, assumed that the United States "cannot continue to live with the Soviet threat. So long as the Soviet Union exists, it will not fall apart, but must and can be shaken apart." Conolly and his team delineated how the United States might take aggressive actions in the near future to subvert the Soviet bloc and erode Soviet power, even if such actions increased the risk of general war.[109]

Eisenhower was impressed by the presentations. He said he had never attended "a better or more persuasively presented staff job." He hoped that the three task forces could meet and integrate their ideas into "a unified policy." Although members of the task forces disagreed with one another strongly, Ike believed that their disparate findings needed to be discussed more systematically by the National Security Council and integrated into an overall national security program.[110]

What was striking in the presentations of the three task forces was the absence of any emphasis on the chance for peace or the pursuit of détente. As discussions proceeded in late July and as the disarray in the Soviet camp became more apparent, hopes mounted that a "climate of victory" could be created. The president and his staff thought they could take more risks because the Soviets seemed more timid and defensive. The United States might even initiate "moderately increased risks of general war by taking some of the aggressive actions against the Satellites proposed by Task Force 'C.' "[111]

Yet their deliberations were confounded by their growing realization that the costs of the national security programs would break the budget. The president kept insisting that national security must be built on sound fiscal policy and domestic economic vitality. "We are in a hell of a fix," he exclaimed at an NSC meeting on 14 July, when he learned of the escalating national deficit that would exceed eight billion dollars in fiscal year 1955 and require congressional action to raise the debt limit.[112] As Soviet strategic capabilities increased and the requirements of continental defense mounted, U.S. capacity to sustain its commitments overseas was squeezed. In July, Ike appointed new men to head the military services and asked them to develop new ideas and concepts that would enable the United States to be secure without bankrupting itself.[113]

In the late summer, the president went on vacation in Denver while the new chiefs of staff designed their plans and presented them to an NSC meeting on 27 August, presided over by Secretary of State Dulles. The chiefs proposed to cut the nation's overseas deployments and to focus on strategic air power and continental defense. This posture would cost more in the short run but would produce significant savings in the long run, said the new chairman of the Joint Chiefs of Staff, Admiral Arthur Radford. After some questioning and discussion, Secretary of the Treasury Humphrey declared that the report was "terrific. . . . This was the most important thing that had happened since January 20." Finally, the NSC had a strategic concept that was new and bold yet fiscally prudent. Unable to contain his excitement, Humphrey insisted that the next move was up to the State Department.

Dulles immediately saw that this new concept would adversely affect U.S. relations with its allies, especially in Europe. He acknowledged that the concept would be wildly popular at home, but "could result in a grave disaster if we were not allowed sufficient time to prepare public opinion abroad for this change." General Matthew Ridgway, the new army chief of staff, added to Dulles's anxieties when he said precisely what the secretary was thinking: should the NATO allies get an inkling of this, they would "construe it as abandonment and the consequences would be terrifying." Yet neither Dulles nor Ridgway could ignore their colleagues' palpable excitement. Suddenly, the National Security Council had a concept, embraced by the JCS, that promised to reconcile security and economy, preserve national solvency, and animate Republican constituencies with new tax reductions.[114]

Cutler flew to Denver to brief the president. Ike was enthusiastic, but stressed that it must never be said that these views were new. He had always regarded the stationing abroad of large numbers of U.S. troops as temporary. He agreed that protecting the homeland from a surprise attack must be an overwhelming priority. The United States must be able to deter an attack and retaliate massively. When Cutler mentioned Dulles's anxieties, Ike said he was eager to hear the secretary's ideas. Ike was very concerned about the recent news of the Soviet hydrogen bomb, clearly reinforcing his worries about homeland defense and underscoring the need to avoid war. It made him wonder about "how much we should poke an animal through the bars of the cage."[115]

Dulles decided to make a quick trip to see the president himself. On 6 September, he flew across the country to spend a few hours in intimate discussions with his boss. Dulles appreciated the need for economy and for continental defense, for "budgetary balance and monetary stability," he said. He realized the anxieties America's allies had because of Soviet possession of a hydrogen bomb. But, he said, the new strategic concept advanced by the JCS would intensify those fears, rekindling allied assumptions that the United States was returning to its isolationist past.

How could the divergent imperatives of U.S. economic, strategic, and foreign policy be brought together? Dulles presented a new view to the president, one that reflected a stunning reversal of his previous inclinations. Perhaps it was time, he acknowledged, to explore "the possibility of taking this occasion to make a spectacular effort to relax world tensions on a global basis and execute . . . mutual withdrawals of Red Army forces and of U.S. forces. . . . The Plan would include limitation of armament and control of weapons of mass destruction." Lest the president think the secretary was totally repudiating his past ideas, Dulles argued that the time was propitious for this. The United States would be negotiating from a position of strength: the Korean armistice had been signed; a radical government in Iran had been overthrown with the aid of covert American and British actions; Adenauer had just won a decisive victory in the West German elections; and France seemed willing to go on the offensive against the Vietnamese communists in Indochina. If ever there was a chance for peace, this was the time, he said.[116]

Eisenhower was supportive. "I am in emphatic agreement," he wrote Dulles after the secretary returned to Washington, "that renewed efforts should be made to relax world tensions on a global basis. Mutual withdrawals of Red Army and United States forces could be suggested as a step toward relaxing these tensions." At the same time, Americans had to be informed of the vastly more dangerous world they were living in as the Russians developed hydrogen weapons and strategic air power. The United States might have to spend more than previously thought to establish a deterrent and defend the homeland; tax cuts might have to be delayed. The trade-offs were excruciatingly difficult. Ruminating on unhappy scenarios, the president speculated that if the country had to maintain a huge defense burden for an indefinite future, it might have to resort to preventive war or accept some "form of dictatorial government." But Ike encouraged Dulles to go ahead and keep an eye on possibilities to advance "the cause of conciliation and understanding." Knowing that it had been trying for Dulles to make the trip to Denver, Ike thanked him profusely for the chance to review "the critical international problems that cry out for study and contemplation and action."[117]

Rational men and women needed to explore whether there was a chance for peace. The State Department's Policy Planning Staff was already grappling with these matters. Over the past six years, the staff had won great influence and earned enormous respect under the leadership of George Kennan and Paul Nitze. Now, Louis Halle, one of its brightest members, argued that it would be a mistake to ignore the significance of developments inside the Kremlin. The future was of course uncertain, and the United States needed to build strength, but it should speak more softly while carrying a bigger stick. "In the present (temporary) state of Soviet history, we might well find ourselves able, if we act wisely, to obtain rather large concessions from Moscow, by negotiation, in return for relatively small concessions on our side."[118]

The overriding problem concerned the future of Germany. "This is the heart of the problem," wrote Dulles's policy planners. "German power and resources added to either scale would be decisive in the balance, and such a shift either way would be adamantly resisted by the side that stood to lose."

Détente, however, might be achieved if the Cold War adversaries could find a way to agree on creating a unified, neutral, peaceful Germany that would enable Soviet and American forces to withdraw from the heart of Europe. The division of Germany might end, and the iron curtain severing Europe might be lifted. By settling the German issue and reducing U.S. forces in Europe, huge sums of money might be saved and the budgetary crunch eased.[119]

Try as they might, policy planners could not find a formula to solve the problem of Germany. A unified, neutral Germany would not relax tensions or enhance U.S. security. For the moment, democracy was working in West Germany. Unlike the Weimar Republic, as Eisenhower wrote French president Joseph Laniel, "the Bonn regime has struck roots. . . . [T]he forces of democracy and common sense have grown considerably in strength."[120] But the trajectory of German politics was uncertain. "The institutions of democracy," said the NSC paper on Germany, "have yet to undergo a real test. Within the population there are maladjusted and, to some extent, disaffected elements which might prove politically unreliable under stress." James Conant, the U.S. high commissioner for Germany, warned Dulles, "The basic German political situation is too unstable and the German governmental structure is too new to trust the final command of a national army to the hands of the unknown German leaders of the future."[121]

Hence Germany had to be integrated, bound, and riveted within a West European community. Ike reminded Laniel that the "spectre of a Germany rapidly increasing its strength outside the ties of Western European unity" was the worst possible scenario.[122] A united, neutral Germany might seek to manipulate Cold War adversaries to serve its own purposes or, worse, be subverted and enticed into a Soviet bloc. Such a scenario was a nightmare because German forces were essential for the defense of Western Europe and for the viability of the NATO alliance. The Joint Chiefs of Staff starkly warned, "Any agreement which would preclude Germany from rearming and aligning itself with the West would be militarily unacceptable."[123]

After very careful assessments, U.S. officials concluded that they had to work for German integration into Western Europe—all of Germany, it was hoped, but at the very least West Germany. They knew they had to stand for German unity because Germans wanted it. The American position vis-à-vis the Adenauer government would be discredited if Washington were seen as opposing unification. But the prerequisite for unification was free elections in both the eastern and western parts of Germany, not the merger of the existing East and West German governments, as the Kremlin seemed to want.[124]

U.S. officials knew that their position made a settlement of the German issue impossible. The Soviets, wanting to sow division among the NATO allies by calling for German unity and a pan-European security pact, feared German power and would never accept a unified Germany linked to NATO. "With the memory of recent German aggression," the NSC acknowledged, "the USSR undoubtedly fears revival of German military power as a threat to its security." The Russians were unlikely to relinquish their position in East Germany lest they jeopardize their access to the uranium resources in Saxony or precipitate a move for independence among all the satellites. "In short," concluded the Policy Planning Staff, "no solution of the German problem seems available so long as Europe remains a theater of rivalry and possible war. [Germany] is so inherently important as an aggregate of power that the only solution would seem to be contingent upon a general East-West détente in this area."[125]

In short, the configuration of power in the international system made a German settlement impossible. Germany was such an important unit within that system, and its future evolution so uncertain, that the United States could not do anything that would jeopardize the integration of German power into the Western alliance. This negotiating posture might prolong the Cold War, but that was more acceptable than running the risks of a prospective settlement. A neutralized Germany simply could not be tolerated.

Nor would unrest in the third world—in Asia, Africa, the Middle East, and Latin America—allow for a settlement. The "forces of unrest and resentment against the West are strong," the president's top advisers agreed. "Among these sources are racial feelings, anti-colonialism, rising nationalism, popular demand for rapid social and economic progress, over-population, the breakdown of static social patterns."[126] Communist ideology, C. D. Jackson wrote, "despite all the evidence of the realities of life in the Soviet system—still has a significant appeal to many peoples outside that system."[127] Eisenhower and Dulles agreed. Eisenhower wrote in his diary,

Nationalism is on the march and world communism is taking advantage of that spirit of nationalism to cause dissension in the free world. Moscow leads many misguided people to believe that they can count on communist help to achieve and sustain nationalistic ambitions. Actually, what is going on is that the communists are hoping to take advantage of the confusion resulting from the destruction of existing relationships . . . to further the aims of world revolution and the Kremlin's domination of all people.[128]

Chances for peace could not be risked so long as revolutionary nationalist movements might be captured by Chinese or Soviet communists. During the early months of his administration, Eisenhower became alarmed by the drift of events in Iran. In Tehran, President Mohammad Mosaddeq was a populist and charismatic leader who had nationalized the British-owned Anglo-Iranian Oil Company in 1951. When London had tightened the economic screws against him, the political situation in the country grew volatile, and Mosaddeq appeared to become dependent on the communist Tudeh Party. Fearing that the communists would outmaneuver Mosaddeq and that Iran's oil resources might slip into the Soviet orbit, Eisenhower decided on 11 July 1953 to authorize an elaborately conceived Anglo-American covert operation to overthrow Iran's leader. As a result of a fortuitous sequence of events, the plot succeeded. Mosaddeq was imprisoned and then put under house arrest. Thousands of his colleagues and communist supporters were arrested, and a few were executed. By the end of 1954, an authoritarian regime under the leadership of Shah Reza Pahlavi was firmly ensconced and beholden to the United States. Iranian oil was placed under the management of a new multinational consortium over which American corporations exerted significant influence. "A year ago," Eisenhower wrote his brother Edgar in November 1954, "we were in imminent danger of losing Iran, and sixty percent of the known oil reserves of the world. . . . That threat has been largely, if not totally, removed."[129]

The success of the covert operation in Iran encouraged Eisenhower and Dulles to employ similar tactics elsewhere. In Guatemala, a reformist government under Jacobo Arbenz Guzman introduced an income tax and promoted land reform that threatened the holdings of U.S. companies in that country, especially the United Fruit Company. Arbenz associated with leftists and brought communists into his administration. He wanted social justice,

President Eisenhower and the Shah of Iran, 1954.
U.S. covert action ensconced the Shah in power.

economic growth, and the autonomy to set Guatemala's priorities without interference from the United States. Louis Halle wrote:

> This typical underdeveloped country is now undergoing the social revolution that typifies underdeveloped countries generally in our time. . . . Social reform and nationalism are its two principal manifestations. We see the same revolution at various stages of development in Asia and Africa. . . . The international communist movement is certainly not the cause of the social revolution in Guatemala, but it has made the same effort there that it has made elsewhere to harness the revolutionary impulses—nationalism and social reform alike—and exploit them for its own purposes.[130]

Eisenhower and Dulles felt they could not tolerate such a regime in their neighborhood, especially when Arbenz defied an American boycott on arms shipments and purchased military supplies from the Soviet bloc. In December 1953, they allocated three million dollars to initiate a covert operation to topple him, and in June 1954 they put it into action. Arbenz, like Mosaddeq, was overthrown.[131]

Ike and his assistants recognized that Moscow and Beijing were not responsible for these revolutionary nationalist movements in the third world, which were the product of backwardness, colonialism, and imperial exploitation. Looking at Indochina, policymakers acknowledged that "with only a modicum of Chinese Communist assistance," the communist-led and nationalist-inspired forces of Ho Chi Minh were successfully contesting French control of the region. Ho's political organization, the Vietminh, had fought the Japanese occupiers of Indochina during World War II and organized an independent government in Vietnam at the end of the war, which officials in Paris had refused to recognize. Since 1946, the Vietminh had been fighting the French for recognition of Vietnam's independence. If elections took place, Ike's assistants recognized, Ho would win not because of external aid but because of indigenous support. This outcome was regarded as unacceptable. There was no alternative, State Department policy planners concluded, but to destroy the organized armed forces of the Vietminh as "a precondition of achievement of U.S. objectives in Indochina."[132]

These officials deemed fighting revolutionary nationalism in Southeast Asia and the Middle East essential because the areas' raw materials and natural resources were indispensable for the economic health and political vitality of Japan and Western Europe. The United States might get along without these resources—although the president did not think so—but America's allies certainly could not. Communist success in Indochina, for example, would encourage all of Southeast Asia to cooperate with China and the Soviet Union and "would equally encourage Japanese political tendencies toward accommodation." Without markets and raw materials in the third world, Japan and Western Europe might be sucked into the Soviet orbit, and the balance of power in the world would move in the Kremlin's direction. Loss of Southeast Asia, concluded the Joint Chiefs of Staff and the State Department, would "result in such economic and political pressures upon Japan as to make it extremely difficult to prevent Japan's accommodation to communism." The president agreed. It is "absolutely mandatory," he emphasized, "that the Japanese nation does not fall under the domination of the

Iron Curtain countries, or specifically the Kremlin. If the Kremlin controls them, all of that great war-making capacity could be turned against the free world."[133]

Eisenhower and Dulles wanted to explore the parameters of détente, but it was immensely difficult to imagine satisfactory terms of peace. Since the Kremlin was populated by men who still fanatically believed in an alternative way of life, the risks of settling with them seemed to outweigh the potential benefits. Although they appeared to want to relax tensions, they might take advantage of any pause in the competition to lure a unified, neutral Germany into their orbit or to subvert nations that possessed vital raw materials or were situated in strategic locations in Southeast Asia, the Middle East, or even Central America. While the Cold War was costly and increasingly risky, and nuclear war was a growing prospect, the clash of ideologies and the dynamics of the international system militated against the chance for peace.[134]

When Ike and his advisers settled on a national security policy statement at the end of October 1953, they acknowledged that the Kremlin might seek a relaxation of tensions. Thus far, however, Malenkov had not demonstrated a "readiness to make important concessions to this end." The Soviet rulers were still basing their policy "on the conviction of irreconcilable hostility between the bloc and the non-communist world." Their basic objective was unchanged: to consolidate and expand their sphere of power and, eventually, gain "domination of the non-communist world."[135]

The United States, therefore, needed to prepare to win the Cold War. The views of all three task forces plus the new JCS concept were integrated into an overall strategy that presumed strategic superiority, deterrence, containment, and a calculated, prudent rollback. The United States had to have a strong military posture "with emphasis on the capability of inflicting massive retaliatory damage by offensive striking power." It also had to "retain the cooperation of our allies" and "seek to win the friendship and cooperation of the presently uncommitted areas of the world, and thereby strengthen the cohesion of the free world." Within the Soviet orbit, the United States should not risk global war, but should take "feasible political, economic, propaganda, and covert measures designed to create and exploit troublesome problems for the USSR, impair Soviet relations with Communist China, complicate control in the satellites, and retard the growth of the military and eco-

Ho Chi Minh, 1954. A communist and nationalist, he typified a generation of postwar leaders in Asia and Africa who wanted independence and rapid modernization for their countries.

nomic potential of the Soviet bloc." Overall, the U.S. aim was to prevent Soviet aggression, end Soviet domination of other nations, and establish an effective arms-control regime with proper safeguards.[136]

The United States should not ignore the prospect of negotiating agreements with the Kremlin, Eisenhower's national security advisers concluded, but those agreements had to comport with U.S. security interests.[137] Otherwise, Eisenhower and Dulles preferred to use America's superior power to win the Cold War rather than settle on terms that might prove dangerous.[138] Rather than agree to a unified Germany, Eisenhower wanted to integrate West Germany into Western Europe, certain that a viable Federal Republic would attract east Germans and East Europeans westward. Rather than accept communist expansion in the third world, Eisenhower and Dulles wanted either to coopt or subvert revolutionary nationalist movements.

It would take time, of course, but perhaps time was not on the communists' side. With its superior power, Eisenhower and Dulles believed the United States could take risks to bring about the type of world it wanted; those risks were more sensible than the risks that inhered in relaxing tensions. Soviet expansion must be stopped, Dulles told his NSC colleagues, "even at the risk of war." The administration's "new look" strategy, based on brinksmanship and massive retaliation, would enable the United States to prevail in a crisis. If the Soviets wanted to choose war, let them do so. Dulles did not think they would. He predicted they would back down, as they had in the past.[139] Shirking his recent pessimism, the secretary of state told his colleagues on 1 October that the most recent evidence suggested that the United States was winning the Cold War, and the Kremlin knew it. The United States, therefore, needed to be smart and tough, bold yet prudent. It should build strength in West Germany and Western Europe, contain Soviet expansion in Southeast Asia and the Middle East, and probe for weaknesses inside the Kremlin's orbit without provoking war. It could win the Cold War without having to fight a hot war.[140]

But the pressures on the president would not cease. Eisenhower realized that he could not allow the chance for peace to slip away. Malenkov and his colleagues were waging a tireless peace campaign. The Russians represented themselves as champions of disarmament, relentlessly seeking to avoid a nuclear holocaust. The effect of their propaganda on peoples reared in war and familiar with hardship could not be disregarded. In the struggle for the soul of mankind, Ike did not want the Kremlin to hold the high ground.

Nor would Prime Minister Churchill permit the president to turn his back on the chance for peace. Since Stalin died, Churchill had been calling for détente and advocating a summit meeting with the new Soviet leaders. He had wanted to come to Washington in the spring to persuade Eisenhower to agree to this, but they could not get their schedules to mesh and then Churchill had been afflicted with a stroke. When he recovered, he resumed his efforts.[141] In early December, Eisenhower and Churchill and their top advisers finally met in Bermuda, along with French premier Joseph Laniel and foreign minister Georges Bidault.

At the first plenary meeting in Bermuda, on 4 December, Churchill emphasized one "supreme" question: "is there a new Soviet look" in the Kremlin? He thought so. U.S. strength and Soviet economic aspirations "may well have brought about a definite change in Russian policy and outlook which may govern their actions for many years to come." Our guard should not be let down, Churchill admonished, but "let us make sure that we do not too lightly dismiss the possibility" that there was a new disposition in Moscow.[142]

But President Eisenhower and his advisers decided that the Kremlin had not changed its mind-set. Under a new "dress," Ike said, there was "the same old girl." "Bath, perfume, and lace" had not changed her. In short, "he did not want to approach this problem on the basis that there had been any change in the Soviet policy of destroying the Capitalist free world by all means."[143]

Rather than discuss means of relaxing tensions, Eisenhower and Dulles wanted to build strength in Europe and shore up vulnerabilities in Southeast Asia. The European Defense Community must be ratified, they kept insisting. Bidault explained why ratification was so difficult, why allowing the West Germans to develop a new army was so hard for the French to stomach, and why integrating West German forces into a European army was causing indigestion. Dulles listened but would not budge. The Russian menace, along with other factors, he said, made it imperative for the French and Germans to heal their "age-old quarrel." "If concrete steps were not taken in the near future to heal the breach that had torn the heart of Western civilization for so many years," Dulles warned, "it would be quite impossible to sustain the interest and support of the American people." Churchill supported Dulles. There was no way that France could prevent the formation of a West German army directly or indirectly incorporated into NATO, he told Bidault. The logic was simple: West German forces were required to defend Western Europe; West Germany had to be integrated into Western Europe; German power had to be harnessed in behalf of western civilization.[144]

Strength had to be built in Asia as well. No more communist advances could be tolerated. Just before the Bermuda conference, Ike's national security advisers agreed that the aim of U.S. policy was to reduce, by means short of war, "the relative power position of Communist China in Asia."[145] If the armistice in Korea were to collapse, Dulles confided to Churchill and Bidault, the United States would strike the Chinese directly, perhaps even with atomic weapons.[146] Likewise, if China were to intervene in Indochina, its regime might face retaliation in China herself.[147] France had to prevail in Indochina, Eisenhower and Dulles believed, because the defense of the "free world" was at stake. The United States, Britain, and France would "work together to restore peace and stability in this area."[148]

Eisenhower and Dulles departed from Bermuda frustrated by Churchill's conciliatory disposition to the new leaders in the Kremlin and by Bidault's indecisiveness over the EDC. Yet Eisenhower immediately went to New York to give one of the most memorable speeches of his presidency. He knew he had to combat the Kremlin's peace campaign and inspire hope that war could be avoided; he knew he had to gain the high ground in world public opinion so that the United States could negotiate from strength.[149] He also knew that Senator McCarthy's anticommunist crusade—his attacks on State Department officials for their alleged disloyalty, his investigation of American libraries abroad for possessing books written by communist authors, or "fellow travelers," and his reckless charges against reputable public servants for their beliefs and behavior—was despoiling America's image abroad and arousing doubts about the vibrancy of American democracy.[150] Eisenhower needed to show the world that America's technological superiority could be harnessed to ameliorate poor living conditions; that its free-enterprise system could bring peace, not war; that its values could inspire liberation, not repression.

"Never before in history," the president told a plenary meeting of the U.N. General Assembly on 8 December 1953, "has so much hope for so many people been gathered together in a single organization," the United Nations. Yet the hopes for universal peace and human dignity were endangered by the progress of science and technology. An atomic age had dawned, and America's arsenal was growing daily. Its stockpile of weapons "exceeds by many times the total [explosive] equivalent of the total of all bombs and all shells that came from every plane and every gun in every theater of war in all of the years of World War II." But that gave the president scant satisfaction. He did not want to contemplate the "hopeless finality . . . that two atomic colossi are doomed malevolently to eye each other indefinitely across a trembling world."

Washington wanted agreements, not war; Americans wanted freedom for themselves and self-determination for others. Now that the Soviet Union had dropped a number of preconditions for a conference, the foreign ministers of the United States, France, Britain, and Soviet Russia could meet to discuss the problems of Germany and Austria, Korea and Indochina. But the president hoped for more. He announced that the United States was willing to meet privately with key nations to discuss solutions to the atomic arms race "which overshadows not only the peace, but the very life, of the world." Wanting to do more than merely reduce or eliminate atomic materials for military purposes, he proposed that the "governments principally involved, to the extent permitted by elementary prudence," make contributions from their atomic stockpiles to an international atomic energy agency. The agency would be established under the auspices of the U.N., and its principal mission would be "to devise methods whereby this fissionable material would . . . serve the peaceful pursuits of mankind." By donating "atoms for peace," the United States and the Soviet Union could join together in a common enterprise to build trust and to enhance the aspirations of humankind for peace and prosperity.[151]

Arms Control, Germany, and Indochina

The Russians appeared interested. On New Year's Day 1954, Prime Minister Malenkov released a statement wishing the American people well and beckoning for peace. "I hold that there are no objective obstacles to an improvement in relations between the Soviet Union and the United States in the New Year, and to the strengthening of the traditional ties of friendship between the peoples of our countries." Nothing was more important, he added, than an agreement not to employ weapons of mass destruction, which was a prerequisite to reaching "an understanding on the complete prohibition of atomic weapons and the establishment of strict international control over the fulfillment of the ban on the use of atomic energy for military purposes." Parallel to these efforts should be negotiations to reduce all other armaments. "All this," he concluded, "would undoubtedly reduce state expenditures for military requirements and would ease the economic condition of the population." Relaxing tensions made sense, Malenkov was indicating, when Soviet priorities were focused on ameliorating domestic living conditions.[152]

The Soviets were ready to talk. When Ambassador Georgi Zarubin met with Dulles a few days later, he was constructive and conciliatory. His government wanted to cooperate, and his own job was to improve relations, he said, but Eisenhower's proposal did not go far enough.[153] It did not ban the use of atomic and hydrogen weapons. In fact, it did nothing to halt the escalation of arsenals. Numbers of weapons could increase even while small amounts of atomic materials were handed over to the proposed international agency. More needed to be done and greater risks for peace taken; the Kremlin was willing to explore all angles.[154]

Yet Eisenhower and Dulles were not prepared to enter a serious round of negotiations to ban the use and prohibit the possession of atomic weapons. In fact, at that very moment, they were reaching consensus on their "new look" strategic posture based on massive retaliatory power. The president would not use atomic weapons in a preventive war and could imagine the eventual outlawry of all weapons of mass destruction.[155] But for the time being his strategic policy depended on the capacity to retaliate with and threaten the use of atomic weapons. "Since we cannot keep the United States an armed camp or a garrison state, we must make plans to use the atom bomb if we become involved in a war," Eisenhower said.[156]

The president and Dulles regarded the shadows cast by American strategic weapons as indispensable for their policy of containment on the Soviet periphery as well as for the defense of Western Europe and the American homeland. This is what strategic analysts meant when they talked about extended deterrence. The consequence was that the United States could not ban nuclear weapons. "Although we are perfectly prepared to listen to anything they may have to say," Dulles emphasized to the president, "we do not intend to let ourselves be drawn into separate negotiations with the Soviet [sic] on the elimination or control of nuclear weapons." Eisenhower concurred. There was, then, no follow-up to the president's U.N. proposal and no serious engagement with the Russians.[157] Trust was the prerequisite to arms control.

To build trust, Soviet officials would have to demonstrate goodwill. Their attitude on Germany was deemed critical. Dulles went to the foreign ministers' conference in Berlin at the end of January 1954 with little anticipation that the Russians would agree to the unification of Germany on terms the United States could accept.[158] Yet from the very first days of the conference, what struck U.S. delegates was Molotov's affability and the evident goodwill of Soviet diplomats. This was the first meeting of foreign ministers in five years, and the new leaders in the Kremlin seemed determined to make it a success. Soviet diplomats—even the habitually taciturn Foreign Minister Molotov—were eager to impress the Americans with their "desire to bring about some tranquility in international relations."[159] The Russians invited the American delegation for dinner at the residence of the Soviet high commissioner. Molotov's humor, C. D. Jackson reported, was sharp and subtle. He "talked quietly," wrote another American diplomat, seeking "to create an appearance of friendly objectivity."[160]

Yet the substance of what Molotov said throughout the conference gave the Americans heartburn. From the first days to the last, he dwelled on the consequences of German power and German militarism and objected to U.S. efforts on behalf of a European Defense Community tied to NATO. "It is well known that German militarism started World Wars I and II. The Soviet peoples cannot forget the sufferings and sacrifices of themselves and others. . . . Attraction of Germany into EDC not only would prevent attainment of German national unity but would also seriously increase the danger of a new world war in Europe." The Soviet Union "felt a grave responsibility," Molotov insisted, to prevent the rebirth of German militarism and to avert another war.[161]

What Molotov said privately resembled what he said publicly. After the Berlin Conference, when he returned to Moscow and reported to his colleagues on the Central Committee of the Party, he recapitulated how Dulles ceaselessly talked about free elections in all of Germany as a prelude to unification, an idea on which he heaped scorn. We all know that not all words about freedom really mean freedom, he said. Some people want freedom that privileges militarists and exploiters. Hitler, too, he recalled, came to power through free elections. The U.S.S.R. had suffered the most from Nazi aggression and could not and would not overlook the revival of German militarism.[162]

Molotov's statements reflected the reports being prepared by the Kremlin's experts on Germany, who meticulously described every sign of German militarism and revanchism. They used reams of statistical data to show the increases in West German coal and steel production. The West Germans, Soviet experts claimed, were developing the industrial infrastructure to produce weapons geared to the strategic requirements of NATO and the EDC. Notwithstanding the prohibitions on the production of weapons of mass destruction, the Soviets thought that West German scientists were developing methods of bacteriological warfare. They were also building strategic roads, reviving their shipbuilding industry, and constructing naval vessels. They were reputed to have plans to build torpedo boats, light cruisers, submarines, tankers, and even an aircraft carrier, all of which would initially sail under an American flag.[163]

In his annual report for 1953, the deputy high commissar in East Germany summarized similar developments, with a particular stress on the preparations to raise a German army, and he made many comparisons to the Nazi period. Four West German ministers in Adenauer's new cabinet were, he alleged, former Nazis. They were preparing to militarize the country and ensconce it firmly in the Western alliance structure either through the EDC or directly in NATO. The composition of the German working class had changed dramatically, now incorporating many former peasants, petit bourgeois, migrants, and former fascist soldiers, all of whom lacked class consciousness and were inclined toward nationalism and revanchism. Overall, the report alleged, the German bourgeoisie was seeking more independence in both internal and external affairs, and would support an army whether or not the EDC were ratified in France. Adenauer was determined to make Germany the decisive factor in world politics, and the Western powers were determined to bring about unification in their own way. They were working, moreover, to subvert the German Democratic Republic.[164]

Ideology and memory dramatically shaped these Soviet perceptions of developments in Germany. The Americans were firmly leading the imperialist camp, Molotov explained. They sought world supremacy. Toward this goal, they had formed NATO, which, he said, resembled the anti–Comintern Pact. From a position of strength, U.S. officials yearned to accrue even greater strength, even though it meant the restoration of German militarism and Hitlerism. When the army was recruited in West Germany, Molotov asserted, it would have Hitlerian generals at its head and would be aggressively revanchist. There was no doubt, he said, that Washington and Bonn were preparing a new war. "It can mean nothing else."[165]

The Russians were not alone in feeling anxious about the trajectory of German politics. The French and Americans also were worried. Nobody could be certain about the future of German democracy. As one American analyst on the Policy Planning Staff pointed out shortly before the Berlin

Conference: "We must recognize that we are dealing with a fluid society [in Germany], an inchoate political community, a people of dynamic and assured purpose but not too sure of their ultimate direction. . . . The Bonn Republic presents an impressive façade to the world but beneath the surface are dynamic forces which may imperil its stability."[166] This made it all the more important to integrate West Germany into the European community, for this would bind German power and help nurture German democracy.

But the Soviets, driven by their Marxist-Leninist axioms, could have no faith in such a community because they postulated the hostile intent of the entire capitalist camp. Molotov explained to his colleagues that his aim at the Berlin Conference had been to thwart Western plans for the EDC, champion the unification of a neutral Germany, and call for the negotiation of an all-European security treaty—aims that conformed with the collective goal of the Kremlin's new leadership: to relax international tensions without capitulating to Western demands. He was pleased to report, moreover, that the Americans had been leveraged into attending yet another conference, to be held in Geneva, on the problems besetting Korea and Indochina. At this meeting, U.S. officials would have to deal with representatives from Beijing notwithstanding their policy of nonrecognition of communist China.[167]

Although Molotov was pleased with the outcome of the Berlin Conference, U.S. officials were not dismayed. Dulles's "virile diplomacy," C. D. Jackson informed President Eisenhower, had thwarted every Soviet move, every possible maneuver to divide the French, British, and Americans. In Jackson's view, the Soviets seemed weak and defensive. Their overriding desire was now to hold East Germany and Eastern Europe. They had nothing positive to offer except their amorphous plan for an all-European security treaty and their call for yet another conference to discuss the problems of Asia.[168]

Their very weakness whetted the American appetite to gather more strength. "If, during 1954, we have the guts and skill to maintain constant pressure at all points of the Soviet orbit, we will get dividends from such a policy," said Jackson.[169] From Moscow, Ambassador Bohlen reported that the Russian disposition to relax tensions offered opportunities the United States should exploit. "If they can be made to recognize that a genuine reduction in tension is only possible by serious concessions on their part, I believe we can present Soviet leadership with a choice which is almost certain to provoke dissension and even real division."[170] By solidifying the integration of West Germany into Western Europe, U.S. officials hoped to get the Kremlin to relax its grip on Eastern Europe. When "there is a really united and strong Western Europe," Dulles told Adenauer, "the Soviets will not be able to maintain their total control of the satellite states by their present methods but will probably have to transform them into buffer states."[171]

Given an ideological foe whose animus toward the West seemed relentless, the United States could not risk the existence of a unified independent Germany in the heart of Europe. This would set back U.S. hopes for a Franco-German rapprochement, for the integration of the West European economy, and for the stability of European politics. The Soviet Union would have more opportunities to divide the West, and communist parties would have more opportunities to exploit social ferment. For Eisenhower and Dulles, relaxing tensions was less important than achieving their objectives in Western Europe. Now was the moment to capitalize on U.S. strength.

But whereas the American position appeared strong in Europe, its vulnerability in Asia seemed palpable. The French were losing the war in Indochina against the Vietminh. In May, they suffered a stunning defeat at Dienbienphu. After that defeat, a new government came to power in Paris under Pierre Mendès-France that was committed to negotiating a peace agreement by the end of July. At the Geneva Conference, France agreed to withdraw from Indochina and to recognize the independent states of Vietnam, Cambodia, and Laos. The Vietnamese communists, under pressure from Moscow and Beijing, agreed to regroup their forces above the seventeenth parallel and accept a temporary division of Vietnam. Free elections were supposed to be held under international supervision within two years.[172]

This outcome of the Geneva Conference was more favorable than Dulles had anticipated, yet he loathed the negotiations. He stayed only a few days at Geneva and left most of the negotiating to Under Secretary Walter Bedell Smith. When Dulles was actually at the meeting, his contempt for the Chinese communists was palpable. He refused to shake the hand of Foreign Minister Zhou Enlai and would not allow himself to be seated near any communist. One British observer commented that Dulles seemed beset "with almost pathological rage and gloom." He sat at the meetings with his "mouth drawn down at the corners, and his eyes on the ceiling, sucking his teeth."[173]

But he was very involved in formulating policy at home. If southern Vietnam was lost, all of Southeast Asia would go communist, he and Eisenhower believed, in which case vital raw materials would be relinquished to the adversary and Japan's position in the Western orbit would be endangered. The Japanese needed markets and raw materials in the free world. If they did not get them there, they would be forced to reach an accommodation with the Chinese communists. The world balance of power would be imperiled. We must not lose Japan, Eisenhower wrote Churchill. "The moral, political, and military consequences" would be calamitous.[174]

The United States could not permit revolutionary nationalist turmoil to follow its natural course. The British might think that the Russian danger was primarily nationalist, but Eisenhower and Dulles thought they were wrong. "Communism, in control of Russia," they were certain, "seeks world domination." They therefore could not tolerate the idea of the Vietminh taking over Indochina because they believed that this would endanger the world balance of power. They did not intervene unilaterally in May 1954 to assist the French or to attack the Vietminh, as Admiral Radford, the chairman of the JCS, wanted them to do, but Eisenhower and Dulles were not prepared to forsake southern Vietnam and the rest of Indochina.[175]

U.S. officials knew they were just beginning to face an era of revolutionary nationalism in the third world. The United States, C. D. Jackson wrote, must not be naïve about the future. "Colonialism is today a moribund duck," but power vacuums must not be allowed to emerge. American officials needed to give careful, serious, sophisticated thought to finding ways to entice or to force nationalist leaders to join the free world. We must get over "our complex," Jackson wrote, "that every little brown or black man with a tommy gun is automatically a 16-carat patriot on his way to becoming a local George Washington."[176] Henry Byroade, assistant secretary of state for Near Eastern, South Asian, and African Affairs, explained:

> This movement toward self-determination is one of the most
> powerful forces in 20th century affairs. When the history of our
> era is finally written it may prove to have been the most signifi-

cant of all. . . . It will be one of the great tragedies of our time if the peoples of Asia and Africa, just as they are emerging from generations of dependence, should be deluded by the fatal lure of the new imperialism and return thereby to an age of slavery infinitely more miserable than they have ever known before.[177]

Eisenhower and Dulles struggled to thwart the Vietminh's triumph in southern Indochina. Publicly, they said that the United States would not undermine the results of the Geneva Conference; privately, they immediately went to work to keep southern Vietnam and the rest of Southeast Asia from falling into communist hands. "The great problem from now on out," Dulles confided to his colleagues on the National Security Council, "was whether we could salvage what the Communists had ostensibly left out of their grasp in Indochina."[178] U.S. officials were under no great public pressure to take this position, nor were allies forcing it on them.[179] Indeed, the British now "seemed complacent about their ability to hold Malaya even if Indochina and Siam are lost," a judgment that Dulles did not share.[180] But Dulles and Ike did share the view that they must "prevent a Communist victory through all-Vietnam elections."[181] In addition, the United States had to be prepared to use force, even unilaterally, to thwart communist advances.[182] But by forming a regional defense alliance in Southeast Asia (SEATO), the Eisenhower administration hoped to be able to work with allies to deter aggression.[183]

In May 1954, just as the situation in Vietnam was unraveling, Eisenhower received another proposal to seek a global settlement with the communists. He talked it over with Dulles, and they decided against it. The time was not ripe. The threats were too great.[184] So long as the United States had superior power, it had to employ it to deter, contain, and roll back communism.

Notwithstanding the new leadership in the Kremlin, U.S. intelligence analysts concluded that the Soviet threat would grow.[185] Yet for the time being, U.S. power far exceeded Soviet power. "As of right now," said Admiral Radford, "and for the next few years . . . a very few years . . . the military posture of the Free nations is strong . . . tremendously strong . . . compared to that of the Soviet."[186] The United States, defense analysts concluded, would reach an era of atomic plenty at around 1955; the Soviets would not reach it until 1959, or later. Until then, the United States had to capitalize on its superior strength, not simply to deter and contain, but also to undermine Chinese communist control of the mainland and capitalize on Soviet weaknesses.[187] But this had to be done carefully, thoughtfully, unprovocatively.

At the end of 1954, Robert Cutler forwarded to the president the most original national security paper he had read since the onset of the administration. Opposition to the Soviet system had to be maintained, it said; it was evil. But the key to victory in the Cold War was to assume an evolutionary approach, not a revolutionary one. The overriding goal was to shape the conduct of communist regimes "and to encourage tendencies that lead them to abandon expansionist policies." Covert actions to subvert them were permissible, but only in conjunction with efforts to alter their overall behavior. Meanwhile, strength needed to be built in Western Europe. Peoples had to see that there were "constructive and attractive alternatives to Communism." In the struggle for the soul of mankind, democratic capitalism had to appear more attractive than the communist alternative.[188]

Over time, if the West could build strength and demonstrate its superiority, the adversary might change.[189] This was not likely in the near future, with the international environment so volatile, the future of Germany so uncertain, and revolutionary nationalist ferment so clearly in its infancy. So long as these conditions were embedded in the international system, there could be no more than an armed truce. The Kremlin would not desist from trying to capitalize on such opportunities. "We must adjust ourselves mentally and physically for a long period of such conditions," wrote Robert Bowie, the influential director of Dulles's Policy Planning Staff.[190]

But the Soviets might change in the long run, when circumstances evolved and ideological competition faded. For the moment, there had been no fundamental transformation in the Kremlin. But the U.S.S.R., said Charles Bohlen, had "entered a new phase with unforeseeable results."[191] In this context, the United States could not take a chance for peace, but it could watch the Kremlin closely, build strength, integrate German power, foment unrest behind the iron curtain, coopt revolutionary nationalism, and become an exemplar of a better way of life. The United States needed to demonstrate that its way was a superior way, that democratic capitalism was not destined for the ashbin of history.

Fear and Power

After Stalin's death, the ray of hope that the Cold War might assume a different trajectory sparkled briefly, but then went out. Ike declared that there was a chance for peace but did little to make it a reality. Why?

Fear and power provide the answers. Eisenhower and Dulles would not take big chances for peace because they worried about the trajectory of German power and because they feared that revolutionary nationalists, such as Ho Chi Minh in Vietnam, would seize power and align with Beijing and/or Moscow.

On the eve of his presidency, Ike had outlined his approach to foreign policy. The "preponderance of the world's resources," he wrote Lewis Douglas, must "not pass into the hands of the Soviets." The United States had to have access to the areas of the world producing vital raw materials. The governments in those areas must be "friendly to our way of life" and believe in free enterprise and open trade. The United States must use its superior power, so long as it lasted, to shape a world order amenable to America's domestic institutions.[192]

Malenkov, wanting to relax international tensions, in March and April 1954 continued to deliver major speeches stressing that every dispute could be settled peacefully. It was not true, he emphasized, that humanity had only two choices, either a new world war or perpetual Cold War. The Soviet government "stands for the further easing of international tension, for durable and lasting peace." Prevailing policies might "spell the destruction of civilization," he warned. "Our position is clear. We stand for the peaceful economic competition of the Soviet Union with all capitalist countries, including, of course, the United States."[193]

Malenkov's motives were unambiguous. The new leaders required time to introduce domestic economic reforms. In their internal deliberations, their discussions in the Central Committee, and the resolutions of their Politburo (or Presidium, as it was then called), they expressed their overriding concern to make more food, clothing, and housing available to the people of the U.S.S.R. Even Foreign Minister Molotov, talking to his domestic audience, stressed that the new leadership would not only accelerate production but also improve the quality and reduce the price of goods.[194]

Yet Stalin's heirs could not yet imagine an end to the Cold War. The documentary record suggests that they believed, as Stalin had, in the fundamental hostility of the capitalist world. Communist ideology postulated a protracted struggle, and Malenkov and the others needed to be no less vigilant than their predecessor in rooting out enemies and thwarting emerging threats. The American imperialists, Molotov told the Central Committee, behaved arrogantly and sought to rearm Germany, build positions of strength, and encircle the Soviet homeland with military bases.[195] Assuming the existence of a formidable foe bent on destroying their way of life, these Soviet leaders could not take big risks for peace. "When necessary," Malenkov explained, "we will negotiate with the imperialists, . . . [but] we will not allow unilateral concessions. . . . We firmly believe in our might."[196]

Of course, U.S. actions reinforced this axiomatic Soviet thinking. The United States would not negotiate a ban on nuclear weapons, would not agree to limit strategic armaments, would not recognize the People's Republic of China, would not accept a communist victory in all of Vietnam, and would not settle the German question except on its own terms. In other words, history and experience seemed to confirm the veracity of Marxist-Leninist thinking. If communists appeared weak, the adversary would seize the opportunity to crush them.[197]

And the new leaders in the Kremlin knew they were weak. They were aware of the problems besetting their system and of the turmoil in their bloc. They knew they needed to reform at home, boost productivity, expand food production, and buttress their allies in the social democracies. Indeed, their claim that Beria had wanted to sell out socialism in East Germany made Malenkov, Khrushchev, and their colleagues all the more determined to make socialism work in the part of Germany they controlled.[198]

Domestic political considerations dictated a relaxation of tensions but also reinforced the Kremlin's commitment to defend socialism and to make it function successfully in their bloc. Soviet leaders deeply resented Dulles's suggestions that their peace overtures reflected weakness, and they thought if they made too many concessions, the Americans would stiffen their demands.[199] And nothing frightened them more than the prospect of revived German militarism, of a strong Germany firmly ensconced in the American camp or acting independently to regain territory lost in the war.[200]

Ideology taught Russian leaders that history was on their side. They believed that socialism represented the future. "More than a third of mankind,"

Malenkov rejoiced, "has forever broken with capitalism."[201] The two world wars had contracted the capitalist sphere. The Chinese revolution had brought hundreds of millions of additional people into the realm of socialist democracy. Revolutionary nationalist turmoil in Asia, Africa, and Latin America portended additional victories. "The forces of Communism grow stronger every day," said Malenkov. "Our Soviet Union, the People's Republic of China, the countries of the People's Democracy, the German Democratic Republic are all a mighty, ever-growing stronghold of people and democracy."[202] While beckoning for peace, Malenkov had no doubt about the trajectory of history. "It is clear to the whole world that aggressive forces will not succeed in turning back the course of history."[203]

Malenkov readily acknowledged that Stalin had made significant errors. Formidable challenges lay ahead. "It would be wrong to forget," he and his comrades agreed, "that we still have unresolved, pressing economic tasks. . . . We still have . . . the giant task of maximally satisfying the ever growing material and cultural demands of the workers."[204] But the Soviet peoples, under the enlightened leadership of the Communist Party, had great recuperative powers. They were building "a new society in which there is no exploitation of man by man, no political and national oppression." They shared similar hopes and aspirations. They wanted "a rapid rise in the material and cultural standards of the people." The leadership of the party, Malenkov assured his listeners in Leningrad on 12 March 1954, would "work tirelessly in order that all Soviet men and women should live better and better." Together they were building a new way of life.[205]

Eisenhower, too, believed he was building a way of life. At meetings of the National Security Council, he talked emphatically about protecting basic values and institutions, which would be endangered if the distribution of power in the international system changed dramatically. Soviet inroads in Southeast Asia, the Middle East, Africa, and Latin America would affect core industrial areas in Japan and Western Europe. If the industrial heartlands of Europe and Asia were pulled into a Sino-Soviet orbit, the world balance of power would be altered and the United States might have to become a garrison state, with its values and institutions compromised.[206]

Eisenhower talked of a chance for peace, and Malenkov yearned to relax international tensions. Yet there could be no real détente or peace so long as ideological presuppositions shaped the two sides' perceptions of threat and opportunity in a dynamic international system. The United States and the Soviet Union possessed the most powerful weapons the world had ever known, but neither of their leaders could liberate himself from his fears or transcend his ideological makeup. The world seemed too frightening; it also seemed too full of opportunity.

III

RETREAT FROM
ARMAGEDDON, 1962-65

Khrushchev, Kennedy,
and Johnson

At the Brink

They went eyeball to eyeball during the missile crisis of October 1962. Nikita Sergeyevich Khrushchev, first secretary of the Communist Party of the Soviet Union and prime minister of the Council of Ministers, tried to slip missiles into Cuba. He was caught when an American surveillance flight over the Caribbean island detected the missiles being constructed. In a dramatic television speech to the nation on 22 October, U.S. president John F. Kennedy said the Kremlin was being "deliberately provocative" and testing American "courage and commitments." The United States would enforce a quarantine around Cuba to prevent any further deliveries of offensive military equipment, he announced. If Soviet ships proceeded and if the missiles were not withdrawn, the United States would stop the vessels. "I have directed the armed forces to prepare for any eventualities," the president declared.[1]

On 24 October, the Joint Chiefs of Staff ordered the Strategic Air Command to its highest level of alert preceding general war. U.S. military officials

Castro and Khrushchev, 1960. Khrushchev heralded the Cuban
revolution and wanted to thwart U.S. efforts to topple Castro.

were prepared to launch America's intercontinental and submarine-based
ballistic missiles. Every available bomber in the U.S. arsenal was put on alert.
Scores of them, loaded with nuclear weapons and with prearranged targets,
flew through the skies, refueled by aerial tankers.[2] "For a week the world was
on the verge of war," the Soviet ambassador to the United States Anatoly
Dobrynin wrote later, and "both our nations were in an excruciating state
of strain."[3]

Tension pulsated through the deliberations and correspondence of the
leaders of both nations. "I see, Mr. President," Khrushchev wrote to
Kennedy on 26 October, "that you too are not devoid of a sense of anxiety
for the fate of the world."[4] Khrushchev masked his own fear with intermit-

tent threats and rash decisions, but he was frightened. "Of course, I was scared," he later reflected. "I would have been insane not to have been scared."[5]

Khrushchev wanted to resolve the crisis without suffering humiliation. "We must not succumb to intoxication and petty passions," he wrote to Kennedy. The Soviet Union did not want war. "I have participated in two wars," he reminded the president. War wrought "death and destruction" that he could not forget or easily contemplate. "Only lunatics or suicides" would initiate offensive war.[6] So he proposed a solution. He had cleared the idea with his colleagues on the Presidium, all of whom deferred to his leadership. On 25 October, they agreed that the crisis should not come to a "boiling point." The game of power politics had to be played, "but without losing your head." Prudence now demanded a sensible settlement. Khrushchev hoped to trade his missiles in Cuba for the withdrawal of America's Jupiter missiles based in Turkey.[7]

But by the next morning, Khrushchev had additional information when the Presidium met. "We have been warned that war could start today," he told his colleagues. Yesterday's proposed letter would have to be revised; the allusion to the trade for the missiles in Turkey ought to be dropped. We must concentrate on the main point, he said. If the Americans promise not to invade Cuba, we will withdraw our missiles. "Otherwise, the situation becomes too dangerous."[8]

But Khrushchev still did not want to blink first. In fact, with luck, he hoped not to blink at all. He wanted to take time to see if the Americans would back down. Kennedy was a coward, Khrushchev told his comrades. The president slept with a wooden knife. Why a wooden knife? asked Anastas Mikoyan, one of the oldest Presidium members and first deputy chairman of the Council of Ministers. Jokingly, Khrushchev retorted, "When a person goes bear hunting for the first time, he takes a wooden knife with him, so that cleaning his trousers will be easier."[9]

But Khrushchev himself was hardly cool and logical. In the rambling, hastily drafted, and confused letter he sent to the president on 26 October, he proposed a deal: "We, for our part, will declare that our ships, bound for Cuba, will not carry any kind of armaments. You would declare that the United States will not invade Cuba with its forces and will not support any sort of forces which might intend to carry out an invasion of Cuba. Then, the necessity for the presence of our military specialists in Cuba could disappear."[10] If Kennedy agreed, Khrushchev told his colleagues, the missiles in Cuba would be dismantled. At that point, he would have established a zone of peace in the Caribbean and secured Fidel Castro's communist regime in Cuba, which the Americans had been trying to topple. Hopes for future revolutionary gains in the region would be preserved, or so Khrushchev contended, as he struggled to save face with his pliant comrades.[11]

Kennedy and his advisers were in no mood for a protracted negotiation. "They're working night and day" on the missile sites, Secretary of Defense Robert McNamara told a meeting of ExComm, the special group of advisers meeting with the president.[12] If the sites were completed, the Soviet Union would have the means to retaliate against U.S. territory if the administration ever decided to take military action against Cuba. Kennedy and his aides continued to insist that the vessels carrying armaments to Cuba turn around and

Nuclear warhead bunker in Cuba, 1962. U.S. intelligence flights detected
Khrushchev's bold gambit to place missiles in Cuba.

the offensive weapons inside Cuba be removed. Khrushchev's most recent letter could be the basis for a settlement, they believed: a noninvasion pledge by Washington in return for Moscow's withdrawal of the missiles.[13]

Before anything could be resolved, Khrushchev sent a second letter to Washington, on 27 October. This letter was a bold gambit, an "effort to snatch victory from the jaws of defeat."[14] "You wish to ensure the security of your country, and this is understandable," he wrote. "But Cuba, too, wants the same thing; all countries want to maintain their security." Khrushchev now revealed what galled him: the American military bases surrounding the Soviet Union. "You are disturbed over Cuba," Khrushchev continued. "You say that this disturbs you because it is 90 miles by sea from the coast of the United States of America. But Turkey adjoins us; our sentries patrol back and forth and see each other. Do you consider, then, that you have the right to de- mand security for your own country and the removal of the weapons you call offensive, but do not accord the same right to us?" The controversy could be ended quickly, Khrushchev concluded, if both sides agreed to withdraw the missiles that loomed so threateningly.[15]

The Soviet leader had upped the ante, reverting to his initial desire of two days before. Not only would the Americans have to pledge not to invade Cuba; they would also have to remove their Jupiter missiles from Turkey. If the Americans liquidated their base in Turkey, Khrushchev had said at a meeting on 25 October, "we will be the winner."[16]

This second letter wrought consternation in Washington. Tension reached its zenith when an American U-2 reconnaissance flight was shot down over Cuba on the morning of 27 October. The military plan was now very clear, said Defense Secretary McNamara. It was "basically invasion." Other presi- dential aides, and not only Kennedy's military advisers, wanted a more mas- sive air assault on Cuba. The invasion force assembled in the southeastern United States was ready, and the Joint Chiefs of Staff, eager to strike Cuba, were preparing, if necessary, to wage all-out nuclear war.[17]

Kennedy decided to ignore Khrushchev's second letter. He wrote Khrushchev that if the Soviet Union removed its weapons systems from Cuba and agreed to U.N. inspection, the United States would terminate the quar- antine measures and pledge not to invade Cuba.[18] But Kennedy feared that the crisis would not end quickly. Sensing that time was running out before the moment when he would feel compelled to authorize military action, he told his brother Attorney General Robert Kennedy to meet again with Ambassador Dobrynin and convey the sense of stark urgency. To avoid catastrophe, the president said he would withdraw the Jupiters if required; the missiles were going to be removed in any case. If telling Khrushchev this secretly could avoid war, the president reasoned, there was no sensible alternative.[19]

Robert Kennedy invited Dobrynin to come stealthily to the Justice Department, where Dobrynin found him looking exhausted. The president's brother was stressed, nervous, and blunt. "The danger of war is great," he told Dobrynin. The president was under great pressure from his military advisers; he did not want war, but it could happen. Khrushchev had to agree by the very next day to remove the missiles from Cuba. Dobrynin asked about the Jupiters in Turkey. Robert Kennedy said they would be withdrawn as a matter of course in a few months. This was not a quid pro quo, but it would happen. Nothing must be said publicly, or the deal would collapse.[20]

As Dobrynin prepared his report for Moscow, the Presidium met again on Sunday morning, 28 October, this time at a dacha outside Moscow. Khrushchev greeted his colleagues without a smile. He was nervous, and the atmosphere was "electric." War seemed imminent. His colleagues listened intently as he summarized the situation. Khrushchev began with allusions to Lenin's decision in March 1918 to sign a peace with Germany and cede most of Russia's borderlands to the enemy. This had been a dramatic diplomatic defeat but a brilliant strategic decision, inasmuch as it enabled the Bolsheviks to concentrate their efforts on vanquishing their domestic adversaries and consolidating their power. "Our interests dictated that decision—we had to save Soviet power," said Khrushchev. Now Soviet power was again at risk because nuclear war loomed. He asked his colleagues for their support in withdrawing the missiles from Cuba in return for the noninvasion pledge from the United States. "In order to save the world, we must retreat."[21]

As he asked for their assent, the telephone rang. The foreign ministry was calling. Dobrynin's report of his meeting with Robert Kennedy had just been received. Oleg Troyanovsky, Khrushchev's aide, took careful notes as the report was read to him over the phone, then summarized it for Khrushchev and his colleagues. Robert Kennedy was more nervous than he had ever seen him, said Dobrynin: there was no doubt "that the time of reckoning had arrived."

Military action was imminent. The Americans expected an answer the very next day, and they wanted Khrushchev to agree publicly to the terms that President Kennedy had laid out in his letter of 27 October. There could be no public mention of the missiles in Turkey.[22]

Khrushchev was not pleased, but he realized it was the best deal he could get. He rambled for an hour, telling his comrades they should trust Kennedy's word. The president would govern for six more years. The Cuban revolution would be saved, and Castro's regime would have time to prosper. Finally, Khrushchev asked his colleagues for their assent. Swiftly, they gave it to him.[23]

Officially, Khrushchev accepted Kennedy's terms. At 5:00 p.m., on 28 October, Moscow radio broadcast the Soviet leader's newest letter to the president of the United States. In order "to eliminate as rapidly as possible the conflict which endangers the cause of peace," Khrushchev wrote Kennedy, the Soviet Union would halt work on the missile construction sites in Cuba, "would dismantle the arms which you described as offensive," would crate and return them to the Soviet Union, and would seek to reach agreement with the Cuban government to allow U.N. verification of the dismantling.[24]

President Kennedy responded even before he read the official text. Events were rapidly "approaching a point" where they could become "unmanageable," he said. They had arrived at a settlement. He was gratified. "Perhaps now," he wrote Khrushchev, "as we step back from danger, we can together make progress" in the vital field of disarmament.[25]

Khrushchev was eager to turn to other matters but was not quite satisfied with the way Kennedy had recapitulated their agreement. He immediately sent another confidential letter to Washington, where Dobrynin handed it to Robert Kennedy. Khrushchev remarked that notwithstanding his silence on the Jupiter missiles, Soviet acceptance of the president's conditions hinged on their being removed from Turkey. Robert Kennedy took the letter, discussed it with his brother, reflected on it overnight, and then returned it to Dobrynin the next day. There would be no quid pro quo, Robert Kennedy insisted, and hence no official record and no exchange of letters. But there was a deal: His brother's word should not be doubted. If Khrushchev wanted more, he would get a public letter that would not make him very happy.[26]

Khrushchev's Retreat

Khrushchev did not demand more. He was intent on moving forward. He wanted no more crises and no war. He "never liked war and was afraid of it—after all, he served on the front," his son Sergei explained in an interview. The fight against the Nazis had been a defining experience of his adulthood. "When they showed war movies on television," Sergei added, "he turned them off—because even the best war movie is a lie."[27]

In his exchange of letters with Kennedy, Khrushchev had emphasized that his people wanted to live in peace. We don't want to destroy your country, he wrote the president. We want to compete on a peaceful basis. "We quarrel with you, we have differences on ideological questions. But our view of the world consists in this, that ideological questions, as well as economic problems, should be solved not by military means, they must be solved on the basis of peaceful competition." Peaceful coexistence was what he sought.[28] Indeed, Khrushchev's reckless move to insert missiles in Cuba appears to have been part of an elaborate plan he had concocted to offset America's preponderance of power and to force it into a comprehensive settlement of outstanding problems.[29]

Sobered by the brush with nuclear war, Khrushchev was now eager to solve those problems. "Evil has brought some good," he again wrote Kennedy in a very long letter on 30 October. "The good is that now people have felt more tangibly the breathing of the burning flames of thermonuclear war and have a more clear realization of the threat looming over them if the arms race is not stopped."[30] "Mr. President," Khrushchev wrote, the "crisis that we have gone through may repeat again. This means that we may need to address the issues" that contain so much "explosive material."[31]

Khrushchev carefully laid out what he wanted to address. The conditions were now ripe for finalizing a nuclear test ban treaty. We already were agreed, he said, on prohibiting nuclear tests in the atmosphere, in outer space, and underwater. Differences still existed on banning underground explosions, but they could be resolved so long as there was no insistence on inspections. More important, the two governments should consider a nonaggression treaty between NATO and the Warsaw Treaty Organization, perhaps even consider abolishing these military blocs. Khrushchev understood that Kennedy would consider such an idea outlandish but invited him nonetheless to begin pondering "norms of conduct which would not generate conflicts."

To avoid war, Khrushchev repeated, it was important to tackle fundamental problems. "Everything in our relations capable of generating a new crisis should be erased now." Talks to bring about genuine disarmament would be beneficial, and so would discussions designed to resolve the German question, guarantee the borders and sovereignty of East and West Germany, and arrange the withdrawal of American, British, and French troops from West Berlin. Peace would be promoted, Khrushchev added, if the United States recognized the People's Republic of China and allowed it to take its rightful place in the United Nations. Tackling these issues, notwithstanding their complexity, was of vital importance. "We, the Soviet people," and the peoples of Asia and Europe, "saw war. War often rolled through our territory." America participated in the two world wars, Khrushchev acknowledged, but had suffered "small losses" and gained "huge profits." Hence perhaps Americans did not quite fully appreciate the need for peace. But the crisis just passed was a Rubicon, alerting all the participants to the truth that they were living on the threshold of nuclear annihilation. The two leaders had been wise to compromise, but they would be even wiser to tackle the problems that might breed another conflict.[32]

President Kennedy did not respond to these broader questions, addressing himself, rather, to the specifics of the current situation. He felt betrayed by Khrushchev, he said. "Your government repeatedly gave us assurances of what it was *not* doing; these assurances . . . proved inaccurate." Relations between the two countries, Kennedy continued, had suffered a "profound shock." Not only had the Soviet actions in Cuba threatened the safety of the Western Hemisphere, but they had been "in a broader sense, a dangerous attempt to change the world-wide status quo." Simply stated, the Russians had lied to him, saying they would never deploy nuclear weapons to Cuba and then proceeding to do so. Before any other issues could be addressed, Kennedy insisted, Khrushchev had to carry out his pledge to remove all offensive weapons from the Caribbean, including the light bombers, the IL-28s, that Khrushchev had sent to Castro.[33]

The president was under the intense scrutiny of political adversaries as well as his military advisers, who were not happy with his negotiated settlement. The Joint Chiefs warned him that the Russians "were preparing the ground for diplomatic blackmail." He should be careful lest he be duped.[34] "We must operate under the assumption that the Russians may try again," Kennedy confided to Secretary of Defense McNamara. Until confidence was restored, détente would have to wait.[35]

Khrushchev responded to Kennedy with his own complaints and mounting frustration. The Americans were slow to lift the blockade. The IL-28s were twelve-year-old planes, incapable of offensive action, and ready to be scrapped; moreover, according to Khrushchev, they had not been part of the deal. Nonetheless, he would remove them, but he needed time. He had pressures of his own. Castro was in a state of total rebellion, refusing Khrushchev's pleas to cooperate. The Americans, in fact, were exacerbating Castro's recalcitrance by violating Cuban airspace and encouraging continuous sabotage.[36]

In the midst of these ongoing recriminations, Khrushchev repeatedly sought to turn Kennedy's attention to the bigger issues. We must "think of some real measures" to ensure security in the world, he wrote the president on 11 November. He sounded chastened: we approached the abyss and then exercised self-control and stepped back. "Next time," he warned, "we might not safely untie the tightly made knot." Rather than focus on the divisive details of the agreement, "let us now give joy to all peoples of the world and show that this conflict really became a matter of yesterday, let us normalize the situation."[37]

During November, the two nations did partly reassure each other. Soviet medium-range missiles in Cuba were dismantled and the light bombers were removed. The American quarantine was lifted, and Kennedy promised yet again that acts of sabotage against Castro would end. He tried to assuage Khrushchev's sensibilities. Thank you for the frank exchanges, he wrote Khrushchev on 14 December. "We are hopeful that once the Cuban crisis is behind us, we shall be able to tackle the other problems confronting us and to find the path to their solution."[38] "The most important" thing, Robert Kennedy quietly told Anastas Mikoyan at a dinner party in Washington, was the relationship between Premier Khrushchev and President Kennedy. "The fate of the world" hinged on whether they could build trust and mutual understanding.[39]

Khrushchev was eager to do so. In early December, he invited Norman

Cousins to the Kremlin. Cousins was the editor of *The Saturday Review*, an advocate of arms control, and a frequent participant in unofficial Soviet-American conferences. Khrushchev was relaxed and amiable. "Now, we will have man-to-man talk," he said. "Please tell me about your family. In Russia we like to hear about families before we talk about business."

After Cousins told Khrushchev about his wife and four daughters, they had a remarkable conversation touching on many matters. Cousins was impressed by Khrushchev's composed demeanor, politeness, and self-reflection. Khrushchev talked thoughtfully, unemotively, yet movingly. Expressing appreciation for the Pope's attempts to improve relations with the Kremlin, Khrushchev said he thought he and Pope John could understand one another. "We both come from peasant families; we both have lived close to the land; we both enjoy a good laugh." Comparing Lenin and Stalin, Khrushchev dryly commented on the very important difference between them: "Lenin forgave his enemies; Stalin killed his friends." The current Soviet economy, Khrushchev claimed, was doing well, especially the industrial sector. But "the bureaucracy made for inefficiency. If something went wrong, it was always someone else who was responsible."

But Khrushchev wanted to focus on foreign policy, as did Cousins. The Soviet premier knew that Cousins had talked to President Kennedy before coming to Russia, and he asked about the president's health. Kennedy was feeling well, Cousins said, and was eager to join with Russia to make a better world. Khrushchev retorted that he, too, was anxious to move forward. The "one thing the President and I should do right away," he added, "is to conclude a treaty outlawing testing of nuclear weapons and then start to work on the problem of keeping these weapons from spreading all over the world." In fact, Khrushchev now denied that he had ever opposed inspections. He had convinced the Presidium to allow a small number of inspections if they were essential for a test ban treaty, but he would not allow inspections to be used for surveillance and espionage, as he believed was the intent of the United States. "We see no reason why it shouldn't be possible for both our countries to agree on the kind of inspection that will satisfy you that we're not cheating and that will satisfy us you're not spying."[40]

On 19 December, Khrushchev followed up this conversation with another letter to President Kennedy, who had asked him for more details about his thinking on the test ban. Khrushchev did so in his usual expansive way.

"The Soviet Union does not need war. . . . Thermonuclear catastrophe will bring enormous losses and sufferings to the American people as well as to other peoples on earth." As an act of conciliation, Khrushchev explained, Soviet negotiators would agree to the idea of allowing the installation of seismic stations. He still did not think they were necessary to monitor underground tests, but he was willing to make this concession. "Thus our proposal on automatic seismic stations includes elements of international control." Since he was told that the U.S. Senate would never ratify a treaty without inspections, he was willing to accept "2–3 inspections a year on the territory of each of the nuclear powers in the seismic areas where some suspicious earth's tremors [sic] might occur." These would be added to the national detection devices that Khrushchev deemed sufficient to monitor a comprehensive test ban treaty, including underground explosions. "We believe now the road to agreement is straight and clear." The "world can be relieved of the roar of nuclear explosions. The peoples are awaiting this." We can now turn our attention, Khrushchev concluded, to more "urgent international problems."[41]

For the Soviet Union, the most urgent international problem was still Germany. In all his interactions with Kennedy, Khrushchev stressed this point over and over again. He worried about the growth of West German power, its economic prosperity, and its attraction to East German workers. Khrushchev now wanted to ensure the permanent division of Germany and force the West to recognize the communist government in East Berlin, since the survival of East Germany was indispensable to the protection of the Soviet sphere of influence in East Europe and the security of the Soviet Union itself.[42] At the Vienna summit meeting in June 1961, he had told Kennedy that the future of Soviet-American relations hinged on settling the German question: "Sixteen years have passed since World War II. The USSR had lost 20 million people in that War and many of its areas were devastated. Now Germany, the country which unleashed World War II, has again acquired military power and has assumed a predominant position in NATO. Its generals hold high offices in that organization. This constitutes a threat of World War III which would be even more devastating than World War II."[43]

Later, during that same summer of 1961, when U.S.-Soviet tensions rose precipitously, Khrushchev had supported the East German government's decision to build a wall dividing Berlin. Initially made of barbed wire and then reconstituted with concrete blocks, the wall stopped the stream of refugees fleeing East Germany. It shored up the communist regime, eased Khrushchev's anxieties about its survivability, and briefly reduced the strain in U.S.-Soviet relations. The wall, thereafter, symbolized the division of not only Germany but all of Europe.[44]

But the wall did not allay Khrushchev's suspicions of West Germany. In December 1962, President Kennedy and British prime minister Harold Macmillan met in Bermuda and announced a nuclear-sharing arrangement regarding Polaris submarines. The agreement allowed for the partial integration of British and American nuclear capabilities in a multilateral force (MLF), which the American and British leaders invited their NATO allies to join. The hope was that the proposed MLF would deter the allies, specifically the Federal Republic of Germany, from trying to build up their own nuclear arsenals.[45] But the Russians immediately saw it as a step toward an independent West German nuclear capability.

Khrushchev's escalating concerns about West Germany were deeply rooted and widely shared among Soviet citizens. Khrushchev told Norman Cousins:

> I can understand how Americans look at Germany somewhat differently than the way we do, even though you had to fight Germany twice within a short time. We have a much longer history with Germany. We have seen how quickly governments in Germany can change and how easy it is for Germany to become an instrument of mass murder. It is hard for us even to count the number of our people who were killed by Germany in the last war. More than twelve million, at least. We have a saying here: "Give a German a gun; sooner or later he will point it at Russians." This is not just my feeling. I don't think there's anything the Russian people feel more strongly about than the question of the rearmament of Germany. You like to think in the United States that we have no public opinion. Don't be too sure about this. On the matter of Germany our people have very strong ideas. I don't think that any government here could survive if it tried to go against it.
>
> I told this to one of your American governors and he said he was surprised that the Soviet Union, with all its atomic

bombs and missiles, would fear Germany. I told your governor
that he missed the point. Of course we could crush Germany.
We could crush Germany in a few minutes. But what we fear is
the ability of an armed Germany to commit the United States
by its own actions. We fear the ability of Germany to start a
world atomic war. What puzzles me more than anything else is
that the Americans don't realize that there's a large group in
Germany that is eager to destroy the Soviet Union. How many
times do you have to be burned before you respect fire?[46]

At the end of 1962, Khrushchev sent warm greetings to the president, expressing his hope for peace and coexistence but at the same time conveying
his disappointment about the MLF. People were disillusioned by yet another
plan for nuclear rearmament, he wrote, and worse yet, a plan that would lead
to the spread of national nuclear capabilities. People "grieved" to see yet

Khrushchev and Kennedy at the Vienna summit meeting, 1961. They
discussed Germany and wars of national liberation without reaching any
accord. Kennedy left feeling very agitated.

more arms, he proclaimed; they yearned for statesmen "to scrap the war machine of states, to destroy all means of annihilation of people."[47]

Khrushchev wanted to constrain arms expenditures and concentrate on lubricating the Soviet economy. Arms control, détente, and a relaxation of tensions were instrumental means to free up more money for Soviet domestic renewal. "Father began talking," said his son Sergei, about "how it was necessary to think primarily about strengthening the country's economy. If it was healthy, no imperialist would frighten us."[48]

Khrushchev lost patience with Soviet military officers who pressed him for more money. Marshal Andrei Antonovich Grechko, commander in chief of the Warsaw Pact, tried to persuade Khrushchev to spend more rubles on tactical nuclear weapons. "Don't try to persuade me," Khrushchev angrily shot back, "I don't have the money. You can't have everything."[49] When Marshal Rodion Yakovlevich Malinovsky tried to argue for more men and longer terms of service in the army and navy, Khrushchev grew even angrier: "Who's serving whom? The army, the people? Or the people, the army? Has it ever occurred to you how many useful things are produced by young men during the third year they *don't* spend in the army? . . . We spend billions training needed specialists, and all you want to do is grab them away, and make them goosestep."[50]

At meetings of the Presidium, in interviews, and in speeches, Khrushchev explained that his overriding priority was to demonstrate the superiority of socialism. He lectured and hectored those of his colleagues who he believed were shirking their responsibilities. They needed to do better, to focus more attention on the organization of the labor force, and to provide more incentives for collective-farm workers. The people demanded more; they deserved more. "This is a serious issue," Khrushchev said to the Presidium. "Now we're saying that we have constructed socialism. What does that mean?" Liquidating private landholding did not suffice. We must "transform private initiative into state initiative so that people will not say, 'You say you built socialism. Go to hell with your socialism! There's no dill, no potato.' "[51]

Khrushchev was certain that in the long run the superiority of communism would be judged by whether it could produce more dill and more potatoes—and more housing, schools, medical care, and consumer goods. For the peoples building socialism and communism, he said to the Central Committee of the Communist Party, "the main policy line . . . is the economic line."

Soviet leaders had to demonstrate "that the socialist and communist economy is superior" in constructing "the living standard of the popular masses—is superior to the capitalist economy in the development of the productive forces of society. And this, in the last analysis, is the main point of controversy between the new world and the old; it is the competition whose result blazes the path to socialism for all mankind."[52]

To achieve these economic goals, Khrushchev wanted to reduce defense expenditures.[53] He delighted in the Soviet Union's scientific advances and weapons technology, and he eagerly developed strategic missiles and powerful warheads. These weapons helped to cast powerful shadows over the imperialist adversaries who, in his mind, were forever seeking to take advantage of a Soviet Union they imagined was weak and vulnerable. He had conceived his gamble to put missiles in Cuba as a quick fix not only to protect Castro's revolution but to redress the strategic imbalance and allow for continued reductions in theater forces and military manpower.[54] If Americans were faced with threats as grave as those facing his own country, he had thought, they would negotiate more seriously about disarmament and Germany.[55] "Father achieved what he was striving for all those years," said his son: "American de jure recognition that the Soviet Union was its equal in destructive power." Now he could move on to the things that mattered most to him: controlling the arms race, reallocating resources, and demonstrating the superiority of socialism.[56]

But in the spring of 1963, Khrushchev's frustration with Kennedy mounted. The test ban negotiations, the essential prerequisite for advances in other areas, were going nowhere. During the 1950s, both the Soviet and American governments had tested nuclear weapons of greater and greater magnitude, thereby contaminating the atmosphere and triggering worldwide protests. Intermittent negotiations to ban the tests had stalled when the Americans insisted on on-site inspections with sophisticated monitoring devices to ensure that the Soviets would not conduct clandestine underground tests. Khrushchev was furious because he had been led to believe that Kennedy would sign a comprehensive test ban treaty if the Kremlin agreed to three inspections. But the president insisted on many more than three, and the inspections were to be conducted with sophisticated monitoring gear in geographically sensitive areas inside the Soviet Union. Khrushchev felt that he once again was being taken to the cleaner's.[57]

On 1 April, he instructed Ambassador Dobrynin to meet with Robert Kennedy to convey his irritation. His long letter, which Dobrynin gave to the attorney general, was filled with aspersions, insults, and disappointments, much of it revealing yet again Khrushchev's own sense of weakness. Don't try to intimidate us, he warned. Don't dare allow the West Germans to get their hands on nuclear weapons. Instead of reneging on his promises (as Khrushchev interpreted them), President Kennedy needed to have the guts to face down his reactionary foes at home. The Soviet leader was sick and tired of the political excuses, of the allegations that a comprehensive test ban with three inspections could not gain Senate approval. Khrushchev wondered if Kennedy really wanted détente. Did the president want nonproliferation? "And what kind of trust can there be when McNamara and Malinovsky take turns speaking, each time annihilating one another?" Yet behind the bluster, which offended Robert Kennedy, was a plea to enter negotiations, perhaps even to convene a summit.[58]

President Kennedy responded in a very conciliatory way, which probably affected Khrushchev's demeanor when he met again with Norman Cousins on 12 April. The editor of *The Saturday Review*, now acting somewhat as a liaison between Kennedy and Khrushchev, was again in the Soviet Union, this time with two of his daughters. Khrushchev invited them down to his residence at Gagra, near the Black Sea. Standing in the driveway by himself as the chauffeured cars arrived from the airport at Sochi, Khrushchev was the perfect host. After a sumptuous lunch, he proudly showed Cousins and his daughters around the estate with its groves of beautiful pine trees. He was especially proud of his hilltop sporting house. When the girls marveled at the pool, Khrushchev encouraged them to go for a swim while he and their father had a quiet talk on the terrace. But first, Khrushchev challenged Cousins to a game of badminton. Cousins was astounded by the agility, reflexes, and competitive spirit of the Soviet leader, who was about to turn sixty-nine.[59]

But when they sat down to talk at a small table on the glass-enclosed terrace, Khrushchev seemed "weighted-down, even withdrawn," quite different from the confident, optimistic leader Cousins had encountered four months earlier. Quickly the conversation turned to the nuclear test ban negotiations, and Khrushchev poured out his feelings of betrayal. Nuclear war, he said, was "sheer madness." But once again he had been made to "look foolish" before his colleagues on the Presidium, whom he had convinced to assent to three inspections. Now he was under pressure from his own military officers and atomic scientists for more testing. "People in the United States seem to think I am a dictator who can put into practice any policy I wish. Not so. I've got to persuade before I can govern." Khrushchev alluded to being under great pressures, especially from the Chinese. "I cannot and will not go back to the Council of Ministers and ask them to change our position in order to accommodate the United States again. Why am I always the one who must understand the difficulties of the other fellow? Maybe it's time for the other fellow to understand my position." When Cousins eloquently explained that President Kennedy did feel there had been an honest misunderstanding and did want an agreement, Khrushchev concurred that something had to be done. But the next move, he insisted, must be up to the United States.[60]

Khrushchev had gotten his point across and was ready to end the conversation, but he politely asked Cousins if he had other things on his mind. Cousins said yes. He wanted to know what Khrushchev thought he should say to critics of the test ban in the United States and to opponents of conciliation and peace who sincerely believed that Khrushchev, as he had said publicly, wanted to bury the United States.

Khrushchev responded "testily":

> What I meant was, not that I will bury you but that history will bury you. Don't blame me if your capitalist system is doomed. I am not going to kill you. I have no intention of murdering two hundred million Americans. In fact, I will not even take part in the burial. The workers in your society will bury the system and they will be the pallbearers. Don't ask me when it is going to happen. It may not happen tomorrow or the day after. But it will happen. This is as certain as the rising sun.

When Cousins defended American capitalism and said that Marx had failed to grasp the fluidity of a free society and the erosion of class consciousness in it, Khrushchev interjected that Marx would not be dismayed by developments in the United States. "I repeat," Khrushchev said, "I have great admiration for the American people. Mark my word, when they become a socialist society, they will have the finest socialist society in the world. They are resourceful, energetic, intelligent, imaginative. What a wonderful thing it will be for them and for the world."[61]

Khrushchev's profound conviction that he represented a system that would prove its superior ability to meet humankind's material and spiritual needs was clear. "Capitalism isn't just an economic system," he told Cousins. "It's a way of life that leads to a corruption of important values." Khrushchev disdained American culture, ridiculed its media, and scorned its concept of freedom. "If the sadism and violence you show [in your films and television] are at all representative of the kind of life you have in America, God help you! All the killing and beatings and cheating and swearing and wife stealing and immorality! A nation can't help being judged by the things it is interested in."[62]

Just a few days after chatting with Cousins, Khrushchev had a long interview with an Italian newspaper editor. "The liquidation of the crisis in the Caribbean," he said, "has truly given rise to great hopes for mankind for a change in international relations." There was the possibility the U.S.S.R. and the West could transcend the Cold War and enter a new era of international relations. "Genuine détente . . . can be created by the joint efforts of all peoples." The different socioeconomic systems should develop trade and scientific and cultural exchanges. "Peoples should get to know each other better. But at the same time," Khrushchev continued, "we communists have never agreed, and never will agree, to the idea of peaceful coexistence in ideologies. In this there can be no compromise."[63]

Khrushchev acknowledged that his nation and his system were encountering many problems. "Of course, we have our problems and certain difficulties in agriculture, but they are the problems of growth and advance. Imagine a young boy who is growing fast and developing his strength literally from one day to another. . . . Either he has grown too big for his trousers, or his coat has split at the seams, or something else happened. But our young boy is, nevertheless, well." Enemies wanted to exaggerate the problems of the Soviet Union, he said, but these problems were small when compared to the troubles of capitalist society. "We are proud of the fact that the society which paves the way into the cosmos for man is the society of victorious socialism which has put an end for good to capitalist exploitation, social injustices, and bondage."[64]

The future rested with socialism, according to Khrushchev. But the transition to socialism would not come about through the use of force, unless capitalists resisted the natural evolution of history.[65] When Indira Gandhi, the daughter of India's prime minister, visited Moscow, Khrushchev explained to her that he had compromised during the missile crisis because history was on the side of communism. It was madness to jeopardize the future and dash the hopes of mankind.[66] Peace had to be maintained. But the battle of ideas would persist, had to persist. "In this sharp struggle of two irreconcilable ideologies, socialist and bourgeois, . . . we have attacked and will continue to attack, to affirm communist ideas."[67]

These ideas, Khrushchev was certain, resonated with the masses of humanity, especially in Asia, Africa, and Latin America. "Our ideas—the ideas of Marxism-Leninism—are conquering the minds of ever new millions of people. They have truly become rulers of the thoughts of progressive mankind."[68] In a private conversation with U Thant, the Burmese secretary general of the United Nations, in August 1962, Khrushchev had amplified his beliefs about the degeneracy of capitalism. Bourgeois values were decadent. In the United States, there was no theater, no great literature, no real freedom of the press. Newspapers were owned by tycoons whose ideas prevailed—not the ideas of the real people, not the views of the workers. And everywhere blacks were discriminated against—in hotels, restaurants, trains, and buses. "It's incredible," Khrushchev exclaimed. "And this is Western Civilization." No, it resembled an "ideology of crazies."[69]

Socialism, on the other hand, resonated with the hopes of mankind. Monopoly capital was not interested in helping the economies of the newly emerging nations, but the socialist countries, with their planned economies, were different. They could help others while satisfying the needs of their own people. Socialist economies did not have crises or recessions. Sure, their managers committed errors, and the planning process was not perfect, but their mistakes were not comparable to the anarchy of free markets in capitalist countries. By 1970, Khrushchev told U Thant, the Soviet Union would equal America's gross national production, and by 1980, surpass it. Lived experience would shape the consciousness of people. Even critics of communism would want to emulate the means by which the Soviet people achieved such material, cultural, and spiritual progress. Planned economies, thought Khrushchev, were the wave of the future.[70]

Leaders throughout the third world agreed with him. From Cuba to Algeria to Ghana to Egypt to India and to Indonesia, new nationalist leaders voiced their support for planning. Most of them were not communists; indeed they sometimes repressed and imprisoned communists. But *planning* was their common vocabulary. "It is inevitable," said the Planning Commission of India in its second five-year plan, that "if development is to proceed at the pace envisaged . . . the public sector must grow." Key decisions "regarding production, distribution, consumption, and investment—and in fact all significant socio-economic relationships—must be made by agencies informed by social purpose."[71]

Khrushchev believed that peoples freeing themselves from imperial exploitation would eventually choose the socialist way of life. He was willing to support them, nurture them, provide them with aid, suffer their insults, and risk recriminations from his own colleagues who were not certain of his judgments, because he was confident that the transformation of the international system and the stirrings of peoples throughout Asia and Africa heralded the future of mankind. As he said after returning from a trip to Egypt, "the fact that [the United Arab Republic] is embarking on the path of socialist development gladdens us, the Soviet people. However, new things are not born at once." There would be trials, tribulations, and wrong turns. But imperialists knew their way of life was being repudiated. "The preponderance of power in the international arena," he said, "is in favor of socialism."[72]

Since Khrushchev believed that the processes of change in the third world could not be thwarted, he resented American invitations to collude in preserving the status quo. At the summit meeting with President Kennedy in Vienna in June 1961, he told the president that "it looked to him as if the United States wanted the USSR to sit like a school boy with his hands on his desk. The Soviet Union supports its ideas and holds them in high esteem. It cannot guarantee that these ideas will stop at its borders."[73] After the Cuban missile crisis, when President Kennedy again asked the Soviet Union "to avoid aggravating the situation in all parts of the globe," Anastas Mikoyan politely retorted, "Revolutions have always been and they will always be."[74]

Moreover, Khrushchev could not easily change Soviet attitudes and policies. He made no secret in his conversations that he was under relentless criticism from the Chinese leadership, which had ridiculed him for backing down in the Cuban crisis, for negotiating a test ban, and for pursuing peace-

Khrushchev and the Indonesian leader Sukarno, 1960. Khrushchev
worked hard to spread Soviet influence in the third world.

ful coexistence. They accused him of withholding arms from revolutionary
nationalists in the third world. They denounced him for ideological heresies.
Their criticisms hurt, for Khrushchev saw them as coming from a government that was itself pursuing irrational economic policies. The Chinese comrades, Khrushchev told his colleagues on the Presidium, were voicing a form
of national egoism. They wanted to be "first violin." They sought to gain
leadership of the communist world. They attacked Moscow rather than the
real enemy, which made no sense. But it meant the Soviet Union could not
for a moment relinquish its efforts to gain friends and allies among revolutionary patriots in the third world.[75]

International conditions were in great flux. The anti-imperial ideology of
Marxism-Leninism resonated, and the ostensible successes of the Soviet
Union's planned economy commanded much respect in the capitals of newly
emerging nations. But the Sino-Soviet rift splintered the communist ideological front and created weaknesses that the capitalist enemy could exploit. Khrushchev and his comrades raged at the Chinese communists, but
also understood that they must try to heal wounds and preserve the prin-

Khrushchev and Brezhnev with Mali's leader, Modibo Keita, 1962.
The Soviets welcomed third world politicians to Moscow.

ciple of unity in their feverish competition for leadership of the communist
world.[76]

Khrushchev would not modulate his ideological fervor or cease the Soviet
Union's competition for the soul of mankind. But the fire in his belly was
tempered by his realization of the dangers in a rivalry that might culminate in
nuclear holocaust. He was a man of paradox: practical yet ideological, impul-
sive yet prudent. The grandson of serfs, the child of peasants, a shepherd in
his boyhood, and a coal miner and machinist in his teens, the untutored and
uneducated Khrushchev had risen to unexpected power as a result of tireless
work, gritty determination, street smarts, earthy wit, and loyalty to a cruel
and vicious leader. He was enormously proud of the civilization he was building, but totally aware of how blemished it was by the experience of Stalinism.
As a party boss in Moscow in the 1930s, Khrushchev had assailed the "enemies of the people," and as party tsar in the Ukraine during the late 1930s
and World War II, he had managed the purges, decimated the intelligentsia,
and destroyed the nationalist opposition. Soaked in the blood of his own victims, Khrushchev nonetheless now wanted to be remembered for his repudi-

ation of Stalinism, for expelling the Stalinist poison from the Soviet system, and for arranging an orderly transition of power. "A man comes to life in his paradoxes," commented Norman Cousins.[77]

Khrushchev was committed to perfecting a superior civilization, as he saw it. The socialist project, to which he and his comrades had dedicated their lives, had nearly been extinguished by Nazi invaders and was still threatened, he believed, by hostile capitalists. And now the communist utopia he hoped to fashion faced an even graver danger: nuclear annihilation. To preserve and nurture that which he most cherished, Khrushchev knew he needed to modulate the competition, avoid miscalculation, negotiate a test ban, limit the arms race, and sign treaties that would guarantee both the existence of two German states and the postwar territorial status quo in Europe.

In the spring of 1963, Khrushchev told his colleagues that they should consider many options in the pursuit of détente, including a limited ban on nuclear testing and even reconciliation with West Germany.[78] But he was not prepared to move boldly in any direction until he discerned that his overtures would be reciprocated.

His bold bluster morphed to impatient prudence. Nobody knew what he would do next. He traveled frenetically inside and outside the Soviet Union. He visited Eastern Europe, Scandinavia, India, and Egypt, often delivering tediously long speeches. In Moscow, he tangled with party bureaucrats and military officials and argued with writers, poets, and painters, whose growing artistic freedom disgusted him and whom he once again started repressing.[79] After the Cuban missile crisis, he was a wounded statesman, still yearning for new breakthroughs and hoping he could find a partner whose passion for peace and human betterment equaled his own, even if that partner represented a civilization doomed to the ashbin of history.

Kennedy Bides His Time

President John F. Kennedy was wary of Khrushchev's overtures. Like Eisenhower in 1953, Kennedy wanted to see Soviet deeds, not hear Soviet words. By secretly deploying missiles to Cuba, Khrushchev had shown his true colors. He "does not wish us well," Kennedy told the American people in an interview at the end of 1962.[80]

Kennedy acknowledged that Khrushchev did not want to use the missiles in Cuba to attack the United States. But their presence in the Caribbean "would have politically changed the [world] balance of power. It would have appeared to, and appearances contribute to reality." The Soviet leader had demonstrated again that he could not be trusted. Through guile and through daring, the Soviets ceaselessly sought to create "a monolithic communist world."[81]

The president was not unwilling, however, to compete peacefully with the communists if they abandoned their expansionist ways and ended their support of wars of national liberation in the third world. Theirs was a system "which really does not suit the desires of the average man."[82] Consequently, the American people welcomed peaceful competition. But the Kremlin, said Kennedy, did not allow people to choose freely. The end of the Cold War was therefore not yet in sight. Communist policy was not likely to change. "A moment of pause is not a promise of peace," he told the Congress in his State of the Union message on 14 January 1963. "The world's prognosis prescribes . . . not a year's vacation for us, but a year of obligation and opportunity."[83]

Opportunity did not mean a meeting with the Soviet leader. Kennedy did not think much would be achieved at another summit conference. Nor did he think that the many signs of division between Beijing and Moscow offered much hope. The "Soviet-Chinese disagreement is over means, not ends," he told Congress. "A dispute over how best to bury the free world is no grounds for Western rejoicing."[84]

Competition was wired into the president's DNA. Born into an Irish Catholic family of great new wealth and extensive political connections, Kennedy had ambition pulsing through his bloodstream. Schooled at elite private institutions and educated at Harvard, he fought in World War II, ran for Congress in 1946, and joined the U.S. Senate in 1952. From early in his career, he aimed to be president. Service and sacrifice were the mantras for his class and generation. Hardened by years of international economic depression, wisened by the failures of appeasement in the 1930s, and toughened by the travail of war, Kennedy and his advisers wanted to fight poverty, combat tyranny, and adjust the United States to an international system transformed by liberation struggles throughout most of the third world. The youthful president, although often ailing from a variety of physical problems, radiated confidence, vigor, and determination. He was witty and intelligent, reflective and analytic, elegant and eloquent. "Let the word go forth," he announced in his inaugural address, that "the torch has been passed to a new generation." Let the world know that Americans would "pay any price, bear any burden, meet any hardship, support any friend, oppose any foe to assure the survival and success of liberty."[85]

Free speech and free enterprise, Kennedy recognized, were beleaguered by an international system undergoing momentous changes. The peoples of Asia, Africa, and Latin America were astir, seeking autonomy, yearning to overcome their backwardness. For Khrushchev, Kennedy knew, these areas of the globe offered opportunities to prove the appeal of communism. For the United States, Kennedy believed, they offered unprecedented challenges. "I do think we have a tendency to think of the world as Communist and free, as if it were two units," he told his fellow Americans. "The fact of the matter is our world is so divided, so poverty stricken, so desperate in many conditions, that we have a full time job strengthening the section of the world which is not Communist."[86] He believed that job needed urgently to be done. The Cold War, wrote Arthur M. Schlesinger, Jr., his friend and adviser, "is a struggle between two different systems trying to show which can deal more effectively with an inexorably changing world."[87]

It was for this reason that Kennedy placed a higher priority on thwarting communist advances in the third world than on responding to Moscow's overtures for détente. Khrushchev's speech of 6 January 1961, rather than his more recent letters, was forever on Kennedy's mind, the speech in which he had conveyed enthusiasm for wars of national liberation—wars that the Kremlin had not caused but would support, that were inscribed in the fabric of history, that signified the repudiation of imperialism and prefigured the triumph of socialism.[88] Prudence demanded that the United States not allow the Kremlin to make gains in the third world. In Latin America, the Soviet Union had hoped to benefit from the great popularity of Castro's revolution and capitalize upon the misery and despair that existed in so many countries; hence, among the president's first foreign policy initiatives in 1961 were his attempts, on the one hand, to overthrow Castro, and on the other, to launch an "Alliance for Progress" to promote economic, social, and political reform in the Western Hemisphere.[89] But Kennedy's concerns stretched around the globe. Throughout Africa, the Soviet Union seemed to be scheming for advantage by offering aid and trying to negotiate new civil aviation agreements.[90] In Southeast Asia, the Kremlin appeared unwilling to stop the renewed fighting in Laos between rightist, centrist, and communist factions, although it had helped to negotiate an agreement to "neutralize" the country in 1962. Everywhere, the Soviets seemed ready to exploit indigenous strife, civil war, and regional unrest. "We cannot permit all those who call themselves neutrals to join the Communist bloc," Kennedy told his advisers in January 1963. If "we lose them, the balance of power could swing against us."[91]

In South Vietnam, the president knew that the Kremlin was not responsible for the ongoing strife that pitted the communist-led and Hanoi-backed National Liberation Front against the government of Ngo Dinh Diem. The Eisenhower administration had put Diem in power in 1954, offered him assistance, and sent military advisers to help train an army loyal to his government. But Diem was never able to muster a great deal of popular support. After rejecting all-Vietnam elections that he knew Ho Chi Minh and the communist leaders of North Vietnam would win, he had faced more and more opposition in South Vietnam. Former communist Vietminh supporters who had remained in the South after the negotiation of the Geneva Accords of 1954 clamored for land reform, equitable taxation, and the end of corruption. Thwarted, they increasingly took up arms, formed the National Liberation Front (the Vietcong), sought assistance from the communist government in North Vietnam, and struggled to overthrow Diem.

President Kennedy was conflicted about the U.S. commitment in Vietnam, but he made decisions in 1961, 1962, and early 1963 that allowed that commitment to grow incrementally. Anticipating that this experiment in counterinsurgency warfare would work, he hoped that he would not have to insert U.S. combat troops or bomb North Vietnam, as many of his advisers were pressing him to do. But he also believed there was "a strong, overwhelming reason for being in Vietnam." If you "lost Vietnam," said Robert Kennedy, "everybody was quite clear that the rest of Southeast Asia would fall." The president assumed, said Robert Kennedy, that such a loss "would have profound effects on our position throughout the world."[92]

President Kennedy's skepticism about Khrushchev's good intentions was reinforced by his conviction that the Soviet leader was doing little to quell Fidel Castro's subversive activities in the Western Hemisphere. The Kremlin, in fact, was slow to remove all its troops, planes, and even tactical nuclear weapons from Cuba. At National Security Council meetings, the Central In-

Ngo Dinh Diem, 1955. Eisenhower and Kennedy supported his government in South Vietnam, but as his position weakened Kennedy came to see him as an impediment to U.S. policy. He was overthrown in early November 1963, with U.S. acquiescence, and killed (to the dismay of the president).

telligence Agency and the Joint Chiefs of Staff remonstrated against Castro and vilified Khrushchev. "We must get the Soviets out," insisted CIA director John McCone, and it was imperative "to prevent any other country from falling to Communism." Kennedy agreed, and continued to authorize covert actions to topple Castro.[93] When the president sent Under Secretary of State W. Averell Harriman to Moscow in late April 1963, Harriman told Khrushchev that he "must realize that Cuba is creating much tension in the whole Caribbean area and if it is not important to the Soviets to have troops in there why don't the Soviets take them out?"[94]

The president realized, of course, that Castro was not Khrushchev's minion, and that in general he was seeking to capitalize on poverty and despair. "I think Latin America is our toughest place," Kennedy told legislative leaders on 8 January 1963, "not really because of Castro but because of all the situation [*sic*]," meaning the social unrest and economic deprivation.[95]

But Castro was not alone in his efforts to exploit volatile socioeconomic conditions. Kennedy was equally concerned about China. China, he knew, would soon test its own atomic bomb.[96] Beijing might then become more inclined to take risks in spreading its own version of Marxism-Leninism. Angered by Soviet neutrality during China's hostilities with India over their border in the fall of 1962, Mao Zedong sought ever greater influence in the third world. "The Chinese will almost certainly continue to attempt to expand their influence at Soviet expense in the underdeveloped areas," said the CIA. They would remain "passionately anti-American."[97]

The Sino-Soviet split, therefore, conjured up additional anxieties for the president and his advisers, and it inclined them to compete with rather than accommodate the U.S.S.R. This was true even though President Kennedy understood that the sources of unrest in the world emanated not so much from Moscow as from the fragmentation of the communist world and the seething unrest in less developed areas of the globe.

But fragmentation was also occurring in NATO. In December 1962 and January 1963, French president Charles de Gaulle challenged America's leadership. He spurned the multilateral force and vetoed Britain's proposed entry into the European Economic Community. He invited German chancellor Konrad Adenauer to Paris, signed a mutual security treaty with the Federal Republic, and reaffirmed the sincerity of the Franco-German postwar rapprochement. De Gaulle reiterated that France would develop its own independent nuclear force and hinted at making a nuclear deal with the West Germans. He and Adenauer distrusted the U.S. commitment to their countries' security and feared the Americans might sign an agreement with Moscow that would reduce the U.S. commitment to Europe in order to ease the financial burden on the American treasury. De Gaulle and Adenauer also worried that American impetuosity, arrogance, and misjudgments in other parts of the globe might drag them into wars that were unrelated to their vital interests. Buoyed by his successes in extricating France from its colonial war in Algeria and in strengthening presidential power in the Fifth Republic,

Charles de Gaulle (left) and Konrad Adenauer shaking hands, 1958. Kennedy feared that their growing friendship might challenge U.S. leadership in Europe.

de Gaulle sought to resurrect French grandeur and presumed to know better than the Americans how to handle a turbulent and uncertain world.[98]

President Kennedy was agitated, even bewildered, by de Gaulle's actions and Adenauer's behavior. De Gaulle, he told his advisers, might try "to run us out of Europe by means of a deal with the Russians." And what, Kennedy mused, did Adenauer mean by his portentous references to a European defense system?[99] He ordered the CIA to give him weekly reports covering every aspect of Franco-Soviet negotiations.[100]

Because Kennedy and his aides recognized they could never alter de Gaulle's policies, they focused their attention on West Germany, which, Kennedy insisted, must remain "aligned with the West." The whole purpose of the MLF was, after all, "to reassure Germany without making Germany a nuclear power." If the West Germans participated in a multilateral nuclear force, Kennedy hoped any enthusiasm they might have for a national force of their own would be quelled or, at least, postponed.[101] But memories of the past and fears about the future shaped Kennedy's and his advisers' thinking. West Germany could not "be relegated indefinitely to an inferior nuclear status," they thought; past attempts to keep it in a subordinate position had been disastrous and must not be tried again. There is no doubt, said Secretary of Defense McNamara, "that within 10–20 years the [West Germans] will have an independent nuclear force unless we tie them within the next 24 months to a multilateral force."[102]

Kennedy understood what the tradeoffs had to be. He knew the Soviets would protest the idea of West German participation in a multilateral nuclear force. "From my talks with Stalin and Khrushchev," Ambassador Harriman reminded Kennedy on 23 January 1963, "I am convinced that the Soviets are really concerned over the possibility of the rebirth of German militarism." Khrushchev did not think Adenauer would ever advocate an aggressive military policy, but he wondered about future German leaders, and so did many of Kennedy's advisers. "I agree with Khrushchev," Harriman wrote, "and do not trust future German developments. . . . A German leader, such as [Franz Josef] Strauss, could really do a de Gaulle on us in developing independent nuclear capabilities."[103]

Notwithstanding these warnings and the MLF's many inherent problems, Kennedy instructed his aides to see if an agreement could be negotiated with the British, West Germans, and other NATO allies. For the moment, actions taken by the French and West Germans, along with the sentiments they expressed and the pressures they exercised, trumped Khrushchev's overtures for peace. In order to keep West Germany out of the clutches of de Gaulle and prevent Bonn from being lured into making an independent deal with Moscow, Kennedy continued to explore some form of a multilateral force and to reaffirm support for German unification within an Atlantic alliance. He was inclined to deflect Soviet overtures until "the Germans were fully in tow."[104] To appease the West Germans, Kennedy acknowledged in a taped conversation with the Joint Chiefs of Staff, "we're opening a [Pandora's] box."[105]

Kennedy never adequately responded to Khrushchev's overtures. The most likely way to begin to relax tensions with the Kremlin was to negotiate a comprehensive nuclear test ban treaty, as Khrushchev felt he had been burned on the issue of inspections.[106] But Kennedy believed that more inspections and more monitoring were needed to overcome the reservations of his domestic political opponents. Republicans, he knew, were eager to pounce on him for his gullibility. With his gaze never far from the 1964 presidential elections and with his priority on domestic tax cuts, the president preferred to keep his options open. Rather than take big chances for peace, he bided his time.[107]

Give Peace a Chance

Nonetheless, on 10 June 1963, President Kennedy delivered one of the most surprising and eloquent addresses of his presidency. The speech was drafted in secrecy by a few close aides in the White House. Neither the JCS nor the CIA nor the State Department was given the opportunity to contest or edit it. The words, we are told by the president's closest confidants, reflected his innermost convictions, his zealous idealism, his fervent hopes, his acute understanding of the dangers faced during the missile crisis, and his determination to transcend them in the future.[108]

Speaking at the annual commencement exercises at American University in Washington, D.C., the president began by introducing a topic "on which ignorance too often abounds and the truth is too rarely perceived." Yet it was "the most important topic on earth: world peace. What kind of peace do we seek?" Kennedy mused aloud:

> Not a Pax Americana enforced on the world by American weapons of war. Not the peace of the grave or the security of the slave. I am talking about genuine peace, the kind of peace that makes life on earth worth living, the kind that enables men and nations to grow and to hope and to build a better life for their children—not merely peace for Americans but peace for all men and women—not merely peace in our time but peace for all time.

Modern weapons, Kennedy explained, made peace imperative. Peace had to be the "rational end of rational men." It had to be seen as "a process—a way of solving problems." Peace "must be dynamic, not static, changing to meet the challenge of each new generation." Peace, Kennedy said, "need not be impracticable, and war need not be inevitable."

But for peace to come, Americans needed to rethink their attitudes toward the Soviet Union. "No government or social system is so evil that its people must be considered as lacking in virtue." As Americans

> we find communism profoundly repugnant as a negation of personal freedom and dignity. But we can still hail the Russian people for their many achievements—in science and space, in economic and industrial growth, in culture and in acts of courage. No nation in the history of battle ever suffered more than the Soviet Union suffered in the course of the Second World War. At least 20 million lost their lives. Countless millions of homes and farms were burned or sacked. A third of the nation's territory, including nearly two-thirds of its industrial base, was turned into a wasteland—a loss equivalent to the devastation of this country east of Chicago.

Let us, therefore, rethink our relationship with the Soviet Union, the president declared. Let us rethink the Cold War. Let us realize that we "can seek a relaxation of tensions without relaxing our guard." Much could be gained. Vast sums of money could be reallocated to "combating ignorance, poverty, and disease." Suspicions could be lessened, resources liberated for constructive purposes, and the arms race constrained. Although the communists' drive "to impose their political and economic system on others is the primary cause of world tension today," this could change if "all nations" respected the rights of peoples to determine their own future and if all nations showed a renewed respect for "world law." Indeed the communist bloc itself could evolve and change. Much could be accomplished by pursuing peace rather than preparing for war.

The president outlined a sequence of steps he proposed to take. He would establish a direct "hot line" to the Kremlin to facilitate communication in times of peril. He would reinvigorate the disarmament talks at Geneva and seek to halt the proliferation of nuclear weapons. He would send a representative to Moscow to join the Soviets and the British in talks that would lead to a comprehensive nuclear test ban treaty. To protect the environment from further pollution, he would halt nuclear testing in the atmosphere so long as other nations did likewise. The United States, Kennedy made clear, would not do anything to endanger its allies or weaken its own interests. But it was time, he concluded, "to do our part to build a world of peace where the weak are safe and the strong are just. . . . Confident and unafraid, we labor on—not toward a strategy of annihilation but toward a strategy of peace."[109]

What caused the president to deliver this message, which Soviet leaders read, pondered, and heralded as the most important American address since World War II?[110] British prime minister Macmillan had had some influence on it. In March, he had sent a thirteen-page letter to the president, beginning, "I am sorry to inflict so long a letter on you, but I feel this very deep personal obligation . . . which in some form or another I must discharge before it is too late." Macmillan wanted to engage Khrushchev, negotiate a test ban, stop the proliferation of nuclear weapons, and "bring the Soviets closer into Europe."[111]

But more important than Macmillan's pleas were Khrushchev's many overtures and his mounting frustration. When Norman Cousins met with the president after he returned from Moscow, he told Kennedy and his advisers that Khrushchev felt embittered. The Soviet leader wanted progress but felt rebuffed. It was critical that the United States seize the initiative and try to end the Cold War, Cousins said.[112] Harriman cabled similar views after seeing Khrushchev at the end of April. Khrushchev "seemed older, less bouncy, and looked tired." He was agitated by the difficulties with China. He wanted to demonstrate that his softer line of approach to capitalist adversaries could reap dividends. Khrushchev "meant what he was saying about peaceful coexistence and cooperation," Leonid Brezhnev, president of the U.S.S.R., told Glenn T. Seaborg, chairman of the U.S. Atomic Energy Commission, when the latter visited Moscow at the end of May. "This is not mere propaganda," Brezhnev stressed. "It is the sincere desire of our government, of our people, and of our party."[113]

Kennedy was increasingly inclined to take these statements and admonitions seriously. The Soviet Union was a formidable adversary whose economy had shown impressive strength over the years, but he knew that trends were now running against it: according to intelligence reports, the Soviet economy was slowing down, and resources available to the Kremlin were "heavily overcommitted." The Soviets, said the CIA, were genuinely fearful of limited war and regarded "the present strategic posture of the USSR as inferior."[114] Khrushchev would try to catch up, but in the aftermath of the missile crisis,

Kennedy knew that the strategic superiority of the United States was not endangered. "I cut his balls off," Kennedy had quipped after Khrushchev blinked in October.[115] Now that Khrushchev wanted to negotiate, Kennedy realized there was an opportunity to talk from a position of strength. "Let us never negotiate out of fear," he had told the American people in his inaugural address, "but let us never fear to negotiate."[116]

Kennedy also calculated that risks in behalf of détente might be taken because Soviet advances in Asia and Africa were in fact minor. While Soviet prestige in the third world was considerable, the Soviet Union was scoring fewer successes than had been feared, and its aid to less developed countries, especially in the Middle East, was winning it little glory and scant influence.[117] "Neutralist leaders, despite their anticolonialist cloaking, were basically nationalist in orientation," U.S. intelligence analysts concluded, and they resisted Soviet efforts to make inroads. In Guinea, Ghana, and Mali, for example, the Russians were encountering difficulties notwithstanding the millions of rubles they had given each in 1962. "Moscow has come to see in aid programs a more limited potential than it previously envisaged," Thomas L. Hughes, director of intelligence and research at the State Department, wrote to Secretary of State Dean Rusk. "Time is on our side," national security aide Robert W. Komer emphasized.[118]

These Soviet setbacks created a possibility, not a certainty, for détente, thought many of Kennedy's closest advisers.[119] But Kennedy's speech at American University was also prompted by concerns about China. A test ban agreement with the Soviet Union and Great Britain might constrain Beijing's quest for atomic weapons. A test ban, it was believed, was the key to nonproliferation. "Our primary purpose in trying to get a treaty with Russia," said the president, "is to halt or delay the development of an atomic capability by the Chinese Communists." They loomed "as our major antagonists of the late 60s and beyond."[120]

Although British pressures, Soviet weakness, and Chinese zealotry inclined Kennedy to take a chance for peace, he would not have done so if the domestic political climate had militated against it. Republican criticisms of his policies were shrill. The president, said Senate Republican leader Everett Dirksen, was making a "grave" mistake in seeking a test ban deal with the Kremlin.[121] Still, public opinion was divided and malleable. Peace groups were ratcheting up their demands, and Americans, according to public opinion polls, believed that their country was getting stronger. When asked if an agreement with the Soviet Union was possible, 49 percent of Americans polled said yes; 37 percent said no.[122] Strong presidential leadership, Kennedy intuited, could swing public opinion, notwithstanding the opposition of his own Joint Chiefs of Staff and his partisan opponents.[123]

Intelligence analysts and presidential advisers carefully examined Khrushchev's motives and policies. They believed that there was a chance for peace, and that the Soviet Union could evolve. The Kremlin had not reappraised its fundamental doctrines, but it might. "Prolonged frustration of Soviets," wrote CIA analysts, "holds some promise over the long run of bringing the USSR around to a view which accepts the permanence of a pluralist world."[124]

Many influential officials in the State and Defense departments thought similarly. They yearned to have the West win the Cold War, but they also saw the advantages of détente. They were torn. They even began to think that they might win the Cold War through an intermingling of détente and containment. "No more important matter can be before us than that of discerning and properly appraising the possibility of shifts in the purposes and direction of the leadership [of the Kremlin]," Secretary of State Rusk and his assistants concluded. "We have been taken by surprise in the past, and often at great costs. We also have doubtless missed some opportunities."[125]

For the moment, Kennedy decided to take a risk for peace, although the pressures, constraints, axioms, and calculations that sustained the Cold War were still operating. The future was contingent when Averell Harriman went to Moscow in mid-July 1963 to meet with Soviet and British officials. By then, Washington, Moscow, and London were aligned in favor of a test ban agreement, if uncertain what would follow from it. They could not agree on how or if inspections of underground nuclear tests would be conducted, but they were prepared to settle for a limited treaty that would prohibit testing in the atmosphere, in space, and beneath the seas. This agreement was reached through intense yet friendly negotiations.[126]

While in Moscow, Harriman met several times with Khrushchev, who was fond of him, as Stalin had been earlier, and joked about hiring the American tycoon as his economic adviser. Harriman usually played along skillfully, exploiting Khrushchev's joviality to elicit information about his thinking and aspirations. Khrushchev was always loquacious, occasionally emotional, and sometimes fuzzy and inscrutable. But in these meetings with Harriman, he was crystal clear about his hopes and aspirations.

He wanted improved relations with the United States. On 21 July, he showed up at a Soviet-American track meet that Harriman was attending at a stadium in Moscow and invited Harriman and Ambassador and Mrs. Foy Kohler to join him and his entourage in his special box at the top of the stadium. Khrushchev talked volubly and amiably about his hopes for Soviet-American relations. Track races, he commented, were far better than arms races. Buoyed by the excellent performance of the Soviet runners, Khrushchev became "quite emotional," wrote Harriman, "when our two flags were carried side by side around the track, with the two teams walking arm-in-arm, one Soviet and one American. Tears seemed to well up in his eyes." Khrushchev received resounding applause from the crowd, and the glow of good fellowship increased. He invited Harriman and Kohler for dinner. "He was most cordial throughout," Harriman wrote back to Washington, "and attempted to impress upon me his desire for closer collaboration in a wider field." When Secretary Rusk came to the Soviet Union to sign the test ban treaty in August, Khrushchev invited him to his residence and "went all out to handle my visit in a friendly and relaxed fashion."[127]

In professional settings as well, Khrushchev and Gromyko made clear that they desired to tackle additional matters; the test ban, they stressed, was simply a beginning. They wanted to negotiate a nonaggression agreement between the Warsaw Pact and NATO. They wanted to freeze military budgets. They hoped to agree on measures to monitor military movements and thereby modulate fears of surprise attacks. They also desired more trade with the West. Trade, Khrushchev said, led to peace. Peace would allow him to ameliorate the Soviet way of life and enhance its living standards. The Soviet people were enjoying economic progress, and wanted more. "Better to have a contest in wheat growing and beef than in atomic weapons," Khrushchev said to Orville Freeman, secretary of agriculture, who also visited Moscow in late July 1963. Despite the contrasting philosophical and political systems, the two nations, Khrushchev said to Rusk, "had the same ultimate goal, namely, development of their resources for the benefit of their people."[128]

But the topic that mattered most to Khrushchev, aside from boosting the productivity of the Soviet economy, was still Germany. "He's really stuck with this," Llewellyn Thompson, the State Department's leading Soviet expert, told President Kennedy. Khrushchev acknowledged that both East and West Germany would like to liquidate the social system of the other, but that was "sheer fantasy." It could not be done without war. "He wondered therefore whether the time had not come when we, mature people who knew life and had seen war, should try [to] move things from rails of war to rails of peace, namely, record situation as it existed now."[129] Khrushchev was not afraid of the Federal Republic per se, Ambassador Dobrynin explained to President Kennedy. But he feared that if there were renewed riots or demonstrations in the GDR, as there had been in 1953, West Germany might intervene, and that would trigger a U.S.-Soviet war. The best way to avoid a collision, Khrushchev fervently believed, was to sign a nonaggression pact and confirm the status quo: the division of Germany into two states with existing borders.[130]

What Khrushchev was saying to the Americans was precisely what he was saying to his own colleagues in public and private. At meetings of the Presidium in the summer and fall of 1963, the Soviet leader hectored them about promoting economic growth, overcoming agricultural difficulties, and redeploying capital to develop the fertilizer and chemical industry. They needed to retune their brains and retool their methods. In addition, they needed to rebut China's criticisms of Kremlin policies. He would not succumb to Chinese slander, nor would he abandon his hope for coexistence. He warned his colleagues that they should not heave insults at the Chinese but advise them, rather, of the harm they were wreaking on the entire world communist movement. Meanwhile, the Kremlin needed to forge ahead with its own efforts to relax tensions and promote peace. The test ban treaty, Khrushchev wanted Kennedy to know, "could lead to a real turning point, and the end of the cold war."[131]

Kennedy appreciated the course Khrushchev was embarked upon, and he, too, wanted to forge ahead. With careful political leadership he secured Senate ratification of the limited test ban treaty, notwithstanding the opposition of several of his own chiefs of military services.[132] When Khrushchev wanted to buy wheat from the United States, Kennedy agreed, despite sharp criticism from prominent Republicans.[133] And at the United Nations on 20 September 1963, Kennedy took another step forward. He proposed that the Soviets and Americans cooperate in the exploration of space and "keep weapons of mass destruction out of outer space." This was a stark turn-around from the year before, when he had ridiculed subordinates for not realizing they had to win the race to the moon no matter the cost. "It was a test of our systems," he had said then. But now he was telling the United Nations that the thaw in relations had to be nurtured with new ideas and new initiatives. If "this pause in the Cold War leads to its renewal and not to its end," Kennedy declared, "then the indictment of posterity will rightly point its finger at us all."[134]

But the constraints were formidable. Neither Adenauer nor de Gaulle was happy with the test ban treaty. The aged, truculent West German chancellor, about to retire after almost fifteen years of imaginative leadership and hardened resistance to communism, told Defense Secretary McNamara that he did not think the Moscow agreement was a great success for the United States. Informed of Adenauer's attitude, Kennedy immediately reassured him that the United States would not be duped, nor would it be "lulled into forgetfulness" by a single limited agreement.[135] When Rusk met with Adenauer a few days later, he reiterated that the United States would not recognize the sovereignty of the German Democratic Republic or withdraw its support for German unification. In late October, after Adenauer left office, Rusk met with Ludwig Erhard, the new German chancellor, conveying to him the same assurances: at the "present time," Rusk said, there was "no détente." West German interests would not be compromised for the sake of a rapprochement with the Kremlin.[136]

If allied pressures militated against a relaxation of Cold War tensions, so did the dynamics of revolutionary nationalism and the turmoil and strife in the third world. The "Family of Man," President Kennedy told a New York audience, was "more than three billion strong. It lives in more than 100 nations. Most of its members are not white. Most of them are not Christians. Most of them know nothing about free enterprise or due process of law or the Australian ballot." Most of them, Kennedy continued, are engulfed in anticolonial wars, or regional strife, or religious and ethnic conflicts. The "Family of Man in the world of today is not faring very well."[137] And these struggles in Africa, Asia, and Latin America created problems for the Great Powers; their wars threatened to suck in the United States and the Soviet Union, often against their will. However well intentioned he and Khrushchev might be, Kennedy knew that neither Moscow nor Washington could control the dynamics of change in the international system. In the third world,

Kennedy's advisers told him, "issues will almost inevitably arise into which the super-powers will be drawn." The Kremlin, in fact, might want to avoid getting involved, as apparently was the case in Vietnam, and might wish to modulate conflict, as apparently was the case in Laos. But Khrushchev could not shape events and was sensitive "to charges of softness already being levied by the Chicoms [Chinese Communists]."[138]

Kennedy was especially aware that Soviet disputes with China created real problems for the Kremlin.[139] Khrushchev needed to stand tall among his communist brethren and support the worldwide march of Marxism-Leninism as robustly as did Mao and his comrades in Beijing. Moscow "has a public opinion problem," wrote Robert Komer.[140]

Kennedy, too, was acutely attuned to criticism, from his domestic political opponents. When the president acted decisively, he rallied public opinion and mustered senatorial support, as happened during the ratification debate over the test ban treaty, but he continued to worry about criticism that he was "soft on communism"; the McCarthy attacks on Democrats were alive in his memory. Both Senator Barry Goldwater and former vice president Richard Nixon, eyeing the 1964 Republican nomination, were already pillorying him for pandering to Khrushchev.[141] The president's advisers knew that Kennedy wanted to cover his "flank against excessive détentism."[142] The hero who fought communists abroad was not quite so valiant when it came to fighting conservatives at home.

Kennedy vacillated. He wanted détente, he yearned for peace, but he also gloried in championing the cause of the free world. "Lift your eyes," he said to a million Berliners on 29 June 1963, "beyond the dangers of today, to the hopes of tomorrow, . . . to the advance of freedom everywhere . . . to all mankind."[143] While he lauded the test ban treaty, Kennedy carefully balanced his evocations of peace with warnings of peril. "The United States," he said, "must continue to seek a relaxation of tensions, but we have no cause to relax our vigilance."[144]

Profound ideological divisions remained. "The United States and the Soviet Union have wholly different concepts of the world, its freedom, its future," said the president. "We still have wholly different views on the so-called wars of national liberation and the use of subversion." These differences, in his view, could not and should not be concealed. "Our conflicts . . . are real."[145] In November, Soviet officials were again growing dismayed that the U.S. president might, in fact, not want, or be able, to give peace a chance.[146]

What, then, was the meaning of détente in a world of ideological rivalry? The president had beckoned for a new relationship with the Soviet Union in his speech at American University, but where it would lead was uncertain. Was détente a strategy to relax tensions, foster peaceful coexistence, and accept a world of diversity, as Kennedy frequently said, or was it a strategy to achieve victory in the Cold War? Would détente make wars of national liberation less dangerous to Washington and enable the United States to ramp down its commitments to countries such as South Vietnam, where almost sixteen thousand U.S. military advisers and special forces were now aiding the South Vietnamese government in its struggle against the communist-led National Liberation Front? Or would détente encourage the communist Chinese to exploit Soviet-American cooperation in behalf of their own revolutionary agenda?

Kennedy's advisers were of two minds. Walt Rostow, director of the State Department Policy Planning Council, argued that "we must dramatize before our own people and the world the limits of the détente," which, he believed, legitimized communism and was of questionable utility. He feared Soviet subversion in Latin America and Southeast Asia and worried about the "insidious effects" of détente on the domestic politics of France, Italy, and Greece.[147] On the other hand, détente could be seen as a sophisticated form of containment, encouraging the Soviets to put down their guard, relax, accept (it was hoped) the unification of Germany, and honor the national sovereignty and independence of the East European nations. A true détente, said Dean Rusk, "was bound to work in favor of the West." The Chinese communists "were probably right in opposing peaceful coexistence as harmful to the Marxist-Leninist system."[148]

Détente could lull the West or evoke change in the Kremlin, legitimate communism or ultimately destroy it. Détente could allow peaceful competition to emerge in a world of diversity or encourage dangerous complacency in a dramatically changing world. Détente could limit the arms race and liberate resources for economic growth and the uplifting of mankind, or allow the Kremlin to take a deep breath, recalibrate its efforts, and demonstrate the superiority of the Soviet way of life.[149]

The future of détente was unclear when bullets struck the young president on 22 November 1963. And now, though the chance for peace was faltering yet still alive, President Kennedy, its most eloquent—if conflicted—champion in America, was dead.

Starting Anew and Ending Abruptly

Foreign Minister Gromyko called Khrushchev at home in the evening to relay the news of Kennedy's passing. Khrushchev was shocked. "A bitter expression was fixed on his face," recalled his son. The Soviet leader had come to admire Kennedy, and he grieved his death. He would always remember the American president with "deep respect," he recalled in his memoirs. Kennedy "didn't let himself become frightened, nor did he become reckless."[150] Together, they had averted nuclear holocaust and moved tentatively toward coexistence. His father, said Khrushchev's son, "trusted Kennedy and felt real human sympathy toward him." Had Kennedy lived, more progress might have been made. "Everything," Khrushchev ruminated, "would be different with Johnson."[151]

He nonetheless tried to start anew with President Lyndon B. Johnson. "There is no need for me to tell you," Khrushchev wrote LBJ, that Kennedy and he had been "people of different political poles." But they both had understood their responsibility "for the destinies of the world." "I do not know how you will react to these words of mine," Khrushchev continued, but Russians saw in Johnson a "comrade-in-arms of the late President" and of President Roosevelt. He hoped that Johnson would join in preserving the peace and nurturing better relations.[152]

Khrushchev and his wife conveyed personal condolences to Mrs. Kennedy, and officially the Kremlin sent Anastas Mikoyan to represent the U.S.S.R. at the funeral. Mikoyan "looked so upset when he came through the line," Jacqueline Kennedy wrote Khrushchev a few days later, that "I was very moved. . . . You and [my husband] were adversaries," Mrs. Kennedy continued, "but you were allied in a determination that the world should not be blown up."[153]

Mikoyan conveyed this very message to the new president and the secretary of state. The Kremlin sought peace and coexistence, Mikoyan emphasized. Khrushchev welcomed the new president's ideas on how to move forward.[154]

Khrushchev's priorities were now clear, spelled out at meetings of the Presidium and in numerous speeches. He would never compromise Soviet power or endanger the security of the Soviet state, but it was time to focus ever harder on the building of socialism. "Comrades, you cannot put a rocket into soup," he exclaimed, "you cannot feed on rockets; rockets are for defense. But in order to develop, to strengthen the life of society it is necessary to toil, to create material values, including bread, potatoes, cabbage, meat, butter—all that is necessary to man."[155]

He launched a new effort to promote the "chemicalization" of industry and agriculture, believing that capital investment in this arena would catapult the Soviet economy forward.[156] Khrushchev admonished everyone to work harder, develop their talents, and apply them. "I dream of the time . . . when all our children in kindergartens and nurseries will be dressed and fed at public expense, when schoolchildren will be fed at public expense. All people want to eat well and substantially, want to dress well, warmly, and beautifully." But to do so, the comrades had to refashion their consciousness and raise their productivity. They had to work and innovate. Ultimately, they would be judged by their deeds and not their words. Their mission was to prove the superiority of the socialism being created in the U.S.S.R. Taking a swipe at Chinese criticisms, Khrushchev declared there was no shame in wanting "the country to be richer and the people to live better. . . . If a man has one suit, please God that he gets two and then three [applause]; let the people have plenty to eat, let all the children study, let all people be able to meet their requirements more fully—this is our dream, which is now coming true."[157]

But the dream could be interrupted by the arms race or turned into a nightmare by nuclear war. The leader who had recklessly deployed missiles to Cuba now incessantly proclaimed the virtues of prudence. This did not mean that Khrushchev had been humbled. "We understand that we cannot plead with the enemies, the imperialists, for there to be no war. We have not begged for peace. We are not striving to prevent war by means of incantations." The Soviet Union believed in a doctrine of deterrence, much as the United States did. The Soviet Union did not want war, Khrushchev repeated, but if "the enemies impose war on us, we will crush the enemies. We have all the means for doing this. Let the aggressors bear that in mind."[158]

Khrushchev knew there were "comrades abroad" who claimed he was "afraid of war." He was not ashamed. He "would like to see the fool who is not afraid of war," he told an assembly of textile workers at Kalinin. It "is only the child and the fool who fear nothing. . . . I have had to experience two wars. . . . I had a son, an airman, who died in the war. And how many fathers, mothers, brothers, and sisters of yours, comrades, died? We know what war is, and what it brings to man. Therefore, we are doing everything so that there should be no war."[159]

In letters to President Johnson, some public, some private, Khrushchev persistently looked for openings. He included the president in a long letter he circulated to many world leaders on New Year's Day 1964, and, more significantly, he communicated with the president directly or indirectly on 28 February, 2 April, 17 April, 20 April, 15 May, and 5 June. They must all "learn to live without quarrels and confrontations," he kept saying.[160] The United States and the Soviet Union were allowing too many incidents and too many opponents of peace to interfere with their mutual desire to be rid of "the shackles of the Cold War." They could take pride in the parallel reductions in the production of plutonium and uranium-235, Khrushchev acknowledged, but they were not acting boldly enough to tackle more fundamental issues.[161]

The Soviet leader reiterated time and again his desire to promote trade and cut military expenditures, to reduce troops in Central Europe, arrange a nuclear-free zone there, sign a German settlement, and complete a non-aggression pact. "As long as John and Ivan, gripping sub-machine guns, are tensely eyeing one another across the boundary between the two German states," Khrushchev wrote Johnson, "the situation will remain dangerous, regardless of what anyone says." For emphasis, he reiterated: "We consider the German question fundamental because it is the source of all existing tension and dangerous developments in the world. . . . If this German question were solved, there would then be no need for you or us to put out such an enormous quantity of troops and of weapons; there would not be, so to speak, the great confrontation of John and Ivan."[162]

In late May 1964, the Soviet Union signed a friendship treaty with the GDR, not the peace treaty with the United States, France, and Britain that Khrushchev so desperately wanted. When Prime Minister Jens Otto Krag of Denmark met with Khrushchev, Krag reported that the Soviet leader "hates Germans viciously."[163] But Khrushchev did not so much hate Germans as fear them, and fear the danger of a Soviet-American conflict over them. In his view, West Germany wanted to absorb East Germany, redraw the borders with Poland and Czechoslovakia, regain territory taken at the end of World War II, and get its hands on nuclear weapons. He thought that the West Germans, led by bourgeois capitalists, yearned for revenge, not for peace.[164]

There were two Germanys, Khrushchev insisted. The status quo had to be confirmed. There could be no unification, not immediately or in the intermediate term; perhaps it would be possible in the long run, but that could not be discussed seriously now. The two Germanys had first to recognize each other, learn to coexist, and settle their own disputes. Otherwise, danger lurked.

Khrushchev himself was willing to deal with West Germany. His son-in-law, Aleksei Adzhubei, a person of growing influence in Moscow, visited the Federal Republic in July 1964, met with many leading politicians and businessmen, and talked indiscreetly about the specter of China and the prospects of a Soviet-German rapprochement. Khrushchev even pondered the possibility of the Soviet Union's acquiescing in the MLF proposal of the United States if he could be certain that West German hands would be kept off the nuclear trigger. Common ground could be found, he believed, if everyone accepted the division of Germany into two social systems, recognized existing borders, and agreed that West Germany would not have a nuclear force of its own. If the German problem were settled, he repeatedly insisted, Cold War tensions would abate, the arms race would slacken, and the chances of a local crisis escalating to nuclear catastrophe would be reduced.[165]

On the other hand, Khrushchev did not shrink from bellicose rhetoric when he addressed non-European issues. "We are against war, I mean aggressive, predatory wars. But there are other wars, wars of national liberation, wars in which oppressed peoples rise against their oppressors—the colonialists and imperialists, such wars are just and sacred."[166] The United States had to respect the national sovereignty of small and large nations alike, he said, and to accept a world undergoing profound change. It had to acclimate itself to communist regimes, as those in China and Cuba, and to revolutionary nationalist movements as in Indochina and the rest of Asia and Africa. "The peoples of the world are awakening to a new life," and the Soviet Union sympathized with them, Khrushchev declared again and again. The U.S.S.R. supported the people of Angola in their struggle against Portuguese fascism, the people of the Congo fighting against "occupationists and traitors," the struggle against racism and oppression in South Africa, and the "patriots of South Vietnam who are struggling for the freedom of their motherland."[167]

Détente, therefore, depended on America's willingness to accept a world in flux, a world evolving toward a new way of life. Socialism is the "fairest of systems," Khrushchev declared, the most productive of systems, the system most attuned to the spiritual needs of humankind. Communism "is paradise on earth," he told the World Youth Forum in Moscow in September 1964.[168] Unabashedly, he wrote President Johnson:

> The fact that mankind is moving toward socialism is recognized now not only by Communists, but by most of the countries of the world. After all, nearly all the countries which today are freeing themselves from colonial enslavement declare their determination to build their lives on a socialist basis. The ideas of socialism have become so popular in the world that even some rather well known leaders in the USA have suggested that some different name be found for capitalism, since capitalism has become synonymous with imperialism, colonialism, and the oppression of peoples.[169]

But Soviet leaders could not simply declare communism's superiority; they had to *demonstrate* it. "Socialism in the whole world is measured by our country," Khrushchev told the Presidium.[170] He hectored Soviet leaders to do better, to organize the Soviet economy more effectively. Winning power was not enough. "The main thing . . . is to be able to wield this power for the purpose of building a new society, of demonstrating the advantages of the socialist system over the capitalist one." This required productive labor, organizational efficiency, scientific creativity, and technical innovation. Everything depended on economic competition. "Communism will defeat capitalism by showing . . . that the communist system is more productive than the capitalist one," he told the World Youth Forum. "That is the crux of the matter."[171]

However much Khrushchev needed détente, the allies and client states of the Soviet Union constrained the Kremlin's behavior. When Khrushchev considered a nuclear nonproliferation treaty seriously—"The Soviet Government has reached the conclusion," the Kremlin informed its allies, "that it is expedient" to move forward so long as it was assured that the West Germans would not gain control of nuclear weapons—Polish prime minister Wladyslaw Gomulka and Walter Ulbricht, the East German leader, staunchly resisted. In their view, West Germany was skillfully manipulating Franco-American differences to gain nuclear autonomy. Moreover, the MLF meant nuclear proliferation and could not be tolerated. The Soviet proposal, Gomulka exclaimed at a Warsaw Pact meeting, must be withdrawn. If not, the Chinese would be angered further and the rift between Moscow and Beijing would widen.[172]

The reluctance of Soviet leaders to exacerbate their difficulties with China was a continuous constraint on their ability to ease tensions with Washington. Mao and Zhou Enlai claimed that the Kremlin was betraying world communism, abandoning Marxism-Leninism, and pursuing détente at the cost of national liberation around the globe. Communists everywhere, they said, had to monitor Soviet behavior vigilantly and prevent recidivism. You see, Mao told a leader of the Laotian communist party, "the Soviet Union has existed for some forty years, and now capitalism has been restored there. The party that was established by Lenin . . . [has] become capitalist and [has] adopted revisionism."[173]

Genuinely agitated by the cleavage in the world communist movement, East European leaders were not averse to using the Sino-Soviet dispute to enhance their own bargaining power vis-à-vis the Kremlin. Remonstrating against giving any concessions to the Federal Republic, Gomulka warned Khrushchev:

> We cannot strive towards a relaxation of the international situation at the cost of our weakness, at the cost of dividing the socialist camp, and a split in the international worker's movement. Such a relaxation would be illusory, in reality it would quickly evolve into an even greater tension, because imperialism, seeing our weakness resulting from the division, would not hesitate to turn its aggressive teeth against the socialist states. Without the unity of the socialist camp, there is not and cannot be a true relaxation [of tensions], there is not and cannot be a possibility of curbing imperialism [and] of safeguarding humanity against the catastrophe of nuclear war.[174]

Khrushchev, Mao, and Ho, 1959. Their relations were fraught
with tension as well as cooperation.

Nor did certain U.S. actions make the pursuit of détente easy for
Khrushchev. Aside from Washington's support of German unification, there
was the threatening posture of the United States toward Cuba, its violation of
Cuban airspace, and its presence at Guantánamo Bay. In South Vietnam, the
United States was acting as a world policeman, according to Khrushchev, and
seeking to crush a genuine national liberation movement. When President
Johnson ordered a retaliatory raid against North Vietnam after American de-
stroyers were allegedly attacked in the Gulf of Tonkin in August 1964,
Khrushchev was infuriated. Since he did not wish to jeopardize détente, his
letter to President Johnson was restrained and expressed merely a sense of
foreboding that events in Southeast Asia might escalate out of control. But
many communists were charging that the Kremlin was doing too little to help
the Vietnamese people, and to them Khrushchev declared publicly that "big
stick" diplomacy with the use of warships must end.[175]

Just a year after the signing of the test ban treaty, Khrushchev feared that
the goodwill between Moscow and Washington was being destroyed, yet he
needed to demonstrate at home and abroad that détente was yielding results.[176] Everyone seemed disillusioned with him: Mao, Fidel, Ho Chi Minh,
the Romanians, the Poles, and the East Germans.[177] Within the U.S.S.R.,

moreover, his claims that détente would liberate resources and buoy the economy were not being borne out. His colleagues grew disaffected and could not stomach his insults and rudeness, his long harangues, and his attacks on their privileges. Officers in the armed forces resented the reductions in their pensions; intelligence analysts and the secret police hated the abolition of supplements to their salaries; party functionaries despised the division of local and regional cadres into industrial and agricultural sections. The nomenklatura resented the restrictions on state-owned cars and the curtailment of their access to high-quality foods at subsidized prices.[178]

Secretly, Khrushchev's colleagues planned to get rid of him. They blamed him, not themselves, for the setbacks the Soviet Union was experiencing. Khrushchev had trumpeted the economic advancement of communism, but his comrades on the Presidium believed they had to look truth in the eye. The Soviet economy was slowing. According to their own estimates, the rate of growth had fallen from 11.1 percent to 5.0 percent between 1956 and 1963. In the past, the great achievement of the socialist planned economy had been its superior growth rate compared with that in the capitalist West, but now the margin was narrowing. So was the pace of scientific and technical advancement, of which Soviet leaders had been so proud in the 1950s, when they launched the first Sputnik. Now, among themselves, they admitted that in a number of fields they were falling behind their capitalist adversaries. Even more disturbing was the performance of the agricultural sector. Demands for meat, butter, vegetables, and grain were not being met. Disaffection was growing. The great advantages of socialist planning were being squandered by Khrushchev's arbitrary meddling and never-ending, whimsical experimentation. They rebelled at all the restructuring; it had to stop.[179]

When Presidium members turned to foreign affairs, their criticisms were equally biting. Khrushchev was impetuous, reckless. He had foolishly deployed missiles to Cuba and imprudently challenged the United States in its own hemisphere. The subsequent retreat had embarrassed the Soviet Union and alienated Castro. Wars of national liberation deserved Soviet aid, but Khrushchev overcommitted the country and intruded in areas where Soviet interests were small. He squandered scarce resources, capriciously offering aid to leaders in the Middle East and Africa who often reneged on their promises or imprisoned communists. Lenin, they said, had advised communists to conduct themselves prudently lest they be lulled into a war with the imperialists. Khrushchev had ignored the great teacher's instructions and endangered everyone.[180] In short, the Soviet leader had acted too adventurously in the third world, and he vested too much importance in getting along with the United States. He had ignored its quest for world hegemony and failed to exploit divisions within the capitalist camp. And by catering to Washington, he had accentuated schisms among communists. Acting sometimes whimsically and sometimes crudely, he had insulted comrades in other countries and embarrassed the Soviet Union in the eyes of the world. He lacked consistency and self-control.[181]

Khrushchev's colleagues called their boss back to Moscow while he was vacationing near the Black Sea in mid-October 1964. He returned, suspecting that something might be amiss. When he arrived at the Presidium, he learned that his performance was to be assessed. He would be obliged to listen, not to intervene. He sat glumly, feeling powerless and isolated. Diverse colleagues, many of whom he had shepherded for decades, presented the case against him. As the proceedings drew to a conclusion, he knew his career was over. "I do not ask for mercy; the question is solved." He acknowledged his rudeness, but not his errors, and he defended his policies. His colleagues had deferred to him in the past. Was it just, he asked them, to fault him now? But he would not mount a struggle. "I am not going to fight."[182]

He wanted to escape with his dignity, indeed with his life. Fortunately, he had squeezed the Stalinist poison out of the system, which meant that a less ominous fate awaited him than had been meted out to others, for example, Beria. Khrushchev would go into retirement. He was pleased, he told his comrades, that the party had matured; it could control its leader. It was time for youth to take over.[183]

But youth did not take over. Leonid Brezhnev, principal orchestrator of the coup, and Aleksei Kosygin assumed leadership of the party and the government. They had been party stalwarts for almost three decades, with Kosygin's expertise being in economic management and Brezhnev's in defense. And notwithstanding their critique of détente and their commitment to a strong military posture, they immediately declared a foreign policy of continuity.

Within days of Khrushchev's dismissal, Brezhnev and Kosygin heralded another Soviet foray into the cosmos and honored the space crew that returned. Their real desire, however, was to inform the world that the policies of the Soviet Union did not wave like straw in the wind, but stayed anchored like a ship in harbor. "The foreign policy of the Soviet Union," said Brezhnev, "is predicated on the Leninist principles of the peaceful coexistence of states with different social systems, tireless struggle for the consolidation of peace, for friendship and cooperation among nations, for the further relaxation of international tension." On 16 October, Ambassador Dobrynin met with President Johnson and reiterated these points. A few days later Kosygin conveyed them yet again to Ambassador Kohler.[184]

Like Khrushchev, Brezhnev and Kosygin had known the hardships of war. A subordinate who knew him well recalled that Brezhnev was not easily convinced of the need for economic reforms or of the value of human rights, but when it came to relations with the West he needed no convincing. He wanted peace. So did Kosygin: "There is no task of greater importance," he proclaimed on the twentieth anniversary of the victory over Nazism, than "that of preventing a worldwide military conflagration."[185]

And like Khrushchev, Brezhnev and Kosygin explained that their mission was to remake Soviet society and ameliorate the conditions of life. "While storming the skies," said Kosygin, "we do not want to forget about the earth . . . the building of new towns and factories, good homes, schools, hospitals, roads; about the fertility of our fields; about the further development of education, science, and art, and of all human culture. . . . There is no loftier and more vital task," he added, "than that of ensuring a steady growth of the living standards and of the welfare of the Soviet people." If Soviet officials could augment labor productivity, spur the creativity of workers, garner the cooperation of all groups in society, and enhance the development of "social democracy," Kosygin declared, they would not only enhance the economic and cultural progress of their country but convince hundreds of millions of people abroad that the "road to the future" rests with Marxism-Leninism.[186]

Was peace possible if détente meant competition as well as coexistence?

Johnson's Agonies and Choices

U.S. officials and policy analysts studied the coup against Khrushchev carefully. They did not know precisely what it portended, but they had a remarkably good grasp of the factors that had prompted Khrushchev's ouster: his impulsiveness, his rift with Mao, and his inability to solve economic problems, overcome resource constraints, and satisfy the Soviet people's growing clamor for consumer goods. "While the precipitating reason for the ouster of Khrushchev may have been the style of his rule, the real causes must be sought not in his personal idiosyncrasy but in the magnitude of problems facing the USSR," concluded the State Department's Intelligence and Research Division.[187]

On 16 October, as the coup in Moscow was studied in the West, communist China tested its first atomic device. This did not come as a shock to U.S. officials, but the meanings of these virtually simultaneous events—the turmoil in Moscow and the successful explosion of a nuclear weapon in China— were perplexing in the extreme. In office for almost a year, President Johnson assembled the executive committee of the National Security Council to explore the implications of these events.[188] He met with Ambassador Dobrynin, telling him that his guard was up but his hand was out. He favored peace and competitive coexistence. The American system was best, he told Dobrynin, but he knew the ambassador felt differently. That was okay; people could choose. After all, not all men liked blondes, Johnson said. Some liked redheads, still others brunettes. The most important thing was to preserve the peace and avoid nuclear war. This had been his mantra since he entered the Oval Office.[189]

Yet as much as he might preach the utility of peace, détente was not a priority for Kennedy's successor. Johnson's attention was fixed on other matters: winning the presidential election that was coming in a matter of days, promoting his domestic agenda of racial equality and poverty eradication, thwarting communist gains in the third world, and avoiding defeat in Vietnam.

Johnson came from a modest family in the Texas hill country not far from Austin. His father was a restless soul, always aspiring, frequently in debt, and sometimes alcoholic. For a decade, he was a local politician with populist sensibilities. Lyndon's mother was a quiet, reserved, somewhat reclusive woman who grew estranged from her husband but was devoted to her children. Through education, she believed, her sons and daughters could transform their lives. Yet the circumstances were not auspicious. Lyndon grew up in a depressed countryside. Young people had limited opportunities, farmers faced bankruptcy, and small businessmen eked out a bare existence. Things got worse after World War I, when farm prices plummeted and foreclosures multiplied.[190]

Lyndon nonetheless struggled to make good. He was always surrounded by an extended, supportive family and a network of friends rooted in community and place. They helped support him through his years at a local teachers college. He was not a particularly good student, but he wanted to get ahead in life. He learned how to cultivate important people, like the president of the college, and began to realize how good he was at persuading and cajoling. He graduated just as the Great Depression struck. Life had never been easy for folks from the Texas hill country, but the Depression wrought misery. It left an indelible imprint on Johnson and his generation.

Johnson became a teacher, but he loved politics. In 1931, after teaching just one year, he secured a job as a staff assistant to a newly elected, wealthy Texas congressman. In Washington, Johnson impressed almost everyone. He labored long hours, ran the congressman's office superbly, networked with other legislative aides, learned the intricacies of the legislative process, and meticulously attended to constituent needs back home. After almost three years, he was eager to run for office himself. In 1934, he became director of the Texas branch of the National Youth Administration, a New Deal program just launched by Roosevelt. But when the congressman in his old home district died, Johnson instantly thrust himself into his first political campaign. In 1937, he won, and his political career was launched.

From the beginning, LBJ churned with ambition. Always insecure, always conscious of his inferior education and modest background, he exaggerated his weaknesses and tried to compensate for them. He voraciously sought information, asked penetrating questions, and worked prodigiously hard. He networked; he flattered; he charmed. Sometimes crude and occasionally patronizing, he was also smart, cunning, and persuasive. He studied people's vulnerabilities and exploited them. He sensed people's fears and tried to allay them. He intuited people's dreams and wanted to transform them into reality. Johnson had embraced the New Deal with enthusiasm and ardently identified himself as a Roosevelt Democrat. He believed that the government had a vital role to play in American life. It could build the infrastructure to spur business recovery. It could provide credit to desperate farmers, housing to urban dwellers, and electricity to people in the countryside. Government could offer opportunity to the young, security to the old, and a semblance of equality to disenfranchised minorities. Government could, in fact, invigorate a capitalist system that had faltered badly but that had the capacity to be revived by a vibrant democratic base. Johnson learned quickly that he could do well for himself by doing good for others. "I wanted power to give things to people," he later reflected, "all sorts of things to all sorts of people, especially the poor and the blacks."[191]

Eking out a victory in his race for the U.S. Senate in 1948, Johnson managed his own rise in the legislative councils of the nation. In 1954, he became the Senate majority leader and led the Democrats brilliantly through the Eisenhower years; he embraced bipartisanship and earned the respect, if not the affection, of almost everyone. Lyndon Johnson was a whirlwind—scheming, dealing, bargaining, imagining, and aspiring. Physically he was big, personally he was imposing, and politically he was powerful. But he was not powerful enough to get the presidential nomination. Although hardly anyone thought a southerner could win the highest office in the land, Johnson believed he might gain the respectability and visibility he needed by obtaining the number two spot on a Democratic ticket. Rebuffed by the Democratic candidate Adlai Stevenson in 1952 and 1956, he made it plain to Kennedy after the primaries in 1960 that he would accept the vice presidential nomination, and he did.[192]

Once Kennedy was elected, Johnson hated his descent into insignificance when he was excluded from the inner circles of decision making in the White House. He felt himself an outcast, impotent and irrelevant. His sense of inadequacy rekindled, he could barely contain his animosity for Kennedy and the people around him—the "Harvards," as he contemptuously, but enviously, called them. Yet when Kennedy was suddenly assassinated and Johnson assumed the reins of power, he declared a policy of continuity. He also retained the late president's top foreign-policy advisers: Secretary of State Rusk, Secretary of Defense McNamara, and McGeorge Bundy, the president's national security adviser.[193]

From the moment he entered the Oval Office, Johnson had his eye on the 1964 presidential election. He yearned for a smashing victory that would legitimize his presidency, give him credibility, and enable him to achieve his domestic goals. His foreign-policy advisers knew his priorities. Ambassador Dobrynin knew his priorities. The men in the Kremlin knew his priorities. Johnson favored peace. But détente was not going to get in the way of his election.[194] Championing peace was good politics, domestically and internationally. But making concessions in behalf of peace threatened to animate critics both at home and abroad.

Yet Johnson happily declared himself in favor of reducing tensions and pursuing peace. In fact, he chided his advisers for not being as creative as Khrushchev in drawing attention to his good intentions. "I don't like to . . . wake up in the morning to see where Khrushchev has sent me another communication for peace," he remonstrated to McNamara in a taped phone conversation. "It makes me appear like a warmonger. When I talk about peace, I've got nothing to talk about. I can't have much substance to my proposals, so I want to be proposing something." Johnson had no idea himself about what to propose or how to respond to the Soviet leader. So he urged Bundy, Rusk, and McNamara to get "the best brains" around Washington and come up with something.[195]

But they could not come up with anything very creative or concrete. The United States had already done all the easy things, Bundy wrote to Johnson on 13 January 1964. Everything else would be tough, and progress might either upset domestic constituencies or antagonize allies that were not inclined to go along with American proposals. Khrushchev, for example, wanted to tackle the German issue, but the government in Bonn was not likely to agree to anything that might satisfy the Kremlin. To overcome the impasse, Dobrynin suggested the possibility of a summit meeting. Bundy, however, thought the idea politically inexpedient. The Kremlin wanted more trade, but Bundy and Johnson believed that commercial talks risked too much controversy at home.[196]

Small steps were taken in behalf of détente that did not antagonize allies abroad or agitate political foes at home, such as reducing the production of fissionable materials, signing a consular treaty, and agreeing to work cooperatively on the desalinization of seawater.[197] Yet for all his good intentions, Johnson did not even meet with the Soviet ambassador until more than four months after he took office. When they did meet, Johnson talked affably about peace but conceded that it was not a propitious time to risk relaxing tensions. Public opinion in America favored steps toward peace, Johnson acknowledged, but his political foes in the Republican Party and their allies in the conservative media were eager to pounce on him. By simply welcoming Khrushchev's overtures, Johnson said, he had been assailed by one newspa-

President Johnson, 1965

per for "publicly hugging a communist." Appearing soft on the Soviet Union, Johnson had said a few months earlier, was like publicly announcing that you had "screwed a girl."[198]

The accidental president did not want the pursuit of détente to compromise his electoral prospects or jeopardize his domestic agenda. In his first State of the Union address, on 8 January 1964, he had boldly announced that he wanted the forthcoming session of Congress to do more for civil rights than had been done during the previous one hundred sessions. Let this Congress, he intoned, be known as the one that declared "an all-out war on human poverty and unemployment in the United States"; let it be known as the one that addressed the health needs of the elderly and the educational requirements of the young; let it be known as the one that "helped to build more homes, more schools, more libraries, and more hospitals than any single session of Congress in the history of our Republic."[199]

Johnson wanted to transform the United States, eradicate poverty, ban discrimination, and enable all Americans to fulfill their dreams. He sought to use his power for the benefit of the young and the elderly, the poor and minorities; to replace "despair with opportunity," to create the great society. "We have in 1964 a unique opportunity . . . to prove the success of our system," he said, "to disprove those cynics and critics at home and abroad who question our purpose and our competence." Nothing was more important than passing civil rights legislation. He later recalled: "I knew that, as President and as a man, I would use every ounce of strength I possessed to gain justice for the black American." Discrimination against black people was America's greatest blemish, a reality that the Kremlin never ceased to exploit in its propaganda. Johnson threw his energy behind the civil rights bill that his predecessor had belatedly introduced in Congress in 1963. If we fail, Johnson acknowledged, history will "judge us harshly."[200]

With so much at stake, the new president could not afford to blunder. Yet he faced formidable problems abroad. "Things are going like hell," he exclaimed to his good friend and mentor Senator Richard Russell in a phone conversation on 20 January 1964. "We're in trouble in Indonesia, and we're in trouble in Tanganyika and we're in trouble in Zanzibar and we're in trouble in Panama."[201] The problems mounted and every week leaped onto the president's desk. One week it was Venezuela or British Guiana; the next week it was Ghana or the Congo; the following week Chile and Brazil; then India and Algeria; and back to Zanzibar or Indonesia.

Regardless of region or country, the same fear resonated through the meetings at the National Security Council and the lunches at the White House: the communists were coming. The aim of U.S. national security policy was to immunize "vulnerable societies" against the threat of communism.[202] "In essence," Bundy wrote Johnson in a memorandum that illustrated the larger challenge, "the problem we face [in Chile] is that a very popular and attractive candidate named Allende, who has thrown in his lot with the Communists, has more than a fighting chance to win [the election]." Bundy wanted LBJ to know that the United States already supported a coordinated program to back Allende's opponents.[203] But in Africa, for example in Zanzibar, Bundy and Rusk urged the president to get the British prime minister to take the initiative to "reverse the present course of events." If not, "we are going to be faced with a center of Communist infection off the East coast of Africa which will give us all endless trouble and expense and danger, not only in East Africa but in all of Southern Africa for a long time to come."[204]

"What Latin American country would go next?" LBJ asked CIA director McCone on 3 February 1964. Throughout Latin America, reported the CIA:

> there is a rising demand for radical change in existing conditions. . . . Backwardness is not in itself a spur to revolution, but rising consciousness of deprivation is. . . . The direction that political change may take remains open. It could as well be democratic or Peronist as Communist. But everywhere the rising demand for change is accompanied by an intensification of nationalistic emotions. Because the predominant foreign presence in the region is that of the US, Latin American ultranationalism has a predominantly anti-Yankee character.[205]

Whatever the sources of anti-Americanism, Johnson felt he could not allow leftist forces to triumph anywhere in the New World. His predecessor had pledged that he would not permit another country in the Americas to go communist, and Johnson was determined to carry out Kennedy's oath.[206] The United States would not invade Cuba if Castro ceased his subversive activities in the hemisphere, Johnson affirmed, but he yearned to be rid of the communist firebrand and ensure that his Cuban experiment not be duplicated elsewhere, whether in Chile, Panama, Brazil, or British Guiana.[207]

His advisers spent enormous amounts of time analyzing hot spots and figuring out ways to thwart revolutionary upheaval and communist advances. Illustratively, again, Bundy wrote Johnson regarding Cheddi Jagan, the leftist leader in British Guiana: "I have always supposed myself that an independent Jagan government would be literally unacceptable to us and that we would have to make sure that it was overthrown, by hook or by crook. The whole object of the present exercise is to avoid having to face this choice in 1964 if possible."[208]

The place where Johnson most wanted to avoid tough choices during the election year of 1964 was Vietnam. He could not abide the notion of defeat, but he wished to avoid escalation and the appearance of warmongering during an election year. Indeed he wanted desperately to present himself as a

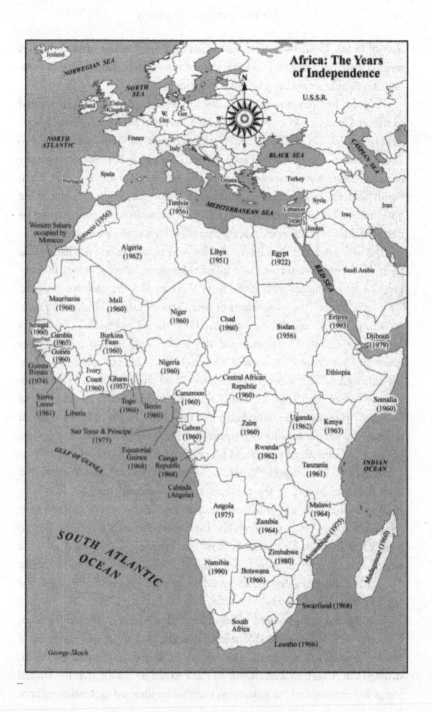

Africa: The Years of Independence

man of peace. In his own mind, he *was* a man of peace. But prudent leaders seeking peace and wanting reelection could not tolerate the advance of communism even in a faraway place like Indochina.

From his first days in office, President Johnson made clear that he wanted to win in Vietnam. On 24 November 1963, just two days after Kennedy's assassination, he met with Rusk, McNamara, Bundy, McCone, ambassador to South Vietnam Henry Cabot Lodge, Jr., and George Ball, the undersecretary of state. Lodge summarized conditions in Vietnam since 2 November, when South Vietnamese generals had overthrown Diem, the longtime leader of the government. Lodge was optimistic that the communist insurrection could be defeated. McCone disagreed, saying that the CIA was more pessimistic.

The new president then interjected his own views. He was not happy that Diem had been overthrown and killed. Moreover, "strong voices in Congress" were calling for withdrawal from Vietnam. But the past was the past. "We have to see that our objectives were accomplished." Inside Vietnam, bickering had to end. Lodge was in charge of all operations. Dissenters "should be removed." Johnson did not believe "we had to reform every Asian into our image." He wanted "to win the war," not reengineer the country, although he fully grasped that economic aid was important to achieving victory.[209] Two days later, he issued a formal memorandum to government agencies: "It remains the central object of the United States in South Vietnam to assist the people and the Government of that country to win their contest against the externally directed and supported Communist conspiracy."[210]

In 1964 no foreign-policy question was more important than Vietnam. No issue consumed more of the president's time. Vietnam trumped détente in spades. Winning the war in Vietnam was far more important to Johnson than relaxing tensions with the Kremlin. He believed that Moscow or Beijing would benefit from an American "loss" in Vietnam. In his mind all these struggles were interconnected, not clearly, not logically, but emphatically. "The world today is a vast battleground between two systems of thought and two philosophies of society."[211]

Johnson was not prepared to negotiate an end to the conflict in Vietnam. President de Gaulle pressed for talks that might lead to the neutralization of South Vietnam. Johnson was not interested. At the end of March 1964, he instructed the American ambassador in Paris to tell de Gaulle that the United States was determined "to assure that communist-directed aggression will not succeed in overthrowing independent states in Asia." Subversion, he believed, posed "a dangerous threat to the . . . stable evolution of developing nations everywhere."[212]

Brushing aside neutralist ideas, Johnson told the Joint Chiefs of Staff that he would do everything they wanted to achieve victory inside South Vietnam, but he could not risk another Korea in an election year. Therefore, he would not approve the bombing of North Vietnam—at least, not yet. After November, new initiatives could be contemplated, but for the present he would approve only prudent measures to bolster the South Vietnamese regime, avoid defeat, and avert Chinese intervention. To the Joint Chiefs of Staff, he also acknowledged one other thing he could not do: ask Congress to pass a resolution in support of an expanded war effort. It would be advantageous to have such a resolution, but "he honestly believed that [Congress] would not give him one that would be useful," at least not then.[213]

Johnson was admitting that neither the Congress nor the public was pressuring him to escalate the war in Vietnam. In 1964, the most influential members of the Senate—Mike Mansfield, the majority leader; William Fulbright, chairman of the Foreign Relations Committee; and Richard Russell, chairman of the Armed Services Committee—opposed escalation of the U.S. commitment or were wary of its implications. Most Americans did not know anything about Vietnam, and of those who did, fewer than 10 percent favored a tougher policy there. "I don't think the American people are for it," Johnson confessed in a long phone conversation on 27 May 1964.[214]

Inner fears and political calculations, not public pressure, animated the president. At a time when only 4 percent of informed Americans thought the United States should take definite military action in Indochina, Johnson was haunted by memories of the vilification of his predecessor Harry Truman over the "loss" of China. We will suffer the same fate, Bundy warned him, "if we should seem to be the first to quit in Saigon." The Republicans, Johnson believed, were eager to use Vietnam against him.[215]

In phone conversations with Senator Russell, Johnson anguished over the choices. He didn't want to fight and he didn't want to have Americans leave Vietnam, either. "I'm in a hell of a shape." But he told Russell that he agreed with the advice of a mutual friend: the American people will "forgive you for anything except being weak." But having U.S. troops stay and fight meant sending American boys to their graves. Mansfield had already warned the

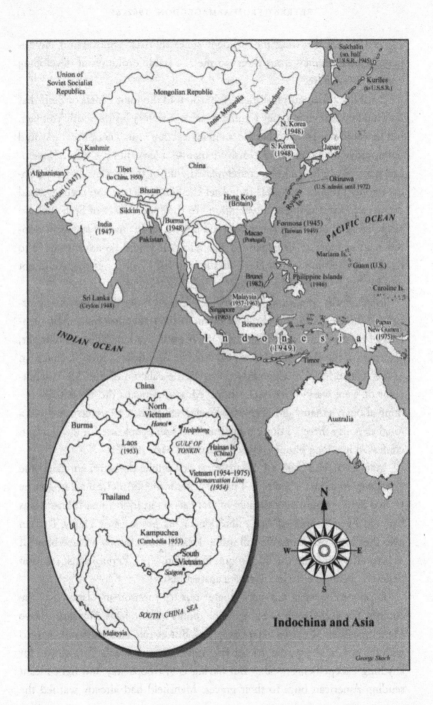

Indochina and Asia

George Skoch

president that if the United States did not cut its losses, a bigger war loomed. Russell said he "shared" some of Mansfield's fears. "I do too," retorted Johnson, "but the fear the other way is more"—meaning the fear of political retribution.[216]

Johnson did not want to "cut and run" from Vietnam. American honor and credibility were at stake. Truman, Eisenhower, and Kennedy had made a commitment, and he would honor it. When U.S. naval vessels were apparently attacked in the Gulf of Tonkin during the first days of August, he exploited the opportunity to ask Congress for a resolution granting him authority to do what was necessary. "America keeps her word," he told Congress. The threat to the entire region and "to us" had to be thwarted. "This is not just a jungle war," he said, "but a struggle for freedom on every front of human activity."[217]

For Johnson, Vietnam was "the face of war in the 1960s." Publicly, he declared that it was the war of liberation that could not be lost. [218] Privately, he was conflicted. Why in the world am I ordering our boys to Vietnam, he mused to Bundy after a night of restless sleep in May 1964. "What in the hell is Vietnam worth to me?" And then he answered his own lament: "Of course, if you start running from the Communists, they may chase you right into your own kitchen."[219]

At a meeting of the National Security Council several months later, Johnson asked each of his top advisers "whether it was worth all this effort." There were no dissenters from the war. The United States could not afford to let Hanoi win, said Maxwell Taylor, former chairman of the Joint Chiefs of Staff and now U.S. ambassador to South Vietnam. If it faltered, America's position in Southeast Asia, indeed in the world, would be jeopardized. "If we should lose in South Vietnam," said General Earle Wheeler, current chairman of the JCS, "country after country on the periphery would give way and look toward Communist China as the rising power of the area." CIA director McCone emphatically concurred. So did Secretary of State Rusk, "with considerable force."[220]

Johnson listened intently and then reiterated his own views. He wanted to shore up "the base" in South Vietnam. He approved the resumption of U.S. patrols in the Tonkin Gulf, as well as limited South Vietnamese raids across the border into North Vietnam. But these were temporary measures, holding actions. When circumstances were more propitious, he would approve at-

President Johnson and Secretary of Defense Robert McNamara, 1964.
They agonized over what to do in Vietnam.

tacks on the North. But for now no money should be spared on improving the situation in the South. It "was necessary not to spare the horses." This "had been his constant view." At the end of the meeting, he said that "money was no object." He "would be ready to do more," he added, "when we had a base."[221]

For the next two months, however, Johnson portrayed himself as a candidate of prudent toughness. When, in the midst of the U.S. election campaign, Khrushchev was ousted from power and Ambassador Dobrynin tried to reassure Johnson that the new Kremlin leadership intended to continue favoring détente, the president responded in kind. "Our mission was peace," Johnson insisted. The United States wanted good relations with Moscow. There were challenges before them, but they could be overcome. "The Soviets," Johnson said, "would have to bend a little bit and so would we."[222]

On Election Day, anticipating the president's smashing victory over Republican candidate Barry Goldwater, Dobrynin visited Rusk at the State Department and gave him a letter from the new Kremlin leaders. The Soviet government reiterated that it wanted improved relations and expanded cooperation. They did "not wish to bury anyone or be buried, and [were] convinced that the difference of views over whose social system is better should not be an obstacle to the development of relations between the Soviet Union and the U.S.A." The Kremlin wanted to reduce the number of Soviet troops in Europe, cut defense expenditures, regularize relations with West Germany, organize security in Europe, promote disarmament, and join with the United States in exploring the galaxies. Brezhnev and Kosygin closed their letter with a touching appeal to past collaboration. The United States and the Soviet Union "were allies in the grim war against the forces of fascism. The Soviet people treasure the memory of the great American President, Franklin D. Roosevelt." They wanted to build upon this tradition and achieve "genuine good-neighborliness and mutually advantageous cooperation."[223]

In subsequent meetings, other Soviet officials conveyed the same message. When Foreign Minister Gromyko met with the secretary of state and the president in early December, he said that the Kremlin wanted to tackle the most important problems that threatened the peace of the world, and once again the future of Germany was at the top of the list. Gromyko proposed that the United States and the Soviet Union recognize the division of Germany, confirm its existing frontiers, and guarantee that neither German state would ever acquire nuclear weapons. The MLF was unacceptable. Notwithstanding U.S. assurances that the West Germans would never get their hands on the nuclear trigger, the Soviet people remained apprehensive. History could not be ignored. German revanchists, although a minority, still hoped to regain the territory in the east that Germany had lost at the end of the war. If they had access to nuclear weapons through the MLF, "that would open up possibilities for FRG adventures."[224]

U.S. officials also worried about the reemergence of an independent German power, and feared it might gravitate toward nuclear weapons. Among themselves, Rusk and his aides acknowledged that "the Germans would seek bigger and better bilateral arrangements with the US [regarding nuclear weapons], but that later they would seek their own." Because U.S. officials worried so much about the future trajectory of the Federal Republic, they worked tirelessly and creatively to harness West German power in behalf of the free world. "We cannot make the Germans second-class citizens," insisted Under Secretary of State Ball.[225]

The Americans would not dare alienate their allies in Bonn by abandoning U.S. support for German unification. President Johnson told Gromyko that he would not sign a peace treaty that recognized the division of Germany.[226] Support for unification was the glue that bonded the Federal Republic to the United States. "Reunification of Germany through self-determination," Johnson said in his State of the Union address on 4 January 1965, "is a great unfinished task."[227]

If this priority dashed the possibility of Soviet-American détente, so be it—though this outcome was not what the president wanted. In the same address, he called for improved Soviet-American relations and broached the idea of an exchange of visits with Soviet leaders. But détente with the Kremlin could not come at the expense of the alliance with the Federal Republic.

President Johnson, of course, preferred not to say these things directly to the Russians. He and his advisers struggled with agonizing tradeoffs. Ambassador-at-large Llewellyn Thompson, the administration's leading Soviet expert, opposed any conciliatory moves. Others saw more opportunities to relax U.S.-Soviet tensions and promote arms control, but they could not advance their agenda effectively. Johnson's staff dawdled for months over what the administration's response should be to the Kremlin's Election Day letter to the president. Bundy knew they had dropped the ball, but he was preoccupied with Southeast Asia. When the president finally wrote Brezhnev and Kosygin on 14 January 1965, he merely reaffirmed his desire for peace and for the nonproliferation of nuclear weapons. He did not inform Moscow that he was backtracking from the MLF, nor did he intimate any willingness to recognize the German Democratic Republic and accept the division of Germany. NATO cohesion was his priority.[228]

So was defeating North Vietnamese aggression and revolutionary nationalism in Southeast Asia. The president and his advisers were convinced that the growing war in South Vietnam was the result of North Vietnamese assistance to the National Liberation Front, and the deployment of growing numbers of North Vietnamese troops in the South lent conviction to their views. With the election over in the United States and conditions deteriorating in South Vietnam, Johnson and his aides focused their attention there. The choices were grave: to escalate the war by bombing North Vietnam and committing U.S. combat troops to Indochina, or to seek to disengage through negotiations. During October, Under Secretary of State Ball wrote a sixty-seven-page memorandum arguing against escalation.[229] Several weeks later, William Bundy, assistant secretary of state for Far Eastern affairs and brother of the president's national security adviser, wrote a forty-two-page memorandum questioning the validity of the domino theory: "The so-called domino theory is over-simplified." In some circumstances, it might apply; in others, it might not. The loss of South Vietnam, Bill Bundy and his colleagues wrote, probably would not affect Asia as the loss of Berlin would affect Europe. But "it could be that bad," so walking away or negotiating from weakness would be dangerous.[230]

At the end of January 1965, McGeorge Bundy and McNamara became convinced that the administration had reached a fork in the road. The United States had to use its "military power in the Far East and to force a change in Communist policy." "Bob and I believe," Bundy wrote LBJ, "that the worst course of action is to continue in this essentially passive role."[231]

The president sent his national security adviser to Vietnam to assess the situation. Johnson was not eager to escalate. He wanted more stability in Saigon. He wanted the South Vietnamese generals to stop feuding. He agonized. He pondered. "A President's hardest task," he said, "is not to *do* what is right, but to *know* what is right."[232]

From Vietnam, Bundy made clear what he thought was right. The situation was horrendous, with a virtual civil war going on within a civil war. Not only were the communist Vietcong gaining ground in their tenacious struggle to overthrow the government, but the generals who succeeded Diem were plotting against one another, and some were even scheming with Buddhist leaders and noncommunist neutralists to open talks with the National Liberation Front. Faced with this chaos, Bundy believed there was no option save to take action to lift morale and strengthen America's commitment to the Saigon regime. "The prospect in Vietnam is grim," he wrote on his way back to Washington. "The energy and persistence of the Viet Cong are astonishing." If the United States pulled out, he said, "there would be a strong feeling" that it had reneged on a commitment to preserve South Vietnam's independence. The consequences in Southeast Asia "would be very large." Elsewhere, "the effect would also be very serious, even to the extent of affecting morale in Berlin."[233]

On 7 February, while Bundy was still in Vietnam, the Vietcong attacked a U.S. Army barracks and helicopter base near Pleiku, in South Vietnam. Eight Americans were killed and 126 were wounded. This unexpected assault accentuated the urgency of deciding whether to make Hanoi pay a penalty for

McGeorge Bundy at Pleiku, South Vietnam, 1965. Bundy visited
Pleiku immediately after a Vietcong attack and recommended
a strong response; a critical escalation in the war ensued.

these events in the South—that is, whether to bomb North Vietnam systematically. Johnson immediately convened his top advisers and a few influential
legislators. Almost everyone was eager to strike back. But there was one com-
plication that Under Secretary Ball highlighted: at that very moment, Premier
Kosygin was in Hanoi. Ball, nonetheless, was in favor of retaliating. Senator
Mansfield was not: "Caution should be our watchword," he said. U.S. actions
might provoke China to intervene, encourage a Sino-Soviet reconciliation, or
antagonize the Kremlin. The results, he said, could be worse than Korea.[234]

Johnson interceded. He had "kept the shotgun over the mantel and the
bullets in the basement for a long time now," as he put it, but his patience
was exhausted. The enemy was killing Americans. "Cowardice has gotten us

into more wars than response has," he said. There was the risk of "involving the Soviets and Chinese but that neither of these are friendly with us and the problem is to face up to them both." At a meeting the next day, the president reaffirmed that he "wanted to impress Kosygin and a number of others in the world." This did not mean that he was abandoning the chance for peace, but nonetheless he ordered the bombing of North Vietnam.[235]

On the first night of the retaliatory raids, Johnson slept restlessly and intermittently was awakened. The next day, his wife recorded in her diary: "In the night, we were waiting to hear how the attack had gone. It came at one o'clock, and two o'clock and three, and again at five—the ring of the phone, the quick reach for it, quiet talk. . . . It was a tense and shadowed day, but we'll probably have to learn to live in the middle of it—for not hours or days, but years."[236]

One decision led to another, and Johnson never stopped agonizing as he ratcheted up the U.S. commitment. Once he approved a systematic, graduated bombing campaign against North Vietnam, known as Rolling Thunder, he was advised that he needed to protect the air bases in South Vietnam with two Marine landing teams. "I'm scared to death of putting ground forces in," he confided to McNamara, whom he trusted and revered, "but I'm more frightened about losing a bunch of planes from lack of security."[237] Johnson's questioning and inner doubts revealed that the answers were far from predetermined.[238] But in April he authorized forty thousand more troops to help defend key enclaves from Vietcong attacks, and in July he sent another fifty thousand soldiers to prove to the enemy that it could not win a quick victory. While seeking to avoid a conflict with China, as had happened in Korea in 1950, he nonetheless promised his military chiefs that he would do more, if necessary, to prevent a communist takeover in South Vietnam.[239]

President Johnson willingly followed a course that his predecessors had established, one fraught with tragedy for more than fifty thousand young American soldiers who would lose their lives, for a million Vietnamese who would perish, for millions more who would suffer incalculable hardship, and for Soviet-American détente, which would falter. In a long (taped) phone conversation with Martin Luther King, Jr., a few months later, Johnson explained his thinking regarding his February decisions. I didn't want "to get into trouble with China and Russia," Johnson said. He waited from

November to February. But they kept coming. They just kept coming and I couldn't stand it any longer. . . . If I pulled out, I think our commitments would be no good anywhere. I think that we'd immediately trigger a situation in Thailand that would be just as bad as it is in Vietnam. I think we'd be right back to the Philippines with problems. I think the Germans would be scared to death that our commitment to them was no good, and God knows what we'd have other places in the world. . . . I think it's the situation we had in Greece and Turkey and Iran, and Truman and Eisenhower and none of these people allowed them to go in and take these peoples' freedom away from them. And I'm trying . . . I didn't get us into this. We got into it in '54. Eisenhower and Kennedy were in it deep.[240]

Fear and power shaped Johnson's decisions. The president feared that a loss in Vietnam would shatter U.S. credibility and erode America's position in the Cold War. He believed he was in a worldwide battle with the communists for the hearts and minds of mankind. Eisenhower said to him: "If we're going to save a nation, we've got to go after their minds and hearts as well as we do at their stomach." Johnson fully agreed, and emphasized that the communists were relentless, ruthless competitors, much as the Nazis had been. "We know, from Munich," he told Everett Dirksen, "that when you give, the dictators feed on raw meat. If they take South Vietnam, they take Thailand, they take Indonesia, they take Burma, they come right back to the Philippines."[241]

This was the much-contested domino theory all over again, which the president and his advisers instinctively fell back on even though they knew the world was more complicated than that. They worried that revolutionary nationalism in the third world would escape their control. McGeorge Bundy's many memoranda justifying escalation regularly invoked the domino theory and affirmed that Vietnam was a test case of America's strength and credibility. Bundy shared the views of Robert Komer, one of his assistants for Asian and African affairs. "I see trouble ahead in Afro-Asia," Komer wrote Bundy in October 1964. "It's the area that Rusk and McNamara understand least, so unless the President gives a strong lead we're in for rough weather ahead. . . . There are enough potential Vietnams, Zanzibars, Congos, etc. to give anyone gray hair." The less-developed countries constituted the chief area of competition between the free and communist worlds precisely "because they are so undeveloped, so unstable, and thus so vulnerable." In this competition, Komer understood, the United States was handicapped by its being perceived as a neocolonial power. Although colonialism was dead, "flogging the dead horse is still the favorite sport of over half the globe." The Soviets and Chinese, Komer stressed, "made massive efforts to promote this line of reasoning, but essentially it springs from the anti-colonial revolution itself."[242]

Time was needed to alter the attitudes of third world leaders. The United States had to be tough and had to be generous, to be willing to allocate massive amounts of economic aid and military assistance, and to be prepared to use military force, if necessary. "Almost every leader in Asia," Komer wrote, "is watching. . . . Our F[ar]E[ast] allies—the Thais, Phils, ROKs [South Koreans], and Chinats [Chinese Nationalists]—are all nervous as cats."[243] In February 1965, when Bundy argued in behalf of sustained air strikes against North Vietnam, his assistants calculated that the United States had only a 25 to 75 percent chance of winning in Vietnam. But the risks were worth taking. "A reprisal policy [against North Vietnam]—to the extent that it demonstrates U.S. willingness to employ this new form of counter-insurgency—will set a higher price for the future upon all adventures of guerilla warfare, and it should therefore somewhat increase our ability to deter such adventures."[244]

Johnson and his advisers believed that the United States possessed the power to cope with the chaos and turbulence in Asia, Africa, and Latin America. The country was stronger today, the president informed Congress on 18 January 1965, "than at any other time in our peacetime history. . . . [We] have a strength of arms greater than that ever assembled by any other nation and greater now than that of any combination of adversaries." Aside from having seen gigantic increases in strategic and tactical nuclear weapons, Johnson stressed, "our forces have been made as versatile as the threats to peace are various." The nation's "Special Forces, trained for the undeclared twilight wars of today, have been expanded eight-fold." The qualitative and quantitative superiority of the United States over the Soviet Union was so great, Secretary of Defense McNamara acknowledged, that he sometimes wondered "why there has not been a Congressional investigation of why we have so much military strength."[245]

There really was no reason to wonder. McNamara, Rusk, and Bundy wanted strategic superiority in order to be able to dominate any escalatory crisis.[246] Yet in early 1965 they did not expect a war with the Kremlin and they did not think the Soviet Union was fomenting trouble in Southeast Asia. "The Soviet Union does not want to be engaged with us in a major struggle over Southeast Asia," said Rusk. "I personally am convinced of that." But a spiraling crisis could occur nonetheless if the United States and communist China became locked in another war in Asia, as during the Korean War, and if the Soviet Union intervened. The overwhelming strength of the United States was designed, therefore, to dissuade the men in the Kremlin from even thinking of such a thing.[247]

At the time they decided to escalate hostilities in Vietnam, U.S. officials believed that the Soviet Union was not contemplating war but seeking to sustain détente. Dobrynin was trying to arrange a series of summits in Moscow and Washington.[248] Kosygin was not in Hanoi to foment trouble but to offer aid, gain influence, and caution restraint. Heretofore, in Vietnam, the Soviets had forfeited influence to the Chinese, but now they were attempting to "smooth irritants," "searching for means of inhibiting the actions of both antagonists," reported the CIA.[249]

When they made their decision to intensify the bombing, Johnson and his advisers pondered the effect that escalation would have on the Kremlin. "We believe that the Soviet Government will feel that it has received a direct insult and challenge because of Kosygin's presence in Hanoi," Assistant Secretary of State William R. Tyler wrote his boss, George Ball. "The Soviets will probably feel that their prestige has been seriously damaged and that they must take some positive actions to save face." From Moscow, Ambassador Kohler sent the same warning: the Russians would feel "increasing pressure not to appear weak and ineffective." At a meeting with Johnson at the White House on 10 February, George Ball and Llewellyn Thompson argued that further bombing should await Kosygin's departure from the Far East. Their caution was not appreciated. Johnson said the air strikes would continue against military installations and infiltration routes in North Vietnam.[250]

Operation Rolling Thunder put détente at risk. Détente was considered less important than combating revolutionary nationalism in the third world, less important than conveying prudent toughness to the leaders in Beijing. "I am convinced," Secretary of State Rusk wrote President Johnson, that "it would be disastrous for the United States and the Free World to permit Southeast Asia to be overrun by the Communist North." If the Chinese "can demonstrate that their course of policy is paying substantial dividends," he told a confidential hearing of the Senate Foreign Relations Committee, it would increase the prospect that the Soviet Union "would attempt to close the gap between Moscow and Peiping by moving toward Peiping's more militant attitude toward the world revolution."[251]

Johnson hoped that détente could survive these actions. The Soviets and the Americans had common interests, especially in limiting the arms race, controlling the spread of nuclear weapons, and containing the expansionism of the Chinese communists. However, believing that the United States and the Soviet Union were locked in a zero-sum ideological contest, Johnson felt he could not show weakness. He had learned as a child "that when you start running from a bully he keeps you running, and if he doesn't respect the line you draw in the pasture he isn't going to respect the line you draw at your front yard. He is going to wind up chasing you right out of your own house."[252]

Johnson said he needed to bolster America's credibility, but allies and neutrals alike expressed dissent, sometimes publicly, more often privately. The French were voluble; the British, more discreet. Japanese prime minister Sato Eisaku wanted the United States to negotiate with the Vietnamese, not fight them. The Canadians were disgusted, as were many Scandinavians. Johnson threatened to "get sick and leave town" rather than listen to more pleas for peace and moderation.[253]

American public opinion followed the president's lead but did not push him. "I don't think the American people are quite ready for us to send our [combat] troops," Johnson had acknowledged in May 1964.[254] Seven months later, in December 1964, a survey showed that more people opposed the deployment of troops than supported it. Even in April 1965, more Americans wanted to get out or negotiate than step up military action or go all out for victory. Nor was congressional opinion significantly more hawkish. In a survey of eighty-three senators in January 1965, only seven favored sending combat troops to South Vietnam or bombing North Vietnam; ten senators wanted to inaugurate immediate negotiations; thirty-one wanted to negotiate when the situation in the South improved.[255]

The public did not want war, but Johnson feared political retribution if Vietnam was lost to the ideological foe. "They'd impeach a president that would run [from Vietnam]," don't you think? he asked Russell. His friend did not think so.[256] But Johnson was not willing to take big risks for peace. Locked in his ideological prism, fearing the turbulence in the third world, and worried about his own reputation and the fate of the Great Society at home, Johnson chose to increase military action against North Vietnam rather than exercise leadership in behalf of détente. Of course, he hoped he could do both. He was wrong.

From Armageddon Back to Cold War

The U.S. actions in Southeast Asia affected decision making in Moscow. Brezhnev and Kosygin hoped to relax tensions with the United States, but they also wanted to preserve harmony among their fellow plotters who had overthrown Khrushchev. They knew they were being watched carefully by Aleksandr Shelepin, Mikhail Suslov, and other Presidium members skeptical of the feasibility and wisdom of trying to improve relations with the United States. While hoping to reassure their colleagues that there would be administrative stability, Kosygin and Brezhnev wanted to tackle domestic economic problems, reconcile relations with the Chinese communists, and preserve unity within the Warsaw Pact.[257] And they were determined to retain the Kremlin's credentials as the fountainhead of an alternative way of life. Moscow, they believed, not Beijing, should be the place to which revolutionary nationalist leaders looked for a glimpse of the future.[258]

In November and December, Brezhnev and Kosygin turned to the economic plan for 1965. They told their colleagues that their primary task was to strengthen the economy and ensure that "the Soviet people live better and better." They looked back with "joy" at their achievements, said Brezhnev, but primarily "we look ahead. We have many unsolved tasks."[259] He and Kosygin wanted to boost national revenue and increase the production of agricultural and consumer goods. To do so, they pondered significant economic reforms. At a Presidium meeting in early December they agreed to small cuts in defense expenditures and allocated the money to domestic priorities instead. In a report to the Supreme Soviet on 9 December, Kosygin said he attached great importance to the parallel cuts being made in the military budgets of the United States and the U.S.S.R., and he hoped for more in the future. He believed the Kremlin should work "persistently and patiently for the settlement of disputable problems," and he expected that improved relations with the West would lead to increased trade. But neither he nor Brezhnev hesitated to say that much would depend on the United States' ending its imperial adventures in Southeast Asia and its covert operations in Africa.[260]

Brezhnev and Kosygin struggled, meanwhile, to contain and coopt the bubbling discontent in Eastern Europe, where Soviet influence was waning. Their Warsaw Pact allies constantly chastised them for disregarding what they saw as the threat emanating from West Germany, failing to heal the split with the People's Republic of China, and minimizing the dangers inherent in U.S. plans to build up conventional capabilities and fight limited wars. At a meeting of the Warsaw Pact in January 1965, Walter Ulbricht warned that more attention had to be given to the "USA-FRG atomic bloc." The FRG was on the verge of acquiring nuclear weapons, he claimed, which "it will use for its revanchist goals." The Polish leader Gomulka agreed. Is the MLF not "a synonym for the term 'proliferation' "? he asked Brezhnev.[261]

Brezhnev shared their concerns. He invoked memories of World War II in speech after speech. "We shall never forget the sufferings of the people. . . . We shall forever remember the millions of courageous patriots of the USSR and Czechoslovakia, Poland, Yugoslavia, France, and many other countries."[262] "Man's memory is not perfect," he told a rally in Warsaw several months later, "and time erases many things, but there are occurrences and events which remain forever in people's minds and hearts and which nobody is able to erase from our memory. Among such events is the immortal deed of the people who destroyed Hitler's fascism."[263] Brezhnev said he agreed with his Warsaw Pact allies: The West Germans yearned for revenge. Wildly distorting the nature of U.S. policy, he said that Americans wanted to exploit "30 million revanchists." Prudent men, he stressed, must not permit German power to rise again.[264]

Nor would Soviet leaders remain indifferent to events in Southeast Asia. Before visiting Vietnam in February 1965, Kosygin sent a message to President Johnson expressing "with all frankness" his "serious concern" that U.S.

actions there might precipitate countermeasures and destroy Soviet willingness to improve relations.[265] Kosygin wanted to improve ties with North Vietnamese leaders who resented Moscow's meager assistance, and he aimed to temper Hanoi's policies and counter the doleful influence of Beijing. He had had no prior knowledge of the attack on the U.S. Army barracks in Pleiku, and was distressed that his North Vietnamese comrades had placed him in an embarrassing position. But when the Americans bombed on the second day of his visit, he was infuriated and lashed out: "U.S. armed forces," he declared, "brazenly attacked the territory of the DRV [North Vietnam]." Imperialist bombs were falling on Vietnamese soil, needlessly spilling Vietnamese blood. The United States, impotent "in the face of the growing liberation movement," he said, was trying to salvage its pride through "military ventures." The situation was "fraught with serious complications." But at the same time he hesitated to delineate any precise initiatives, except to promise support to North Vietnam.[266]

Kosygin's hapless situation was magnified when he stopped in Beijing on his way back to Moscow. While he hoped to mend relations with Mao Zedong, he did not want to abandon Moscow's desire to modulate the arms race and nurture détente. Kosygin tried hard to convince Mao that these policies were not betrayals of socialism. We seek "to accommodate you, as comrades would do, we are treating you with respect," he implored, for ideological unity was indispensable in the peaceful struggle with capitalism. This fact was so obvious to Kosygin that it was hard for him to grasp why the comrades in Beijing and Moscow were feuding incessantly with one another. "What ties us together is greater than what keeps us apart," he said.

Mao did not agree, and did not hide his contempt for Kosygin. Chinese communists, Mao said, were dogmatists; "we are bellicose," "[a] combative people"; they did not believe in general and complete disarmament. Moscow's policies, Mao insisted, were defeatist and backward. "We think that you are doing too little to support the revolutionary struggle of nations." He was not interested in mending fences. Rather than attend a conference of communist parties that Moscow was championing to restore unity (and the Kremlin's leadership), Mao claimed that "an entire era" would be needed to see which leading communist nation was right. In the interim, Beijing would not withhold its criticisms.

Kosygin grew angry. Mao, he said to his face, was all words. "You only talk, and you do little," whereas the Soviet Union was fully committed to the revolutionary project. "The Americans would like to plant capitalism everywhere, and we would like that communism was everywhere." The Soviets need unity, not war, Kosygin reiterated. They opposed both revisionism and dogmatism. "We are no less combative Marxist-Leninists than you," Kosygin said toward the end of their long conversation, but we "are against creating a war situation."[267]

When Kosygin returned to Moscow, he delivered a speech on Soviet television in which he attacked the United States for widening the war and bombing North Vietnam. The "imperialists are trying to take revenge on all the Vietnamese people for the determination of the Vietnamese patriots to attain freedom."[268] The Kremlin would not abandon their communist comrades. They would provide aid and encourage negotiations, but they would not force Hanoi to make concessions nor betray the revolution in South Vietnam. They could not do so. Their standing in the world communist community was at risk. If they faltered, they would be scorned by the Chinese and ridiculed by communists and revolutionary nationalists everywhere. "In this situation," declared Brezhnev, "it is a matter of honor, an international duty of socialist countries, to render effective support" to a fraternal country. Our hands were tied, Dobrynin wrote, "by our own ideological loyalties," much as were Johnson's.[269]

What the United States was doing in Vietnam did not shock Moscow. Capitalists were acting like capitalists. The imperialists were once again manifesting their "hopeless desire to turn back the course of history and suppress people struggling for their freedom and independence," said Brezhnev.[270] They would fail. "Mighty colonial empires" were collapsing. "Socialist ideas are conquering the minds of the liberated peoples more and more," he exclaimed. "Many states in Asia and Africa are entering on the path of Socialist reforms. . . . They see that communists are in the vanguard of the revolutionary struggle." And communism, Brezhnev continued, was "the most influential political force" in the world today. "It brings to people real freedom and equality, fraternity and peace. Without communists, there would be no modern world, no movement forward, no progress. The future is for communism."[271]

But the present was still fraught with peril. To an audience of six thousand veterans, commanders, workers, and scientists gathered at the Kremlin to commemorate the twentieth anniversary of the victory over Nazism, Brezhnev reverted to the familiar theme of German revanchism:

> Time can change much but the main culprits responsible for the past war, the German militarists, live outside time; the crushing defeat did not make them come to their senses. To their minds, history apparently can travel in but one and the same circle, namely, war, defeat, regrouping of forces, and then a fresh war. After Versailles, Germany required more than 15 years to create a framework for its armed forces. The present-day German militarists, with the active support of imperialists of the United States and other NATO countries, did the same thing in 9 years. They now have in their hands a Bundeswehr of a half-million men and an officer corps to build up a massive army. The strategic plans for forming and training the West German armed forces are based on the calculation that they will obtain nuclear-armed weapons. The aim of the political and military leaders of the German Federal Republic is to lay their hands on these weapons and with such backing to revise the results of World War II.[272]

Twenty years lapsed as a shooting star. From the Soviet perspective, not much had changed: great fears remained, and still greater opportunities beckoned. When Averell Harriman visited Moscow in July, Kosygin talked to him at great length about Soviet disappointments and hopes. He and his colleagues, Kosygin joked, "had voted for Johnson against Goldwater, although their ballots could not be counted." They hoped "that trust and confidence . . . could be developed." But they were disillusioned. There were "dangerous forces" at work, most especially the specter of German power. According to Kosygin, the multilateral nuclear force "was aimed at Soviet Union and US was thereby protecting German revanchism." Worse yet, in continuing to support the long-term goal of German unification, the United States set "West Germans against East Germans and this puts us into conflict." Nobody in Europe really wanted German unification, said Kosygin. The German problem might be solved if the United States recognized the division of Germany and guaranteed that Bonn would never possess nuclear weapons.[273]

But the possibility of tackling these issues hinged on Washington's willingness to abandon its struggle against the Vietnamese revolution. Brezhnev and Kosygin had not solidified their leadership positions, and they were under great pressure from defense officials and party ideologues to stiffen Soviet resistance to American "adventurism" in Southeast Asia and Central America.[274] The United States, said Kosygin, "was trying to strangle national liberation movements everywhere in the world." Washington would fail. Meanwhile, opportunities to defuse the Cold War would evaporate.[275] "Don't you think your relations with the USSR are of high priority?" Dobrynin asked Vice President Hubert Humphrey. "If you do, then why do you bomb North Vietnam? Why do you test us?"[276]

The answer was clear: for U.S. officials, leftist uprisings and liberation movements were part of an inchoate but foreboding worldwide phenomenon, and communists must not be allowed to advance anywhere. In late April 1965, for example, when turmoil mounted and violence flared in the Dominican Republic, the president sent twenty-three thousand U.S. troops to preserve order and prevent a government coup that might turn out to be hostile to the United States. Although the situation was terribly murky, and the president's advisers were divided on what should be done, Johnson's mind-set was strikingly evident. In a taped phone conversation with Bundy, he said, "I am seeing the pattern and I just cannot be silent. . . . What they are doing in La Paz, Bolivia, what they are doing in Mexico City, and what they are doing in Vietnam and the Dominican Republic is not totally unrelated."[277]

Johnson and his advisers believed that faltering in Vietnam was especially dangerous because it would invigorate China's version of communism.[278] All communists were America's ideological foe, but the Chinese variety was deemed virulent. Mao and his comrades were dedicated, even fanatic, communists. Belief in "the righteousness of their cause, the correctness of their doctrine, and the certainty of eventual victory sustained them through the arduous and bloody 28-year struggle which brought them to control the vast land and population of mainland China." Their ultimate aim, wrote the CIA, was "to establish a Communist world according to Peiping's militant revolutionary brand of Marxism-Leninism." Of course, their behavior also was shaped by their "strong sense of the centrality of their nation, history, and culture," and these influenced the trajectory of Chinese policy, especially the feud with Moscow. According to U.S. intelligence analysts, the energy, militancy, and tenacity of the Chinese communists enabled them to have a greater impact on the international environment than their

> military and economic power would seem to justify. . . . This results less from the potency of Chinese policy than from the peculiar vulnerability of the international order in present circumstances. The rapid dissolution of colonial empires in Africa and Asia has left a political vacuum, marked by uncertain and shifting national alignments and chronic instability. The new nations with their weak, inexperienced governments are highly vulnerable to Peiping's line. With large expectations and small capabilities, their people are frustrated by the status quo and naturally inclined to blame their woes on such external factors as colonialist exploitation and racial domination. It is not too hard to sell them radical "solutions" to their problems.[279]

Johnson and his advisers had to demonstrate that the Vietnamese and the Chinese communists were not part of a forward wave that would engulf the third world. If Beijing "shows profit from its militancy," said Secretary Rusk, "if they demonstrate that this is the way of the future, . . . then I think this gives an enormous impetus to the more militant doctrine of communism . . . and that Moscow would be sorely tempted to move in that direction." If the communists were not stopped in Vietnam, he said, Cambodia would be next "to complete the journey to the other side," followed swiftly by Thailand. Communists everywhere, said Rusk, from Indonesia to South America, were observing events in Indochina closely, seeking clues for the future.[280] If stopping the march of communism in the third world meant sacrificing détente, that was a regrettable but acceptable consequence. "We were determined to improve relations [with the USSR]," Bundy told the columnist Drew Pearson, but "we could not let Vietnam go under just for this purpose."[281]

Johnson, Rusk, Bundy, Harriman, and their colleagues wanted the Kremlin to prod Hanoi to abandon its revolutionary agenda in South Vietnam but understood that if Soviet leaders did this, they would be repudiating their leadership of a movement "of worldwide historical significance."[282] The Kremlin could not allow Mao and his comrades to claim to be the lone champions of worldwide liberation. Kohler wrote from Moscow on 5 April that if Soviet officials had to choose, they would place priority on retaining influence in the communist world rather than nurturing détente with the United States.[283]

Nonetheless, Johnson and his advisers decided on a major escalation of the war in Vietnam. They were inspired by fear but empowered by a sense of their superior strength. Eventually, American analysts estimated, "the urgent requirements of domestic economic reform and growth" would force Soviet leaders to accommodate the United States.[284] Weakness would mellow them. In addition to the stagnancy of the Soviet economy, Brezhnev and Kosygin faced dissent in Eastern Europe and the intensifying rivalry with Beijing. Conflicting pressures and impulses would beleaguer them for a long time to come. They, too, might be sucked into third world quagmires, often against their own better judgment. But eventually they would seek to defuse the competition with the United States so as to meet the growing demands of their own people. "We think," judged the CIA, "that important pressures in the Soviet scene and the international setting will eventually favor the chances for a new Soviet effort to make the relaxation of tensions with the West the basis of the USSR's foreign policy."[285]

Soviet weakness spelled opportunity for the United States, notwithstanding the deteriorating situation in Vietnam. America was healthier than the Soviet Union, Johnson's advisers believed. If only they could triumph in Vietnam, they could position themselves for additional gains throughout the third world, exploit the ferment within the Soviet bloc, and eventually win the Cold War. Power, they all agreed, was dispersing, but if they operated adroitly and mended their own fraying alliance in Western Europe, they could handle the new world order far better than their adversary.[286] The national liberation moment in world history, so portentous in its immediacy, would soon end; the fervor of anticolonialism would erode; the opportunities for communist gains would decline. "The process of decolonization is practically over," Komer wrote Bundy. And once it was over, he predicted, "we can capture the anti-colonial revolution."[287]

Indeed, the Soviet model of national development, beguilingly attractive as a fast track to modernization, was showing its flaws, and, in time, the shortcomings would grow. In Eastern Europe, there were persistent rumblings of discontent and growing experimentation and decentralization. The iron curtain was getting rusty; cracks were appearing. Johnson supported more trade with the Eastern bloc, in the hope that this would promote more fragmentation.[288] The United States, American officials hoped, could build bridges to Eastern Europe, gradually erode Soviet domination, *and* compete effectively in the third world. In fact, if they could build the Great Society and eradicate racism at home, they would prevail in the competition for the soul of mankind around the globe.

When Johnson chose to escalate in Vietnam, Vice President Hubert Humphrey warned him that he was making a "fateful" decision. "I have nothing but sympathy for you," he wrote the president. He understood "the burden and the anguish." But it was mistaken to think that Americans wanted to get embroiled in a war in Vietnam. It might become a quagmire, erode America's reputation abroad, and disrupt the creation of the Great Society at home. Speaking as one able politician to another, Humphrey told him they had a chance to disengage from Vietnam without negative political consequences. The Democrats had won a decisive victory in 1964, campaigning on their prudence rather than their opponents' warmongering. "It is the first year," wrote Humphrey, "when we can face the Vietnam problem without being preoccupied with the political repercussions from the Republican right."[289]

Johnson did not agree. "We don't need all these memos," he wrote his vice president, and then shut him out of the policymaking process.[290] He would not undo the commitment of three predecessors or risk the repudiation of the American people. He would not appear weak or admit error. He would not allow dominos to fall or the communists to advance.

Lyndon Johnson could not transcend the ideological shibboleths he had adopted or overcome the political lessons he had learned. He would agonize and torment himself, worrying always that he needed just a few more smart, loyal, and hardworking people to help salvage the situation. But he could not and would not turn back. He had a mission, he explained in his inaugural address on 20 January 1965, "to inspire the hopes of all mankind" and to promote "the liberation of man."[291] If he failed to show courage abroad, failed to honor "the American Covenant," he feared that his political opponents might defeat him at home and thwart his efforts to create a Great Society that would serve as the exemplar of a superior way of life for all humankind.

Nor could Soviet leaders transcend their past. The "great Lenin" had laid down markers they felt obliged to follow. History was flowing in their direction, they believed. The Americans were seeking "to turn back the course of history" by suppressing the Vietnamese people's quest for freedom and independence.[292] The "revolutionary struggle of the working people has never before known such sweep," exclaimed Brezhnev. "Socialist ideas are conquering the minds of the liberated peoples more and more. Many states in Asia and Africa are entering on the path of socialist reforms. . . . They see that communists are the vanguard of the revolutionary struggle."[293]

· Although opportunity loomed in the third world to advance the Soviet way of life, danger forever lurked in the Old World. "At this very moment," said Brezhnev on 8 May 1965, "with the blessing of the Western powers, the West German Bundestag has risen from its habitual seat and illegally gone off to West Berlin to hold a session there." The "revanchist itch" persisted.[294] Vigilance was imperative. After leveling off and even decreasing in the early and middle 1960s, Soviet defense expenditures resumed their upward spiral.[295]

Revolutionary nationalism in the third world, the fear of German nationalism in the Old World, and Chinese xenophobia in East Asia loomed portentously over the global international order (or disorder). The men who made policy in Washington and Moscow viewed developments through ideological prisms and historical memories that made détente extremely difficult to sustain. They could not transcend their past, overcome their fears, modify their aspirations, escape the pressure of allies, or ignore domestic political adversaries. They felt peril and they glimpsed salvation. They had nowhere to go once they escaped from Armageddon but back to Cold War.

IV

THE EROSION
OF DÉTENTE, 1975–80

Brezhnev and Carter

Brezhnev and Détente

"It was show time in Helsinki," with an "all-star cast," reported *Time* magazine on 4 August 1975. The week's summit spectacular in the capital of Finland might be called "Goodbye to World War II." "The star was unquestionably that durable ex-heavy Leonid Brezhnev."[1]

Time might have thought that a mocking, playful tone was appropriate for introducing American readers to the "Final Act" of the Conference on Security and Co-operation in Europe. This one-hundred-page, thirty-thousand-word agreement, signed by thirty-three heads of European states plus the president of the United States and the prime minister of Canada, was not a treaty. It did not have the force of law. Nonetheless, for Brezhnev, it represented the high point of his career as a statesman, the culmination of the effort begun by Malenkov and Molotov in 1954 to get European and American leaders to acknowledge the legitimacy of the territorial borders in Central and Eastern Europe that came about at the end of World War II, notably the Oder-Neisse frontier between Poland and the GDR. It also meant affirmation of the division of Germany into two states, acknowledgment of the German Democratic Republic, and validation of Stalin's land grabs at the expense of his East European neighbors. In short, it meant legitimation of Soviet frontiers, security for their homeland, and acceptance of their way of life in half of Europe—and, as such, the indispensable framework for détente.[2]

At the time of the Helsinki meeting, Brezhnev's health was beginning to decline, but he was at the height of his influence in the Kremlin. After orchestrating the coup against Khrushchev in 1964, he had shared power for several years with Premier Alexei Kosygin. Gradually they had rid themselves of opponents in the Politburo; gradually Brezhnev had elevated himself to unquestioned leadership, though he always consulted his colleagues and acted with their concurrence. He was a master of Kremlin intrigue, sensitive to slights but not vindictive in victory. He prized collegiality, hated turmoil, and sought stability and tranquility.[3]

Brezhnev was a Communist Party man, too young to have participated in the Bolshevik revolution but just the right age to have benefited enormously from the career opportunities triggered by Stalin's bloody purges. Born in 1906 in the mill town of Kamenskoye, in eastern Ukraine, he was the son of a steelworker. "Everything gravitated towards the [steel mill]," Brezhnev later recalled in his ghostwritten memoir, "and I knew . . . that I would be going to the mill . . . in my father's footsteps. No other fate in the settlement was thinkable."[4]

But World War I and the ensuing revolution enveloped the region in conflict. "Great was the complexity of social existence in the years of my youth," remembered Brezhnev. "Things were not easy" as Kamenskoye passed from the clutches of one warring faction to another, Belgian and French capitalists and their hired managers were driven out, and a new era began. His town was a workers' town, "the greater part of the population was working class," wrote Brezhnev, "and so we always thought of the proletarian revolution as ours!"[5]

Brezhnev's parents were literate and wanted their son to have a good education. They sent Leonid to the Kamenskoye Boys' Classical Grammar School when it began to admit a few working-class children before the revolution, and Leonid himself was motivated and disciplined. Brezhnev's father was not a member of the Communist Party but he allegedly supported the Bolsheviks and rejoiced when Leonid joined the Komsomol, the communist youth organization, at the age of seventeen. Although a deep economic depression settled on Kamenskoye in the years following World War I and the family was forced to move to Kursk, the revolution opened opportunities for young Leonid he never could have contemplated. In 1924, he enrolled in a technical school, where he studied land management and reclamation.[6]

Brezhnev lent his newly acquired talents to the party in its drive to collectivize the countryside. "Those were hard times when the old, outworn forms of existence were falling apart, and the shoots of the new were just poking through and one had to search for, support and cultivate them persistently." He helped erase old property boundaries, uniting "on the maps all the broken up, individual strips of land into one collective field." Notwithstanding private misgivings over the barbaric treatment of family friends and neighbors, he forced people to pool their land, cattle, farm implements, and dwellings. He was thrilled, his ghostwriter maintained, to be "in the thick of events of the greatest social revolution in the country." Landowners remonstrated and resisted. "And even more decisively and daringly we led the offensive against [them]."[7]

In these early years of his adulthood, Brezhnev began to earn his spurs as a party loyalist and devoted follower of Stalin. But he sensed an even greater battle on the horizon, the struggle to industrialize the country. He returned to Kamenskoye, now called Dneprodzerzhinsk, to help revive Ukraine's steel industry. He worked in the factories, went back to school, educated himself as an engineer, and began moving up party ranks after officially joining in 1931. In the mid-1930s he was drafted into the Red Army and assigned to a tank battalion, where he quickly impressed his superiors and was made a platoon commander and political instructor.

Released from service in 1936, Brezhnev returned to Dneprodzerzhinsk, where he served first in the town council (or local soviet) and then as propaganda secretary for the provincial committee of the Communist Party of the Ukraine. More important, he took responsibility for the production of metals in the region and for the coordination of its defense industries. In these years, Brezhnev got to know Nikita Khrushchev, who was overseeing party affairs throughout the Ukraine. They worked together and with other Stalinists to purge the region of prospective Nazi collaborators and liquidate the Ukrainian intelligentsia. With the German invasion in 1941, Brezhnev's task became that of disassembling the furnaces and factories and shipping them eastward before the advancing German armies could capture them.[8]

During the war, Brezhnev served as a political commissar on the southern front, where his job was to encourage, motivate, and instill discipline. Soviet troops, he insisted, had to stand and fight. Although the Nazi onslaught seemed at first merciless and unstoppable, "every man must be made to realize," Brezhnev said, "that further retreat is impossible. He must realize with his mind and heart that this is a matter of the life and death of the Soviet state, of the life and death of the people of our country. . . . The Nazi troops must be stopped now, before it is too late."[9]

The war was the defining experience of Brezhnev's life.[10] He loved to recount the story of a conversation with his father just before the war: What is the highest mountain in the world? his father asked. Everest, said Leonid. How high is the Eiffel Tower? About three hundred meters, said Leonid. We should build a steel tower on the top of Everest and hang Hitler and a dozen of his accomplices for all the world to see, his father told him. This conversation "left an indelible impression on him, on his policies, his ideology, his psychology—indeed, his whole way of life."[11]

After World War II, Brezhnev helped to oversee the reconstruction of the industrial infrastructure of Ukraine. Afterward, Stalin sent him to Moldova, newly annexed from Romania, to help consolidate the Kremlin's hold there, then rewarded him by naming him to the Central Committee in 1952. After Stalin's death, Brezhnev hitched his future to Khrushchev. Although demoted briefly from the Presidium, he played a key part in Khrushchev's efforts to develop the uncultivated lands of Kazakhstan. More important, he became ever more closely associated with the military-industrial complex of the Soviet Union, first as head of the political directorate of the army and navy, and then, in 1956, as a candidate member of the Politburo, with substantial authority over defense manufacturing, heavy industry, the space program, and capital construction. Among other things, he helped oversee the production of nuclear weapons and the building of missile silos. After supporting Khrushchev against his foes and enjoying enormous prestige from Soviet space successes, he was selected as president of the Supreme Soviet in May 1960. Khrushchev was grooming Brezhnev as his successor when Brezhnev helped orchestrate the coup that toppled Khrushchev from power.[12]

Brezhnev was elected first secretary of the CPSU immediately after Khrushchev's ouster but did not dominate foreign-policy decision making, which was conducted by an inner circle of the Politburo, including Alexei Kosygin, Party Secretary Mikhail Suslov, and Nikolai Podgorny, chairman of the Presidium. In the late 1960s and early 1970s, Yuri Andropov, head of the KGB, Defense Minister Marshal Andrei Grechko, Foreign Minister Andrei Gromyko, and Boris Ponomarev, head of the International Department of the CPSU, played increasingly important roles. On military issues, the armed forces and the defense industry shaped policy under the broad supervision of the Defense Council, which Brezhnev chaired; on relations with the United States, major West European nations, Japan, and China, the foreign ministry predominated; on interactions with many nonruling communist parties, less-developed countries, and third world guerilla movements, Ponomarev, Suslov, Andropov, and their assistants were influential; on ties with Eastern Europe, a separate Central Committee department reported directly to the Secretariat and Politburo.[13]

At first, Soviet goals and strategies were far from clear. Humiliated by Khrushchev's blunders during the Cuban missile crisis and angered by Johnson's bombing of North Vietnam and his intervention in the Dominican Republic, the Kremlin embarked on a major military buildup. Between 1965 and 1970, defense expenditures increased by more than a third and, according to some estimates, came close to doubling. The numbers of strategic weapons in the Soviet arsenal—intercontinental ballistic missiles, submarine-launched ballistic missiles, and long-range bombers—soared, from approximately 472 in 1964 to 1,470 in 1969. The annual production of tanks rose from 3,100 in 1966 to more than 4,250 in 1970; armored vehicle production grew during these same years, from 2,800 to 4,000. Yet Brezhnev and his colleagues did not want to wage war. They yearned for American respect, despised America's strength, and demanded equal security. They bristled at the expansion of U.S. influence in Southeast Asia when the Indonesian army overthrew President Sukarno in 1965 and slaughtered three hundred thousand communists; they felt even more humiliated in 1967, when the Israeli army routed the Kremlin's Arab friends (Egypt and Syria in particular) in the Six-Day War. Brezhnev and his associates dreamed of extending their influence around the globe, yet they felt they were being tested by U.S. actions and challenged by the Chinese. Mao Zedong was building a nuclear arsenal, meddling in Eastern Europe, and, most daringly, raising questions about the Sino-Soviet border and the status of Mongolia, a former Chinese province that was now an independent state subservient to the Kremlin.[14]

Brezhnev faced the defining crisis of his career in 1968. In January, the Czechoslovak Communist Party chose Alexander Dubček to be its leader. He quickly instituted economic reforms, permitted political liberalization, and appointed new people to top positions in the interior and military ministries. Political clubs arose, newspapers multiplied, and citizens freely discussed their country's future. The "Prague Spring," as it came to be called, sent tremors through the Eastern bloc. Polish and East German leaders voiced their worries to Brezhnev. Soviet leaders felt similar anxieties about the spread of antisocialist tendencies, the looming challenge to the Communist Party's monopoly of power, and the threat to the Kremlin's sphere of influence in Eastern Europe. Petro Shelest, first secretary of the Ukrainian Communist Party and a member of the Politburo, warned Brezhnev that events in Czechoslovakia were "causing unsavory phenomena" in Ukraine.[15] Much as Johnson had done during the early months of 1965, Brezhnev agonized and procrastinated. He did not want to deploy troops to crush the reform movement. But he, too, worried about falling dominos. Although Dubček did not threaten to leave the Warsaw Treaty Organization, top generals in his military establishment questioned Soviet strategic thinking and called for greater independence. As reformers gained additional influence in Prague during May and June, Brezhnev came under increasing pressure to take decisive action. His nerves were shaken, and colleagues noted that he appeared grim and pale. "I may look soft," he commented, "but I can strike so hard that afterwards I feel sick for three days." He began taking tranquilizers and sleeping pills, a habit he would never overcome. In August, he authorized Soviet troops to intervene. In what became known as the Brezhnev Doctrine, the Kremlin declared:

> The sovereignty of individual socialist countries cannot be set against the interests of world socialism and the world revolutionary movement. . . . Each Communist party is free to apply the principles of Marxism-Leninism and socialism in its own country, but it is not free to deviate from these principles if it is to remain a Communist party. . . . The weakening of any of the

links in the world system of socialism directly affects all the socialist countries, and they cannot look indifferently upon this.[16]

Soviet intervention in Czechoslovakia had profound ramifications. The
resentment of the Czech and Slovak people was palpable. China denounced
Soviet actions and reinforced its troops along the Sino-Soviet border. Albania
severed its last ties with the Warsaw Pact, and Romania ridiculed the invasion. Polish, East German, and Hungarian leaders were pleased and assigned
troops to the invading force, but their people resented Soviet action. The use
of brute force across sovereign borders evoked widespread condemnation
throughout the West. In Western Europe, the left was deeply disillusioned;
the invasion spurred the growing autonomy of the French, Italian, and Span-
ish communist parties from Moscow's control, a trend subsequently referred
to as eurocommunism. In many parts of the third world, nationalist leaders
began questioning Moscow's credentials as the champion of anti-imperialism.
In Russia itself, reformers were dismayed, and rulers were less tempted to
listen to experts who encouraged new thinking with regard to the Soviet
economy. Restructuring, Brezhnev realized, might mean eroding the party's
monopoly of power.[17]

Crushing the Prague Spring marked a critical turning point in the evolution of Brezhnev's foreign policy. He and his advisers had calculated that the
West would do nothing more than protest the use of force, and they were
right. Neither the United States nor West Germany threatened serious retaliation. Not long ago, Gromyko had proudly told his aides, "the Politburo had
to think carefully, time and again, before taking any foreign policy step—
What would the US do? What would France do? This period is over. . .
Whatever noise they can make, the new correlation of forces is such that ey
no longer dare to move against us." Brezhnev's self-confidence grew. "Fm
the crucible of Czechoslovakia emerged a different Brezhnev," commend
Alexander Bovin, one of his speechwriters.[18]

Brezhnev and his colleagues now felt they had the strength to bargaif-
fectively. "Nobody wants to talk to the weak," Andropov quipped.[19] ie
U.S.S.R. worked collaboratively with the United States to complete the st
treaty to thwart the proliferation of nuclear weapons. They were wod
not only about the nuclear aspirations of West Germany, but also at
the mounting capabilities of China. As Soviet troops clashed with Che

soldiers along their ill-defined border in 1968 and 1969, Kremlin leaders thought more about their rivalry with China. Even as they justified their intervention in Prague, they unequivocally denounced Beijing's "leftist adventurist conception of 'exporting revolution,' of 'bringing happiness' to other peoples."[20]

Above all, Brezhnev and Kosygin wanted peace and stability in Europe. They wanted West Germany to recognize the formal existence of East Germany and to accept the Oder-Neisse border—in short, to confirm the postwar territorial status quo. Hence when Willy Brandt, leader of the West German Social Democrats, put together a new coalition government in October 1969 and communicated a readiness to deal with East Germany, Brezhnev glimpsed an opportunity to achieve the Kremlin's long-term goals. At a meeting of the Warsaw Pact on 7 January 1970, he said he would begin diplomatic talks with Brandt. He would be cautious and prudent, for he was not convinced there had been any fundamental change in West Germany, but it would be folly, he added, not to take advantage of the positive turn of events.[21]

Brandt's policy of opening relations with the East, his *Ostpolitik*, did indeed precipitate dramatic change. Brandt wanted to ease the tension, ameliorate the everyday life of Berliners, and facilitate travel between East and West Germany. He sought to promote the unification of German families rather than dwell on seemingly futile efforts to unify the German nation. His allies in Washington, London, and Paris had accepted the division of Germany, neither challenging the construction of the Berlin wall nor reacting strongly to the Soviet invasion of Czechoslovakia. If change were to be brought about, it would have to come through rapprochement with the Kremlin. In a remarkable series of treaties and agreements, the West German government renounced the use of force to bring about territorial revision, accepted the existence of the GDR, recognized prevailing borders, supported the nuclear nonproliferation movement, and nurtured diplomatic and economic relations with all the Warsaw Pact nations, most especially with the Soviet Union. Brezhnev, in turn, achieved what had long eluded his predecessors: a sense of security in Europe based on German acceptance of the territorial status quo.[22]

In March 1971, Brezhnev put the full imprimatur of the party leadership behind the policy of relaxing tensions with the West and negotiating arms-reduction treaties with Washington and NATO. He could not have done so without the assent of key colleagues in the Politburo, but gaining their approval, or acquiescence, was not easy. Podgorny, Shelest, Suslov, and Grechko had serious reservations. Nonetheless, Brezhnev used his considerable skill to forge a consensus. In these years, before his health declined, Brezhnev impressed associates as "a dynamic, lively, energetic, agile man." Although he had no intellectual curiosity, he possessed common sense and political shrewdness; he "knew how to please people," writes the historian Vladislav Zubok. He allowed party ideologues and military bureaucrats to have their way on many issues. He did not reduce their perks or threaten their jobs, as had Khrushchev. In exchange, he asked for their loyalty and their support of détente, which he cared about more than any other policy.[23]

Brezhnev embraced détente because he wanted to lessen the chances of nuclear war and encourage trade with the West, and because he was worried about frontier clashes with China and the burden of defense expenditures. Although military spending grew rapidly between 1965 and 1970, from about nine to thirteen billion rubles in official figures, and from thirty to forty-two billion rubles according to some outside experts, Brezhnev and Kosygin believed that a relaxation of tensions, premised on strategic parity with the United States, might enable the Soviet Union to gain access to Western technology and credit and shift resources gradually toward the production of consumer goods, thereby satisfying growing demand among frustrated Soviet citizens.[24]

In his report to the twenty-fourth Congress of the CPSU in March 1971, Brezhnev emphasized that the aim of the party was to "bring about a radical turn towards détente and peace on this continent." The next step was to "ensure the convocation and success of an all-European [security] conference."[25] Previously, the Kremlin had supported holding such a conference *without* the United States, believing that such a meeting would foment division in the West and promote the dissolution of NATO, a long-term Soviet goal. But Brezhnev changed course in 1972, becoming enamored of the pomp and ceremony of great-power summitry. President Richard M. Nixon impressed him when in a private meeting at their first summit in Moscow, in May 1972, he said straightforwardly to Brezhnev, "Let's leave systems aside, and let's talk about how to improve our relationship."[26] Brezhnev was mightily taken with these words and prized his relationship with the American president. And he

came to see that it was advantageous to have the United States as a participant in the Conference on Security and Co-operation in Europe. Should they
achieve an agreement, it would represent American acceptance of the postwar status quo and serve as the peace treaty that had eluded Stalin and Truman and all their successors.[27]

At the Moscow summit, Brezhnev and Nixon signed the first Strategic
Arms Limitation Treaty (SALT), an anti–ballistic missile (ABM) treaty, and
numerous other accords regarding trade, science, health, and the environment. Very important to the Kremlin was the agreement on basic principles
for conducting bilateral relations. Despite ideological differences, the United
States and the Soviet Union agreed to conduct their relations according to
the principles of "sovereignty, equality, non-interference in one another's internal affairs, and mutual advantage."[28] The Soviet government, Brezhnev
told his comrades, now had everything it needed to speak firmly and clearly
to the Americans, but also respectfully.[29]

In a major party address in December, Brezhnev explained that détente
affirmed the Leninist policy of peaceful coexistence but did not put an end to
class struggle. "The world outlook and class aims of socialism and capitalism
are opposite and irreconcilable." But the United States and the Soviet Union
would now "strive to shift this historically inevitable struggle on to a path
free from the perils of war, of dangerous conflicts and an uncontrolled arms
race. This will be a tremendous gain for world peace, for the interests of all
peoples, of all states."[30]

Brezhnev hoped that he and Nixon would take additional steps to curb
the arms race. SALT I was an interim agreement that froze for five years each
side's land-based intercontinental ballistic missiles and submarine-launched
ballistic missiles. It did not specify numbers, but the understanding left the
Soviets with about 2,400 launchers and the United States with 1,700. Although the disparity in numbers triggered much opposition to SALT I in
the United States, Soviet military leaders were none too happy, either. The
agreement did not limit America's strategic air force, much superior to the
Russians', or the number of missiles the United States could equip with independently targeted warheads. Nor did it restrict the number of weapons in
U.S. forward bases around the periphery of the Soviet Union and, most especially, in Western Europe. Brezhnev championed détente because it promised
to provide equal security, strategic parity, and economic dividends, but he

Nixon and Brezhnev, 1973. Brezhnev delighted in his summitry with Nixon.

knew he would not be able to negotiate a more permanent treaty if he did not
have the concurrence of the Soviet generals and defense managers who were
his traditional allies.

Many Soviet military officers and defense officials were prepared to accept the SALT process if they could shape future agreements to serve Soviet
national security goals and constrain America's lead in the arms race. "We
in the Soviet Union understood," said General Viktor Starodubov, chief
SALT II adviser to the Soviet General Staff, "that for us trying to catch up to
the United States would be too costly, too difficult, in terms of the economy
and so forth." Notwithstanding the great quantitative gains they had been
making, Soviet military leaders acknowledged the superiority of U.S. technology, the greater accuracy of American weapons, and the high quality of its
submarine force. They wanted to use the SALT process to erode these advantages, and they did not think that SALT I had achieved this goal.[31] In any
subsequent strategic arms limitation treaty Brezhnev had to allay the concerns of these generals and ease the burden on the Soviet economy. He was
determined to do so.

Brezhnev loved the pageantry of the summit meetings and the attention he received there. In 1973–74, however, he became dismayed by growing U.S. criticism of détente and by the erosion of Nixon's stature because of Watergate. He was disappointed when the U.S. Congress limited the president's authority to lower tariffs and extend credits and when it made expanded economic intercourse contingent on the Kremlin's willingness to allow Jews to emigrate from the Soviet Union. Liberal legislators in Washington were ridiculing Nixon for his callous disregard of Soviet human rights violations and for his alleged indifference to the plight of Jews seeking to flee the U.S.S.R. Conservative senators and congressmen were disgruntled by the president's failure to secure a better deal on strategic weapons. An unlikely coalition of liberals and conservatives, led by Democratic senator Henry Jackson of Washington, joined together to circumscribe the administration's ability to offer the Soviet Union most-favored-nation status.

Détente did not yield the economic rewards that Brezhnev had hoped for, yet he was not prepared to abandon it. Increasingly, he vested his domestic legitimacy in this policy. Unwilling to support domestic reform, he skillfully represented himself as the champion of peace and stability, both of which resonated with millions of Soviet citizens whose memories of war remained vivid. When Nixon resigned in disgrace in the summer of 1974, Brezhnev immediately pressed for a meeting with the new president, Gerald Ford.[32]

On 23 November, the Soviet general secretary traversed the broad expanse of the Soviet Union and met Ford in Vladivostok, the Soviet port city on the Pacific. Brezhnev was upbeat and cordial, eager to get to know the new president, and always ready to exchange banter with Henry Kissinger, the influential secretary of state and former national security adviser to Nixon. Most of all, Brezhnev wanted to convey his intentions and determine whether progress could be made toward another SALT agreement. "Let us speak not as diplomats but as human beings," he said to Ford. "Both you and I fought in World War II. That war was child's play as compared to nuclear war."[33]

Disdaining the technical details, Brezhnev said he had more important points to convey to the American president: "We want friendly, stable, mutually advantageous relations with the United States. Not only I but our entire party, government, and all our people want friendly relations with the United States."[34] The technical details, he exclaimed, obscured a larger truth: "we don't intend ever to attack you."[35] The world "is looking at us," Brezhnev emphasized, and the world wanted the great powers to ensure "that there will be no nuclear war."[36] Had they been making progress? "We have not achieved any real limitation, and in fact we have been spurring the arms race further and further. That is wrong. Tomorrow science can present us with inventions we cannot even imagine today, and I just don't know how much farther we can go in building up so-called security. . . . We are spending billions on all these things, billions that would be much better spent for the benefit of the people."[37]

Brezhnev was content to make these larger points, but Ford wanted to discuss details. The Soviet leader had to understand the political exigencies and legislative constraints the accidental president was facing. During a six-hour negotiating session on the evening of 23 November, Brezhnev tired of hearing these explanations for the failure of the United States to compromise on key issues. Time and again, he voiced misgivings over the tough U.S. negotiating position. He, too, had problems. "The military," he told Ford, "always want as much as they can get. I don't think there are any holy people in the military."[38]

But he also wanted to move forward. "I don't want to create an impasse," he said. "I want to find a solution."[39] He suggested a break in the discussion and telephoned Moscow to speak to Grechko, his defense minister. Brezhnev wanted to make concessions; Grechko opposed them. Angrily, Brezhnev told his old friend to convene a Politburo meeting; he, the party's general secretary, would fly back to Moscow to attend it. Grechko backed down. He did not want to fight Brezhnev before the whole Politburo.[40]

When Brezhnev returned to the negotiating table, he insisted that he and Ford find solutions and not belabor problems. He said he appreciated the president's dedication to the policy of détente. "We will do everything to support a United States President who wants to follow this course." Saying they must not waste time on trivia, he proposed that each country be allowed to have 2,400 launchers and 1,320 missiles that could be armed with multiple warheads. Ford concurred, emphasizing that Congress insisted on equivalence in numbers.[41]

Brezhnev made substantial concessions in other areas covered in the talks—for example, allowing America's forward base systems to be excluded from the agreement—but he believed he was gaining acknowledgment of the principle of equal security. As the late-evening conversation wound up, he observed, "the primary question is not that of missiles, the main point is peaceful cooperation between our two countries." The details of SALT II, Brezhnev said, could be worked out over the next six months. He expected a final agreement by June or July 1975. He was already looking forward to his trip to the United States.[42]

The next morning he and Ford met again. They reviewed some of the issues from the night before and then discussed the situation in the Middle East and preparations for the European security conference.[43] Some discord on these matters did not sour Ford's feelings. "I was euphoric," he wrote in his memoir.[44] At the close of the session, he expressed his appreciation and expectations to Brezhnev:

> I heard from Mr. Nixon and Dr. Kissinger about your dedication to peace on the basis of détente between our two countries. Everything Mr. Nixon and Dr. Kissinger said has been borne out in these 24 hours. This gives me great hope that in the future we will be able to develop détente and do what I believe both our countries need. Everything I heard about your humanitarian approach proved to be true on the basis of my personal encounter. Of course, we have some differences philosophically and politically but I hope they can be overcome.[45]

Brezhnev felt equally elated. Impulsively, after a late lunch, he gave Ford a quick tour of Vladivostok. They sat together in the back of a limousine and drove through the city. Then, as they headed back to the airport, Ford remembered, "the strangest thing happened. Brezhnev reached over and grabbed my left hand with his right hand. He began by telling me how much his people had suffered during World War II. I do not want to inflict that upon my people again, he said." Ford reassured him that they had made significant progress and more would be accomplished during the forthcoming year. "His grip on my hand tightened, and he turned to look me in the eye. 'We have accomplished something very significant and it's our responsibility, yours and mine, on behalf of our countries, to achieve the finalization of the document. . . . This is an opportunity to protect not only the people of our two countries, but, really, all mankind.' " Ford was so touched that, as he

Ford and Brezhnev, 1974. Their summit in Vladivostok
created a bond between the two men.

prepared to board Air Force One, he took off his new Alaskan wolfskin coat
and handed it to the general secretary. Brezhnev put it on and "seemed truly
overwhelmed."[46]

Shortly after his meeting with Ford, Brezhnev had a stroke. He was seriously incapacitated for several months and never totally recovered.[47] For him
and his colleagues, however, the SALT talks with the United States formed
only part of their strategy of détente, only a milestone on the way to an all-
European security conference and the consummation of decades of Soviet
diplomacy.

Preliminary negotiations for this conference, the Helsinki Conference,
had been going on for several years, and Soviet diplomats focused on the issues covered in what became known as "Basket One" of the Helsinki Agree-

ment. They wanted the Final Act to recognize the inviolability of existing European borders. West European diplomats and officials from the neutral and nonaligned states were determined to elicit Soviet concessions in exchange for recognition of the territorial status quo. In Basket Two of the proposed agreement, they called for the increased flow of trade and information, which Soviet and East European diplomats also wanted, needing Western technology and credit as they did to invigorate their countries' economic performance. But West European and neutral negotiators insisted on inserting a set of human rights principles into Basket Three of the Final Act. All signatories, they said, must "respect human rights and fundamental freedoms, including freedom of thought, conscience, religion, or belief"; must agree to "promote and encourage the effective exercise of civil, political, economic, social, cultural and other rights and freedoms all of which derive from the inherent dignity of the human person." The Soviets chafed at these demands. Party ideologues such as Suslov and Ponomarev staunchly opposed the human rights provisions. Foreign Minister Gromyko and KGB director Andropov did not like them, either, but after trying to weaken and deflect them during numerous rounds of negotiation, they had to decide whether to accept the tradeoff: recognition of human rights in return for recognition of the territorial status quo. The fate of the all-European security conference hung in the balance.[48]

Brezhnev resolved to go ahead with the conference. Nixon and Kissinger had promised him that the United States would not interfere in the internal affairs of other nations. This principle—respect for the sovereignty of nations—was also inscribed in the Helsinki Final Act. In Brezhnev's view, the excessive demands of some Western and neutral governments had been rebuffed, and did not represent a serious threat to the internal life of communist states. He said this on 18 March 1975, when he had recovered enough to attend a meeting with Warsaw Pact leaders. But he sounded weary. "I have been slightly sick in recent months," he acknowledged. Deflecting their pleas for more economic aid, he said he came "with empty pockets. . . . We have to state honestly that we are faced with a number of difficult problems. . . . We have to think seriously about how to make our economy more profitable." But he did want them to know that he was pushing ahead with the all-European security conference. He was aware of the dangers. Referring to the millions of Germans who had fled Poland and East Germany after the end of

World War II and to the politicians who represented them, he said, "influential forces in the FRG put forward demands [for] . . . voluntary changes of borders." They want "to gobble up [Erich] Honecker," chairman of the East German Socialist Unity [Communist] Party. "Those revanchists are insatiable," he remonstrated. "Lessons of history mean nothing to them. Tens of millions of people who died are not enough for them. This is the danger, which we should always remember and which we should always counter." We "must monitor the West German situation constantly."[49]

Notwithstanding the dangers, Brezhnev wanted agreement quickly. "Europe's bloody history tells us a lot and puts many tasks before us." He asked for Warsaw Pact leaders' cooperation: "All of us . . . should work skillfully and with great energy to bring this conference to completion successfully." If capitalists and communists could agree on the principles governing relations among European states, "it would be a great political victory. It would give new power to all proponents of peace and progress." He did not favor a military parade to commemorate the thirtieth anniversary of the victory over fascism: "There's no necessity rattling tanks and rockets on the Square at a time of an intensive struggle for peace."[50]

During the first half of 1975, Foreign Minister Gromyko continued to work with Secretary of State Kissinger to complete the final arrangements for the Helsinki Conference. Kissinger tried to allay Soviet worries about mounting U.S. criticism of détente. A "long-term perspective" was essential, he told Gromyko. "I am convinced that by the 1980s the identity of interest will become self-evident. Now it is self-evident with regard to nuclear weapons; by the 1980s it will be true of many political issues. We shouldn't lose sight of this fact."[51]

President Ford reiterated these views in a long conversation with Brezhnev on 30 July, the day before the conference convened. There were critics of détente on the right and the left whom he could not disregard. But he was convinced that détente was the right policy. "I can tell you very forcefully I am committed to détente, and the American people agree with me."

As they parted, Brezhnev took the president aside. Appreciating the ties he had forged with the incumbent administration and hoping to make future progress, Brezhnev said quietly, "I wish to tell you confidentially and completely frankly that we in the Soviet leadership are supporters of your elec-

tion." "I expect to be elected," Ford replied, "and I think that that meets ...
the cause of strengthening détente."⁵²

When Brezhnev rose on 31 July to deliver his address to the heads of state
assembled in Helsinki, he represented the Soviet Union at the peak of its
power and influence. But his aim was not to trumpet its strength or affirm the
superiority of its way of life but to herald the cause of peace and détente.
"Those who belong to the generation which experienced the horrors of
World War II most clearly perceive the historic significance" of this day.
"The soil of Europe was drenched with blood in the years of the two world
wars." Now was the time to transcend the past. He expressed satisfaction
that the Final Act constituted "a summing up of the political results of World
War II." But the theme of his message was forward-looking. "What has been
achieved is not the limit. Today it is the maximum possible, but tomorrow it
should become the starting point for a further advance along the lines
charted by the Conference."⁵³

Brezhnev was never eloquent, but he tried to convey his sense of a
brighter future. "Possibilities for cooperation now extend to areas where it
was inconceivable in the years of the cold war." Governments must do their
best to augment the exchange of information among states and peoples. They
must not interfere in one another's internal affairs. They must nurture the
well-being of their peoples, providing more education, supporting better
health, and ensuring that they can live their lives in peace and with confidence. Toward this end, he declared, his country "unswervingly supports the
idea that the Conference should be followed by a further advance of military
détente." He wanted to complete a SALT II agreement and reduce forces
and armaments in Central Europe.⁵⁴ A few days before, he had told President Ford, "Relaxation of tensions doesn't stop with Europe, the U.S. and
Canada. . . . [D]etente is useful not only for Europe but for all the world."⁵⁵

When they met privately at the end of the conference, Ford congratulated
Brezhnev on his "outstanding speech." He liked "the tone" and welcomed
the emphasis on strategic arms limitations and conventional arms reductions
(known as the Mutual and Balanced Force Reduction negotiations, and concurrently going on in Vienna). Ford insisted that the United States, too,
wanted to make progress in these areas. He said he looked forward to Brezhnev's visit to America in the autumn, when they would sign the second SALT

agreement, whose framework they had designed at Vladivostok. Brezhnev agreed wholeheartedly, stressing their moral obligation to transcend the technical details. There was too much talk about throw weight, launching weight, size of silos, cruise missiles, and strategic bombers, he said. The two nations had different weapons systems and used different fuels. "A cup of tea is not a cup of mercury," said the general secretary. "But if missiles are used, the result will be the same: Brezhnev dies and Kissinger dies."[56]

Yet an agreement eluded them. In the United States, President Ford was engulfed in controversy for signing the Helsinki Agreement and pursuing détente. He saw the Final Act as an opportunity to enlist Soviet support for human rights and peaceful change, but ethnic groups denounced him for selling out Eastern Europe, and many conservative and liberal politicians criticized him for ignoring the plight of Soviet dissenters and Russian Jews. Ford was coddling the Kremlin and disregarding its ominous military buildup, they charged. Defense experts inside and outside of government reevaluated Soviet defense expenditures and military programs and came to gloomy conclusions about the nature of the military balance between the United States and the Soviet Union. The Soviets were outspending the Americans by significant sums—by approximately thirty-five billion dollars in 1976 alone—and their growing capabilities appeared to have whetted the Kremlin's appetite and expanded its reach. Moreover, Soviet weapons were being used by North Vietnamese forces as they overran South Vietnam, finalizing the defeat of the U.S. crusade to contain communism in Indochina. Worse, the U.S.S.R. was now intervening in Africa—transporting Cuban troops to Angola, where civil war had broken out in the Portuguese colony, a potentially rich and valuable territory. According to Ford's critics, the Kremlin was flagrantly violating the rules that called for each of the great powers to eschew unilateral advantage.[57]

The United States was astir with discontent, and the policy of détente was under siege. Nixon's lying during the Watergate investigation had bred distrust of government, as had Ford's pardon of the disgraced president in September 1974. Revelations about CIA misbehavior at home and abroad accentuated widespread cynicism among the American people. The secrecy with which Kissinger conducted his negotiations—whether about Vietnam or nuclear weapons—sowed further suspicion. His diplomatic accomplishments lost luster as the United States withdrew from Vietnam, accepting a commu-

Female North Vietnamese troops entering Saigon, 1975. North
Vietnam's victory seemed to symbolize the erosion of U.S. power.

nist victory, and as American economic and financial power waned. High oil
prices, declining productivity, and a weakening dollar precipitated the worst
recession since World War II. California's governor, Ronald Reagan, a presidential aspirant, pummeled Ford for his naïveté and ridiculed him for signing
the Helsinki Agreement. Responding to these attacks in March 1976, Ford
said he would no longer talk of détente and would pursue "peace through
strength."[58]

The Soviet leaders, meanwhile, did their best to rebut the attacks on their
actions and policies. Brezhnev bitterly resented the allegations that the Soviet

Union was seeking nuclear superiority over the United States. No matter how much it was spending, Soviet officials believed the U.S.S.R. was still the weaker nation, and was only striving to overcome its entrenched position of inferiority. "We had the psychology of an underdog," explained General Starodubov to a group of historians in 1994. "Our leaders were old," emphasized General Nikolai Detinov, a member of the commission that recommended policy on strategic arms limitations. They "approached problems with attitudes formed during World War II." Experience mandated vigilance against imperialist and fascist aggressors. History could recur. The Soviet Union could be attacked again. "On no account should we ever forget this," wrote Marshal Grechko.[59]

For Brezhnev, greater and greater Soviet military strength was the key to détente. When the Soviet Union had been weak, the Americans had been unwilling to bargain or compromise; in Brezhnev's view, the real aim of the United States was to intimidate or blackmail rather than deter. In order to transcend the Cold War, Kremlin leaders felt they had to destroy their adversary's sense of superiority. Soviet power would convince the Americans that "not brinksmanship but negotiation . . . not confrontation but peaceful cooperation is the natural course of things."[60] Strength was a prerequisite for détente, and Brezhnev still associated himself with the quest for peace, arms restraint, and cooperation with the United States. He waited impatiently for the 1976 presidential elections to see if the SALT talks could be revived and détente rekindled.

Meanwhile, the Kremlin rebuffed American criticism of Soviet intervention in Angola. When Kissinger protested Soviet transport of ten thousand Cuban troops to the former Portuguese colony, Gromyko replied that the U.S.S.R. was responding to South Africa's earlier intervention in the Angolan civil war. The apartheid regime in Pretoria, he said, had deployed troops across its borders and was trying to affect the outcome of the indigenous conflict in the newly emerging nation. In November 1975, Augostinho Neto, the leader of the leftist-oriented Popular Movement for the Liberation of Angola (MPLA), had declared Angola's independence and asked Cuba for military aid and supplies. According to Gromyko, Castro was responding to Neto's legitimate requests for assistance. The Kremlin, Gromyko insisted, was not despoiling détente and was doing nothing wrong in assisting Angolan independence. It acted much like the United States, which also had been allocating supplies and distributing funds to its friends and clients. "It is a tragedy because the Soviet Union has nothing to gain in Angola," Kissinger retorted. "We have nothing to gain in Angola. Five years from now it will make no difference." Gromyko warned Kissinger not to return to Washington and cast aspersions on Soviet-American relations; he might kill détente. "I cannot believe that this meets the interests of the world situation."[61]

In fact, Kremlin leaders had not orchestrated these developments in Angola. The Soviet Union had given tiny amounts of assistance to the MPLA prior to mid-1975. But the Cubans had responded promptly to Neto's requests, seized the initiative, and maneuvered the Kremlin into giving more aid than Soviet leaders had intended. Then, as Gromyko had indicated, South African military intervention (as well as Chinese assistance to an opposing group) spurred the Soviets forward. Kremlin leaders came to believe that if they did not act, the forces of national liberation they favored—the MPLA—would be crushed by the racist regime in Pretoria. During critical months in late 1975 and early 1976, Soviet military supplies and Cuban assistance were decisive to Neto's success.[62]

Yet Brezhnev did not want Soviet embroilment in Africa to jeopardize détente. Soviet actions in Angola were expedient, he stressed, required by the imperialism "of South African racists."[63] Normally, there was no need to intervene actively because the world was moving inexorably toward a socialist future.[64] The lessons of Vietnam, he said, attested to "the all-conquering force of Marxist-Leninist ideas."[65] Newly liberated countries in Asia and Africa were shifting their industrial production to the state sector and nationalizing foreign enterprises. The capitalist nations were floundering. Their social welfare reforms were failing. Capitalism, Brezhnev said, was "a society without a future."[66]

Although much has been written about the complacency and stagnation of the Brezhnev era, the general secretary and his comrades took their communism seriously. So did the Soviet people, even when their everyday practices transgressed official ideology. "For great numbers of Soviet citizens," writes the anthropologist Alexei Yurchak, "many of the fundamental values, ideals, and realities of socialist life . . . were of genuine importance."[67] Communists were creating "a new society," Brezhnev liked to say, "the likes of which mankind [had] never known before."[68]

Brezhnev was a true believer, certain that communism would prove its superiority if only it had the chance to compete peacefully. Under the leadership of the Communist Party, he said, "the anarchy of production gave way to scientific, planned economic management."[69] "Centuries-long backwardness" had been overcome "within the lifespan of one generation."[70] Soviet leaders now had a historical responsibility to promote people's well-being, nurture justice and equality, and ameliorate living standards. Their aim, he emphasized, was "to do everything necessary for the welfare of man, for the sake of man."[71]

Defense expenditures, Brezhnev told his comrades at a party plenum in October 1976, should be no more than were "necessary to assure the Soviet Union's security." Military spending should not interfere with the party's desire to raise people's living standards.[72] He was angered, as Khrushchev had been, by the demands of military officials for more and more rubles. What could he do, he complained to his speechwriters, when his minister of defense told him that U.S. initiatives endangered Soviet security. "Should I give them 140 billions or 156 billions? And I do give them money, again and again—money that disappears into the funnel." As chairman of the Defense Council, he rhetorically asked, could he deny his military advisers the funds they deemed necessary to guarantee Soviet security?[73]

Brezhnev recognized the problems besetting the Soviet economy. Although living standards were still improving, growth rates were declining, from approximately 4.8 percent a year during the 1960s to 2.9 percent annually between 1970 and 1975.[74] He was aware of the food shortages, low productivity, shoddy goods, and technological stagnation. He feared popular discontent and dreaded the accusation that he was failing to meet the needs and expectations of the Soviet people.[75] In speech after speech, Brezhnev recounted the economic achievements of socialism, the improvement in wages, and the gains in housing, education, and health care. But he knew these were not enough. "You will say that more flats are needed, more schools and kindergartens, more goods in stores," he told the people of Tula, after there were rumblings of discontent in that city. "Well, you are right. Our requirements are outrunning our possibilities. But we are not marking time, we are advancing."[76]

To advance further, much still had to be done. Progress, Brezhnev acknowledged, would not be easy. He prodded and hectored, not as stridently as Khrushchev had, but more than most historians suggest. People had to work harder, increase their efficiency, experiment and innovate. "To live better, to earn more, one must work better. This is an old but not an aging truth." The state, for its part, had to manage resources more effectively, stimulate scientific innovation, promote agricultural production, develop resource-rich regions, and foster trade and technological and scientific exchange with the West.[77] "The new society needs peace," said Andropov, Brezhnev's close adviser. "To make détente irreversible is the task history has set mankind."[78]

In September 1976, Averell Harriman met with Brezhnev for three hours at the Kremlin to tell the general secretary about a new personality on the American political scene. Governor Jimmy Carter of Georgia, Harriman said, had an even chance of being elected president of the United States. The Democratic candidate wanted Brezhnev to know that he favored peace, détente, trade, and nuclear force reductions, and that should he win, he hoped to meet the Soviet leader. Kind words from the Kremlin, Harriman added, might help pave the way to improved relations no matter who was elected.

Brezhnev listened attentively. He expressed disappointment that the SALT talks had been frozen for many months. He had been reading Carter's speeches, he said, and although he was not altogether pleased by them, he was not abandoning hope. With considerable emotion, he told Harriman that he "had dedicated his life to prevent nuclear war." If one bomb fell, there would be world war. Such being the case, Harriman interjected, might the general secretary communicate a few apt words that would help relieve tension and promote trust?[79]

Shortly after the U.S. presidential election, Soviet ambassador Anatoly Dobrynin called on Harriman in Washington. Brezhnev, he said, wanted President-elect Carter to know that "we are ready to cooperate fully." Together, they could complete SALT II and pursue a Middle East settlement. Through other intermediaries, Brezhnev sent word to Carter that the Soviet Union would do nothing to embarrass or intimidate the new administration.[80]

Two days before Carter took office, Brezhnev delivered a long public speech. Invoking memories of World War II, he stressed that the Soviet Union was wholeheartedly committed "to the tireless struggle for peace" and to "eliminating the danger of war." It did not seek strategic superiority or crave first-strike capabilities, but wanted to reduce nuclear arsenals, first by finalizing the understandings reached at Vladivostok and then by progressing forward. "We will never embark on the road of aggression, will never raise the sword against other nations." This was why détente remained the policy of the Soviet government. "Détente means first of all the overcoming of the cold war and the transition to normal, stable relations among states. Détente means willingness to resolve differences and disputes not by force. Détente means a certain trust and ability to take into consideration each other's legitimate interests."[81]

Brezhnev's words augured well for a new beginning with a new American administration. But intentions cannot always be realized. International turbulence interceded. The North Vietnamese communists were consolidating their victory over the South and beginning to flaunt their power throughout Indochina. In the Middle East, two recent wars—in 1967 and 1973—had left the region in greater turmoil than before and threatened to suck in the great powers. Arab governments refused to recognize Israel's right to exist within secure borders, and Israel would not relinquish territories it had conquered from Syria, Jordan, and Egypt. Beyond the Middle East, the entire African continent seethed with unrest. After radical military officers seized power in Lisbon in 1974 and overthrew the authoritarian government that had ruled Portugal for more than forty years, they announced their intent to free Portugal's possessions, thereby ending the era of European colonialism in the third world. The strife in Angola was one direct consequence of the resulting power vacuum, but turmoil spread well beyond the former Portuguese territories. In southern Africa, particularly in Rhodesia, black liberation movements struggled to gain power, and in South Africa, the African National Congress did not abandon hope that someday it would topple the racist apartheid regime. Elsewhere, in the Horn of Africa, a radical group of Marxist-Leninist military officers in Ethiopia, led by Mengistu Haile Mariam, had toppled Emperor Haile Selassie in 1974 and was struggling to consolidate its regime. Ethiopia's neighbor, Somalia, already ruled by a radical-talking leader, Siad Barre, glimpsed opportunities for territorial gain at Ethiopia's expense. In all these places, racial injustice and the legacy of colonialism mixed with regional rivalries, tribal strife, and economic backwardness.

For Moscow, vigilance was imperative in the third world because imperialism and counterrevolution might revive and show their ugly faces. But where there was danger, there was also opportunity: if allowed to express their own volition, the developing nations of the world would emulate the Soviet Union, "which opened the road to a new life for mankind." The "countries of victorious socialism and the forces of national liberation," Kremlin leaders never stopped saying, "are natural and reliable allies in the anti-imperialist struggle."[82]

Officially, the Kremlin's position could not have been more correct. "The Soviet Union does not interfere in the internal affairs of other countries and peoples. It is an immutable principle of our Leninist foreign policy to respect the right of every people, every country, to choose its own way of development."[83] But whether the Soviet Union would resist temptation or prudently assess danger was uncertain. On such calculations, the future of détente hinged. For although the U.S.S.R., according to Brezhnev, "does not look for advantages, does not hunt for concessions, does not seek political domination, and is not after military bases," it nevertheless acted according to its revolutionary conscience and communist convictions.[84]

A New Face in Washington, an Old One in Moscow

Jimmy Carter was a new face on the American political scene. Raised in rural southwest Georgia on a farm during the Great Depression, he sought more opportunity and more scope for his talents than the land and community could provide. He attended the U.S. Naval Academy, became an engineer, helped to design the first U.S. nuclear submarines, and then, surprisingly, in 1953, quit the navy and returned to the farm on which he grew up, when his father died of cancer. Jimmy's parents were not wealthy, but they lived in comfort compared with the black laborers and sharecroppers who worked their land and with whose children Jimmy had played, fished, and hunted as a child. Like his father, Jimmy aimed to succeed in farming, yet he cared deeply about the well-being of the larger community. Also like his father, he participated on local boards of education and then entered politics. He served in the Georgia Senate in the early 1960s, ran for and lost the governorship in 1966, and then ran again in 1970, becoming chief executive of one of the poorest states in the union. As Carter matured, he recognized the deep inequities and racial injustices that made a mockery of the American dream for African Americans. They deserved their rights; poor people, whether white or black, merited the opportunity to succeed. Government had an important role to play, but Jimmy Carter had no love for big government or for inefficient bureaucracy.[85]

Jimmy Carter was characterized by paradox. He was modest yet self-confident, humble yet ambitious. He was a man of deep faith, a born-again Christian, yet secular and humane in his outlook. He prayed several times a day but privately and unobtrusively. He had gone to the Naval Academy, but he eschewed militarism and was averse to the nation's use of force. He was affable and radiated cheerfulness, yet he craved solitude and was often cold in his personal relations with people. He read several books a week yet sought intense exercise and liked competitive sports. He appreciated contrasting ideas, but once he made up his mind he was not inclined to reexamine. If there was one political attribute that accounted for his success, he would later reflect, it was his "tenacity. Once I get on something, I'm awfully hard to change."[86]

Jimmy Carter had no real background in foreign-policy matters, and he frequently declared that the country's success in foreign policy depended on getting its domestic house in order.[87] Yet from day one his advisers knew that he intended to be the decision maker in foreign-policy matters, leaving domestic issues to cabinet officials, whom he encouraged to run their own departments. His managerial style was to set a broad direction for his top executives and let them organize, coordinate, and execute.[88] He preferred to master a few priority issues. And master them he did.

Jimmy Carter was disciplined, curious, industrious, and, yes, tenacious. "I'm an engineer at heart and I like to understand the details of things," he subsequently recalled.[89] But immersion in detail did not divert him from the big picture. Zbigniew Brzezinski, the Columbia University professor of Soviet history and politics who became Carter's national security adviser, commented: "His memory was phenomenal, his reading voracious, and his thirst for more knowledge unquenchable."[90] Cyrus Vance, a lawyer who was Carter's choice for secretary of state, described his new boss in much the same way, adding that the incoming president always preferred "bold, comprehensive" approaches rather than "modest, incremental building on past agreements."[91]

Carter's election had been a matter of circumstance. After Watergate, Vietnam, and the CIA scandals, he represented something new in American politics, something that Americans appreciated as never before. He was an outsider from national politics, untainted by the corruption, lies, and failures of his predecessors, whether Democrats or Republicans. He prided himself on his integrity and competence. "Why not the best?" he asked the American people. Why not choose a person who represented their deepest values and reflected their honesty and decency; who believed, as they did, in the importance of an efficiently administered and open government that nurtured opportunity for everyone but remained fiscally responsible and circumscribed in its authority; who was both realistic and idealistic? For Carter, "the demonstration of American idealism was a practical and realistic approach to foreign affairs, and moral principles were the best foundation for the exertion of American power and influence."[92]

Before taking office, Carter asked Vance and Brzezinski to submit memoranda outlining the new administration's goals and priorities, and the president-elect discussed these aims with each in great depth. "First," wrote Brzezinski, "I felt it important to increase America's ideological impact on the world and to infuse greater historical optimism into our outlook." He wanted "to restore America's political appeal to the Third World," and to "improve America's strategic position . . . in relationship to the Soviet Union." Brzezinski worried that the Soviet Union's growing military capabilities might tempt the Kremlin "to exploit Third World turbulence or to impose its will in some political contest with the United States."[93]

Vance talked to Carter about these issues, too. He hoped to reduce tensions with the Soviet Union, "while vigorously defending our global interests and maintaining an unquestioned military balance." He wanted to sustain détente, but insisted that it be "reciprocal." He also advised Carter that we "must not become so preoccupied with U.S.-Soviet and East-West relations" that we fail to address the more pressing problems besetting the third world.[94]

Vance and Brzezinski were men of different backgrounds, sensibilities, and inclinations. Brzezinski had a deep sense of his Polish identity and, like many Poles, harbored a deep distrust of Soviet Russia. Widely read and widely published, he was ambitious and intelligent. Eager to gain as much influence as he could, he wanted easy access to the president and maximum control over the coordinating mechanisms of the National Security Council, which he quickly reorganized into two subcommittees, the Policy Review

Zbigniew Brzezinski and Cyrus Vance, 1977. Carter's most
influential advisers often feuded with each other.

Committee and the Special Coordination Committee. "Coordination is predominance," he wrote in his memoir.[95]

Vance was a quiet, methodical, thoughtful lawyer who had had considerable experience serving in the Kennedy and Johnson administrations. During
the presidential campaign, when Vance was an adviser, Carter came to like,
admire, and trust him. Vance did not seek fame or glory. He was quiet and
discreet, an able negotiator, a careful tactician. Sensitive to the new crosscurrents in the international political economy and the seething unrest in the
third world, he was as eager as the new president to move beyond the traditional shibboleths of the Cold War.[96]

Although Vance and Brzezinski were to clash in the future, the friction
between them initially was minimal. Carter was not worried about their differences. He felt comfortable with them and with his extraordinarily able
and accomplished secretary of defense, Harold Brown, and his affable and
knowledgeable vice president, Walter Mondale. In fact, the president's favorite time of the week was Friday mornings, when he would discuss the
most pressing issues with his foreign-policy team. He did not fear conflicting
views. He was self-confident and liked to listen to disparate advice, sift

through the facts, and come to his own decisions. Hamilton Jordan, Carter's longtime and most trusted political confidante and administrative assistant, neatly summed up the president's attitude: "Zbig would be the thinker, Cy would be the doer, and Jimmy Carter would be the decider."[97]

Carter intended to make human rights a central, if not *the* central, theme of his foreign policy. In his inaugural address, a speech he drafted himself, Carter outlined a new direction for the United States. Rather than Kissinger's affinity for balances of power, or Kennedy's invocation of strength, or Truman's quest for containment, Carter aimed to restore faith in an "old dream—the dream of human liberty." This dream "endures." As the world experienced rapid change, peoples everywhere yearned for "their place in the sun." They demanded their basic human rights. "The passion for freedom is on the rise. . . . Because we are free, we can never be indifferent to the fate of freedom elsewhere."[98]

These words reflected his deepest convictions. "I know how easy it is to overlook the persecution of others," he wrote, alluding to the segregated society in which he had been raised and which he had taken for granted until adulthood. But injustice no longer could be tolerated. Human rights constituted "the new reality of our time," he believed, "the new historical inevitability of our time."[99]

Carter was profoundly aware that the international system was fragmenting and disorder was spreading. U.S. allies, especially West Germany, France, and Japan, were growing in strength and often unhappy with American decisions. They were incensed by American monetary policy during the Nixon years, when the United States unilaterally suspended the convertibility of the dollar and forced them to deal with the consequences of U.S. balance-of-payment deficits. Carter now needed those allies' assistance and collaboration, especially given the new challenges posed by the Organization of the Petroleum Exporting Countries (OPEC), the oil cartel that included Saudi Arabia, Iraq, Iran, and Venezuela. After the defeat of Egypt and Syria in the 1973 Yom Kippur War, OPEC had quadrupled petroleum prices and thrown the capitalist West into disarray. Inflation soared, economic growth rates dropped, and unemployment in Western Europe, Japan, and the United States reached its highest levels since 1945.[100]

The new power of the OPEC nations reflected the aspirations of the southern part of the globe. Although most governments in Asia, Africa, the

Middle East, and Latin America did not have OPEC's leverage, their clamor for national autonomy, unrestricted sovereignty, higher raw material prices, and a fairer distribution of wealth created a new discourse and a new agenda for the capitalist West. The demands of these nations intensified as the last colonial empire, that of the Portuguese, disintegrated, and as national liberation movements competed for power throughout southern Africa. Their rhetoric was laced with appeals for justice, remonstrations against racism, and threats of retribution. They distrusted the laws of the free marketplace. They hoped that purposeful state action could overcome the legacy of imperialism and the iron laws of capitalism. And they had champions in Moscow and supporters in Beijing, where the attentiveness of the leaders of the two great communist states was advanced by their own competition with each other.[101]

"Can Capitalism Survive?" was the cover story in *Time* magazine about a year before Carter was elected. Everywhere in the Western world, *Time* pointed out,

> There is a gnawing fear that capitalism has no way to cure inflation except deep recession, and that any concerted attempt to lift an economy rapidly out of recession will only fan inflation. . . . Inflationary recession is only the most imminent danger; there are longer-range subtler perils, too. Within many a capitalist country, the free market is being steadily hemmed in by the power of omnipresent government regulators, mass unions, and giant corporations.

Seven Nobel Prize winners signed a declaration condemning corporate greed and called for an "intensive search for alternatives to the prevailing Western economy." This was expressive of the general mood in the United States as prosperity waned, prices soared, and real wages ended their steep postwar incline.[102]

Not since 1947 had American officials worried so much about turmoil in Western Europe. "The Western Allies have been in a protracted period of political stagnation and economic decline," Brzezinski warned the president on 11 March 1977. Communist parties, increasingly critical of Moscow's policies, were gaining strength. European elites feared that their peoples were losing "faith in the liberal democratic political and economic system that has provided both prosperity and social stability." "Every major government in Europe is a near political minority (FRG, France, Britain, Italy)," said Brzezinski, "and neither Japan nor Canada can be considered in good shape. This political weakness has been aggravated by economic stagnation. . . . Communist parties and those of the extreme right have growing public acceptance and legitimacy."[103]

If Europe was shaky, conditions elsewhere were even more so. "Explosive forces of change in the developing world" had to be reckoned with, Vance felt. Africa "is a morass," Brzezinski wrote Carter on 1 April 1977. The continent "is in the midst of social-political upheaval, with post-colonial structures collapsing." Pro-Western and pro-Soviet regimes and factions were contesting for power. The situation was "grave," portending a "rather dark future." Looking forward ten or twenty years, "it is clear that the United States needs desperately to fashion a comprehensive and long-term North-South strategy."[104]

"It is a new world, but America should not fear it," Carter said in a major speech at Notre Dame University after being in office a few months. "It is a new world, and we should help to shape it. It is a new world that calls for a new American foreign policy—a policy based on constant decency in its values and on optimism in its historical vision."[105]

Carter's advisers had to design a foreign policy that comported with the president's commitment to a "moral base." This was not a problem for Brzezinski. At a time "when the Soviet Union was saying that the scales of history were tipping in favor of socialism" and when the Kremlin was declaring that the "triumph of communism was only a decade away," he knew that Carter's commitment to human rights constituted a good geopolitical strategy and admirable idealism.[106] The president's intentions were "coherent and consistent," Brzezinski wrote Carter. Attentive to the "emerging consciousness of mankind," Brzezinski said he would implement the president's wishes:

> (1) We will seek to coordinate more closely with our principal allies in order to provide the foundations for a more stable international system; (2) We will engage in a North-South dialogue in order to deal with wider human needs; (3) We will

seek accommodation on the East-West front in order to avoid war and to widen trans-ideological cooperation. In addition, we will seek to halt the spread of arms, both conventional and nuclear.[107]

Undaunted, Carter sought to address the many looming problems, but did not make his priorities clear. To shore up relations with allies and mend West-West relations, he sent Vice President Mondale to Western Europe and Japan. To set a new tone in North-South relations, he appointed Andrew Young, a black American and a former mayor of Atlanta, as ambassador to the United Nations and sent him on a mission to southern Africa. To reinvigorate Middle East diplomacy, he sent Vance to Tel Aviv and Cairo. And to resolve the long-festering and potentially explosive dispute with Panama, he appointed a special representative to renegotiate the canal treaty. We "needed to correct an injustice," Carter maintained. Panama's demand to regain sovereignty over the canal had "become a litmus test throughout the world, indicating how the United States, as a superpower, would treat a small and relatively defenseless nation."[108]

Carter wrote his first letter to Chairman Brezhnev on 26 January 1977: "I want to confirm that my aim is to improve relations with the Soviet Union on the basis of reciprocity, mutual respect and advantage. I will pay close personal attention to this goal, as will Secretary Vance." He emphasized that he wanted to avoid a new arms race—"the elimination of all nuclear weapons is my firm goal"—and to move ahead on the SALT talks. He hoped to conclude a "properly verifiable agreement on the universal banning of all nuclear tests" and anticipated progress on the "balanced reduction of military forces in Central Europe." He also expressed a desire to improve economic ties, adding, "At the same time we can not be indifferent to the fate of freedom and individual human rights."

Toward the end of the letter, Carter explicated his general approach to bilateral relations, one that was not very different than Brezhnev's own:

> We represent different social systems, and our countries differ from each other in their history and experience. A competition in ideals and ideas is inevitable between our societies. Yet this must not interfere with common efforts towards formation of a

more peaceful, just, and humane world. We live in the world, which to a greater and greater extent demands collective answers to the main human questions, and I hope that our countries can cooperate more closely to promote the development, better diet and more substantive life for the less advantaged part of mankind.[109]

Although Brezhnev answered in a businesslike manner, saying he was looking forward to Secretary Vance's visit, relations quickly took a turn for the worse.[110] In a meeting with Ambassador Dobrynin and in a second message to Brezhnev, Carter said he was seeking much larger cuts in nuclear arsenals than had been envisioned at Vladivostok.[111] On 5 February, moreover, he responded to a letter from Andrei Sakharov, the eminent Soviet physicist and renowned critic of the Soviet regime. The president tried to craft his response tactfully, but repeated his inaugural statement: "Because we are free, we cannot be indifferent to the fate of freedom everywhere."[112]

Brezhnev and his colleagues were indignant. Washington seemed to be altering the terms of the deal negotiated with President Ford. Brezhnev did not oppose the idea of additional reductions, but he felt a sense of ownership about the Vladivostok understandings, for which he had taken a risk, overruling his military officials. He did not want to make changes now that might provoke dissent. He and Carter needed to proceed in an orderly manner. He regarded Carter's leap into the future as a "slap in the face."[113]

The Soviet leaders were even more upset by Carter's letter to Sakharov. Andropov and Defense Minister Dmitri Ustinov demanded that Brezhnev convene a special meeting of the Politburo. Carter was intervening in their internal affairs, precipitating a "drastic" change in direction and launching "unwise" policy. They understood their own situation in starkly different terms than did U.S. officials, seeing human rights conditions in the Soviet Union as improving, not deteriorating. The Western press, the Kremlin claimed, talked of tens of thousands of prisoners, "whereas in reality" very few people were serving sentences for crimes against the state. Some people—Sakharov, Yuri Orlov, Anatoly Shcharansky, and Aleksandr Ginzburg—were being persecuted, "but it was nothing like the massive repressions we used to have before," reflected reformist foreign-policy expert Georgi Shakhnazarov.[114]

Andropov reported to the Politburo regularly on the treatment of dissidents. Between 1971 and 1974, the KGB warned about sixty-three thousand people to cease their activities—hiding pamphlets, circulating literature, conspiring with foreigners. Few of these warnings, however, led to imprisonment. In late 1975, there were about 850 political prisoners in the country, 261 incarcerated for disseminating anti-Soviet propaganda. In that same year, the year of the Helsinki Final Act, 76 people were tried in criminal courts; in 1976, there were 69 trials; and, in 1977, there were 48. In 1974, 178 dissidents were jailed; in 1975, there were 96; and in 1976, the number was 60. When the Moscow Helsinki Watch Group was formed in May 1976, members were under continuous KGB surveillance, but the organization was permitted to function (and was shut down only in 1982). Repressive as was the regime's behavior, "the constant monitoring," concludes historian Svetlana Savranskaya, "was a very mild treatment by Soviet standards."[115]

After Helsinki, Brezhnev and his colleagues found themselves on the defensive, and they were angry.[116] Since Khrushchev's "thaw," the regime had backtracked in its openness to cultural innovation and free political discourse. But the leaders were working on a new constitution and believed they were constructing a superior way of life, a society, in Brezhnev's words, "which would enable every man to develop himself more fully and more usefully."[117] They could accept criticism but not efforts to undermine the basic premises of their way of life. In their view, the prominent dissidents whom Washington focused on were not friendly critics but "enemies of the regime."[118] The KGB arrested Orlov, Ginzburg, and Shcharansky in 1977, and gave them heavy sentences; other dissidents were forced into exile. But until the invasion of Afghanistan and the collapse of détente, the repression was restrained: between 1976 and 1980, 347 people were sentenced for political crimes.[119]

The elderly men who ran the Kremlin, most of whom had lived through the revolution and all of whom had survived the Great Patriotic War, wanted their critics to understand the challenges they had faced and the magnitude of their achievements. The Kremlin instructed its ambassadors abroad to emphasize that for the first time in history human rights were being defended in the Soviet Union in deed and not just in word. Soviet people had free medical care and education, the right to vote, to work, and to be elected to key administrative positions. In contrast, Americans did not have employment rights or guarantees of security in their old age. Dobrynin was told to ask Vance how Carter would like it if the Soviet government decided to make dé- tente contingent on the elimination of race discrimination or unemployment in the United States.[120]

Soviet leaders acknowledged that more needed to be done in their society, but they demanded vigilance against any foes who tried to topple their noble if imperfect enterprise. After all, they had transformed a backward land into a modern industrial state and now were grappling with the attendant chal- lenges. Their task, they knew, was to make things better if only they could fig- ure out how to do so. Among other things, they were working on a new constitution whose aim, said Brezhnev, was to deepen socialist democracy.[121] As his colleagues collaborated on a response to Carter's letter and prepared for the talks with Vance in Moscow, Brezhnev told trade union leaders that socialism and democracy were inseparable. "In building communism, we will develop democracy. One speaks, of course, about socialist democracy, that is a democracy that covers the political, social and economic spheres, a democ- racy that, above all, ensures social justice and social equality."[122]

Even while arresting leading dissidents, the Kremlin tried to defuse the human rights issue in Soviet-American relations. Brezhnev instructed Do- brynin to invite Henry Jackson—the hawkish, defense-minded Democratic senator who championed the rights of Jews and dissidents in the Soviet Union—to Moscow if Carter thought that would ease the president's political difficulties.[123] At the same time Andropov allegedly tried to make a deal with Sakharov that would restrict his activities but allow him to stay out of jail. The KGB director also told his subordinates to resolve specific human rights cases that the Americans deemed important.[124] Brezhnev himself had given President Ford a year-by-year accounting of Jewish émigrés, claiming that 98.4 percent of all requests to emigrate had been granted.[125]

The men in the Kremlin thought they were genuinely trying to meet American concerns in order to promote détente and finalize a second strate- gic arms treaty. But they were incensed when Vance came to Moscow at the end of March 1977 and focused on making more significant cuts in nuclear arsenals than the Vladisvotok framework had envisioned. "What you are bringing is a complete non-starter," Dobrynin warned him. Brezhnev did not want new proposals. He wanted to complete the accord he had designed with President Ford. His colleagues told him that Washington was trying to intimidate him, to test him. Before Vance arrived, they said: "Leonid Ilych, show the Americans how we are strong and they are not serious."[126]

Brezhnev's feelings turned from anger to "disgust" when Vance discussed human rights. "Suddenly, right there in Moscow—in Brezhnev's office—to talk about human rights!" recalled Brezhnev's interpreter. "To talk about Soviet violations of somebody's human rights! Unheard of! It was a personal affront. It was taken very, very, very personally by Brezhnev and Gromyko. On the human plane, that's how it was."[127]

Yet Vance and his subordinates were equally aggrieved. They left Moscow agitated. "We got a wet rug in the face," Vance reflected. The Russians, he complained, had not negotiated in good faith, had not come back with counterproposals. He knew Soviet officials were agitated by the Americans' disregard of the Vladivostok framework, but Carter himself had insisted upon this new position, wanting a bold departure from the past, and Brzezinski had made no effort to dissuade him.[128] In fact, Brzezinski had prodded the U.S. delegation to "take a firm and unyielding stand in Moscow," hoping Brezhnev would bow to American demands.[129]

Carter, Vance, Brzezinski, and Secretary of Defense Brown subsequently acknowledged that the opening gambit in Moscow was ill advised, but they did not act that way at the time.[130] After Gromyko attacked the U.S. position publicly, Brezhnev wrote Carter, privately restating his desire for a strategic arms treaty and reaffirming his hopes for constructive interaction and cooperation.[131] But U.S. officials were in no hurry to move forward. Brzezinski believed that they had put the Soviets on the defensive. By appearing to champion far-reaching arms reductions, the United States had captured the high ground before the eyes of the world. "My view," wrote Brzezinski, "was that the ball was in the Soviet court and we should sit tight and wait for a counterproposal." "It is a time for inflexibility," Carter scribbled on a memorandum.[132]

Carter tenaciously held to his own vision of a strategic arms treaty, yet he still wanted détente. "It is my hope," he wrote Brezhnev in June, "that I can welcome you to our nation at an early date so that you and I can pursue personally our goals of disarmament, peace, trade, and increasing cooperation and friendship."[133] But time was working against the president. As the months passed, U.S. sentiment against the Soviet Union was growing, while turmoil in the international arena seemed to be increasing. Influential Democrats such as Senator Jackson and John C. Stennis, chairman of the Senate Armed Services Committee; arms control experts such as Paul Nitze; former members of the Ford administration such as Defense Secretary James R. Schlesinger; and prominent military officials such as Admiral Thomas H. Moorer, former chairman of the Joint Chiefs of Staff, all assailed Soviet behavior and demanded that the U.S. administration negotiate from a position of strength.[134] Carter was unable to manage U.S. domestic opinion or guide events in Africa and the Middle East. "The currents of history were running against us," said Vance.[135]

"You need incredibly gifted and disciplined leadership to run against historical tides," reflected Leslie Gelb, one of Vance's influential aides.[136] Yet neither in Moscow nor in Washington did such gifted leaders govern. Carter was disciplined and had noble goals. He "was trying to do great things" but "without preparation for doing them," Gelb reminisced.[137] Buffeted by events in the third world that he could not control, a domestic energy crisis that he could not master, and public ridicule that he could not deflect, Carter was nonetheless lured by a sense of self-confidence. He had faith in himself and in his God, faith in his abilities to get what he wanted through doggedness and determination, faith that the American way of life was more attractive than that of its rival. Notwithstanding all the talk about Soviet military prowess, he sensed that if he persevered, the Soviet Union would bow to American pressure.[138]

The leaders in the Kremlin were aged, Brzezinski told Carter. They needed détente more than the United States did. Long-term trends favored the United States. There was "a rough overall asymmetrical equivalence in military capabilities," but the Soviet Union's economy was faltering, its dissident groups were growing, its rivalry with China was unremitting.[139] Unrest in Eastern Europe was mounting and would increase with détente, which was nonetheless an inescapable choice for Brezhnev, given the Soviet Union's economic problems. The "basic fact is that the West in general, and the U.S. in particular, has the power to greatly aggravate the Soviet dilemma," Brzezinski wrote Carter on 24 June 1977. "And it is this consciousness that, in the end, will bring Brezhnev back to a foreign policy of moderation."[140]

But whether Brezhnev could remain in power and navigate the tides of history was uncertain. In May 1977, he orchestrated the removal of Nikolai Podgorny from the Politburo and assumed the title of president of the

Supreme Soviet as well as general secretary of the Party. This move attested to his ongoing resourcefulness when it came to Kremlin intrigue. Yet those close to him were well aware of the steady decline in his health and vigor and the steady growth of his vanity and greed. Brezhnev loved his comforts, collected more and more cars, and never ceased to appreciate the medals and awards his colleagues bestowed on him. He still liked to play dominoes, hunt, and swim. But the robust and handsome man who had impressed so many with his zest and appearance in the 1950s and 1960s was becoming a sad shadow of himself.

Brezhnev had had a stroke in November 1974, and a second one in early 1976. He suffered from arteriosclerosis. He had trouble sleeping at night and experienced frequent bouts of nervous exhaustion. He mustered his energy for major occasions, such as meetings with Vance and other visiting dignitaries, but took more and more days off. His dependency on tranquilizers grew. He went to sleep late and got up late. He read less and less. He missed more and more meetings. He spoke haltingly. The speeches drafted for him contained shorter and shorter phrases and were written in larger and larger letters. He had trouble seeing and hearing. His ability to concentrate waned. He depended more and more on a few close friends and associates, such as Konstantin Chernenko, Andropov, and Ustinov, who sheltered and protected him and who, in turn, benefited greatly from the general secretary's patronage.[141]

Brezhnev's poor health made it difficult for him to stay focused on his priorities, and he could not control events. He cared not "a damn" about the Horn of Africa, said Dobrynin, but he could not resist the pleas of revolutionaries fighting imperialism and racism, or squelch the ardor of independent-minded clients, such as Fidel Castro. Nor could he dampen the fervor of party ideologues or thwart the pressures of defense officials eager to employ the growing Soviet military capabilities. Turbulence in the international system created opportunities they found hard to resist, and Brezhnev's failure to rein them in created problems he could not have imagined. The sick and aged general secretary had more medals, more titles, and more authority than ever before, but his capacity to shape events was severely circumscribed.[142]

Clients, Hegemons, and Allies

In the spring of 1977, Fidel Castro made a goodwill trip to Africa, where he was welcomed as a hero. For more than a decade he had been supporting liberation movements there, sending doctors, nurses, and military advisers, and finally, in the case of Angola, combat troops.[143] Castro acted out of conviction, believing he, too, was part of the contest for the soul of mankind. Fighting imperialism, capitalism, and racism, he went to the Horn of Africa in March and met sequentially with Mohammad Siad Barre, the ruler of Somalia, and Mengistu Haile Mariam, the military officer who ran Ethiopia after the assassination of Emperor Haile Selassie.

Castro tried to mediate the conflict between Somalia and Ethiopia. Somalia wanted to regain territory, the Ogaden, that had been incorporated into the Ethiopian empire in the late nineteenth century. Siad wanted to take advantage of the civil strife in Ethiopia while Mengistu was struggling to consolidate his power, having murdered many friends as well as foes. In the early 1970s, Siad had struck up an alliance with the Soviet Union, secured substantial aid, and allowed the Kremlin to build a military base at Berbera, on the Indian Ocean. Equipped with Russian guns and tanks, Siad readied to attack Ethiopia. Castro tried and failed to keep the peace.

Castro next flew to Berlin in early April to talk with Erich Honecker, the leader of East Germany, and then on to Moscow, to meet Brezhnev and his comrades. "I developed the impression that there was a real revolution taking place in Ethiopia," Castro said. Land was being redistributed. Reforms were taking place in the cities. "Rightists" fought back, but Mengistu arrested and shot them. He "strikes me," Castro continued, "as a quiet, honest and convinced leader who is aware of the power of the masses." In his view, the dictatorial and murderous Mengistu merited support far more than Siad Barre, who was a chauvinist and a fraud, feigning "a socialist face" in order to get aid from the Soviet Union. Siad had rebuffed Castro's mediation efforts and was trying to grab Ethiopian land and endanger Mengistu's revolution.

"The socialist countries are faced with a problem," Castro told Honecker. If they help Ethiopia, they will lose Siad Barre's friendship. If they don't, "the Ethiopian Revolution will founder." That would be a pity, he said, because revolutionary fervor was spreading across black Africa. Castro had just been to Mozambique and Angola, and was thrilled with the work being

Castro and Brezhnev (center), with Podgorny (extreme left), Carlos Rodriguez, and Kosygin (far right), 1977. After visiting Africa, Castro went to Berlin and Moscow to champion the revolution in Ethiopia.

done by Soviet and Cuban advisers. "The revolution in Ethiopia is of great significance. . . . In Africa we can inflict a severe defeat on the entire imperialist policy. We can free Africa from the influence of the USA and of the Chinese. . . . Ethiopia has a great revolutionary potential."[144]

In Moscow, where Castro was welcomed warmly—"Dear Comrade Fidel Castro," said Brezhnev, "all Soviet people express feelings of friendship, love and respect for you"—Cuba's revolutionary hero pressed the case for Mengistu, and Soviet leaders listened sympathetically. The Ethiopians, they said, having "experienced enormous sufferings and humiliations during imperialist domination," were acting naturally, "departing from the capitalist roads and setting their bearings on socialism."[145] Brezhnev talked in Moscow, much as his colleagues did when they visited Africa. "We Soviet people," they liked to say, recognized "our youth" in the struggle of Africa's nationalist leaders to liberate their people. Their effort to "advance towards a new life is reminiscent in a way of our own road."[146]

Responding to Castro's importuning and to the advice of the Soviet embassy in Addis Ababa, Kremlin officials welcomed Mengistu to their capital

Mengistu Haile Mariam, 1977. The Ethiopian
revolutionary leader impressed Castro and
garnered huge amounts of aid from Moscow.

in May 1977. Just before arriving, he had closed down American bases and
research centers in Ethiopia. In Moscow, Mengistu declared, as he had many
times before, that he was a Marxist-Leninist. His revolution, he told Brezhnev, was part of "the world revolutionary process." He pleaded for economic
aid and military supplies. He said he faced an invasion from Somalia, a sepa-
ratist rebellion in Eritrea, and incessant opposition from domestic rightists.[147]

Having been slow to meet Mengistu's previous requests, Soviet leaders
now offered significant aid, estimated at $350–450 million, and signed a dec-
laration of friendly relations between the two nations. They had no great
plans, no strategic vision. Some Politburo members and influential military
officers were opposed to getting embroiled in Ethiopia. But Defense Minister
Ustinov and Communist Party Secretary Ponomarev could not resist tempta-

tion. Flush with hard currency from Soviet exports of oil and natural gas and embarrassed by the loss of Soviet influence in Egypt after the Yom Kippur War, they were eager to project Soviet power and influence. Their decision making was "primitive," reflected General Anatoli Gribkov, who at the time had been deputy commander in chief of the Warsaw Pact joint armed forces. As soon as Mengistu and leaders of other African countries mentioned the word *socialism*, Gribkov sneered, Kremlin elders would succumb to their entreaties. "They wanted that country to instantaneously exchange their donkeys for Mercedes or Fords."[148]

Even as they decided to support Mengistu, top leaders in the Kremlin reaffirmed their support for détente. Sending weapons and advisers abroad, in their view, did not breach détente. This was no different from what Washington did when opportunity beckoned. Soviet arms sales were increasing but were still much smaller than those of the United States.[149] For Brezhnev and his colleagues, the Horn of Africa was a sideshow. They did not want Soviet actions there to undercut détente. Détente, they liked to say, "should spread to all parts of the earth so that peoples all over the world . . . should be able to avail themselves of its fruits."[150]

Carter and his advisers did not think the Soviets meant what they said. The president distrusted the Soviet moves in the Horn of Africa and despised the brutality of Mengistu's regime. Although Carter was told that Soviet assistance to Mengistu was limited and that the Horn of Africa was "not of great strategic importance to the United States," he regarded the Soviet maneuverings as portentous.[151] His statecraft was being tested, Brzezinski wrote Carter on 8 July 1977. "Everyone is taking our measure."[152]

Still, the United States had an opportunity, said a presidential review memorandum, to advance its "influence in the [Horn] as a whole by consolidating our position in neighboring countries now friendly to us, e.g., Sudan and Kenya, and in advancing our position in Somalia."[153] Brzezinski advised Carter not to cooperate with the Soviets if they invited the United States to join them in efforts to end Somalia's aggression. The Kremlin was in "a quandary," caught between its former alliance with Siad and its new fondness for Mengistu, and the United States should exploit the Soviet predicament, insisted Brzezinski.[154] Washington hoped the Russians would "fall off both horses," Secretary Vance told the Chinese when he visited Beijing in August.[155] Thinking that Mengistu's regime might not survive and hoping that the Soviets might be ensnared in their own Vietnam, Carter's advisers wanted to position the United States to advance its influence throughout the Horn while reminding the Soviets that they must stay loyal to the spirit of détente.[156]

In September 1977, the future of events in the Horn was contingent as was the fate of détente. Somalia was attacking Ethiopia; Mengistu's regime was tottering; the Cubans seemed to be hesitating; Brezhnev was giving aid to Mengistu yet appealing for peace in the region.[157] Both Moscow and Washington appeared to want to extend their reach and expand their influence without jeopardizing possibilities to cooperate when it was in their interest to do so. When the Soviets uncovered information that the South African apartheid regime was developing nuclear weapons, they invited the United States to join in a collaborative demarche. And when they focused their attention on a Middle East settlement between Israel and its Arab neighbors, they presented Washington with a "remarkably balanced" document.[158]

Vance was very interested in keeping détente alive, and he labored to collaborate with Gromyko on a joint statement regarding the Middle East.[159] On 1 October, the United States and the Soviet Union announced their intention to reconvene in Geneva for another conference. Together, the Soviet and American governments would seek to arrange a Middle East settlement. Together, they would work for Israeli evacuation of occupied territory and for Arab recognition of Israel's right to exist within secure borders. Together, they would promote normal relations between Arabs and Israelis and seek to gain respect for the rights of the Palestinian people.[160]

Gromyko and Vance also resumed their work on a strategic arms treaty. The president still wanted the Soviet Union to reduce its nuclear arsenal below the levels envisioned at Vladivostok. He sought to limit the Kremlin's most formidable intercontinental ballistic missiles (ICBMs) and constrain the number of ICBMs that could carry multiple warheads. At the same time, he hoped to equip America's heavy bombers with air-launched cruise missiles and to restrict the numbers of Soviet Backfire aircraft, which the United States regarded as a strategic weapon, not an intermediate-range aircraft, as the Soviets insisted it was.[161]

When the Soviet foreign minister met Carter on 27 September, agreement was reached on many but not all of these issues. "There was a good spirit about this session," wrote the president. He and Gromyko agreed that

SALT I, due to expire in October, would be extended, providing time to complete work on SALT II and to begin designing the parameters of a SALT III. Détente still had life. "My overall assessment," Carter wrote Brezhnev on 4 November 1977, "is that progress is being made toward a more cooperative and harmonious relationship between our two countries."[162]

But the two most powerful nations on earth were not in control of events. The Jewish community in the United States and the government of Menachem Begin in Israel ridiculed the proposals laid out by Gromyko and Vance.[163] While the Israelis elicited new concessions from Washington, the Egyptian president Anwar Sadat decided to seize the initiative. Seeking to break the impasse in Arab-Israeli relations, he announced that he would visit Jerusalem and try to strike a deal with the Israelis. "We were stunned by Sadat's decision," Vance recalled.[164]

While the president moved quickly to work with Sadat and Begin, the Soviets felt excluded from the ongoing drama. Brezhnev wrote Carter on 16 December: "The present moment is extremely serious and crucial." Washington should not shut the Kremlin out of the peace process. Nor should it exclude representatives from the Palestinian Liberation Organization from the conference table. There was still a chance to work collaboratively.[165]

Carter responded that the United States had neither conspired with Sadat nor orchestrated the dramatic turn of events. The president invited the Kremlin to encourage radical Arab states, such as Syria, to stop attacking Sadat. Trying to reassure Brezhnev, Carter repeated that all the parties eventually would make their way to Geneva, where the Kremlin would most definitely have a role to play.[166]

But the resentment of Soviet officials simmered. They were no fools. They correctly intuited that Carter was backtracking from his promise to treat the Soviet Union as an equal partner in the Middle East peace process. They were right. "The Soviet Union should not be deeply involved," wrote Brzezinski.[167]

If Sadat was the prime mover of events in the Middle East, Siad Barre played a similar role in the Horn of Africa. He continued his aggression against Ethiopia and supported the Eritrean independence movement. He severed his alliance with the Kremlin, threw the Soviets out of their base in Berbera, and looked to the West and to conservative Arab states, such as Saudi Arabia, for assistance. In late October, Mengistu secretly made his way back to Moscow. "Revolutionary Ethiopia," Mengistu implored, had found itself encircled and desperately required the support of the "first of all the socialist states."[168]

The Soviets could not rebuff a revolutionary comrade. The Chinese would mock them and maneuver for advantage in the region, while the Cubans would be disillusioned and might be tempted to act on their own, as they initially had done in Angola. Kremlin policymakers acted decisively. They gave more than a billion dollars in military equipment to Mengistu's army. They also deployed about a thousand Soviet officers and advisers to Ethiopia, coordinated the Ethiopian army's moves, and helped to transport more than seventeen thousand Cuban combat troops and technical experts to the region. The top military brass in Moscow liked jousting with American imperialists and demonstrating their military prowess so long as the rivalry did not get out of hand.[169]

While this was a dramatic manifestation of the Soviet Union's power projection capabilities, Gromyko emphasized to Deputy Secretary of State Warren Christopher that the Kremlin would seek to control its new client. It would not allow the Ethiopians to cross into Somalia. Ethiopian actions were purely defensive, Gromyko insisted. Siad was the aggressor. Gromyko invited joint Soviet-American efforts to stop the fighting. "If we could pool our efforts this would be a good example of U.S.-Soviet cooperation."[170]

On 12 January 1978, Brezhnev again wrote to Carter. "Now that we stepped over the threshold of the new year," it was a propitious time to review overall trends. He noted with satisfaction that both sides had shown flexibility in the strategic arms talks, but he complained about U.S. plans to develop a new type of nuclear weapon—the neutron bomb—whose purpose was to kill people and reduce damage to surrounding property. He also lamented how long SALT II was taking, even though the Kremlin had gone a long way to meet the American position. "In all candor," Brezhnev continued, "we do not see equivalent steps from the US side towards us." The number one task for the new year, he insisted, was to conclude a strategic arms limitation treaty. He then complained once again about unilateral American actions in the Middle East and called for the restoration of a collaborative approach. As for the Horn of Africa, where "the USSR does not seek any advantages for itself," he agreed with Carter that peace must be restored. A just solution based on the cessation of hostilities and the withdrawal of Somali troops from Ethiopian territory was imperative. Last, Brezhnev reiterated his hopes for a relaxation of tensions in Europe and the promotion of commercial, scientific, and cultural exchanges. Overall, the agenda for the new year was formidable, but he was not discouraged.[171]

Carter's response ten days later expressed his gratification that the "predominant trend" in Soviet-American relations was constructive. He hoped to move swiftly to wrap up the SALT negotiations because he was worried about mounting public opposition to an agreement. He thought that Soviet rhetoric and Soviet actions were doing harm; the campaign against the neutron bomb seemed hypocritical when the Kremlin was deploying a far more destructive generation of intermediate-range missiles in Europe, the SS-20s. Moreover, Soviet claims of being excluded from the Middle East peace negotiations struck a false chord because the United States was not repudiating the idea of a conference in Geneva where Soviet officials could participate fully. Most of all, Carter stressed, the Kremlin's use of proxies to advance its interests in the Horn of Africa was stirring unease. Carter concluded: "I discuss these difficult matters frankly in the earnest desire for a more cooperative relationship between our two countries."[172]

But when Carter went before Congress to give his State of the Union message, he paid little attention to Soviet-American relations. "The state of our Union is sound," he began. "For the first time in a generation, we are not haunted by a major international crisis or by domestic turmoil, and we now have a rare and a priceless opportunity to address persistent problems and burdens." The most overriding challenge was the energy shortage. "Every day we spend more than $120 million for foreign oil." Underproduction and overconsumption sapped the nation's financial strength and fueled inflation. "Our main task at home this year, with energy a central element, is the Nation's economy."[173]

Only after addressing the need for tax cuts, fiscal prudence, regulatory reform, and a comprehensive energy program did Carter finally deal with the country's foreign policy. He was optimistic. The American people were strong, peaceful, and resilient. "We've restored a moral basis of our foreign policy. The very heart of our identity as a nation is our firm commitment to human rights." His administration sought security, peace, and economic growth. The United States could compete with the Soviet Union if it had to but preferred to cooperate when it was opportune to do so. "We are negotiating with quiet confidence," he said, "without haste, with careful determination, to ease the tensions between us." But his mind was on more enduring values. His recent trip to India, Egypt, Poland, France, and Belgium had "crystallized for me the purposes of our Nation's policy: to ensure economic justice, to advance human rights, to resolve conflicts without violence, and to proclaim in our great democracy our constant faith in the liberty and dignity of human beings everywhere."[174]

The president was still seeking to transcend the Cold War, but there were obstacles abroad and at home. Exchange fluctuations and monetary disorders were causing "growing concern," wrote Helmut Schmidt, chancellor of West Germany, not only in his country but among all the NATO allies. These problems were not "transitory"—they resulted from the energy shortage and OPEC price hikes—and they portended a "crisis of considerable dimensions." The whole world economic system was at risk, Schmidt warned. "This gives the problem a crucial political significance."[175]

Brzezinski admonished Carter that they needed to work harder on alliance cohesion. The NATO allies were also worried about the buildup of Warsaw Pact conventional forces and the deployment of SS-20s, and they feared that the Americans might negotiate an agreement with the Kremlin at their expense. "Political trends in Western Europe are ominous," Brzezinski wrote. Italian moderates were cutting a deal with Italian communists; the left coalition of communists and socialists in France might win in the forthcoming elections; West German politics were manifesting neutralist tendencies. "In sum," Brzezinski wrote, by the end of March "we could see major Communist advances in Europe, and then an important backlash at home with the administration being criticized for doing too little too late."[176]

Brzezinski tirelessly warned Carter that domestic support for his foreign-policy goals was fading. Carter was seen as "soft," he wrote bluntly. Conservatives blasted Carter for wanting to reestablish relations with Cuba and for trying to heal wounds with Vietnam. They ridiculed him for his cancellation of important weapons programs, such as the B-1 bomber, and for cutting back U.S. forces in Korea. They scorned his negotiation of a canal treaty with Panama, his reaching out to Red China, and his bargaining with the Kremlin over strategic arms. Carter's political advisers echoed Brzezinski, emphasizing to the president that it would be "very difficult" to get Senate approval of a strategic arms treaty.[177]

Carter searched for help. Hoping to sustain détente, he tried to enlist the assistance of French president Valery Giscard d'Estaing and Marshal Broz Tito, the president of Yugoslavia. "It is important for Soviet leaders to understand the gravity of the situation," he wrote Tito. "As you know, it is my earnest hope that we will be able to promote détente and to work with Soviet leaders in promoting mutual objectives in important areas of arms control. It would be regrettable if Soviet actions in Ethiopia made pursuit of those objectives more difficult, and complicated the process of reducing tensions and building a firmer basis for East-West relations."[178]

Not all the president's advisers were happy with the link he was making between détente and the Horn of Africa. At a series of high-level meetings at the end of February and early March 1978, Secretary of State Vance expressed his disapproval. "Zbig, you yesterday and the President today" suggested that a SALT agreement was connected to Soviet behavior in Africa. "I think it is wrong to say that," he admonished. "We will end up losing SALT and that will be the worst thing that could happen. If we do not get a SALT treaty in the President's first four years, that will be a blemish on his record forever."[179]

Brzezinski tenaciously defended his position. Ten thousand Cuban troops were moving into the Horn, and the Soviets were delivering arms and supplies estimated to be worth a billion dollars. "The Soviets should be made aware of the fact that they are poisoning the atmosphere." They were exploiting a local conflict "for larger purposes. They are frightening more countries in the region and they are creating a precedent for more involvement elsewhere. . . . If we allow the Soviets to send expeditionary forces to resolve territorial conflicts in ways that are beneficial to them, then we are going to have more and more problems."

Brzezinski wanted the United States to take action. He wanted to send a naval task force to the Red Sea to convey political signals, to demonstrate to critics at home and friends abroad that the United States meant business. Friends and allies, such as Saudi Arabia and Iran, were watching closely. They should be made to see that the United States would not permit the Soviets to fish in troubled waters. Washington must raise the costs of the Soviets' and Cubans' African interventions. "We should get the regional powers to act and make the Soviets and Cubans bleed."[180]

The "conundrum," as Vice President Mondale pointed out, was that in

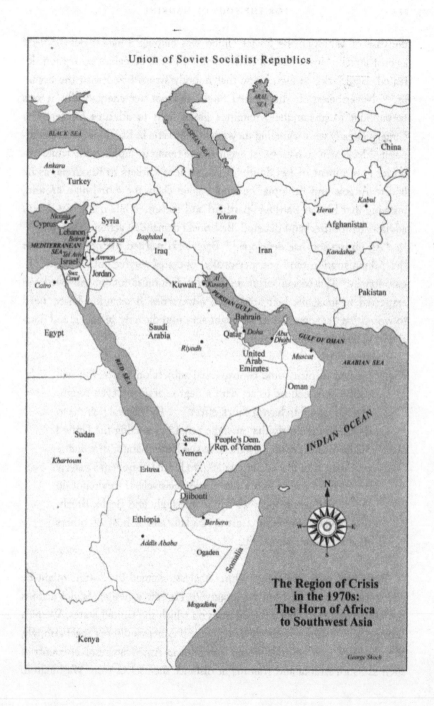

Union of Soviet Socialist Republics

BLACK SEA

CASPIAN SEA

ARAL SEA

China

Ankara

Turkey

Kabul

Herat

Afghanistan

Cyprus

Nicosia

Lebanon

Beirut

Damascus

Syria

Tehran

Kandahar

MEDITERRANEAN SEA

Tel Aviv

Baghdad

Iran

Pakistan

Israel

Amman

Iraq

Jordan

Kuwait

Al Kuwayt

Cairo

Suez Canal

PERSIAN GULF

Egypt

Saudi Arabia

Riyadh

Bahrain

Qatar

Doha

Abu Dhabi

GULF OF OMAN

United Arab Emirates

Muscat

ARABIAN SEA

Oman

RED SEA

INDIAN OCEAN

Sudan

Sana

Yemen

People's Dem. Rep. of Yemen

Khartoum

Eritrea

Djibouti

Ethiopia

Berbera

N

Addis Ababa

Ogaden

W   E

Somalia

S

The Region of Crisis
in the 1970s:
The Horn of Africa
to Southwest Asia

Kenya

Mogadishu

George Skoch

the case of Ethiopia, the Soviet Union was helping a nation defend itself against attack. Most of black Africa wanted to see Somalia's aggression defeated. Brzezinski, in fact, knew that nobody sympathized with the Somalis.[181] Nevertheless, if the United States did not act energetically, it was tantamount to giving the Kremlin a green light to advance farther. The Cubans already were signaling they might intervene in Rhodesia, where competing black African nationalist groups were trying to supplant the white minority government of Ian Smith. If Castro sent soldiers to Rhodesia, as he had to Angola and Ethiopia, he would again claim the moral high ground, insisting that he was battling apartheid and racism. While many of Carter's advisers temporized and debated, Brzezinski demanded action.[182]

"An impression has developed," Brzezinski warned the president, "that the Administration (and you personally) operates very cerebrally, quite unemotionally." This was unfortunate. "A president must not only be loved and respected; he must also be feared." U.S. adversaries, Brzezinski advised, need to worry that "at some point, we might act unpredictably, in anger, and decisively." The time might be ripe

> for you to pick some controversial subject on which you will deliberately choose to act with a degree of anger, even roughness, designed to have a shock effect. . . . The central point is to demonstrate clearly that at some point obstructing the United States means picking a fight with the United States in which a president is prepared, and willing, to hit the opponent squarely on the head and to knock him down decisively. If we do not do this soon to somebody, we will increasingly find Begin, Brezhnev, Vorster, Schmidt, Castro, Qadafi, and a host of others thumbing their noses at us.[183]

Brzezinski was unrelenting. Other analysts claimed the Soviets might be acting opportunistically, but he disagreed. He saw a design. Soviet actions portended a plan to choke the oil lanes on which the United States, Western Europe, and Japan were sorely dependent. If America did not react strongly, friends, allies, and neutrals would lose faith in American resolve; countries such as Saudi Arabia and Iran might distance themselves from Washington.

"If the Soviets do not conclude that we are prepared to stand up to them, you can only anticipate worsening difficulties in the years ahead."[184]

Carter scribbled on one of Zbig's memos: "I'm concerned but we mustn't overreact."[185] He bided his time. He was preoccupied trying to get the Senate to ratify the Panama Canal Treaty. "It's hard to concentrate on anything except Panama," he jotted in his diary.[186] SALT was just one of many matters on his agenda, and it did not have high priority. No longer was he waging a Cold War, but neither was he lusting for détente.

The delays in the SALT talks and the carping over the Horn of Africa exasperated the Soviet Union. Brezhnev dearly wanted progress. On 27 February, he wrote Carter, again emphasizing that a strategic arms treaty must be a top priority. He reiterated his concerns about American intentions to develop a neutron bomb and his country's alleged exclusion from the Middle East peace process. "No less puzzling," he said, were allegations that the Soviet Union was seeking unilateral gain in the Horn of Africa. Soviet policy, Brezhnev insisted, has "the sole purpose of restoring justice and peace in that region. . . . If Somalia withdraws its troops from Ethiopia, . . . then the cause of the conflict would cease to exist." I address these issues, he concluded, "not for the sake of polemics," but because "practical constructive measures in Soviet-US relations is becoming ever more urgent."[187]

Ambassador Dobrynin reinforced all these points with Secretary Vance. The leadership in Moscow was genuinely upset that nothing was being accomplished. Brzezinski's "Polish temperament made him strongly anti-Soviet," Dobrynin told Harriman.[188] Kremlin officials were not, in fact, pursuing any grand design but acting as a great power, extending their strategic reach and their diplomatic influence, not orchestrating developments, seeking confrontation, or manipulating Mengistu. Among friends, Soviet officials acknowledged not only that Mengistu was hard to control but that his brutality was appalling. They would not allow him to use Soviet equipment to cross into Somali territory. They also tried to persuade him to accept Eritrea's autonomy. Even the Cubans were struggling to contain, rather than encourage, Mengistu's ambitions.[189]

At a secret meeting in Havana on 16 March 1978, Vice President Carlos Rafael Rodriguez explained the Cuban perspective to Thomas L. Hughes, president of the Carnegie Endowment for International Peace. Hughes, a former head of the Intelligence and Research Division of the State Department, was conveying an unofficial message from Carter, objecting to Soviet and Cuban behavior in Africa as deeply disappointing, since it was colliding with the administration's hopes to remove the Cold War from Africa and normalize relations with Cuba.

Rodriguez, now the number three person in the Cuban hierarchy, just below Fidel and his brother, Raul, listened intently. He "was alert, intelligent, suave, at times witty and charming," wrote Hughes, "very much the self-confident, consummate political ideologue and international strategist which he (and others) consider him to be." Rodriguez systematically enumerated the degrees to which he believed American officials were exaggerating Cuba's role in Libya, Sierra Leone, and Mozambique. He gave a long account of Fidel's interactions with Siad and Mengistu. Siad had violated his promise not to invade, and then tried to justify his aggression based on Cuba's intervention. "When Siad Barre said we had 20,000 Cuban troops in Ethiopia, we had no more than 300 specialists." Cubans were not seeking to stir up trouble in Africa, Rodriguez insisted. They were trying to constrain Mengistu and get him to settle with the Eritreans. "Our African involvements have often been against our wishes and have been undertaken knowing that they complicate our general political aims. We are not agitating Africa. Indeed in Ethiopia . . . we are acting as conservatives responding to government requests, defending borders, preserving the established status quo. We do this for principle's sake."

Castro believed he had revolutionary obligations, said Rodriguez. But he was not looking for trouble. He wanted to normalize relations with the United States. But he, too, was responding to circumstances he could not control, to the dynamics of local revolutionary forces, and to the breakdown of imperial and racist rule in Africa. The United States government did not want to face reality, Rodriguez suggested. Fidel was beleaguered with requests from African heads of state for assistance, bombarded with requests for aid to revolutionary movements fighting apartheid in southern Africa. "We keep turning down requests which are difficult for us to do."

Cuba did not want to intervene further, said Rodriguez, and did want détente with Washington. The United States was a great capitalist power, he acknowledged. "We don't like that, but we are realists. . . . Convergence of interest produces international détente." But if white racists attack Mozambique or Zambia, Cuba would be asked "by all progressive forces in Africa . . . to send military support. Times change. In March of 1977, a year ago, we did not think we would be in Ethiopia either. No idea we would be." What happened in the future could not be predicted. The normal processes of history could not be thwarted.[190]

While Carter could not control events, he could try to persuade the Kremlin not to exploit them.[191] On 17 March, the day after the first of his two Panama treaties squeaked through the Senate, he delivered a major speech at Wake Forest University. "Our potential adversaries have now built up massive forces armed with conventional weapons—tanks, aircraft, infantry, mechanized units," he warned. "These forces could be used for political blackmail, and they could threaten our vital interests unless we and our allies and friends have our own military strength and conventional forces as a counterbalance." The Kremlin was displaying "an ominous inclination" to use its military power to intervene in local conflicts. The United States had to strengthen its military forces, enhance its deterrent capabilities, and augment its strategic reach. The country needed forces that could be deployed rapidly to the Middle East, Indian Ocean, and Persian Gulf, said Carter. "We, like our forefathers, live in a time when those who would destroy liberty are restrained less by their respect for freedom than by their knowledge that those of us who cherish freedom are strong."[192]

The new face in American politics was sounding like his predecessors. He still preferred cooperation to competition with the Soviet Union, but he needed to be prudent. Indeed he *had* to be prudent, given the boldness of the Kremlin's clients and the anti-Soviet feelings among the American public, given the pleas of allies and the worries of friends.

Doubts about the American way of life were rife, Carter acknowledged. "Voices in the developing world ask whether notions of free speech, personal liberty, freely chosen governments should not be pushed aside in the struggle to overcome poverty. Voices in the industrialized world ask whether democracy equips us for the frenzied pace of change in our own modern lives."[193]

Skeptics could question, but Carter was not inclined to despair. Americans must "proclaim our faith in the values of a democratic society," he said. Liberty would empower developing nations to "achieve their full economic and political potential." Democracy, he emphasized in a speech in Paris on 4 January 1978, "is not merely right and just. It's also the system that is most consistent with human nature. It's the most effective way to organize society for the common good."[194] The challenge, as he understood it, "was to defend our values fearlessly, while tirelessly working to prevent war."[195]

To meet the challenge, he would try something new. On 16 March 1978, Carter informed Secretary of State Vance and Vice President Mondale that he was sending his national security adviser to Beijing to talk to Mao's heirs.

The China Card

During a very contentious discussion among Carter's advisers on 2 March 1978 about Ethiopia, Secretary of Defense Brown suddenly interjected: "I have an idea re China. The Chinese are less concerned about [who is] the aggressor. Why don't we get together with the Chinese . . . and issue a joint statement of concern about the Horn and append to it a statement that we will consult on other areas where we have a joint interest? That would get the Soviets' attention."

Vance objected. "That would get their attention but we are at the point where we are on the brink of ending up with a real souring of relations between ourselves and the Soviet Union and it may take a helluva long while to change and may not be changed for years." We should think carefully "before we go down that road," he admonished.[196]

Brzezinski relentlessly pushed Carter down that road. From the outset, he had believed the United States and China "had parallel strategic interests against the Soviet Union" that made them natural partners. "We have failed to use the China card against the Soviets," he noted to Carter in a particularly strident weekly analysis on 21 April 1978.[197] Carter, of course, had been thinking of normalizing relations with China since the first days of his presidency, and had sent Vance to China in August 1977 to explore possibilities. But the Chinese insisted that the United States must sever its ties with Taiwan before opening formal diplomatic relations, which Carter knew would cause political acrimony at home and endanger ratification of the Panama Canal treaties. So he had put China on a back burner. Détente had priority. Panama had priority.[198]

But having won a landmark legislative victory with the ratification of the first Panama treaty and facing growing public disillusionment with the Soviet Union, Carter decided that it made sense to try again to normalize relations

with China. Like Vance, he did not want this rapprochement to damage relations with the Kremlin. In fact, he hoped that establishing formal diplomatic
ties with Beijing would make the Soviet Union more tractable while also po-
sitioning the United States to compete more effectively in the third world.
"We all agreed that a better relationship with the PRC would help us with
SALT," he wrote in his diary. Vance concurred. Normalization might
"strengthen our hand in securing ratification of SALT II."[199]

Vance did not want Brzezinski to be the administration's emissary to Beijing, but the national security adviser convinced the president that he was the
right man for the mission. Brzezinski conferred with Carter and then drafted
his own instructions, which the president reviewed carefully and issued in his
own name. His visit was not tactical, said Carter. "The United States and
China . . . have parallel, long-term strategic concerns. The most important of
these is our common opposition to global or regional hegemony by any single
power."[200]

Brzezinski went to China feeling "exhilarated." He had outmaneuvered
Vance and now had the chance to compete with Kissinger for the fame and
glory that surrounded a reestablishment of normal diplomatic relations with
China after more than two decades of nonrecognition. "The opening of
China in 1972 had been a bold stroke, of the greatest geopolitical significance," wrote Brzezinski, "and I was determined to succeed in transforming that still-tenuous relationship into something more enduring and more
extensive."[201]

Between 20 and 22 May 1978, Brzezinski spent many hours in Beijing
talking to Foreign Minister Huang Hua, Vice Premier Deng Xiaoping, and
Party Chairman Hua Guofeng. China was going through a period of remarkable change after the death of Mao in 1976. Among the leaders, there was
much internecine strife, and Deng was about to consolidate his power.
Brzezinski immediately liked him. He "was tiny in size, but great in his boldness." "Bright, alert, and shrewd," Deng "was quick on the uptake, with a
good sense of humor, tough, and very direct." He spoke much less than
Brzezinski but made his points clearly, as Brzezinski had anticipated. "In the
relations between our two countries," Deng declared, "the question of normalization is of fundamental importance." The United States had to reaffirm
the commitments already made by Kissinger, state that there was but one
China, terminate diplomatic relations with Taiwan, sever its defense treaty,

and end its arms shipments. China would not renounce its right to liberate Taiwan, as the United States had wanted, maintaining that it was an internal matter. The United States could, however, make a unilateral statement of its own expectations. Working out these arrangements would not be too difficult, said Deng. It was a question of resolve. It was up to President Carter to determine whether he really wanted to take the requisite steps to establish normal ties with the People's Republic. And once formal diplomatic relations were established, Chinese officials would then gladly visit the United States and collaborate in "coping with the Polar bear." Deng sneered at U.S. efforts to relax tensions with the Kremlin. He scorned détente. "Soviet strategy is fixed and will not change. They will try to squeeze in wherever there is an opening." The United States, he said flatly, "is not strong enough in its actions."

"President Carter is a very unusual person," Brzezinski assured Deng, "one who is decisive, who likes challenges, whose entire political career has involved taking on causes where he started behind and where he ended on top." He now had made up his mind. He wanted the United States to have normal diplomatic relations with China. But Brzezinski did not want to focus on the details of normalization or on the future of Taiwan. He much preferred to focus on grand strategy. He defended the U.S. policy of détente as tough-minded and realistic.

> The American-Soviet relationship will remain for a very long time to come fundamentally a competitive and in some respects a hostile relationship, but there are also some cooperative aspects to it which stem from mutual interest and particularly from the need to restrict or to confine the dangers of a nuclear war. Accordingly, American policy toward the Soviet Union must be one which combines sustained political competition with occasional willingness to cooperate and to accommodate. Unfortunately, the occasional accommodation and cooperation is misunderstood by some people as termination of the rivalry.

Luckily, Brzezinski went on to say, Soviet actions in Africa and elsewhere were now strengthening the influence of those officials in the United States who insisted that "Soviet designs are fundamentally aggressive and . . . must be resolutely resisted. This brings me to the question of more tangible cooperation between China and the U.S."[202]

On the next day, 22 May, Party Chairman Hua told Brzezinski that the United States "should not use China as a pawn in order to improve its relations with the Soviet Union. You should have a long-term strategic viewpoint." Brzezinski assured him that the United States did indeed have strategic vision, and he knew the Soviet Union was basically hostile. He wanted to discuss how the United States and China could begin to cooperate in commercial, military, scientific, and cultural matters. Recognizing that the Chinese were reluctant to arrange details before the issue of Taiwan was resolved, Brzezinski simply repeated to China's head of state, "President Carter has made up his mind." "We will observe the actual action," retorted Hua.[203]

The flavor of the discussions is best captured by the toasts offered by Brzezinski and Foreign Minister Huang at their formal dinner on the first night, 20 May. "Though China and the United States," said Huang,

> have different social systems and ideologies and though there
> are fundamental differences between us, our two countries do
> hold common or similar views on a number of questions in the
> present international situation. . . . The present-day world is
> full of contradictions, and the international situation is marked
> by turbulence and drastic change. The struggle for hegemony is
> the main source of global intranquillity. [sic] The shadow of
> social-imperialism can be seen in almost all the changes and
> disturbances in every part of the world. . . . Hegemonism,
> though blustering and menacing, is a paper tiger.

Thanking the Chinese for their hospitality, Brzezinski responded:

> Our two societies are rooted in different traditions and are
> based on different views about the nature of man and the purposes of government. But one does not have to share in your
> ideology to respect your civilization, your history, and your determination to defend your nation, to develop your country
> and to promote the welfare of your people.
> The admiration and friendship which the American people

feel toward the Chinese is part of our historical tradition. Ours is a nation of immigrants.... Because of our diverse origins, we naturally welcome a world of diversity. President Carter repeatedly has voiced his conviction that a pluralistic world order would best express the manifold aspirations, traditions, cultures, and beliefs of mankind.

We recognize—and share—China's resolve to resist the efforts of any nation which seeks to establish global or regional hegemony....

In many regions in today's world, the U.S. and China can contribute to peace and deter imperialist designs....

Together, we can promote the common aspirations of all mankind for dignity, self-respect, freedom, a decent life, and the enjoyment of the fruits of one's labor.[204]

Brzezinski returned from China euphoric. Carter warmly congratulated him but then told his national security adviser that he had been seduced by the Chinese. Carter wanted to normalize relations with Beijing, but he was not willing to set aside détente. When Brzezinski gave a series of interviews revealing his distrust of the Kremlin, Carter was displeased. The president smiled—it was a smile, recalled Brzezinski, that said, "I like you but I'm really burning inside." "You're not just a professor, you speak for me," said Carter. "And I think you went too far in your statements. You put all of this responsibility on the Soviets. You said they were conducting a worldwide vitriolic campaign encircling and penetrating the Middle East, placing troops on the Chinese frontier. All this simply just went a little too far."[205]

Carter told his advisers that after the November elections they should work toward a normalization agreement with the Chinese, and should also pursue the elusive SALT agreement.[206] In a major speech at the Naval Academy commencement, he chided the Kremlin for its aggressiveness, military buildup, and attempts to exploit unrest in Africa. But he also beckoned for cooperation. "Our long-term objective must be to convince the Soviet Union of the advantages of cooperation and of the costs of disruptive behavior."[207] When the president's message was criticized by the media as reflecting the tug of war between Brzezinski and Vance, he tried to clarify his views during a news conference on 26 June:

We want to be friends with the Soviet Union. We want to have rapid progress made on the SALT negotiations, the comprehensive test ban, increased trade, better communication. Some of the things the Soviets do cause us great concern. The human rights questions within the Soviet Union in violation of the Helsinki agreement, their intrusion, along with the Cubans, into Africa. . . . But I have a deep belief that the underlying relationship between ourselves and the Soviets is stable and that Mr. Brezhnev, along with myself, wants peace and wants to have better friendship.[208]

At the end of May, Carter and Vance talked to Gromyko in Washington, and in mid-July Vance met him again in Geneva. These exchanges were characterized by tough, sometimes brutally frank accusations, yet they illuminated the deeper desire on both sides to resolve their differences and reach a SALT II agreement. Vance told Gromyko the Soviets were setting fires in Africa. Gromyko indignantly denied it. The Soviet Union was not intervening in Rhodesia, Namibia, or Zaire, he insisted. That it had an ideological influence on Africa was true. This was natural, inevitable, "because for many years the Soviet Union had argued against colonialism and racism." Carried away, Gromyko denied meddling even in Ethiopia. "There was no Soviet Napoleon in Africa," he told Carter. Nor were the Soviets aiming for military superiority; they merely desired security, like the United States. When Vance reiterated that U.S. officials wanted peace and détente, Gromyko asked for deeds, not words.[209]

Two issues dogged the SALT negotiations other than Soviet actions in Africa and American diplomacy in the Middle East. Brezhnev and Gromyko despised the renewed American emphasis on human rights and hated U.S. efforts to play the China card. On 21 July, President Carter released a statement: "I speak today with the sadness the whole world feels at the sentence given Anatoly Shcharansky." Shcharansky, a Russian Jew, had been officially charged with espionage and treason. Sentenced to three years in prison and ten years in a labor camp, he had been allegedly conspiring with the CIA to foment dissent, encourage Jewish emigration, and stir up trouble among Jews who had been refused permission to leave the Soviet Union.[210] "We are all sobered," said Carter, "by this reminder that, so late in the 20th century, a person can be sent to jail for asserting his basic human rights."[211] When the president raised Shcharansky's case directly with Gromyko, the Soviet foreign minister barely controlled his furor. "I never saw Gromyko so mad as at that time. Never in my life," recalled Dobrynin. Gromyko was a cultured man, said the Soviet ambassador, an able diplomat, usually very controlled, very self-disciplined, occasionally displaying a sardonic wit. But on this occasion, he was almost apoplectic. Why in the world, he exclaimed to Dobrynin, was Carter dwelling on human rights rather than discussing matters they could resolve, like SALT?[212]

Soviet authorities were trying to quell the unanticipated efforts of dissidents in their own country and in Eastern Europe to enforce the Final Act of the Conference on Security and Co-operation in Europe. The Helsinki Agreement was fast becoming a rallying point for proponents of freedom and self-determination throughout the communist .world. In Czechoslovakia, writers, intellectuals, and former supporters of the Prague Spring formed Charter 77 and appealed to their government to honor the Final Act. In Poland, the Workers' Self-Defense Committee, the KOR, protested the rise in food prices, pressed for the right to organize, and clamored for higher wages. In the republics of the Soviet Union, nationalists in Georgia, Armenia, Ukraine, and Lithuania struggled to revive their cultural and ethnic identity in the face of Russian domination. Soviet authorities wanted to thwart these groups without engaging in widespread repression. They arrested key leaders, and then deeply resented American expressions of sympathy for the dissidents.[213]

Criticism of the prison sentences was coming at a time when thousands of people were being executed in China, and Soviet leaders saw the U.S. position as hypocritical—scolding Moscow while embracing Beijing. Brzezinski told the president that a previous estimate of executions in China had been updated, and the new figure was as high as twenty thousand, an estimate "based on reports by foreign travelers in China" and relying on notices posted at twenty courts "well distributed around the PRC. The final figure was then extrapolated from the fact that more than 2,000 Chinese courts had the power to impose the death sentence." Carter jotted on Brzezinski's weekly message: "Keep me informed."[214]

Yet this new information did not deflect the process of normalizing relations with the People's Republic of China. Gromyko warned Carter and

Vance not to play a "dirty game," not to collude with China against the Soviet Union.[215] But Brzezinski kept pushing in this direction, often flagrantly excluding State Department officials who needed to be informed and end-running Secretary Vance, who wanted progress with China to advance in tandem with progress on SALT.[216]

Brzezinski recognized the Soviet sensibility, but he was not swayed by it. The Chinese were "leaning to one side, this time toward the U.S.," he informed Carter on 1 September 1978. "By doing so, the Chinese hope to accentuate strains in the U.S. détente process. . . . The implications for the Soviet Union are profound." The United States, he reiterated, could reap "beneficial security and economic dividends." The opportunity must be grasped.[217]

While President Carter was focusing on mediating an agreement between Menachem Begin and Anwar Sadat at Camp David, Brzezinski's focus never wandered from America's strategic competition with the Soviet Union. He cited new intelligence reports outlining further increments in Soviet military capabilities and lambasted the State Department for leaks regarding China and for its efforts to normalize relations with Vietnam, a move bound to antagonize the Chinese, who now viewed Vietnam as a Soviet client. Brzezinski was alarmed by the unrest in Iran and the drift of events in Afghanistan, and he was ever more determined to move ahead on China. The president sought to cool his ardor. In Carter's view, his national security adviser was "exalting" the China issue. But Brzezinski would not let it go, and worked deliberately to finalize arrangements while Vance was traveling in the Middle East and preparing for another round of talks with Gromyko on SALT.[218]

On 15 December, Brzezinski told Ambassador Dobrynin that Washington and Beijing would immediately announce the establishment of formal diplomatic relations between their two countries and that Deng would visit the United States in January. Dobrynin "looked absolutely stunned," recalled Brzezinski. "His face turned kind of gray and his jaw dropped." In fact, Dobrynin was not stunned, just angry. In Geneva, where Vance was meeting Gromyko, the Soviet foreign minister was even angrier at the news. "There was a violent anger," recalled Marshal Shulman, Vance's expert on Soviet affairs.[219]

The opening with China came just after Carter had mediated a stunning agreement at Camp David between Begin and Sadat providing for, among

Vice Premier Deng Xiaoping and President Carter, 1979. Carter welcomed
Deng to the White House, hoping to improve Sino-American relations
and exert pressure on the Kremlin.

other things, the withdrawal of Israeli troops from the Sinai in exchange for
Egyptian diplomatic recognition of Israel. Together, these initiatives infused a
spirit of optimism in U.S. policymaking circles—notwithstanding soaring inflation, growing domestic demoralization, and mounting disorder in Africa
and Asia. "I believe that as we enter 1979," Brzezinski wrote Carter, "you,
quite literally, have a historic chance to start shaping a new global system,
with the United States as its predominant coordinator if no longer the para-
mount power."[220]

Brzezinski prepared meticulously for Deng's historic visit to Washington
in January. Elaborate briefing memos that he and Vance sent the president
emphasized that the aim of U.S. policy was to forge a new world order based
on respect for diversity and a collaborative battle against hegemony. Toward
this end, the United States would begin to forge commercial ties with its new
partners in Beijing, to work out scientific exchanges, technology transfers,
and arms sales. If Soviet leaders wanted to join this new world order, Brzezinski maintained, they would not be excluded. But it would be a world order
that served America's purposes, not theirs.[221]

Brzezinski's optimism, rather than the gloomy mood of American public opinion, infused Carter's State of the Union address on 23 January 1979. There were problems, to be sure—energy, inflation, and unemployment—but they could be solved through creative effort, an ingenious private sector, and a fiscally prudent government that did not overreach. "America has the greatest economic system in the world," exclaimed the president. "Let's reduce government interference and give it a chance to work." Confidence was growing again, he insisted. The nation was strong militarily but needed to get even stronger. National security "requires more than just military might." The peoples of the world were astir with new demands, new needs, new yearnings. "This demand for justice and human rights is a wave of the future." Neither superpower could dominate the world, but values would compete, and America's would prevail. "Our way of life, and what we stand for as a nation, continue to have magnetic international appeal."[222]

Carter was not giving up on détente. In a personal message he tried to reassure Brezhnev that normalization of ties with China "has no other purpose but to promote the cause of world peace. . . . There is no greater priority in my government than the strengthening of relations between our two countries."[223] In his State of the Union address, he reiterated: "The new foundation of international cooperation that we seek excludes no nation. Cooperation with the Soviet Union serves the cause of peace, for in this nuclear age, world peace must include the superpowers—and it must mean the control of nuclear arms."[224] When a reporter noted that "Brezhnev is getting older and visibly more feeble," and asked what would happen if the Soviet leader disappeared from the scene, Carter answered: "I'm determined that our relations with the Soviet Union will improve as we go into the next two years."[225]

Brezhnev, too, was not giving up hope. He had met with Averell Harriman at the Kremlin on 13 December 1978, even when he had not been well. He read from prepared notes, though occasionally he lifted his eyes and ad-libbed. The Soviet Union was not seeking military superiority, he had insisted, but the United States was not accustomed to equality and wanted to reestablish its predominance—that was the essential problem. Yet the arms race made no sense, affording neither side additional security, and was conducted at the expense of all peoples. Speaking extemporaneously, Brezhnev denied that the Kremlin was fomenting unrest around the world; allegations of this sort were preposterous. When Harriman fulsomely expressed goodwill, Brezhnev was vividly moved. Tears welling in his eyes, he repeated to Harriman that he wanted to improve ties with the United States. He eagerly awaited a meeting with Carter once the strategic arms agreement was finalized.[226]

Among his Warsaw Pact comrades, Brezhnev spoke more candidly, but his message was much the same. Overlooking Carter's desire to halt the arms race and constrain new weapons programs, like the B-1 bomber, Brezhnev said the Americans could not stomach the Soviet Union's great strategic gains. Officials in Washington found it hard to accept parity. They wanted to overturn the existing correlation of forces and "impose their will [and] their ways on the rest of the world." They were spending huge sums on modernizing their arsenal and seeking new weapons of mass destruction. They were angling to apply economic leverage and scheming to sunder the unity of the Warsaw Treaty Organization. At the same time, "They have already begun to feed China, to supply it with weapons, and to push it toward hostile excursions against the socialist countries, as was done some time ago in Europe during the years of the shameful Munich policies."

Capitalism faced a severe crisis, Brezhnev said. The imperialists could not deal with their energy shortages, unemployment, or soaring inflation. They were choking with anger about the contraction of their imperialist domain in Asia and Africa. Laos was taking a socialist turn, revolutions were occurring in Angola, Ethiopia, and Afghanistan, struggles for independence were escalating in Rhodesia and Namibia, and the racist regime in South Africa was beginning to founder. There was turbulence in Iran and Nicaragua, stirring even greater alarm. Around the globe, imperialists saw evidence of their own demise, but as they had since 1917, they claimed that Moscow was fomenting the unrest. They refused to acknowledge the ineluctable workings of their own system. They refused to admit that revolutions ripen and grow on domestic turf.

Imperialists would seek to thwart the flow of history. Some imperialist politicians would try to clamp down on workers' movements, reconcile divisions among themselves, and lash out at détente. Danger must not be ignored. "Our sacred duty to our own peoples," said Brezhnev, "to the cause of socialism, is not to allow imperialism to break the correlation of forces, which has been achieved at the price of so many sacrifices, and which in itself represents the most important guarantee against nuclear war in the present times."[227]

Although vigilance was always necessary, Brezhnev made clear to his allies that he was not abandoning his quest for a SALT agreement and other forms of arms control. Since the West was alarmed by the growth of Soviet SS-20s in Europe, Brezhnev said he would discuss this matter on the basis of equality and reciprocity. "We oppose the arms race," he told his Warsaw Pact allies. We "do not plan to attack anybody, and we are always prepared to dissolve the military blocs." During the forthcoming year, he hoped to meet with Carter, sign a strategic arms treaty, and inject "a positive current into the development of Soviet-American relations once again."[228]

Brezhnev would not abandon hope that relations with the United States could be improved. "The task set by life itself—[is] to put an end to the unrestrained arms race." Responding to questions from *Time* magazine reporters, he emphasized, "Goodneighborliness—regardless of differences in political system and views—is the best line in interstate relations. And I am deeply convinced that Soviet-American relations can be not just normal, but truly good."[229]

Iran and Afghanistan

Few places on earth experienced more political turbulence in 1978 than southwest Asia. In Iran, Shah Mohammad Reza Pahlavi had sat on the throne since 1941. He had consolidated his authority over the country in 1953, after the CIA helped topple Mohammad Mosaddeq, the populist and nationalist prime minister. For the next twenty-five years, the Shah became a major U.S. ally, receiving economic aid, technical assistance, and military hardware and providing the United States with Persian Gulf oil and surveillance capabilities on the very border of the Soviet Union. During the middle 1970s, the Shah's control of his country started to unravel. His long-term efforts to modernize Iran, curb the influence of Islam, accelerate industrial development, build military prowess, and operate as a regional powerhouse bred opposition. Islamic clergymen and large landowners despised his efforts to promote land reform and alter traditional customs. Professionals and middle-class people grew disillusioned when his economic initiatives were not ac-

Iranian demonstrators burning the U.S. flag in Tehran, 1979.
The revolution in Iran quickly turned intensely anti-American.

companied by political reforms. Workers and students were disaffected when
rapid economic growth subsided in the mid-1970s and unemployment and
inflation eroded their opportunities. Moreover, the Shah's violent yet spo-
radic repression of political foes intensified opposition. Leftists, moderates,
and Islamic reformers focused their wrath on the Shah while competing for
support in urban streets and rural towns.

From exile in Iraq and then in Paris, Ayatollah Ruhollah Khmeini spat
forth his hatred of the Shah, of America, and of modernity. Like he communists, he called for justice and blamed the woes of humankind on capitalist
greed; unlike the communists, whom he detested, he called for the restoration of God's law, the Sharia. Political Islam had found a voice.[2]

Carter observed these developments with growing consternation.
Throughout 1978, there were strikes, demonstrations, and riots in Iran. Ten
to twelve thousand people were killed, and another forty-five fifty thousand, injured. "The country was literally afire," writes James Bill, a scholar
of Iran who visited the country at the end of 1978.[231] But not til the fall of

that year did Carter and his advisers recognize the full dimensions of the crisis. They did not blame the Soviet Union—the Shah's problems were of his own making—but the implications for U.S. economic, strategic, and diplomatic interests were profound.[232] Iranian oil fueled the economies of Western Europe and Japan; its monitoring sites and airfields enabled the United States to gather critical information on Soviet missile developments and strategic capabilities; the Shah's friendship was believed to enhance Washington's prestige and influence throughout the Persian Gulf and was of invaluable assistance to Israel. "The disintegration of Iran," Brzezinski wrote the president on 28 December 1978, "would be the most massive American defeat since the beginning of the Cold War, overshadowing in its real consequences the setback in Vietnam."[233]

Brzezinski wanted Carter to take more determined action to buck up the Shah or to align the United States behind a military coup, either policy designed to sustain America's long-term influence in the country. In early December, he asked the Defense Department to make contingency plans for deploying U.S. forces to Iran to guard the oil fields. He wrote President Carter on 2 December:

> If you draw an arc on the globe stretching from Chittagong (Bangladesh) through Islamabad to Aden, you will be pointing to the area of currently our greatest vulnerability. . . .
> There is no question that we are confronting the beginning of a major crisis, in some ways similar to the one in Europe in the late 40's. Fragile social and political structures in a region of vital importance to us are threatened with fragmentation.
> The resulting political vacuum might well be filled by elements more sympathetic to the Soviet Union. . . .
> If the above analysis is correct, the West as a whole may be faced with a challenge of historic proportions. A shift in Iranian/Saudi orientation would have a direct impact on trilateral cohesion [meaning the United States, Western Europe, and Japan], and it would induce in time more "neutralist" attitudes on the part of some of our key allies. In a sentence, it would mean a fundamental shift in the global structure of power.[234]

The Kremlin anticipated the possibility of U.S. intervention in Iran. It monitored developments there carefully, realizing its own incapacity to shape events, but knowing it would be the winner if the Shah were toppled and the Americans ejected. On 17 November, Brezhnev informed Carter that he had received information about an impending U.S. military intervention. "We would not want to believe it," he wrote, "but, unfortunately, it is difficult for us to judge the real intentions of the United States." Conveniently forgetting the Kremlin's actions in Czechoslovakia in 1968, he emphasized that U.S. intervention would violate the U.N. Charter and endanger Soviet security. He suggested that the Soviet and American governments issue statements renouncing intervention. Such declarations would comport with the U.N. Charter and help the cause of "universal peace and international security."[235]

Carter replied that the United States would not intervene in Iran, but that he still supported the Shah and intended to retain a "strong bilateral political, economic, and security relationship" with his country. Worried that the Kremlin might use rumors of American action to justify its own intervention, Carter told Brezhnev to stay out of Iran. "I am sure you appreciate that any such interference would be a matter of the utmost gravity to us."[236]

In January 1979 the Shah left Iran, transferring power to a coalition government. "Millions of Iranians took to the streets in an ecstasy of personal and political celebration that demonstrated the depths of their disaffection [with the Shah]," writes James Bill.[237] The trend of events now portended the ascendancy of a radical Islamic government, headed directly or indirectly by Ayatollah Khomeini. Brzezinski, however, minimized the threat of political Islam and kept his focus on Iran's communist left, which, in his view, was tied to Moscow. But Carter possessed greater insight. Events in Iran, he said, demonstrated that a "relatively few militants, who had deep and fervent commitments," could succeed "against an all-powerful military force and an entrenched government. . . . I think this would tend to inspire or to instigate uprisings among the Palestinians, for instance, or other militant groups, in the future, to assert their authority."[238]

Yet Carter was deeply committed to nonintervention. All through the Iranian crisis, Vietnam was much on his mind. American military embroilments in foreign civil wars were bound to fail and were incompatible with U.S. beliefs.[239] Détente required self-discipline in the face of strategic setbacks. "In our generation, we've had a hundred new nations formed. And they go through a traumatic experience when they shake off colonialism or establish their own government. Quite often they turn to the Soviet Union . . . but eventually they turn to a more stable interrelationship and they become more nationalistic in spirit." Patience, therefore, was imperative. The "most important single responsibility on my shoulders is to have peace, an improved understanding, consultation, communication with the Soviet Union, because on the super powers' shoulders rests the responsibility for peace throughout the world."[240]

The question was whether the Soviet government agreed. If it did, would it exert the same self-discipline? At the very time that Carter was making these remarks, officials in the Kremlin faced a similar crisis in Iran's neighbor to the east, Afghanistan. In that country, Soviet hopes about an unexpected opportunity were rapidly shifting to anxieties about inchoate danger.

At the end of April 1978, the Afghan Communist Party, formally known as the People's Democratic Party of Afghanistan (PDPA), had seized power in Kabul. Prime Minister Mohammed Daoud had earlier arrested several members of the party, and the communists had decided to strike back before they were wiped out. Soviet ambassador Aleksandr Puzanov was told about the coup shortly before it occurred. He opposed it, as did the Kremlin. The U.S.S.R. had cultivated cordial relations with Daoud's government and was not eager to see the PDPA come to power.[241]

The PDPA was divided into two factions, the Parchams and the Khalqs, who hated each other. Nur Mohammad Taraki, the Khalq leader, now became head of the government; Babrak Karmal, a leader of the Parchams, took the number two position; Hafizullah Amin, another Khalq, became a second vice prime minister and minister of foreign affairs. From the outset, Taraki and Amin worked closely, if suspiciously, with one another. Within days, they arrested thousands of people, among them many Parchams.

Taraki and Amin were exhilarated by their success but understood their vulnerability. They needed help. The day after seizing power, they reproached the Kremlin for not supporting their revolutionary ardor but reaffirmed their commitment to Marxism-Leninism. They said they would build socialism in Afghanistan, and they requested military and economic aid. They told Ambassador Puzanov that they intended to conceal their true aims as

Hafizullah Amin, 1979. Afghanistan's communist leaders,
Amin and Nur Muhammad Taraki (next page), feuded and
schemed until Amin killed Taraki.

long as possible. Moscow could be assured, however, that in the conduct of
their foreign policy they would stay nonaligned yet would cooperate with the
Soviet Union.[242]

The American embassy did not believe that the Soviet Union had played
any role in the coup, and U.S. diplomats were initially uncertain about the
identity of the new leaders, many of whom seemed young, leftist, and nationalistic. Then, on 6 May, Taraki asked U.S. ambassador Theodore Eliot to
meet with him. Taraki "greeted me with a warm handshake and a friendly
smile," Eliot reported. The new head of state was a slim, white-haired, and
engaging man with a professorial bent, and seemed older than his sixty-one
years. He had spent several years in the United States as a young man, and
spoke English. Taraki recalled his years in America happily, wrote Eliot, and
said that Americans and Afghanis shared similar traits.

Taraki's real intent was to convey the magnitude of his ambitions, and he

Nur Muhammad Taraki, 1978

talked passionately, his eyes fiercely intense. A revolution would occur in
Afghanistan, he said. Unlike their predecessors, Taraki and his colleagues
"really care about the poor people of this country and have no interest in
putting money in Swiss banks." They wanted to provide bread, clothing, and
shelter to those in need, to modernize and industrialize, to create good jobs
and attract back to Afghanistan the many thousands of émigrés who, like him
and Amin, had studied abroad. His government, Taraki said, "would judge
other Governments by their willingness to help Afghanistan."[243]

There was no doubt about Soviet willingness to help a new revolutionary
government in Afghanistan. The KGB and the International Department
long had had ties with Taraki, Amin, and Karmal, although Karmal and his
Parcham followers were their favorites. When Taraki and Amin shunted Karmal aside, the Kremlin was dismayed but not deterred. Suslov, Ponomarev,
and Andropov were eager to capitalize on events. Quickly, they sent military
supplies and economic aid; party ideologues and military specialists flocked
to Kabul.[244] By mid-June, the U.S. embassy in Kabul reported to Washington
that the new government "was overwhelmingly dependent on the Soviet
Union. It cannot stay in power without Soviet help. It relies one hundred
percent on the Soviet Union for military supplies and equipment, and increasingly on the Soviet Union for economic assistance . . . and for trade."[245]

But Soviet leaders quickly became displeased. Taraki and Amin purged their Parcham opponents in the government and terrorized the Islamic opposition in the countryside. Soviet ambassador Puzanov ridiculed their methods and criticized their actions. Friends of Karmal escaped to Moscow, where they pled for Soviet intervention.[246] In September, the Politburo sent Ponomarev to Kabul to persuade Taraki and Amin to stop persecuting their adversaries. They were fueling the opposition and endangering the fate of the revolution. They should improve the conditions of their people rather than destroy the lives of their foes, said Ponomarev. Taraki defended his actions and appealed for more assistance. Westerners and Americans, he explained, were tempting them with promises of aid. Ponomarev warned them not to be lured into a trap; the KGB was already receiving reports that Taraki and Amin might have ties with U.S. intelligence services.[247]

In December 1978 the Kremlin invited Taraki and Amin to Moscow, where Brezhnev warmly welcomed them. Their revolution meant a "turning point in the age-old history of Afghanistan," and relations would now assume a "qualitatively new character . . . permeated by a spirit of comradeship and revolutionary solidarity." The new treaty of friendship and cooperation between the two governments, Brezhnev said, was designed to translate the goals of the April revolution into reality.[248]

Soviet officials told the Khalq leaders that they needed to rule with better judgment and more sophistication. They must garner support in the countryside, curtail their repression, accommodate local customs, and build ties with district leaders. Taraki and Amin said they would act with more wisdom, but they needed more aid. Brezhnev and Kosygin assured them they would get it. In February 1979, they sent I. V. Arkhipov, a deputy chairman of the Council of Ministers, to Kabul to work out the details of a generous aid package that would help build infrastructure, promote modernization, and satisfy consumer needs.[249]

Brezhnev emphasized that his support of the Afghan revolution meant no diminution in his quest for peace. He hoped to deepen détente and expand it to the most populous continent on earth—Asia. Preventing conflict needed to be everybody's goal, he said, for if war erupted anywhere on the globe it "would be a terrible calamity for all of mankind."[250]

But in Kabul, Taraki and Amin pursued their own agenda. They continued to act like ruthless thugs, spying on their friends and killing their foes. Aiming to impose a secular, collectivist, centralizing, and modernizing program, they paid little heed to the Islamic sensibilities, local traditions, kinship loyalties, and ethnic ties of their countrymen. In less than a year, insurgencies mounted in many parts of Afghanistan. Islamic fundamentalists of different stripes had already been mobilizing support for more than a decade, first to struggle against Daoud and now, even more fiercely, to rid themselves of the communists in Kabul. They gained inspiration from the success of Ayatollah Khomeini's revolution in Iran and received assistance from backers in Pakistan. On 15 March 1979, they launched a major insurrection in the city of Herat, near the Iranian border. Taraki and Amin appeared unable to put it down. Their soldiers deserted, their regime was endangered, their revolution imperiled. They appealed to Moscow for help.[251]

Late at night on Saturday, 17 March, the senior Politburo member, A. P. Kirilenko, convened his colleagues for an emergency meeting. Brezhnev was at his dacha, too ill to attend. Kirilenko summarized developments: "Bands of saboteurs and terrorists" had "infiltrated from the territory of Pakistan." They had been "trained and armed not only with the participation of Pakistani forces but also of China, the United States of America and Iran." They were committing "atrocities" in Herat. Insurgents from Pakistan and Iran had aligned with domestic counterrevolutionaries who were mostly religious fanatics.

He reported that during the day, a subcommittee—comprised of Gromyko, Ustinov, and Andropov—had worked out a set of recommendations, which now required full Politburo approval. He had talked to Amin earlier in the day and was dumbfounded by his relaxed demeanor, notwithstanding the desertion of infantry and artillery regiments. In Kirilenko's view, the situation was dire, the need for action imperative.

Gromyko took over the meeting. He made it clear that a major decision loomed. Taraki had appealed for military equipment, ammunition, rations, and ground and air support. "This must be understood to mean that the deployment of our forces is required, both land and air forces." In grappling with these requests, Gromyko insisted that the Politburo obey a fundamental axiom: "under no circumstances may we lose Afghanistan. For 60 years now we have lived with Afghanistan in peace and friendship. And if we lose Afghanistan now and it turns against the Soviet Union, this will result in a sharp setback to our foreign policy."

Ustinov and Andropov then presented additional information from military advisers and KGB agents inside Afghanistan. About three thousand in-surgents "are being directed into Afghanistan from Pakistan. These are, in main part, religious fanatics from among the people." While the actual situa-tion was unclear, many ordinary people seemed to be involved in the insur-rection. Kosygin sensed that Amin and Taraki were hiding the true state of affairs. Nevertheless, he then summarized the types of economic assistance and military supplies the Soviet Union could deliver without delay. The Kremlin, he insisted, must provide everything that was needed, but he won-dered aloud what would happen if Soviet troops were required. Whom would they be fighting? "They are all Mohammedans, people of one belief, and their faith is sufficiently strong that they can close ranks on that basis."

Kosygin rightly believed that they needed to talk more fully with Taraki and Amin, ascertain the facts, and persuade them that their own mistakes in Kabul had contributed to their predicament. "They have continued to exe-cute people that do not agree with them; they have killed almost all of the leaders—not only the top leaders, but also those of the middle ranks—of the Parcham party."

The men in the Kremlin possessed only a fraction of the information they needed. Yet they felt impelled to act lest Afghanistan be lost. They blanched, however, at the idea of deploying troops, preferring to take other steps first: economic aid, military supplies, advisers, and maybe even a political settle-ment. If we are talking about deploying forces, said Kirilenko, "the question must be considered thoroughly." Kosygin, they decided, should speak to Taraki and ascertain his will. But Taraki "must be instructed to change his tactics. Executions, torture and so forth cannot be applied on a massive scale." Religious questions and relations with religious communities had to be worked out.

The Politburo discussion on Saturday night, 17 March, led to a clear ob-jective but a murky strategy. Toward the end of the meeting, Gromyko said, "Today the situation in Afghanistan for now is unclear to many of us. Only one thing is clear—we cannot surrender Afghanistan to the enemy. We have to think how to achieve this. Maybe we won't have to introduce troops."[252]

The next day Kosygin called Taraki, who was clear and insistent. "The sit-uation is bad and getting worse." He needed Soviet troops to put down the insurrection in Herat. The population around Herat was not supporting the revolution: "It is almost wholly under the influence of Shiite slogans." We need your arms, your people, Taraki implored. "It is a very complex matter," retorted Kosygin. But complexity was not what Taraki wanted to hear. "Iran and Pakistan are working against us, according to the same plan," he explained. "Hence, if you now launch a decisive attack on Herat, it will be possible to save the revolution." Kosygin saw problems: "The whole world will immediately get to know this. The rebels have portable radio transmitters and will report it directly."

But Soviet assistance was vital, repeated Taraki. His own troops, including Afghan officers trained in the Soviet Union, had turned out to be what he called "Moslem reactionaries. . . . We are unable to rely on them, we have no confidence in them." He wanted Soviet deployments. "We want you to send us Tajiks, Uzbeks, and Turkmens. . . . They could drive tanks. . . . Let them don Afghan costume and wear Afghan badges and no one will recognize them."

Again, Kosygin hesitated: "You are, of course, oversimplifying . . . a complex political and international issue." Any Soviet intervention could not be concealed. "Two hours later the whole world will know about this. Everyone will begin to shout that the Soviet Union's intervention in Afghanistan has begun." But Kosygin assured Taraki that more consultations would go on in Moscow. "We are comrades and are waging a common struggle."[253]

Later that day, 18 March, the Politburo reconvened. Kosygin described his phone conversation. "Almost without realizing it, Comrade Taraki responded that almost nobody does support the government." But Kosygin did convey the essence of Taraki's message: "if Herat falls, then the revolution is doomed." Defense Minister Ustinov reported on his own conversation with Amin, who, like Taraki, insisted that the survival of the revolution depended on Soviet action. Ustinov was frustrated: "What is the problem? Why is this happening? The problem is that the leadership of Afghanistan did not sufficiently appreciate the role of Islamic fundamentalists. It is under the banner of Islam that the soldiers are turning against the government, and an absolute majority, perhaps only with rare exceptions, are believers."

Andropov interceded, and set the tone of all further discussion:

> I have considered all these issues in depth and arrived at the
> conclusion that we must consider very, very seriously, the ques-
> tion of whose cause we will be supporting if we deploy forces
> into Afghanistan. It's completely clear to us that Afghanistan is

not ready at this time to resolve all the issues it faces through socialism. The economy is backward, the Islamic religion predominates, and nearly all the rural population is illiterate. This is not a revolutionary situation.

The Soviet Union must not intervene with Soviet bayonets, he insisted. That "is utterly inadmissible. We cannot take such a risk."

Gromyko strongly agreed. If Soviet troops were used against the Afghan people, the Kremlin would be deemed the aggressor. "All that we have done in recent years with such effort in terms of détente, arms reduction, and much more—all that would be thrown back. China, of course, would be given a nice present. All the nonaligned countries will be against us. In a word serious consequences are to be expected from such an action." Afghanistan "has not been subject to any aggression," Gromyko concluded. "This is its internal affair."

Kirilenko summed up. Yesterday, the Politburo was tempted to intervene. Today "we are all adhering to the position that there is no basis whatsoever for the deployment of forces." All other possible aid would be forthcoming, but the Soviet Union would not intervene. We must not deploy troops, Ustinov repeated. There "are no plusses for us at all" in doing so, Kosygin agreed. Scores of countries would "come out against us."[254]

The next day, the Politburo met again, with Brezhnev attending. He put his imprimatur on what his comrades had decided. "The time is not right for us to become entangled in that war [in Afghanistan]." Taraki would be invited to Moscow, and Brezhnev himself would explain the situation to him.

Gromyko recapitulated the most recent events around Herat, which now looked more favorable. Yet vigilance was required: "We may assume with full justification that all these events, not only in Afghanistan but in the neighboring governments, including those in China, are being directed by the hand of the USA," Gromyko said. "China, Pakistan, and Iran are playing a role here that is not all that far behind."

But vigilance did not mean junking détente. Too much was at stake. Should the Soviet Union send troops to Afghanistan, declared Gromyko:

We would be largely throwing away everything we achieved with such difficulty, particularly détente, the SALT-II negotiations would fly by the wayside, there would be no signing of an agreement (and however you look at it that is for us the greatest political priority), there would be no meeting of Leonid Ilych with Carter, . . . and our relations with Western countries, particularly the FRG, would be spoiled.

Andropov concurred: "To deploy our troops would mean to wage war against the people, to crush the people, to shoot at the people. We will look like aggressors, and we cannot permit that to occur."[255]

Taraki was summoned to the Kremlin to meet with Kosygin, Gromyko, Ustinov, and Ponomarev. Afterward, Brezhnev saw him. Our friendship is "calculated for [the] ages," said Kosygin, but Taraki needed to "widen the social support" of his regime and stop alienating the people. Then Kosygin broke the news: "The deployment of our forces in the territory of Afghanistan would immediately arouse the international community and would invite sharply unfavorable multipronged consequences."[256] Brezhnev reiterated these themes. The main thing, he stressed, "is political work among the masses." Repression was a "sharp weapon," he added, and "must be applied extremely cautiously, and only in the case when there are serious legal grounds for it."[257]

The Vienna Summit

During the winter and spring of 1979, Brezhnev and Carter were both fighting an uphill battle. They were profoundly wary of each other's moves, and they both struggled with defense officials, military chiefs, intelligence analysts, and personal advisers whose main goal was to ensure that the prospective foe not gain a strategic advantage or first-strike capability. Yet they believed that détente was in their nations' interests. They shared a similar view: they should contain the arms race, expand the purview of their cooperation, and allow their systems to compete peacefully for the soul of mankind. Each believed his system would prevail.

Brezhnev suspected that the Americans were carrying out a deviously Machiavellian diplomacy. Imperialists did that type of thing. He was angry that the Chinese had attacked Vietnam, Russia's ally, shortly after the Chinese leaders visited the United States. He warned Carter against colluding with Beijing.[258]

Brezhnev was also aggrieved by Carter's recent trip to the Middle East and his mediation of an Israeli-Egyptian peace agreement that disregarded the Palestinian issue. "What kind of peace is that if more than three million people who have the inalienable right to have a roof over their heads, to have their own . . . small state, are deprived of that right?" The rest of the Arab world was agitated, and Brezhnev predicted that peace would not come to the Middle East. Worse yet, he chastised Carter for operating "on the sly, by-passing the Soviet Union" in a region of the world that was so close to the U.S.S.R.[259]

In other letters to the president, Brezhnev complained about American military exercises and the prospective deployment of a new, land-based inter-continental ballistic missile, the MX, which not only carried multiple war-heads but could also be launched from mobile vehicles, making it much less vulnerable to a preemptive attack. The construction of new silos for these missiles, said Brezhnev, "would be absolutely incompatible with the corre-sponding provision of the [SALT] draft treaty."[260]

Brezhnev's military advisers exerted unrelenting pressure on Soviet diplo-mats and on Brezhnev himself to guard against American efforts to outsmart the Soviet negotiators on the complex technical issues involved in the strate-gic arms talks, fearing that not even Gromyko and Dobrynin could grasp the details or even the underlying concepts.[261] The Soviet general staff originated the responses to U.S. arms control initiatives that were then vetted by experts on two interdepartmental committees in Moscow dominated by high-level officials with a defense mind-set. The foreign ministry was often sidelined and ignored. But the committee members were not indifferent to the benefits of arms control for Soviet self-interest. They wanted to thwart the develop-ment of U.S. weapons, such as cruise missiles, and get rid of the U.S. forward base systems in Europe. In return, they knew they had to make reciprocal concessions. But in hammering out policy recommendations, they faced for-midable technical and definitional matters, many of which got more compli-cated as the negotiations advanced. For example, what precisely constituted a "new" missile? What information was essential for verification? To what ex-tent could they encrypt, or scramble, electronic data sent back to earth dur-ing test flights? These questions baffled even the best-intentioned officials. The military experts, at least in their view, tried to comply with Brezhnev's position that the Soviet Union was aiming not for superiority but for parity.

But they saw U.S. proposals "as a direct attempt to destroy the parity which we had just achieved," said General Detinov.[262]

Suspicions of this sort were embedded in the psyche of Soviet officials like Brezhnev. How could Americans think that he wanted Soviet military superiority? "I repeat again and again that we do not seek military superiority." But he believed that the Americans would not take him seriously or respect his sensibilities, interests, and goals unless he, too, could bargain from a position of strength.[263] Strength, however, was always a relative concept, blurred by rapidly evolving concepts of opportunity and threat in a turbulent world.

Brezhnev's conception of prudent strength made Carter's life miserable. The president invited Dobrynin to his office on 27 February 1979, and reiterated his hopes for a SALT agreement.[264] But Brzezinski and Defense Secretary Brown warned the president that the military balance was tipping in favor of the Soviet Union. "The trend in strategic forces has favored the Soviet Union since the mid-1960s," Brzezinski wrote Carter a month later. "Since January 1977, however, this trend has become significantly more pronounced."[265] Six weeks later, a net assessment conducted by the Defense Department was even more ominous. After Brown discussed the numbers with the Joint Chiefs and with officials in the State Department, Brzezinski informed the president that the administration could not fulfill its strategic objectives. Given current trends, the United States could not maintain essential equivalence with the Soviet Union or respond effectively to a Warsaw Pact attack or defend the Persian Gulf. "No matter what program decisions we make to modernize our strategic forces, in the early 80's we are likely to be perceived as having less than essential equivalence with the Soviets."[266]

Brzezinski bluntly told Carter that he was seen as weak. "Unfairly, the mass media have stimulated the widespread perception of this Administration as being indecisive in regard to foreign policy issues."[267] This view jeopardized the chances for the SALT treaty to be ratified. Public opinion polls showed that the American people favored SALT but were worried about the Soviet Union's mounting strength and frustrated by the oil shortages and price hikes. Powerful senators, meanwhile, were lining up against SALT, most notably Henry Jackson. The president's personal popularity plummeted, with his favorable ratings dropping to 33 percent. Patrick Caddell, his main pollster, was shocked. "Frustration with the President is moving toward personal hostility," he warned. "This suggests a qualitative change in public attitude that can only be viewed with alarm."[268]

Yet Carter pushed forward, circumspectly to be sure, but forward still. He would not shape his foreign policy by poll numbers. If nothing else, he was dogged, determined, tenacious. Tenacity had enabled him to achieve Senate ratification of the Panama Canal treaty and had paid off in a Middle East breakthrough and an Egyptian-Israeli peace agreement. SALT, he believed, made sense. He would push for it.

Not indifferent to the formidable military machine that the Soviets were putting together, he was determined to keep up. He approved the MX, even though he found it "nauseating" to think about the waste of money. He bowed to JCS and CIA insistence that he demand limits on the Backfire bomber and that he prevent Soviet encryption of data necessary for verification. He knew there would be no Senate ratification of SALT if there were doubts about U.S. capabilities to monitor Soviet compliance.[269]

Nor was he indifferent to Soviet activities in the third world, but he did not think the Kremlin was gaining undue influence there. The United States had normalized relations with China; improved relations with India; preserved good ties with Japan; won a new friend in the Middle East, Egypt; and reconciled differences with its NATO allies. Vietnam and Iran were setbacks, but they were not decisive.[270]

In Carter's view, the United States was not losing the competition with the Kremlin. The Soviet economy was faltering. For the first time since World War II, U.S. growth, despite problems afflicting the American economy, surpassed that of the Soviet Union.[271] "We see every reason to believe that a continued decline in the rate of economic growth of the Soviet Union is inevitable through most of the 1980s," said Admiral Stansfield Turner, director of the CIA. Eventually, the Kremlin would face agonizing choices. "The low growth rates we envision for the mid-1980s could squeeze their resources to the point where something has to give." Turner did not say that excessive Soviet defense spending would change in the short term, but he suggested that it could not be sustained in the long run.[272]

Carter did not believe in American weakness. The United States was much stronger than the Soviet Union, he told Bill Moyers in an interview in late 1978. He wanted cooperation, but he was undaunted by competition so long as it was peaceful. He had as much faith in American values as Brezhnev had in his own. "Our values and our democratic way of life have a magnetic appeal for people all over the world." A "materialistic and a totalitarian philosophy" could never match America's, he said.[273]

When the details on the SALT agreement were finally hammered out by Vance and Dobrynin in May 1979, Carter began preparing carefully for the long-awaited summit conference scheduled to take place in Vienna the next month. Brezhnev's health would be a limiting factor, and Carter was advised not to interrupt the Soviet leader when he read his statements; whether Brezhnev could or would engage in a real conversation after he spoke was unknown. The president's expectations should be modest, Vance cautioned. "Actual negotiations on central issues" were not likely to occur. "He is old, human, and emotional," Harriman told Carter. Yet Brezhnev was not as frail as some people contended, and he would be fully in charge of the Soviet delegation. He would seek to discern the president's motives and he would be influenced by Carter's personal style. The president should deal with him warmly, informally, Harriman advised. Brezhnev was not interested in details. His one consuming preoccupation was to spare his people the agony of another invasion, or worse, a nuclear war.[274]

Carter went to Vienna with conflicting impulses. He knew he had to appear tough lest domestic critics skewer him for his meekness and timidity. He had to be unyielding on the Backfire and on encryption in order to please his intelligence and defense advisers. Yet his overriding goal, as Vance put it, was to establish a rapport with Soviet leaders that would sustain détente after Brezhnev was gone. He "wanted the Soviets to know that the United States was driven by a desire for peace," that he would treat them as equals, that neither nation could achieve nuclear superiority, and that, in his view, the arms race made no sense. He wanted them to know that he was prepared to commence work immediately on SALT III, which must encompass restrictions on intermediate-range missiles in Europe as well as greater reductions in intercontinental missiles. He wanted them to know that if détente was to survive, the Soviet Union had to exercise restraint in Africa and Southeast Asia and recognize that the Persian Gulf was a vital interest to the United States and the Kremlin must not intervene there.

When he met with Brezhnev in Vienna, he conveyed these views cogently and directly, even sharply at times.[275] In contrast, Brezhnev was weak and fragile. His hair was slicked back, his face puffed up. He read his prepared text out loud, and his interpreter, when necessary, picked through his notes and pointed out what else he needed to say. Brezhnev could not discuss anything at length, but he occasionally expressed his strong views. When issues got complicated, Gromyko intervened. The sessions had to be short, not more than two hours. Informal conversation was not easy. Brezhnev could no longer discuss matters late into the night, as he had with Nixon and Ford. Dinners could not be delayed. He retired early. He was an old man who took offense easily. He complained that the menu for the meal at the U.S. embassy had been printed only in English. The Soviets were more sensitive, he said, printing their menus in English as well as Russian. But sick and old as he was, the Americans could not mistake that Brezhnev's colleagues still deferred to him.[276]

Brezhnev emphasized to the Americans that the Kremlin might support national liberation movements but did not foment them. It was simply a "fairy tale" to think Moscow could orchestrate these movements. They were inscribed in the fabric of history. Nor did the Soviet Union seek military supremacy. As chairman of the Defense Council, Brezhnev told Carter, he could say with certainty that the Soviet Union did not want war, any war. The Kremlin rejected the first use of nuclear or conventional weapons. Détente, Brezhnev emphasized, must rest on the principles of equal security, respect for each other's legitimate interests, and noninterference in internal affairs—nothing more, nothing less. He did not understand why the Americans were launching a rearmament program. He objected to the modernization of NATO's forces and to the retention of American forward-based nuclear systems in Europe. The president might dwell on an arc of crisis stretching from southwest Asia through the Persian Gulf and the Middle East to East Africa, but Brezhnev wanted Carter to understand that Europe was of primary importance to the U.S.S.R. "It was the chief concern of the Soviet leadership that neither the Soviet people nor any other people in Europe ever live through what the Soviet people had experienced in the years of World War II as a result of the Hitlerite aggression."[277]

These largely predictable exchanges were carefully scripted. Brezhnev and Carter did not deviate significantly from any position that their diplomats had been presenting for the prior two years. The state of play between the two governments was vividly illuminated when Secretary of Defense Brown and his Soviet counterpart, Marshal Ustinov, met in a special session to try to break the long-standing deadlock in negotiations on the reduction of conventional troops in the heart of Europe, the Mutual and Balanced Force Reduction (MBFR) negotiations. Brezhnev and Gromyko had given Ustinov a set of concessions to put on the table, but when Brown and Ustinov started talking they arrived at the same impasse where their subordinates had been stuck for years. Brown insisted that the Soviets either clarify their data regarding existing force structures or accept the U.S. numbers. Ustinov said that he had no obligation to examine the disputed data but wanted to discuss force reductions. He then conveyed the Kremlin's new position. The Soviet Union "is offering to reduce twice as many troops as the U.S. side," emphasized Marshal Nikolai Ogarkov, Ustinov's associate. Brown was not impressed. He wanted data. The frustration of Soviet officials was palpable. Ogarkov snapped, "You are military people. Be specific. Make a proposal." Brown would not budge. The American people seem to be "interested in the balance of forces," commented Ustinov, "the Soviet people . . . in the relaxation of tensions." They got nowhere.[278]

As the heads of state of the two most powerful nations on earth, Carter and Brezhnev shared a special burden that no one else could really appreciate. Each wanted the other to know that he had a unique responsibility to control the arms race, avoid nuclear war, and sustain détente. Carter went out of his way in the first session to "salute" Brezhnev "for initiating the concept of détente."[279] And Brezhnev made his personal attitudes clear. Before the negotiating sessions began, the two paid their respects to the president of Austria, and as they left his office they exchanged a few personal words. Brezhnev put his hand on the president's shoulder and said, "If we do not succeed, God will not forgive us." Carter was touched. "As we walked down a few steps to leave the building," he remembered later, "Brezhnev kept his hand on my arm or shoulder to steady himself. This simple and apparently natural gesture bridged the gap between us more effectively than any official talk."[280]

At the conference table, Brezhnev repeated the official Soviet position on almost every issue but made it clear that détente meant a great deal to him personally. He said he did not like it when U.S. officials called the Soviet Union an adversary. American and Soviet values might compete, but his own purpose was to expand cooperation.[281] At the closing ceremony, he hugged Carter, a gesture that had not been scripted. Carter was "quite a nice guy, after all," he whispered to his comrades.[282]

Brezhnev and Carter at the Vienna summit, 1979. Brezhnev,
by then very frail, took Carter's arm for support—a gesture
Carter felt had real significance.

Carter sensed Brezhnev's warmth even while he felt the heat of his domestic critics. Hamilton Jordan, Carter's most intimate political adviser, warned
Ambassador Dobrynin that Carter must avoid "looking like a leader who
flung himself carelessly into the embrace of the Russians."[283] But the president thought he had established a good rapport with Brezhnev, that he
understood him. After Vienna, he recalled, "there were strong feelings of
cooperation between us." He gave Brezhnev a handwritten note: "I look forward . . . to our next meeting, when we will be able to build on this new
foundation which we have established."[284]

Nicaragua and Afghanistan

The world was not kind to Brezhnev and Carter, however.

Back in the United States, Carter delivered a speech to a joint session of Congress. Failure to ratify SALT, he warned, would intensify the strategic arms race, impose huge burdens on the U.S. budget, increase the danger of nuclear proliferation, and accentuate tensions between East and West. The treaty was not a panacea to all the world's problems, Carter acknowledged. It "will not end the competition between the United States and the Soviet Union. That competition is based on fundamentally different visions of human society and human destiny," but SALT regulated the competition and channeled it in peaceful directions, much to America's advantage. "The ultimate future of the human race lies not with tyranny, but with freedom," Carter assured Congress, "not with war, but with peace." With SALT ratified and the Cold War reconfigured, the American people could shift their focus to domestic priorities, such as the energy crisis.[285]

Turbulence abroad undercut the president's plans. Just days before Carter had gone to Vienna, Brzezinski told him that Central America "now demands our highest attention." There was increasing violence and political polarization throughout the area. The Alliance for Progress that Democratic administrations had touted in the 1960s had not made a dent in the region's poverty; nor had it ended U.S. military assistance to numerous right-wing authoritarian leaders and murderous despots. In Nicaragua, "Communist guerillas could seize power," Brzezinski now warned Carter. He was alluding to the Sandinista National Liberation Front, which had been struggling to overthrow the dictatorship of President Anastasio Somoza Debayle, whom the United States had long supported. At a meeting of top U.S. officials on 11 June, Frank Carlucci, deputy director of the CIA, reported that Somoza would not last out his term, which would expire in 1981. Businessmen, clergymen, and liberal reformers wanted to get rid of him, as did many impoverished peasants, rural workers, students, and urban laborers, who rallied behind the Sandinista movement. The moderate center "is being chewed up," said Carlucci. "The left is much stronger than before." And Cuba's involvement was escalating.[286]

By the time Carter returned from Vienna, the worrisome situation in Nicaragua had become an acute crisis. For two years, he had been trying to throw U.S. support behind the moderate center, seeking to champion human rights without risking a radical takeover. But now his options were narrowing. On 23 June, Brzezinski said he faced a grave decision in Nicaragua: "either a Castroist Sandinista victory" or a "US military intervention." The latter would "destroy the credibility" of U.S. policies toward the third world and provoke "universal condemnation."[287]

Brzezinski did not believe Somoza would last another week, but he, Vance, Brown, and Turner still tried to design viable options to stop the Sandinistas from gaining power.[288] Their efforts failed. By the time Carter's diplomats arranged for Somoza to step down in mid-July 1979, the Sandinistas were in control of a coalition government. More pressing issues now arose. Robert A. Pastor, the Latin American expert on Brzezinski's staff, starkly outlined them: "how can we keep Nicaragua from becoming another Cuba, and how can we keep the rest of Central America from becoming another Nicaragua?"[289]

Secretary of Defense Brown highlighted these concerns to the president. The administration must consider "what we might do to prevent the destabilization of neighboring countries, especially El Salvador, Guatemala, and Honduras." If the Sandinistas consolidated their power in Nicaragua and followed a Marxist-Leninist course, leftist forces in neighboring countries would be emboldened and the rightists would be terrified. More civil strife would ensue, and America's vulnerability would grow. Brown recommended that the administration relax its support for human rights and back moderate military leaders in Guatemala, Honduras, and El Salvador.[290]

Pastor objected. Brown's arguments, Pastor wrote Brzezinski, rested "on a weak and perhaps erroneous premise: that U.S. support is necessary and sufficient to stabilize these regimes." He emphasized that the crisis in Central America stemmed from the "increasingly widespread alienation of the people of Central America from their governments; we are witnessing the wholesale delegitimization of narrow-based military governments." The United States needed to promote elections, human rights, and reforms, he insisted, and different options must be tried in different countries "until we find the one that works." The United States must not become discouraged and withdraw. "And we need to counter everything the Cubans do."[291]

On 20 July, the National Security Council met to discuss the crisis in Central America. "The issue is whether El Salvador, Honduras, and Guatemala can gradually and peacefully broaden their bases of support by making the kinds of reforms necessary to deal with the inequities and inadequacies of the socio-economic and political structures. The alternative is revolution as just occurred in Nicaragua."[292] Brown's concerns were not ignored, and everyone agreed that the current leaders of these countries had to be supported. But support depended on reform, as Pastor urged. Summing up the meeting, Brzezinski wrote Carter, "We must get in back of the forces of change in El Salvador and Honduras, and to a lesser extent in Guatemala in order to prevent a repetition of the Nicaragua crisis."[293]

This advice accorded with the predilections of the president. He hated dictatorships. He would not support them unconditionally. Nor would he intervene militarily to defend them against the forces of change. Right-wing critics might claim that Castro was fomenting unrest and seeking to topple America's traditional allies, but Carter thought otherwise. "It's a mistake" to think that Castro was responsible for the revolution in Nicaragua, he told a press conference. Somoza had "lost the confidence of the Nicaraguan people." U.S. policy must allow the Nicaraguan people to choose their own leaders. His administration, Carter declared, would try to improve relations with the Sandinistas. On a special flight carrying emergency food and medicines, the U.S. ambassador returned to Managua to offer his credentials. In the fall of 1979, Carter asked Congress to appropriate seventy-five million dollars for assistance to the new government.[294]

The region was astir with revolutionary unrest, and the Kremlin knew it had new opportunities to exploit. Carter, however, did not lose sight of his own priorities. In the midst of the Nicaraguan crisis, he addressed the nation on 15 July:

> I want to speak to you first tonight about a subject even more serious than energy or inflation. I want to talk to you right now about a fundamental threat to American democracy. . . .
>
> The threat is nearly invisible. . . . It is a crisis of confidence. It is a crisis that strikes at the very heart and soul and spirit of our national will. We can see this crisis in the growing doubt about the meaning of our own lives and in the loss of a unity of purpose for our Nation.

The erosion of our confidence in the future is threatening to destroy the social and the political fabric of America.[295]

President Carter now was very clear about his overriding priority: The United States must deal with the energy crisis. It must cut its consumption of foreign oil and boost its production of alternative energy sources. The American people must overcome drift, stagnation, and paralysis, and regain their self-confidence by tackling their most difficult challenge. If they needed a more streamlined, focused, and disciplined leadership, Carter would provide it. He soon outlined a number of changes in his cabinet and staff. But he did not blame the country's angst on foreign foes or hostile ideologies, nor hold his national security team responsible for the Sandinista revolution in Nicaragua or the Islamic upheaval in Iran. Ferment, he knew, was sewn into the seams of the international system.

His equanimity in the face of growing turbulence abroad stirred the passions of political adversaries and animated the concerns of his national security advisers. The administration, Brzezinski warned Carter on 27 July, would be foolish to ignore Cuba's growing subversive activities, which were becoming a political issue inside the United States. "Castro's successes abroad, and Soviet sponsorship of his activities, now confront us with an increasingly difficult foreign policy problem."

Brzezinski wanted more information on Soviet military deliveries to Cuba and on Cuban activities in Central America and Africa, which he was sure were provocative. "Whether Cuba is acting as a Soviet surrogate, partner or (in my view least likely) simply dragging the USSR along, the result is clear: Castro's foreign activities have well served Soviet interests and created far-reaching problems for us—not the least of which has been a crisis of confidence among our friends (e.g., Saudi Arabia, Sudan, several Latin American governments) as to whether we can or will counter Cuban/Soviet interventionism." The United States had to make it clear by deeds as well as words "that we hold the Soviet Union accountable for Cuba's intensified activity. The Soviets otherwise have an absolutely cost-free and risk-free device for increasing our difficulties."[296]

Once U.S. intelligence homed in on Cuba, it illuminated something ominous there—a "combat brigade" of Soviet soldiers. Information about this brigade was quickly disseminated among high-level officials in the Carter administration, who feared that a news story about its existence would jeopardize Senate ratification of the SALT II agreement. Vance and Under Secretary of State David Newsom learned that the news had already been leaked and would appear in the press. They contacted interested senators, such as the Democrat Frank Church, chairman of the Senate Foreign Relations Committee, and Richard Stone, a Democrat from Florida, hoping to modulate congressional and public reaction to the worrying report. News of a Soviet combat brigade in Cuba would be seen as another sign not only of Soviet audacity but also of Soviet mendacity, Vance said, a violation of the promise Khrushchev had made to Kennedy in 1962 to remove offensive Soviet military capabilities from the Caribbean island.[297]

Notwithstanding Vance's hopes, senators Church and Stone used the information to boost their popularity in their home states rather than support the administration's battle for SALT ratification. Facing a very tough reelection campaign and ridiculed by right-wingers for his dovish positions, Church inflamed the situation by saying that SALT hearings could not continue until the Soviet Union allayed U.S. concerns about Cuba. On Labor Day weekend, the story was plastered on the front pages of the country's newspapers. Carter's opponents gleefully used it to revive their charges of presidential meekness and U.S. weakness. Vance had to spend a month seeking clarification from the Kremlin, and Carter a month figuring out how to handle the matter.[298] Did the brigade amount to a significant threat? Did it constitute a breach of previous Soviet commitments? Should SALT be sandbagged?

Brzezinski launched a ferocious private campaign to get Carter to toughen up. He wanted the president to consider why his administration got so little credit for genuine foreign-policy accomplishments, why "public opinion in the world at large, notably in allied countries, [views] this Administration as perhaps the most timid since World War II." Everywhere, the Soviet Union was seen as "assertive" and the United States as "acquiescent," he wrote. And now much of the world "is watching to see how we will behave on the Soviet/Cuban issue." In Latin America, "revolutionary fervor is on the rise, and we have not been able to give those who want to rely on us a sense of security." People at home and abroad were waiting to see Carter exercise effective leadership. The country "craves, and our national security needs, both a more assertive tone and [a] more assertive substance to our foreign policy," Brzezinski insisted. He listed options, including sending Defense Secretary Brown to China to discuss technology transfer and arms sales, maximizing Cuban economic problems, and accelerating U.S. broadcasts to Soviet national minorities, especially Ukrainians and Muslims.[299]

Carter's national security adviser did not want a confrontation over the Soviet brigade in Cuba. From the start, Brzezinski sensed this was a phony issue, more important for its domestic political fallout than for its actual military implications. But he insisted that Carter exploit the opportunity to demonstrate strength and impress his political foes at home, including Senator Ted Kennedy, who was preparing to run against Carter for the Democratic nomination. I know it will "irritate you" to read this, Brzezinski wrote Carter, but it was necessary to build up U.S. defenses, work on a rapid-deployment force, and convey a real determination to use force when necessary. The French had a saying, the cosmopolitan Brzezinski wrote his provincial boss, "*c'est le ton qui fait la chanson* (it's the tone that makes the song)."[300]

Irritate the president he did, but he did not convince him. Brzezinski assailed the incompetence of the State Department, but Carter nonetheless followed the course advised by Vance, and throughout September, Vance demanded that the intelligence agencies review their previous data regarding Soviet troops in Cuba. As they did, it became increasingly clear that Soviet ground forces had been in Cuba for years, probably since 1962, and that previous Democratic and Republican administrations had simply accepted their presence without alarm. No "combat brigade" had recently been inserted; there was no new threat.[301] But a month of adverse publicity about this boded ill for Senate ratification of SALT II.

In a speech to the American people on 1 October, Carter acknowledged that the brigade issue "was not a simple or easy subject." It was a "serious matter" that had to be put in larger perspective. The important philosophical differences between the Soviet Union and the United States had to be recognized, and while competition between the two would continue, the need for cooperation on matters of mutual interest, such as controlling the arms race, trumped other concerns. The Kremlin had provided appropriate assurances that its ground forces in Cuba would not be increased or its mission, which was solely to train the Cuban armed forces, altered. This was good news, but Carter announced he was taking measures of his own, creating a joint Caribbean task force with military headquarters in Key West to monitor the situation and, if necessary, take swift action. He would authorize military exercises to be conducted in the Caribbean; provide additional economic assistance to the Caribbean region to help "troubled peoples . . . resist social turmoil and possible communist domination"; reinforce the U.S. naval presence in the Indian Ocean; and augment the capabilities of America's rapid-deployment forces.

But Carter's major point was that the brigade issue was certainly no reason for a return to the Cold War. "A confrontation might be emotionally satisfying for a few days or weeks for some people, but it would be destructive to the national interest and to the security of the United States." Toward the end of his speech, he emphasized, "We must not play politics with the security of the United States[,] . . . with the survival of the human race[,] . . . with SALT II. It is much too important for that—too vital to our country, to our allies, and to the cause of peace."[302]

In a world brewing with danger, Carter remained steadfast. He did not ignore the many warnings of Soviet military aggrandizement, but he refused to be alarmed by them. He would spend more on defense, deploy the MX missile, and configure a force for missions in the Middle East and Persian Gulf. He would send Defense Secretary Brown to China to signal the further evolution of a new strategic orientation and would ask his NATO allies to accept a new generation of nuclear weapons, including cruise missiles and Pershing IIs. But he would not lose sight of détente or abandon SALT II.

He was delighted when he met the new Pope. Imbued with a hatred of communism and a love of God, the former cardinal of Krakow Karol Wojtyla was an omen of the times. In the struggle for the soul of mankind, the president and the Pope knew that atheistic communism could not meet the yearnings of people seeking meaning, fulfillment, and opportunity. "The Soviets subjugate the rights of an individual human being to the rights of the state," Carter told a news conference on 9 October. "We do just the opposite. The Soviets are an atheistic nation; we have deep and fundamental religious beliefs. . . . So, I don't have any fear or any trepidation" about competing with the Soviets peacefully.[303]

Carter was well aware of the increasing ferment in Eastern Europe, notably in Poland. Developments there, Brzezinski informed him, represented "a significant change in the Soviet world and a sign of decreasing Soviet control." Despite its formidable military capabilities, the Soviet Union was internally weak and bureaucratically stagnant, and it was experiencing a "dramatic drop in its ideological appeal." These weaknesses could be capitalized on, argued Brzezinski, and with shrewd policies, the United States might be able to drive a wedge between the Kremlin and some of its satellites.[304] Hard times inside the Soviet Union made it a propitious moment to "aggravate ethnic conflict," "erode the authority of the party, and raise questions about the efficacy of the Soviet economic system," the CIA reported. According to U.S. intelligence analysts, Marxist-Leninist ideology was "waning as a force capable of mobilizing the population to make personal sacrifices for the sake of loftier social goals."[305]

But "malaise" also afflicted Western societies. Carter's willingness to dwell on this reality elicited nothing but scorn from his many critics, who blamed him for the malaise.[306] His approval ratings continued to be dismal, hovering around 30 percent. The pollster Patrick Caddell warned him that he was significantly trailing Ted Kennedy in the polls. While Americans admired his character, Caddell said, they deplored his leadership. "People make the judgment everyday . . . *that events dominate us, that we react to, not lead events.*" Unless Carter demonstrated more boldness and exercised more leadership, he would lose the next election. "I implore you to take action," Caddell wrote.[307]

Just as Caddell was finishing his analysis, events in Iran took a dramatic turn for the worse. For months, the Iranian revolution had been following a more radical Islamic course, and invective against America had soared. Revolutionary leaders warned Washington not to allow the exiled and now dying Shah to enter the United States for medical treatment, but Carter finally assented to pleas from the Shah's many influential friends. Iranians were incensed. On 1 November, more than two million demonstrators marched through the streets of Tehran shouting, "Death to America!" Three days later, young Islamic radicals seized the U.S. embassy, and Ayatollah Khomeini did nothing to stop them. The days and weeks passed, but the fifty-two hostages were not freed. America's impotency and Carter's weakness became ever more glaring. Hamilton Jordan, now serving as the president's chief of staff, wrote to him, "The American people are frustrated at our country's inability to do anything to free the prisoners and retaliate in a fashion that makes us feel better about ourselves."[308]

Carter grasped "the gravity of the situation" and appealed to the Iranian government to free the hostages. He froze Iranian assets in the United States and suspended the importation of Iranian oil. The United States, he said, "will never allow any foreign country to dictate any American policy," and he warned that "grave consequences" would ensue if the hostages were harmed. When he heard that the Ayatollah might put Americans on trial for spying, he grew angry. He assailed the Islamic fundamentalists who ruled Tehran:

> The actions of Iran have shocked the civilized world. For a government to applaud mob violence and terrorism, for a government actually to support and, in effect, participate in the taking and the holding of hostages is unprecedented in human history. This violates not only the most fundamental precepts of international law but also the common ethical and religious heritage of humanity. There is no recognized religious faith on earth which condones kidnapping. There is no recognized religious faith on Earth which condones blackmail.[309]

Iranians marching U.S. hostages, 1979.
The hostage crisis highlighted U.S. vulnerabilities.

The American people rallied behind their president but yearned for bolder leadership. Hamilton Jordan was taken aback when his twelve-year-old nephew told him that his "friends at school say that Jimmy Carter doesn't have the guts to do anything." Carter knew what people were thinking. If "I asked the people of Plains [his hometown] what I should do, every last one of them would say, 'Bomb Iran!' "[310]

Yet Carter appealed for calm. He asked Americans not to mistreat Iranians residing in the United States and to reduce oil consumption. When taunted at a news conference—Khomeini "doesn't believe you have the guts to use military force"—Carter responded with restraint. All options were open, he said, but he preferred to resolve the crisis peacefully. Americans had learned in Vietnam, he said on 13 December, "that to become unnecessarily involved in the internal affairs of another country when our own security is not directly threatened is a serious mistake."[311] But he did not rule out the use of force.

Brzezinski and Brown prodded him to explore military options. Brzezinski was not so worried about the hostages as about the erosion of America's position in the Persian Gulf. "I recommended a number of steps designed to enhance our security presence in the region and to place greater pressure on Iran, including the possibility of assisting efforts to unseat Khomeini."[312] On the bottom of one of Brzezinski's memos, Carter wrote that his advisers should consider everything "that Khomeini would not want to see occur and which would not incite condemnation of U.S. by other nations."[313]

The president was sorely tempted to take action, yet he was a man of tenacious self-discipline, and he wanted détente to survive. He held his fire and waited. He was still hoping to welcome Brezhnev to Washington after SALT II was ratified.[314]

Carter expected the Kremlin to share his priorities and show equal self-restraint. He was wrong. Brezhnev and his colleagues were eager to capitalize on America's distress both in Central America and in the Persian Gulf. Brezhnev sent a telegram to the new Sandinista government in Managua congratulating the leadership on its heroic victory. On 8 August, an Aeroflot IL-76 landed in Nicaragua with medical supplies and baby food donated by Soviet trade unions.[315] In an emblematic speech on 18 September, Mikhail Suslov, the Kremlin's leading ideologue, endorsed SALT, embraced peace, and heralded the "defeat of imperialist and neocolonialist forces" in Angola,

Ethiopia, Mozambique, Afghanistan, Kampuchea, and Nicaragua. "In the midst of the complex processes of world development one can distinctly see the chief trend of the modern era—the growth of [socialism] . . . and the steady development of revolutionary processes in the world."[316]

But decolonization, revolutionary nationalism, and capitalist disorder bred danger as well as opportunity. Vigilance was a hallmark of Marxism-Leninism, and Soviet leaders never ceased reminding one another that they must be vigilant.[317] The insurgency in Afghanistan made them wary. The truculence, incompetence, and undependability of their new comrades in Kabul heightened their sense of threat. Moreover, political Islam might become a contagion. On 12 June 1979, Ayatollah Khomeini told the Soviet ambassador in Tehran, "We hope that Afghanistan, which is an Islamic country, will solve its problems through Islamic means. Soviet interference there will have an effect on Iran. We demand that the USSR should not interfere in Afghanistan."[318]

The Kremlin did not want to intervene militarily. Brezhnev assigned responsibility to a committee of the Politburo composed of Gromyko, Ustinov, Andropov, and Ponomarev. Their reports endorsed military assistance and economic aid, and called for more Soviet advisers to work with the Afghan army and for more Soviet experts to staff the Afghan government ministries. But they knew that success depended on the Kabul government's willingness to widen its political base, distribute land, and foster economic growth. The Kremlin wanted Taraki and Amin to institute reforms and stop their murderous actions. Soviet officials called for more "law and order, based on revolutionary legality." Repressive measures must be constrained. "A person's fate should not be decided on the basis of circumstantial and unverifiable evidence." The Muslim clergy should be handled adroitly. Their "influence could be diminished by encouraging religious freedom and demonstrating that the new power does not persecute the clergy as a class, but only punishes those who act against the revolutionary system."[319]

But Taraki and Amin continued to want more than economic aid and military assistance from the U.S.S.R. In repeated meetings with Soviet officials, they requested paratroop divisions and combat units because, they said, Iran and Pakistan as well as Saudi Arabia, China, and the United States were supporting the insurrectionists.[320] Soviet officials declined. They did not think that the risks were worth the sacrifices or that Taraki and Amin merited such bold measures. The problems of the Afghan government, concluded Andropov, Ustinov, Gromyko, and Ponomarev, were only "becoming more intense" because of the abuses committed by its leaders. "In the Party and the government a collegial leadership is lacking, all power in fact is concentrated in the hands of N. M. Taraki and H. Amin, who none too rarely make mistakes and commit violations of legality."[321]

In late August 1979, Kremlin officials decided that Amin had to be removed from power. He was conspiring against Taraki and behaving treacherously. KGB officers in Kabul had tired of dealing with him. He was regarded as the person most responsible for repressing the people and employing military means to tackle problems that were essentially political, economic, and social.[322] On his way to a conference of heads of state of "non-aligned" nations in Havana in September, and on his way back to Kabul, Taraki stopped in Moscow and talked to Kremlin leaders. On 10 September, Brezhnev read to him from notes prepared by the KGB and approved by Andropov, Ustinov, Gromyko, and Ponomarev. "The concentration of excessive power in the hands of others, even your closest aides, could be dangerous to the fate of the revolution," said Brezhnev. As he continued, the message became unmistakably clear: Taraki must get rid of Amin.[323]

An elaborate plot was concocted in the Kremlin. Upon his arrival in Kabul, Taraki and a number of co-conspirators tried to carry it out. It backfired. Amin survived, took Taraki prisoner, and killed him.[324]

Leaders in the Kremlin then made a fateful decision: to work with Amin, though they knew he lusted for power and dealt ruthlessly with his foes. "We are not pleased by all of Amin's methods and actions," Brezhnev admitted. He was "very power-driven" and exhibited "disproportionate harshness." But one could not "ignore the currently existing situation." Soviet officials explained to their comrades in East Germany that they hoped they could control Amin's excesses. They wanted him to collaborate with "real revolutionaries" in Afghanistan whose dedication to Marxism-Leninism could not be questioned. Meanwhile, they would watch him carefully, "observing whether he is keeping his promises."[325]

But Amin was impossible to deal with. He repeatedly asked the Kremlin for more aid. Soviet officials could not control him and did not trust him. On 29 October, Andropov, Ustinov, Gromyko, and Ponomarev issued another report to Brezhnev expressing their disaffection, but acknowledging that they were not yet ready to give up on him. Amin's oppression had widened. His "actions are provoking growing unrest among progressive forces." His attitudes and actions toward the Soviet Union "ever more distinctly expose his insincerity and duplicity." Outwardly he feigned agreement with the Kremlin but in practice he fomented anti-Soviet sentiments. Worse, he was beginning to make overtures to the United States. But the Soviets still had leverage over him and would try to exert it, for their fundamental premise "was not to allow the victory of counter-revolution."[326]

The specter of defeat hovered ever more ominously with each passing week, however. Soviet military advisers and KGB operators in Afghanistan were producing meager results. Andropov and Ustinov grew warier and more agitated. On 2 December, Andropov sent a handwritten note to Brezhnev: "we have been receiving information about Amin's behind-the-scenes activities which might mean his political reorientation to the West."[327] Afghanistan's April revolution was endangered; Soviet security was endangered.

A few days later a key meeting took place in the Walnut Room of the Kremlin, attended by Andropov, Ustinov, Gromyko, and Suslov. They saw danger. They discussed the absence of effective air defenses along the southern border of the Soviet Union, explored the implications of having Pershing II missiles in Afghanistan, should the United States gain a foothold there, and speculated about the prospective use of Afghan uranium by Iran or Pakistan. Aware of the ethnic rivalries in the region, they ruminated about the fragmentation of Afghanistan and the expansion of Pakistan. They even talked about alleged American plans to create a "New Great Ottoman Empire" that would absorb the southern republics of the U.S.S.R.[328] "We were concerned," recalled Valentin Varennikov, who then headed operational planning in the General Staff, "that if the United States were forced from Iran, they would move their bases to Pakistan and grab Afghanistan. . . . We thought that they would try to put intelligence centers in the north of Afghanistan."[329]

Brezhnev's closest advisers concluded that they had to get rid of Amin. They planned to replace him with Babrak Karmal, who would be more reliable and more responsive to their concerns and interests, but they knew Karmal would need help to consolidate power and establish order. Reluctantly, they agreed that, if necessary, they would deploy combat troops to assist him. Ustinov, Andropov, and their colleagues did not contemplate a prolonged intervention or a protracted war. Their troops would ensure an orderly transition after a bloody coup. Karmal would institute the reforms they had long envisioned. Order would return. The troops would then leave. "Do not worry, Anatoly," Brezhnev said to Dobrynin, "we will end this war in three or four weeks."[330]

Ustinov's top generals advised against intervention. They feared a protracted guerrilla war that would sap the Soviet army's morale and erode its strength. Marshal Ogarkov, chief of the General Staff, attended a meeting of top decision makers on 10 December. Intervention, he exclaimed, would unite all Muslims against the Soviet Union and embarrass the Kremlin in the eyes of the world. Andropov cut him off and told him to stick to military affairs. Ogarkov persisted, but his was a lone voice. Chernenko, Suslov, Ustinov, and Kirilenko would not listen. Andropov, Brezhnev said, should be supported.[331]

Preparations began for the deployment of troops, the removal of Amin, and the installation of Karmal. But the decision makers were uneasy. Andropov was tenser than his doctor had ever seen him. Brezhnev was angry, feeling that Amin had betrayed Moscow's friendship.[332] When the final decision was made on 12 December, Andropov, Ustinov, and Gromyko were its key proponents; Brezhnev, in a quivering hand, signed the directive to send in combat troops. Dissenters, such as Kosygin, did not attend the final meeting. After months of hesitation, equivocation, uncertainty, and anxiety, the fateful decision was made. Afghanistan "must not be given to the Americans," said Brezhnev's closest aide, Andrei Aleksandrov-Agentov.[333]

When they made their decision to intervene in Afghanistan, Soviet leaders saw threat, not opportunity. Imperialists could not be trusted. The United States and its NATO allies had just resolved to deploy new nuclear forces in Europe. This decision, in the Kremlin's view, jeopardized the principle of equal security on which détente was premised. Brezhnev had warned against another escalation of the arms race and even offered to reduce the number of Soviet SS-20s if the West would talk and not act. But NATO leaders moved ahead on 12 December, saying they were willing to talk but would not stop their plans to deploy 464 ground-launched Tomahawk cruise missiles in Western Europe and 108 Pershing II intermediate-range ballistic missiles. Brezhnev and his colleagues were dismayed. The Americans were again seeking to negotiate from strength. Washington lusted for first-strike capabilities in order to blackmail the Soviet Union. "After the [NATO] decision to station medium-range missiles in Europe," Soviet leaders concluded, "there was nothing to lose."[334] Feeling vulnerable, Brezhnev and his colleagues decided to take no chances in Afghanistan.

The Soviets also expected the United States to intervene in Iran. They could not imagine that a great power would allow its diplomats to be held captive for long. Gromyko warned the Americans not to use force on the Soviet periphery. They should stay composed, act calmly, and keep their emotions from boiling over. Dobrynin went to see Brzezinski: "We could not remain indifferent if the United States interfered militarily in our southern neighbor," he said. But the Kremlin still thought Carter "would do something."[335]

Turbulence in Iran was portentous. Ayatollah Khomeini hated communists only slightly less than he did Americans. "There were two Satans," remembered the chief KGB agent in Tehran, "the greater one was the United States, the lesser one was the Soviet Union." The Soviets continued to worry that Islamic fervor would spill over into Afghanistan, where its consequences could not be predicted, especially when Amin could not be trusted. The Americans could end up lodging themselves on Soviet frontiers.[336]

Brezhnev was discouraged. His own body was failing him, and his colleagues were disappointing him. He trusted the party cadres to do their job, but they were underperforming. Sick as he was, he grasped the dismal realities. On 27 November, he addressed the plenum of the party's Central Committee. Ritually, he summarized the achievements of the most recent five-year plan but then he launched into a long critique. There were bottlenecks and shortages, inefficiencies and incompetence. Vast sums were being invested, "and yet the final result which we obtain is smaller than it should be, and smaller than our possibilities permit." More attention must be focused on transportation, fuel, power, and metallurgy. But Brezhnev was especially distressed by the party's inability to satisfy the basic needs of Soviet citizens. Complaints were pouring in about shortages of medicines, soap, washing powders, toothbrushes, toothpaste, needles, thread, and so on. "This, comrades, is inexcusable." In designing the next five-year plan, Brezhnev told party officials, they had to be more creative and more disciplined. They must satisfy "growing public demands." Those who could not perform adequately, he warned, would lose their jobs. Mismanagement could not be tolerated.

The "centralism we need is democratic centralism, which opens a wide vista for initiative from below."[337]

Brezhnev's body was weak, but his mind was not fuzzy when he sent the combat troops to Afghanistan.[338] His system was underperforming at home and facing danger abroad. Détente, if it worked, would enable Soviet leaders to address their domestic problems more easily. The arms race, they knew, "swallows up the most colossal resources, undermines healthy economic development and places a heavy burden on the shoulders of hundreds of millions of people."[339] But domestic needs could not trump security concerns. Vigilance against external foes was the lesson that Brezhnev's generation could never forget. It constituted the heart of their ideology and the core of their experience.

Shortly before approving the deployment of troops to Afghanistan, Brezhnev shared his frustrations and fears with Erich Honecker. Washington and Bonn were playing a "dangerous game," Brezhnev said to him. Their plan to deploy a new generation of intermediate-range nuclear weapons in Europe was "a severe blow to détente." Worse, it was now unlikely that SALT II would be ratified, since the hysteria over the alleged Soviet brigade in Cuba had practically killed its chances. The Americans wanted "to blackmail" the Kremlin, hoping to "coerce concessions." They also wanted to play their "Chinese card," encouraging Beijing to attack Soviet allies in Indochina. We must "watch out," Brezhnev stressed.[340]

Gloomy and sick, determined and resentful, Brezhnev made his fateful decision. As Christmas 1979 dawned in the West, détente faded.

The End of Détente

Leonid Brezhnev killed détente with the United States, the policy he had helped to launch a decade before. And while he agonized about the decision, Jimmy Carter did not agonize about his reaction to Brezhnev's move. This "is deliberate aggression that calls into question détente and the way we have been doing business with the Soviets for the past decade," he told Hamilton Jordan over the phone. "It raises grave questions about Soviet intentions and destroys any chance of getting the SALT Treaty through the Senate. And that makes the prospects of nuclear war even greater."[341]

In his letter to Brezhnev on 28 December Carter did not mince words.

Soviet actions were a clear threat to the peace, violated the principles of dé-tente, and flouted "all the accepted norms of international conduct." Military intervention in a nonaligned nation "represents an unsettling, dangerous and new stage in your use of military forces. . . . Unless you draw back from your present course of action, this will inevitably jeopardize the course of U.S.-Soviet relations throughout the world."[342]

Brezhnev shamelessly defended Soviet actions. Moscow, he said, was an-swering the requests of the Afghan government, and the intervention had but one purpose: to help Afghanistan defend itself against external aggression. Soviet troops would not stay long, Brezhnev assured Carter. Meanwhile, he advised the president to be calmer. The "immoderate tone" of the American message had "hit us squarely between the eyes." The previous work together should not be in vain. The U.S.S.R. did not want to abandon détente and hoped the United States would see its continued advantages.[343]

But for Carter, there was no more temporizing. As long as Soviet troops were in Afghanistan, détente was dead. He recalled the U.S. ambassador from Moscow and reduced diplomatic contacts. He asked the Senate to sus-pend consideration of SALT II. He cut trade, stopped the sale of high-technology items, imposed an embargo on grain sales, and limited Soviet fishing rights off U.S. shores. American athletes, he said, would not partici-pate in the summer Olympic games to be held in Moscow in 1980. He boosted defense appropriations and accelerated the development of a rapid-deployment force. He beefed up military assistance to Pakistan and encour-aged Saudi aid to that country.[344]

In a series of interviews, statements, and speeches, Carter explained his thinking, motives, and fears. "The last 2 months have not been happy days for our Nation. . . . No one knows the ultimate outcome of these chal-lenges."[345] "The Soviet invasion of Afghanistan is the greatest threat to peace since the Second World War."[346] Soviet troops in Afghanistan were in strik-ing distance of the Indian Ocean and the Strait of Hormuz. They could gain control of the petroleum resources of the Persian Gulf and Middle East, the source of more than two-thirds of the world's exportable oil. Soviet actions, therefore, constituted "a threat to an area of the world where the interests of our country and those interests of our allies are deeply imbedded."[347] The U.S. position must be absolutely clear, Carter told the American people. "An attempt by any outside force to gain control of the Persian Gulf region will be regarded as an assault on the vital interests of the United States of America, and such an assault will be repelled by any means necessary, including military force." The Carter Doctrine was born, containment revived, and the Cold War resurrected.[348]

"The 1980s have been born in turmoil, strife and change," Carter stated.[349] Opportunities for Soviet expansion abounded; threats to American interests and values were indisputable and incalculable. Fritz Ermath, the Soviet expert on Brzezinski's staff, vividly summed up the sense of danger:

> the invasion sharply increases the prospect of eventual Soviet military domination of the greater Middle East and US exclusion from the region, except perhaps from Israel. Next we shall very probably see civil strife in Iran with direct Soviet involvement, a [communist] PDRY take-over of North Yemen, increased Soviet efforts to destabilize Turkey and Pakistan, and intense Soviet pressure on other states in the region to line up with Soviet interests.[350]

The American assessment of Soviet motivations was as flawed as the Soviet perception of danger. When Ambassador Dobrynin returned to Washington from Moscow after the Soviet invasion, Vance asked him earnestly: Are Soviet troops going to move into Pakistan or Iran? For Dobrynin, the question was preposterous. Nobody in the Politburo was even thinking of deploying troops to those countries. Far from possessing a grand design of his own, Brezhnev in fact had queried Dobrynin, "Where is the 'Arc of Crisis,'" where is that region of the world that Brzezinski claimed was the target of Kremlin designs?[351] The Soviets could not fathom American fears; the Americans could not fathom the Soviet perception of threat. "You were thinking," said Dobrynin, "that we were going to seize the Middle East oil fields; we were thinking that you wanted to press us militarily—to force us into a new arms race, and to press us from a position of strength."[352]

In a turbulent world, fear shaped policy. Of course, the Soviets had a real interest in guarding their periphery and the Americans had a real interest in protecting the oil fields of the Persian Gulf, but the Americans were not seeking to lodge themselves inside Afghanistan and the Soviets were not angling to capture the petroleum of the Middle East. The fears that haunted Soviet and American leaders did not stem from accurate assessments of actual intentions but from deeply embedded ideological axioms about motives and aims.

Although Carter and Brezhnev believed their systems would capture the allegiance of peoples around the globe, they each governed societies whose confidence was waning at a time of economic turmoil and political strife. Détente was a respite to lessen the burdens of the arms race while Soviet and American leaders tackled domestic priorities and insured their countries against the dangers of nuclear war. For Brezhnev and Carter, détente offered glimpses of a more rational world where their two nations could compete peacefully and progress economically. It did not dampen their hopes nor ease their fears. And so it foundered when forces of inexorable change in a dynamic world accentuated their sense of vulnerability and vindicated domestic opponents, who from the outset had never believed that détente was a suitable framework to compete for the soul of mankind.

V

THE END OF
THE COLD WAR, 1985–90

Gorbachev, Reagan,
and Bush

On 13 March 1985, Vice President George H. W. Bush, Secretary of State George Shultz, and Ambassador Arthur Hartman met the new Soviet leader, Mikhail Gorbachev, in the Kremlin for the first time. Konstantin Chernenko, Gorbachev's predecessor, had just been laid to rest. Gorbachev thanked the Americans for paying their respects and then delivered a sweeping statement of his government's aims. "The USSR has no expansionist ambitions. . . . The USSR has never intended to fight the United States and does not have any intentions now. There has never been such madmen in the Soviet leadership, and there are none now. The Soviets respect your right to run your own country the way you see fit. . . . As to the question of which is the better system, this is something for history to judge."

Bush responded, and then asked Shultz to say a few words. "President Reagan told me to look you squarely in the eyes and tell you: 'Ronald Reagan believes that this is a very special moment in the history of mankind,' " the secretary of state said to Gorbachev. "You are starting your term as general secretary. Ronald Reagan is starting his second term as president. . . . President Reagan is ready to work with you." He invites you "to visit the United States at the earliest convenient time. . . . If important agreements can be found, the sooner the better."

Gorbachev then said: "this is a unique moment; I am ready to return Soviet-U.S. relations to a normal channel. It is necessary to know each other, to find time to discuss outstanding problems, and to seek ways to bring the two countries closer together."[1]

Morning in America

For four years President Ronald Reagan had been seeking a negotiating partner in the Kremlin. Few suspected this was the case because his sharp rhetoric, ideological convictions, and defense buildup had made him appear as the coldest of cold warriors. During the 1970s, long before the Soviet invasion of Afghanistan, he had been one of the harshest critics of détente. He had assailed the second strategic arms limitation treaty negotiated by President Carter and denounced Soviet adventurism in the third world. But he was not simply hostile to Soviet conduct. He detested the Soviet system. "When a disease like communism hangs on as it has for half a century or more," he wrote in notes prepared for a radio broadcast in 1975, "it's good now and then, to be reminded of just how vicious it really is. . . . Communism is neither an ec[onomic] or a pol[itical] system—it is a form of insanity—a temporary aberration which will one day disappear from the earth because it is contrary to human nature."[2]

Nor was this rhetoric reserved simply for the campaign trail. In his first press conference as president of the United States, he was asked about the long-range intentions of the Soviet Union. Its goals, he said, were well known: "the promotion of world revolution and a one-world Socialist or Communist state." And to this end, Reagan went on, "they reserve unto themselves the right to commit any crime, to lie, to cheat."[3] The communists believed in "treachery, deceit, destruction, & bloodshed."[4] They denied the existence of God and the sanctity of human life. They vitiated the human spirit. "Let us be aware," Reagan said in one of his most famous speeches as president, "that while they preach the supremacy of the state, declare its omnipotence over individual man, and predict its eventual domination of all peoples on the Earth, they are the focus of evil in the modern world."[5]

Although Ronald Reagan hated communism, he did not fear it, not nearly as much as many of his predecessors. He was supremely confident of the superiority of American values and of the American way of life. "The West won't contain communism," he told the graduating students at the University of Notre Dame on 17 May 1981, "it will transcend communism."[6] His adversaries in the Kremlin might trumpet its inevitable victory, but Ronald Reagan saw a different reality. Speaking to the British parliament in June 1982, he rephrased Winston Churchill's 1946 iron curtain speech: "From Stettin on the Baltic to Varna on the Black Sea, the regimes planted by totalitarianism have had more than 30 years to establish their legitimacy. But none—not one regime—has yet been able to risk free elections. Regimes planted by bayonets do not take root."[7]

The tide of history was moving in a direction that belied the beliefs of Marxist-Leninists. "Democracy is not a fragile flower," Reagan declared, nor was capitalism a decaying system. "We are witnessing today," he said in 1982, "a great revolutionary crisis, a crisis where the demands of the economic order are conflicting directly with those of the political order. But the crisis is happening not in the free, non-Marxist West, but in the home of Marxism-Leninism, the Soviet Union. It is the Soviet Union that runs against the tide of history by denying human freedom and human dignity to its citizens."[8]

There were new dynamics in the international system. The era of decolonization was over, having expired with the breakup of the Portuguese empire in the 1970s. No longer could the Soviet Union exploit the evils of Western imperialism or present itself as the embodiment of a successful model of development. Revolutionary nationalists were no longer flocking to Moscow to learn the secrets of economic modernization and technological innovation. The Soviet economy was sputtering, the Chinese communist economy was being reimagined, and those of Eastern Europe, deeply indebted to Western creditors, were floundering. Outraged by the rising cost of meat, Polish workers went on strike in the summer of 1980 and demanded the right to form independent trade unions and to express themselves freely. Garnering widespread support among the Polish people, the Solidarity movement, as it was called, challenged the Communist Party's monopoly of power and demanded that the Polish government comply with the human rights provisions inscribed in the Helsinki Final Act. Although the movement was suppressed after the Kremlin threatened to intervene militarily and after the Polish government declared martial law in December 1981, Solidarity's resonance was considerable. "Around the world, the democratic revolution is gathering new strength," Reagan declared. Humankind was rejecting "the arbitrary power of the state." Everywhere, peoples were refusing to "subordinate the rights of the individual to the superstate"; everywhere, they were recognizing that "collectivism stifles all the best human impulses." If given the choice, Reagan predicted, people would always choose democracy over dictatorship. They would "leave Marxism-Leninism on the ash-heap of history," as they had left other tyrannies that had stifled the freedom and muzzled the voice of the people.[9]

Reagan's confidence in the superior appeal of Western values meant that he welcomed peaceful competition with the Kremlin. He was not a warmonger, as so many of his critics claimed, but he believed sincerely in peace through strength, and even more sincerely in his capacity to deal with the Kremlin. Reagan's unique contribution to the end of the Cold War was not his ideological convictions, because they did not depart from those of Truman, Eisenhower, Kennedy, Johnson, and Carter, nor his conviction that the United States must negotiate with the Soviet Union from strength, a policy that Truman and Acheson had made axiomatic during the formative years of the Cold War and that Eisenhower and Dulles had perpetuated until the era of détente. What was unique about Reagan was his willingness to reach out to a leadership he abhorred, men whose values he detested; to appreciate the concerns of his adversary; and to learn from experience. What was unique about Reagan was his confidence in himself and his capacity to effectuate change. "We meant to change a nation," he said, "and instead, we changed a world."[10] Of course, this was made possible by time, circumstance, and the personal qualities and beliefs of the new man who ruled the Kremlin. But Reagan had his own gifts: personal charm, a core set of convictions, and optimism about himself and the way of life he represented.

It was no accident that Reagan entitled his autobiography *An American Life*. For him, America was a special place, a city on a hill, because it gave all its citizens "the freedom to reach out and make our dreams come true." In America, individuals "could determine their own destiny; their ambition and work determine their fate in life." Every day was "Morning in America," Reagan's campaign theme in 1984, because every day every man and every woman could shape his or her destiny through hard work, self-discipline, entrepreneurship, and personal creativity. Reagan thought his mission in politics was to preserve the America of his imagination, the institutions and values that nurtured individual opportunity and personal freedom. He thought his own life embodied the American odyssey, from rags to riches, from obscurity to eminence. He loved his life story. He loved being president. His optimism was inbred, but the trajectory of his life proved, at least to himself, that the America of his imagination was the America of lived experience.[11]

"He wasn't a complicated man," said Nancy Reagan, his second wife, the person who knew him best. "He was a private man, but he was not a complicated one." He was also the most optimistic man she had ever known. "If he worries, you'd never know it. If he's anxious, he keeps it to himself. Depressed? He doesn't know the meaning of the word."[12]

The sources of Reagan's basic disposition are somewhat hard to fathom, but not inexplicable. He grew up in a poor, if not impoverished, family. His father was an unsuccessful shoe salesman, moving frequently from one small Illinois town to another, with a brief stint in Chicago. He was also an alcoholic, periodically going through bouts of inebriation and fighting with Reagan's mother, who preached tolerance.[13]

As a child, Reagan had a wandering existence until the family settled down in Dixon, Illinois, when he was nine years old. He loved Dixon; it was "heaven"—a small community where people knew and cared for one another. Yet Reagan was not popular. "I was a little introverted," he recalled, "and probably a little slow in making really close friends."[14] Ronnie was "a loner," Nancy explained in her memoir. "There's a wall around him. He lets me come closer than anyone else, but there are times when even I feel that barrier."[15]

Ronald Reagan's optimism, serenity, and patience were most clearly shaped by his mother. From his father he learned the "value of hard work and ambition, and maybe a little something about telling a story. From my mother, I learned the value of prayer, how to have dreams and believe I could make them come true."[16] His mother, wrote Nancy Reagan, "was a very religious woman whose faith saw her through bad times. She was also an incredible optimist. . . . Ronnie once said, 'We were poor, but I never knew it.' "[17]

Reagan's mother told him that "everything in life happened for a purpose. She said all things were part of God's Plan, even the most disheartening setbacks, and in the end everything worked out for the best." She taught her boys not to let bad things get them down. "You stepped away from it, stepped over it, and moved on."[18] Those who knew him well knew that Reagan's faith ran deep. "Ronald Reagan believed that God had a plan for everything."[19]

Not many boys in Dixon went to college in those days. Reagan's father could not afford to pay tuition, but Dutch, as Reagan was known in his youth, followed his dream and enrolled in Eureka College, a small liberal arts institution affiliated with the Disciples of Christ, situated not far from his hometown. Reagan was able to secure a football scholarship and a part-time job. He preferred sports and acting to studying economics, his major.[20]

Reagan graduated in 1932, during the depths of the Great Depression. He struggled to find a job, as did all his contemporaries, and finally landed a position as a radio sports announcer in Des Moines, Iowa. He worked hard at perfecting his rhythm and delivery and enjoyed broadcasting college football and professional baseball games. When he began to vote, he voted Democratic, following his father's political loyalties. Dutch Reagan "idolized" FDR. He loved the president's fireside chats. Roosevelt's "strong, gentle, confident voice . . . reassured us that we could lick any problem."[21]

In the mid-1930s, Reagan went to southern California each year to report on the Chicago Cubs during spring training for the baseball season. In 1937, he used the opportunity to schedule a screen test at a Hollywood studio. The studio liked his voice, if not his looks, although he was a strong, tall, handsome man in splendid physical condition. He got a contract, began an acting career, and repossessed his birth name, Ronald. Within a couple of years, Ronald Reagan was a minor star, making popular movies and earning a very substantial income. He won no Academy Awards, but producers, directors, and actors liked him. He was modest, reliable, and hardworking. He had a great memory and learned his lines quickly. His career was flourishing when the Japanese attacked Pearl Harbor. As a reserve officer, he was quickly assigned to active duty, but because of his terrible eyesight he was not shipped overseas and spent the war years making training films for the air force.[22]

After the war, Reagan resumed his film career and became active in the

Screen Actors Guild. These were critical years in his political maturation. He was still "a New Dealer to the core," and joined a host of political organizations. Although he knew little about communism and almost nothing about the Soviet Union, he quickly became suspicious of communist sympathizers. When a labor dispute erupted in 1946 that threatened to shut down a number of studios, Reagan wanted to have the Screen Actors Guild mediate the tangled conflict, which involved producers as well as unions. "More than anything else, it was the Communists' attempted takeover of Hollywood . . . that led me to accept the nomination as president of the Screen Actors Guild, and indirectly at least, set me on the road that would lead me into politics." Although his grasp of these events was less than perfect, they shaped his understanding of the postwar world. "Now I knew from firsthand experience how Communists used lies, deceit, violence, or any other tactic that suited them to advance the cause of Soviet expansionism. I knew from the experience of hand-to-hand combat [in Hollywood] that America faced no more insidious or evil threat than that of Communism."[23]

In the late 1940s, Reagan's acting career floundered and his first marriage collapsed. Not long thereafter he met Nancy Davis, and they were married in March 1952. A few months later, he and Nancy took the train to Fulton, Missouri, where an old friend had arranged for Reagan to give the commencement address at tiny William Woods College. Reagan's speech, entitled "America the Beautiful," presaged much that he would be saying for the next forty years. He said that America was less a place than an idea. The idea "is nothing less than the inherent love of freedom in each one of us." America, he told the audience, "was set aside as a promised land." He exhorted the new graduates to join in the struggle against "totalitarian darkness" and urged them to ensure that "this land of ours is the last best hope of man on earth."[24]

Soon thereafter, Reagan realized that his acting career was over. He could not get the roles he wanted, and he faced growing financial difficulties. He took a job as host of a new television drama series sponsored by the General Electric Corporation. The program was a great success in the early days of the new medium, and Reagan became a household presence in millions of homes every Sunday evening. He also went around the country delivering speeches for his new corporate employer.[25]

During the 1950s, Reagan's political beliefs shifted. He became a staunch foe of government regulation and opposed the progressive income tax, which in his view throttled business enterprise and personal initiative. He shifted parties, registered as a Republican, and in 1964 eagerly accepted the co-chairmanship of Barry Goldwater's presidential campaign in California. His speaking was polished and effective. Toward the end of the campaign, some of Goldwater's leading backers asked Reagan to prepare a half-hour address to be presented on national television the week before the election.[26]

"The Speech," as it became known, was nothing more than a compilation of the ideas that Reagan had been articulating for a decade. The American people, he warned, faced a stark choice between individual freedom and creeping totalitarianism as embodied in Lyndon Johnson's Great Society programs. "You and I have a rendezvous with destiny," he concluded. "We will preserve for our children this, the last best hope of man on earth, or we will sentence them to take the last step into a thousand years of darkness."[27]

Among Republican conservatives, the speech was a smashing success and it transformed Reagan's life. He was encouraged to run for governor of California, and in November 1966 he defeated the incumbent, Pat Brown. He served two terms in Sacramento and in 1976 challenged President Gerald Ford for the Republican nomination. Although he lost in a very close contest, he spent the next four years delivering speeches and perfecting his messages for a run against Jimmy Carter in 1980.

Reagan was one of the oldest men ever to campaign for the presidency, but his message was one of spiritual renewal. America's greatest years lay in the future, he said. He assailed Carter's talk of malaise. The American people were not to blame for the country's difficulties, for they were optimistic, energetic, innovative, and resilient. The Democrats, not the American people, were the source of the problem. For decades, Democrats had been taxing and spending the American people's money, triggering huge deficits, causing runaway inflation, and eroding personal incentives to work and invest. The Democrats' arms negotiations and defense programs had tied America's hands and eroded American power. "We had to recapture our dreams, our pride in ourselves and our country, and regain that unique sense of destiny and optimism that had always made America different from any other country in the world." Vote for Reagan and there would be a new "morning in America."[28]

Reagan won a decisive victory over Carter in November 1980, and the Republicans captured a majority in the Senate for the first time since 1954, although the Democrats still controlled the House of Representatives. In his inaugural address on 20 January 1981, Reagan reemphasized his most fundamental convictions: "government is not the solution to our problem; government is the problem. . . . It is time to reawaken this industrial giant, to get government back within its means, and to lighten our punitive tax burden." Under his leadership, the United States would recapture its greatness. "We have every right to dream heroic dreams," he told the American people. Adversaries should take heed: "our reluctance for conflict should not be misjudged as a failure of will. . . . We are a nation under God, and I believe God intended us to be free."[29]

Reagan's priorities were clear: to restore the nation's economic vitality and augment its military strength. His staff worked feverishly to push through Congress his program of tax and spending cuts. The defense budget skyrocketed—12 percent in fiscal year 1981, and 15 percent in 1982. Military officials envisioned spending $2.7 trillion during the 1980s. Increased funds were allocated for training, for preparedness, for command and communications, for the B-1 bomber, for one hundred MX intercontinental ballistic missiles, for fifteen Trident submarines, and for research and development of the B-2 Stealth bomber and the Trident II missile.[30]

Reagan's most fundamental axiom on national security policy was that the United States must negotiate from strength. The Soviets, he believed, respected "only strength." The United States had been negotiating with its hands tied behind its back. Greatly distorting what had happened during the 1970s, he claimed that Washington had unilaterally disarmed, providing little incentive for the Kremlin to negotiate in good faith. "[W]e're going to be far more successful," Reagan declared, "if [the] adversary knows that the alternative is a buildup."[31]

Critical to Reagan's way of thinking was his conviction that the Soviet system was in rotten shape. State Department officials, national security advisers, and intelligence analysts conveyed abundant information about Soviet economic problems, popular malaise, and ethnic discontent. "The Soviet people are no longer confident that their standard of living will continue to improve," reported the CIA's directorate of intelligence. "Popular dissatisfaction and cynicism seem to be growing." Corruption was rampant. Economic productivity was declining. Ethnic discontent was mounting.[32] None of this surprised President Reagan. Among his core beliefs was the inefficiency of a command economy, and its fundamental incapacity to satisfy the aspirations of people who wanted a better way of life. "We could have an unexpected ally," he said as early as 1977, "if Ivan is becoming discontented enough to start talking back."[33]

Reagan wanted to squeeze the Soviet Union. The United States would do whatever was necessary to stay ahead of the Kremlin in the arms race, he insisted. "[W]e could outspend them forever." The men in the Kremlin knew "that if we turned our full industrial might into an arms race, they cannot keep pace with us."[34]

To negotiate from strength, however, meant a willingness to talk. Reagan grasped this fundamental reality and wanted to engage the Soviets in a dialogue:

> I wanted to let them know that we realized the nuclear standoff was futile and dangerous and that we had no designs on their territories. . . . Somewhere in the Kremlin, I thought, there had to be people who realized that the pair of us standing there like two cowboys with guns pointed at each other's heads posed a lethal risk to the survival of the Communist world as well as the free world. Someone in the Kremlin had to realize that in arming themselves to the teeth, they were aggravating the desperate economic problems in the Soviet Union, which were the greatest evidence of the failure of Communism.[35]

After Reagan was badly wounded in an assassination attempt on 30 March 1981, he lay in bed mulling over these issues. "Perhaps having come so close to death made me feel I should do whatever I could in the years God had given me to reduce the threat of nuclear war; perhaps there was a reason I had been spared."[36] He told Secretary of State Alexander Haig that he wanted to lift the grain embargo and write a personal letter to Brezhnev. Haig opposed both ideas, which agitated Reagan, who desired to engage with the Soviet leader "as a human being." In his typically compromising way, the president allowed Haig to write Brezhnev a formal letter that represented the tough-minded attitude of the administration, but Reagan stubbornly went ahead with his own letter, which he wrote in longhand to underscore its authenticity.[37]

In this letter, the president emphasized the hopes the Soviet leader had kindled when Brezhnev first met President Richard Nixon, a decade earlier. "Those meetings had captured the imagination of all the world." At the time, Reagan reminded Brezhnev, they had met one another at Nixon's home in San Clemente. "You took my hand in both of yours and assured me . . . that you were dedicated with all your heart and mind to fulfilling those hopes and dreams." The peoples of the world, Reagan continued, still retained those dreams. Regardless of race and ethnicity, they shared similar aspirations for themselves and their children:

> They wanted the dignity of having some control over their individual destiny. They wanted to work at the craft or trade of their own choosing and to be fairly rewarded. They wanted to raise their families in peace. . . . Governments exist for their convenience, not the other way around. . . . Is it possible that we have permitted ideology, political and economic philosophies and governmental policies to keep us from considering the very real, everyday problems of peoples?

Reagan concluded by saying he hoped that lifting the grain embargo would catalyze "meaningful and constructive dialogue which will assist us in fulfilling our joint obligation to find lasting peace."[38]

Nothing came of this letter, partly because Brezhnev replied coolly and was by then physically and mentally incapable of taking any new initiative, partly because Reagan did not know how to move his administration forward. His national security team had been in disarray from the moment he took office, and things got worse before they got better. The president's style of decision making, his aloofness, his aversion to conflict, his disdain for facts and detail, and his penchant for ideological verbiage contributed greatly to the disorder. Those who knew him best, whether admirers or detractors, agreed on the way he operated. "He made no demands, and gave almost no instructions," explained Martin Anderson, a longtime admirer and one of Reagan's most influential economic advisers. "Essentially, he just responded to whatever was brought to his attention and said yes or no, or I'll think about it." According to David Stockman, the president's first budget tsar, Reagan "gave no orders; no commands; asked for no information; expressed

The final days of Brezhnev, 1982. The Soviet leader was
as pathetic as he looked, and incapable of responding to
Reagan's private overture.

no urgency." At some meetings of the National Security Council, according
to Richard Pipes, the Soviet expert who served on the NSC staff, the president seemed "really lost, out of his depth, uncomfortable." "Unlike some of
his predecessors," wrote Haig, "Reagan made no decisions on the spot, and
gave little indication of his own position on the issues."[39]

His advisers on foreign and defense policy feuded, sometimes for personal reasons, sometimes because of institutional rivalries, and sometimes
over policy. Secretary of State Haig, a former general and NATO commander, believed he was entitled to shape policy as he pleased. He was never
on intimate terms with the president. Reagan's closest advisers and friends
in the White House—Edwin Meese, Michael Deaver, and James Baker—
disliked Haig, and he reciprocated their feelings. Haig and Defense Secretary
Caspar Weinberger, an old associate of Reagan's, also were at odds, the strife
being as much departmental rivalry as personal antipathy. Theoretically, the
president's national security adviser, Richard Allen, should have been able to
ease these feuds, but he lacked both intellectual stature and a personal tie to
the president—indeed, he did not even have direct access to him. Moreover,
Allen had staffed the National Security Council with many hard-line anti-

communists who regarded State Department officials with disdain, if not
contempt. "The entire first year and a half of the administration passed in
an atmosphere of unremitting tension between the NSC and State," wrote
Pipes.[40]

The feuding bureaucracies took more than a year to produce a strategy
statement for the new administration. On 20 May 1982, President Reagan approved it. Times were treacherous, the document stressed:

> The growing scarcity of resources, such as oil, increasing ter-
> rorism, the dangers of nuclear proliferation, uncertainties in
> Soviet political succession, reticence on the part of a number of
> Western countries, and the growing assertiveness of Soviet for-
> eign policy all contribute to the unstable international environ-
> ment. For these reasons, the decade of the eighties will likely
> pose the greatest challenge to our survival and well-being since
> World War II.[41]

But there was no reason to despair. The Soviet Union had significant vulnerabilities. "The economies and the social systems of the Soviet Union and
of most Soviet allies continue to exhibit serious structural weaknesses. The
appeal of communist ideologies appears to be decreasing throughout much
of the world, including the Soviet bloc itself." Soviet military difficulties in
Afghanistan after their intervention in December 1979 demonstrated the
limits of the Kremlin's power-projection capabilities. Unrest in Poland revealed weaknesses in the Warsaw Pact. Inside the Soviet Union, the growth
of non-Russian nationalities posed a latent threat to "the dominant Russian
population."

The strategy statement also stipulated that the administration's policy
should be designed to nurture the economic well-being of the nation,
strengthen its industrial and technological base, and promote access to
foreign markets and resources. The United States should maintain and
strengthen alliances and "wherever possible" encourage and reinforce "freedom, the rule of law, economic development and national independence
throughout the world." With regard to the Soviet Union, the United States
had to be able to deter attack and prevail in war. The strategy statement explained that the Soviet leaders did not want war but would be inclined to en-

gage in aggressive risk-taking in light of their mounting military capabilities, believing they could intimidate or blackmail the United States. The aim should be to "neutralize" these efforts and "to contain and reverse the expansion of Soviet control and military presence throughout the world, and to increase the costs of Soviet support of proxy, terrorist, and subversive forces."[42]

William Clark, an old friend of Reagan's and perhaps his closest confidant other than his wife, claimed that the president focused much attention on this document.[43] On 1 January 1982, the president had made Clark his national security adviser when a minor scandal discredited Allen. Clark was a virulent anticommunist but knew little about international affairs. His task was to improve communication among the departments and with the White House. Like many other Reagan advisers, he believed this goal could be achieved if Haig were removed as secretary of state. In June 1982, Reagan, who loathed controversy among his advisers and hated firing anybody, dismissed Haig and appointed George Shultz as secretary of state. A man of great ability and experience in business, government, and the academy, Shultz had been a professor of economics at the University of Chicago, served as secretary of labor and secretary of the treasury in the Nixon administration, and was currently president of the Bechtel Corporation.[44]

But Shultz's arrival did not ease the difficulties besetting the national security process. He immediately sensed that "a cult of secrecy verging on deception had taken root in the White House and NSC staffs." He agreed with all the basic Reagan doctrines. The challenge, in Shultz's view, was "to use freedom and open markets as the organizing principles for economic and political development, and to do so long enough to allow communism's failures to be fully recognized and to play themselves out." But Shultz also believed that the United States should negotiate with the Soviet Union to nurture a more constructive relationship. He knew the president shared this view, but was convinced that Clark, Weinberger, CIA director William Casey, and their staffs were obstructing implementation of the president's wishes.[45]

Shultz thought that he alone among Reagan's top advisers actually had experience dealing with the Soviets. As secretary of the treasury, he had conducted extensive trade talks with Nikolai Patolichev, then Soviet minister of foreign trade, a hardened old communist who during World War II had been in charge of tank production. On a trip to Moscow in 1973, Patolichev had taken Shultz to a Leningrad cemetery where more than a million dead soldiers lay buried. Shultz and Patolichev walked solemnly among the graves as Patolichev vividly described the fighting around Leningrad. The experience left an indelible impression on Shultz:

> I had learned something of the human dimension to the Soviet Union. I learned that World War II—the Great Patriotic War against fascism, the Soviets called it—was a matter of deep significance to them. I also learned that the Soviets were tough negotiators but that you could negotiate successfully with them. In my experience, they did their homework and had skill and patience and staying power. I respected them not only as able negotiators but as people who could make a deal and stick to it. . . . Their willingness to engage seriously would depend entirely on how they perceived their interests. Such occasions would come, I felt, when the Soviets concluded that we were not only strong and determined but also willing to make agreements that were mutually advantageous.[46]

Bill Clark's NSC staff did not see things in quite this way. Richard Pipes and his colleagues labored during 1982 on a new document more precisely defining American policy toward the Soviet Union. NSDD-75, "U.S. Relations with the USSR," specified that the Reagan administration would seek to achieve three broad objectives: "to contain and over time reverse Soviet expansionism"; to promote, "within the narrow limits available to us, the process of change in the Soviet Union toward a more pluralistic political and economic system"; and "to engage the Soviet Union in negotiations . . . consistent with the principle of strict reciprocity and mutual interest."[47] Clark explained to Reagan that what was distinctive about the document was the second goal, "namely encouraging antitotalitarian changes within the USSR."[48] Nothing transformative was expected in the short term. Neither Pipes nor Clark believed this was a strategy to dismantle communism in the Soviet Union. Although their expectations were modest, they were nonetheless significant: "the prospect for major systemic change in the next few years is relatively low, [but] the likelihood of policy shifts is much higher, and some of these could set the scene for broader changes in the system over the long term."[49]

What separated Clark and Pipes from Shultz was their relative indifference to the importance of negotiations. When Brezhnev died in November 1982, and Yuri Andropov succeeded him, Shultz warned Reagan that the new Soviet leader would inject more dynamism into Soviet policy. "There is already evidence of greater foreign policy energy and sophistication under Andropov," Shultz wrote Reagan on 15 January 1983, "and the Soviets will clearly be on the offensive." The United States needed to react with "strength, imagination, and energy." It needed to revitalize its economic and military capabilities, promote alliance cohesion, stabilize relations with China, compete briskly in the war of ideas, and mediate regional conflicts in the Middle East, Central America, and elsewhere. But to be successful, Shultz emphasized, America also needed to enter a dialogue with Andropov. The Soviet Union was not about to collapse nor lose its capacity to compete. "While recognizing the adversarial nature of our relationship with Moscow, we must not rule out the possibility that firm U.S. policies could help induce the kind of changes in Soviet behavior that would make an improvement in relations possible."[50]

Reagan endorsed Shultz's policy, but he then proceeded to intensify his rhetorical and programmatic onslaught against the Kremlin. The president was angered by the declaration of martial law in Poland. He assailed the Soviets for aiding Castro, supporting the Sandinistas, indirectly fomenting insurrection in El Salvador, and escalating the fighting in Afghanistan. He denounced them for their arms buildup, religious persecution, restrictions on Jewish emigration, and violations of the Helsinki Agreement on human rights. Reagan's vitriol reached new heights in a speech he gave to evangelical Christians on 8 March 1983, when he called the Soviet Union an "evil empire." "Let us pray for the salvation of all of those who live in totalitarian darkness," he said, "pray they will discover the joy of knowing God." "Religion," he believed, might "turn out to be the Soviets' Achilles heel."[51]

Shultz shared the president's disgust with Kremlin policies, but he thought Reagan's rhetoric was getting out of hand. White House officials had not told him that the president would denounce the Soviet Union as an "evil empire," and Shultz felt that he was being excluded from the decision-making loop. He met with Reagan at the White House on 10 March determined to present a new approach and to persuade the president, who he believed had become a "prisoner of his own staff," to shift gears. Reagan, however, assured him that he supported Shultz's ideas, and he encouraged him to go ahead with his efforts to engage the Kremlin in a constructive dialogue.[52]

Reagan was no one's prisoner. He possessed his own complex and protean ideas about the nation's security, however inept he was in thinking them through or finding the means to implement them. On 23 March, with little consultation with either his secretary of defense or his secretary of state, he announced his intention to launch a program "which holds the promise of changing the course of human history." He wanted to build a shield to protect the United States and its allies from incoming missiles with nuclear warheads, something he had been thinking about for several years. He knew it would take a long time, knew he needed to reassure allies and adversaries alike that this initiative would not endanger their security or contravene previous treaties. But the president firmly believed that relying on the doctrine of mutual assured destruction (MAD) to preserve peace was mad. It was also irresponsible, and a conventional wisdom whose time had passed. Purposefully avoiding discussion with advisers who he knew would oppose it, Reagan announced that he was initiating a "long-term research and development program" designed "to achieve our ultimate goal of eliminating the threat posed by strategic nuclear missiles. This could pave the way for arms control measures to eliminate the weapons themselves. We seek neither military superiority nor political advantage. Our only purpose . . . is to search for ways to reduce the danger of nuclear war."[53]

Reagan did not want his support of "Star Wars," as the Strategic Defense Initiative (SDI) came to be called, to ratchet up the arms race or intensify Cold War tensions. He insisted that he would be willing to share the anticipated technology—space-based lasers, mirrors, particle beams, and kinetic-energy weapons—with the Soviet leaders so that they, too, could gain reassurance.[54] According to Jack Matlock, the experienced foreign service officer who at this time succeeded Pipes as the Soviet expert on the NSC staff, Reagan did not want to torpedo diplomatic negotiations with the Kremlin; he wanted to engage the new Soviet leadership. Matlock later recalled:

From the time I joined the NSC staff in 1983 my main duty
[was] to devise a negotiating strategy for dealing with the Soviet Union. Many in his administration . . . doubted that the
Soviet leaders would conduct negotiations in good faith, but
Reagan was an optimist. For all his distaste for the Soviet system, he nevertheless believed that it could change if subjected
to sufficient pressure and his personal negotiating skill.[55]

Throughout 1982 and 1983, Reagan repeated that he wanted to talk with
Soviet leaders. He was ready and willing to attend a summit conference with
Andropov, notwithstanding the Soviet leader's KGB background and aura of
toughness. On learning of Brezhnev's death, Reagan told a press conference:
"I want to underscore my intention to continue working to improve our relationship with the Soviet Union."[56] The United States, he insisted, was accruing strength not to wage war, but to negotiate more effectively. We want "to
discuss practical steps that could resolve problems." Talks would improve if
the Soviets ended the bloodshed in Afghanistan and permitted reform in
Poland, but "we do not insist that the Soviet Union abandon its standing as a
superpower or its legitimate national interests."[57]

Reagan exchanged letters with Andropov reiterating his desire to preserve
the peace and eliminate the nuclear threat. "You and I share an enormous responsibility for the preservation of stability in the world. I believe we can
fulfill that responsibility but to do so will require a more active level of exchange than we have heretofore been able to establish. We have much to talk
about. . . . Historically, our predecessors have made better progress when
communicating has been private and candid. If you wish to engage in such
communication you will find me ready. I await your reply."[58]

Andropov's written responses were hopeful, but Soviet actions belied his
words.[59] On 1 September 1983, Soviet fighter planes shot down a Korean
civilian airliner wandering through Soviet airspace, killing 269 people. Reagan was "outraged." Cutting short his summer vacation in California, he returned to Washington on Labor Day weekend and wrote a speech conveying
his "unvarnished" feelings: the downing of the plane "was an act of bar-
barism, born of a society which wantonly disregards individual rights and
the value of human life and seeks constantly to expand and dominate other
nations."[60]

Yet Reagan refused to cut off talks with the Soviets. Secretary of Defense Weinberger and others insisted that Shultz cancel a meeting he had scheduled with Foreign Minister Gromyko in Vienna. Weinberger wanted arms-control talks to cease until the world got an honest explanation for the destruction of the airliner. Reagan "brushed aside" this idea. "I could see that [the president] wanted to take a hard position with the Soviets," Shultz remembered, "but he was not about to break off from important dealings with them."[61]

While Reagan wanted to keep talking, he did not want to ease pressure on the Kremlin. In the fall of 1983, he did everything he could to get Great Britain, West Germany, and Italy to deploy the new intermediate-range nuclear weapons that had been envisioned since 1979. He rebuffed all talk of freezing the current stock of American and Soviet nuclear weapons, insisting that he wanted reductions, not the status quo (which, in his view, favored the U.S.S.R.).[62] Since the Soviets had rejected his proposal to eliminate all intermediate-range missiles in Europe, the so-called zero-zero option, Reagan insisted on NATO deployment. In mid-November, the first U.S. ground-launched cruise missiles were sent to Britain; a week later the first Pershing II missiles arrived in West Germany.

Reagan also approved Able Archer 83, a military exercise to test command and communications procedures for firing nuclear weapons in wartime—a scenario, said the president, "that could lead to the end of civilization as we know it."[63] Able Archer was only one of a series of increasingly provocative tests. U.S. aircraft "tested" the Kremlin's defensive systems, explained one of the CIA's leading Soviet experts; the U.S. Navy probed its territorial waters; the Pacific Fleet conducted its largest exercise in history around Soviet waters.[64]

On 24 October 1983, without consulting Congress, Reagan deployed U.S. forces to the tiny Caribbean island of Grenada to thwart a takeover by leftists even more radical than the incumbent leader, who had just been murdered. The motive was ostensibly to rescue American students and to respond to the overtures of Grenada's neighbors, who feared the growth of Castroism. But Reagan's real intent was to show strength. Two hundred and forty-one Americans had just been killed by a terrorist assault on U.S. Marine headquarters in Beirut. Defense officials wanted to pull American forces out of Lebanon, where they were terribly exposed to attacks and where their mission was inchoate, but nobody in the administration wanted to seem weak. In Lebanon, U.S. officials were grappling with civil strife and regional conflict; in the Caribbean, they thought they were dealing with Cuban adventurism. Reagan was determined to overcome the Vietnam syndrome and not allow one inch of additional territory to fall within the Soviet sphere of influence. The United States, he later recalled, "couldn't remain spooked forever by this [Vietnam] experience to the point where it refused to stand up and defend its legitimate national security interests."[65]

At the same time, Reagan began to wage proxy wars against the Soviet Union in the third world. He had a rationale. Whereas in the past, the third world had presented endless opportunities for communist advancement, this was no longer the case. The U.S.S.R. was no longer an economic model for developing societies.[66] With the breakup of the last colonial empire in the 1970s, Marxist-Leninist rhetoric no longer resonated in quite the same way. Now, guerrilla forces waged war against Soviet-backed governments, for example, in Nicaragua and Afghanistan, and the United States could support these insurgencies, much as the Soviets had supported revolutionary nationalist movements against colonial or neocolonial regimes. In December 1981, Reagan had signed a presidential directive approving covert aid to a tiny group of counterrevolutionaries (or Contras) in Nicaragua, who were battling to overthrow the radical Sandinista government.[67] At the same time, he began ratcheting up U.S. aid to the Mujahedin and other insurgent groups in Afghanistan who were struggling to unseat the Soviet-imposed government in Kabul and who were bloodying Soviet combat forces in Afghanistan.[68]

Soviet leaders despised Reagan's rhetoric and feared American initiatives. When Foreign Minister Gromyko summoned Ambassador Hartman for a meeting on 19 October 1983, he was reflective and philosophical yet unusually passionate. The president's discourse seemed to be exceeding the bounds of propriety, Gromyko insisted. Reagan was attacking the very legitimacy of the Soviet system. Soviet leaders could not grasp the reasons for the president's inflammatory invective. They did not understand that their evasion of responsibility for the destruction of the civilian airliner had infuriated Americans and discredited the Soviet Union with most of the world. In a speech commemorating the anniversary of the Bolshevik revolution on 5 November, Soviet Politburo member Grigory Romanov declared that the global atmosphere had not been so bad since the end of the Great Patriotic War. "Comrades, the international situation at present is white hot, thoroughly white hot."[69]

Andropov summoned aides to his hospital bed, where he was close to death. "The international situation is very tense," he said, tenser than at any time since the Cuban missile crisis of 1962. "The United States wants to change the existing strategic situation and they want to have the opportunity of striking the first strategic strike."[70] The Soviet Union must prepare itself for every possible contingency in the short run, and boost its economic capabilities in the long run. Believing that domestic proponents of human rights were collaborating with foreign intelligence organizations and scheming to undermine the Soviet regime, the Politburo cracked down more strenuously on dissent and disbanded the Moscow Human Rights Group.[71] The American threat was no illusion, stressed Defense Minister Ustinov. His subordinates were instructed to accelerate the training of troops.[72] When Able Archer got under way in November, KGB officials watched it with trepidation. Some Soviet intelligence analysts believed it portended a real attack.[73]

U.S. intelligence analysts tracked Soviet behavior. "What's going on here?" they wondered. "Are these people nuts?"[74] Initially, they could not fathom why the Soviet Union had gone on heightened alert; they could not imagine the level of Soviet fear. But when they grasped that it was real, they reported it to the White House.[75]

Reagan wrote in his diary: "I feel the Soviets are so defense minded, so paranoid about being attacked that without being in any way soft on them, we ought to tell them no one here has any intention of doing anything like that." He instructed retired general Brent Scowcroft, who was going to Moscow, to convey privately his hopes to improve relations and reduce the level of armaments.[76]

Reagan was learning. "Three years had taught me something surprising about the Russians," he recollected later. "Many people at the top of the Soviet hierarchy were genuinely afraid of America and Americans. Perhaps this shouldn't have surprised me, but it did." But as he raised these matters with foreign leaders and his own advisers, his education grew. He met with President Mika Spiljak of Yugoslavia in early 1984, and then jotted in his diary: "I picked his brains about the Soviet Union. He was the ambassador there for a time. He believes that coupled with their expansionist philosophy, they are also insecure and genuinely frightened of us. He also believes that if we

THE END OF THE COLD WAR, 1985-90

opened them up a bit, their leading citizens would get braver about proposing changes in their system. I'm going to pursue this." And a few weeks later, Reagan talked to West German chancellor Helmut Kohl and on 5 March noted in his diary: "He confirmed my belief that the Soviets are motivated at least in part by insecurity and a suspicion that we and our allies mean them harm."[77]

The president still wanted strength, but the purpose of strength was to talk, reduce tensions, promote change in the Soviet Union, discourage Soviet adventurism, and, most of all, avoid nuclear war. On 10 October 1983, he had seen a preview of the ABC movie *The Day After*, which was going to be televised nationally on 20 November. In the film, Lawrence, Kansas, is wiped out in a nuclear war with Russia. "It is powerfully done and left me greatly depressed," Reagan commented. He was sobered even more a few days later when Secretary Weinberger and the Joint Chiefs of Staff briefed him on the American plan for nuclear war, the famous Single Integrated Operational Plan (SIOP), which, for Reagan, seemed to foreshadow "a sequence of events that could lead to the end of civilization as we knew it." He was appalled that there were still men in the Pentagon "who claimed a nuclear war was 'winnable.' I thought they were crazy," and so were their Soviet counterparts.[78]

Reagan, meanwhile, had changed his national security adviser again. Shultz and Clark simply could not get along, and Deaver and Nancy Reagan believed that Clark's hard-line attitudes were not only influencing Reagan but eroding his popularity. The president promoted Robert (Bud) McFarlane, a former Marine officer who had been Clark's assistant. McFarlane had worked for Henry Kissinger and served on congressional staff committees before joining Haig's team in the State Department and then moving to the White House in 1982. His attitudes were those of the traditional cold warrior. But he also believed, like Reagan and Shultz, that the United States could bargain with the Soviet Union from strength, and could squeeze it because of its economic vulnerability. McFarlane collaborated with Shultz and Vice President Bush to help Reagan communicate more clearly his desire to negotiate with the Soviets as well as compete with them. Given the popularity of the antinuclear movement, whose numbers had multiplied in response to the spiraling arms race and the deployment of new intermediate-range missiles in Europe, Reagan's aides knew that public opinion at home and abroad would welcome a softer message from the White House.[79]

On 16 January 1984, Reagan addressed the nation and the world. We live

in a time of challenge and of opportunity, he began. "Neither we nor the Soviet Union can wish away the differences between our two societies and our
philosophies." But the "fact that neither of us likes the other system is no reason to refuse to talk. Living in this nuclear age makes it imperative that we do
talk." Henceforth he would pursue "a policy of credible deterrence, peaceful
competition, and constructive cooperation." He emphasized, "we want more
than deterrence. We want genuine cooperation. We seek progress for peace.
Cooperation begins with communication."[80]

Communication, however, was difficult. Andropov died on 9 February
and was succeeded by Konstantin Chernenko, one of Brezhnev's closest
cronies. Representing the United States at Andropov's funeral, Vice President Bush and Senator Howard Baker met Chernenko. Bush found him "less
hard-nosed and abrasive than Andropov." Baker agreed. "General Secretary
Chernenko is a man with whom we can deal," he wrote the president. Reagan
recorded in his diary: "I have a gut feeling that I'd like to talk to him about
our problems man to man."[81]

Reagan immediately launched into a correspondence with Chernenko,
one far more extensive than was known at the time. "I have no higher goal
than the establishment of a relationship between our two great nations characterized by constructive cooperation," Reagan wrote on 11 February. He
hoped they could make progress in reducing strategic and conventional armaments and in "reducing the dangers of wider confrontation" in regional or
local disputes stretching from Afghanistan to southern Africa. "The United
States fully intends to defend our interests and those of our allies," he concluded, "but we do not seek to challenge the security of the Soviet Union and
its people."[82]

In subsequent letters, Reagan reiterated many of the same points. We
"should look for specific areas in which we can move our relationship in a
more positive direction," he wrote, citing various arms control initiatives, regional imbroglios, and bilateral discussions where he thought progress could
be made. Vice President Bush told me, Reagan wrote to Chernenko, that it
was your hope that history would recall "us as leaders known to be good,
wise, and kind. Nothing is more important to me, and we should take steps
to bring this about."[83] Again, on 16 April, he wrote that he looked forward to
a productive working relationship. "As for myself, I am prepared to consider
your concerns seriously, even when I have difficulty understanding why they

are held." But Reagan was trying to understand better. He added a handwritten postscript to the six-page letter:

> In thinking through this letter, I have reflected at some length on the tragedy & scale of Soviet losses in warfare through the ages. Surely those losses which are beyond description, must affect your thinking today. I want you to know that neither I nor the American people hold any offensive intentions toward you or the Soviet people. . . . Our constant & urgent purpose must be . . . a lasting reduction of tensions between us. I pledge to you my profound commitment to that end.[84]

Shultz and McFarlane kept nudging Reagan forward. They wanted to educate the president. On 28 January, McFarlane had forwarded to Matlock an article by James Billington, the renowned historian of Russia and the Soviet Union. McFarlane asked Matlock to summarize it for the president. "I would like to infuse the president with an historical appreciation of where we stand in relationship and what we can expect in the way of Soviet leadership (goals and strategy)." Even if progress was not likely with Chernenko, McFarlane wanted to "keep alive the hope of an alternative future among the successor generation."[85] Over the next couple of years, McFarlane had Matlock write more than two dozen memoranda on Soviet history, strategy, and politics for the president. Reagan read them avidly, commented on them, and circulated them among his advisers. He hated reading dry briefs presented in large loose-leaf notebooks and was renowned for ignoring them, but he was genuinely interested in learning more about his adversary.[86]

He needed to, because he was bombarded with conflicting views from Weinberger, Casey, and their top aides. According to the secretary of state, Casey and Weinberger "wanted no dealings with the Soviets and were reluctant to make any changes in our negotiating positions once they had been laid down."[87] As Reagan began to think about a second term, McFarlane advised him to make some personnel changes. The acrimony was unbearable. Weinberger and Shultz "were like oil and water." The president had to choose one or the other. Reagan did not agree. "They are both my friends. I don't want to fire either one of them," he told McFarlane. "You're going to have to work harder."[88]

Shultz would not let the matter rest, however. He told the president, "To succeed, we have to have a team: right now there isn't one. Cap Weinberger, Bill Casey, Jeane Kirkpatrick [ambassador to the United Nations], and I just don't see things the same way." Shultz said he was fed up with the leaks, end runs, and delaying tactics. It was impossible to get anything done. "I'm frustrated," he told Reagan, "and I'm ready to step aside."[89]

Reagan would never fire Cap Weinberger, a longtime friend and associate, but he knew he had to make a choice. "Cap was not as interested as George in opening negotiations with the Russians," Reagan recalled, "and some of his advisors at the Pentagon strongly opposed some of my ideas on arms control that George supported, including my hope for eventually eliminating all nuclear weapons from the world." Weinberger and his conservative allies in Congress told Reagan that Shultz "had gone soft on the Russians." Reagan knew this was nonsense, but he also knew that he had to resolve the differences between McFarlane and Shultz on the one hand and Weinberger, Casey, and Ed Meese on the other. The "dispute is so out of hand that George sounds like he wants out. I can't let that happen," Reagan wrote in his diary right after his victory in the 1984 presidential election. "Actually, George is carrying out my policy. I'm going to meet with Cap and Bill and lay it out to them. Won't be fun but has to be done."[90]

The exchanges with Chernenko were not leading anywhere, but Reagan's mind was made up. He had learned a great deal during his first four years as president and believed he could pursue a peace agenda with the Russians when the opportunity presented itself. "Hang tough and stay the course," he said to himself and his advisers. "America was back," and the Soviets knew it. Eventually, they would be more forthcoming.[91] Reagan was a patient, stubborn man. He wanted to bargain, but from strength. He seemed very much like Harry Truman when Truman had said that he wanted to cooperate with the Russians, so long as he could get his way 85 percent of the time.[92]

Reagan had tremendous faith in his own negotiating skills, disarming friends and foes alike with his relaxed, calm, modest, and self-effacing manner. He was sentimental yet unemotional, a "warmly ruthless man," wrote Martin Anderson.[93] Reagan had the gift "of setting you utterly at ease," wrote David Stockman. He was a "master of friendly diplomacy," said Shultz, and "was easy to like."[94] He was often short on facts and devoid of knowledge but, according to Richard Pipes, "had irresistible charm."[95] But he was no pushover. He was calculating, competitive, tough-minded, and disciplined. He instinctively grasped the rhythm of negotiations. His stubborn patience was a powerful weapon, as were his apt use of humor and anecdote, simple language, and strong convictions.[96]

By 1984, Reagan was eager to apply his negotiating skills to the Russians. "There is renewed optimism throughout the land," he said in his State of the Union message on 25 January. "America is back, standing tall, looking to the eighties with courage, confidence, and hope." He had great plans for the new year and for a new presidential term, a term that he was determined to win through a decisive electoral victory. "America has always been greatest when we dared to be great." He now invited the Soviet people to join him in his dream to make a safer world, "to preserve our civilization in this modern age." "A nuclear war cannot be won and must never be fought," Reagan declared. Speaking to the members of Congress who sat before him, but explicitly directing his remarks across the oceans, he asked the "People of the Soviet Union" to join America in a quest for peace. "If your government wants peace, there will be peace. We can come together in faith and friendship to build a safer and far better world for our children and our children's children."[97]

Reagan's tough actions and increasingly mellow talk sat well with the American people. His defense buildup, deployment of intermediate-range missiles, intervention in Grenada, and aid to the Mujahedin in Afghanistan were popular, even while his support of the Contras in Nicaragua and his indifference to human rights violations in El Salvador and Guatemala triggered virulent opposition. His wife and some of his political advisers, such as Michael Deaver, nurtured the president's more conciliatory rhetoric, wanting to dispel the warmongering image the Democrats liked to employ against him. But Reagan did not cater to the polls. He hated arguments based on politics, and he believed he could read the temperature of the American people better than anyone.[98]

Reagan won a smashing victory in the 1984 elections. His opponent, former vice president Walter Mondale, won only his home state and the District of Columbia. Reagan promised throughout the campaign that "morning in America" meant more of the same: smaller government, less regulation, and more freedom. In his second inaugural address, on 21 January 1985, he proposed an "opportunity society" at home "in which all of us—white and

black, rich and poor, young and old, will go forward together, arm in arm."
He thought a "new beginning" had been achieved during his first administration domestically, and freedom was on the march internationally. He promised an unwavering quest for peace based on strength. Through negotiations with the Kremlin, he was determined to reduce the number of nuclear weapons and seek their "total elimination . . . from the face of the earth." He insisted that his Star Wars "security shield" was an eminently sensible way to proceed. "It wouldn't kill people; it would destroy weapons. It wouldn't militarize space; it would help demilitarize the arsenals on earth."[99]

Chernenko and his aides did not know quite what to make of Reagan's new public rhetoric. Through most of 1984, Chernenko had sent friendly replies to Reagan.[100] He authorized the renewal of talks that had been suspended when the Pershing IIs had been deployed in West Germany. These discussions bogged down quickly, but Gromyko accepted an invitation to meet with Reagan in the White House at the end of September 1984. As Reagan put it in his diary, the president opened "with my monologue and made the point that perhaps both of us felt the other was a threat." Both men acknowledged that both sides had mountains of nuclear weapons that were getting higher and more dangerous. "I tried to let him know," Reagan recalled, "that the Soviet Union had nothing to fear from us." To Reagan, Gromyko appeared "hard as granite." To Shultz, he seemed "comfortable with the Cold War." But Gromyko nonetheless took Nancy Reagan aside at a reception before lunch and whispered playfully, "Does your husband believe in peace?" Nancy replied that he did. "Then whisper 'peace' in your husband's ear every night," Gromyko said.[101]

Shultz and McFarlane kept nudging Reagan to push forward with his overtures to Chernenko, but on 10 March 1985 Chernenko died. He was the third Soviet leader to pass away on Reagan's watch. The president had tried to engage each of them but had had little success, partly because of their reluctance, partly because they could not discern the American president's real intentions when his rhetoric and actions often seemed so threatening.[102]

Yet Reagan's and Shultz's hopes for the future were lucidly outlined in the talking points prepared for Vice President Bush when he headed to Moscow to attend Chernenko's funeral and talk to the new Soviet leader, Mikhail Gorbachev. "I bring with me a message . . . of peace," Bush was scripted to tell Gorbachev. "We know this is a time of difficulty; we would like it to be a time of opportunity." The Soviet and American systems were different, and the differences would not disappear soon. "Our relationship is bound to be essentially competitive. But it is in the interest of both countries to compete and resolve problems in peaceful ways, and to build a more stable and constructive relationship. We know that some of the things we do and say sound threatening or hostile to you. The same is true for us." But the point Bush was supposed to stress was that "neither the American government nor the American people has hostile intentions toward you." They recognized that "you have suffered a great deal, and struggled a great deal, throughout your history." They recognized that World War II was a great triumph for the Soviet Union and a great tragedy. The triumph opened up possibilities for a more peaceful world; the tragedy was that the opportunities were squandered. Now there was a new chance. "We are ready to embark on that path with you. It is the path of negotiations." A number of agreements had already been signed, but there could be more. "We think it is a time to be more energetic, to tackle larger issues, to set higher goals. . . . [W]e should strive to eliminate nuclear weapons from the face of the earth." Both nations should aim for a "stable deterrence based on non-nuclear defense. . . . [W]e should approach the other issues between us with the same energy and vision. We should seek to rid the world of the threat or use of force in international relations."[103]

Bush did not actually say these words at the meeting, but wandered instead into a discussion of regional issues and human rights. But then Secretary Shultz looked directly at Gorbachev and conveyed the president's message: "President Reagan told me to look you squarely in the eyes and tell you: 'Ronald Reagan believes this is a very special moment in the history of mankind.' "[104]

Twilight in Moscow

Mikhail Gorbachev impressed Shultz and Bush. He was lively, energetic, and intelligent. He listened, asked questions, and probed. He liked to talk. He was smart and self-confident. "He has a deep and sharp mind," Gromyko had said at the Politburo meeting that elected Gorbachev general secretary, and was a man who could "distinguish the primary from the secondary. . . . He dissects every issue to see its structure. But he doesn't leave it at that—he generalizes and draws broader conclusions. He's a man of principle and conviction. . . . He's straightforward with people . . . can say things not to your liking but . . . get along with different people."[105] Shultz saw precisely these traits. "In Gorbachev we have an entirely different kind of leader in the Soviet Union than we have experienced before," he told Bush. Gorbachev was quick, fresh, engaging, and wide-ranging. "I came away genuinely impressed with the quality of thought, the intensity, and the intellectual energy of this new man on the scene," Shultz recalled.[106]

Mikhail Gorbachev was born in the village of Privolnoe in the Stavropol region of southern Russia on 2 March 1931. His grandparents were peasants. His mother's father was an ardent supporter of the Bolshevik revolution, a member of the Communist Party, and an organizer of a collective farm; his father's father, Andrei Gorbachev, wished to farm independently. Andrei and his family suffered terribly during the great famine of 1933, and he was arrested the following year for failing to meet the government's sowing quota. During the 1930s, both grandfathers at different times were declared "enemies of the people" and incarcerated in concentration camps before returning to Stavropol, where they then worked diligently and productively on collective farms. Gorbachev's grandmothers, meanwhile, were deeply religious, as was his own mother. Gorbachev himself was secretly baptized. "Under the icon on a little home-made table stood portraits of Lenin and Stalin," he remembered.[107]

Gorbachev was ten when the Nazis invaded. "Wartime impressions and experiences remain engraved in my mind," he wrote. In August 1941 his father, along with all the other men in the village, was conscripted. "Entire families would accompany their men, profusely shedding tears and voicing parting wishes all the way. We said goodbye at the village center. Women, children, and old men cried their hearts out, the weeping merging into one heart-rending wail of sorrow."[108]

Only women and children remained in the village. Mikhail had to take over his father's household chores and cultivate the vegetable patch that provided the family food. "The wartime children skipped from childhood directly to adulthood," he wrote. In late summer 1942, German armies occupied the village. "Rumours of mass executions in the neighboring towns circulated, and of machines that poisoned people with gas." Mikhail and his mother and grandparents feared for their lives. But they were saved when Soviet troops returned in early 1943 and drove the Germans westward. During that year everything in the village had been destroyed—"no machines were left, no cattle, no seeds. We ploughed the land by hitching cows from our individual households. The picture is still fresh in my memory," Gorbachev continued, "the women crying and the sad eyes of the cows." Famine raged. His mother sold his father's clothes and boots for a sack of corn. They planted seed. The rains came. They lived.[109]

In late summer 1944, they received a letter saying Mikhail's father had been killed. But the news was wrong. He had survived. He had fought at Rostov, Kursk, and many other battlefields; in his brigade alone, 440 soldiers were killed, 120 wounded, and 651 missing. But he survived, returning home in mid-1945 after being wounded.[110]

War meant devastation; war meant trauma. Those who were too young to fight were spared some of the worst pain and suffering, but they occasionally caught shocking glimpses of the meaning of war. Roaming the countryside in March 1943, when the snows were beginning to melt, young Mikhail and his friends "stumbled upon the remains of Red Army soldiers." They beheld "unspeakable horror: decaying corpses, partly devoured by animals, skulls in rusted helmets. . . . There they lay, in the thick mud of the trenches and craters, unburied, staring at us out of black, gaping eye-sockets. We came home in a state of shock." Mikhail would never forget. "I was fourteen when the war ended. Our generation is the generation of wartime children. It has burned us, leaving its mark both on our characters and our view of the world."[111]

Life in the postwar Russian countryside was hard. Drought struck. Harvests were poor. Famine wracked the villages in 1946 and 1947. "There was nothing but hard labor and the belief that once reconstruction was complete, we would finally be able to lead a normal life," Gorbachev wrote. "Hope inspired the most laborious, humiliating work."[112]

Gorbachev was ambitious. In school, he compiled an exemplary record. He also joined the Komsomol, the Young Communist League. He was socialized. The school system, he later commented, "played an enormous role in forming our ideas about the world; it sought to convince us by all means at its disposal that we were living in the most just form of society. Thus we developed the outlook . . . that no alternative was possible."[113]

Of course, he grasped that the realities around him did not correspond to the theories that were inculcated in him. But the ideals were inspiring. "The impulse provided by the revolution had a powerful effect: freedom, land, . . . human dignity for those who had been humiliated—the belief in all those values was, in spite of everything, something quite positive."[114] He was motivated, moreover, by his father's becoming a communist at the battlefront. For Gorbachev, as for so many others, "the war was not only a great victory over fascism but proof that our country's cause was the right one. And by the same token," he reminisced, "so was the cause of Communism." After the victory over the Nazis, "there existed a truly positive subjective attitude toward Soviet society on the part of entire generations who connected their dearest hopes and plans in life with the success of that society."[115]

As a teenager, Gorbachev labored in the fields during the summer with his father, a machinist and tractor driver, whom he greatly admired for his intelligence, industry, courage, and intellectual curiosity. In 1948, working together and with another father-and-son team, they produced a record harvest, five or six times the average. Gorbachev's father won an Order of Lenin prize and Mikhail the Order of the Red Banner of Labour. The young Gorbachev greatly valued this award, which was instrumental in winning him admission to Moscow State University, an unprecedented opportunity for a peasant lad from the boondocks whose grandfathers had been enemies of the people.[116]

Studying law transformed Gorbachev's life. Initially, he felt inadequate. His preparatory education had not been on a par with that of the more urbane students from Moscow and Leningrad. But he was hardworking, ambitious, curious, and intellectually gifted. He loved delving into topics he had not previously explored. The curriculum presumed that in order to study law you needed to understand the socioeconomic and political processes that undergirded the law. Gorbachev preferred the courses in history, diplomacy, political economy, and philosophy to the more practical legal courses. Although much brainwashing went on, he was exposed to new ideas, new students, and stimulating faculty. "The lectures revealed a new world, entire strata of human knowledge hitherto unknown to me."[117]

When, in 1953, Stalin died, it was "a heavy blow that we found hard to endure," Gorbachev acknowledged many years later. "All night long we were part of the crowd going to his coffin." But university life changed for the better after the dictator's death. Lectures became more interesting, seminars livelier. "Doubts were expressed—warily at first, but gradually more outspoken." Traditional interpretations were challenged. Gorbachev learned "how to think. . . . Before the university I was trapped in my belief system in the sense that I accepted a great deal as given, as assumptions not to be questioned. At the university I began to think and reflect and to look at things differently."[118]

He met his soul mate, Raisa Titorenko, at the university. An accomplished student of philosophy, she also came from a family that had experienced the purges and terror of the 1930s. With Raisa, Gorbachev found somebody with whom he could discuss his concerns and share his ambitions. They were married in 1953. She did not have his social skills, but she was smart, incisive, and committed to ameliorating the many ills of the Soviet system, including the position of women and the backward conditions of the peasantry, subjects she studied while her husband pursued his career.[119]

After graduating from Moscow State University, Gorbachev returned to Stavropol. For the next two decades, he moved steadily up the ranks, first of the Komsomol and then of the local and regional Communist Party. As he worked on party and agricultural issues and traveled around the region, he learned much about the poverty and backwardness of his country. The infrastructure of Stavropol—health care, education, transport, and water supply—was in miserable shape. "Sewage often poured into the open gutters lining the streets." He was dismayed by the sterility of thought of local officials. All directives emanated from Moscow. He, like everybody else, "was bound hand and foot by orders from the center." Gorbachev longed for enlightened leadership from Moscow, but the hopes initially inspired by Khrushchev's thaw quickly faded. Kosygin's economic reforms floundered. "All eyes were fixed on the center," Gorbachev recalled, "and it rejected any kind of innovation, or else it drained the energy and vitality out of any kind of initiative. My first doubts about the effectiveness of the system were born at that time."[120]

These doubts were reinforced by foreign travel. As he moved up the party ranks, Gorbachev gained the right to travel abroad, for example to the German Democratic Republic and Bulgaria. In 1969, only months after the Soviet invasion of Czechoslovakia, he visited Prague and was shocked by the hostility he encountered. In 1971 he went to Italy, in 1972 to Belgium and Holland. Later in the 1970s, he went on trips to Italy and West Germany and traveled extensively in France. As a provincial official in Stavropol, he knew little about the world, so he relished these trips as opportunities to learn. The trips themselves reflect how highly he was regarded by his superiors, since very few Soviet officials received the right to travel in the West during those years. Gorbachev liked talking to foreigners, exchanging ideas, and making comparisons between his way of life and theirs. He felt pride in the Soviet educational system. He believed his countrymen had better access to medical care and a superior public transport system. But his travels abroad bred doubt:

> [M]y previous belief in the superiority of socialist democracy over the bourgeois system was shaken as I observed the functioning of civic society and the different political systems. Finally, the most significant conclusion drawn from the journeys abroad: people lived in better conditions and were better off than in our country. The question haunted me: why was the standard of living in our country lower than in other developed countries?[121]

Doubts about the system did not mean rejection of it. Gorbachev was a devoted communist. He saw that Soviet communism functioned badly, but he nonetheless believed deeply in its values and appreciated its achievements. He later reflected:

> For many years people experienced an extraordinarily high rate of industrial growth, the tangible and undeniable change from a backward country into an industrialized country. People came from remote villages to work in new factories, which they took pride in as their own accomplishment. . . . The eradication of illiteracy, access to education, and visible improvement in living conditions for the masses after ominous destruction and starvation—all this was not just propaganda, but people's actual experience.

Inefficiencies proliferated and corruption grew, but basic needs were provided and society was not polarized. At "the lowest levels of the social

ladder," Gorbachev later recalled, "people did not live in such hopeless circumstances that lack of social mobility was transferred from generation to
generation, as is typical for those living in poverty in many countries with
capitalist economies."[122]

As the party chief in Stavropol, Gorbachev's aims were to accelerate economic growth and ameliorate living conditions. He was energetic, personable, and adaptable. He tried to appoint young people who were talented
and creative. "I considered it my duty to support whatever was new and to
encourage the development of a democratic atmosphere in our region." He
struggled to raise agricultural productivity "not by administrative methods"
but by encouraging local autonomy and embracing scientific and technological innovation. He tried to spur the independence of local enterprises.[123]

His vigor and determination captured the attention of patrons in
Moscow. Fedor Kulakov, minister of agriculture; KGB head Andropov; and
Mikhail Suslov, the ideology tsar and party secretary, came to know him.
They had close ties with the Stavropol region and liked to vacation there at
the numerous spas. Gorbachev had worked under Kulakov when the latter
was regional first secretary. When Suslov and Andropov visited Stavropol,
Gorbachev found ways to meet with them and ingratiate himself. Andropov
liked him. In 1970 Gorbachev was designated first secretary of the Stavropol
region. The next year, at the age of forty, he became a full member of the
Central Committee. When Kulakov died in 1978, Brezhnev brought Gorbachev to Moscow and appointed him party secretary in charge of agriculture. Shortly thereafter, he was asked to join the Politburo, first as a
candidate member and then as a full member. In his late forties, he was
nearly twenty-five years younger than his average colleague.[124]

In Moscow, Gorbachev was eager to bring about change. He met with
agricultural economists and other experts, visited various policy institutes,
asked questions, listened, and probed. He wanted to decentralize authority,
give farmers more responsibility for organizing their work, and pay them according to their productivity.[125] Yet, as long as Brezhnev lived, he was able to
accomplish little. By now old and sick, Brezhnev could not organize the work
of the government or the party, communicate effectively, or consider new approaches or initiatives. The Politburo, according to Gorbachev, was in "total
disarray." Top party leaders were insulated from the people and isolated from
one another. At regular meetings in the early 1980s, they talked little about

their work and rarely explored new ideas. There was a need to reallocate resources away from the defense establishment, but "the problem could not even be analyzed. All statistics concerning the military-industrial complex were top secret, inaccessible even to members of the Politburo."[126] For leaders with reformist instincts, there was little to do but wait for Brezhnev to die.

Meanwhile, Gorbachev kept developing himself. As a high party official, he now had access to books not previously available to him. He was exposed to new ways of thinking about socialism as he perused articles by Willy Brandt and François Mitterrand.[127] He also initiated contacts with experts on foreign policy and atomic weapons. He met scientists like Yevgeni Velikhov, academicians like Georgi Arbatov, and international relations experts like Anatoli Chernyaev and Georgi Shakhnazarov. On a trip to Canada, he renewed his acquaintance with Alexander Yakovlev, the Soviet ambassador in Ottawa. The two men discovered they were "kindred spirits." "We spoke completely frankly about everything," Yakovlev recalled; "the main idea was that society must change, it must be built on different principles."[128]

When Brezhnev died and Andropov became general secretary, there was a palpable change in the atmosphere. The former KGB chief wanted to invigorate the system and accelerate industrial production. He looked to Gorbachev to help spearhead overall economic reform. And knowing he was ill, he began grooming the younger man as his successor. He assigned Gorbachev the task of preparing the major address commemorating the sixtieth anniversary of Lenin's death and encouraged him to think more broadly about all issues: "act as if you had to shoulder all the responsibility . . . ," said Andropov.[129]

Andropov set a course that greatly appealed to Gorbachev. He "resolutely denounced all the features commonly associated with Brezhnevism, that is, protectionism, in-fighting and intrigues, corruption, moral turpitude, bureaucracy, disorganization and laxity."[130] He called for the perfection of "developed socialism." Qualitative changes, he insisted, must occur not only in the productive forces of society but also in the superstructure. He meant that labor productivity must increase and new technologies must be embraced, including computers and robots. Like his predecessors, Andropov stressed that the quality of goods must be enhanced. He reminded his comrades that the "ultimate objective of our efforts in the economic field is to improve the living conditions of the people." Even while he demanded stricter discipline, he also believed that socialist democracy must be broadened, that the "activities of the party and state bodies [must be brought] closer to the needs and interests of the people."[131]

Andropov did not hesitate to say that the challenges were daunting. "Frankly speaking we have not yet studied properly the society in which we live and work, and have not yet fully revealed the laws governing its development, particularly economic ones," he acknowledged in a speech to the party plenum on 15 June 1983. "This is why we have to act at times empirically, so to speak, by the quite irrational trial-and-error method." Life constantly interjected new problems, and scientific study was required. But science and technology conjured up new challenges and threats, too.[132]

No threat was greater than that of nuclear war. "An unprecedented sharpening of the struggle between the two world social systems has taken place," said Andropov. "[But] an attempt to solve the historical dispute between the two systems through a military clash could be disastrous to mankind." Preserving the peace was therefore his main objective. So important was it, he insisted, that one had to "reappraise the principal goals . . . of the entire communist movement." Fighting "oppression and the exploitation of man by man" had always been an overriding concern, but nowadays communists "must also struggle for the preservation of human civilization, for man's right to life." Capitalism was facing ever graver crises, besieged as it was by "internal and interstate antagonisms, upheavals, and conflicts." But within the capitalist world were factions and movements that realized the necessity of peaceful coexistence. Andropov wanted them to know that he shared their hope for peaceful coexistence, which met "the interests of the peoples on both sides of the social barricades dividing the world."[133]

Andropov still "believed that the future belongs to socialism. Such is the march of history." But this did not mean that "we are going to engage in the 'export of revolution.' " Socialism would "ultimately prove its advantages precisely in the conditions of peaceful competition with capitalism. And we by no means advocate competition in the military field, which imperialism is foisting on us." Although he would never sacrifice the security of the U.S.S.R. or its allies and was prepared to enhance the combat power of the nation's armed forces, he preferred "to reduce the level of armaments and military spending on both sides and embark on disarmament, which we are actively seeking." The goal of the Soviet Union, he concluded, was not merely to avert war but to seek a radical improvement in international relations.[134]

These ideas appealed to Gorbachev, but they were put on hold when Andropov died in early 1984. Gorbachev briefly thought he might be elected general secretary, but the old guard united behind Konstantin Chernenko, who led the country for a year. Seventy-three years old, sick, and infirm, he was an embarrassment to those who yearned for dynamism and innovation. Although he talked about proceeding in the direction set by Andropov, he lacked the vigor, imagination, and determination to shake up the party cadres, catalyze economic change, spur production, or reconfigure relations with the United States. Since Chernenko often was too sick to attend Politburo meetings, Gorbachev grew accustomed to running them. Then, as Chernenko's death grew near—he died on 11 March 1985—Gorbachev mobilized his supporters. Eager to take command, he was not to be outfoxed a second time by his opponents. He wanted to reform and revitalize the system, and he had developed his own ideas about how to move forward. "We can't go on living like this," he whispered to Raisa on the eve of assuming power. He thought the "system was dying away; its sluggish senile blood no longer contained any vital juices."[135]

The next day, at the meetings of the Politburo and the Central Committee, he was unanimously elected general secretary. Applause greeted the choice.[136] It was twilight in Moscow, but Gorbachev offered a glimpse of a new dawn.

Arms Reductions

At the Central Committee meeting that officially designated him the new general secretary, Gorbachev outlined his vision. Without repudiating the past, he emphasized that the Soviet economy must be rejuvenated and its society revitalized. He wanted to accelerate production, restructure economic management, and promote openness and democracy.[137] "Accelerate" meant to incorporate scientific and technological innovations promptly into Soviet industry, to heighten labor productivity, and to combat alcoholism. Socialist democracy must be nurtured along with more discipline and more order, Gorbachev said. Individual workers had to be reengaged in production, develop a sense of ownership in the process. More self-management demanded more transparency (glasnost).[138] Gorbachev believed that more democracy in the workplace meant more socialism. And more socialism meant more social justice, the feature that distinguished socialism from capitalism and made it more likely to satisfy man's quest for personal fulfillment and creativity.[139]

Turning to foreign affairs, Gorbachev stated unequivocally that the arms race must be curbed. "Never before has such a terrible danger hung over the heads of humanity in our times," he told his comrades. "The only rational way out of the current situation is for the opposing forces to agree to immediately stop the arms race—above all, the nuclear arms race."[140]

The mounting stockpiles of nuclear weapons made no sense to Gorbachev. They did not contribute to national security, and he believed a nuclear war could not be won and must never be waged. "In the atomic-cosmic era," he would say in May 1986, "world war is an absolute evil."[141] Nor did he think that nuclear weapons could be used politically to blackmail or intimidate an adversary in a crisis. Risk-taking of this sort could be suicidal, as war might arise through miscalculation if the adversary did not back down. Nuclear weapons "must stop being used in a political role because it's impossible to achieve our goals using [them]."[142]

The greatest danger to Soviet communism, however, did not arise from external threats. Gorbachev "did not think anyone was going to attack us," said Anatoli Chernyaev, one of the foreign-policy experts who became an aide to the new Soviet leader in February 1986. Soviet military capabilities were sufficiently great "to repulse the desire for aggression."[143] However, Gorbachev did consider the Soviet Union imperiled by internal decay. The arms race had to be tamed and international relations defused because these steps were indispensable for the success of his domestic program. "[W]e understood that if nothing was changed in our foreign policy, we would get nowhere with regard to the internal changes we had in mind," Gorbachev recalled. Chernyaev emphasized that there was an intimate connection "between every important domestic issue and foreign policy."[144]

Gorbachev's thinking adumbrated a radical shift in ideology. Imperialism was still to be worried about; vigilance was necessary.[145] The United States, Gorbachev would say over and over again during his first years in office, was trying to exhaust the Soviet Union, "waiting for us to drown."[146] He would not allow his country to be intimidated by superior American power, and he was initially prepared to shift more resources to modernize Soviet defense capabilities. Military preparedness is "for us the sacred of the sacred."[147] But the primary threat emanated from within, from the communist system's failure to fulfill the expectations of the Soviet people, to produce the goods people wanted, and to ensure the way of life they anticipated.

Restructuring was the key to a revival of socialism's appeal. "Contemporary world politics [was] a struggle for the minds and hearts of people," Gorbachev believed.[148] In this contest, socialism offered a glorious vision of social justice and individual fulfillment. But "the international impetus of socialism had lessened."[149] By restoring its dynamism at home, he could increase its attractiveness abroad. When he was elected general secretary, he made it clear that he wanted to focus on domestic issues. On 15 March 1985, he told a conference of party secretaries that the U.S.S.R. "should emphasize domestic issues and solving the economic and social problems of our country's development." In his report to the twenty-seventh Party Congress on 25 February 1986, he would reiterate that the main "international duty" of the party was to ensure the success of the revolution at home.[150]

Gorbachev recognized from the outset, however, that his domestic goals could not be achieved without readjusting Soviet foreign policy. He understood, according to Chernyaev, that "in order to pursue some sort of transformation, to improve Socialism, nothing could be done unless you stop the arms race." The purpose of foreign policy, Gorbachev said a year after taking over leadership, was to "do everything . . . to weaken the grip of expenses on defense." He was to be even more explicit at a Politburo meeting in October 1986, when he discussed his strategy for his forthcoming meeting with President Reagan at Reykjavik, Iceland. "Our goal is to prevent the next round of the arms race. If we do not accomplish it, . . . [w]e will be pulled into an arms race that is beyond our capabilities, and we will lose it, because we are at the limits of our capabilities." Gorbachev's comrades agreed, even most of the military officers, if not the civilian managers in the defense industries.[151]

To defuse international tensions and promote an atmosphere conducive to arms cuts, Gorbachev wanted to transform the image of the Soviet Union. "From the very beginning," Chernyaev stressed, "he . . . knew that you could not change society if you did not first change the attitudes of other countries toward the Soviet Union." The "image of our country . . . when Gorbachev

came to power was actually the worst it [had] ever been in the eyes of international society," said Sergei Tarasenko, another influential foreign-policy adviser. For almost a decade the country had been run by a group of elderly,
infirm men who seemed out of touch with contemporary needs at home and
abroad. The invasion of Afghanistan, the escalation of the arms race, the declaration of martial law in Poland, the incessant wrangling with China, the destruction of the Korean civilian airliner, and the stagnation of the economy
had soiled the Kremlin's reputation and discredited its leaders. "[O]ne of the
first concerns of the Gorbachev administration," Tarasenko continued, "was
to repair this image so the Soviet Union wouldn't be viewed as the 'evil empire.' "[152]

Gorbachev immediately went to work trying to alter the image of the
Soviet Union and to promote better relations with the United States. On
24 March 1985, a few days after speaking forcefully to Vice President Bush
and Secretary of State Shultz about the need for a new beginning, he sent his
first letter to President Reagan:

> Our countries are different by their social systems, by the ide-
> ologies dominant in them. But we believe that this should not
> be a reason for animosity. Each social system has a right to life,
> and it should prove its advantages not by force, not by military
> means, but on the path of peaceful competition with the other
> system. And all people have the right to go the way they have
> chosen themselves, without anybody imposing his will on them
> from outside.

The two countries, Gorbachev continued, had one overriding interest uniting
them: "not to let things come to the outbreak of nuclear war which would inevitably have catastrophic consequences for both sides." The leaders needed
to stop "whipping up animosity," to assess their differences calmly, and to
"create an atmosphere of trust between our two countries." Gorbachev welcomed a personal meeting with the U.S. president.[153] Like Reagan, he believed that "normal relationships" across ideological lines must be built on "a
human basis."[154]

Reagan wrote back swiftly and warmly, asking Gorbachev to meet with
Congressman Thomas P. ("Tip") O'Neill, Speaker of the House of Represen-

tatives, and other legislators visiting Moscow. Gorbachev readily complied. On 10 April, he said candidly to O'Neill: "The relations between our countries are presently in a kind of ice age," but they did not have to remain frozen. "A fatal conflict of interest between our countries is not inevitable." There was "a way out, namely, peaceful coexistence, the recognition that each nation has the right to live as it wishes. There is no other alternative."[155]

To achieve this goal, Gorbachev needed to plow new ideological ground. He was already beginning to embrace "common security," or "equal security," a concept extensively discussed among European socialists and theorists of international relations and a core ingredient of Gorbachev's "new thinking," which moved the Soviet conception of international relations away from class conflict.[156] Of course, words were cheap, and Gorbachev knew that deeds needed to match his rhetoric. He started to explore ways to withdraw Soviet troops from Afghanistan.[157] He told the Warsaw Pact allies that he would negotiate to reduce intermediate-range nuclear missiles in Europe "or, better yet, to reciprocally rid Europe of both intermediate-range and tactical nuclear weapons altogether."[158] In July 1985 he announced a unilateral moratorium on Soviet nuclear testing and expressed hope that the United States would reciprocate.[159]

The seriousness of Gorbachev's intentions began to impress foreigners when at the end of June 1985 he dramatically removed Andrei Gromyko as foreign minister, a post he had held for more than twenty years. The able, tough-minded veteran diplomat was, in Gorbachev's view, "rigid," his ideas "locked in concrete."[160] Gromyko was burdened, as his son later acknowledged, by the memory of Nazi aggression, the "June 22 Syndrome," and by the belief that the Soviet Union was forever encircled and besieged by imperialist enemies.[161]

In his place, Gorbachev appointed Eduard Shevardnadze, a young Politburo member from Georgia with no foreign-policy experience. Gorbachev knew Shevardnadze well. They were of the same generation, had both endured the hardships of war on the home front, and had moved up the ranks of the party hierarchy simultaneously, Shevardnadze in Georgia and Gorbachev in Stavropol. They had met at meetings and had come to regard one another as kindred spirits. Gorbachev knew that in appointing Shevardnadze he was selecting a foreign minister who would embrace his new thinking.[162]

World War II had powerfully shaped Shevardnadze's views, though not as permanently as it had those of the generation of 22 June. "The war shaped me as it did millions of my contemporaries," he recalled. "It formed my convictions and purpose in life." His brother died in the first days of the war; his other brother was immediately summoned to the front. "My mother dressed in mourning for all present and future losses." The Nazi attack confirmed that "outsiders wanted to destroy us, to annihilate us physically. My choice [of communism] was determined by the death of friends and relatives, by the grief, suffering, and privations of millions of people." For Shevardnadze, "the war with fascism became a personal battle. . . . The fascists were attacking communism, and communism was my religion."[163]

When appointed foreign minister, he had not grown ashamed of his commitment. "The collectivism that I served with all my might was literally working miracles, transforming barren land, defeating fascism, raising the country from ruins, and therein lay its great authority." But like Gorbachev, Shevardnadze could see the flaws in the system—its lawlessness, its penchant to reduce "a person to a cog who could be crushed with impunity." As party leader in Georgia, Shevardnadze had tried to gain more autonomy, get around the command system, and unleash local initiative, but he was frustrated. "Everything is rotten," he had confided to Gorbachev in late 1984.[164]

Shevardnadze was flabbergasted by the offer to be foreign minister. He knew little of the world and spoke no foreign language. Georgian was his native tongue, and he spoke Russian with a pronounced accent. But Gorbachev implored him to take the job, for he wanted innovation, courage, and dynamism. He wanted someone, like himself, who could deal with the Americans on a human basis, who could transcend the ideological chasm.[165]

When Shevardnadze met Secretary of State Shultz in Helsinki at the end of July 1985, he knew little of the details of the arms-control negotiations that had been going on for so many years. He did not hide his ignorance. He told Shultz that he would simply read the talking points that had been prepared for him. His candor and openness impressed Shultz, which was precisely Shevardnadze's intention. His primary goal was to eradicate the "image of the enemy." "We and the Americans were divided by walls built out of the rubble of distrust and stones of ideology," he recalled.[166]

Shevardnadze's speech in the Finnish capital commemorating the tenth anniversary of the Helsinki Agreement contained the seeds of the new Soviet thinking. The Kremlin, Shevardnadze said, now wanted to defuse international tension and focus on domestic life. Soviet leaders wanted to accelerate social and economic development, promote citizens' well-being, and create the conditions for the "harmonious development of the individual." Soviet foreign policy sprang from these domestic requirements. "In order to carry out its large-scale plans," Shevardnadze concluded, "the Soviet Union needs a lasting peace in Europe, a lasting peace all over the world."[167]

Gorbachev communicated the same message. In early October 1985, he told a French television audience that his highest priority was "to develop the economy, social relations, and democracy." Answering journalists' questions with vibrant self-confidence, he remarked, "We have different political systems. We have different views of human values. But we also have much in common." Since "we live in the same house, we need to cooperate." When asked about whether the Soviet Union had four million political prisoners, he bristled and said it was "absurd" to talk about numbers of this sort. "We know what has to be done in order to open up even more the best aspects of this social system. And at the center of all our aspirations is man and his needs."[168]

He made the same points when he met with leaders of the Warsaw Pact on 22 October, though in that setting he also denounced what he saw as American attempts to accelerate the arms race. "They are planning to win over socialism through war or military blackmail." His hostility to SDI was unreserved: "Its militaristic nature is obvious. . . . Its purpose is to secure permanent technological superiority of the West, not only over the socialist community, but over [the US] allies as well." If necessary, the Kremlin would counter the American initiative and was already pouring more resources into military research and strategic defense. But he preferred not to do so; it was costly. "We need to force imperialism to undertake concrete steps toward disarmament and normalization of the situation in the world." His aim was to eradicate the Western image of a "Soviet military threat."[169] But the new tone was distinctive and the larger message clear: the Soviet Union and the United States obviously had substantial differences, as he wrote to Reagan, but must "proceed from the objective fact that we all live on the same planet and must learn to live together."[170]

Reagan eagerly anticipated his first encounter with the new general secretary, scheduled for mid-November. The president's "juices were flowing. In a very real sense," he recalled, "preparations for the summit had begun five years earlier, when we began strengthening our economy, restoring our national will, and rebuilding our defenses. I felt ready."[171]

He and Shultz knew that Gorbachev wanted to focus on arms reductions and stop the SDI program.[172] Report after report from intelligence analysts in the State Department and CIA stressed that the Soviet Union was "a society in trouble." Although it was not likely to collapse anytime soon, it could no longer serve as a model for restless peoples and revolutionary nationalists seeking rapid modernization and social transformation. In fact, the Americans believed the Soviet regime would be unable to fulfill its people's expectations or to muster the resources to meet Gorbachev's ambitious economic goals.[173]

Knowing all this, Reagan aimed to extract concessions on matters that interested him: the state of human rights inside the U.S.S.R., the war in Afghanistan, and the turmoil in Central America, southern Africa, and other regional hotspots. To him, arms negotiations were linked to these matters. The tension and animosity between the U.S. and the U.S.S.R. were, in his view, a result not of armaments but of mistrust. If the Soviet Union wanted arms reductions, as did he, they would have to remove the distrust, help settle regional disputes, and allow some of their dissidents to speak more freely and emigrate more easily.[174]

President Reagan was willing to bargain—except on the Strategic Defense Initiative. He wrote in his diary on 11 September 1985: "I won't trade our SDI off for some Soviet offer of weapon reductions."[175] He hoped to settle other matters—just not right away. Unlike his secretary of defense, director of central intelligence, and head of the Arms Control and Disarmament Agency, he was eager to talk to Gorbachev.[176] But Shultz advised him to modulate his expectations; Gorbachev was extremely personable and engaging, but he was also tough and intelligent. The most important thing was to establish a personal rapport, to begin a process.[177] Reagan agreed completely. He believed he knew how to negotiate. "You're unlikely to get all you want; you'll probably get more of what you want if you don't issue ultimatums and leave your adversary room to maneuver; you shouldn't back your adversary into a corner, embarrass him, or humiliate him; and sometimes the easiest way to get things done is for the top people to do them alone and in private."[178]

Ronald and Nancy Reagan flew to Geneva on 16 November 1985 to meet

Mikhail and Raisa Gorbachev. Their excitement was palpable. "As we shook hands, I had to admit . . . there was something likeable about Gorbachev," the president recalled. "There was warmth in his face and his style." Reagan immediately suggested they chat without advisers, an idea he had been carefully planning. He wanted to establish a sense of intimacy. Together, with only their interpreters, they talked for about an hour.[179]

"The fate of the world" was in their hands, Reagan began. They could bring peace to the world, if only they could allay the deep suspicions that separated their countries. The president suggested that they focus, first, on building trust; solutions to specific problems would follow if only they could build confidence. Reagan tried to be empathetic, mentioning his understanding of the impact of World War II on the Soviet Union, but he also expressed apprehensions about Soviet efforts to spread Marxism-Leninism by brute force. The U.S.S.R. and the United States, Reagan said, should work together to settle the problems besetting third world countries.[180]

Gorbachev wanted to build a rapport, too, but he was far more eager than Reagan to reach an agreement on reducing nuclear armaments and pre-

Reagan and Gorbachev at the Geneva summit, 1985. Their
conversation led to a remarkable relationship.

venting an arms race in space. He spoke with warmth and sincerity, and told the president that his intention was to talk quietly and with respect. The Soviet peoples bore no grudges and wished America no harm. He was convinced that they could improve relations but stressed that they had an obligation to solve the overriding question of war and peace. The way to begin was to reduce armaments. Though he shared Reagan's concern about the strife and turmoil in the third world, the Soviet Union was not responsible for the unrest, he argued. Moscow was not "omnipotent." He did not wake each morning thinking about "which country he would now like to arrange a revolution in." Revolutions had their own indigenous causes; the Kremlin supported self-determination, and did not want to impose its way of life on anybody.[181]

This initial conversation immediately created a bond between the two men. What was obvious was that they both wanted to build a human relationship, to transcend the ideological divide without abandoning their principles. As they joined the larger delegations, they continued to elaborate on many of the key themes they had introduced in this first talk.

Each leader expressed his concerns about the other's expansionist tendencies. Gorbachev, however, picked up on Reagan's initial theme about building trust. But he wanted more than trust: he wanted Reagan to disavow SDI. The Soviets regarded Star Wars as an American effort to gain supremacy, and as an offensive, not defensive, measure. SDI could not effectively shield America against a premeditated Soviet attack involving thousands of missiles; its utility, therefore, must be to thwart Soviet retaliation should the Americans launch a preemptive strike on the Soviet homeland.

Gorbachev said he knew that some Americans relished a chance to demonstrate technological superiority and ratchet up the arms race, thinking it would wear down the Soviet economy. This strategy, he insisted, would not work: if necessary, "we will build up in order to smash your shield." Yet that was not what he wanted to do. He wanted—and he was surprisingly candid in explaining his thinking—to rechannel money from the arms race into the civilian economy. In both their countries, the military was "devouring huge resources."[182]

Over the next day and a half, Reagan repeatedly accused the Soviets of sponsoring revolution around the world, crushing human rights, and building up a gigantic nuclear arsenal. Gorbachev needed to remove American anxieties about these developments, Reagan said. In turn, the U.S. president wanted to allay Soviet fears about Star Wars, which, he maintained, was not part of an offensive strategy; he had no intent to catalyze an arms race in space. To prove American goodwill, Reagan said the United States would share the SDI technologies with the Soviet Union. With both sides having the same defensive capabilities, substantial cuts in strategic weapons, perhaps even the elimination of all nuclear warheads, would be possible.[183]

Gorbachev and his advisers were baffled by the American position. When Reagan and Gorbachev went off for another private chat in the afternoon, Shevardnadze told Shultz that the president's ideas about Star Wars were a form of "fantasy." Deputy Foreign Minister Georgi Kornienko explained that the Kremlin could never agree to such proposals. How could Soviet officials know for sure that subsequent American presidents would honor Reagan's commitments? "Unfortunately, we knew from history examples of treaties which were signed and then thrown into the wastebasket." The whole idea was "naïve."[184]

Over the two days of conversations, SDI became the great stumbling block. Gorbachev kept explaining why SDI was unacceptable, and Reagan kept insisting that it was being designed for defensive purposes. Why could the Soviets not trust him? "With some emotion," Gorbachev emphasized that verification of space-based technologies would be exceedingly difficult, and he appealed to the president to rethink his attitude. "What was the logic of starting an arms race in a new sphere?"[185]

The discord over SDI meant that there could be no meeting of minds on the limitation of strategic, intermediate-range, or conventional weapons. Nor was there any agreement on regional disputes. Nonetheless, both Reagan and Gorbachev gained confidence in one another and agreed to meet again, first in Washington and then in Moscow. Gorbachev was disappointed that he left Geneva without concrete understandings, but he sensed that Reagan "was a man you 'could do business with.' "[186] In turn, Reagan liked Gorbachev. Already at the end of the first day, Nancy Reagan recalled, "I noticed an unmistakable warmth between them."[187]

The warmth was most conspicuous during the evening dinners and toasts, when Gorbachev greatly impressed the president and his wife. He was relaxed, asked questions, and had a good sense of humor. "He could tell jokes about himself and even about his country," Reagan wrote, "and I grew to like him more."[188] In one of Gorbachev's warm, evocative toasts, he recalled a biblical story about "a time to throw stones, and . . . a time to gather them; now is the time to gather stones which have been cast in the past." Reagan, in turn, reminded the guests that they were dining on the forty-third anniversary of the Soviet counterattack at the battle of Stalingrad, the turning point in the Great Patriotic War. He hoped, he said, that this meeting might be "yet another turning point for all mankind—one that would make it possible to have a world of peace and freedom."[189] At the end of dinner on the second night, when both leaders reflected on their failure to achieve concrete results, they nevertheless voiced optimism. "We will not change our positions, our values, or our thinking," said Gorbachev, "but we expect that with patience and wisdom we will find ways toward solutions." The president agreed. Previous summits had led nowhere, he mused, but " 'To hell with the past,' we'll do it our way and get something done."[190]

Gorbachev intrigued the president. "I don't know, Mike," Reagan confided to his former aide, Michael Deaver, when he returned to Washington, "but I honestly think he believes in a higher power."[191] To his good friend the actor George Murphy, Reagan summed up his feelings: the meeting "was worthwhile but it would be foolish to believe the leopard will change his spots. [Gorbachev] is a firm believer in their system (so is she [Raisa]), and he believes the propaganda they peddle about us. At the same time, he is practical and knows his economy is a basket case. I think our job is to show him he and they will be better off if we make some practical agreements, without attempting to convert him to our way of thinking."[192]

Hoping for quick progress, Reagan sent a long handwritten letter to Gorbachev a week after their meeting. The message was vintage Reagan: glowing with warmth yet tough in substance. "I found our meeting of great value," he wrote. They had spoken frankly, ascertained that "there are many things on which we disagree and disagree very fundamentally." But they both recognized that they must manage their relations in a peaceful fashion. He then defended SDI and reiterated that it had nothing to do with achieving first-strike capabilities. "[W]e should be able to find a way, in practical terms, to relieve the concerns you have expressed." They must instruct their negotiators in Geneva to "face up" to the tough issues and make certain that neither nation achieved a one-sided advantage. Reagan then shifted to regional issues. Once again, seeking to show Gorbachev he had listened, Reagan stressed, "I can assure you that the United States does not believe that the Soviet Union is the cause of all the world's ills," but it had "exploited and worsened local tensions." It could allay American anxieties and show its true intentions by withdrawing its forces from Afghanistan. He concluded with another personal touch, urging Gorbachev to collaborate with him to achieve noble goals that only they could reach. "Both of us have advisors and assistants, but . . . the responsibility to preserve peace and increase cooperation is ours. Our people look to us for leadership."[193]

Gorbachev was eager to provide the leadership, but he wanted Reagan to make the concessions. He was frustrated by the president's intransigence on SDI. "Believe me, Mr. President," Gorbachev replied, also in a handwritten letter, "we have a genuine and truly serious concern about U.S. nuclear systems." And his government also worried about U.S. actions in many third world regions. Both Washington and Moscow offered military assistance to countries around the globe. "Why apply a double standard and assert that Soviet assistance is a source of tension and U.S. assistance is beneficial?" The Soviet Union was assisting legitimate governments that came to it for aid when beleaguered by outside interference. The United States often "incites actions against governments and supports and supplies weapons to groups which are inimical to society and are, in essence, terrorists." He mentioned Washington's actions in Nicaragua and, implicitly, U.S. support of the Mujahedin in Afghanistan. However noble were the president's intentions, he could not ignore U.S. capabilities. But like Reagan, Gorbachev wanted to take the sting out of his letter: Please accept this letter, Gorbachev concluded, "as another one of our 'fireside talks.' I would truly like to preserve not only the spirit of our Geneva meetings, but also to go further in developing our dialogue."[194]

Gorbachev recognized that Reagan was trying to use Soviet weaknesses to wring concessions on SDI, regional struggles, and human rights. Gorbachev wanted to get out of Afghanistan.[195] He also was sensitive to Reagan's accusations about the human rights situation in the Soviet Union, and was not averse to easing emigration restrictions.[196] But he was most eager to break the impasse over SDI and press forward with arms reductions. This was critical to the success of perestroika, his program to restructure domestic economic and social life, which he was preparing to present at the forthcoming meeting of the twenty-seventh Party Congress in February.

Gorbachev maneuvered deftly to put more of his own people into positions of influence in the International Department of the CPSU and in the foreign ministry. He promoted innovative thinkers like Yakovlev and brought experts like Chernyaev into his office. In these early years of his rule, his control of the party machinery was masterful. His talks with foreign statesmen, his vigor, and his confidence in handling Western journalists added to his stature in the Kremlin. At Politburo meetings, he did most of the talking, and his colleagues deferred to him. Some winced at his long-winded monologues, but most grasped the need to change in order to revitalize the system. They accepted his determination to modulate the arms race and, eventually, shift expenditures away from the military, so long as Soviet security was not jeopardized and its prestige not damaged.[197]

Gorbachev knew, of course, that he could not disregard the sensibilities of his military advisers and the defense industry managers. He dealt craftily with them, trying to win them over and allowing them to think they were using him. He wanted his generals to devise a viable strategy to solve the problem of intermediate-range missiles in Europe. Marshal Sergei F. Akhromeyev, chief of the General Staff, endorsed a comprehensive program for nuclear disarmament that was generated in the foreign ministry, believing that eventually the program would turn out to be nonnegotiable and that military officers would be able to avoid the cuts they opposed. Gorbachev, however, embraced the idea of this comprehensive package, as it accorded with his predilections and offered a huge opportunity to alter the Soviet image. At a key meeting at the end of 1985, the Politburo approved the new initiative, giving Gorbachev wide room to maneuver. "Once you have a document in your pocket approved by the Politburo about the total destruction, down to zero, of all nuclear armaments, then you are justified in continuing in this policy direction," reflected General Nikolai Detinov, a leading arms-control expert. "It is easier to speak to the military once you have such a document."[198]

On 15 January 1986, Gorbachev proposed a bold vision to advance the cause of nuclear disarmament, calling upon key statesmen to abolish all weapons of mass destruction by the year 2000. Many of Reagan's advisers felt nothing but contempt for this, and many of Gorbachev's admirers thought he had been hoodwinked by his own armed forces and was offering nothing but platitudes. But Gorbachev took it seriously. "My impression is that he's really decided to end the arms race no matter what," Chernyaev wrote in his diary. "He is taking this 'risk' because, as he understands, it's no risk at all— because nobody would attack us even if we disarmed completely. And in order to get this country on solid ground, we have to relieve it of the burden of the arms race."[199]

Reagan's advisers told him to dismiss Gorbachev's initiative. General Edward Rowny, an arms-control expert, told the president not to take Gorbachev's proposal seriously. The Soviet Union would not change; it would cheat. Rowny shouldn't worry, the president said reassuringly. "I'm not going soft. . . . But . . . I have a dream of a world without nuclear weapons. I want our children and grandchildren particularly to be free of these terrible weapons."[200]

Gorbachev's dream coincided with Reagan's, but both leaders were pragmatists as well as dreamers. Gorbachev's primary goal was to promote perestroika and accelerate economic growth. At the end of February, he presented his program to the twenty-seventh Party Congress, as always a major event in the Soviet Union. The general secretary outlined his vision in a (tediously) long report that began with a paean to socialism and went on to a discussion of capitalism, its animosity toward socialism, and its inherent contradictions—all traditional pablum. Gorbachev then shifted gears and mused: "Will the ruling elites of the capitalist world" make sober assessments? "Maybe yes and maybe no," he continued. But "we cannot take no for an answer to the question: Will mankind survive or not? We say: The progress of society, the life of civilization, must and will continue. . . . The course of history, of social progress, requires ever more insistently that there should be constructive and creative interactions between states and peoples." Such interactions were essential to avoid nuclear catastrophe and tackle other challenges. "The realistic dialectics of present-day development consist in a . . . growing tendency towards interdependence of the countries of the world community. This is precisely the way, through the struggle of opposites . . . [toward an] interdependent and in many ways integral world."[201]

This was a shift in communist thinking—to argue that history would lead to interdependence and peace—but it was a prerequisite to the elaboration of Gorbachev's program. What is "acceleration"? he asked. "Its essence lies in the new quality of growth: The all-around intensification of production on the basis of scientific and technical progress, a structural reshaping of the economy, and efficient forms of managing, organizing, and stimulating labor." Administrative changes were imperative; corruption must end. Workers must become engaged in self-management, and their self-discipline and productivity must improve. Enterprises must gain more autonomy. Food shortages must end. Consumer goods must proliferate. People must live better. Social justice must be promoted. Society must change, and socialist democracy must grow "in all its aspects and manifestations." This was a summary of what Gorbachev called Perestroika—a term that literally means "restructuring" but that he used as a label for his whole economic-social program.[202]

The country's economic and social agenda must shape its international strategy, Gorbachev then emphasized. The goal was straightforward: peaceful coexistence must "become the supreme and universal principle of interstate relations." The ideological chasm must be crossed, the two systems must coexist and compete peacefully, and "a comprehensive system of international security" must be designed. All societies must have the right to choose their own social systems, and regional disputes must be resolved justly.[203]

In Politburo meetings after the Party Congress Gorbachev reiterated these themes. "The idea of acceleration and the idea of preserving peace" must proceed together, he said. They were mutually reinforcing.[204] Thereafter, he and Shevardnadze tried to improve ties with West European governments and transform the image of the Soviet Union. But they never lost sight of the fact that the indispensable partner was the United States. Agreement with Washington was the ultimate prize, the key to reconfiguring international politics, effectuating arms cuts, shifting resources to domestic priorities, and revitalizing socialism within the U.S.S.R. On 3 April, Gorbachev told the Politburo, "Notwithstanding all the ambiguity in our relations with the United States, reality is such that we cannot do anything without them, nor they without us. We live on one planet. And we cannot preserve peace without America."[205]

But Gorbachev was frustrated. The arms-control talks in Geneva had bogged down, and Reagan had shown no inclination to budge on Star Wars. They "are putting pressure on us—to exhaust us," Gorbachev told the Politburo on 24 March.[206] Nor was he satisfied with the pace of change at home. He went around the country making speeches, trying to generate support for his initiatives, sometimes hectoring, sometimes pleading. Soviet citizens must not tolerate obsolete practices that "are holding back our movement, . . .

blackening and darkening our conditions, our life, our socialist system," he told party loyalists in Khabarovsk. They needed "fewer words, chatter, conceit and empty theorizing, and more down-to-earth concern about real matters and satisfying the demands and requirements of people."[207]

Gorbachev was infuriated and embarrassed by the explosion on 26 April at the nuclear power plant in Chernobyl, Ukraine, which killed more than 30 people and required the evacuation of 116,000 local residents. Although he tried initially to conceal its dimensions, he soon realized he could not. The fire raged for days, catalyzing fears of a massive nuclear meltdown. Radiation clouds wafted across Europe carrying more radioactive material than had been released from the bombings of Hiroshima and Nagasaki. The accident was a catastrophe, costing billions of rubles, ruining the lives of tens of thousands of citizens, and endangering the food chain throughout Central and Western Europe.[208] Gorbachev was disgusted with the incompetence of his managers, yet another indication of the rot in the Soviet system, but he was also angered by the way Westerners used the accident to heap contempt on the U.S.S.R. and stymie progress on arms talks. Still, the overall lesson was

The nuclear disaster at Chernobyl, 1986. The explosion at the nuclear power plant intensified Gorbachev's commitment to tamp down the international arms race.

clear: "it is another sound of the tocsin, another grim warning that the nuclear era necessitates a new political thinking and a new policy." He announced that he would extend the moratorium on Soviet nuclear tests, and again asked the United States to reciprocate. Chernobyl had illuminated "what an abyss will open if nuclear war befalls mankind. . . . The nuclear age demands a new approach to international relations, the pooling of efforts of states with different social systems for the sake of putting an end to the disastrous arms race."[209]

In August, Gorbachev vacationed in the Crimea. He was worried and agitated. "[W]hen we spent our vacation together," Chernyaev reflected, "Gorbachev was really concerned . . . that Perestroika was starting to slow down, that all his efforts to make the Party pursue Perestroika, to try to awaken society, that this was all going to collapse."[210] He felt he was being tested, squeezed. The Americans "were using our sincere desire to disarm [as a tool against us]."[211] When the Politburo met again on 4 September, Gorbachev poured forth his spleen. The Americans, he said, wanted to exhaust the Soviet Union, to keep the Kremlin trapped in regional imbroglios, like the one in Afghanistan. They yearned for superiority and sought to intimidate. Their aim, he suspected, was to undermine perestroika. They did "not want to let us increase the dynamism of our system." They must not be permitted to gain superiority.[212]

But while he fumed, he did not retreat from his strategy. He was tenacious, and he believed that perestroika at home depended on progress abroad. He decided not to go to Washington, as had been initially planned, because it might be interpreted as a sign of weakness. Instead, he would ask Reagan to meet again on neutral ground. On 15 September, he wrote another letter to Reagan. "We still have not moved one inch closer to an agreement on arms reductions." The Kremlin had tried to be accommodating, but American negotiators were intransigent. Events since their Geneva meeting "all give rise to grave and disturbing thoughts." (He was referring to the arrest of Soviet spies in the United States and the Soviet imprisonment of an American journalist, Nicholas Daniloff, for espionage.) The two governments, Gorbachev said, needed to proceed calmly, temper their rhetoric, and focus on solutions. Knowing that Reagan would not change his mind on Star Wars, Gorbachev proposed that they strengthen the anti–ballistic missile treaty of 1972 in a way that would permit research on SDI but confine it to the laboratory for fifteen years; if that were acceptable, the Kremlin would be willing to make large reductions in its stockpile of strategic weapons. And he repeated that he would eliminate all Soviet intermediate-range missiles in Europe if the Americans reciprocated. Last, Gorbachev once again challenged Reagan to accept a moratorium on nuclear testing. Negotiations had been floundering for almost a year. "They will lead nowhere unless you and I intervene personally."[213]

Reagan wanted to move forward, but he demanded that Daniloff first be set free. To Shevardnadze, he denounced the Kremlin's disregard for individual freedom, and he again chastised the Soviets publicly for their military intervention in Afghanistan, their assistance to leftist factions in local conflicts in southern Africa and Central America, and their callousness about human rights. Reagan's aim was to sustain the pressure, to make the Kremlin blink first, and to set forth his own prerequisites for any agreement. He believed he was negotiating from strength; they, from weakness.[214]

His advisers were divided. Shultz agreed with Reagan's impulses and was pleased that the "Soviets were now talking from our script."[215] But Secretary of Defense Weinberger and his influential assistant secretary for national security policy, Richard Perle, were wary of any attempt to reach agreement. Would the Soviets really change? They doubted it. Were Gorbachev's reforms significant? Intelligence analysts did not think so. And if, in fact, Gorbachev succeeded at reform, might he make the Soviet Union into a stronger adversary? They worried that the president might be lured into a foolish deal. Reagan hated nuclear weapons and believed that once the world was rid of them, Star Wars might shield America against rogue states cheating on an agreement. Skeptical of his idiosyncratic view yet knowing they had to support him, Weinberger and Perle proposed that Reagan offer Gorbachev a deal that would eliminate *all* ballistic missiles. (This plan sounded transformative, but Weinberger and Perle knew the Soviets would reject it because it would mean the elimination of a category of weaponry in which they were superior.) By doing so, Reagan could capture the high ground yet kill the negotiating process—precisely what Weinberger and Perle hoped to accomplish.[216]

On 11 and 12 October, Gorbachev and Reagan met for the second time. "At Reykjavik my hopes for a nuclear-free world soared briefly, then fell during one of the longest, most disappointing—and ultimately angriest—days of my presidency," Reagan wrote.[217]

The two leaders began their talks privately, agreeing that progress had been slower than they had hoped. Reagan expressed disappointment about the Soviet record on human rights. It would be easier to reach an agreement with the Kremlin on matters it deemed important, he said, if American public opinion were not "aroused by things that happen in the countries [like Russia and Poland] where people came from." But Gorbachev swiftly shifted the conversation to the arms race. "The Soviet side was in favor of proposals which were aimed at total elimination of nuclear arms, and on the way to this goal there should be equality and equal security for the Soviet Union and the United States." Reagan expressed overall agreement with this goal, provided there was proper verification: "Doveryay no proveryay (trust but verify)," he said with a smile.[218]

After summoning Shevardnadze and Shultz to join them, Gorbachev presented the concrete Soviet proposals: cutting strategic offensive arms by 50 percent; eliminating all U.S. and Soviet intermediate-range nuclear forces in Europe without regard to British and French weapons, a major Soviet concession; and freezing short-range (less than a thousand kilometers) missiles. With regard to SDI, Gorbachev said it could go forward so long as research was confined to laboratories, and so long as both governments agreed not to withdraw from the existing anti–ballistic missile treaty for ten years. In addition, they should ban nuclear testing and agree on verification procedures, including on-site inspections.[219]

Reagan was encouraged by Gorbachev's proposals, but then dwelled on SDI. He proposed that both sides stay "within the ABM limits, and when the point was reached when testing was required beyond the limits of the ABM treaty, the US would go forward with such testing in the presence of representatives of the other country. . . . If testing showed that such a defense could be practical, then the treaty would call for the US to share this defense system. In return for this there would be a total elimination of strategic missiles."[220] As they talked more, Reagan clarified that he was stressing cuts in ballistic missile warheads, not all strategic nuclear arms. He also made clear that his intent was for the United States to proceed with SDI testing for the next ten years within the existing ABM treaty, whose meaning was hotly contested and, in the view of U.S. defense officials, did not restrict research to laboratories.

On the morning of the second day, their discussion became testy. To Gorbachev, the Americans did not seem to want to make any concessions. In turn, Reagan was upset that Gorbachev mistrusted his commitment to share Star Wars technology. Communists, he said, were always full of mistrust, even though their own intention—except for Gorbachev—had been to seek world domination. Gorbachev denied any intention to gain supremacy, accused Reagan of rhetoric more virulent than that of his Soviet predecessors, and insisted that he was not ashamed to discuss human rights in their respective countries. Shultz had to intercede to calm them down.[221]

Gorbachev and Reagan seemed at loggerheads, with no resolution possible. On the afternoon of the twelfth, their last scheduled meeting, they struggled to break the impasse. Gorbachev insisted that "the Soviets were not trying to bury SDI," which, he agreed, the Americans could work on so long as their research was confined to laboratories for ten years, and there were no tests in space. Meanwhile, both sides could proceed with big cuts in strategic weapons, confident that the ABM treaty would "be observed during the period of the process of eliminating them."[222] But then the two leaders got into a wrangle about whether they were talking about eliminating all ballistic missiles or all strategic arms. Reagan said he was talking about offensive ballistic missiles. Gorbachev insisted he wanted to ban all strategic offensive weapons, in the air, under the seas, and on land.

Finally, Reagan said, okay, "it would be fine . . . if we eliminated all nuclear weapons." "Let's do it," interjected Shultz.[223] Excited, Gorbachev exclaimed that he was ready to sign an agreement in two minutes provided they concur on one last matter—that SDI testing be confined to laboratories for ten years. Reagan insisted that the United States must preserve the right to test in space. Gorbachev told him that "greatness" was three steps away if only they could agree on this point. The whole world "would cheer." Saying he wanted to talk to Gorbachev as one political leader to another, Reagan explained that "If he did what Gorbachev asked, he would be badly hurt in his own country." He would be condemned by conservative critics. Gorbachev retorted that if *he* gave in, his own colleagues would call him a "dummy (durak)." He assured Reagan again that he was not against SDI, "but the research had to be in the laboratories." Reagan implored: he was asking "a favor." He was willing to abide by the ABM treaty for ten years, but could not agree to restricting the research to laboratories. The Soviet leader "was asking him to give up the thing he'd promised not to give up." He was asking "a favor," Reagan reiterated. Gorbachev said he could not do it.[224]

Both men left the meeting looking profoundly dismayed. Watching the news on television in Washington, Nancy Reagan saw the expression on her husband's face and knew "something had gone wrong. He looked angry, very angry. His face was pale and his teeth were clenched."[225] "The stress was incredible," remembered Chernyaev. Gorbachev seemed very unhappy. Yet, before parting, the two leaders turned to one another and hugged. "They put their hands on each other's shoulder," said Chernyaev, and he could see that the bond between the two leaders remained. Reagan went off in his car, but Gorbachev strolled into a conference room two hundred meters away, where reporters from around the world wanted to know what had happened. He declared, "It's not a failure; it's a breakthrough." With these words, Chernyaev explained, "Gorbachev preserved hope, gave hope to all humankind."[226]

Reagan and Shultz were distraught. Their assistants, however, saw matters differently. "Why in the world are you calling this a failure?" Deputy Secretary of State John Whitehead asked Shultz. The meeting, Whitehead insisted, "was a success." The Soviets had moved closer to the American position on almost every arms-control issue. Jack Matlock said much the same thing to Reagan's closest White House aides. His major reservation was Gorbachev's failure to resolve regional disputes and allay the president's human rights concerns.[227]

Gorbachev returned to Moscow and immediately met with the Politburo. He was defiant. "Success was near. Had we adopted the decision to reduce and liquidate nuclear armaments, this would have become a turning point in the evolution of international affairs." More important, the agreements would have empowered the Soviet Union to move ahead domestically with the new plans to accelerate its social and economic development. Reagan, however, had insisted on SDI, and the Americans believed that "because of [our] internal difficulties we would have to accept their proposals." "We are dealing with political dregs," said a frustrated Gorbachev on 1 December. He would not be intimidated. He would remain calm, aware that the Kremlin now had a great opportunity to capitalize politically on Reagan's intransigence. It could win a great propaganda victory in Western Europe.[228]

Meanwhile, Gorbachev would stay the course, even accelerate it. He talked more and more about not only economic modernization but also polit-

Reagan and Gorbachev at Reýkjavik, 1986. Their looks reveal
their dismay after failing to reach agreement.

ical democratization. The Americans, he confided to Chernyaev, wanted "to
see us get stuck, to fall. It is not our foreign policy that interests them, but
what would happen with socialism. . . . There is no other option left for our
generation but to restructure the country. . . . Our task is to learn how to lead
280 million people to socialism."[229]

Gorbachev grew increasingly confident that the Americans would have
difficulty developing SDI. Even if they succeeded, the Soviets could counter
it at much less cost.[230] But Gorbachev was angry at his generals for raising

objections to his plans. He told the Politburo that it must not "become like the generals," who were "trying to scare us," "hissing among themselves." They complained about the resources allocated to them, while "25 million [Soviet citizens] live under the minimum which we officially pronounced as poverty level."[231] In May 1987, when a private German aircraft glided into Soviet airspace and landed in Red Square, Gorbachev was humiliated by the seeming incompetence of his defense establishment to protect the heart of Moscow. He used the ensuing inquiries about the incident as an opportunity to shake up the ranks and promote officers who, he thought, would be more amenable to his way of thinking, his policy and goals.[232]

The security of the Soviet Union, Gorbachev believed, was not at risk. "I'm not going to war," he told his colleagues.[233] "In this nuclear age," the "world has become too fragile for war and power politics," he told a meeting of the Warsaw Pact. He would never initiate war, never contemplate a nuclear first-strike.[234] All that was needed, he declared, was enough weapons to ensure a "reliable guarantee of defense of our country." There was no need, he insisted to the Politburo, to count "a gun there, and a gun here." If they did not change their ways, they would have to "stop building socialism." They must not turn their country into a military camp, nor steal "from our people." They must not play into the hands of the Americans who wanted to exhaust them in an arms race. They must not be made to seem like fools. His comrades concurred.[235]

After Reykjavik, Gorbachev instructed his defense chiefs to reconfigure Warsaw Pact strategy and focus on defense. He also decided to separate the discussions regarding an agreement on intermediate-range nuclear weapons from the strategic talks involving Star Wars. Defying his military advisers, he was even willing to get rid of the Oka missile, the SS-23, which the Americans were saying had to be included in any intermediate nuclear force (INF) treaty.[236] "We start from the assumption" that as difficult as it is to do business with the United States "we are doomed to do it," he told the Politburo. "We have no choice. Our main problem is to remove confrontation." In February 1987, he invited Shultz back to Moscow to resume their talks.[237]

After Reykjavik, however, the Reagan administration was totally absorbed in a scandal consuming the attention of everyone in Washington. The president was accused of clandestinely and illegally selling arms to moderates in Iran in return for the release of hostages in Lebanon, and then using the

funds, again illegally, to support the Contras in Nicaragua (who were still battling to overthrow the Sandinistas). Reagan denied that he had sold arms for
hostages, but even Secretary Shultz acknowledged privately that the evidence
was irrefutable. Shultz turned in anger on the CIA, the NSC, and the Defense
Department, where, he believed, the plans had been hatched and implemented. A "wounded president" made it harder to resume dialogue with
Gorbachev and Shevardnadze, and Shultz believed that the efforts he was
making to reach an agreement on intermediate nuclear forces were being
thwarted by Weinberger. Reports, largely exaggerated, that the Soviets had
secretly penetrated the U.S. embassy in Moscow created an uproar in Washington and played into Weinberger's hands. "The mood of the town [in
March 1987] was boiling hot," Shultz recalled. Yet Reagan, once again, made
the decision to move forward. He instructed Shultz to go to Moscow, albeit
with circumscribed authority.[238]

On 13 April, Shultz arrived in Moscow carrying a letter to Gorbachev
from Reagan. "It has been a long time since you and I last communicated directly," Reagan acknowledged. The president had not abandoned hope that
they could "make a difference in the future course of world events." He was
"encouraged by the many steps you are taking to modernize your own country and by the improved dialogue on arms reductions." More could be accomplished if the two governments could remove distrust, such as that
created by the news of Soviet spying in the U.S. embassy. Reagan encouraged
Gorbachev to withdraw Soviet troops from Afghanistan and to curb Soviet
support for Moscow's clients in Central America, southern Africa, and southeast Asia.[239]

Shultz was exhilarated by his talks with both government officials and opposition figures in Moscow, where he saw signs of significant change. He was
gratified when Gorbachev assured him that reports of Soviet actions in the
American embassy had been greatly exaggerated.[240] The secretary of state attended a Passover seder with Jews who had been denied permission to leave
the country, and he met with Soviet dissidents. Gorbachev complained about
these meetings, but accepted them. He and Shultz heatedly debated human
rights in socialist and capitalist countries, and Shultz seized the opportunity
to lecture his Soviet host about the benefits of free markets in the information
age. Gorbachev's perestroika, Shultz said, would not succeed if restructuring
failed to nurture human creativity and individual initiative. Gorbachev was

more inclined to think that his domestic agenda required progress on arms cuts, and he again homed in on these issues. He wanted to conclude an agreement eliminating intermediate-range nuclear forces in Europe. NATO's Pershing II missiles were "like a pistol to our head," he said, and the Soviet SS-20s "swallowed up" critical resources. When Shultz responded that the United States wanted to destroy all INF weapons, including those deployed in the Asiatic part of the Soviet Union, Gorbachev did not reject the possibility.[241]

Shultz called the president from Moscow. "It's not been peaches and cream," he told Reagan. Gorbachev was tough, but there was no doubt that "the Soviet Union is changing." The strong policies "you've kept in place have made a real difference," Shultz emphasized. He was hoping to pave the way to another summit, and Reagan told him he could speak positively about holding such a meeting in Washington toward the end of the year, during which an INF treaty might be signed.[242]

When the secretary of state returned to Washington, the national security bureaucracy was still in turmoil over the Iran-Contra scandal, and congressional hearings about it were still consuming the attention of the president and most of his top advisers. CIA and Defense Department officials cast doubt on Gorbachev's intentions. Defense-minded Democrats, such as Senator Sam Nunn of Georgia, sneered at the deal Shultz was contemplating, and architects of realpolitik, such as Henry Kissinger, claimed that Reagan was undermining NATO cohesion. Robert Gates, deputy director of the CIA, wrote a memo to the president saying that Gorbachev and his fellow reformers were seeking not to ameliorate the lives of Soviet citizens but "to strengthen the USSR at home, to further their own personal power, and to permit the further consolidation and expansion of Soviet power abroad."[243]

Shultz interpreted Gorbachev's motives differently, but he was puzzled on a return trip to Moscow in October when he found Gorbachev testy and argumentative. The Soviet leader intimated that he would not come to Washington simply to sign an INF treaty. He also wanted both sides to cut long-range strategic forces and to agree to prohibit the militarization of space. With this renewed challenge to Reagan's Star Wars initiative, Gorbachev seemed to be imperiling the summit both leaders had claimed they favored.[244]

But Gorbachev quickly changed his mind and sent Shevardnadze back to

Washington with a letter for Reagan that spelled out his thinking. The meeting in Reykjavik, he wrote, had been a "landmark" in the struggle to reduce nuclear armaments, and the opportunity it created must be grasped. Why, then, was Washington hardening its view and upholding positions "which are clearly one-sided?" This made no sense to Gorbachev, who pointed out that he had embraced the U.S. position on most issues: he was willing to ignore the number of British and French nuclear weapons; he agreed to the destruction of all intermediate- and short-range weapons in the Asiatic part of the Soviet Union as well as in Europe, thereby accepting, in effect, the global zero-zero deal Reagan had long said was his ideal accord. "Our position is clear and honest: we call for the total elimination of the entire class of missiles with ranges between 500 and 5,500 kilometers and of all warheads for those missiles. The fate of an agreement on intermediate- and short-range missiles now depends entirely on the U.S. leadership and on your personal willingness, Mr. President, to conclude a deal."[245]

Shultz thought the letter was promising. The president now had a chance to consummate a historic agreement to eliminate an entire category of armaments. He told Reagan it could be done without compromising the U.S. position on Star Wars and strategic weapons.[246] "I felt that a profound historic shift was under way," he later recalled. "The Soviet Union was, willingly or unwillingly, consciously or not, turning a corner: they were not just resting for round two of the cold war." They were bowing to U.S. strength. "[W]e can continue to let [Gorbachev be] the innovator as long as he keeps innovating in our direction," Shultz told Reagan on 18 November.[247]

Gorbachev came to Washington in mid-December to sign the INF treaty and to expedite progress on a strategic arms agreement between the U.S. and the U.S.S.R. Exuding confidence and conveying goodwill, he talked of peace and international harmony. Russians and Americans together, he suggested, must envision a brighter future where common sense and mutual understanding supplanted political rivalry and national egotism.[248] The effect of his words was astonishing. "The things he said were almost too good to be true," said the distinguished American writer Joyce Carol Oates. He preached a "beautiful picture of the world in which we were all brothers," commented Billy Graham, the renowned evangelist.[249]

In meetings with Reagan and Shultz, Gorbachev was not flustered when they challenged him to settle regional disputes, withdraw from Afghanistan, tear down the Berlin wall, and allow more freedom of expression inside the Soviet Union. The Soviet leader talked with poise and intelligence about all these difficult issues. "Mr. President, you are not a prosecutor and I am not on trial here. Like you, I represent a great country and therefore expect our dialogue to be conducted on a basis of reciprocity and equality."[250] He insisted that he, too, wanted to reach agreement on all regional issues, especially Afghanistan. He was especially eager to make headway on a strategic arms treaty, an agreement that he hoped he and the president might sign at their next meeting, to be held in Moscow in the late spring. Together, Gorbachev declared, the United States and the Soviet Union must build "a bridge to the future."[251]

Good feelings infused the concluding sessions of the Washington summit. The warmth that Reagan and Gorbachev felt for one another grew as they took pride in their mutual achievement. The INF treaty, in Reagan's view, was a "landmark in postwar history," the first agreement to reduce nuclear weapons.[252]

But the president was not complacent. Though wary of growing criticism among conservatives, he made clear that he wanted progress "on a far broader agenda," which included not just arms-control issues but also "Soviet expansionism, human rights violations, as well as our own moral opposition to the ideology that justifies such practices."[253] "Between us, there has also been a profound competition of political and economic philosophy, making us the protagonists in a drama with the greatest importance for the future of all mankind," he said to Gorbachev.[254] But it was time, he emphasized, "to move from confrontation to cooperation. . . . We can coexist as do two wrestlers in a ring if necessary, but we would much prefer to coexist as partners and as friends."[255]

In order for them to have the friendship that Reagan envisioned, the Soviet Union would need to change still more at home and abroad. At the Brandenburg Gate in June, he had challenged Gorbachev: "If you seek peace, if you seek prosperity, . . . tear down this wall!"[256] However unlikely it might seem, Reagan hoped such changes would occur. The future, he told the American people, "belongs not to repressive or totalitarian ways of life but to the cause of freedom." This cause still required U.S. strength. Reagan asked Americans to support the administration's defense programs and foreign policies. More could be accomplished if Congress stopped cutting the military budget, ceased placing constraints on Star Wars research, and championed "freedom fighters" from Nicaragua to Afghanistan. But he felt the summit had been a great success, and he expressed "hope and optimism" for the future.[257]

Gorbachev drew similar conclusions, telling the Soviet people, "The accords reached represent a historic opportunity for all mankind to begin to throw off the heavy burden of militarism and war, which have not only claimed monstrous human sacrifices, but also retarded economic development and material culture." He was not yet prepared to say there was a "fundamental turning point," but he was encouraged.[258]

To his comrades in the Politburo, he also was prudently upbeat. In Washington he had understood, "maybe for the first time . . . the importance of the human factor in international politics." Responsible leaders could represent "the interests and hopes of most common people." He and Reagan were such leaders, "motivated by . . . normal human desires and feelings."[259] And the Washington summit, moreover, confirmed the wisdom of recent Soviet policies. Perestroika at home and relaxation of tensions abroad went hand in hand:

> We saw with our own eyes for the first time how much interest
> there was in everything that was happening in our country, to
> our perestroika. And the friendly atmosphere, even enthusiasm
> to some degree, with which straight-laced Washington met us,
> was a sign of the changes that have begun to transpire in the
> West, and which meant that the "enemy image" had begun to
> erode, and that the myth of the "Soviet military threat" was un-
> dermined. It was very special for us. And it was noticed in the
> entire world.[260]

Gorbachev explained to news reporters that the INF treaty was just a beginning. More needed to be done to reduce strategic armaments and conventional forces. The Soviet Union should be prepared for "drastic reductions." As for Afghanistan, Gorbachev said, "[W]e do not strive for a pro-Soviet regime [there]. But the U.S. side must just as clearly state that it is not striving for a pro-U.S. regime there." To reach a settlement, more work needed to be done. He would not shirk his duty. The Americans regarded Soviet withdrawal from Afghanistan as critical to their future relationship.[261] Perestroika could not succeed without withdrawal.

The Troops Come Out

On 8 February 1988, Gorbachev announced publicly that the Soviet Union would withdraw its troops from Afghanistan over the next year, provided an agreement could be signed. Regional conflicts, he said, "are bleeding wounds capable of causing spots of gangrene on the body of mankind." More than a hundred thousand Soviet troops were then in Afghanistan. From his first days in office Gorbachev had recognized that the war imposed too heavy a burden on the Soviet Union, required too many sacrifices from his people, blemished the reputation of the U.S.S.R. in the eyes of neutral and non-aligned leaders throughout the third world, and poisoned relations with the West, especially the United States. He had wanted for years to get out of Afghanistan. But this was easier said than done.[262]

On 14 March 1985, just days after he became general secretary, Gorbachev had had his first talk with Babrak Karmal, the communist leader of Afghanistan whom Gorbachev's predecessors had installed in Kabul. Expressing sympathy with Karmal's struggle against the counterrevolutionaries, Gorbachev nonetheless made himself clear: "Soviet troops cannot remain in Afghanistan forever." Karmal explained that the insurgency was being supported by Pakistan and Iran, and was also receiving help from the United States and China, but Gorbachev nonetheless insisted that Karmal must mend relations with his own people, broaden the social-class basis of his government, unite his party, and coopt the insurgency.[263]

Gorbachev and the Politburo were being bombarded with letters from grieving mothers and wives. They wanted to know why their sons and husbands were being sacrificed in Afghanistan. "Why do we need [this war] and when will it end?" they asked.[264] From the outset, the war had not gone as anticipated. Although Brezhnev had expected a quick intervention and rapid withdrawal, the mission of Soviet troops kept expanding, from interdicting the flow of supplies to the insurgents, to protecting the periphery of major cities and bases, and, finally, to engagement in major combat operations. But the insurgency kept growing, catalyzed by widespread hatred of the Soviet occupation, inspired by Islamic religious fervor and ethnic and clan loyalties, and abetted by the support of Pakistan, China, Saudi Arabia, and the United States. The fighting inside Afghanistan was fierce, leading to the deaths of almost a million Afghans and causing millions more to flee, especially to Pakistan. By the early 1980s, more than a half-dozen Mujahedin groups were operating out of Pakistan, intriguing against one another as well as battling communist infidels and the Soviet invaders.[265]

The experts to whom Gorbachev turned for advice—Georgi Arbatov, Georgi Shakhnazarov, Anatoli Chernyaev, Karen Brutents, Aleksandr Yakovlev, and Vadim Medvedev—saw nothing to be gained by prolonging the conflict in Afghanistan. It was wasting billions of rubles and costing thousands of Soviet lives. Embroilments in the third world, particularly Afghanistan, drained Soviet resources and distracted the Kremlin from its internal priorities. Since the 1970s, Soviet opportunities to capitalize on revolutionary nationalist processes had withered while the risks and dangers had increased. Soviet troops should withdraw from Afghanistan, they advised.[266]

On 17 October 1985, Gorbachev met again with Karmal to tell him that Soviet troops were going to leave Afghanistan:

[B]y the summer of 1986 you will have to learn to defend your revolution on your own. For the moment we will assist you, but not with soldiers—only with aviation, artillery and equipment. If you want to survive you must broaden the social base of the regime. Forget about socialism, and share real power with those who enjoy real influence, including the warlords, who are now hostile to you. Restore the status of Islam. Restore popular customs and traditions, seek the support of those who have traditionally enjoyed moral authority, and try to give people a chance to see that they can benefit from the revolution.

Karmal was stunned, Gorbachev told the Politburo. "[W]ith or without Karmal we will firmly stay the course that will result in our withdrawal from Afghanistan as quickly as possible."[267]

When Gorbachev met Reagan in Geneva a month later, the Soviet leader emphasized that he wanted to modulate disputes in the third world. "You could help. The U.S., however, does not help. You say the U.S.S.R. should withdraw its troops [from Afghanistan], but actually you want them there, and the longer the better."[268] Gorbachev believed that the United States wanted the Soviet Union to be entrapped in a protracted guerrilla conflict that would drain its resources and morale, much as U.S. vigor and strength had been sapped in Vietnam. Nonetheless, he proposed a package solution "involving a non-aligned Afghanistan, Soviet troop withdrawal, the return of refugees, and international guarantee of no outside interference." Karmal's government would cooperate, but nothing could be accomplished if the Mujahedin and other insurgents continued to fight. Gorbachev assured Reagan that the Soviet Union had "no plan for using Afghanistan to gain access to a warm water port, to extend its influence to the Persian Gulf, or to impinge on U.S. interests in any way."[269]

The Soviet war in Afghanistan, Reagan retorted, was the Kremlin's fault. The Russians had invaded a neighbor, imposed a communist government, and forced three million refugees to flee. Perhaps the United Nations could help to effectuate a settlement. "Specifically," he mused, "how about bringing about the mutual withdrawal of all outside forces, then forming a coalition of Islamic states to supervise the installation of a government chosen by the people of Afghanistan?"[270]

This proposal was not serious, and Gorbachev knew it. The U.S. administration was not eager to arrive at a settlement in Afghanistan. Reagan and his aides were happy to see Soviet armies bloodied there. CIA director Casey was a strong proponent of the Afghan insurgency, and he mustered support among key congressmen who championed covert aid to the Mujahedin. He told an assistant in early 1984 that "the Soviet Union is tremendously overextended and they're vulnerable." If America challenged the Soviets at every turn and ultimately defeated them "in one place," their prestige would be shattered and their empire would start to unravel. As Soviet troops got bogged down in 1983 and 1984, Casey's enthusiasm for the insurgency grew. "Here is the beauty of the Afghan operation," he told his aides. "Usually it looks like the big bad Americans are beating up on the natives. Afghanistan is just the reverse. The Russians are beating up on the little guys. We don't make it our war. The Mujahedin have all the motivation they need. All we have to do is give them help, only more of it."[271] President Reagan agreed. To help the Mujahedin, the CIA collaborated with the monarchy in Saudi Arabia and with the Pakistani intelligence agency, the ISI; increased its secret funding to $300 million in 1985 and to $470 million in 1986; and provided

Mujahedin soldiers on a destroyed Soviet helicopter in Afghanistan, 1980.
The CIA helped to finance and support the Mujahedin's resistance
to the Soviet invasion of Afghanistan.

more advanced weapons, such as Stinger ground-to-air missiles, and sophisticated intelligence support. Casey even wanted to allow the Mujahedin to extend their operations across the Afghan-Soviet border into the Soviet Union itself. Shultz was more restrained, but in February 1985 the secretary of state publicly declared that it would be a "shameful betrayal" to abandon "freedom fighters" in places like Afghanistan.[272]

U.S. actions made it more difficult for Gorbachev to withdraw. "The situation is not simple," he told the Politburo. "Now we're in, but how to get out racks one's brains." Washington had "set itself the goal of obstructing a settlement in Afghanistan by any means," he claimed. He wanted to leave without a loss of credibility (much as the Americans had tried to disengage from Vietnam without humiliation). "We could leave quickly, not thinking about anything," he acknowledged. "But we can't act that way. India would be concerned, and they would be concerned in Africa. They think this would be a blow to the authority of the Soviet Union. . . . And they tell us that imperialism will go on the offensive if you flee from Afghanistan."[273]

Nonetheless, Gorbachev was determined to get out. When Babrak Karmal objected and obstructed, the Soviet leader arranged to have him replaced with Muhammad Najibullah, an ambitious, intelligent, and well-educated man from a wealthy Pashtun family. Not yet forty years old, Najibullah had joined the Parcham faction of the Afghan Communist Party in 1965, when he was an eighteen-year-old medical student at Kabul University. For a brief period after the coup in 1978, he had been part of the government's revolutionary council. He then went into exile and returned when Soviet forces intervened in 1979. Between 1980 and 1986, Najibullah had directed the Afghan state security apparatus and worked closely with Soviet KGB agents in Kabul. When the Kremlin arranged for his elevation to the top party post in May 1986, it hoped for a client more collaborative than Karmal had been.[274]

Speaking to the Politburo on 13 November 1986, Gorbachev poured out his frustration: "Karmal's policy was simple: sit and rule and leave the fighting to us [the Soviets]." Gorbachev would not tolerate this attitude. "Our strategic goal is to end the war and to withdraw the troops within a year, two years at the most." He heard no dissent. "We cannot resolve this problem through military means," said Viktor Chebrikov, head of the KGB. "We need to end this war," insisted Shevardnadze. "We have lost," declared Marshal Akhromeyev. "Most Afghans today support the counterrevolutionaries." Gorbachev concurred. In his view, Afghanistan's communist clique had to be largely reconstituted. "After all, it is not socialism that we want there" but a peaceful, nonaligned, independent nation that was not ruled by Islamic fundamentalists. To accomplish that end, he was ready to initiate talks with Pakistan.[275]

Throughout 1986 and 1987, Gorbachev struggled to shape a realistic exit strategy. Although several Politburo colleagues and military advisers believed that the war would go on forever if they continued to support Najibullah, Gorbachev did not want "to cut and run," and he argued that Najibullah should not be abandoned. "We will leave there with bruises no matter what, but we should try to get fewer and make them less painful." He favored a political settlement. The Americans, he maintained, needed to be brought into the process; they had to become part of the solution.[276] Meanwhile, he wanted to step up Soviet military action in order to gain political leverage in the negotiating process. Soviet troops, in fact, briefly went on the offensive, aiming to stop the flow of supplies into Afghanistan and to intimidate Pakistan with air and artillery strikes across the border.[277]

Gorbachev kept insisting that Najibullah change the policies of the revolution. He must realize that "without Islam there can be no Afghanistan." Representatives of opposition parties, Gorbachev said, must constitute at least 50 percent of a new government. Najibullah would find it hard to follow this recipe for peace, but he had to learn to govern without Soviet help. "Warn him again," Gorbachev said to Shevardnadze and other colleagues dealing with Najibullah. "Do as you yourself think and ask us less often."[278] Shevardnadze went back and forth to Kabul trying to persuade Najibullah to accept Soviet strategy, and then Gorbachev met with him in Moscow on 20 July 1987. "The future of Afghanistan can only be secured through national reconciliation," Gorbachev stressed. "It is impossible to jump to socialism without a stage of national democratic reforms. We and the Chinese had 'great leaps.' We know how they end." In the circumstances, the Afghan Communist Party must broaden its appeal, embrace pluralism, and form a coalition government with Najibullah at its head. Only with such a strategy, Gorbachev reiterated, could the party survive and compete in the future.[279]

When Najibullah returned to Moscow in November for the seventieth anniversary celebration of the Bolshevik revolution, Gorbachev met with him to recapitulate the Kremlin's current thinking. In order to implement perestroika at home, the Kremlin needed a quiescent international environment. "Our domestic interests are compatible with common human interests. We need a normal international situation."[280]

Najibullah tried to reassure Gorbachev. He was taking steps toward national reconciliation. "In a month we plan to hold a Loya Jirga [grand national council] at which we will adopt a constitution for the country and elect a president," he told Gorbachev. "Afterwards it is intended to hold elections to a National Council." Najibullah was seeking the "constructive participation of all political forces and all sectors of the population." It was essential to respect the peasantry, Gorbachev told him, and he would not survive if he did not placate his foes and win over part of the opposition. If this policy were followed, the Kremlin would support him even while Soviet troops were withdrawn.[281]

Gorbachev mentioned to Najibullah that he was trying to secure U.S. cooperation. Shevardnadze had already told Shultz in September that the Soviet Union was going to pull out of Afghanistan, and Kremlin leaders wanted the Americans to dissuade Islamic fundamentalists from seizing power as the Soviets withdrew.[282] Gorbachev admitted that he was not sure if the Americans would do this, but he told Najibullah to form a coalition government regardless of U.S. actions.[283]

This reshaping of Soviet policy in Afghanistan had the effect of reconfiguring the zero-sum game of power politics in the third world. Gorbachev knew the international appeal of socialism had waned and "new thinking" at home required the end of old rivalries abroad.[284] In November, Soviet experts on Africa told State Department officials that they wanted to resolve problems in Namibia and Angola, one of the regional disputes that had long preoccupied policymakers in Washington.[285] When Nicaragua's president, the Sandinista leader Daniel Ortega, visited Moscow that month, Gorbachev encouraged him to allay American anxieties. "Let's act as one," Gorbachev said. "When I meet with Reagan, I'll tell him that neither do you want to transform Nicaragua into a Soviet base, nor are we intending to create one there." When Ortega pleaded for more aid, Gorbachev was candid: he could not offer additional loans. The fall in oil prices meant huge cuts in anticipated revenues. "[W]e have much internationalism, but not enough means," he said. Indeed, even the Soviet Union's own five-year plan was "under threat."[286]

By the end of 1987 Gorbachev's focus was on injecting new dynamism into his domestic initiatives. Reform at home, not adventurism abroad, was on his mind.[287] But to make reform work at home, he needed to reassure the United States that the Kremlin was not seeking to take advantage of local strife and regional disputes to expand Soviet influence. When Reagan said in December 1987 that Afghanistan was his number one priority, Gorbachev told him that the Soviet Union wanted to cooperate on all regional issues—in Central America, Kampuchea, the Middle East, and Afghanistan. When Reagan said he had heard enough promises and wanted action, not words, Gorbachev declared that Soviet troops could withdraw within twelve months, even less, if a coalition government were agreed upon and the United States ceased financing the anti-Soviet resistance. "The Soviets were realists," Gorbachev said. "They did not want to try to make Afghanistan socialist. . . . Moscow had no intention of seeking to leave behind a regime acceptable to itself alone. It would have no problem with a nonaligned and independent government." Gorbachev suggested a gentleman's agreement: "the Soviets would talk to Najib[ullah], and the U.S. to the opposition."[288]

Yet on 8 February 1988, when Gorbachev announced that Soviet troops would withdraw from Afghanistan, he did this despite many signs that the United States was going to continue its support of the Mujahedin. Gorbachev expressed his disappointment to Shultz in Moscow: "I feel you have maintained a negative attitude," ignoring "our genuine desire to work with you in solving these problems." He repeated that Afghanistan was not going to serve as a Soviet springboard toward warm-water ports or the Persian Gulf: "This is nonsense."[289]

When Shultz showed no inclination to alter the U.S. position, Gorbachev had to reassess the decision to withdraw. He worried that Najibullah's government might collapse and that Islamic fundamentalists might gain control of Afghanistan as they already had in Iran.[290] And he worried that his nation's credibility with its friends and clients would be shattered. Their thinking was simple, he said: "you're abandoning Afghanistan; it means you're abandoning us."[291] Nonetheless, he decided to proceed with withdrawal. "It is difficult to overestimate the political significance of solving the Afghanistan problem," he told the Politburo. "It will confirm our new approach to solving international problems. In this way, we deprive our enemies and opponents of their most powerful argument."[292]

Najibullah was not happy with the Soviet decision. He was a vulnerable client whose very weakness gave him considerable leverage. Gorbachev wanted the communist government in Kabul not to collapse, but to survive. He wanted it to defeat the die-hard Islamists. He wanted Najibullah to expand his coalition and embrace moderate elements of the resistance, and he wanted a peaceful, non-Islamist neighbor allied with neither the Americans nor the Pakistanis. As the day approached, in mid-April 1988, to sign the agreements committing the Soviets to withdrawal, Gorbachev met with Najibullah in Tashkent. He promised him aid, money, and military advisers. He encouraged him to persevere. But he would not change his mind. Soviet troops must leave.[293]

On 14 April, the Soviet Union, the United States, Pakistan, and Afghanistan signed the Geneva agreements. The Soviet Union would withdraw its forces, Pakistan would cease interfering, the Afghan government would allow refugees to return to Afghanistan, and Washington, along with Moscow, would guarantee noninterference. Of all the parties to this agreement, only Gorbachev intended to match words with deeds. Pakistan's president, Mohammed Zia ul-Haq, assured Reagan that Pakistan was not going to stop supplying the Afghan rebels. "We'll just lie about it. That's what we've been doing for eight years. . . . Muslims have the right to lie in a good cause." Reagan did not object. Shultz stated publicly, "it is our right to provide military aid to the resistance. We are ready to exercise that right, but we are prepared to meet restraint with restraint."[294]

The Americans saw an opportunity to capitalize on Soviet weakness. They believed that when the Soviet Union withdrew its forces and stopped aiding Kabul, Najibullah's government would collapse. Conservative supporters in Congress did not want Reagan to abandon the Mujahedin just because Soviet troops were being driven out of Afghanistan. Najibullah must fall in any case. They did not care that anti-Soviet forces were increasingly dominated by Islamic fundamentalists with wildly different aspirations from their own.[295]

Institutional forces in the U.S. government, especially the CIA and the Defense Department, also had much invested, materially and psychologically, in overthrowing Najibullah's government. They were not interested in efforts the Afghan communist leader might make to incorporate his erstwhile opponents in a coalition government. As long as Najibullah headed the government, the Soviet Union would have a friend in Kabul, a minion it had installed, a symbol of totalitarianism on the march. Although Reagan and Shultz wanted to reach out to Gorbachev, encourage reforms, and sign agreements, they wanted to do so on their own terms. "We should continue to maintain our strength while seeking agreements that serve our interests," Shultz told Reagan.[296]

Najibullah understood his predicament. He returned to Moscow and implored Gorbachev not to abandon him. He wanted to achieve "a decisive turning point in the psychological mood of the population . . . by launching decisive strikes on irreconcilable groups." To succeed, he needed more aid and some Soviet troops, which he would deploy in the "second and third echelons" to boost his soldiers' morale. Victory would infuse his supporters with "confidence in their ability to defeat the enemy by themselves."[297]

Gorbachev was sympathetic, and he knew the Pakistanis were flagrantly breaching their promise not to funnel aid to the Islamic fundamentalists.

A Soviet soldier in Afghanistan leaving for home, 1989. The eventual failure
of the Soviet invasion of Afghanistan was deeply demoralizing.

Gorbachev wanted Najibullah to keep working at national reconciliation.
Since the insurgents were badly divided and slaughtering one another as well
as attacking the government, he encouraged Najibullah to peel off factions
among them who might be enticed into his coalition. And he should tell
friends and foes alike that the Soviet Union had no selfish designs on
Afghanistan and would respect the traditions and customs of the Afghan
people. The Kremlin's goal was simple: "a loyal neighbor at the southern borders of the Soviet Union with whom our country has a long-standing friendship." Gorbachev assured Najibullah that he would not be abandoned. The
Kremlin's aid would increase, but Soviet troops must leave. He could not violate his word.[298]

Gorbachev also wanted Najibullah to grasp what was going on in the Soviet Union. "[W]e are passing through a critical stage in Soviet history. And
we can not lose it," he emphasized. The Afghan leader assured Gorbachev
that he understood: "We consider the policy of national reconciliation to be
part of the policy of perestroika. . . . The ideas of perestroika have international importance and go far beyond national boundaries."[299]

Yet Najibullah would not stop complicating Gorbachev's domestic agenda. As the date neared for full withdrawal of Soviet troops, scheduled for February 1989, he asked permission to use a Soviet brigade to break the insurgents' blockade of Kandahar. Shevardnadze, who dealt with Najibullah on a continual basis, supported this request, but Gorbachev's closest aides were incredulous. "Is he [Shevardnadze] crazy?" exploded Chernyaev. "Doesn't he understand that Najib[ullah] is setting a trap to prevent us from leaving, to set us against the Americans and the whole world? Or is he [Shevardnadze] such a wimp that he can't turn down a request?" At a Politburo meeting on 24 January, Gorbachev scorned Shevardnadze's position: "From Eduard Shevardnadze here we have heard baby talk and the vain screech of a hawk." Vladimir Kriuchkov, the KGB chief, and Chebrikov, now secretary of the CPSU Central Committee, supported Gorbachev, as did others.[300]

Shevardnadze had developed a personal attachment to Najibullah, and he believed the Kremlin was betraying a loyal client. The Soviet Union must not abandon its friends, he declared at a Politburo meeting on 2 March, when it was considering another request from Najibullah, this time for air strikes from Soviet territory. "What will they say in the 'Third World'?" Shevardnadze rhetorically asked his colleagues. This time his view elicited support, but Gorbachev interceded. He "was red in the face and angry," Chernyaev recorded in his diary. "I am absolutely against all such air strikes or anything like them," Gorbachev declared. "And while I am general secretary here, I will not let anybody break a promise that we have given before the entire world."[301]

Gorbachev was not indifferent to Shevardnadze's claim that Soviet credibility was at risk, nor was he callous to Najibullah's predicament. But his overriding concern was revitalizing socialism at home, not spreading it abroad. The greatest threats to Soviet communism were within, not without. At a Politburo session on 23 March, he explained his policy toward Afghanistan: "Our most important goal is to prevent the emergence of a hostile state there. As for the rest of it . . . let it be any type of government—it is none of our business."[302]

When Najibullah demonstrated unanticipated staying power after Soviet troops withdrew in February 1989, Gorbachev did not abandon him. He believed that the Afghan's efforts during 1989 and 1990 to widen the coalition and coopt former adversaries continued to be the wisest strategy. When they met for the last time, on 23 August 1990, Gorbachev was tired and worried about the growing instability in his own country. "[T]he load is great," he said to Najibullah. "Possibly in some respects it is now quieter in Afghanistan than here [Moscow]." Perestroika had exposed both new socioeconomic problems and old ethnic conflicts. But Gorbachev was not apologetic. Reliance on leftist radicalism and war communism, he told Najibullah, had "not stood the test of time." To work for the "revolutionary renewal of society within the framework of the socialist choice" was the correct course to follow notwithstanding the turbulence it precipitated.

The Americans, he added, were not being helpful. Officials in Washington, though they recognized the looming threat of Islamic fundamentalism, could not resist the opportunity to topple Najibullah and incite tens of millions of Muslims in the Soviet Union. Americans "were and will remain Americans." Their intention, Gorbachev told Najibullah, was to weaken the Soviet Union. They hoped to "attain much else [by] exploiting our difficulties."[303]

But he would not turn back.

New Thinking, Old Thinking

Gorbachev would not reverse himself because he was determined to reshape the image of the Soviet Union. "We are proposing and willing to build a new world," he explained to the Politburo at the end of 1988. His aim was to shatter Western assumptions about Soviet aggressiveness. There were dangers in this approach. The Americans, thinking that Soviet leaders were bowing to U.S. power rather than to Moscow's own assessment of the need for change, might try to wring additional concessions, and American adventurism might grow. But the risks appeared acceptable to Gorbachev, given his mounting determination to achieve domestic reform and his evolving perception of threat.[304] The Soviet Union, he had said proudly in February 1987, "is a modern state which has immense achievements. . . . But it is a society which has many problems. . . . We are not giving up on socialism; we want to make it better."[305]

As Gorbachev prepared to celebrate the seventieth anniversary of the Bolshevik revolution in November 1987, he wrestled with his country's past and tried to envision its future. His assistants prepared a long report that

Afghan president Najibullah and Gorbachev in Moscow, 1990.
Gorbachev kept supporting him but withdrew Soviet troops and
lamented U.S. policies that he deemed shortsighted.

tried to put the tarnished yet, in their view, heroic past of the Soviet Union in
historical perspective, and the Politburo discussed the report at a meeting on
15 October 1987. Criticism was muted, except for that emanating from Boris
Yeltsin, and Gorbachev thoughtfully defended almost every word of the document.

He wanted to acknowledge but not exaggerate errors in their past. For
the last few years he had been struggling, within a Leninist mind-set, to reconcile the market and the state, the individual and the collective, pluralism
and planning, communism and democracy. Socialism could not realize its
potential without democracy, but democracy remained a unity of rights and
responsibilities. This sounded vague, and Gorbachev acknowledged that he
was grappling with elusive concepts and an uncertain trajectory. He had not
worked out all the answers, but what was indisputable was that World War II
had proved the worthiness of their system. However "immense and unpar-
donable" was Stalin's mass repression and however long it would take to
overcome the stagnation that had set in during the late Brezhnev years, Gorbachev emphasized, "We have gone on the correct path—that is the conclusion."[306]

On 2 November, he delivered an address to the Soviet people and to a huge assemblage of guests. He began, "Today, we turn to the October days that shook the world . . . for spiritual support and instructive lessons." The "main meaning of October was the creation of a new life." And what that new life meant, he concluded several hours later, was "Collectivism instead of selfishness, freedom and equality instead of exploitation and oppression, genuine people's power instead of the tyranny of a minority, an increasing role for common-sense and humanity instead of the elemental and harsh interplay of social forces, and general human unity and peace instead of discord, dissension and wars." Now socialism needed perestroika, needed restructuring.

> The objective of restructuring is to fully restore, both theoretically and practically, the Leninist conception of socialism, in which priority is given to the man of labor, to his ideals and interests. . . . As a result of restructuring, socialism could and should fully realize its capabilities as a system of real humanism, serving man and elevating him. It is a society for people, . . . a society in which man feels himself to be completely in charge.[307]

As Alexander Yakovlev explained it, "Today we are reconstructing the person and the souls of people."[308]

To realize this vision, Gorbachev proclaimed, peace and coexistence were indispensable. "Despite the profoundly contradictory nature of the modern world and fundamental differences of the states which comprise it, it is mutually connected, mutually dependent, and forms a definite integral whole."[309] The task of Soviet foreign policy was to shape the international environment to allow perestroika to flourish.[310] And the overriding ideological question was whether capitalism would allow a competitive system to achieve its potential.

Gorbachev's answer to that question reconfigured Soviet ideological thinking about the nature of capitalism, the functioning of the international system, and the requisites of Soviet security. He did not change his conviction that communism constituted a superior system, but he did change Soviet threat perception. Buried in the middle of his long speech was a somewhat tortured but highly significant discussion of whether capitalism could live with socialism. He himself regarded this analysis as hugely important, and stressed its significance the next day at another public meeting. The issues went to the very root of communist thinking about dialectical materialism, historical inevitability, and class conflict. Could technology, science, and the threat of nuclear warfare alter the nature of an imperialist social system? Could capitalism free itself from militarism? Could capitalism do without neocolonialism?[311] The answers to these immensely complicated questions were contingent on circumstances that nobody could predict. But Gorbachev drew conclusions that would be momentous for the future conduct of Soviet foreign policy and the eventual end of the Cold War.

Basically he said that capitalism was changing. "The postwar period has provided evidence of a profound modification of contradictions which have determined the main processes in the world economy." He was impressed that West Germany and Japan had enjoyed enormous growth with minimum military expenditures. More than anything else, he believed that the nuclear age had "brought to the forefront the problem of the very survival of mankind." Not all capitalists were ready to acknowledge the new realities, he stressed, but their numbers were growing. They understood that humanity's fate depended on reconfiguring the relationships between states with contrasting social systems: "What we are counting on is that life will compel [our class enemy] to take realities into account and to become aware that we are in the same boat and we must behave in such a way that it does not capsize."[312]

The Soviet Union had to convince capitalists that they had nothing to fear from it. Imperialist militarism was not based primarily on laws of the capitalist marketplace or exigencies of class strife. "Contradictions in this sphere, too, yield to modifications."[313] Militarism in the West, Gorbachev explained, enjoyed support mainly as a result of the Soviet military threat.[314] If Soviet leaders allayed that perception of threat, they could reshape their foes' foreign policies. If the Kremlin demonstrated that shared values united, rather than divided, mankind, it could relax tensions and nurture more peaceful relationships. But Kremlin leaders could take these risks only if they, too, believed their security was not threatened.

And they did believe they were safe. Gorbachev did not think the United States would attack the Soviet Union. Soviet leaders now, unlike in the 1950s and 1960s, said Shevardnadze, felt confident that their country's security was not endangered.[315] The Americans would not risk retaliation and self-destruction. In a nuclear world, added Marshal Akhromeyev, chief of the Soviet General Staff, "war is an anachronism."[316] Nor were intracapitalist wars that might engulf the Soviet Union likely. Capitalists were able to demilitarize their economy and retain it on a "civilian footing."[317] So the new Soviet intention must be to focus on the matters that would lessen tensions, promote peace, allow for a reduction of military expenditures, and assist reform and restructuring. "We will not forgo, not by one iota, the real values of socialism," Gorbachev declared. "On the contrary, we will enrich and develop them, ridding ourselves of all that which distorted the humanistic essence of our system."[318]

By redefining the nature of threat and focusing on the humanistic values of communism—"serving man and elevating him"—Gorbachev arrived at a discourse that allowed him to communicate more and more effectively with President Reagan. Their capacity to talk to and understand one another was vividly displayed during Reagan's trip to Moscow in May 1988. Here was the president in the capital of what he had called the "evil empire," yet he found an interlocutor in Mikhail Gorbachev the likes of which he never could have anticipated when he became president in 1981. It was not Reagan who had changed; it was Gorbachev. His "new thinking" had transformed his approach to international relations and to the United States of America.

At their first meeting at the Kremlin on the afternoon of 29 May, the president "said that both sides had come a long way since he first wrote to Gorbachev in 1985," and he praised the Soviet exit from Afghanistan: "The whole world approved the courage he was showing." Gorbachev said, "It had been a difficult but necessary beginning. . . . But it was also evident that no problems in the world could be solved by military means. War made things too unpredictable." Contrasting ideologies had to live together peacefully.[319]

Gorbachev then gave Reagan a statement of principles that he believed should govern their nations' future relations:

> Proceeding from their understanding of the realities that have
> taken shape in the world today, the two leaders believe that no
> problem in dispute can be resolved, nor should it be resolved,
> by military means. They regard peaceful coexistence as a
> universal principle of international relations. Equality of all

states, non-interference in internal affairs and freedom of socio-
political choice must be recognized as the inalienable and
mandatory standards of international relations.

Reagan liked it, and said his advisers would examine it carefully. He then
asked Gorbachev to look at a list of human rights cases. He had done this on
previous occasions, he noted, because he assigned great importance to these
matters. He had a "dream," he told Gorbachev. He would never talk about it
publicly, and if it were leaked to the press, he would deny ever having mentioned it. But could not Gorbachev rule

that religious freedom was part of the people's rights, that people of any religion—whether Islam with its mosque, the Jewish faith, Protestants or the Ukrainian Church—could go to the
church of their choice. . . . If Gorbachev could see his way clear
to do what the President had asked, he felt very strongly that
he [Gorbachev] would be a hero, and that much of the feeling
against his country would disappear like water in hot sun.[320]

The president's boldness was extraordinary. He temperately phrased an
audacious request to subvert key elements of the Soviet way of life by prod-
ding Gorbachev to live up to the rhetoric of his "new thinking" and his
self-proclaimed ideals.[321] Equally remarkable was the general secretary's tem-
perate yet tough and self-assured response. "Gorbachev said with a smile that
he felt it was incumbent upon him to respond." He did not want the president or anybody else to think he was being pressed "in a corner" when it
came to discussing human rights. He was prepared for a dialogue, not only
between the two of them, but on a much wider basis—even with the U.S.
Congress. He "was calling for a seminar, on a continuous basis, involving officials, legislators and academics of the two sides." The United States, Gorbachev said, had plenty of human rights problems of its own, especially
concerning blacks and people of color, but not limited to them. What about
social and economic rights, the treatment of antiwar protesters, and other
matters? "He did not want to teach lessons to the United States on how to
run America," but the president should not presume to think he knew all
there was to know about the Soviet Union. "Recently, the Soviets had be-

come much more self-critical, but the U.S. had not." Perhaps not everything was "alright" in the United States. They should talk more. There was much to accomplish. It was too bad the president would soon leave office.[322]

During the next few days, Gorbachev was disappointed that the statement of principles he had handed to the president was deemed unacceptable. Reagan's advisers had convinced the president that he should not sign a document that mentioned peaceful coexistence, a phrase they said "carried political baggage." His domestic political supporters would not like phrases that implied the legitimacy of an alternative system, invoked memories of détente, or underscored the class nature of international relations on which the idea of peaceful coexistence (in the Soviet vocabulary) had always been anchored.[323]

Gorbachev was irritated but not diverted from his path. Within the Kremlin that spring, he faced growing criticism, not widespread or virulent, but criticism nonetheless. Yegor Ligachev and others in the Politburo were carping that he was going too far in repudiating the command economy and the class base of international politics. Gorbachev did not think so. Apparatchiks in the party fiercely resisted the changes he was proposing, yet he wanted to initiate still more radical political ones. The party needed to be democratized. Elections had to occur. He advocated the creation of a Congress of People's Deputies, partially selected by ballot. The people had to be empowered so that mid-level functionaries would be more responsive to their needs. Among his advisers—Chernyaev, Medvedev, Shakhnazarov, and Yakovlev—Gorbachev confided that they must finally sever "the umbilical cord tying us to the command-administrative system and the whole legacy of Stalinism."[324]

This was easier said than done, but the aspiration itself inspired even greater efforts to reshape Soviet foreign policy. On 20 June, the same day they discussed far-reaching political reforms, Gorbachev told the Politburo that the arms race was a "stupid" dialectic. "[W]e got wound up. . . . [W]e were always catching up, and we did not use political methods to achieve our objectives in a proper manner." Mathematical parity made no sense. It was foolish to "to race with the whole world in the volume of armaments: cannon by cannon, plane by plane." The leadership had turned the Soviet Union into a military camp. New thinking was imperative. A few weeks later, Gorbachev again told Warsaw Pact leaders that they must transform the "the image of the enemy as cultivated in the West."[325]

If this required a new vocabulary, so be it. If Reagan and his advisers found the language of peaceful coexistence unacceptable, Gorbachev and Shevardnadze would reassure them that they were not preaching a covert form of class warfare. In a highly publicized speech to the U.N. General Assembly at the end of September 1988, the Soviet foreign minister emphatically stated that his government was renouncing an ideological approach to international relations. "In our vision of peaceful coexistence as the universal principle of international relations," declared Shevardnadze, "it does not appear as a special form of class struggle." Three months later, Gorbachev appeared before the same body and proclaimed his commitment to the self-determination of nations, the rule of law, and the exercise of military self-restraint. "The de-ideologization of interstate relations has become a demand of the new stage," he said. "We are not giving up our convictions, philosophy, or traditions. Neither are we calling on anyone else to give up theirs. Yet we are not going to shut ourselves within the range of our values. That would lead to spiritual impoverishment."[326]

Because his own perception of threat had changed and because he was seeking to alter how the West perceived threat, Gorbachev used his appearance at the United Nations to electrify the world with an announcement of the Soviet Union's unilateral reduction in its stock of conventional arms. Over the next two years, it would cut its armed forces by 500,000 persons, 10,000 tanks, 8,500 artillery pieces, and 800 combat aircraft. Six tank divisions would come out of the Warsaw Pact nations of Eastern Europe. This reduction meant that 50,000 soldiers, 5,000 tanks, and other offensive weaponry would be pulled out of East Germany, Hungary, and Czechoslovakia. The remaining Soviet divisions in Eastern Europe would be reorganized along defensive lines. More cuts would occur in Asia. "The world has changed," Gorbachev declared. For too long, international relations "were built under the banner of confrontation," but now people everywhere could feel relieved as Washington and Moscow reconfigured their relationship along more normal lines.[327]

The speech was a sensational success, "as remarkable as any ever delivered at the United Nations," wrote Robert Kaiser in *The Washington Post*. The point of it, Gorbachev told the Politburo, was to eradicate the image of the iron curtain engraved in the imagination of the West by Winston Churchill in his speech in Fulton, Missouri, in March 1946. It was Fulton in reverse.[328]

Right after the address, on 10 December, a devastating earthquake in Armenia killed forty-five thousand people and displaced as many as a half million more. Gorbachev was forced to return promptly to the Soviet Union, but he did meet briefly with the president-elect, George H. W. Bush, and took time to say his good-byes to the outgoing president. He and Reagan had forged a remarkable relationship. They had shared a sense of optimism, an appreciation of human agency, and a sense of destiny. They had brought warmth, humor, and candor to their interactions. They could listen to one another and learn from one another. They understood the principles that separated them and appreciated the values that united them, most particularly their aversion to nuclear weapons and their yearning for peace. Reagan had begun his presidency with a desire to contain and transform an evil empire, but he ended with an understanding of Soviet fears, an appreciation of perestroika, and a belief that he and Gorbachev shared a commitment to make "a better world."[329] Gorbachev had begun with a wish to accelerate Soviet economic growth and a conviction that he had to reshape the image of the Soviet Union. He had progressed to a point where he was seeking to democratize socialism, reconceptualize threat perception, and transcend the Cold War. Ronald Reagan had become an indispensable partner.[330]

On the eve of the new year, 1989, Gorbachev told his countrymen that "a new vision of the world was being established. . . . The Cold War is starting to retreat." The Soviet people must seize the opportunity to forge a new future. In pursuing "radical reform in the political sphere," his aim was to establish "a law-governed socialist state, where the interests of the individual will serve as the yardstick of all and everything, where citizens' rights and freedoms will be ensured." The challenge was formidable. "We are not expecting and do not promise manna from heaven. We are well aware that the burden of unresolved questions is heavy. Our road is difficult. But the choice has been made."[331]

But he was not certain if the new American president shared his new thinking. Meeting with the Politburo after his trip to New York, Gorbachev did his best to modulate their expectations. He did not think the new president would aggravate relations with the Soviet Union. Nor would he be inclined to carry on adventures abroad. But at the same time, Gorbachev doubted that Bush was ready for a "serious turn in relations . . . which would

Bush, Reagan, and Gorbachev in New York City, 1988. Gorbachev said a
last goodbye to President Reagan and departed, feeling that Bush was
not ready for a serious relaxation of tension.

correspond to the steps our side has taken." U.S. officials, he thought, would
"drag their feet."[332]

Gorbachev was right. The new president was prudent and cautious. Born
into a patrician New England family and educated at Yale, George H. W.
Bush had dedicated much of his adult life to public service as a congressman,
emissary to the People's Republic of China, and director of the CIA before

becoming Reagan's vice president. For most of his career, he had been a typical cold warrior—fearful of communist expansion, alarmed by Soviet military power, and committed to alliance cohesion and political bipartisanship on foreign policy. He believed in peace through strength. Like Reagan, Bush was convinced that a democratic revolution was sweeping the globe. "We know what works," he said in his inaugural address. "We know how to secure a more just and prosperous life for man on earth: through free markets, free speech, free elections, and the exercise of free will unhampered by the state."[333]

Bush appreciated the changes that Gorbachev was making and wanted to build a positive relationship with him, but he was uncertain of Soviet intentions and felt the United States had to be cautious. Three weeks after taking office, he addressed a joint session of Congress: "The fundamental facts remain that the Soviets retain a very powerful military machine in the service of objectives which are still too often in conflict with ours. So, let us take the new openness seriously, but let's also be realistic. And let's also be strong."[334]

Bush chose Brent Scowcroft, a former general with abundant experience in the executive branch, as his national security adviser. Having served as an assistant to Henry Kissinger, Scowcroft became national security adviser to Gerald Ford; then, during the Reagan years, he served on many advisory committees. But he had come to feel that Reagan had been seduced by Gorbachev's charm and charisma. When Scowcroft agreed to join the new administration, he did not believe "the forty-year confrontation between East and West" had come to an end. "I was suspicious of Gorbachev's motives and skeptical of his prospects," he wrote later. The Soviet leader was simply more sophisticated and imaginative than his predecessors: "he was attempting to kill us with kindness rather than bluster." Scowcroft chose as his top aide Robert M. Gates, a Soviet analyst and former deputy director of the CIA, who distrusted Gorbachev even more than his boss.[335]

James A. Baker III, Bush's secretary of state, looked more benignly on Gorbachev's domestic policies, but was not persuaded that any fundamental change had occurred. He quickly grew wary of the debates about Soviet intentions, regarding them as "academic theology. . . . What mattered to me were what actions we could take . . . to maximize our diplomatic gains while minimizing risks." Like his colleagues, Baker feared that Gorbachev was seizing the foreign-policy initiative and controlling the agenda. He resented Gorbachev's celebrity status and worried about his capacity to split the Western alliance.[336]

Most skeptical of Gorbachev was Bush's secretary of defense, Richard Cheney. He, too, was a man with considerable experience, having served as Gerald Ford's chief of staff in the White House. At the time of his appointment to the Pentagon, Cheney said, "There are those who want to declare the Cold War ended. They perceive a significantly lessened threat. . . . But I believe caution is in order. . . . We must guard against gambling our nation's security on what may be a temporary aberration in the behavior of our foremost adversary."[337]

Nor did the messages from Ambassador Jack Matlock in Moscow promote "new thinking" in Washington. Matlock reported that Gorbachev's changes were real and substantive. "The Soviet Union has, in effect, declared the bankruptcy of its system, and . . . there is no turning back." Matlock wanted to continue to press the Soviets for more and more economic and political reform, but perestroika was not likely to produce "marked improvements" in the Soviet economy over the next few years. Matlock cautioned, however, that the Kremlin's preoccupation with its domestic agenda "will not preclude an activist foreign policy . . . but will mean that foreign policy will be heavily—and often decisively—influenced by domestic needs and imperatives."[338] Gorbachev wanted a reduction in international tension so that he could turn his attention, energy, and resources to solving domestic problems, which would lessen the Soviet threat in the short and intermediate term, but not necessarily in the long term. "The potential long-term Soviet capacity to use force for political ends will not disappear," Matlock explained.

Nor was the Kremlin's influence likely to wane because of the Soviet Union's political confusion and economic disarray. Matlock warned that Soviet prestige might grow as the Kremlin appeared less threatening and more cooperative. Gorbachev and his colleagues were learning that they could go "a long way on a smile and a shoeshine. . . . They expect the smile to translate into political benefits." Their peace offensive, unilateral arms cuts, and defensive military strategy were "designed to maintain Moscow's great power status and influence during a period of military and economic retrenchment." The United States might find "that the smiling face will have a more divisive effect than the belligerent growl."[339]

Matlock advised Washington that the United States had a "historic opportunity" to use its leverage not to help Gorbachev or the Soviet Union but rather "to promote U.S. interests." In the case of the Soviet Union, the overriding U.S. interest was the "transformation of the Soviet political system into one with effective structural constraints on the use of military force outside Soviet borders." Toward that end, Matlock urged that the new administration not get bogged down on arms-control issues but should press the Soviets to end their military involvement in Central America and scale back their presence in Cuba. Although Washington "could not force them to give up the store," and should not give Moscow any economic aid, he advised that the United States "offer significant incentives for the Soviet leaders to develop a decentralized, pluralistic, and civilian-oriented economy."[340]

Bush, Scowcroft, Baker, and their colleagues were eager to put their own imprint on U.S. national security policy. They launched a comprehensive study, but it got ensnared in the bureaucracy. "What we received was mush," wrote Baker.[341] Scowcroft's staff, led by the Soviet expert Condoleezza Rice, seized control of the agenda and outlined a foreign-policy framework: the administration should solidify the NATO alliance, challenge Soviet domination of Eastern Europe, demand Soviet disengagement from Central America, and seek the Kremlin's collaboration to stabilize other troubled areas in the third world. If the U.S.S.R. needed economic aid, the administration should use the opening to set "our sights literally on transforming the behavior of the Soviet Union at home and abroad."[342]

In a series of speeches in May, President Bush presented the new strategy:

> We are approaching the conclusion of an historic postwar struggle between two visions: one of tyranny and conflict and one of democracy and freedom. . . . Our goal is bold, more ambitious than any of my predecessors could have thought possible. . . .
> [I]t is time to move beyond containment to a new policy for the 1990s—one that recognizes the full scope of change taking place around the world and in the Soviet Union itself.

The U.S. goal was "much more than simply containing Soviet expansionism. We seek the integration of the Soviet Union into the community of nations."[343] The Cold War could end, Bush was saying, if the Kremlin accepted and integrated itself into a democratic capitalist world order.

"We are witnessing the end of an idea: the final chapter in the Communist experiment," Bush said in a speech at the Coast Guard Academy. "What is it that we want to see?" he asked rhetorically. "It is a dynamic community of democracies anchoring international peace and stability, and a dynamic free-market system generating prosperity and progress on a global scale." The Soviet Union should embrace the principles of free markets and free peoples. Perestroika would receive his staunch support so long as it evolved in this direction. But the Kremlin had to earn the right to participate in this new configuration of international politics. It needed to act, not talk. "The national security policy of the United States is not predicated on hope," he declared. "It must be based on deeds, and we look for enduring, ingrained, economic and political change."[344]

In National Security Directive 23, President Bush outlined the "deeds": "fundamental alterations in Soviet military structure, institutions, and practices." Soviet military forces must get smaller and become less threatening. The U.S.S.R. must renounce class conflict as a "source of international tension" and act in a way that is consistent with that pledge; allow self-determination in Eastern Europe and repudiate the Brezhnev Doctrine; demilitarize Soviet foreign policy in other areas of the globe and make a serious effort to "ameliorate conflict"; exert pressure on its clients to cease their aggressive behavior; stop the proliferation of ballistic missile technology; show willingness to cooperate with the United States in solving global problems like terrorism and the international drug trade; and institutionalize "democratic internal laws and human rights practices, political pluralism, and a more market-oriented economic structure." If Moscow embraced these conditions, it would "find the United States a willing partner in building a better relationship."[345]

In short, if Gorbachev reconfigured his military establishment, renounced his ideological heritage, and adapted his "new thinking" to an international order based on traditional American principles of democratic capitalism, the Cold War would end.

The Wall Comes Down

The new administration in America knew it could not ignore the arms-control agenda; the idea of reducing the gigantic stockpiles of nuclear weapons was hugely popular, especially in Western Europe and most particularly in West Germany. But Bush, Baker, Scowcroft, and Cheney wanted to finesse arms control and concentrate on issues they regarded as more important. They wanted to forge cohesion in Western Europe and liberate Eastern Europe from communist rule and Soviet domination. "Our overall aim," Bush declared, "is to overcome the division of Europe and to forge a unity based on Western values."[346]

At their initial strategy meetings, they discussed the great ferment underway in Poland and Hungary. The Kremlin was showing unusual tolerance for the opposition to the regimes there, but it was hard to know how much self-restraint it would continue to exercise. Since Gorbachev had proposed to cut conventional forces in Europe, Bush and his advisers wanted to exploit this overture to reduce the military capabilities of the Warsaw Pact and erode Soviet power. "Our principal goal should be to try to lift the Kremlin's military boot from the necks of the East Europeans," Scowcroft insisted.[347]

To outmaneuver the Kremlin and deflect another popular Gorbachev initiative—the abolition of tactical nuclear weapons in Europe—Bush and his advisers designed a proposal to highlight conventional arms reductions. They challenged the Soviets to sign an agreement that, in their view, would reshape the military landscape and terminate both sides' fear of a surprise attack. Believing that Gorbachev had not gone far enough to show his goodwill, they proposed that, to correct the imbalance, Gorbachev reduce Soviet troops in central Europe by 325,000 in return for a cut of 30,000 U.S. soldiers, leaving about 275,000 Americans there. This "revolutionary" proposal, as Bush called it, allayed a contentious dispute among America's German and British allies and lobbed the ball back onto the Soviet side of the court.[348]

Bush and his advisers were exhilarated by their ability to reassert U.S. leadership of NATO. During their first months in office they had been severely criticized for their lassitude and vacillation. By June, however, they were reveling in their talk about a foreign policy that looked beyond containment, embraced Western European economic integration, and envisioned a Europe whole and free.[349] Their aim was to contest Gorbachev's appeal for the hearts and souls of Europeans.

Gorbachev's popularity was by then unraveling at home but surging abroad. His domestic political reforms fragmented opinion inside the Politburo and opened possibilities for the public contestation of his policies. But outside his country, Gorbymania reigned. In June and July, he went to France and West Germany and addressed the Council of Europe at Strasbourg. Wherever he went, he was thronged by cheering crowds. He inspired his listeners by championing a common European home, the elimination of tactical nuclear weapons, and promises to respect the rights of all peoples to choose their future. Gorbachev believed that his talk of glasnost, democracy, and common human values would reignite enthusiasm for socialism. The Soviet Union, he said, would not insist on its way of life, but bourgeois society alone did not represent "eternal values." Peoples should be free to choose.[350]

Bush was delighted to take up the challenge, and in July he traveled to Poland and Hungary. Spectacular changes were occurring in both countries. In Poland, economic hardship, huge debts, and spiraling inflation had forced the communist government to seek the collaboration of the long-repressed opposition led by the Solidarity labor union movement. After "roundtable discussions," the two sides agreed on a new electoral law that provided for the open constestation of about a third of the seats in the Sejm, the lower house of the legislature. The Polish people voted freely in June and dealt the

Gorbachev visiting Prague, 1987. Wherever he traveled abroad, he was greeted with enthusiasm.

communists a humiliating defeat. Yet the configuration of Polish politics and
the degree of real power-sharing were still far from clear in July, when Bush
arrived in Warsaw.

In Hungary, the future was also impossible to discern. The Communist
Party there was reforming itself, tolerating open discussion, nurturing private
markets, allowing free elections, and then suddenly, in May, opening Hungary's borders. This meant that East Germans vacationing in Hungary could
cross the frontier and move to Austria and the West. Thousands of them
were doing so, and the Hungarians were ignoring the pleas of East German
leaders to stop the exodus that was so embarrassing to Erich Honecker's
communist government.

Poles and Hungarians were enthralled by the rebirth of civil society and
their own self-empowerment. Yet their future still hinged, at least in part, on
the intersection of local dynamics and great-power interactions. How much
change would Gorbachev allow? How much risk would he accept? How
much aid would Western nations provide to abet the transition away from
communism?

Bush was eager to remind Poles and Hungarians that there was an alternative to their lived experiences, but he did not want to antagonize Gorbachev, provoke Soviet intervention, or encourage unrealistic expectations.
The president remembered 1956, when Soviet troops had entered Budapest
and extinguished a previous generation's yearning for freedom. Just weeks
before, on 4 June 1989, the Chinese army had brutally shot several hundred
civilians protesting in Beijing's Tiananmen Square. This massacre was a vivid
reminder that even communist "reformers" were not ready to accept the
American interpretation of history's trajectory. As Erich Honecker said at the
time, "we took power in order to keep it forever."[351]

Bush therefore measured his words to reporters in Warsaw and Budapest.
"He did not want to poke a stick in the eye of Mr. Gorbachev." The United
States "ought not to overpromise, ought not to overexhort for others to be
like us." He was there not to interfere but to support the Polish and Hungarian people. They were their own agents of change. Their future was in their
hands. Nor did he want to "drive wedges between the Soviet Union and
Eastern Europe." In fact, he liked Gorbachev's concept of a common European home, "but let's be sure a guy can move from room to room. Let's be

sure it's open." Let's be sure that countries "can continue to move towards what works, and what works is freedom, democracy, market economies."[352]

In a speech to the Polish National Assembly, Bush alluded to the dramatic events transpiring across the globe. "A profound cycle of turmoil and great change is sweeping the world from Poland to the Pacific. It is sometimes inspiring, as here in Warsaw, and sometimes it's agonizing, as in China today. But the magnitude of change we sense around the world compels us to look within ourselves and to God to forge a rare alloy of courage and restraint."

The turmoil and volatility, the risks and opportunities, reminded the president of the dramatic events before and after World War II. "The divided world of the modern age began here—right here, in Poland—fifty years ago this summer." But after a heroic victory over fascism, Americans and Poles alike anticipated a bright future. The Atlantic Charter outlined the framework of a new world order based on self-determination and freedom from fear. Peoples were promised the right to choose their way of life. But Stalinism had been imposed on a third of the continent and the Cold War had begun. "You have been a crucible of conflict," Bush told the Polish people; "now you're becoming a vessel for change." Quoting Gorbachev, the president reminded the Poles that all peoples had a right to "choose either capitalism or socialism." Poland's fate must reside in the hands of the Polish people. Although no nation's security should be put at risk—meaning that the Soviet Union should not fear change—Poland should have the right to forge whatever ties it wanted with the rest of Europe. The moment was laden with great opportunity, said Bush. "Democracy has captured the spirit of our time. . . . [It is] the destiny of man."[353]

The Soviet leader was annoyed by these public pronouncements. Bush seemed to be standing back, hoping that Soviet power would disintegrate. To Gorbachev, Bush's professions of support for perestroika did not ring true. Nor did Gorbachev like the fact that Bush had said he would welcome the withdrawal of Soviet troops from Poland. That statement seemed "very strange," Gorbachev said to French president François Mitterrand.[354]

Yet when Gorbachev spoke to the Warsaw Pact leaders at a meeting in early July, he was upbeat. He stressed that the Cold War was winding down. In his view, regional strife in the third world was abating and "trust [was] being created in relations between East and West." Warsaw Pact forces must be cut and reconfigured to comport with the new strategic doctrine of defensive sufficiency. The Warsaw Treaty Organization itself should become more a political, rather than a military, alliance. "By changing ourselves, we are inspiring the rest of the world to change," he said. His hope was that NATO, too, would change. Eventually, the two blocs would disintegrate, and a common European home would evolve, with rooms for different socioeconomic systems.[355]

But not all his allies shared his vision of domestic reform and international reconciliation. Erich Honecker and Nicolae Ceausescu, general secretary of Romania's Communist Party, voiced their anxieties. They attacked imperialists for seeking to destabilize and overturn socialism. "We have reason to be proud of our accomplishments," Ceausescu insisted. He did not regard bourgeois parliamentarism as a model his country should emulate. Gorbachev was not saying that it was. Although the Soviet leader supported change, his hope was that it would proceed along socialist lines.[356]

There was "something schizophrenic about this [Warsaw Pact] conference," wrote the East German defense minister, Heinz Kessler.[357] He thought that Gorbachev was reluctant to face facts: Hungary and Poland were already veering toward bourgeois parliamentarism and free markets. But Gorbachev was facing facts: the Poles and Hungarians, he understood, wanted change. In August, when asked for his views, he advised the Polish communists to accept a minority status in a new government in Warsaw. In September, he told the Hungarians that he would not object if they opened their borders, a move that would lead to the exodus of tens of thousands of East Germans and place great strain on Honecker's government.[358]

Gorbachev's disaffection with Honecker was palpable. East Germany was the Soviet Union's most valued ally, its economy the most highly regarded in the socialist camp. Yet Honecker's intractability and dogmatism exasperated the Soviet leader. East Germans were seething with discontent, and over the summer had begun to rally peacefully in the streets of Leipzig and other cities. An opposition group, New Forum, did not challenge the fundamentals of a socialist society but called for political reform and the rectification of abuses. More boldly, other organizations sprang up—the Social Democratic Party and Democracy Now—and more forthrightly championed political pluralism, free trade unions, and a market economy. These groups were inspired by developments in Budapest and Warsaw, and by the reforms insti-

Gorbachev and Erich Honecker (right), 1989. Gorbachev's disaffection with Honecker was clear when he visited Berlin for the fortieth (and last) anniversary of the German Democratic Republic.

tuted in Moscow by Gorbachev himself. When the Soviet leader went to Berlin in early October to attend the fortieth anniversary of the founding of the East German communist regime, he was met with adulation in the streets. In his public remarks, he celebrated the achievements of the East German Communist Party, the SED, but not its leadership. Privately, without criticizing Honecker directly, he invited change, intimating that Honecker's truculent defense of the status quo was not only counterproductive but also a betrayal of socialism. Gorbachev's attitudes and actions, however vague, probably encouraged the SED leaders in Berlin to topple Honecker on 18 October.[359]

Egon Krenz, Honecker's successor and close associate, could not escape the turmoil he inherited. He was beleaguered by unrest in the streets, demoralization in the party, and the government's impending bankruptcy. On 1 November he went to Moscow to apprise Gorbachev of the regime's ghastly financial situation. By the end of 1989 the East German government would owe $26.5 billion to the West; its current annual payments deficit was more than $12 billion. Taken aback, Gorbachev encouraged Krenz to seek loans from West Germany, but to be wary of making too many concessions. Krenz worried that demonstrators might try to break through the Berlin wall. He emphasized that he wanted to act prudently, and that he and his colleagues were thinking of recognizing the New Forum, with whom they had been negotiating for several weeks. Gorbachev encouraged tolerance and frowned upon the use of force. He made clear that Soviet troops in East Germany could not be used to bolster the regime and advised that the people not be regarded as the enemy. But he prescribed no recipe for success. Advocating reform, he rather aimlessly discussed the problems engendered by perestroika. In his own country, he said, "the horse had been saddled but the ride not completed. One could still be thrown off."[360]

Krenz and his comrades decided to take action. On 9 November, they agreed to renounce the monopoly of power held by the SED since the late 1940s. They said they would accept free elections and allow East Germans to travel abroad more easily.

On the same day, West German chancellor Kohl was in Warsaw talking to Lech Walesa, the Solidarity leader. Walesa worried that developments in East Germany were getting out of control. What would happen if the "GDR completely opened its border and tore down the wall?" Would it mean the unification of Germany? Poles still feared their German neighbors, Walesa reminded Kohl. The situation was fraught with danger. Kohl did not disagree. He noted: "if one shoots, everything would be over."[361]

On that same day, 9 November, the Politburo met in Moscow, where Gorbachev discussed the growing turmoil, not in East Germany, but in the Soviet Union. His glasnost policies had unleashed long-repressed feelings of resentment among submerged nationalities. From the Baltic to the Crimea and beyond, they could now express their desire for autonomy and independence as well as their antipathy toward one another. The inner empire of the Soviet Union was at risk, and Kremlin leaders faced revolutionary nationalist impulses akin to those they had previously exploited throughout the third world. Gorbachev reported to his colleagues that Latvia and Estonia wanted to leave the U.S.S.R. and were blackmailing him. The Kremlin must show them, he said, that those who seek independence face economic ruin. But he wanted to retain the initiative and keep them loyal with a series of positive steps toward federation, price reform, and property guarantees. His remarks spurred dissent. As soon as local elections occurred in the Baltic republics, said Prime Minister Nikolai Ryzhkov, they would leave the Soviet

East and West Berliners celebrating New Year's together, 1990.
The Germans' desire for unification was overwhelming.

Union and chaos would ensue. The repercussions would reach far beyond Latvia, Estonia, and Lithuania. "What we should fear is not the Baltics, but Russia and Ukraine," Ryzhkov said. "I smell an overall collapse."[362]

That night, 9–10 November, in Berlin, the German people tore down the wall—literally.

West German chancellor Kohl telephoned President Bush the next day to describe events. He could hardly contain his euphoria. "I've just returned from Berlin. It is like witnessing an enormous fair. It has the atmosphere of a festival." The frontier between East and West Berlin was completely open, and people were joyously walking back and forth. Hundreds of thousands were in the streets of Berlin, Leipzig, and Dresden. "I hope they will continue to be calm and peaceful." So did Bush. "I want . . . to avoid hot rhetoric that by mistake might cause a problem." Bush and Kohl congratulated each other on their prudence and on the achievements they had witnessed. The wall was down, the Poles and Hungarians were free, and the winds of freedom were spreading to Czechoslovakia and Bulgaria. Kohl's mind was already spinning with dreams of German unification, but Bush urged continued prudence.[363]

"The Berlin Wall has collapsed," wrote Chernyaev in his diary that very same day. "This entire era in the history of the Socialist system is over. . . . This is the end of Yalta [and] the Stalinist legacy. . . . This is what Gorbachev has done. And he has indeed turned out to be a great leader. He has sensed the pace of history and helped history to find a natural channel."[364]

Gorbachev's sense of history was inextricably linked to his perception of threat. Capitalism and communism, he liked to say, were changing. Although Washington and Moscow might disagree and compete, he had a strong "inner conviction" that the United States would never attack the Soviet Union. Much had changed since the 1950s and 1960s, when "there was no firm sense of national security, and the threat of war was seen as an immediate and even inevitable reality." What had changed most was the Kremlin's capacity to inflict unimaginable damage on the adversary should war erupt. Our "existing nuclear means guarantee us from a direct aggression," wrote Gorbachev's trusted adviser Georgy Shakhnazarov.[365]

Even Gorbachev's strident critics in the military and defense establishment agreed. None of them pressed him to use force in Poland, Hungary, or East Germany. So long as Germany was divided, there was little reason to fear the unfolding of developments in Eastern Europe. "Thanks to nuclear parity, we could live in peace," Defense Minister Yakov recollected.[366]

Gorbachev did not believe that the peace and security of the Soviet Union would be endangered by developments in Eastern Europe. In early 1989, several of his advisers in the International Department of the CPSU and in prominent policy institutes had calculated that the socialist countries of Eastern Europe were redefining their priorities and placing economics at the top of their agendas. Poles and Hungarians were likely to adopt a multiparty system, embrace private markets, and repudiate their ideological heritage. "The European socialist countries [find] themselves in a powerful magnetic field of the economic growth and social well-being of West European states. Against this background, on the one hand, their own achievements [grow] dim, and on the other hand, the real problems and difficulties that exist in the West, are practically imperceptible."[367]

Nonetheless, Gorbachev's experts did not think the Kremlin should intervene. The security of the Soviet Union would be affected only if foreign governments interfered in Eastern Europe. "By itself the fact of a transfer of power to alternate forces does not mean an external military threat to our country." Since neither Poland nor Hungary was likely to leave the Warsaw Pact in the short run, Soviet security was not threatened. The old specter of Western encirclement had been eliminated "once and for all and irreversibly" by the prospect of nuclear holocaust. "[W]e need to liberate ourselves from some persistent ideological stereotypes," Gorbachev's new thinkers wrote, "for instance from the assumption that only a communist party in power can provide guarantees of the security of Soviet borders."[368]

Gorbachev did liberate himself from this assumption. He did not intervene to preserve the communists' monopoly of power in Poland or Hungary (or elsewhere) because employing force would clash with his overriding goal of transforming the image of the Soviet Union in the West. He was seeking to build a common European home where the rules barred the use of force and required respect for the will of the residents. If the rival alliance structures were to be dissolved, which was a long-term goal, force must be abjured.[369]

Nor could he contemplate using force outside the Soviet Union when he was totally absorbed with preserving unity within it. Day in and day out, he faced one internal crisis after another. Nationalistic passions were raging; blood was being spilled; dissent was spreading from one region to another. In the Politburo, Gorbachev faced severe criticism for what his opponents thought was timidity in the face of this unrest. Yet using force at home would destroy his image almost as much as would employing it abroad. After Soviet troops brutally suppressed demonstrators in Tbilisi, Georgia, on 9 April, leaving twenty people dead, he insisted that this not happen again.[370]

Gorbachev's foreign policy continued to be shaped by his domestic agenda. Talking to students five days after the fall of the Berlin wall, he began, "let's start with the main thing, perestroika." "Through restructuring we want to give socialism a second wind and to unveil in all its plentitude the vast humanist potential of the socialist system." Man was not to be viewed as a cog in that system, but the system was to be reconfigured for the benefit of man. Gorbachev made it clear that he was going to launch a new round of economic reforms. The Soviet Union had to leap into a new "technological epoch" grounded in microelectronics, information science, and biotechnology. Funds had to be freed up for these areas and investments made in order to generate the immense advances in productivity and efficiency that would lead to more food, consumer goods, and services.[371]

Given these priorities, Gorbachev could not possibly intervene in Eastern

Europe when he saw no security imperatives endangered. Poland and Hungary owed enormous sums to Western creditors. He could not rescue them from drowning in their own indebtedness when his own economy was buffeted by the fall in oil and raw material prices.[372] Nor could he think of intervening abroad when his troops were returning from Afghanistan bloodied and demoralized and when Najibullah was still pleading for more trucks, fuel, ammunition, and weapons.[373]

When Chancellor Kohl called on 11 November to assure him that West Germany did not want to destabilize East Germany, Gorbachev was grateful. He and Kohl agreed that they needed to stay in close contact. "Deep changes are underway in the world," said Gorbachev. They could take different forms in different countries, and "be more or less deep." But stability must be preserved and all sides must "act in a responsible way."[374] Yet he was uncertain how Kohl would behave. Three days later, Gorbachev telephoned French president Mitterrand. The flow of events did not disturb him except in one respect, he said. "I have in mind all the excitement . . . in the FRG around the issue of German unification."[375]

On 17 November, Foreign Minister Shevardnadze spoke more clearly on this subject to the Supreme Soviet. The processes occurring in Eastern Europe, he said, "are natural and historically conditioned. Democratization, the renewal of socialism, and the exercise of the peoples' right to free choice are under way." But the postwar territorial status quo must not be upset; two Germanies must remain. "The past must never be repeated. Europe and the world paid a high price for past mistakes. The Soviet people have not forgotten and never will forget history's lessons."[376]

Soviet leaders regarded the division of Germany as a fundamental requisite of Soviet security.[377] Over time, the division of Germany had mitigated their perception of threat. The absence of threat, in fact, enlarged the opportunities for reform, and the desire to reform reinforced their determination to lessen the threat they posed to others. But suddenly the specter of German power had reemerged.[378] It "was obvious that the German question . . . touched emotional chords other European issues did not," wrote Secretary of State Baker.[379]

Two Countries Become One

On 28 November 1989, Chancellor Helmut Kohl of West Germany strained those chords. In a speech to the German Bundestag he outlined a ten-point road map to German unification. He talked about regulating travel and sharing technology. But he stressed that West German economic aid to East Germany would be forthcoming only if the East German regime agreed to hold free elections and dismantle its centralized planning. Once these steps were taken, the two Germanys could establish a "treaty community" and then design confederative structures that would eventually culminate in a federal system for all Germany. These steps should be coordinated with efforts to enhance pan-European structures and reduce armaments. "Nobody knows today what a re-united Germany will ultimately look like," he said. "I am sure that the unity will come if the people of Germany want it."[380]

Hardly anyone else wanted German unity. Memories of the past haunted Europe. British prime minister Margaret Thatcher made clear to President Bush that she opposed it. So did the Dutch and Italian foreign ministers. Mitterrand was displeased with Kohl's initiative but hesitated to voice his opposition openly lest he antagonize a West German friend whose collaboration he needed to promote further European integration.[381]

President Bush was an exception. He despised the East German regime and believed German nationalism was a natural impulse that could not be thwarted. "While Thatcher, Mitterrand, and others feared that Germany might cause more trouble and tragedy," Bush recalled, "I did not." A newly reunited Germany, in Bush's view, "would be different." It would be democratic; respect existing borders; be anchored to the NATO alliance; be integrated into other supranational institutions; and collaborate with Washington. The day after Kohl's speech, Bush called the German chancellor. A unified Germany, Kohl promised, would remain in NATO. Bush was reassured and said he would support Kohl. Over the next few months, he and Kohl spoke frequently on the phone. Their friendship grew as they labored to transform the landscape of Europe. Bush knew what he wanted and where he was heading. He was happy for Kohl to take the lead.[382]

Not all of Bush's advisers were enthusiastic. They worried about dangers and imponderables. "Suppose that [Kohl] decided he could get unification only by trading it for neutrality," thought Scowcroft. The specter of a neutral, powerful, unified Germany in the middle of Europe had been a recurrent nightmare of American and European statesmen since the very beginning of the Cold War. Bush, of course, was determined that there would be no neutral Germany. But how could they be sure?[383]

They worried, in part, about how the Soviet Union would react to Kohl's initiative. It would be hard for Gorbachev to swallow a unified Germany, let alone a unified Germany inside NATO, which would, wrote Baker, "alter the fundamental geostrategic, political, and economic architecture of Europe." The loss of East Germany and its absorption into NATO, Scowcroft realized, "would be fatal to post-war Soviet military strategy and tantamount to a shift in the tectonic plates of the alliances themselves. East Germany was the prize of World War II. . . . Losing it, and accepting that loss, would mean acknowledging the end of Soviet power in Eastern Europe and the complete erosion of Moscow's security buffer of satellite states, the very core of its security planning."[384]

Kohl was thrusting the issue of German unification on the international scene just as Bush and Gorbachev were readying for their first meeting, in early December in Malta. Notwithstanding the breathtaking events of the preceding months and the ongoing transformation of governments in Bulgaria and Czechoslovakia, U.S. officials were still wary of Gorbachev. They did not think his reforms would succeed, and they still were uncertain of his intentions. "I still believed Gorbachev remained a communist," recalled Scowcroft, "perhaps not inevitably wedded to the notion of inevitable conflict between the two systems, but quite prepared to take advantage of us whenever the opportunity arose." Gorbachev might simply be lulling the West into complacency. He was making a virtue of necessity, Richard Nixon wrote Bush, and that did not make him a virtuous leader. Beware![385]

Bush was more optimistic, but still unsure. He prepared carefully for his meeting with the Soviet leader, wanting to put Gorbachev on the defensive. As their respective ships anchored in Malta's harbor, a terrible storm raged. Inside, the atmosphere, "while friendly, was not relaxed." Bush assured Gorbachev that he supported perestroika and wanted to plan for another summit in June. He raised some Soviet human rights cases, discussed the possibilities for expanded trade, and then pressed the Soviet leader to support free elections in Central America and to constrain Castro's adventurism.[386]

Gorbachev presented a more philosophical overview of the Cold War.

"Today all of us feel we are at a historic watershed." New problems must be addressed. A new world was evolving. Cooperation had to supplant competition. "The United States and the USSR are doomed to cooperate for a long time, but we have to abandon the images of an enemy." The Soviet Union would never attack the United States.

Gorbachev then turned to Germany. "Mr. Kohl is in too much of a hurry. . . . This is not good," he said. Gorbachev still hoped that a reformed and reconstituted East German regime would survive. There "are two states mandated by history," he told Bush. "So let history decide the outcome." Bush promised that the United States would not act recklessly, but he did not oppose German unification. How did Gorbachev want to proceed? The Soviet leader talked vaguely about adhering to the principles agreed upon at Helsinki: preserving stability, respecting the balance of power in Europe, and reconfiguring their military alliances along more political lines. But he had no blueprint.[387]

On the German question there was no meeting of minds, but at Malta there was a meeting of hearts. Gorbachev and Bush talked candidly and openly to each other. Gorbachev felt that Bush was ready to cooperate, expand trade, and assist his initiatives at home. Bush felt that Gorbachev talked straight, even about the most sensitive topics, such as the turmoil in the Baltic republics, where Bush felt that Soviet use of force would "create a firestorm" and wreck possibilities of cooperation. Baker sent a cable to American ambassadors in NATO capitals: "We believe [that Gorbachev is] firmly committed to perestroika—that gives us a very good chance to improve dramatically—even transform—the East-West relationship."[388]

Gorbachev returned to Moscow to face unprecedented problems. His economic initiatives were floundering—worsening, rather than improving, people's living conditions. His political reforms were sparking dissent and eroding his prestige. His attempts to accommodate the demands of subject nationality groups were scorned by ethnic patriots in the Baltic and the Crimea and ridiculed by Russian nationalists. His closest associates were losing faith in him.[389]

And now he could not escape dealing with the future of Germany. His frustration, indeed his anger, flared when he and Shevardnadze met with Hans-Dietrich Genscher, the West German foreign minister, on 5 December. Gorbachev felt betrayed, he told Genscher. In previous meetings, he and

Kohl had built an understanding: they had talked about how World War II had affected their lives and shaped the destiny of their countries; they had reflected on the obligation they shared to heal old wounds, and the opportunity they had to plan a more hopeful future. Now Kohl had shattered these expectations by spouting a plan for German unification without consulting him. East Germany was still a sovereign state, Gorbachev insisted, and Kohl was crudely interfering in its domestic affairs, treating the people of the GDR as if they were his own citizens. This was "blatant revanchism." "Even Hitler did not allow himself anything like that," Shevardnadze interjected. When Genscher tried to explain, Gorbachev snapped: don't even try to defend him. Kohl's plan for unification was a "political miss," he declared, and warned: "[Y]ou can spoil everything that we have created together. . . . You have to remember what mindless politics led to in the past. . . . Everybody can see that Chancellor Kohl is rushing."[390]

"The German issue is a painful one," Gorbachev said to Mitterrand in a meeting the next day. But not even Gorbachev could deny reality. East Germans wanted unification. "The majority of the people in the German Democratic Republic no longer support the idea of two German states," Hans Modrow, the East German communist leader, told him at the end of January.[391]

Gorbachev and Shevardnadze had talked for years about their respect for self-determination. They now had to decide if they would use force to thwart the will of the German people. Should they do so, they would violate their most fundamental principles and besmirch perestroika. Secretary of State Baker witnessed the "emotional weight" of this wrenching issue as he dealt with Shevardnadze. "You know how proficient the Germans are," Shevardnadze said to him. "They have tremendous creative potential. But they also, as we have seen in the past, have tremendous destructive potential." He could not forget "the memory of two world wars unleashed by Germany, especially the last war, which cost our country 27 million lives." Nor could he forget the personal anguish of that war, the deaths of his brother and uncles.[392]

At a four-hour meeting with their closest associates on 28 January 1990, Gorbachev and Shevardnadze wrestled with the issue of German unification. Grudgingly, they acknowledged it could not be stopped. Instead of opposing it in principle, they would try to work with Kohl. He was projecting unification as an integral part of an all-European vision, a concept championed by French president Mitterrand and comporting with their own ideas about a common European home. The Soviet leaders decided that the World War II allies—Britain, France, the United States, and the Soviet Union—should establish a process, along with the Germans, Kohl and Modrow, to determine the future of Germany.[393]

In February, Gorbachev and Shevardnadze told Secretary of State Baker that they were ready to participate in what came to be known as the Two Plus Four process. The task was to reconcile Germans' legitimate right to self-determination with the other four nations' security requirements. In a speech to the Canadian parliament, Shevardnadze lucidly outlined the challenge of dealing with "two truths": "No one doubts the right of the Germans in the GDR and the FRG to self-determination. But equally certain is the right of Germany's neighbors and the European states to have guarantees that a united Germany, if it is created, will not be a threat to them, that it will not raise the question of a review of European borders, and that Nazism and fascism will not revive in it."[394]

Soviet and U.S. leaders agreed that a united Germany needed to be bound by supranational institutions and structures. "[W]e needed a safety net which would protect us and the rest of Europe from any 'surprises' from the Germans," Gorbachev told Baker. But the appropriate security mechanisms, he stressed, "should be provided not by NATO but by new structures created within a pan-European framework." What he meant by this was unclear: he had no real plan.[395]

The issue of German unification cast a pall over Soviet politics. Old-line communists charged that Gorbachev was intending to destroy the leading position of their party, institute a multiparty system, embrace private property and a free-market economy, and allow the breakup of the Soviet Union itself. In the Politburo and the Central Committee, opponents of change attacked Gorbachev and Shevardnadze mercilessly. The German issue was particularly disquieting because it had such a loud resonance. "We should not overlook the impending danger of the accelerated reunification of Germany," said Yegor Ligachev, an influential member of the Politburo, who was increasingly disaffected with Gorbachev. "It would be unpardonably short-sighted and a folly not to see that on the world horizon looms a Germany with a formidable economic and political potential." There must not be another Munich, he intoned. "I believe the time has come to recognize this new danger of our era and tell the party and the people about it in a clear voice."[396]

This criticism shook Gorbachev and Shevardnadze. In May, they rebuffed a package of security assurances that Secretary of State Baker brought to Moscow. A unified Germany within NATO, Baker said, would not be allowed to develop or possess any nuclear, chemical, or biological weapons. Its army would be limited in size. Its existing border with Poland would be guaranteed. In addition, NATO would be reorganized into a more political than military alliance, and NATO forces would not enter former East German territory for a number of years. German-Soviet economic ties would be nurtured, and new pan-European structures would be created through procedures that comported with the Helsinki Final Act.[397] Although these security assurances were significant, they did not satisfy Gorbachev and Shevardnadze, who continued to be assailed by officials in the foreign ministry and the Soviet military establishment. In May, while Gorbachev celebrated the anniversary of the victory over Nazism, many hard-liners and some moderates quipped "that the Soviet Union was capitulating to Germany forty-five years after the end of the war."[398] Baker left Moscow on 19 May

> with an overriding impression that Gorbachev was feeling squeezed. . . . Germany was over-loading his circuits. I had believed that Shevardnadze was more emotional and less logical on Germany than his boss, but . . . both of them were having trouble squaring the circle. I felt they trusted us and trusted the German leadership and oftentimes seemed on the verge of accepting Germany in NATO, only to have their political sense or historical memories pull them back.[399]

Gorbachev flew to the United States at the end of May for his summit with President Bush. He now had more friends in Washington than he had in Moscow, and he needed American help, badly. Over a number of days, including a relaxed interlude at Camp David, he talked with great candor about his problems. He wanted his American interlocutors to understand just how far he had gone and how much farther he hoped to travel to reshape socialism and nurture democracy in the Soviet Union. He was caught in a terrible vise by Lithuania's threat to secede and his opponents' demand that he preserve the unity of the Soviet Union. Personally, he was of two minds—understanding a people's right to self-determination but despairing over the impending disintegration of the nation he governed. He elicited Bush's empathy and invited his assistance. He wanted a trade treaty. He looked for progress on the strategic and conventional arms-reduction agreements. Nobody listening to Gorbachev could think that he regarded the United States as an enemy or doubt that he believed the shared interests of the two nations trumped their differences. But he was negotiating from a position of weakness, and he desperately needed diplomatic achievements to sustain perestroika. "The phase of perestroika that we are now going through is probably decisive," he told Bush. "The difficulties will be fundamental. . . . Different republics may have different relationships, but our basic decision is for a market economy."[400]

Gorbachev's desperation was most apparent when the two leaders turned their attention to the German question. "Germany could be in both alliances or neither," Gorbachev said. "Either would be acceptable to the Soviet Union, but a Germany only in NATO would unbalance Europe." Bush tried hard to dissuade Gorbachev, employing one line of argument after another. Did he not agree that peoples could determine their own future? Did he not agree that the Helsinki Final Act permitted nations to choose their alliances? Did he not think that the people of a united Germany should have the right to choose what they wanted to do?[401]

"To my astonishment," Bush recollected, "Gorbachev shrugged his shoulders and said yes," the Germans should have the right to choose. The room fell silent, and Bush repeated his inquiry. Gorbachev assented a second time. A din arose as Gorbachev's advisers started whispering angrily to one another. The "dismay in the Soviet team was palpable," wrote Bush. "Akhromeyev's eyes flashed angrily." As Gorbachev continued to speak to Bush, members of his delegation snapped at one another. "It was an unbelievable scene," Bush remembered. "I could scarcely believe what I was witnessing," commented Scowcroft.[402]

As the dissent flared, Gorbachev tried to qualify his position. He did not repudiate his statement but instead talked about a long transition period and the need to assuage Soviet insecurities about the rebirth of German power, whether as an autonomous nation or linked to a hostile alliance.[403] Such thinking recalled Soviet fears at the onset of the Cold War.

But much had changed. Gorbachev's mind-set was not that of Stalin, or Malenkov, or Khrushchev, or Brezhnev. He did not assume that all capitalists were mortal enemies, nor did he regard the United States as a future adversary. Like Shevardnadze, he had liberated himself from ideological stereotypes. "Pseudo-ideology" had impoverished his nation.[404] The United States needed to be viewed as a potential partner rather than as an inveterate foe. Accordingly, Gorbachev reversed himself. It was in the interest of the Kremlin, he said, to have U.S. troops stay in Europe. His subordinates might shudder at such an idea, but he now regarded NATO as an instrument to keep the United States involved in Europe, an insurance policy against the latent power of a unified Germany.[405]

Gorbachev's thinking about Germany had evolved in significant ways. This was apparent in his meetings with Chancellor Kohl and Foreign Minister Genscher and in his conversations with Bush. Gorbachev had fumed when Kohl made his statement to the Bundestag on 28 November, but now he could talk sharply to Genscher precisely because he believed trust had developed between them, though he worried that the trust might be very slim. Still, it endured, sustained by Kohl's and Gorbachev's recognition of their mutual interests and by Gorbachev's capacity to recast his perception of threat and imagine a different historical trajectory. "Germany can be trusted," Bush had assured Gorbachev. "For fifty years there has been democracy in Germany. This should not be ignored." The Germans had learned from history, Gorbachev acknowledged. A bourgeois, democratic neighbor, however powerful, could be peaceful, could resist its militarist past.[406]

Kohl traveled to Moscow in mid-July 1990 to see if he could negotiate a treaty governing relations between a unifying Germany and a rapidly changing Soviet Union. During the previous weeks, NATO leaders had agreed to recast the alliance along more political and defensive lines, and the governments of the Western industrialized nations had decided to make credits available to East European governments and the Soviet Union if they continued to make the transition to free-market economies and open societies. Kohl, therefore, had more leverage to deal with Gorbachev than Bush had had in May. But Gorbachev's position also had been strengthened, at least momentarily. At a stormy meeting of the twenty-eighth Congress of the CPSU in early July, his comrades endorsed Gorbachev's political changes and reaffirmed his leadership of the party.[407] When Kohl met with him, Gorbachev conveyed more self-confidence than he had for many months.

His confidence was not arrogance. He and Kohl chatted emotionally about transcending their pasts and overcoming traditional hostilities. "A special responsibility falls to our generation, to people of our age," said Kohl. "We did not fight in the war, . . . but we remember the war, we saw its horrors." Gorbachev agreed: "The current generation . . . [has] a unique experience. We have felt the chance that has opened. Our generation can still make a statement in history. . . . We have felt that we are one civilization." Later on, he repeated: "We can't forget the past. Tragedy entered each one of our families. . . . But it's time to turn our faces toward Europe, to take the path of cooperation with the great German nation."[408]

Talking to Kohl, Gorbachev reaffirmed his new attitude toward the presence of U.S. troops in Europe. They could play a stabilizing role. He was pleased, moreover, that the NATO powers had agreed to restructure the alliance. "The transformation of NATO is apparent," said Gorbachev, "as is its emphasis on a political accent in its activities. A great step towards casting off the fetters of the past [has been taken]. . . . The fact that the West does not see the Soviet Union as an enemy has great importance for the future."[409]

Recasting the enemy image meant that Soviet leaders had more room to maneuver at home, more ability to pursue reform, and more leeway to shift resources from the military establishment to civilian sectors. The "basic mission" of Soviet foreign policy, Shevardnadze reminded his colleagues in April 1990, was to create "the conditions most conducive to internal transformations in the country." Their goal was to ensure that external circumstances "are nowhere an impediment to our perestroika."[410]

This attitude shaped Gorbachev's approach to the treaty negotiations with Kohl. He wanted to protect Soviet security, deflect domestic criticism, gain financial assistance, and most of all, sustain his floundering perestroika economic reforms. He agreed to a united Germany in NATO. In return, Kohl promised that Germany and NATO would provide the assurances that Baker had outlined months before: German troops would be limited in size; the sphere of NATO activities would be restricted to the former West Germany, so long as Soviet troops remained in the eastern part of the country before their withdrawal over three or four years. Germany would forswear weapons of mass destruction and promise to respect the prevailing border with Poland, and new pan-European institutions would be forged to ensure security in the common European home. Germany would also provide Gorbachev with significant financial aid.[411] Gorbachev's concessions were huge: the Soviet leader assented not only to the unification of Germany along democratic capitalist lines, but also to its incorporation into an alliance whose very purpose had been the containment of the Soviet Union. "For me, the Cold War ended when the Soviets accepted a united Germany in NATO," said Brent Scowcroft.[412]

The Cold War was over because Gorbachev previously had withdrawn Soviet troops from Afghanistan, de-ideologized international politics, ceased competing in many third world trouble spots, accepted free-market ideas and democratic political reforms at home, and permitted the overthrow of communist governments in Eastern Europe. The Soviet Union no longer had the capacity or will to compete ideologically or militarily for the soul of mankind. Gorbachev recast his government's approach to international affairs and retracted its power nearly to its prewar borders. Shortly, that power would shrink further as one republic after another, including Ukraine, seceded from the Union. In 1948, George F. Kennan, the architect of containment, had said that the Cold War would end when such happenings occurred—and they had.

Gorbachev, Reagan, and Bush

It was Gorbachev who ended the Cold War. Among all the leaders we have examined, it was his thinking that shifted most fundamentally. He came to feel that Soviet security was not endangered by capitalist adversaries. Nor were there many opportunities for communist advances abroad. He could focus, therefore, on restructuring communist society in the U.S.S.R.

Gorbachev would not have persevered had he not found empathetic interlocutors in Washington. Ironically, Reagan's greatest contribution to ending the Cold War was not the fear he engendered but the trust he inspired. At the time Gorbachev took office he was told that America's rearmament effort had reached its peak and was likely to be constrained thereafter by economic woes, fiscal exigencies, and political partisanship.[413] Gorbachev was not awed by America's power or Reagan's ideological zealotry, but he was impressed

Eurasia After the Cold War

Gorbachev in power, 1985–1991
U.S.S.R. dissolved, 1991

German reunification, 1990

Yugoslavia breaks up, 1991

with the president's personal character, political strength, and desire to eliminate nuclear weapons. Reagan seemed to want to get to know us personally,
Shevardnadze recalled. While "adhering to his convictions," Gorbachev
wrote, the president "was not dogmatic." He wanted to negotiate and cooperate. Most of all, Reagan had the trust of the American people. The Soviet
leader knew that if he struck a deal with Reagan, it would stick.[414]

To his relations with Reagan, America's most renowned ideologue, Gorbachev could apply his own considerable personal skills. He could try to
shatter the image of the evil empire, and to a considerable degree, he did.[415]
But the substantive outcomes were always on American terms, since Reagan
did not compromise much. Yet Gorbachev was not unhappy with the relationship because the summitry had bestowed a more benign image on himself and his country. With time, he hoped, he would gain the opportunity to
shift resources, nurture his perestroika, and create a system of democratic socialism worthy of example.

Gorbachev wanted continuity with Reagan's successor and welcomed
Bush's victory in the 1988 elections. Although he was irritated by Bush's policy reassessment, the two men subsequently developed a rapport with one another. Bush was not the ideologue that Reagan was, nor did he have the same
political base. But Gorbachev liked Bush's cautious, prudent demeanor. The
new president did not rub Gorbachev's nose in his defeats. He did not talk
flamboyantly or arrogantly. "I have conducted myself in ways not to complicate your life," Bush said to Gorbachev. "That's why I have not jumped up
and down on the Berlin Wall." "Yes, we have seen that," retorted Gorbachev,
and "appreciate" it.[416]

The affection that characterized Gorbachev's relations with Bush and,
even more, the warmth that developed between Baker and Shevardnadze
were conditioned by the weakness of the Soviets' position domestically and
internationally.[417] They were supplicants. Gorbachev and Shevardnadze
made most of the concessions. At the outset of the Cold War, Truman had
said that there could be cooperation between Moscow and Washington if the
United States got its way 85 percent of the time. Now that was happening.
Rather than compete for the soul of mankind in a global competition, Gorbachev wanted mostly to rekindle the real promise of communism, now
reconceived as democratic socialism, in the Soviet Union. To do so, he
needed to end the Cold War.

CONCLUSION

The Cold War was not predetermined. Leaders made choices. During the Second World War, Franklin D. Roosevelt, Joseph Stalin, and Winston Churchill were besieged by competing impulses and clashing priorities. They distrusted one another. Yet as allies they labored diligently at wartime conferences to modulate their differences and plan for victory and peace. As the most horrible war in history came to an end, leaders in Washington and Moscow, including the untutored and provincial Truman and the evil and paranoid Stalin, recognized that cooperation was preferable to conflict. So did their successors.

Cooperation might mean collaboration in preserving the peace when the advent of atomic weapons made war even ghastlier than before. It might mean collaboration in punishing and controlling foes whose eventual revival was taken for granted and whose long-term behavior was a frightening imponderable. It might mean collaboration in reconverting wartime economies and reconstructing devastated areas. Moscow might receive reparations from the western zones of Germany and might get credits from Washington in exchange for its acceptance of a liberal peace based on open markets and self-determination. If conflict could be avoided and an arms race modulated, American and Soviet leaders might be able to focus on their domestic priorities and direct funds to meet the needs of their societies as defined by their respective political cultures. Stalin and Truman; Malenkov and Eisenhower; Kennedy, Johnson, and Khrushchev; Brezhnev and Carter; and Reagan, Bush, and Gorbachev never doubted that they represented alternative ways of organizing human society. But the question they faced was whether they could identify and pursue common interests notwithstanding their ideological differences.

Until the mid- and late 1980s, they were unable to do so. The Cold War emerged and persisted for four decades because these leaders were trapped by their ideas and ideals and beleaguered by the dangers and opportunities that lurked in the international system. Their beliefs heightened their sense of danger and accentuated messianic impulses. Their rhetoric and programs mobilized domestic constituencies and empowered interest groups and bureaucracies that opposed policy changes and made them increasingly difficult. Foreign allies and clients often developed their own stakes in the bipolar system, manipulated the United States and the Soviet Union in behalf of their own interests, and made it harder for the two powers to relax tensions and reconfigure their relationship. Leaders in both countries often glimpsed the mutuality of their interests but became hostages to their ideas and constituents rather than agents of change. It took an exceptional man, Gorbachev, to reconceive the nature of threat and to focus on domestic resurrection rather than external opportunity. It took an exceptional man, Reagan, to muster the inner conviction, personal charm, and domestic political strength to leverage his opponent's concessions into a framework that preserved and institutionalized his own nation's global hegemony.

The Cold War lasted as long as it did because of the ways in which American and Soviet ideas intersected with evolving conditions of the international system. U.S. and Soviet leaders thought they represented superior ways of organizing human existence. The men in the Kremlin sincerely believed they were reconfiguring human society and eradicating human exploitation. By eliminating private property and a marketplace economy, they thought they could supplant human greed as the driving force behind human progress.

Planning would replace the anarchy of the marketplace. Workers would no longer be at the mercy of their employers, and oppressed peoples would no longer be subject to imperial domination. The Communist Party would serve as the vanguard of the proletariat and the liberator of colonial peoples. The trajectory of history envisioned the end of capitalism, perpetual peace, universal justice, and the emancipation of mankind.

The men in the White House had a different vision of how history should unfold. Their aim was to fashion a world order along the lines of democratic capitalism. They wanted people to be free and markets to be open. Political parties should compete for power in governments that represented their citizenry. Individual rights and private property were the keys to human advancement and personal opportunity. God, they often said, intended people to be free. Certainly, men and women could not worship as they pleased if they were not free.

These contradictory visions of mankind's future were inseparable from Soviet and American ideas about the past. Historical memories and ideological assumptions shaped perceptions of fear and opportunity. For Soviet leaders, from Stalin to Brezhnev, capitalist countries could neither escape conflict with one another nor resist the temptation to crush an ideological foe. History since 1917, as they understood it, confirmed the implacable hostility of capitalists, the volatility of the international capitalist economy, and the enmity of other powers like Germany and Japan, whose governments were controlled by fascists and militarists. Notwithstanding the immense suffering that Soviet citizens had endured, their utopian experiment had survived and, allegedly, demonstrated its superiority. If the Kremlin remained vigilant, history's trajectory portended a glorious future for communism.

U.S. officials, no less than their counterparts in Moscow, were inspired by their ideals and shaped by their experience. For Americans, their past confirmed that totalitarian governments, whether fascist, Nazi, or communist, were likely to expand and to crush human freedom—the freedom to speak, to practice religion, to own property, and to trade. Americans had learned from the interwar years that freedom and liberalism could not be safe at home if they were at risk abroad; the United States could not be secure if a totalitarian adversary controlled the human resources, raw materials, industrial infrastructure, and technological know-how of Eurasia and used those assets to challenge the American way of life.

The international environment posed danger and opportunity to leaders in Moscow and Washington. In Europe, the suffering bequeathed by the years of depression, war, and genocide was almost beyond human comprehension. Almost forty million Europeans had perished during the war, but the suffering did not end when the guns fell silent. The anguish, the turmoil, the hunger, the upheaval, were just beginning for millions and millions. As Europeans yearned for a better future, communism and communists competed vigorously for their allegiance, especially in France and Italy. Stalin's reputation was not tarnished by his brutality but exalted by his wartime victories. Europeans wanted change, security, welfare, peace. "They have suffered so much," Dean Acheson acknowledged, "that they will demand that the whole business of state control and state interference shall be pushed further and further."[1] For Stalin, opportunity beckoned in Western Europe; for Truman there was peril—in the prospect not that Soviet armies would march to the Atlantic but that demoralized peoples would choose alternative ways of organizing their societies.

While U.S. officials worried about the configuration of West European politics, Stalin could not relax about his East European periphery. Everywhere his armies went, they marauded. Soviet troops raped and despoiled, intensifying the distrust that traditionally existed between Russia and many, if not all, of its neighbors. Proximity to Soviet behavior usually meant revulsion; lived experience was very different from utopian imagination. In Romania, Hungary, and Poland, communist partisans were few; in Bulgaria and eastern Germany, they had no chance of triumphing in free elections. Free elections in the lands occupied were not likely to lead to governments friendly to the Soviet Union. These countries had assisted the enemies of the Soviet Union in the past and might do so in the future. Even Soviet minions and clients were susceptible to capitalist blandishments, like the Marshall Plan. Nobody could be trusted in a world beset by capitalist adversaries who neither controlled their own penchant for conflict nor resisted the temptation to surround, squeeze, or maybe even crush Stalin's utopian project to remake mankind. For him, the postwar Soviet occupation of other countries in Eastern and Central Europe offered an opportunity to gain defense in depth, as the Americans liked to call their own security perimeter, which stretched across the oceans and included all of the Western Hemisphere.[2]

Security could not be entrusted to others when the future of Germany was so uncertain. And the international configuration of power depended on the future of Germany. On this fact, American and Soviet leaders agreed. They also agreed for many decades that Germans, left to themselves, could not be trusted. From Stalin to Gorbachev, German power was feared; from Truman to Bush, German power had to be harnessed in behalf of the West. Tension in Europe abated when the wall that divided Berlin seemed to resolve the German question and when the sovereignty of two German nations was recognized, one bourgeois and democratic, the other communist; the Helsinki Final Act in 1975 confirmed this understanding. To the extent that it allayed the fears of Brezhnev and his colleagues about German revanchism, the Helsinki Agreement was the high point of détente and, in Soviet eyes, worth the price of agreeing to reconfirm the legitimacy of human rights. Thereafter, Kremlin leaders could focus on negotiating strategic arms agreements and expanding trade with the West. But to their chagrin, Brezhnev's comrades would learn that the security of their way of life was far more endangered by the human rights provisions of the Helsinki Final Act than by the resolution of the German question—a fine illustration of how their vision of the morrow was buried in fears of the past rather than in any understanding of the future.

The same could be said about U.S. officials in the 1970s. After Helsinki and SALT I, their apprehensions did not wane and the Cold War did not end. The growth of Soviet military capabilities and ferment in the third world continued to conjure fears they could not overcome. They were haunted by the threat of Soviet gains in the Horn of Africa, the Persian Gulf, and southwest Asia; an arc of crisis defined that part of the globe, said Zbigniew Brzezinski. If U.S. officials did not calm regional turbulence and thwart Soviet inroads, critical sources of petroleum and other raw materials might fall outside Western control, and the industries of Western Europe and Japan would be at risk. As the great economic advances of the 1950s and 1960s slowed—as cheap oil disappeared, unemployment mounted, and inflation soared—social peace showed signs of unraveling and people wondered, as *Time* magazine put it, "can capitalism survive?"[3]

The aging men in the Kremlin were heartened. Systemic conditions appeared to be confirming their idea of history's trajectory. Their own society was advancing more slowly than it had in the past, but they could take heart in the travails of Western capitalism. For a brief while in the 1970s, there were even fleeting hopes for communist gains in Europe as Spain and Portugal threw off their neofascist governments, leftist parties competed vigorously for power, and the souls of Europeans as well as Asians, Africans, and Latin Americans seemed up for contestation once again. Upheavals in Afghanistan, Angola, Ethiopia, Indochina, Mozambique, Nicaragua, and Yemen tantalized the Kremlin. New leaders from these and other nations genuflected before their patrons in Moscow, spouted Marxist-Leninist rhetoric, and enticed ever more aid out of aging military leaders and party ideologues who saw a chance for vindication and reincarnation.

The Cold War lasted through the 1960s and 1970s because these revolutionary nationalist upheavals and regional turbulences engendered exaggerated hopes in Moscow and aroused exaggerated fears in Washington. In Moscow, defense managers and party ideologues were eager to exploit new opportunities, and for a few years Kremlin leaders were awash in petrodollars that financed foreign adventure. They sent arms, deployed agents, and empowered surrogates in faraway places like Angola, Ethiopia, and Yemen. In the United States, there was a political groundswell against this perceived Soviet adventurism. Disaffected liberals—soon to become the intellectual forefathers of neoconservatism—joined with traditional conservative groups, ethnic blue-collar workers in the Northeast, defense industrialists and business entrepreneurs in the South and Southwest, and evangelical Christians. These business, ethnic, and religious groups had little in common but their fear of Soviet power, their antipathy to atheistic communism, and a desire to redirect what they regarded as a wrongheaded liberal tendency in American politics. They believed strongly that the United States had to rebuild its military strength. Jesus "was not a sissy," asserted Jerry Falwell, the emerging leader of America's so-called Moral Majority. For these groups—and their representatives in the Congress—the contest for the soul of mankind abroad was related to the struggle to fight feminists and gays at home, preserve traditional culture, stifle the growth of big government, and maintain the underpinnings of an interconnected global economy open to the free movement of goods, capital, and people.[4]

The hopes and fears of politicians, bureaucrats, defense managers, and ideologues in Moscow and Washington obscured the subterranean crosscurrents in the international system. For while the oil crisis of the 1970s eroded the strength of Western capitalism and brought huge revenues to Moscow, it diverted attention from the profound technological changes imperceptibly transforming capitalism in the United States, Japan, and Western Europe. Electronics, microprocessors, pharmaceuticals, and biotechnology were creating knowledge-based industries and services that would not only rejuvenate economic productivity in the United States but also refashion and refurbish its military capabilities. But for the time being in the 1970s, the United States seemed vulnerable. Its economy was battered by stagflation, its relative military power was diminished, its alliances were shaky, and its position in the third world was more vulnerable than ever before.

Systemic developments seemed to be playing to the advantage of Moscow. "The global swing away from democracy in the 1960s and 1970s was impressive," writes the renowned political scientist Samuel Huntington.[5] Soviet leaders talked with pride about their accomplishments and aspirations. "The world is changing before our very eyes, and changing for the better," Brezhnev declared to the twenty-fifth Congress of the CPSU Central Committee in February 1976. "We have created a new society, a society the like of which mankind has never known before. It is a society with a crisis-free, steadily growing economy. . . . [I]t is a society governed by the scientific materialist world outlook. It is a society of firm confidence in the future, of radiant communist prospects. Before it lies boundless horizons of further all-around progress."[6]

But for Soviet leaders vigilance was forever necessary because capitalists were forever seeking to undo Moscow's mighty achievements and thwart the trajectory of history. The Americans had tried and failed to set back revolutionary forces in Indochina. The imperialists had been dislodged from Iran when the Shah was overthrown, and they were being challenged in Central America by the Sandinistas. But the Americans nonetheless were scheming with the Chinese renegades to encircle the Kremlin, and plotting to insert themselves in Afghanistan where the People's Democratic Revolution of 1978 was devouring itself in incompetence, repression, and corruption. Détente between the superpowers began to founder on these Soviet perceptions of threat. Soviet leaders deployed troops to Afghanistan not because they aimed to seize oil in the Persian Gulf but because they dreaded the prospect of encirclement. If the communist revolution were reversed in Kabul, where would the forces of reaction stop?

Ideology shaped perceptions—this is one of the great lessons of the Cold War—accentuating fears, highlighting opportunities, and warping rational assessments of interests in Washington and Moscow. And in the early 1980s, the relationship of fear to opportunity evolved. U.S. officials sensed that the Kremlin was growing more vulnerable. The Soviet Union's economic growth rate was slowing to a trickle.[7] The appeal of the Soviet model of development was waning. The Chinese were abandoning it. Almost everywhere "the vogue of revolution" was disappearing. "There was a sweeping loss of faith throughout Latin America, the Middle East, Africa, and Asia in the promise of revolution and in the dominant revolutionary ideology—socialism."[8] In India, for example, socialism and planning were seen as failures that had created enormous inefficiencies. As the first generation of revolutionary nationalist leaders passed from the scene in Asia and Africa, the "force of anti-colonial and nationalist sentiments" declined. New leaders were willing to open their economies and learn from the West.[9] The colossal failure of governmental human-engineering projects, like Mao Zedong's attempts to re-make China's economy, society, and culture, made people aware that "certain kinds of states, driven by utopian plans . . . [were] a mortal threat to human well-being."[10] Among Western intellectuals, the light generated by communist utopianism and the Soviet Union's heroic defeat of Nazism finally disappeared after fading for almost two decades. Asians and Africans studying in Paris and London in the 1970s and 1980s were receiving different cues and learning vastly different lessons than had the previous generation.[11]

The optimism of official Soviet rhetoric was belied by confidential reports and internal memoranda from Soviet experts and officials, especially during the Polish crisis of 1980–81, when it became clear that the Poles could no longer tolerate their communist government and wanted change, and when the Polish pope, John Paul II, championed human rights and positioned the Church as the guardian of individual freedom and personal conscience. When he visited Poland in June 1979, his trip commanded enormous attention. "Christ cannot be kept out of the history of man in any part of the globe," he exclaimed. The huge crowd in Warsaw's Victory Square cheered rhythmically, "We want God, we want God."[12]

The men in the Kremlin did not want God, but they understood the popularity of the Pope and the enthusiasm for Solidarity. Fearing that the movement would "spur workers in the Soviet Union . . . to press for improved living conditions, greater freedom, and an independent trade union of their own," they knew that Solidarity had to be thwarted. Recognizing that military intervention would be costly and self-defeating, they orchestrated the Polish government's imposition of martial law, but the communist hold on Poland and Eastern Europe would never be the same.[13]

Soviet leaders now worried less about their security and more about their vision. From Malenkov to Brezhnev, the justification for the existence of the Soviet regime and one-party rule was that the Bolsheviks projected the best and boldest vision for the future. It is customary to trivialize their rhetoric and mock their vision. The Soviet nomenklatura was corrupt, complacent, and self-referential. But Soviet leaders were not cynics; they were "authentic true believers," writes Martin Malia, the eminent scholar of Soviet politics and ideology. The archival materials recently brought to light underscore the importance of taking their *public* rhetoric seriously.[14] In speech after speech, whether by Malenkov or Khrushchev, Kosygin or Brezhnev, or even Andropov or Chernenko, Soviet leaders pronounced that they would promote the welfare of Soviet peoples and bring about a more humane society guided by social justice. In November 1961, at the twenty-second Party Congress, they declared improvements in social welfare and increases in distributive equality to be their central policy goals.[15] "As Lenin taught us," declared Andropov in a typical speech in 1979, "the ultimate goal of socialism is to secure the 'complete well-being and free all-around development of all members of society.' "[16]

Although they stepped back from Khrushchev's boast that communism would surpass capitalism in a generation, and although they constantly reformulated the stages they were traversing toward communism, Brezhnev and his colleagues always spoke in heroic terms about the need to accelerate economic development, technological innovation, and agricultural output.[17] They were excited by their ability to turn out military hardware to protect "Great October," and they gloried in statistics showing substantial gains in Soviet coal, steel, and electrical production. But the revolution also was designed to deliver more dill and more potatoes for Soviet consumers, as Khrushchev once put it at a Presidium meeting.[18] In fact, Soviet leaders never ceased talking about their obligation to provide more housing, more food, better health care, and more education to the Soviet people. And "most people," writes the historian Stephen Kotkin, "simply wanted the Soviet regime to live up to its promises."[19]

But the regime fell short of its promises. The Soviet economy gained relative to the United States in the 1950s and 1960s, advancing from about a quarter to a little more than a third of per capita U.S. production, but by 1980 it was falling behind. In fact, many other nations, including Italy, Spain, Japan, and South Korea, narrowed the gap between their per capita production and the American level better than did the Soviet model.[20]

More important for Soviet peoples themselves, increases in per capita consumption slowed noticeably in the late 1970s. Growth rates for consumption had peaked in the late 1960s, when advances per year were at a hefty rate of about 5 percent. Although in the mid-1970s most Soviet citizens (about 74 percent) thought life was improving, the government's expenditures on social consumption—education, health care, social security, and housing—were taking a turn for the worse; soon spending on education and health care barely increased to keep up with the times. The food supply was not improving. Soviet consumers ate far more bread and potatoes and much less meat and fish than did Americans, British, Spaniards, Italians, or Japanese. Workers began expressing their discontent. In the last years of Brezhnev's rule, strikes, theoretically forbidden, "became larger and more frequent," particularly at major automotive plants in Gorky, Togliatti, and Cheliabinsk. Many Soviet citizens had once been willing to accept or acquiesce to one-party rule and authoritarian government in return for employment security, health care, educational opportunity, and better and more equal living conditions. But when the regime faltered in carrying out its side of the deal, people's disaffection grew.[21] The Kremlin could not compete for the soul of mankind when it could not win the trust of its own citizens—another great lesson of the Cold War.

Gorbachev understood this growing demoralization. He did not want to retract Soviet power, but he believed the first priority was to refashion communism at home so that it could have a demonstrative appeal elsewhere. In order to do this, he needed to shift resources from the military to the civilian sector, which he could not do so long as his own society felt beleaguered by an intractable, formidable foe.[22] Changing the zero-sum game of the Cold War was Gorbachev's great challenge and his greatest achievement. He accepted the argument that the U.S.S.R. must reduce the threat perception of the adversary; to accomplish this he had to make wrenching changes in his own perception of threat.

Basically, Gorbachev came to feel that Soviet security was not threatened by capitalist adversaries; it was far more endangered by communist functionaries, economic managers, and demoralized workers than by any external foe. Rigid controls, leveling practices, and alcoholism had sapped individual creativity, eroded productivity, and interfered with the potential of national planning. When he made his decisions to modulate the arms race, he did so because he was scared of his society's growing impoverishment. "We are encircled not by invincible armies but by superior economies," he said.[23]

While altering his conception of threat and changing his views about the functioning of capitalist systems, Gorbachev never ceased to believe that communism represented something better than capitalism. But capitalists need not be seen as intractable foes. Nor was it necessary to believe that economic conflicts with the United States were more salient than the mutual interests that bound the U.S.S.R. to its antagonist as well as to socialist economies. Common human interests, Gorbachev and Shevardnadze came to feel, transcended class ties.

Gorbachev's achievement was a uniquely personal one, although he was not alone. He was general secretary of a party with a monopoly of power; traditions of deference were ingrained. When he made his fateful decisions to de-ideologize international politics, to let the Berlin wall come down, to agree to the unification of Germany, to withhold force against secessionist republics within the U.S.S.R., and to end regional disputes in southern Africa and Central America, he rarely asked the Politburo for advice or consulted with the Defense Council. He did confer with experts, advisers, and other officials in an ad hoc fashion, but he had no process and no blueprint. He twisted and turned. Rather than implement a policy, he followed a vision that, however blurry at first, became clearer as he trekked forward.

Strong as was his position as general secretary (and then president), Gorbachev was not unassailable. Malenkov and Khrushchev had both been pushed aside. Indeed, Gorbachev perhaps at times exaggerated his vulnerability. From 1985 to 1989, he worked to remove opponents from key positions and to promote people who held a more flexible disposition. But he could never satisfy some of his allies, who tired of what they saw as his ambivalence. His vacillation, however, was a reaction to an unpredictable environment where so much was contingent on the responses of friends and foes. As the man most responsible for Soviet affairs, he appreciated the formidable obstacles he faced and understood the daunting nature of the enterprise he was contemplating. His acceptance, however grudging, of a unified Germany within NATO suggests how profound were the changes he was willing to tolerate even when they awakened tortured memories and infuriated political foes. In a functioning democracy, Gorbachev might not have been able to make these changes; in fact, he could do so in Soviet Russia only so long as he functioned as general secretary of the party representing the dictatorship of the proletariat. When he altered the structures of Soviet domestic governance in 1989, he vastly complicated his own efforts to bring about the changes he wanted. But he felt he had no choice, given the ends he pursued.[24]

Gorbachev would not have persevered with his reforms had he not found sympathetic listeners in Washington. Reagan's greatness was not his buildup of force but his inspiring of trust. In March 1985, when Gorbachev became general secretary, the rearmament phase had peaked in Washington and Reagan was constrained by new budget deficits, growing antimilitarism in Congress, and mounting skepticism about the practicality of Star Wars. Unlike so many of his predecessors, however, Reagan could persuade the American people and the American Congress to appreciate the changes under way in the Soviet Union. Reagan, thought Gorbachev, would have the strength and might have the will not only to convince his countrymen to accept arms-reduction treaties but also to imagine the possibility of transcending the Cold War. Although Gorbachev frequently ranted to the Politburo about Reagan's inflexibility, he nevertheless appreciated a partner who could help him to reconfigure the image of the Soviet Union in the West and thereby allow him to concentrate on reforms at home.

The many conversations that Reagan and Shultz had with Gorbachev and Shevardnadze about human rights, religious freedom, and democratic practices had an impact. Gorbachev and Shevardnadze frequently responded favorably to the American requests to intervene in certain cases because they wanted to make headway on issues they deemed more important, such as arms reductions. But they also responded positively because they were embarrassed by the cases, which revealed flaws in a system they continued to regard as superior to capitalism. Dissidents such as Andrei Sakharov upset

Gorbachev because he felt they were aberrations and got too much attention. Accusations of mass repression in the Soviet Union incensed him because he considered them untrue, part of a Stalinist past that had been disavowed. When Gorbachev learned from the KGB just how many political prisoners there were (only 250–300), he did not mind jousting with Reagan and Shultz about the virtues of their respective systems.[25] Still, in tactful and respectful yet forceful ways, Reagan and Shultz never let Gorbachev forget the gap between the promise and the reality of communism in the Soviet Union.

Reagan's ideological fervor was very important in bringing about the end of the Cold War because it gave him tremendous confidence about the appeal of his way of life. His predecessors had also believed that democratic capitalism worked well in the United States and represented the best system of political economy, yet they were not sure that others agreed. They worried incessantly about communism and eurocommunism, state planning and nationalized industries, Marxist-Leninist rhetoric and revolutionary nationalist impulses. But by the late 1970s and early 1980s, the world economy was changing and Reagan's beliefs meshed with evolving international realities. Shultz spoke frequently about the trend toward economic globalization and the pace of technological innovation. Planned economies would never keep abreast of the changes wrought by the information and communications revolutions, he said. Only free men and free women operating in democratic societies and motivated by free markets and personal incentives could harness the new technology and employ it to generate economic growth and material advancement. Command economies and nationalized industry might have generated impressive results when the output of steel and coal were benchmarks of success, but not when electronics, computers, data processing, and biotechnology had redefined the meaning of modernity in production. Command economies and national ownership might have seduced revolutionary nationalists in the third world during the era of decolonization, and communist rhetoric might have appealed to demoralized and hungry Europeans in the wake of depression and war, but the world was changing dramatically. Men and women around the globe were discovering, Reagan declared, that "Democracy, the profoundly good, is also the profoundly productive."[26]

Reagan believed that if people had a choice, they would always choose personal freedom, private markets, and entrepreneurial opportunity. In this respect, he expressed what most Americans thought. He was a salesman for the American way of life, certain that he offered salvation for the souls of mankind everywhere. Consequently, he was afraid neither to compete with nor to talk to his opponents. He knew, moreover, that most Americans were sure he would not betray their interests or their ideals. Reagan *could* talk to the men from the evil empire with less fear of partisan recriminations and conservative criticism. Unlike Truman, he was not facing a Congress dominated by the virulent anticommunism of an opposition party; unlike Eisenhower, he did not have to deal with an American political culture aroused by McCarthyism; unlike Kennedy and Johnson, he was not haunted by fears that his domestic policies would be undercut by the appearance of weakness in foreign policy; unlike Carter, he did not have to worry that he would be accused of temerity. Reagan could lead the American people to accept the end of the Cold War—on American terms, of course.

Reagan's legacy is instructive. He believed in strength. Strength tempered the adversary's ambitions and tamped down its expectations. But the purpose of strength was to negotiate. Even while he denounced the tyrants who ran an evil empire, he reached out to talk to them. In one of his most famous speeches, he asked the American people to imagine what Ivan and Anya would say to Jim and Sally if they should discover one another in a waiting room. "Would they debate the differences between their respective governments?" Or would they talk about their hobbies, their children, and their careers? All people "want to raise their children in a world without fear and without war," Reagan said. "They want to have some of the good things over and above bare subsistence that make life worth living. They want to work at some craft, trade, or profession that gives them satisfaction and a sense of worth. Their common interests cross all borders."[27]

Reagan believed that leaders were obliged to work in behalf of these common interests. "The fact that neither of us likes the other system is no reason to refuse to talk," he said. "Living in this nuclear age makes it imperative that we do talk."[28] Moreover, as he tried to find opportunities to talk, he discovered that the fears of the adversary were not feigned and that the dreams of the enemy were not dissimilar to some of his own—for example, the abolition of nuclear weapons.[29] With patience and determination, with dignity and grace, Reagan crossed the ideological divide without altering his principles or ideals. "Tell the people of the Soviet Union," he said to Gorbachev on

2 June 1988, "of the deep feelings of friendship felt by us and by the people of our country toward them."[30] In his "farewell address" to the American people a few months later, he advised, "We must keep up our guard, but we must also continue to work together to lessen and eliminate tension and mistrust."[31]

Reagan's shrewdest insight was his understanding that the Cold War would be won by the system that could respond most effectively to people's wish for a decent living, a peaceful environment, and an opportunity for free expression, religious piety, and individual advancement. After World War II, it had been far from certain that democratic capitalism would have the capacity to avoid another depression, sustain the peace, and satisfy the yearnings of Asians and Africans for autonomy and self-determination. The Cold War tested the capacity of two alternative systems of governance and political economy to deal with the challenges of a postcolonial and postindustrial age.

The overriding achievement of Cold War America was that its leaders usually remained patient and prudent in dealing with the Soviet Union. Although ideology and historical experience accentuated their sense of threat and tempted them to overreach when danger loomed or opportunity beckoned, they recognized that nuclear weapons made any armed great power conflict irrational. They realized they had to achieve their overriding strategic goal—a favorable correlation of power in Eurasia—without war. They were most successful at this during the early postwar years, when they calculated interests carefully, rebuilt Germany and Japan, helped to reconstruct Western Europe, forged the North Atlantic military alliance, and avoided embroilment in China's civil war. They did less well in the 1960s and 1970s, when they allowed fears of revolutionary nationalism and regional turbulence to overcome any reasoned assessment of national interest. Forever worried that their adversary would seek to blackmail them in a crisis, exploit opportunities in the third world, and shrink the world capitalist market, they built up and maintained a nuclear arsenal that exceeded U.S. needs, got sucked into conflicts (like the one in Vietnam) that drained U.S. resources, and supported authoritarians (like the Shah in Iran) and insurgents (like the Mujahedin in Afghanistan) who disdained U.S. ideals. These Cold War policies did not cripple America's ability to compete with a much weaker adversary—in the case of Afghanistan, American policy actually worked to America's short-term advantage—but they inflicted misery on millions of people in Asia, Africa, and Central America who were having difficulty enough dealing with the problems of modernization and industrialization.

Like the men in the Kremlin, U.S. leaders recognized that the ultimate proof of the superiority of their system would be measured by its capacity to give security, opportunity, and a high standard of living to its people. Yet, unlike the men in the Kremlin, they had to contend with a well-established democratic culture and a host of democratic political processes. At critical moments during the Cold War, public opinion—real and imagined—and legislative intentions complicated the presidents' efforts to modulate conflict and reduce tensions. But in the final phase of the Cold War, in the middle and late 1980s, something like the opposite happened: Congress reined in defense and intelligence officials when it thought Reagan was overspending on defense, exaggerating the potential value of Star Wars, overreacting to a perceived communist threat in Central America, and in fact disobeying the law (as in the Iran-Contra scandal). Although Reagan fumed at this, his efforts to reach out to the Kremlin may well have been aided by the legislative constraints: his rearmament programs and interventionist proclivities had in fact been playing into the hands of Gorbachev's foes and making it harder for Gorbachev to reach his goals.

No one, then, was more responsible for ending the Cold War than the Soviet leader. Reagan was critically important, but Gorbachev was the indispensable agent of change. Without losing his political faith, he transcended the Marxist-Leninist ideological postulates that defined the nature of threat and opportunity in the international system. He used his authority to retract Soviet power in ways that his predecessors had considered unimaginable. He understood how nuclear weapons had transformed the traditional security imperatives of the Soviet Union and how economic shortcomings required the government to reconfigure Soviet priorities. His predecessors had occasionally recognized this, but their unchanged perception of threat and of opportunity, as well as their sense of mission, prevented them from shifting course and sticking to a new direction.

Gorbachev believed that external threats to the Soviet Union were small and external opportunities even smaller. Success, for him, depended on democratizing socialism and making it work more productively for Soviet citizens. He failed miserably in these efforts, but he realized that ensuring the well-being of his people and letting them have a voice in shaping their destiny were more important tasks than pressing the universal claims and millennial aspirations of the Soviet way of life. As a result, he neither sought foreign enemies nor thought they were necessary to preserve totalitarian rule at home. Instead, he needed friendly governments and foreign aid to buttress his attempts at socialist renewal. For him, a geopolitical world with a relaxation of tensions at its core would be the key to a successful reformation of socialism with the well-being of Soviet people as its centerpiece. This nexus brought together geopolitics and ideology in ways that could not have been imagined when the Allies met at the Elbe River in 1945, and when Stalin and Truman first pondered the risks and opportunities of the postwar world.

NOTES

Introduction

1. George H. W. Bush, "Introduction," *At the Abyss: An Insider's History of the Cold War*, by Thomas C. Reed (New York: Ballantine Books, 2004), 1.

I: The Origins of the Cold War, 1945–48: Stalin and Truman

1. Quoted in Roman Brackman, *The Secret File of Joseph Stalin: A Hidden Life* (London: Frank Cass, 2001), 73. The same quotation, with slight differences in translation, appears in Robert Service, *Stalin: A Biography* (Cambridge, Mass.: Harvard University Press, 2005), 70; and Hiroaki Kuromiya, *Stalin* (Harlow, England: Pearson, 2005), 18.

2. Robert Conquest, *Stalin: Breaker of Nations* (New York: Penguin, 1991), 14; Alfred J. Rieber, "Stalin, Man of the Borderlands," *American Historical Review* 106 (December 2001): 1651–91.

3. For the young Stalin and the impact of these religious schools, see Service, *Stalin*, 13–31; Kuromiya, *Stalin*, 207; Conquest, *Stalin*, 16–26; Dmitri Volkogonov, *Stalin: Triumph and Tragedy* (New York: Grove Weidenfeld, 1988), 7, 229.

4. Svetlana Alliluyeva, *Only One Year* (London: Hutchinson, 1969), 341.

5. Service, *Stalin*, 13–101; Kuromiya, *Stalin*, 1–25; Conquest, *Stalin*, 16–49; Adam B. Ulam, *Stalin: The Man and His Era* (New York: The Viking Press, 1973), 16–126.

6. Conquest, *Stalin*, 22; Kuromiya, *Stalin*, 6.

7. Sergo Beria, *Beria: My Father: Inside Stalin's Kremlin*, ed. by Françoise Thom, trans. by Brian Pearce (London: Gerald Duckworth, 2001), 148; Volkogonov, *Stalin*, 235.

8. Alliluyeva, *Only One Year*, 341; also see Kuromiya, *Stalin*, 7.

9. Service, *Stalin*, 43–112; Volkogonov, *Stalin*, 5–12, 225–36; Conquest, *Stalin*, 27–57; Alliluyeva, *Only One Year*, 45; Moshe Lewin, *The Soviet Century*, ed. by Gregory Elliott (London: Verso, 2005), 19–20.

10. Service, *Stalin*, 113–53; Ulam, *Stalin*, 47–157; Alliluyeva, *Only One Year*, 27–57.

11. Service, *Stalin*, 150–85; Ulam, *Stalin*, 167–91; Conquest, *Stalin*, 72–95.

12. Volkogonov, *Stalin*, 78–82; for strong antipathy between Lenin and Stalin, see Lewin, *Soviet Century*, 12–18; for a more nuanced view of their relationship, see Service, *Stalin*, 190–218.

13. Service, *Stalin*, 219–50; Kuromiya, *Stalin*, 50–100; Conquest, *Stalin*, 96–170; Robert C. Tucker, *Stalin in Power: The Revolution from Above, 1928–1941* (New York: W. W. Norton, 1990), 25–145; Ulam, *Stalin*, 192–358.

14. Conquest, *Stalin*, 69; for a more praiseworthy view that also stresses his zealotry and pragmatism, see Service, *Stalin*, 94.

15. Quoted in Roy A. Medvedev, *On Stalin and Stalinism* (New York: Oxford University Press, 1979), 34.

16. Central Committee of the CPSU (B), *History of the Communist Party of the Soviet Union (Bolshevik): Short Course* (New York: International Publishers, 1939), 355–58; Stalin, "The Foundations of Leninism," in Bruce Franklin, ed., *The Essential Stalin: Major Theoretical Writings, 1905–1952* (New York: Anchor Books, 1972), 102–105.

17. Stalin, "Foundations of Leninism," 104–106; Service, *Stalin*, 93–94.

18. Stalin, "Foundations of Leninism," 121.

19. John Gooding, *Socialism in Russia: Lenin and his Legacy, 1890–1991* (Houndmills: Palgrave, 2002), 142; Lewin, *Soviet Century*, 37.

20. CPSU, *Short Course*, 273.

21. Stalin, "Foundations of Leninism," 122–26, 172–83.

22. *Ibid.*, 157.

23. CPSU, *Short Course*, 314.

24. *Ibid.*, 276–77; Service, *Stalin*, 253–64; Kuromiya, *Stalin*, 74–100.

25. Ethan Pollock, "Conversations with Stalin on Questions of Political Economy," Cold War International History Project (CWIHP) Working Paper No. 33 (Washington, D.C.: Woodrow Wilson International Center, 2001), 6.

26. CPSU, *Short Course*, 314.

27. Kuromiya, *Stalin*, 101–17; Volkogonov, *Stalin*, 159–73; Conquest, *Stalin*, 156–65.

28. Service, *Stalin*, 297; for a superb account of the death of Stalin's wife and the dictator's reaction, see Simon Sebag Montefiore, *Stalin: The Court of the Red Tsar* (London: Weidenfeld and Nicolson, 2003), 1–18; the quotation is on page 18. See also Rosamond Richardson, *Stalin's Shadow: Inside the Family of One of the World's Greatest Tyrants* (New York: St. Martin's Press, 1993), 119–35.

29. Conquest, *Stalin*, 171–209; Kuromiya, *Stalin*, 122–28; Anne Applebaum, *Gulag: A History of the Soviet Camps* (London: Allen Lane, 2003), 68–72, 103–18; Hugh Ragsdale, "Comparative Historiography of the Social History of Revolutions: English, French, and Russian," *Journal of the Historical Society* 3 (Summer/Fall 2003): 348–52.

30. J. Arch Getty and Oleg V. Naumov, *The Road to Terror: Stalin and the Self-Destruction of the Bolsheviks, 1932–39* (New Haven, Conn.: Yale University Press, 1999), 573.

31. *Ibid.*, 11.

32. *Ibid.*, 557.

33. See the essays by Oleg Khlevniuk, "The Reasons for the 'Great Terror': the Foreign-Political Aspect"; Geoffrey Roberts, "The Fascist War Threat and Soviet Politics in the 1930s"; and Andrea Romano, "Permanent War Scare: Mobilisation, Militarisation and Peasant War," in Silvio Pons and

Andrea Romano, eds., *Russia in the Age of Wars, 1914–1945* (Milan, Italy: Fondazione Giangiacomo Feltrinelli, 2000); Kuromiya, *Stalin*, 121–28; Service, *Stalin*, 346–56.

34. Getty and Naumov, *Road to Terror*, 447, 490; Albert Resis, ed., *Molotov Remembers: Inside Kremlin Politics: Conversations with Felix Chuev* (Chicago: Ivan R. Dee, 1993), 256, 265, 339.

35. Richard Overy, *Russia's War* (London: Penguin, 1997), 34–72; Silvio Pons, *Stalin and the Inevitable War, 1936–1941* (London: Frank Cass, 2002), 180–81, 222–23, quotation on 181; Lennart Samuelson, "Wartime Perspectives and Economic Planning: Tukhachevsky and the Military-Industrial Complex, 1925–1937," in Pons and Romano, *Russia in the Age of Wars*, 207–10.

36. CPSU, *Short Course*, 274; Service, *Stalin*, 399–409; Geoffrey Roberts, *Stalin's Wars: From World War to Cold War, 1939–1953* (New Haven, Conn.: Yale University Press, 2007), 30–60.

37. Jan Gross, *Revolution from Abroad: The Soviet Conquest of Poland's Western Ukraine and Western Belorussia* (Princeton, N.J.: Princeton University Press, 1988); Overy, *Russia's War*, 52–53; Geoffrey Roberts, "Stalin and the Katyn Massacre," in *Stalin and His Times*, ed. by Geoffrey Roberts (Cork: Irish Association for Russian and East European Studies, 2005); also see Steven Merritt Miner, *Stalin's Holy War: Religion, Nationalism, and Alliance Politics, 1941–1945* (Chapel Hill, N.C.: University of North Carolina Press, 2003), 27–89; Geoff Swain, *Between Stalin and Hitler: Class War and Race War on the Dvina* (London: RoutledgeCurzon, 2004).

38. Overy, *Russia's War*, 34–72; for the most definitive account, see Gabriel Gorodetsky, *Grand Delusion* (New Haven, Ct.: Yale University Press, 1999); for a not altogether convincing argument stressing preemption, see Constantine Pleshakov, *Stalin's Folly: The Tragic First Days of World War II on the Eastern Front* (Boston: Houghton Mifflin, 2005), 56–57, 81–83; for a fine historiographical essay, see Teddy J. Uldricks, "The Icebreaker Controversy: Did Stalin Plan to Attack Hitler?" *Slavic Review* 58 (Fall 1999): 626–43; for recent syntheses, Service, *Stalin*, 406–14; Roberts, *Stalin's Wars*, 61–81; John Lukacs, *June 1941: Hitler and Stalin* (New Haven, Conn.: Yale University Press, 2006).

39. Pons, *Stalin and the Inevitable War*, 150–85; Overy, *Russia's War*, 34–72.

40. Stalin's errors are described in David E. Murphy, *What Stalin Knew: The Enigma of Barbarossa* (New Haven, Conn.: Yale University Press, 2005); Pleshakov, *Stalin's Folly*; for an excellent short synthesis, see Kuromiya, *Stalin*, 133–52.

41. Pons, *Stalin and the Inevitable War*, 175–81; Erik Van Ree, *The Political Thought of Joseph Stalin: A Study in Twentieth-Century Revolutionary Patriotism* (London: RoutledgeCurzon, 2002), 211; David Brandenberger, *National Bolshevism: Stalinist Mass Culture and the Formation of Modern Russian National Identity, 1931–1956* (Cambridge, Mass.: Harvard University Press, 2002).

42. "Fmert' detoubiytsam" ["Death to the Baby-Killers"], *Pravda*, 14 August 1942. My appreciation to Dmitry Pobedash and Tatiana Leonova for bringing this article to my attention. The article also appeared in provincial newspapers, such as *Uralskiy Rabochiy* [The Uralian Worker], the following day, 15 August 1942.

43. Catherine Merridale, *Night of Stone: Death and Memory in Twentieth Century Russia* (New York: Vintage, 2001), 227–28; Geoffrey P. Megargee, *War of Annihilation: Combat and Genocide on the Eastern Front, 1941* (Lanham, Md.: Rowman and Littlefield, 2006).

44. Anna Krylova, "Healers of Wounded Souls: The Crisis of Private Life in Soviet Literature, 1944–1946," *Journal of Modern History* 73 (June 2001): 308–309; Catherine Merridale, *Ivan's War: Life and Death in the Red Army, 1939–1945* (New York: Metropolitan Books, 2006); Antony Beevor and Luba Vinogradova, ed. and trans., *A Writer at War: Vasily Grossman with the Red Army, 1941–1945* (New York: Pantheon Books, 2005); Jeffrey Brooks, *Thank You, Comrade Stalin: Soviet Public Culture from Revolution to Cold War* (Princeton, N.J.: Princeton University Press, 2000), 163; Elena Zubkova, translated and edited by Hugh Ragsdale, *Russia After the War: Hopes, Illusions, and Disappointments, 1945–1957* (New York: M. E. Sharpe, 1998), 20*ff*.

45. Quoted in Merridale, *Night of Stone*, 222–23.

46. Quoted in Overy, *Russia's War*, 78–79; Volkogonov, *Stalin*, 405–12.

47. For a very critical day-by-day accounting, see Pleshakov, *Stalin's Folly*.

48. Overy, *Russia's War*, 78–80; Kuromiya, *Stalin*, 152.

49. Overy, *Russia's War*, 79.

50. Alliluyeva, *Only One Year*, 352.

51. Overy, *Russia's War*, 117; Merridale, *Night of Stone*, 227.

52. Uwe Garternschlager, "Living and Surviving in Occupied Minsk," in Robert W. Thurston and Bernd Bonwetsch, *The People's War: Responses to World War II in the Soviet Union* (Urbana: University of Illinois Press, 2000), 21; Overy, *Russia's War*, 107.

53. Svetlana Alliluyeva, *20 Letters to a Friend*, trans. by Priscilla Johnson McMillan (New York: Harper & Row, 1967), 185; Overy, *Russia's War*, 80–81; Kuromiya, *Stalin*, 152–54.

54. Overy, *Russia's War*, 73–124; Roberts, *Stalin's Wars*, 82–117; for Stalin and Zhukov, see also Pleshakov, *Stalin's Folly*, 188–89, 250–53.

55. Oleg A. Rzheshevsky, ed., *War and Diplomacy: The Making of the Grand Alliance: Documents from Stalin's Archives* (Amsterdam: Harwood Academic Publishers, 1996), 204; Geoffrey Roberts, "Ideology, Calculation, and Improvisation: Spheres of Influence and Soviet Foreign Policy, 1939–1945," *Review of International Studies* 25 (1999): 657–65.

56. Quoted in Brooks, *Thank You, Comrade Stalin*, 170; Richard Stites, "Soviet Russian Culture: Freedom and Control, Spontaneity and Consciousness," in Thurston and Bonwetsch, *People's War*, 180–82.

57. Stalin's speech on the twenty-sixth anniversary of the October Revolution, 6 November 1943, in Franklin, *Essential Stalin*, 401–402.

58. V. O. Pechatnov, "Averell Harriman's Mission to Moscow," *Harriman Review* 14 (July 2003): 26–27; also see Kuromiya, *Stalin*, 159–63.

59. Stalin's speech, 6 November 1943, in Franklin, *Essential Stalin*, 403.

60. "Record of the Conversation of Comrade I. V. Stalin and Comrade V. M. Molotov with the Polish Professor Lange," 17 May 1944, in "Conversations with Stalin," document collection disseminated by CWIHP at conference at Yale University, "Stalin and the Cold War, 1945–1953" (New Haven, Conn.:, September 1999), 16–17. These documents can be located at the CWIHP (Woodrow Wilson International Center, Washington, D.C.); "Account of General De Gaulle's Meeting with Marshall Stalin," 2 December 1944, *ibid.*, 88; for the theme of cooperation, see Roberts, *Stalin's Wars*, 165–91.

61. Silvio Pons, "In the Aftermath of the Age of Wars: The Impact of World War II on Soviet Security Policy," in Pons and Romano, *Russia in the Age of Wars*, 277–307; V. O. Pechatnov, "The Big Three After World War II: New Documents on Soviet Thinking About Post-War Relations with the United States and Great Britain," CWIHP Working Paper No. 13 (Washington, D.C.: Woodrow Wilson International Center, 1995); Roberts, "Ideology, Calculation, and Improvisation," 665–73.

62. Pons, "In the Aftermath of the Age of Wars," 305; also see Kuromiya, *Stalin*, 180–91; Roberts, *Stalin's Wars*, 118–253; for Stalin's operating procedures, also see Jonathan Haslam, "The Making of Foreign Policy Under Stalin," in *Empire and Society: New Approaches to Russian History*, ed. by Teruyuki Hara and Kimitaka Matsuzato (Sapporo, Japan: Slavic Research Center, Hokkaido University, 1997), 167–79.

63. Quoted in Ree, *Political Thought of Joseph Stalin*, 211–12.

64. For an excellent example of this process, see Bradley F. Abrams, *The Struggle for the Soul of the Nation: Czech Culture and the Rise of Communism* (Lanham, Md.: Rowman and Littlefield, 2004).

65. Ulam, *Stalin*, 358–62. These themes emerge clearly in the most recent analysis of Soviet policy in Bulgaria. See Vesselin Dimitrov, *Stalin's Cold War: Soviet Foreign Policy, Democracy, and Communism in Bulgaria, 1941–1948* (Hampshire, UK: Palgrave Macmillan, 2007).

66. Quoted in Eduard Mark, "Revolution by Degrees: Stalin's National Front Strategy for Europe, 1941–47," CWIHP Working Paper No. 31 (Washington, D.C.: Woodrow Wilson International Center, 2001), 22; "Record of the Conversation of Comrade I.V. Stalin with the General Secretary of the CC French Communist Party, Comrade Thorez," 19 November 1944, "Conversations with Stalin," 84, CWIHP; Ivo Banac, ed., *The Diary of Georgi Dimitrov, 1933–1949* (New Haven, Conn.: Yale University Press, 2003), 350–51; Silvio Pons, "Stalin, Togliatti, and the Origins of the Cold War in Europe," *Journal of Cold War Studies* 3 (Spring 2001): 3–27; also see Kuromiya, *Stalin*, 182–84; Norman M. Naimark, "Cold War Studies and New Archival Materials on Stalin," *The Russian Review* 61 (January 2002): 5–6; Dimitrov, *Stalin's Cold War*.

67. "From the Record of I. V. Stalin's Conversation with A. Hebrang," 9 January 1945, *Cold War History* 1 (April 2001): 161–62.

68. "Notes of V. Kolarov from a Meeting with J. Stalin," 28 January 1945, "Conversations with Stalin," 130, CWIHP; "Notes on Stalin's Statement from a Meeting with a Bulgarian Delegation," [late August 1945], *ibid.*, 247–48; "Report of the Labor Party on its Goodwill Mission to the USSR," [late July 1946], *ibid.*, 330–31; "Report to Central Committee of Communist Party of Czechoslovakia on Meeting with Stalin," 26 September 1946, CWIHP Collection; Roberts, "Ideology, Calculation, Improvisation"; Norman M. Naimark, "The Soviets and the Christian Democrats: The Challenge of a 'Bourgeois' Party in Eastern Germany, 1945–1949," *East European Politics and Society* 9 (Fall 1995): 369–92.

69. Pons, "Stalin, Togliatti, and the Origins of the Cold War in Europe," 15; Dimitrov, *Stalin's Cold War*.

70. "Notes of Stalin's Speech during a Reception at the Kremlin to Celebrate the Achievement of the Agreement to Create the Polish Provisional Government of National Unity," 23 June 1944, "Conversations with Stalin," 21, CWIHP.

71. "Notes of V. Kolarov," 28 January 1945, *ibid.*, 130; "Notes of Stalin's Speech during a Reception at the Kremlin," 23 June 1944, *ibid.*, 21; "Record of a Conversation of Comrade I. V. Stalin and Comrade V. M. Molotov with the Polish Professor Lange," 17 May 1944, *ibid.*, 15; for Stalin's preoccupation with Germany, see Roberts, *Stalin's Wars*, 165–91.

72. "Record of a Conversation of Comrade I. V. Stalin and Comrade V. M. Molotov with the Polish Professor Lange," 17 May 1944, *ibid.*, 18.

73. Quoted in Mark Kramer, "The Soviet Union and the Founding of the German Democratic Republic: 50 Years Later—A Review Article," *Europe-Asia* 51 (1999): 1097–98.

74. John Mearsheimer, *The Tragedy of Great Power Politics* (New York: W. W. Norton, 2001), 198.

75. Georgi Arbatov, *The System: An Insider's Life in Soviet Politics* (New York: Random House, 1992), 168. Most historians examining the Soviet archives agree. In the complex mix of Bolshevism and nationalism, the nationalist component grew. See, for example, Pons, "In the Aftermath of the Age of Wars"; Roberts, "Ideology, Calculation, and Improvisation"; Brandenberger, *National Bolshevism*; Kuromiya, *Stalin*, 180–87; Dimitrov, *Stalin's Cold War*.

76. "Record of Meeting between T. Soong and Stalin," 30 June 1945; 2, 7, 9, 11 July 1945; 10 August 1945; "Conversations with Stalin," 207, 145, 148, 157, 173, 179, 207, 225, CWIHP.

77. For Stalin's objectives in eastern Europe, based on new archival materials, see Mark, "Revolution by Degrees"; Roberts, *Stalin's Wars*; Vojtech Mastny, *The Cold War and Soviet Insecurity: The Stalin Years* (New York: Oxford University Press, 1996), 11–29; Francesca Gori and Silvio Pons, eds., *The Soviet Union and Europe in the Cold War* (New York: St. Martin's Press, 1996); Norman Naimark and Leonid Gibianskii, eds., *The Establishment of Communist Regimes in Eastern Europe, 1944–1949* (Boulder, Colo.: Westview Press, 1997); Odd Arne Westad, Sven Holmsmark, and Iver B. Neumann, eds., *The Soviet Union in Eastern Europe, 1945–1989* (New York: St. Martin's Press, 1994); for the emphasis on security, see Tony Judt's recent survey, *Postwar: A History of Europe*

Since 1945 (New York: The Penguin Press, 2005), 117–21; for a recent assessment of Stalin and the Greek communists, see John O. Iatrides, "Revolution or Self-Defense: Communist Goals, Strategy, and Tactics in the Greek Civil War," *Journal of Cold War Studies* 7 (Summer 2005): 3–33.

78. Ree, *Political Thought of Joseph Stalin*, 243; for recent analyses, see Kuromiya, *Stalin*, 169–200; Roberts, *Stalin's Wars*; Dimitrov, *Stalin's Cold War*.

79. Norman M. Naimark, *The Russians in Germany* (Cambridge, Mass.: Harvard University Press, 1996), 114–16.

80. Ilya Ehrenburg, *The War, 1941–1945* (London: McGibbon & Kee, 1964), 187–88.

81. Overy, *Russia's War*, 280; Hiroaki Kuromiya, *Freedom and Terror in the Donbas: A Ukrainian-Russian Borderland, 1870s–1990s* (London: Cambridge University Press, 1998), 297–98.

82. Ehrenburg, *The War*, 187–92.

83. S. Beria, *Beria*, 142–43; Brooks, *Thank You, Comrade Stalin*, 205; Service, *Stalin*, 438, 461–68.

84. Alliluyeva, *Only One Year*, 162–63; Alliluyeva, *20 Letters*, 199–207; Yoram Gorlizki and Oleg Khlevniuk, *Cold Peace: Stalin and the Soviet Ruling Circle, 1945–1953* (New York: Oxford University Press, 2004), 49; Montefiore, *Stalin*, 454–71.

85. S. Beria, *Beria*, 145–46; Gorlizki and Khlevniuk, *Cold Peace*; Montefiore, *Stalin*, 435–577; Service, *Stalin*, 521–40.

86. Montefiore, *Stalin*, 455; Kuromiya, *Stalin*, 184.

87. These contradictions appear in the many conversations assembled by the CWIHP. See the collection "Conversations with Stalin," for example, pp. 272, 248; for Stalin's inscrutable nature and ambiguous language, also see Steven Kotkin, "A Conspiracy So Immense," *New Republic* 234 (13 February 2006): 28–34; also see Dimitrov, *Stalin's Cold War*.

88. Overy, *Russia's War*, 312; also see Service, *Stalin*, 478–87.

89. Roberts, *Stalin's Wars*, especially chap. 7; Brooks, *Thank You, Comrade Stalin*, 207; Arbatov, *The System*, 35–36; Service, *Stalin*, 467–68.

90. The emphasis on Stalin's trying to reconcile security and cooperation has emerged in the writings of many who have seen the new Russian documents. See, for example, Roberts, *Stalin's Wars*; Marks, "Revolution by Degree"; Pons, "In the Aftermath of the Age of Wars"; Kuromiya, *Stalin*, 161; Dimitrov, *Stalin's Cold War*.

91. Margaret Truman, ed., *Letters from Father: The Truman Family's Personal Correspondence* (New York: Arbor House, 1981), 106; Elizabeth Edwards Spalding, *The First Cold Warrior: Harry Truman, Containment, and the Remaking of Liberal Internationalism* (Lexington, Ky.: University Press of Kentucky, 2006), 16.

92. For the quotation, see Alonzo L. Hamby, *Man of the People: A Life of Harry S. Truman* (New York: Oxford University Press, 1995), 293.

93. Robert H. Ferrell, *Dear Bess: The Letters from Harry to Bess Truman, 1910–1959* (New York: W. W. Norton & Company, 1983), 213, 215; Arnold Offner, *Another Such Victory: President Truman and the Cold War* (Stanford, Calif.: Stanford University Press, 2002), 9.

94. Offner, *Truman*, 9.

95. For influential books on Truman, see Hamby, *Man of the People*; David McCullough, *Truman* (New York: Simon and Schuster, 1992); Robert Ferrell, *Truman and Pendergast* (Columbia, Mo.: University of Missouri Press, 1999); Offner, *Another Such Victory*.

96. Ferrell, *Dear Bess*, 293, 285; for the most recent assessment, see Wilson D. Miscamble, *From Roosevelt to Truman: Potsdam, Hiroshima, and the Cold War* (New York: Cambridge University Press, 2007), 1–33.

97. *Ibid.*, 277.

98. Harry S. Truman, *Truman Speaks* (New York: Columbia University Press, 1960), 32.

99. Ferrell, *Dear Bess*, 451.

100. Michael C. Adams, *The Best War Ever: America and World War II* (Baltimore, Md.: The Johns Hopkins University Press, 1994), 114, 131, 136, 126–27; for the astounding prosperity that no one anticipated, see David M. Kennedy, *Freedom from Fear: The American People in the Depression and War, 1929–1945* (New York: Oxford University Press, 1999), 785–86.

101. Richard J. Overy, *Why the Allies Won* (London: Jonathan Cape, 1995), 192; Paul M. Kennedy, *The Rise and Fall of the Great Powers* (New York: Random House, 1987), 357–58, 369.

102. Robert H. Ferrell, ed., *Off the Record: The Private Papers of Harry S. Truman* (New York: Harper & Row, 1980), 49; Ferrell, *Dear Bess*, 516, 518.

103. Ferrell, *Dear Bess*, 519; Miscamble, *From Roosevelt to Truman*, 87–96.

104. See, for example, John M. Blum, ed., *The Price of Vision: The Diary of Henry A. Wallace, 1942–1946* (Boston: Houghton, Mifflin, 1973), 437, 440–41, 448–51.

105. Ferrell, *Dear Bess*, 515, 522.

106. Davies Diary, 15 and 16 July 1945, box 18, Joseph Davies Papers, Library of Congress, Washington, D.C.

107. Harry S. Truman, *Memoirs: 1945, Year of Decisions* (New York: Signet, 1955), 72.

108. Ferrell, *Dear Bess*, 520.

109. *Ibid.*, 522; for the emphasis on continuing Roosevelt's policies and getting along with the Russians, see Miscamble, *From Roosevelt to Truman*.

110. Truman, *Truman Speaks*, 67–68.

111. Ferrell, *Dear Bess*, 519; for Truman and Byrnes, see Robert L. Messer, *The End of an Alliance: James F. Byrnes, Roosevelt, Truman, and the Origins of the Cold War* (Chapel Hill, N.C.: University of North Carolina Press, 1982).

112. M. Truman, *Letters from Father*, 178.

113. Davies Diary, 16 July 1945, box 18, Davies Papers.

114. Ferrell, *Dear Bess*, 522.

115. Davies Diary, 28 and 29 July 1945, box 19, Davies Papers.

116. For the end of the war, see Tsuyoshi Hasegawa, *Racing the Enemy: Stalin, Truman, and the Surrender of Japan* (Cambridge, Mass.: Harvard University Press, 2005).

117. For Byrnes's thinking about the atomic bomb, see Brown Log, 16 July–1 August 1945, James F. Byrnes Papers, Clemson University Library, Clemson, S.C.

118. For information on Stalin, Molotov, and the meeting of the council of foreign ministers, see V. O. Pechatnov, " 'The Allies Are Pressing on You to Break Your Will . . .': Foreign Policy Correspondence between Stalin and Molotov and Other Politburo Members, September 1945–December 1946," CWIHP, Working Paper No. 26 (Woodrow Wilson International Center, 1999), 18–32; Gorlizki and Khlevniuk, *Cold Peace*, 19–23.

119. For insight into Byrnes's thinking, see Messer, *End of an Alliance*, 137–55; Gregg Herken, *The Winning Weapon: The Atomic Bomb in the Cold War* (New York: Knopf, 1980), 66–94; Eduard Mark, "American Policy Toward Eastern Europe and the Origins of the Cold War, 1941–46: An Alternative Interpretation," *Journal of American History* 68 (September 1981): 313–36.

120. Ferrell, *Off the Record*, 72; Blum, *Price of Vision*, 512–13; Minutes of Cabinet meetings, October–December 1945, Matthew J. Connelly Papers, box 1, Harry S. Truman Library (HSTL), Independence, Mo.

121. Clark Clifford Oral History, pp. 180–84, HSTL.

122. "Address on Foreign Policy," 27 October 1945, Harry S. Truman, *Public Papers of the Presidents, 1945* (Washington, D.C.: Government Printing Office, 1961), 431–38 (hereafter cited as *PPP: HST, year*, page).

123. For the quotation, see Diary of William Leahy, 27 October 1945, William L. Leahy Papers, Library of Congress, Washington, D.C.

124. Ferrell, *Off the Record*, 79–80; Messer, *End of an Alliance*, 156–66; Spalding, *First Cold Warrior*, 24–35.

125. Pechatnov, "Harriman's Mission to Moscow," esp. 26–27; Geoffrey Roberts, "Sexing Up the Cold War: New Evidence on the Molotov-Truman Talks of April 1945," *Cold War History* 4 (April 2004): 105–25.

126. Montefiore, *Stalin*, 445; Vladislav Zubok and Constantine Pleshakov, *Inside the Kremlin's Cold War: From Stalin to Khrushchev* (Cambridge, Mass.: Harvard University Press, 1996), 42–43; Jonathan Haslam, "The Cold War as History," *Annual Review of Political Science* 6 (2003): 92–93; Pechatnov, " 'The Allies Are Pressing on You,' " 31.

127. Joseph Stalin, "New Five Year Plan for Russia," 9 February 1946, *Vital Speeches of the Day* 12 (1 March 1946): 300–304.

128. Banac, *Diary of Georgi Dimitrov*, 358.

129. David Holloway, *Stalin and the Bomb* (New Haven, Conn.: Yale University Press, 1994), 168.

130. Joseph Stalin, *For Peaceful Coexistence: Postwar Interviews* (New York: International Publishers, 1951), 11–12.

131. Transcript of interview between Stalin and Byrnes, 24 December 1945, G. P. Kynim and Y. Laufer, eds., *SSSR i germanski vopros, 1941–1949: documenty iz arkhiva vneshnei politiki Rossiiskoi federatsii [USSR and the German Question: Documents from the Foreign Policy Archives of the Russian Federation], Vol 2: May 9, 1945–October 3, 1946* (Moskva: Mezhdunarodnye, otnosheni, 2000), 335–36; Pechatnov, " 'Allies Are Pressing on You,' " 10–11.

132. Memorandum, by Litvinov, 5 July 1945, in Kynim and Laufer, *USSR and the German Question*, 171–75; Litvinov to Stalin, 25 May 1946, *ibid.*, 517–19; draft statement prepared by Litvinov and I. M. Maiskii, 12 June 1946, *ibid.*, 596–98.

133. Jeffrey Burds, "The Early Cold War in Soviet West Ukraine, 1944–1948," *The Carl Beck Papers in Russian and East European Studies*, No. 1505 (Pittsburgh, Pa.: University of Pittsburgh Press, 2001), 25–30; Kuromiya, *Freedom and Terror in the Donbas*, 251–323.

134. Burds, "Early Cold War in Soviet West Ukraine"; Jeffrey Burds, "The Soviet War Against 'Fifth Columnists': The Case of Chechnya, 1942–4," *Journal of Contemporary History* 41(2): 309–14; Eduard Mark, "The War Scare of 1946 and Its Consequences," *Diplomatic History* 21 (Summer 1997): 406–407, 410–11; Richard J. Aldrich, *The Hidden Hand: Britain, America, and Cold War Secret Intelligence* (New York: The Overlook Press, 2002), 142–45; Kuromiya, *Freedom and Terror in the Donbas*, 313–16; Irina Mukhina, "New Revelations from the Former Soviet Archives: The Kremlin, the Warsaw Uprising, and the Coming of the Cold War," *Cold War History* 6 (August 2006): 397–411.

135. Odd Arne Westad, *Cold War and Revolution: Soviet-American Rivalry and the Origins of the Chinese Civil War, 1944–1946* (New York: Columbia University Press, 1993), 55; also see Haslam, "Making of Foreign Policy under Stalin"; for most recent assessments, see Norman M. Naimark, "Stalin and Europe in the Postwar Period, 1945–1953: Issues and Problems," *Journal of Modern European History* 2 (2004): 28–56; Roberts, *Stalin's Wars*; Vladimir O. Pechatnov, "The Soviet Union and the Outside World, 1944–1953," *Cambridge History of the Cold War*, ed. by Melvyn P. Leffler and Odd Arne Westad, 3 vols. (London: Cambridge University Press, forthcoming).

136. Naimark, "Stalin and Europe in the Postwar Period," 36.

137. Gomulka's Memorandum of a Conversation with Stalin, third quarter of 1945, in "Conversations with Stalin," 272, CWIHP.

138. Walter Bedell Smith to Secretary of State, 5 April 1946, *ibid.*, 293–94; "Report of the Labour Party on Its Goodwill Mission to the USSR," [Summer 1946], *ibid.*, 330–32; "Answers to the Questions Posed by A. Werth," 17 September 1946, *ibid.*, 339–40; "Answers to the Questions of Mr. H. Bailey," 26 October 1946, *ibid.*, 341–44; for the theme of cooperation, also see esp. Roberts, *Stalin's Wars*; Pechatnov, "The Soviet Union and the Outside World."

139. Pechatnov, "Harriman's Mission to Moscow," 45–46; "Answers to the Questions of Mr. H. Bailey," 26 October 1946, in "Conversations with Stalin," 344, CWIHP.

140. Stalin's concern with Japan emerges clearly in all the recent research. See, for example, Pechatnov, " 'The Allies Are Pressing on You,' " 11–16.

141. These generalizations have been shaped by Naimark, *The Russians in Germany*; Naimark, "The Soviets and the Christian Democrats"; Roberts, *Stalin's Wars*, 228–45, 350–55; Vladimir K. Volkov, "German Question as Stalin Saw It," draft paper for the conference "Stalin and the Cold War, 1945–1953" (New Haven, Conn.: Yale University, 1999); Wilfried Loth, *Stalin's Unwanted Child: The Soviet Union, the German Question and the Founding of the GDR* (New York: St. Martin's Press, 1998).

142. Csaba Bekes, "Soviet Plans to Establish the Cominform in Early 1946: New Evidence from the Hungarian Archives," CWIHP *Bulletin* 10 (March 1998): 135. These generalizations emerge from my reading of the many documents assembled in "Conversations with Stalin," CWIHP; Roberts, *Stalin's Wars*, 245–53; Mark, "Revolution by Degree"; Zubok, *Inside the Kremlin's Cold War*; Holloway, *Stalin and the Bomb*; Mastny, *Cold War and Soviet Insecurity*; Pechatnov, " 'The Allies Are Pressing on You' "; Pechatnov, "The Soviet Union and the Outside World."

143. The "Long Telegram" can be found in George F. Kennan, *Memoirs, 1925–1950* (New York: Bantam, 1967), 583–98.

144. W. Averell Harriman and Elie Abel, *Special Envoy to Churchill and Stalin, 1941–1946* (New York: Random House, 1975), 535–36.

145. For U.S. policy in Germany, see especially Carolyn Eisenberg, *Drawing the Line: The American Decision to Divide Germany, 1944–1949* (New York: Cambridge University Press, 1996), 71–276; for Soviet espionage, see Katherine A. S. Sibley, *Red Spies in America: Stolen Secrets and the Dawn of the Cold War* (Lawrence, Kansas: University Press of Kansas, 2004); Allen Weinstein and Alexander Vassiliev, *The Haunted Wood: Soviet Espionage in America—The Stalin Era* (New York: Random House, 1999).

146. These generalizations about Truman's policies in 1945 and 1946 are elaborated upon in my book *A Preponderance of Power: National Security, the Truman Administration, and the Cold War* (Stanford, Calif.: Stanford University Press, 1993), 25–181; for different interpretations, see Offner, *Another Such Victory*, 1–184; Marc Trachtenberg, *A Constructed Peace: The Making of the European Settlement* (Princeton, N.J.: Princeton University Press, 1999), 3–65; McCullough, *Truman*; Hamby, *Man of the People*; Deborah Welch Larson, *Origins of Containment: A Psychological Explanation* (Princeton, N.J.: Princeton University Press, 1985); John L. Gaddis, *The United States and the Origins of the Cold War, 1941–47* (New York: Columbia University Press, 1972).

147. Memorandum for the president, by McCloy, 26 April 1945, box 178, President's Secretary's File (PSF), Harry S. Truman Papers (HSTP), HSTL; Diary of Henry L. Stimson, 19 April 1945, Henry L. Stimson Papers, Yale University.

148. Acheson testimony, 12 June 1945, U.S. Senate, Committee on Banking and Currency, *Bretton Woods Agreements*, 79th Cong., 1st sess., (Washington, D.C.: Government Printing Office, 1945), 1–51, esp. 19, 20, 21, 48–49.

149. Quoted in Igor Lukes, "The Czech Road to Communism," in Naimark and Gibianskii, eds., *Establishment of Communist Regimes in Eastern Europe*, 249; for an elaboration of this idea, see Abrams, *Struggle for the Soul of the Nation*.

150. A.J.P. Taylor, "The European Revolution," *Listener* 34 (22 November 1945): 576; see Judt, *Postwar*, 215–19.

151. Adam Westoby, *Communism Since World War II* (New York: St. Martin's Press, 1981), 14–15; Roberts, "Ideology, Calculation, and Improvisation," 671; Abrams, *Struggle for the Soul of the Nation*, 9–38.

152. Acheson testimony, 8 March 1945, U.S. Senate, Committee on Banking and Currency, *Bretton Woods Agreements*, 1: 35.

153. Acheson testimony, 13 March 1946, U.S. Senate, Committee on Banking and Currency, *Anglo-American Financial Agreement*, 79th Cong., 2nd sess. (Washington, D.C.: Government Printing Office, 1946), 306.

154. "Statement by the President," 6 February 1946, *PPP: HST, 1946*, 106; Cabinet Minutes, January–March 1946, Connelly Papers, box 1.

155. Stimson to Truman, 16 May 1945, box 157, PSF, HSTP; Joseph Grew to Truman, 27 June 1945, Department of State, *Foreign Relations of the United States, Potsdam*, 1: 267–80 (hereafter cited as *FRUS*); Central Intelligence Agency, "Review of the World Situation," 26 September 1947, box 203, PSF, HSTP.

156. Memorandum, by Will Clayton, 5 March 1947, Frederick J. Dobney, ed., *Selected Papers of Will Clayton* (Baltimore, Md.: The Johns Hopkins University Press, 1971), 198.

157. Harry S. Truman, *Memoirs: Years of Trial and Hope, 1946–1952* (New York: Signet, 1956), 124–25.

158. "Special Message to the Congress," 12 March 1947, *PPP: HST, 1947*, 176–80.

159. For Marshall's speech, see Department of State *Bulletin* 16 (15 June 1947): 1159–60; Clayton to Acheson, 27 May 1947, *FRUS, 1947*, 3: 230–32; Howard C. Petersen to Robert P. Patterson, 12 June 1947, box 8, general decimal file, Robert P. Patterson Papers, Record Group 107, National Archives (NA), Washington, D.C.

160. "Address on Foreign Economic Policy," 6 March 1947, *PPP: HST, 1947*, 170–71.

161. "Special Message to the Congress," 19 December 1947, *ibid.*, 516–17.

162. "Radio and Television Address," 6 March 1952, *ibid.*, 1952–1953, 194–95; also see "Special Message to the Congress," 6 March 1952, *ibid.*, 189.

163. Kennan, "Russia's National Objectives," 10 April 1947, box 17, George F. Kennan Papers, Seeley Mudd Library, Princeton University, Princeton, N.J.

164. Directive to Dwight D. Eisenhower, 26 July 1945, *FRUS, Potsdam*, 2: 1028–30; Jean Edward Smith, ed., *The Papers of General Lucius D. Clay: Germany, 1945–1949*, 2 vols. (Bloomington: Indiana University Press, 1974), 1: 44.

165. Memoranda, by John Foster Dulles, 26 February and 7 March 1947, box 31, John Foster Dulles Papers, Mudd Library, Princeton University.

166. Memorandum of Conversation, 15 April 1947, *FRUS, 1947*, 2: 339–44; Robert H. Van Meter, "Secretary of State Marshall, General Clay, and the Moscow Council of Foreign Ministers of 1947: A Response to Philip Zelikow," *Diplomacy and Statecraft* 16 (2005): 139–67.

167. Meeting of the secretaries of state, war, and navy, 3 July 1947, box 3, safe file, Robert P. Patterson Papers, Records of the Office of the Secretary of War, RG 107, NA.

168. Minutes of a Visit to Generalissimo J. V. Stalin, by Czech delegation, 9 July 1947, in "Conversations with Stalin," 395–99, CWIHP; Geoffrey Roberts, "Moscow and the Marshall Plan: Politics, Ideology, and the Onset of the Cold War," *Europe-Asia* 46 (1994): 1371–85.

169. For the quotation, see "Stenographic Record of a Speech by Comrade J. V. Stalin at a Special Session of the Politburo," 14 March 1948, in "Conversations with Stalin," 432, CWIHP; Mastny, *Cold War and Soviet Insecurity*, 23–46; Zubok and Pleshakov, *Inside the Kremlin's Cold War*, 50–52, 104–108; Kramer, "Soviet Union and the Founding of the GDR," 1099–1102.

170. "Stenographic Record," Stalin speech, 14 March 1948, "Conversations with Stalin," 429, CWIHP.

171. Record of a Meeting of Comrade I. V. Stalin with the Secretary of the CC French Communist Party Thorez, 18 November 1947, *ibid.*, 403–405.

172. Report of Milovan Djilas about a Secret Soviet-Bulgarian-Yugoslav Meeting, 10 February 1948, CWIHP *Bulletin* 10 (March 1998): 128–34.

173. Stalin, "Foundations of Leninism," 110.

174. "Stenographic Record," Stalin speech, 14 March 1948, "Conversations with Stalin," 429–32, CWIHP.

175. Memorandum by chief of staff, ND [July 1947], ABC 471.6 Atom (17 August 1945), section 6-A, American-British Conversations, Records of the War Department General and Special Staffs, RG 165, NA; also see Walter Millis, ed., *The Forrestal Diaries* (New York: Viking, 1951), 350–51.

176. For Clayton's statement, see Dabney, *Selected Papers*, 208; for Marshall's views, see Marshall to Caffery, 26 May 1948, *FRUS, 1948,* 2: 284.

177. Marshall statement, in cabinet meeting, 23 July 1948, box 1, Connelly Papers; for Clay, see Smith, *Clay Papers,* 2: 708; for the views of Kennan and Bohlen, see *FRUS, 1948,* 3: 152–54, 157–58, 177, 186; Kennan to Lauris Norstad, 4 May 1948, box 33, Records of the Policy Planning Staff, RG 59, NA.

178. Randall B. Woods and Howard Jones, *Dawning of the Cold War: The United States' Quest for Order* (Athens: University of Georgia Press, 1991), 98–102; Meg Jacobs, *Pocketbook Politics: Economic Citizenship in Twentieth-Century America* (Princeton, N.J.: Princeton University Press, 2005), 222–31.

179. Memo, by Clayton, 5 March 1947, Dabney, *Selected Papers,* 198; Minutes of the First Meeting of the Special Committee to Study Assistance to Greece and Turkey, 24 February 1947, *FRUS, 1947,* 5: 47; Dean Acheson, *Present at the Creation: My Years at the State Department* (New York: Norton, 1969), 218–19; Joseph M. Jones, *The Fifteen Weeks* (New York: Viking, 1955), 129–70.

180. Truman, *Memoirs: Years of Trial and Hope,* 128.

181. Jonathan Bell, *The Liberal State on Trial: The Cold War and American Politics in the Truman Years* (New York: Columbia University Press, 2004), 80.

182. *Ibid.,* 46–120; Richard M. Freeland, *The Truman Doctrine and the Origins of McCarthyism: Foreign Policy, Domestic Politics and Internal Security, 1946–48* (New York: New York University Press, 1985); Thomas J. Christensen, *Useful Adversaries: Grand Strategy, Domestic Mobilization, and Sino-American Conflict, 1947–1958* (Princeton, N.J.: Princeton University Press, 1996), 49–69; Melvin Small, *Democracy and Diplomacy: The Impact of Domestic Politics on U.S. Foreign Policy, 1789–1994* (Baltimore, Md.: Johns Hopkins University Press, 1996), 84–86.

183. Christensen, *Useful Adversaries,* 52.

184. Richard Gid Powers, *Not Without Honor: The History of American Anti-Communism* (New York: The Free Press, 1995), 217.

185. *Ibid.,* 223; Bell, *Liberal State on Trial,* 92.

186. For Knowland's quotation, see *Appendix to the Congressional Record,* vol. 93, p. A4915; for Kennan's view, see Policy Planning Staff Paper No. 20, "Effect Upon the United States If the European Recovery Plan Is Not Adopted," *Policy Planning Staff Papers,* ed. by Anna Kasten Nelson, 3 vols. (New York: Garland, 1983), 2: 78–79; for Truman, see "Special Message to Congress," 6 March 1952, *PPP: HST, 1952–53,* 189.

187. Ehrenburg, *The War,* 124; Merridale, *Night of Stone,* 213–14; Overy, *Russia's War,* 329.

188. Donald Filtzer, *Soviet Workers and Late Stalinism: Labour and the Restoration of the Stalinist System After World War II* (Cambridge, Eng.: Cambridge University Press, 2002), 46–47, 76; Kuromiya, *Freedom and Terror in the Donbas,* 300–308.

189. Vladislav Zubok, "Limits of Empire: Stalin and the Lean Year of 1946," unpublished paper; for slightly different renditions of this conversation, see Kuromiya, *Stalin,* 177; Robert Service, *A History of Twentieth-Century Russia* (London: Penguin, 1997), 299.

190. Burds, *Early Cold War in Soviet West Ukraine;* Kuromiya, *Stalin,* 174–80; Kuromiya, *Freedom and Terror in the Donbas,* 310–20; Swain, *Between Stalin and Hitler.*

191. Service, *Russia,* 299; Applebaum, *Gulag,* 516–20; Gorlizki and Khlevniuk, *Cold Peace,* 31–43;

Werner G. Hahn, *Postwar Soviet Politics: The Fall of Zhdanov and the Defeat of Moderation* (Ithaca, N.Y.: Cornell University Press, 1982).

192. Service, *Russia*, 301; Gorlizki and Khlevniuk, *Cold Peace*, 1–65; J. Eric Duskin, *Stalinist Reconstruction and the Confirmation of a New Elite* (Houndsmills, Eng: Palgrave, 2001).

193. Service, *Stalin*, 531–40; Gorlizki and Khlevniuk, *Cold Peace*, 45–65; Naimark, "Soviets and the Christian Democrats," 370–71; Kotkin, "A Conspiracy So Immense."

194. Ree, *Political Thought of Joseph Stalin*, 282–83; Brandenberger, *National Bolshevism*.

195. For the quotations, see Kuromiya, *Stalin*, 188; Service, *Russia*, 308; also see Volkogonov, *Stalin*, 531, 534; Zubok and Pleshakov, *Inside the Kremlin's Cold War*, 50–51, 104–108.

196. For Stalin's negotiations with T. V. Soong, see the many documents in "Conversations with Stalin," 144–246, CWIHP; for Stalin's reflections on his own actions, see "Report of Milovan Djilas about a Secret Soviet-Bulgarian-Yugoslav Meeting," 10 February 1948, CWIHP *Bulletin* 10 (March 1998): 131; for Stalin and Mao, see S. N. Goncharov, John W. Lewis, Xue Litai, *Uncertain Partners: Stalin, Mao, and the Korean War* (Stanford, Calif.; Stanford University Press, 1993); Jung Chang and Jon Halliday, *Mao: the Unknown Story* (New York: Alfred A. Knopf, 2005), 175–89, 281–92, 337–55; Michael J. Sheng, *Battling Western Imperialism: Mao, Stalin, and the United States* (Princeton, N.J.: Princeton University Press, 1997); Chen Jian, *China's Road to the Korean War: The Making of the Sino-American Confrontation* (New York: Columbia University Press, 1994), 66*ff.*

197. Shuguang Zhang and Jian Chen, *Chinese Communist Policy and the Cold War in Asia: New Documentary Evidence, 1944–1950* (Chicago, Ill.: Imprint Publications, 1996), 54; Ilya V. Gaiduk, *Confronting Vietnam: Soviet Policy Toward the Indochina Conflict, 1954–1963* (Stanford, Calif., and Washington, D.C.: Stanford University Press and Woodrow Wilson Center Press, 2002), 3.

198. Quoted in Ree, *Political Thought of Joseph Stalin*, 252.

199. Record of the Meeting of Stalin and Thorez, 18 November 1947, "Conversations with Stalin," 403–406; also see Pons, "Stalin, Togliatti, and the Origins of the Cold War"; Judt, *Postwar*, 139–45.

200. This is abundantly clear in the collection of documents "Conversations with Stalin," CWIHP; also see Banac, *Diary of Georgi Dimitrov*, 421–23, 437–40; Pons, "Stalin, Togliatti, and the Origins of the Cold War"; Iatrides, "Revolution or Self-Defense?"; for Stalin's relations with Mao, see citations in note 196 above.

201. Banac, *Diary of Georgi Dimitrov*, 439–440; "Report of Djilas," 10 February 1948, CWIHP *Bulletin* 10 (March 1998): 129–33; Leonid Gibianskii, "Stalin's Policy in Eastern Europe, the Cominform, and the First Split in the Soviet Bloc," 17–22, paper prepared for the conference "Stalin and the Cold War."

202. Loth, *Stalin's Unwanted Child*, 84–94; Roberts, *Stalin's Wars*, 354–55.

203. Leffler, *Preponderance of Power*, 182–286.

204. William Hitchcock, *France Restored: Cold War Diplomacy and the Quest for Leadership in Europe, 1944–54* (Chapel Hill, N.C.: University of North Carolina Press, 1998); Geir Lundestad, "Empire by Invitation? The United States and Western Europe, 1945–1952," *Journal of Peace Research* 23 (September 1986): 263–77; Mark Lawrence, *Assuming the Burden: Europe and the American Commitment to War in Vietnam* (Berkeley, Calif.: University of California Press, 2005).

205. Conversation between Wladyslaw Gomulka and Stalin, 14 November 1945, CWIHP *Bulletin* 11 (Winter 1998): 136.

206. *Ibid.*

207. "Annual Message to the Congress on the State of the Union," 5 January 1949, *PPP: HST, 1949*, 6.

208. "Special Message to the Congress," 6 March 1952, *ibid.*, *1952–53*, 189.

209. Kennan to Marshall and Robert Lovett, 17 December 1948, box 33, Records of the Policy Planning Staff, RG 59, NA.

210. NSC 20/4, "U.S. Objectives with Respect to the USSR to Counter Soviet Threats to U.S. Security,"

23 November 1948, in Thomas H. Etzold and John L. Gaddis, eds., *Containment: Documents on American Policy and Strategy* (New York: Columbia University Press, 1978), 208.

211. *Ibid.*, 204–209.

II: The Chance for Peace, 1953–54: Malenkov and Eisenhower

1. Dmitri Volkogonov, *Stalin: Triumph and Tragedy* (New York: Grove Weidenfeld, 1988), 572; for details surrounding Stalin's death, see Simon Sebag Montefiore, *Stalin: The Court of the Red Tsar* (London: Weidenfeld & Nicolson, 2003), 555–77; William Taubman, *Khrushchev: The Man and His Era* (London: The Free Press, 2003), 236–41; Vladimir Shamberg, "Stalin's Last Inner Circle," *Harriman Review* 10 (Spring 1997): 38–39.

2. Montefiore, *Stalin*, 567.

3. *Ibid.*, 569–72.

4. Shamberg, "Stalin's Last Inner Circle," 39; Albert Resis, ed., *Molotov Remembers: Inside Kremlin Politics: Conversations with Felix Chuev* (Chicago, Ill.: Ivan R. Dee, 1993), 236; Strobe Talbott, ed., *Khrushchev Remembers* (Boston: Little, Brown & Co., 1970), 316–20; Volkogonov, *Stalin*, 567–76; Taubman, *Khrushchev*, 236–40; Amy Knight, *Beria: Stalin's First Lieutenant* (Princeton, N.J.: Princeton University Press, 1993), 176–80.

5. Volkogonov, *Stalin*, 574; Taubman, *Khrushchev*, 238.

6. Andrei Sakharov, *Memoirs* (New York: Alfred A. Knopf, 1990), 164.

7. Catherine Merridale, *Night of Stone: Death and Memory in Twentieth-Century Russia* (New York: Viking, 2001), 260–61.

8. Sakharov, *Memoirs*, 163–64; also see Georgi Arbatov, *The System: An Insider's Life in Soviet Politics* (New York: Random House, 1992), 37.

9. Ted Hopf, *Social Construction of International Politics: Identities and Foreign Policies, Moscow, 1955 and 1999* (Ithaca, N.Y.: Cornell University Press, 2002), 46; Robert Service, *Stalin: A Biography* (Cambridge, Mass.: Harvard University Press, 2005), 299–309.

10. Sakharov, *Memoirs*, 165.

11. Svetlana Alliluyeva, *Only One Year* (London: Hutchinson, 1969), 369, 355.

12. Merridale, *Night of Stone*, 260–61.

13. Taubman, *Khrushchev*, 249.

14. Talbott, *Khrushchev Remembers*, 392.

15. Sergo Beria, *Beria, My Father: Inside Stalin's Kremlin* (London: Gerald Duckworth & Co., 2001), 251.

16. Mark Kramer, "The Early Post-Stalin Succession Struggle and Upheavals in East-Central Europe: Internal-External Linkages in Soviet Policy Making (Part 2)," *Journal of Cold War Studies* 1 (Spring 1999): 18.

17. Taubman, *Khrushchev*, 246; Beria, *My Father*, 251–67; Kramer, "Post-Stalin Succession Struggle," part 2, 15.

18. Beria, *My Father*, 253, 262.

19. Talbott, *Khrushchev Remembers*, 392–93; Kramer, "Post-Stalin Succession Struggle," part 2, 19.

20. Quoted in Taubman, *Khrushchev*, 243–44.

21. Beria, *My Father*, 262 (quotation), also 261–65; Taubman, *Khrushchev*, 242–44; Kramer, "Post-Stalin Succession Struggle," part 2, 18–19.

22. "Funeral Orations by Malenkov, Beria, Molotov," *Current Digest of the Soviet Press* 5, no. 7, 1953: 7–8.

23. From Beria's speech, *ibid.*, 9.

24. Resolution, USSR Council of Ministers, with draft letters from Soviet Government to Mao Zedong and Kim Il Sung and directive to Soviet delegation at United Nations, 19 March 1953, Cold War

International History Project (CWIHP) *Bulletin* 6–7 (Washington, D.C.: Woodrow Wilson International Center, 1995/1996), 80–81.

25. Speech, by Malenkov, 16 March 1953, *Current Digest of the Soviet Press* 5, no. 8, 1953: 5.

26. Quoted in Taubman, *Khrushchev*, 242.

27. Shamberg, "Stalin's Last Inner Circle," 30; Beria, *My Father*, 161–62.

28. Talbott, *Khrushchev Remembers*, 313, 322–23; Resis, *Molotov Remembers*, 233.

29. For the quotations, see Beria, *My Father*, 160–64; for Malenkov, also see Shamberg, "Stalin's Last Inner Circle"; "Malenkov," by Norma C. Noonan, *The Modern Encyclopedia of Russian and Soviet History* (Gulf Breeze, Fla.: Academic International Press, 1989), vol. 50 (Supplement): 16–22; Eddy Gilmore, "A Report on Russia: Mr. Malenkov Takes Over," *Vital Speeches of the Day* 20 (November 1953): 85–90; Resis, *Molotov Remembers*, 337–38; Yoram Gorlizki and Oleg Khlevniuk, *Cold Peace: Stalin and the Soviet Ruling Circles, 1945–1953* (New York: Oxford University Press, 2004). For portraits of Malenkov, I am indebted to the incisive analyses of two research assistants, Pierre DuQuesnoy and Isaiah Gruber.

30. For Malenkov's friendship with Khrushchev, see Shamberg, "Stalin's Last Inner Circle," 33–34; for Malenkov's closeness with Beria, see Talbott, *Khrushchev Remembers*, 315–41; for Malenkov's underestimation of Khrushchev, see Taubman, *Khrushchev*, 236–66. Because of the subsequent struggle among Stalin's successors, all participants later stressed their differences, but Kramer persuasively illuminates the similarity of views in the first weeks after Stalin's death. See Kramer, "Post-Stalin Succession Struggle," part 2, 15–21; also see Taubman, *Khrushchev*, 248–49.

31. Stephen E. Ambrose, *Eisenhower*, 2 vols. (New York: Simon & Schuster, 1983 and 1984); Robert F. Burk, *Dwight D. Eisenhower: Hero and Politician* (Boston: Twayne Publishers, 1986); Chester J. Pach, Jr., and Elmo Richardson, *The Presidency of Dwight D. Eisenhower* (Lawrence: University Press of Kansas, 1991); Fred I. Greenstein, *The Hidden-Hand Presidency: Eisenhower as Leader* (New York: Basic Books, 1982).

32. William B. Pickett, *Dwight David Eisenhower and American Power* (Wheeling, Ill.: Harlan Davidson, 1995), 4.

33. Eisenhower to Swede Hazlett, 19 July 1947, in Robert W. Griffith, ed., *Ike's Letters to a Friend, 1941–1958* (Lawrence: University Press of Kansas, 1984), 40.

34. For Eisenhower's career, see citations in notes 31 and 32 of this chapter.

35. For background, see Melvyn P. Leffler, *A Preponderance of Power: National Security, the Truman Administration, and the Cold War* (Stanford, Calif.: Stanford University Press, 1992), 312–518; William W. Stueck, *The Korean War: An International History* (Princeton, N.J.: Princeton University Press, 1995); Chen Jian, *China's Road to the Korean War: The Making of the Sino-American Confrontation* (New York: Columbia University Press, 1994); Ernest R. May, ed., *American Cold War Strategy: Interpreting NSC-68* (Boston: Bedford Books, 1993).

36. For background on McCarthyism, see, for example, Robert S. Griffith, *The Politics of Fear: Joseph R. McCarthy and the Senate* (Lexington: University of Kentucky Press, 1970); David M. Oshinsky, *A Conspiracy So Immense: The World of Joe McCarthy* (New York: The Free Press, 1983); Richard Gid Powers, *Not Without Honor: The History of American Anticommunism* (New York: The Free Press, 1995).

37. "Inaugural Address," 20 January 1953, Dwight D. Eisenhower, *Public Papers of the Presidents: Dwight David Eisenhower*, 1953 (Washington, D.C.: Government Printing Office, 1960), 1–8 (hereafter cited as *PPP: DDE, year* page).

38. Diary entry, 22 January 1953, Louis Galambos, ed., *The Papers of Dwight David Eisenhower: NATO and the Campaign of 1952* (Baltimore, Md.: The Johns Hopkins University Press, 1989), 13: 897.

39. Eisenhower to A. F. Lorenzon, 9 September 1953, Dwight David Eisenhower Papers (DDEP), Ann

Whitman File (AWF), Diary Series, box 3, folder 2 (Dwight David Eisenhower Library [DDEL], Abilene, Kans.).

40. Eisenhower to George Arthur Sloan, 20 March 1952, Galambos, *Papers of DDE*, 13: 1103; Robert H. Ferrell, ed., *The Eisenhower Diaries* (New York: W. W. Norton, 1981), 136-37, 143-44.

41. For background on Dulles, see Richard H. Immerman, *John Foster Dulles: Piety, Pragmatism, and Power in U.S. Foreign Policy* (Wilmington, Del.: Scholarly Resources, 1999); Ronald W. Pruessen, *John Foster Dulles: The Road to Power* (New York: The Free Press, 1982).

42. For Dulles as a moralist, see Townsend Hoopes, *The Devil and John Foster Dulles* (Boston: Little, Brown, and Company, 1973); for Dulles as a realist, see Michael A. Guhin, *John Foster Dulles: A Statesman and His Times* (New York: Columbia University Press, 1972); for Dulles's religious views, see Mark G. Toulouse, *The Transformation of John Foster Dulles: From Prophet of Realism to Priest of Nationalism* (Macon, Ga.: Mercer University Press, 1985); for more synthetic yet critical views, see Immerman, *Dulles*; and the essays in Richard H. Immerman, ed., *John Foster Dulles and the Diplomacy of the Cold War* (Princeton, N.J.: Princeton University Press, 1990); for corporate internationalism, see Robert W. F. Griffith, "Dwight D. Eisenhower and the Corporate Commonwealth," *American Historical Review* 87 (February 1982): 87-122; for a wonderful illustration of this attitude, see Eisenhower to Sloan, 20 March 1952, Galambos, *Papers of DDE* 13: 1097-1104.

43. John Foster Dulles, *War or Peace* (New York: Macmillan, 1950), 163, also 74-78; Immerman, *Dulles*, 1-34.

44. David L. Snead, *The Gaither Committee, Eisenhower, and the Cold War* (Columbus: Ohio State University Press, 1999), 20; Memorandum of Meetings of the National Security Council (NSC), 25 March 1953, 24 September 1953, Department of State, *Foreign Relations of the United States, 1952-54* (Washington, D.C.: Government Printing Office, 1984), 2: 261, 469 (hereafter cited as *FRUS, year*, volume, page); Eisenhower to Lewis W. Douglas, 20 May 1952, Galambos, *Papers of DDE*, 13: 1230.

45. Emmet John Hughes, *The Ordeal of Power: A Political Memoir of the Eisenhower Years* (New York: Atheneum, 1975), 101; Minutes of Cabinet meeting, 6 March 1953, DDEP, AWF, Cabinet Series, box 1.

46. William J. Morgan, to H. S. Craig, 4 March 1953, DDEL, White House Office, NSC Staff: Papers, 1948-1961, Psychological Strategy Board, Central Files, box 8, file 1, folder 2; Frank G. Wisner to George Morgan, 9 March 1953, *ibid*.

47. "Supporting Thinking for Message to Soviet Government and Russian Peoples," 11 March 1953, W. W. Rostow, *Europe After Stalin: Eisenhower's Three Decisions of March 11, 1953* (Austin: University of Texas Press, 1982), 87-90; Gregory Mitrovich, *Undermining the Kremlin: America's Strategy to Subvert the Soviet Bloc* (Ithaca, N.Y.: Cornell University Press, 2000), 126-32.

48. Smith to C. D. Jackson, Allen Dulles, George M. Morgan, and Harold Stassen, 11 March 1953, DDEL, WHO, NSC Staff, PSB, Central File, box 8, file 2, folder 3; Charles Bohlen to Hughes, 9 March 1953, National Archives (NA), Record Group (RG) 59, Records of the Department of State, Lot 74 D 379, Charles Bohlen Papers, box 9.

49. Memorandum for Jackson, by James S. Lay, 12 March 1953, NA, RG 273, Records of the National Security Council, P Papers, P 31, box 1; Samuel Lubell to Bernard Baruch, 7 March 1953, DDEL, John Foster Dulles Papers, White House Memo Series, box 1, folder 5.

50. Special Estimate (SE) 39, "Probable Consequences of the Death of Stalin and of the Elevation of Malenkov to Leadership in the USSR," 10 March 1953, in Rostow, *Europe After Stalin*, 96-101.

51. Hughes, *Ordeal of Power*, 102-105; Memo of Conversation with the President, by Dulles, 16 March 1953, DDEL, Dulles Papers, Telephone Conversation Series, White House Telephone Calls, box 10.

52. I have conflated quotations from Hughes's book and diary. See Hughes, *Ordeal of Power*, 103–105. The statements are even stronger in Hughes's diary, 16 March 1953, Emmet Hughes Papers, Seely Mudd Library, Princeton University, Princeton, N.J.; see also "Telephone Conversation with Emmet Hughes," 16 March 1953, DDEL, Dulles Papers, Telephone Conversation Series, White House Telephone Calls, box 10.

53. "Marginal Suggestions for Secretary's Use in Presentation Before House Appropriations Committee," [no signature], 18 March 1953, NA, RG 59, Lot 64 D 563, Records of the Policy Planning Staff (PPS), 1947–1953, box 42.

54. Memorandum to the president, by Jackson, 2 April 1953, DDEL, C. D. Jackson Papers, box 50, folder 2.

55. Memorandum, by Carlton Savage, 1 April 1953, *FRUS, 1952–54* (Washington, D.C.: Government Printing Office, 1988), 8: 1138.

56. Louis Halle to Paul Nitze, 8 April 1953, NA, RG 59, Lot 64 D 563, Records of the PPS, box 42.

57. Allen W. Dulles to Morgan, 2 April 1953, enclosing "Malenkov: Some Biographical Highlights," 20 April 1953, DDEL, WHO, NSC Staff, PSB, Central Files; Morgan to Craig, "Malenkov Test Case," 26 March 1953, Declassifed Documents Reference System (DDRS), electronic access, declassified 20 May 1997.

58. Memorandum of meeting of NSC, 8 April 1953, DDEL, Eisenhower Papers, AWF, NSC Series, box 4; for Allen Dulles's allusions to encirclement, see diary entry, 16 March 1953, Hughes Papers.

59. *Ibid.*

60. Memorandum of conversation, by Walter Stoessel, 1 April 1953, *FRUS, 1952–54*, 8: 1139.

61. For quotation, see diary entry, 17 March 1953, Hughes Papers; Hughes, *Ordeal of Power*, 106–107; Mitrovich, *Undermining the Kremlin*, 128–29; PSB D-40, "Plan for Psychological Exploitation of Stalin's Death," 20 March 1953, DDEL, WHO, NSC Staff, PSB, Central Files, box 8.

62. Abbot Washburn to Jackson, 6 April 1953, DDEL, Jackson Papers, box 7.

63. Jeffrey Brooks, "Stalin's Ghost: Cold War Culture and U.S.-Soviet relations," in *The Cold War After Stalin's Death: A New International History*, ed. by Kenneth A. Osgood and Klaus Larres (Lanham, Md.: Rowman and Littlefield, 2006), 125; George H. Gallup, *The Gallup Poll: Public Opinion, 1935–1971*, 3 vols. (New York: Random House, 1972), 2: 1136.

64. Peter G. Boyle, ed., *The Churchill-Eisenhower Correspondence, 1953–1955* (Chapel Hill: University of North Carolina Press, 1990), 30–45, quotation on p. 41.

65. Diary entry, 16 March 1953, Hughes Papers; Hughes, *Ordeal of Power*, 102. For more critical views of Eisenhower's intentions, see Klaus Larres, "Eisenhower and the First Forty Days After Stalin's Death: The Incompatibility of Détente and Political Warfare," *Diplomacy and Statecraft* 6 (July 1995): 431–69; Kenneth A. Osgood, "Form Before Substance: Eisenhower's Commitment to Psychological Warfare and Negotiations with the Enemy," *Diplomatic History* 24 (Summer 2000): 405–33.

66. Address, "The Chance for Peace," 16 April 1953, *PPP: DDE*, 1953, 179–88.

67. See the discussion of the response to the speech at the NSC meeting on 22 April 1953. Memorandum of meeting of the NSC, 22 April 1953, DDEP, AWF, NSC Series, box 4 (omitted from *FRUS, 1952–54*, 2: 291–305).

68. Dulles's speech is conveniently reprinted in Rostow, *Europe After Stalin*, 122–31.

69. The *Pravda* editorial also appears in *ibid.*, 151–62.

70. Kennan to Allen [Dulles?], 25 April 1953, NA, RG 59, Records of Intelligence and Research, Subject Files, 1945–1960, Lot 58 D 776, box 14.

71. Bohlen's letter can be found in Rostow, *Europe After Stalin*, 162–64.

72. Memorandum of NSC meeting, 28 April 1953, DDEP, AWF, NSC Series, box 4.

73. For the conversation between Dulles and Eisenhower, see "Solarium Project," [no signature], 8 May 1953, NA, RG 59, PPS, Lot 64 D 563, box 64; Immerman, *Dulles*, 59–62.

74. Memorandum of NSC Meeting, 13 August 1953, *FRUS, 1952–54* (Washington, D.C.: Government Printing Office, 1986), 7: 502.

75. "Statement on Policy of United States Position with Respect to Germany," by Perry Laukhuff, 24 June 1953, NA, RG 59, PPS, Lot 64 D 563, box 42; Intelligence Estimate No. 51, "Long-Term Trends in Germany," 8 May 1953, *ibid.*, Intelligence and Research, Office of Director, 1950–59, Lot 58 D 528, box 65.

76. For Germany as a magnet, see Eisenhower to Bernard Law Montgomery, 14 July 1953, Galambos, *Papers of DDE: The Presidency: The Middle Way* (Baltimore, Md.: Johns Hopkins University Press, 1996), 14: 383–84.

77. Memorandum of NSC Meeting, 31 March 1953, *FRUS, 1952–54*, 2: 271–72.

78. Dulles to Eisenhower, 17 May 1953, DDEL, AWF, Dulles-Herter Series, box 1; Memorandum of NSC meeting, 1 June 1953, DDEP, AWF, NSC Series, box 4.

79. Jackson to Henry Luce, 19 May 1953, DDEL, Jackson Papers, box 70; Jackson to Robert Cutler, 11 May 1953, WHO, Office of Special Assistant for National Security Affairs (OSANA), NSC Series, Briefing Notes Subseries, box 8.

80. Eisenhower to Jiang Jieshi, 5 May 1953, Galambos, *Papers of DDE*, 14: 209.

81. L. A. Minnich, "Notes on Legislative Leadership Meeting," 30 April 1953, DDEP, AWF, Legislative Meetings Series, 1.

82. For the quotations, see Memorandum of NSC meeting, 25 March 1953, *FRUS, 1952–54*, 2: 261; Eisenhower to Alfred M. Gruenther, 4 May 1953, DDEP, AWF, Diary Series, box 3; also see *FRUS, 1952–54*, 2: 237–386.

83. Eisenhower to Jiang Jieshi, 5 May 1953, Galambos, *Papers of DDE*, 14: 210.

84. See, for example, Malenkov's opening remarks at the plenum of the Central Committee dealing with Beria. Minutes, 2 July 1953, D. M. Stickle, ed., *The Beria Affair: The Secret Transcripts of the Meetings Signalling the End of Stalinism* (New York: Nova Science Publishers, 1992), 3.

85. Kramer, "Post-Stalin Succession Struggle," part 2, 9–21; Taubman, *Khrushchev*, 245–46.

86. Beria, *My Father*, 161.

87. Quoted in Taubman, *Khrushchev*, 250.

88. Mark Kramer, "The Early Post-Stalin Succession Struggle and Upheavals in East-Central Europe: Internal-External Linkages in Soviet Policy Making (Part 1)," *Journal of Cold War Studies* 1 (Winter 1999): 3–55.

89. Transcript of conversation between the Soviet leadership and a Hungarian Workers' Party delegation in Moscow, 13 and 16 June 1953, in Christian F. Ostermann, ed., *Uprising in East Germany, 1953* (Budapest and New York: Central European University Press and the National Security Archive, 2001), 144–51.

90. *Ibid.*, xxxiii–iv; Kramer, "Post-Stalin Succession Struggle," part 1, 50–55.

91. Otto Grotewohl's notes of meetings between East German and Soviet leaders in Moscow, 2–4 June 1953, in Ostermann, *Uprising in East Germany*, 137; Hope M. Harrison, *Driving the Soviets Up the Wall: Soviet-East German Relations, 1953–1961* (Princeton, N.J.: Princeton University Press, 2003), 12–31.

92. USSR Council of Ministers Order, "On Measures to Improve the Health of the Political Situation in the GDR," 2 June 1953, in Ostermann, *Uprising in East Germany*, 134; also see *ibid.*, 67–71, 82–85, 90–109, 133–36.

93. Pavel Sudaplatov and Anatoli Sudaplatov, with Jerrold L. and Leona P. Schecter, *Special Tasks: The Memoirs of an Unwanted Witness—a Soviet Spymaster* (Boston: Little, Brown and Company, 1994), 363–64.

94. Andrei Gromyko, *Memoirs* (New York: Doubleday, 1989), 317; Resis, *Molotov Remembers*, 334–35.

95. Beria, *My Father*, 262.

96. Kramer, "Post-Stalin Succession Struggle," part 2, 27–34.

97. "Resolution on the Criminal Anti-Party and Anti-Government Activities of Beria of the Plenum of the Central Committee CPSU," 7 July 1953, Stickle, *The Beria Affair*, 187–88; also see Malenkov's remarks, 2 July 1953, *ibid.*, 3–13.

98. For Khrushchev's and Bulganin's comments, see *ibid.*, 22, 44–45.

99. Molotov's comments, 2 July 1953, *ibid.*, 29.

100. For the quotations, see Malenkov's comments on 5 July 1953 and the CPSU final resolution regarding Beria, *ibid.*, 178–79, 189; for policy regarding East Germany and East Europe, see Mark Kramer, "The Early Post-Stalin Succession Struggle and Upheavals in East-Central Europe: Internal-External Linkages in Soviet Policy Making (Part 3)," *Journal of Cold War Studies* 1 (Fall 1999): 3–66; Harrison, *Driving the Soviets Up the Wall*, 38–48.

101. Beria to Malenkov, 1 July 1953, Ostermann, *Uprising in East Germany*, 155–57.

102. Kramer, "Post-Stalin Succession Struggle," part 2, 37; Taubman, *Khrushchev*, 256–57.

103. Malenkov's closing remarks on 7 July 1953 and the CPSU final resolution regarding Beria, in Sickle, *The Beria Affair*, 178, 190.

104. For Malenkov's speech on 8 August 1953, see *Vital Speeches of the Day* 19 (1 September 1953): 679–91.

105. Memoranda of the meetings of the NSC, 25 June 1953 and 9 July 1953, DDEP, AWF, NSC Series, box 4; Minutes of Cabinet meeting 10 July 1953, DDEP, AWF, Cabinet Series, box 2.

106. NSC 158, "United States Objectives and Actions to Exploit the Unrest in the Satellite States," 29 June 1953, in Ostermann, *Uprising in Eastern Europe*, 332–34; Mitrovich, *Undermining the Kremlin*, 132–34.

107. Ostermann, *Uprising in East Germany*, 321–24.

108. Memorandum prepared in the Department of State, 1 October 1953, FRUS, *1952–54*, 8: 84; Ostermann, *Uprising in East Germany*, 325.

109. For the overall review of national security policy known as Project Solarium—named after the Solarium room in the White House where Eisenhower and Dulles conceived the project—see FRUS, *1952–54*, 2: 323–28, 349–54, 360–66, 387–434; also see "Project Solarium: Summary of Basic Concepts of Task Forces," 30 July 1953, NA, RG 59, Records Relating to the State Department Participation in the Operations Coordinating Board (OCB) and the NSC, 1947–1953, Lot 66 D 148, box 122.

110. Memorandum, by Cutler, 16 July 1953, FRUS, *1952–54*, 2: 397–98.

111. Memorandum, by Cutler, 31 July 1953, *ibid.*, 440–41.

112. Memorandum of the meeting of the NSC, 14 July 1953, DDEP, AWF, NSC Series, box 4; also see "Statement of Policy of the NSC," 10 June 1953, FRUS, *1952–54*, 2: 379–80.

113. Editorial Note, FRUS, *1952–54*, 2: 394; Robert J. Watson, *History of the Joint Chiefs of Staff: The Joint Chiefs of Staff and National Policy, 1953–1954* (Washington, D.C.: Government Printing Office, 1986), 14–21; Richard M. Leighton, *Strategy, Money, and the New Look, 1953–1956: History of the Office of the Secretary of Defense* (Washington, D.C.: Government Printing Office, 2001), 65–204.

114. Memorandum of the meeting of the NSC, 27 August 1953, FRUS, *1952–54*, 2: 443–55; for Humphrey's previous criticisms of strategic planning, see, for example, Memorandum of the meeting of the NSC, 14 July, DDEP, AWF, NSC Series, box 4; also see Watson, *JCS and National Policy, 1953–1954*, 17–21.

115. Memorandum, by Cutler, 3 September 1953, FRUS, *1952–54*, 2: 455–57.

116. Memorandum, by Dulles, 6 September 1953, *ibid.*, 457–60.

117. Eisenhower to Dulles, 8 September 1953, *ibid.*, 460–63.

118. Halle to Bowie and Jacob Beam, 27 July 1953, NA, RG 59, Records of the PPS, Lot 64 D 563,

box 42; Edmund A. Gullion, "Principles for Exploitation of the Situation in the Soviet Union and Follow-Up of President Eisenhower's April 16 Speech," *ibid.*; Rostow to Jackson, "Some Notes on American Policy," [ND], DDEL, Jackson Papers, box 6.

119. "Possible Accommodation with the Soviets in Europe," 3 October 1953, [no signature], included in Bowie to Dulles, 3 October 1953, NA, RG 59, Records of the PPS, Lot 64 D 563, box 43; also see Leon Fuller, "Possible Soviet-Western Agreement on International Status and Power Position of a Unified Germany," 21 July 1953, *ibid.*, box 42.

120. Eisenhower to Joseph Laniel, 20 September 1953, Galambos, *Papers of DDE*, 14: 527–28.

121. NSC 160/1, "United States Position with Respect to Germany," 17 August 1953, *FRUS, 1952–54*, 7: 511; Fuller to Beam and Bowie, 20 November 1953, NA, RG 59, Records of the PPS, Lot 64 D 563, box 43; James Conant to Dulles, 28 October 1953, *FRUS, 1952–54*, 7: 551–52.

122. Eisenhower to Laniel, 20 September 1953, Galambos, *Papers of DDE*, 14: 528.

123. For JCS view, see JCS to Secretary of Defense, 30 September 1953, NA, RG 330, CD 350.05 (Europe), box 29; for NSC conclusion, see NSC 160/1, "United States Position with Respect to Germany," 17 August 1953, *FRUS, 1952–54*, 7: 515; see also "Possible Accommodation with the Soviets in Europe," 3 October 1953, NA, RG 59, Records of the PPS, Lot 64 D 563, box 42.

124. NSC 160/1, "United States Position with Respect to Germany," 17 August 1953, *FRUS, 1952–54*, 7: 510–20.

125. For NSC assessment, see *ibid.*, 513; for view of PPS, see "Possible Accommodation with the Soviets in Europe," 3 October 1953, NA, RG 59, Records of the PPS, Lot 64 D 563, box 42; also see Leon Fuller, "Establishment of an All-German Government," 13 August 1953, *ibid.*; Beam to Bowie, 22 September 1953, *ibid.*, box 43; Bowie, "Bases for Settlements," 3 October 1953, *ibid.*; Fuller, "Soviet Concept of Security," 17 July 1953, *ibid.*, box 42.

126. NSC 162/2, "Basic National Security Policy," *FRUS, 1952–54*, 2: 587.

127. The President's Committee on International Information Activities, "Report to the President," 30 June 1953, pp. 10, 19, 27–28, NA, RG 273, P Papers, box 1.

128. For the quotation, see Ferrell, *Eisenhower Diaries*, 223; also see, for example, Eisenhower to Margaret Winchester Patterson, 15 June 1953, Galambos, *Papers of DDE*, 14: 293; for Dulles, see Memorandum of meeting of NSC, 9 June 1953, *FRUS, 1952–54*, 2: 377.

129. Eisenhower to Edgar Newton Eisenhower, 8 November 1954, Galambos, *Papers of DDE*, 15: 1387; for an excellent set of essays analyzing the overthrow of Mossadeq, see Mark J. Gasiorowski and Malcolm Byrne, eds., *Mohammad Mosaddeq and the 1953 Coup in Iran* (Syracuse, N.Y.: Syracuse University Press, 2004).

130. Memorandum, by Halle, 28 May 1954, *FRUS, 1952–54*, 4: 1140–41.

131. Nick Cullather, *Secret History: The CIA's Classified Account of Its Operations in Guatemala, 1952–1954* (Stanford, Calif.: Stanford University Press, 1999); Piero Gleijeses, *Shattered Hope: The Guatemalan Revolution and the United States, 1944–1954* (Princeton, N.J.: Princeton University Press, 1991); Stephen G. Rabe, *Eisenhower and Latin America: The Foreign Policy of Anticommunism* (Chapel Hill: The University of North Carolina Press, 1988), 42–63.

132. For Indochina, see Fuller, "Settlement in the Far East," 3 October 1953, NA, RG 59, Records of the PPS, Lot 64 D 563, box 43; for the Middle East, see F. Wilkins, "Problem: How to Create a Position of Strength in the Middle East," 17 September 1953, *ibid.*, box 65.

133. For the quotation by policy planners, see F. Wilkins, "Building Strength in Regional Groupings in the Far East," 18 September 1953, *ibid.*, box 65; also see "Settlement in the Far East," [no signature], 3 October 1953, *ibid.*, box 43; for the JCS and the State Department, see the quotation in Michael Schaller, *Altered States: The United States and Japan Since Occupation* (New York: Oxford University Press, 1997), 97; for Eisenhower's view of the importance of Japan, see Editorial Note, *FRUS, 1952–54*, 14: 1663; Minutes of Cabinet meeting, 6 August 1954, *ibid.*, 1693–95; for Eisen-

hower's thinking about the interconnections between the industrial core of the world and the underdeveloped periphery, see Eisenhower to George Arthur Sloan, 20 March 1952, Galambos, *Papers of DDE*, 13: 1097–99; also see, for example, Eisenhower to Douglas, 20 May 1952, *ibid.*, 1229–30; "Summary of Points," 16 July 1953, *FRUS, 1952–54*, 2: 433.

134. In addition to citations in preceding notes, see the Memorandum of the meeting of the NSC, 1 October 1953, DDEP, AWF, NSC Series, box 4.

135. NSC 162/2, "Basic National Security Policy," 30 October 1953, *FRUS, 1952–54*, 2: 579, 584.

136. *Ibid.*, 578–95, with quotations on 582, 591–92, 595.

137. *Ibid.*, 594–95; also see the discussion at the meeting of the NSC on 7 October 1953, in *ibid.*, 514–34.

138. For the emphasis on winning the Cold War, also see Kenneth Osgood, *Total Cold War: Eisenhower's Secret Propaganda Battle at Home and Abroad* (Lawrence: University Press of Kansas, 2006).

139. Memorandum of meeting of the NSC, 9 June 1953, *FRUS, 1952–54*, 2: 374, 377; also "Review of Basic National Security Policy," 30 September 1953, *ibid.*, 494.

140. Memorandum of meeting of the NSC, 1 October 1953, DDEP, AWF, NSC Series, box 4; Jackson to Eisenhower, 21 September 1953, DDEL, Jackson Papers, box 50.

141. For Churchill's efforts, see Boyle, *Churchill-Eisenhower Correspondence*, 30–110; Klaus Larres, *Churchill's Cold War: The Politics of Personal Diplomacy* (New Haven, Conn.: Yale University Press, 2002), 189–317.

142. First Plenary Tripartite Meeting of the Heads of Government, 4 December 1953, *FRUS, 1952–54* (Washington, D.C.: Government Printing Office, 1983), 5: 1758–59.

143. *Ibid.*, 1761; for background paper for the Bermuda meeting, see Bowie, "Analysis of Soviet Positions," NA, RG 59, Papers of the PPS, Lot 64 D 563, box 43; Bowie, "Outline of U.S. Policies," 2 December 1953, *ibid.*

144. For discussion of the EDC at the Bermuda meeting, see *FRUS, 1952–54*, 5: 1770–71, 1780–82, 1796–1804, 1835–36, 1843.

145. NSC 166/1, "U.S. Policy Toward Communist China," *FRUS, 1952–54* (Washington, D.C.: Government Printing Office, 1985), 14: 281.

146. Second Restricted Meeting of the Heads of Government, 7 December 1953, *ibid.*, 5: 1810–13.

147. NSC Staff Study on U.S. Policy Toward Communist China, 6 November 1953, *ibid.*, 14: 303–304.

148. Communiqué of the Bermuda Conference, 7 December 1953, *ibid.*, 5: 1839.

149. For similar, but more critical, accounts of Eisenhower's motives, see Osgood, *Total Cold War*, 153–80; Ira Chernus, *Eisenhower's Atoms for Peace* (College Station: Texas A & M Press, 2002).

150. Jeff Broadwater, *Eisenhower and the Anti-Communist Crusade* (Chapel Hill: University of North Carolina Press, 1992), 54–136.

151. "Address Before the General Assembly," 8 December 1953, *PPP: Eisenhower, 1953*, 813–822.

152. Replies by Malenkov to an American journalist, 1 January 1954, in Denise Foliot, ed., *Documents on International Affairs, 1954* (London: Oxford University Press, 1957), 263–64 (hereafter cited as *DIA, year*, page).

153. Draft memorandum of conversation, by Livingston Merchant, 11 January 1954, *FRUS, 1952–54*, 2: 1335–36.

154. Statement by Russian government, 22 December 1953, in Foliot, *DIA, 1953* (London: Oxford University Press, 1956), 122–25; Communiqué by the Russian government, 6 January 1954, in *DIA, 1954*, 263–64.

155. Eisenhower to Jackson, 31 December 1953, *FRUS, 1952–54*, 2: 1321–22; Summary of meeting with the secretary of state, 6 January 1954, *ibid.*, 1325–26.

156. Memorandum of meeting of NSC, 3 December 1953, *ibid.*, 2: 805–6; Eisenhower-Churchill Meeting, 5 December 1953, *ibid.*, 5: 1768.

157. Summary of meeting in the White House, 16 January 1954, *ibid.*, 2: 1342–43; also see Memorandum of meeting of the NSC, 26 February 1954, *ibid.*, 1364–65; for the absence of follow-up, see McGeorge Bundy, *Danger and Survival: Choices About the Bomb in the Past Fifty Years* (New York: Random House, 1988), 293–95; for Eisenhower's antipathy for real disarmament, see Ira Chernus, "Operation Candor: Fear, Faith, and Flexibility," *Diplomatic History* 29 (November 2005): 791–92, 804; Osgood, *Total Cold War*, 153–89.

158. Memorandum, by Dulles, 20 January 1954, DDEL, Dulles Papers, White House Memo Series, box 1 (Meetings with the president, folder 4).

159. Memorandum, by Bohlen, 28 January 1954, *FRUS, 1952–54*, 7: 854–55.

160. Memorandum of conversation, 29 January 1954, *ibid.*, 880–85; Dulles to Eisenhower, 1 February 1954, *ibid.*, 916–17; Memorandum, by Jackson, 22 February 1954, *ibid.*, 1215–16.

161. For the reports on Molotov's speeches, see U.S. Delegation to the Department of State, 25 January 1954 and 2 February 1954, *ibid.*, 815, 913–16.

162. Statement, by Molotov, in Rossiiskii gosudarstvennyi arkhiv noveishei istorii (RGANI), "Plenumy Tsentral'nogo Komiteta Kommunisticheskoi partii Sovetskogo Soiuza, 1941–1990," *fond* 2, *opis'* 1, *delo* No. 77 ("Stenogramma odinnadtsatogo zasedaniia 2 marta 1954 g. Nepravlennaia"), list 38–68 [Russian State Archives of Contemporary History, "Plenums of the Central Committee of the Communist Party of the Soviet Union, 1941–1990," collection 2, catalog 1, item no. 77 ("Uncorrected Stenographic Records of the 11th Session of the Plenum of the Central Committee of the CPSU)," 2 March 1954, leaves, 36–68], Lamont Library, Microforms, Film A1059, Harvard University, (hereafter cited as "Plenums of the Central Committee of the CPSU, 1941–1990").

163. Biulleten' ekonomicheskoi informatsii po Zapadnoi Germanii, Nos. 6 & 7 (Berlin: Apparat Verkhovnogo Komissara SSSR v Germanii, 1953), in Rossiiskii gosudarstvennyi arkhiv noveishei istorii (RGANI), "Obshchii otdel Tsk KPSS, 1953–1966 gody, *fond* 5, *opis'* 30, *delo*" no. 35 ("Proekt postanovleniia prezidiuma Soveta Ministrov SSSR . . . biulleteni ekonomicheskoi informatsii po Zapadnoi Germanii I dr."), *listy* 66–191 [Bulletin of Economic Information on West Germany, Numbers 6 and 7 (Berlin: Apparatus of the High Commissar of USSR in Germany, 1953), in Russian State Archive of Contemporary History, "The General Department of the Central Committee of the CPSU, 1953–1966," collection 5, catalog 30, item no. 35 ("Draft Resolution of the Presidium of the Council of Ministers of the USSR, Bulletins of Economic Information on West Germany, etc."), leaves 66–191], Lamont Library, Microforms, Film A1046, Harvard University.

164. *Ekonomicheskoe I politicheskoe polozhenie Germanii v 1953 godu* (Berlin: Verkhovnyi Komissar SSSR v Germanii, 1954), in Rossiiskii gosudarstvennyi arkhiv noveishei istorii (RGANI), "Otdel TsK KPSS po sviaziam s inostrannymi Kompartiiami (Mezhdunarodnyi otdel TsK KPSS), 1953–1957 gody," *fond* 5, *opis'* 28, *delo* no. 53 ("Otchet Verkhovnogo komissara SSSR v Germanii ob ekonomicheskom I politicheskom polozhenii GDR v 1953 g."), *listy* 1–151 [*The Economic and Political Situation of Germany in 1953* (Berlin: USSR High Commissar in Germany, 1954), in Russian State Archive of Contemporary History, "Department of the Central Committee of the CPSU for Relations with Foreign Communist Parties (International Department of the Central Committee of the CPSU), 1953–1957," collection 5, catalog 28, item no. 53 ("Account of the USSR High Commissar in Germany on the Economic and Political Situation of the GDR in 1953"), leaves 1–151], Lamont Library, Microforms, Film A1050, Harvard University.

165. For the quotation, see Statement, by Molotov, 2 March 1954, in "Plenums of the Central Committee of the CPSU, 1941–1990," no. 77, leaf 22; see also leaves 13–19, 36–37, 56–59.

166. Fuller to Beam and Bowie, 20 November 1953, NA, RG 59, Records of the PPS, Lot 64 D 563, box 43. In the early 1950s, 40 percent of the officials in the foreign ministry, 42 percent in the interior ministry, and 75 percent dealing with German refugees from the east were former officials of the Nazi government. Jeffrey Herf, "Amnesty and Amnesia," *New Republic*, 10 March 2003, 33–35; for

an illumination of the powerful influence and expansionist aspirations of the migrants from else-where in Eastern Europe, see Pertti Ahonen, *After the Expulsion: West Germany and Eastern Europe, 1945-1990* (New York: Oxford University Press, 2003), 1-154.

167. Statement, by Molotov, 2 March 1954, "Plenums of the Central Committee of the CPSU, 1941-1990," no. 77, leaves 37-81.

168. Jackson to Eisenhower, 22 February 1954, *FRUS, 1952-54*, 7: 1215-20.

169. *Ibid.*, 1220; Jackson to Frank Wisner, 27 February 1954, DDEL, Jackson Records, box 50 (Eisenhower correspondence, folder 2); Jackson to Eisenhower, 1 March 1954, *ibid.*, box 50.

170. Bohlen to Department of State, 20 January 1954, *FRUS, 1952-54*, 8: 1223-25.

171. Memorandum of conversation, by Douglas MacArthur, II, 20 February 1954, *ibid.*, 7: 1210.

172. Gareth Porter, *Perils of Dominance: Imbalance of Power and the Road to War in Vietnam* (Berkeley, Calif.: University of California Press, 2005), 32-40.

173. Immerman, *Dulles*, 93. In contrast, Molotov was relaxed, confident, and conciliatory. See Ilya A. Gaiduk, *Confronting Vietnam: Soviet Policy Toward the Indochina Conflict, 1954-1963* (Stanford, Calif.: Stanford University Press, 2003), 45-53.

174. Eisenhower to Churchill, 14 December 1954, Galambos, *Papers of DDE*, 15: 1444; for the evolution of U.S. policy, also see NSC 5405, "United States Objectives and Courses of Action with Respect to Southeast Asia," 16 January 1954, *FRUS, 1952-54*, 12: 367-80; NSC 5429/2, "Review of U.S. Policy in the Far East," 20 August 1954, *ibid.*, 769-76; NSC 5429/3, "Current U.S. Policy Toward the Far East," 19 November 1954, *ibid.*, 973-80; NSC 5429/5, "Current U.S. Policy Toward the Far East," *ibid.*, 1062-70.

175. "Specific Problems with the UK," 16 May 1954, DDEL, White House Memo Series, General Foreign Policy Subseries, box 8; Memorandum of Conversation, by Cutler, 5 May 1954, *FRUS, 1952-54*, 12: 446-50; Memoranda of meetings of the NSC, 6 May 1954, 3 June 1954, 9 June 1954, *ibid.*, 452-59, 532-37, 552-55; Dulles to Eisenhower, 28 May 1954, *ibid.*, 527-28; Conference in the President's Office, by Cutler, 2 June 1954, *ibid.*, 529-31; for Radford's views, see the documents in NA, RG 218, Records of the Joint Chiefs of Staff, Radford Files, box 10, folder 091 Indochina.

176. Jackson to Luce, 11 August 1954, DDEL, Jackson Papers, box 70.

177. Henry Byroade, "The World's Colonies and Ex-Colonies: A Challenge to America," Department of State *Bulletin*, 29 (16 Nov 1953): 655-56.

178. Quoted in Robert J. McMahon, *The Limits of Empire: The United States and Southeast Asia Since World War II* (New York: Columbia University Press, 1999), 66.

179. See, for example, Eisenhower's remarks at a White House meeting on 2 June 1954. He wanted to know how he could get the American people to support strong action against Communist China should it attack Indochina. See Conference in the President's Office, 2 June 1954, *FRUS, 1952-54*, 12: 530-31.

180. "Specific Problems with the UK," 16 May 1954, DDEL, Dulles Papers, White House Memo Series, General Foreign Policy Subseries, box 8, folder 2.

181. Memorandum of Meetings of the NSC, 12 and 18 August 1954, *FRUS, 1952-54*, 12: 730, 756-57; Minutes of a Meeting on Southeast Asia, 24 July 1954, *ibid.*, 666-67.

182. Memorandum of Meeting of the NSC, 18 August 1954, *ibid.*, 756; NSC 5429/2, "Review of U.S. Policy in the Far East," 20 August 1954, *ibid.*, 769-76.

183. Memorandum, by Cutler, 2 June 1954, *ibid.*, 529-31; Minutes of Meeting on Southeast Asia, 24 July 1954, *ibid.*, 665-69ff.

184. Memorandum of Luncheon Conversation with the President, 11 May 1954, DDEL, Dulles Papers, White House Memo Series, box 1 (Meetings with the President, 1954, folder 3); Memorandum for the President, by Dulles, 12 May 1954, *ibid.*; Dulles, "United States Foreign Policy," 16 May 1954,

ibid., General Foreign Policy Matters, box 8, folder 2; Dulles to Eisenhower, 17 May 1954, *ibid.*, box 1 (White House Correspondence, 1954, folder 3).

185. See, for example, Office of Intelligence and Research and Division of Research for the Soviet Union and Eastern Europe, "Soviet Intentions and Capabilities," 8 September 1954, NA, RG 59, Intelligence and Research Subject Files, Lot 58 D 776, box 14; NIE 11-5-54, "Soviet Capabilities and Main Lines of Policy through Mid-1959," 7 June 1954, *FRUS, 1952–54*, 8: 1235–38; NIE 11-4-54, "Soviet Capabilities and Probable Courses of Action Through Mid-1959," 14 September 1954, *ibid.*, 1248–52.

186. Draft of speech, "Our Armed Forces," by Radford, 8 June 1954, NA, RG 218, Radford Files, box 29, 337 Quantico.

187. Charles E. Wilson, "A Review of the United States Policy on the Regulation, Limitation, and Balanced Reduction of Armed Forces and Armaments," esp. pp. 110–25, 11 December 1954, NA, RG 330, Records of the Secretary of Defense, 1954, box 58, CD 388.3.

188. Cutler to Eisenhower, 17 December 1954, DDEP, White House Office, OSA/NSA, NSC Series, Policy Paper Subseries, box 14; NSC 5505/1, 31 January 1955, "Exploitation of Soviet and European Satellite Vulnerabilities," 31 January 1955, *ibid*. Although employing the rhetoric of liberation, Ike and his advisers were embarking on a more prudent, long-term policy that sought to avoid the risk of war in the short term but effectuate liberation in the long term. The policy was fraught with internal contradictions. See Ronald R. Krebs, *Dueling Visions: U.S. Strategy Toward Eastern Europe Under Eisenhower* (College Station: Texas A & M University Press, 2001); Lazlo Borhi, "Rollback, Liberation, Containment, or Inaction? U.S. Policy and Eastern Europe in the 1950s," *Journal of Cold War Studies* 1 (Fall 1999): 91–95; Chris Tudda, *The Truth Is Our Weapon: The Rhetorical Diplomacy of Dwight D. Eisenhower and John Foster Dulles* (Baton Rouge: Louisiana State University Press, 2006).

189. In addition to the citations in note above, see Mitrovich, *Undermining the Kremlin*, 163–71.

190. Bowie, "Analysis of Soviet Position," p. 9, NA, RG 59, Records of the PPS, Lot 64 D 563, box 43.

191. Summary Minutes of the Chiefs of Mission, 22–24 September 1953, *FRUS, 1952–54*, 8: 96; also see Bowie, "Analysis of the Soviet Position," NA, RG 59, Records of the PPS, Lot 64 D 563, box 43.

192. Eisenhower to Douglas, 20 May 1952, Galambos, *Papers of DDE*, 13: 1229–31.

193. Speech, by Malenkov, 12 March 1954, *U.S. News & World Report*, 26 March 1954, 125–28; Address, by Malenkov, 26 April 1954, *Current History* 26 (June 1954): 372–73.

194. Speech, by Molotov, 11 March 1954, *U.S. News and World Report*, 26 March 1954, 128–31; Plenums of the Central Committee, 1953–54, Lamont Library Microforms, A 1059.

195. See his report to the Central Committee on the Berlin Conference, 2 March 1954, No. 77, Lamont Library Microforms, A 1059.

196. Malenkov's closing remarks to the Central Committee regarding Beria, 7 July 1953, in Stickle, *Beria Affair*, 179.

197. *Ibid.*, 178–79; Malenkov's speech, 9 August 1953, *Vital Speeches of the Day* 19 (September 1, 1953): 688.

198. For awareness of their many problems, see Malenkov's remarks to the Central Committee, 7 July 1953, Stickle, *Beria Affair*, 173–80.

199. Malenkov's opening comments to the Central Committee, 2 July 1953, *ibid.*, 3; Malenkov's speech, August 1953, *Vital Speeches of the Day* 19 (September 1, 1953): 688–89.

200. Fear of Germany is a pervasive theme throughout the meetings of the Central Committee regarding Beria. See Stickle, *Beria Affair*.

201. See his speech, 26 April 1954, *Current History* 26 (June 1954): 372.

202. Malenkov's closing remarks, 7 July 1953, Stickle, *Beria Affair*, 178.

203. Malenkov's speech, 8 August 1953, *Vital Speeches of the Day* 19 (September 1, 1953): 691.

204. "Resolution on the Criminal Anti-Party and Anti-Government Activities of Beria," 7 July 1953, Stickle, *Beria Affair*, 190.

205. Malenkov's speech, 12 March 1954, *U.S. News & World Report*, 26 March 1954, p. 128; Malenkov's speech, 8 August 1953, *Vital Speeches of the Day* 19 (September 1, 1953): 691.

206. For illustrative comments, see, for example, Eisenhower to Hazlett, 19 July 1947, Griffith, *Ike's Letters to a Friend*, 40; Diary entry, 6 January 1953, Ferrell, *Eisenhower Diaries*, 222–24; Notes, by Minnich, 14 December 1954, *FRUS, 1952–54*, 2: 825–26.

III: Retreat from Armageddon, 1962–65: Khrushchev, Kennedy, and Johnson

1. For Kennedy's speech, see Ernest R. May and Philip D. Zelikow, eds., *The Kennedy Tapes: Inside the White House During the Cuban Missile Crisis* (Cambridge, Mass: Harvard University Press, 1997), 276–81; for background, also see Dino A. Brugioni, *Eyeball to Eyeball: The Inside Story of the Cuban Missile Crisis* (New York: Random House, 1991); James G. Blight and David A. Welch, eds., *On the Brink: Americans and Soviets Reexamine the Cuban Missile Crisis* (New York: Noonday Press, 1990); Max Frankel, *High Noon in the Cold War: Kennedy, Khrushchev, and the Cuban Missile Crisis* (New York: Ballantine Books, 2004); Sheldon M. Stern, *The Week the World Stood Still: Inside the Secret Cuban Missile Crisis* (Stanford: Stanford University Press, 2005).

2. Philip Zelikow and Ernest R. May, eds., *John F. Kennedy: The Presidential Recordings: The Great Crises*, 3 vols. (New York: W. W. Norton & Company, 2001), 3: 183–84.

3. Anatoly Dobrynin, *In Confidence: Moscow's Ambassador to America's Six Cold War Presidents* (New York: Random House, 1995), 111.

4. Nikita S. Khrushchev to John F. Kennedy, 26 October 1962, Department of State, *Foreign Relations of the United States, 1961–1963: Kennedy-Khrushchev Exchanges* (Washington, D.C.: Government Printing Office, 1996), 6: 172 (hereafter cited as *FRUS, years*, volume: page).

5. Norman Cousins, *The Improbable Triumvirate: John F. Kennedy, Pope John, Nikita Khrushchev* (New York: W. W. Norton & Company, 1972), 46.

6. Khrushchev to Kennedy, 26 October 1962, *FRUS, 1961–1963*, 6: 172–74.

7. Minutes no. 61, 25 October 1962, Vladimir Malin's notes of the Presidium meetings, in A. A. Fursenko et al., ed., *Prezidium TsK KPSS, 1954–1964: Chernovye protokol'nye zapisi zasedanii, stenogrammy, postanovleniia* [The Presidium of the CC of the CPSU, 1954–1964: Draft Records of Session Proceedings, Stenographic Transcripts, Resolutions], vol. 1 (Moscow: ROSSPEN, 2003). A revised and expanded version was printed in 2004. I have used the Miller Center translation of Malin's notes, by Timothy Naftali, who has collaborated with Fursenko on two books (hereafter cited as Malin Notes). These transcripts are now accessible on the website of the Miller Center of Public Affairs at the University of Virginia, http://millercenter.virginia.edu/scripps/gigitalarchive/kremlin. Also see Oleg Troyanovsky, "The Making of Soviet Foreign Policy," in *Nikita Khrushchev*, edited by William Taubman, Sergei Khrushchev, and Abbott Gleason (New Haven, Conn.: Yale University Press, 2000), 234–38; for Khrushchev and the missile crisis, also see Aleksandr Fursenko and Timothy Naftali, *"One Hell of a Gamble": The Secret History of the Cuban Missile Crisis* (New York: W. W. Norton & Company, 1997); William Taubman, *Khrushchev: The Man and His Era* (New York: The Free Press, 2003), 529–77.

8. Sergei N. Khrushchev, *Nikita Khrushchev and the Creation of a Superpower*, trans. by Shirley Benson (University Park: Pennsylvania State University Press, 2000), 584.

9. Minutes no. 61, 25 October 1962, Malin Notes.

10. Khrushchev to Kennedy, 26 October 1962, *FRUS, 1961–1963*, 6: 176–77; S. Khrushchev, *Superpower*, 584, 588.

11. Nikita S. Khrushchev, *Khrushchev Remembers: The Glasnost Tapes*, trans. and ed. by Jerrold L.

Schecter with Vyacheslav V. Luchkov (Boston: Little, Brown & Company, 1990), 170–73; S. Khrushchev, *Superpower*, 578–95; Fursenko and Naftali, *"One Hell of a Gamble,"* 259–60; Taubman, *Khrushchev*, 566–69; Aleksandr Fursenko and Timothy Naftali, *Khrushchev's Cold War: The Inside Story of an American Adversary* (New York: W. W. Norton and Company, 2006), 482–87.

12. Zelikow and May, *Kennedy*, 3: 360.

13. *Ibid.*, 355.

14. Fursenko and Naftali, *"One Hell of a Gamble,"* 274; Fursenko and Naftali, *Khrushchev's Cold War*, 487–88.

15. Khrushchev to Kennedy, 27 October 1962, *FRUS, 1961–1963*, 6: 178–81.

16. Minutes no. 61, 25 October 1962, Malin Notes; Fursenko and Naftali, *"One Hell of a Gamble,"* 274; Taubman, *Khrushchev*, 569–70.

17. Stern, *The World Stood Still*, 163, 188; Fursenko and Naftali, *"One Hell of a Gamble,"* 266, 280; Zelikow and May, *Kennedy*, 3: 387–88*ff.*

18. Kennedy to Khrushchev, 27 October 1962, *FRUS, 1961–1963*, 6: 181–82.

19. Stern, *The World Stood Still*, 157–88; Fursenko and Naftali, *"One Hell of a Gamble,"* 281–82; Arthur M. Schlesinger, Jr., *Robert Kennedy and His Times* (Boston: Houghton Mifflin Company, 1978), 520–21.

20. S. Khrushchev, *Superpower*, 617–20; Dobrynin, *In Confidence*, 86–88; for Theodore Sorensen's acknowledgment that Dobrynin's account was more accurate than Robert Kennedy's memoir, *Thirteen Days*, see Cold War International History Project (CWIHP) *Bulletin 5* (Spring 1995): 78; Jim Hershberg, "More on Bobby and the Cuban Missile Crisis," *ibid.*, 8–9 (Winter 1996/1997): 274, 344–47.

21. Taubman, *Khrushchev*, 574; S. Khrushchev, *Superpower*, 621–22; Fursenko and Naftali, *"One Hell of a Gamble,"* 284–86.

22. Taubman, *Khrushchev*, 575; Fursenko and Naftali, *"One Hell of a Gamble,"* 285; Troyanovsky, "Making of Soviet Foreign Policy," 237.

23. Nikita Khrushchev, *Khrushchev Remembers*, trans. and ed. by Strobe Talbott (Boston: Little, Brown and Company, 1970), 498; Taubman, *Khrushchev*, 574–75; Dobrynin, *In Confidence*, 87–88; S. Khrushchev, *Superpower*, 622–24.

24. Khrushchev to Kennedy, 28 October 1962, *FRUS, 1961–1963*, 6: 183–87; Dobrynin, *In Confidence*, 89–91.

25. Kennedy to Khrushchev, 28 October 1962, *FRUS, 1961–1963*, 6: 187–88.

26. Dobrynin, *In Confidence*, 90; Dobrynin to U.S.S.R. Foreign Ministry, 30 October 1962, CWIHP, *Bulletin 8–9* (Winter 1996/97): 304; Schlesinger, *Robert Kennedy*, 523; James W. Hilty, *Robert Kennedy: Brother Protector* (Philadelphia, Pa.: Temple University Press, 1997), 450–51. In their new book, Fursenko and Naftali claim that Khrushchev had not expected Kennedy to trade the U.S. missiles in Turkey for Soviet missles in Cuba, and hence the tacit deal pleased Khrushchev. See Fursenko and Naftali, *Khrushchev's Cold War*, 490.

27. Interview with Sergei Khrushchev, "Khrushchev byl v 20 minutakh ot voiny s SShA," [Khrushchev Was 20 Minutes Away from War with the USA], *Argumenty i fakty* 49 (8 December 2004): 1258; S. Khrushchev, *Superpower*, 582.

28. Khrushchev to Kennedy, 26 October 1962, *FRUS, 1961–1963*, 6: 174.

29. For the most recent analysis of Khrushchev's motives, see Fursenko and Naftali, *Khrushchev's Cold War*, 409–37, 539–45.

30. Khrushchev to Kennedy, 30 October 1962, *FRUS, 1961–1963*, 6: 196.

31. Khrushchev to Kennedy, 28 October 1962, *ibid.*, 190.

32. Khrushchev to Kennedy, 30 October 1962, *ibid.*, 190–98.

33. Kennedy to Khrushchev, 6 November 1962, *ibid.*, 201–204, quotation on 202; also see Kennedy to

Khrushchev, 15 November 1962, *ibid.*, 212–15; Dobrynin to U.S.S.R. Foreign Ministry, 5 November 1962, CWIHP *Bulletin* 8–9 (Winter 1996/1997), 326; V. V. Kuznetsov and V. A. Zorin to U.S.S.R. Foreign Ministry, 6 November 1962, *ibid.*, 327–28.

34. Zelikow and May, *Kennedy*, 3: 517; Fursenko and Naftali, *"One Hell of a Gamble,"* 287; Dobrynin to U.S.S.R. Foreign Ministry, 12 November 1962, CWIHP, *Bulletin* 8–9 (Winter 1996/1997): 331–32.

35. Quoted in Robert Dallek, *An Unfinished Life: John F. Kennedy, 1917–1963* (Boston: Little, Brown and Company, 2003), 571; also see Kennedy to Khrushchev, 15 November 1962, *FRUS, 1961–1963*, 6: 212–15.

36. Khrushchev to Kennedy, ND [11 November 1962], *FRUS, 1961–1963*, 6: 204–208; Minutes no. 68, 21 November 1962, Malin Notes; see the many Soviet documents in James G. Hershberg, "New Evidence on the Cuban Missile Crisis: More Documents from the Russian Archives," CWIHP *Bulletin* 8–9 (Winter 1996/97): 270–343; Vladislav M. Zubok, "New Evidence on the Cuban Missile Crisis," CWIHP *Bulletin* 5 (Spring 1995): 59, 89–109, 159.

37. Khrushchev to Kennedy, ND [11 November 1962], *FRUS, 1961–1963*, 6: 204–208.

38. Kennedy to Khrushchev, 14 December 1962, *ibid.*, 232; also Kennedy to Khrushchev, 21 November 1962, *ibid.*, 223.

39. Mikoyan, Memorandum of Conversation with Robert Kennedy, 30 November 1962, CWIHP *Bulletin* 8–9 (Winter 1996–97): 335.

40. Cousins, *Improbable Triumvirate*, 39–57, quotations on 39, 44–45, 42–43, 54.

41. Khrushchev to Kennedy, 19 December 1962, 7 January 1963, *FRUS, 1961–1963*, 6: 234–37, 247–49; Record of a Meeting between V. V. Kuznetsov and Kennedy, 9 January 1963, Russian Archives Documents Database (RADD) 208, National Security Archive (NSA); Fursenko and Naftali, *Khrushchev's Cold War*, 504–13.

42. Fursenko and Naftali, *Khrushchev's Cold War*, 358.

43. Memorandum of Conversation, 4 June 1961, *FRUS, 1961–1963: Soviet Union* (Washington, D.C.: Government Printing Office, 1998), 5: 217.

44. Hope M. Harrison, *Driving the Soviets Up the Wall: Soviet-East German Relations, 1953–1961* (Princeton, N.J.: Princeton University Press, 2003), 172–223; Fursenko and Naftali, *Khrushchev's Cold War*, 374–75.

45. For the Nassau Agreement and the Multilateral Force concept, see *FRUS, 1961–1963: Western Europe and Canada* (Washington, D.C.: Government Printing Office, 1994), 13: 1088–1123; Marc Trachtenberg, *A Constructed Peace: The Making of the European Settlement, 1945–1963* (Princeton, N.J.: Princeton University Press, 1999), 305–306, 355–67.

46. Cousins, *Improbable Triumvirate*, 54–55.

47. Khrushchev to Kennedy, 29 December 1962, and Khrushchev and Leonid Brezhnev to Kennedy, 30 December 1962, *FRUS, 1961–1963*, 6: 241–43.

48. S. Khrushchev, *Superpower*, 673; also see Fursenko and Naftali, *Khrushchev's Cold War*, 513.

49. S. Khrushchev, *Superpower*, 670.

50. Quoted in Taubman, *Khrushchev*, 586; also see Khrushchev, *Khrushchev Remembers*, 515–20.

51. "The Statements Made by Khrushchev at the Session of the Presidium of the CC," 10 September 1963, Malin Notes.

52. Khrushchev Speech to the CPSU Central Committee Plenum, 14 February 1964, esp. p. 56, located in box 217, USSR, National Security Files (NSF), Lyndon Baines Johnson Library (LBJL), University of Texas (Austin, Texas). What Khrushchev said to the presidium in private was what he said publicly in many speeches. See, for example, his speech at the Moscow election meeting, 27 February 1963, FBIS, 28 February 1963, BB 1–22.

53. Khrushchev Speech to the CPSU Central Committee Plenum, 14 February 1964, pp. 53–55, box 217, USSR, NSF, LBJL; Khrushchev, *Khrushchev Remembers*, 515–20. The CIA understood

Khrushchev's intentions. See, for example, NIE 11-4-63, "Soviet Military Capabilities and Policies, 1962–1967," Donald P. Steury, ed., *Intentions and Capabilities: Estimates on Soviet Strategic Forces, 1950–1983* (Washington, D.C.: Central Intelligence Agency, 1996), 147–67; Fursenko and Naftali, *Khrushchev's Cold War*, 543.

54. For the insertion of the missiles in Cuba, see Troyanovsky, "Making of Soviet Foreign Policy," 234–37; Taubman, *Khrushchev*, 529–77; Fursenko and Naftali, "*One Hell of a Gamble*"; for reductions in theater forces and military manpower, see NIE 11-4-63, "Soviet Military Capabilities and Policies, 1962–1967," 162–66; also the charts and figures, in Noel E. Firth and James H. Noren, *Soviet Defense Spending: A History of CIA Estimates, 1950–1990* (College Station: Texas A & M University Press, 1998), 111; U.S. Arms Control and Disarmament Agency, *World Military Expenditures and Arms Trade, 1963–1973* (Washington, D.C.: Government Printing Office, 1975), 56.

55. Fursenko and Naftali, *Khrushchev's Cold War*, 388–437.

56. S. Khrushchev, *Superpower*, 656; Khrushchev, *Khrushchev Remembers*, 515–20; Troyanovsky, "Making of Soviet Foreign Policy," 238.

57. Lawrence S. Wittner, *Resisting the Bomb: A History of the World Nuclear Disarmament Movement, 1954–1970* (Stanford, Calif.: Stanford University Press, 1997), 335–421; for background see Robert A. Divine, *Blowing on the Wind: The Nuclear Test Ban Debate, 1954–1960* (New York: Oxford University Press, 1978).

58. Message from Soviet Foreign Ministry to Dobrynin, 1 April 1963, *FRUS, 1961–1963*, 6: 250–62, quotation on 261; for Robert Kennedy's reaction, see Robert Kennedy to John Kennedy, 3 April 1963, *ibid.*, 262–65.

59. Cousins, *Improbable Triumvirate*, 81–90.

60. *Ibid.*, 90–101.

61. *Ibid.*, 101–102.

62. *Ibid.*, 105.

63. Khrushchev interview with editor in chief of *Il Giorno*, 23 April 1963, FBIS, 24 April 1964, esp. BB 14 and 15, located in box 188, USSR, NSF, John F. Kennedy Library (JFKL), Boston, Mass.

64. *Ibid.*, BB 10, 6.

65. *Ibid.*, BB 14.

66. For a transcript of the conversation between Khrushchev and Indira Gandhi, in late July 1963, see CIA, Information Report No. EO 12958, 1 October 1963, located in box 188, USSR, NSF, JFKL.

67. Khrushchev interview, 23 April 1963, FBIS, 24 April 1963, BB 15, *ibid.*

68. *Ibid.*, BB 18.

69. Conversation between Khrushchev and U Thant, 28 August 1962, *Istochnik* 6 (2003): 150–59, quotations on 155–56.

70. *Ibid.*, 155–57.

71. Government of India, Planning Commission, *Second Five-Year Plan* (New Delhi, 1956), 23, 22; also see David C. Engerman, "The Romance of Economic Development and New Histories of the Cold War," *Diplomatic History* 28 (January 2004): 23–54; Odd Arne Westad, *The Global Cold War: Third World Interventions and the Making of Our Times* (Cambridge, Eng.: Cambridge University Press, 2005), 73–109; Forrest D. Colburn, *The Vogue of Revolution in Poor Countries* (Princeton, N.J.: Princeton University Press, 1994).

72. Khrushchev's Radio Speech, 27 May 1964, FBIS, 28 May 1964, BB 13; Khrushchev Speech, 16 September 1964, FBIS, 17 September 1964, BB 13; Khrushchev's remarks to the presidium of the CC of the CPSU, 27 June 1964, *Istochnik* 6 (2003): 182–84; Khrushchev to Fidel Castro, 31 January 1963, RADD 326, NSA.

73. Memorandum of Conversation, 3 June 1961, *FRUS, 1961–1963*, 5: 174–78, quotation on 177.

74. Dobrynin, *In Confidence*, 92.

75. Stenographic Notes of the Session of the CC of the CPSU, 7 June 1963, Malin Notes; Cousins, *Improbable Triumvirate*, 96; conclusion of Khrushchev's speech to the presidium of the CC of the CPSU, 13 December 1963, RADD 1437, NSA; Speech by B. N. Ponomarev, 13 December 1963, RADD 1434, NSA; Thomas L. Hughes to Dean Rusk, 4 June 1963, box 2, Undersecretary of State for Political Affairs, Subject Files, 1961–1963, Records of the Department of State, Record Group (RG) 59, National Archives (NA); for background on the Sino-Soviet split, see, for example, Odd Arne Westad, ed., *Brothers in Arms: The Rise and Fall of the Sino-Soviet Alliance, 1945–1963* (Washington, D.C.: Woodrow Wilson International Center, 1998).

76. Speech by Ponomarev, 13 December 1963, RADD 1434, NSA; B. N. Ponomarev, *Selected Speeches and Writings* (Oxford: Pergamon Press, 1981), 82–104.

77. See Khrushchev's very revealing remarks to Cousins, *Improbable Triumvirate*, 108–10; for Khrushchev's background, see especially Taubman, *Khrushchev*, 72–207; Iurii Shapoval, "The Ukrainian Years," in *Nikita Khrushchev*, ed. by Taubman, S. Khrushchev, and Gleason, 8–43. "My arms are up to my elbows in blood. That is the most terrible thing that lies in my soul," Khrushchev said in retirement. See William Taubman, "How a Speech Won the Cold War," *New York Times*, 25 February 2006.

78. Stenographic Notes of the Presidium of the CC of the CPSU, 25 April 1963, Malin Notes; Minutes no. 101a, 13 June 1963, *ibid.*; Fursenko and Naftali, *Khrushchev's Cold War*, 522–26.

79. Taubman, *Khrushchev*, 578–619; Roy Medvedev, *Khrushchev: A Biography*, trans. by Brian Pearce (Garden City, N.Y.: Anchor Books, 1984), 213–22.

80. "Television and Radio Interview," 17 December 1962, *Public Papers of the Presidents: John F. Kennedy, 1962* (hereafter cited as *PPP: Kennedy, year*, page) (Washington, D.C.: Government Printing Office, 1963), 900.

81. *Ibid.*, 898.

82. *Ibid.*, 900.

83. "Annual Message to the Congress on the State of the Union," 14 January 1963, *PPP: Kennedy, 1963*, 15.

84. *Ibid.*, 17–18; for the Sino-Soviet split, see CIA, OCI No. 0581/63, "Sino-Soviet Relations at a New Crisis," 14 January 1963, box 180, USSR, NSF, JFKL.

85. For the quotation, see Kennedy's inaugural address, *PPP: Kennedy, 1961*, pp. 1–3; for illuminating accounts of Kennedy and his administration, see Dallek, *An Unfinished Life*; Michael O'Brien, *John F. Kennedy: A Biography* (New York: Thomas Dunne/St. Martin's Press, 2005); Robert D. Dean, *Imperial Manhood: Gender and the Making of Cold War Foreign Policy* (Amherst: University of Massachusetts Press, 2000); Richard Reeves, *President Kennedy: Profile of Power* (New York: Simon and Schuster, 1993); Nigel Hamilton, *JFK: Reckless Youth* (New York: Random House, 1992); John D. Fair, "The Intellectual JFK: Lessons in Statesmanship from British History," *Diplomatic History* 30 (January 2006): 119–42.

86. "Television and Radio Interview," 17 December 1962, *PPP: Kennedy, 1962*, 900.

87. Arthur M. Schlesinger, Jr., to Theodore Sorensen, 2 January 1963, box 327, Meetings and Memoranda, NSF, JFKL.

88. For key parts of Khrushchev's speech, see Jussi Hahnimaki and Odd Arne Westad, eds., *The Cold War: A History in Documents and Eyewitness Accounts* (Oxford, Eng.: Oxford University Press, 2003), 358–60; for Kennedy's preoccupation, see, for example, "Summary of Kennedy's Remarks to the National Security Council (NSC)," 18 January 1962, *FRUS, 1961–1963: National Security Policy* (Washington, D.C.: Government Printing Office, 1996), 8: 239–40; for the resonance of Khrushchev's remarks, see Memorandum for the Record, regarding Robert Kennedy's remarks to students and faculty of the interdepartmental seminar, 22 April 1963, box 315, Meetings and Memoranda, NSF, JFKL.

89. Stephen C. Rabe, *The Most Dangerous Area in the World: John F. Kennedy Confronts Communist Revolution in Latin America* (Chapel Hill: University of North Carolina Press, 1999).

90. See the many documents in boxes 1 and 2, Records of the Under Secretary for Political Affairs, Subject Files, 1961–1963, HM 1993, Records of the Department of State, RG 59, NA.

91. For the quotation, see "Record of Meeting of NSC," 22 January 1963, *FRUS, 1961–1963*, 8: 460; for background to Kennedy's statement, see Memorandum for the President, by Komer, 19 January 1963, box 314, NSF, JFKL; for the importance of the contest in less developed countries, see "Highlights from the Secretary of State's Policy Planning Meeting," 26 March 1963, *FRUS, 1961–1963*, 5: 658.

92. For Robert Kennedy's discussion of his brother's views on Vietnam, see Edwin O. Guthman and Jeffrey Shulman, eds., *Robert F. Kennedy in His Own Words* (New York: Bantam Books, 1988), 394–95; for background on Kennedy and Vietnam, see especially David Kaiser, *American Tragedy: Kennedy, Johnson, and the Origins of the Vietnam War* (Cambridge, Mass.: Harvard University Press, 2000), 1–212; Gareth Porter, *Perils of Dominance: Imbalance of Power and the Road to War in Vietnam* (Berkeley: University of California Press, 2005), 141–79; Howard Jones, *Death of a Generation: How the Assassinations of Diem and JFK Prolonged the Vietnam War* (New York: Oxford University Press, 2003).

93. "Summary Record of NSC Meeting," 13 March 1963, *FRUS, 1961–1963: Cuban Missile Crisis and Aftermath* (Washington, D.C.: Government Printing Office, 1996), 11: 715–18; "Summary Record of Meeting of the Standing Group of the NSC," 23 April 1963, *ibid.*, 780–81; Memorandum for the Record, by Desmond Fitzgerald, 19 June 1963, *ibid.*, 837–38; Memorandum for the Record, 12 November 1963, *ibid.*, 883–85; Sherman Kent, Memorandum for the Director [of the CIA], "Cuba a Year Hence," 22 April 1963, box 315, Meetings and Memoranda, NSF, JFKL; also see Don Bohning, *The Castro Obsession: U.S. Covert Operations Against Cuba, 1959–1965* (Washington, D.C.: Potomac Books, 2005).

94. Memorandum of Conversation, 26 April 1963, box 187, USSR, NSF, JFKL.

95. Tape, "Briefing on Foreign Policy for Legislative Leaders," 8 January 1963, Presidential Recordings Project, Miller Center, University of Virginia (hereafter cited as PRP, MC).

96. *Ibid*; William Burr and Jeffrey T. Richelson, "Whether to 'Strangle the Baby in the Cradle': The United States and the Chinese Nuclear Program, 1960–1964," *International Security* 25 (Winter 2000/2001): 54–99.

97. National Intelligence Estimate (NIE) 13–63, "Problems and Prospects in Communist China," 1 May 1963, box 4, NIEs, NSF, LBJL.

98. Erin Mahan, *Kennedy, DeGaulle, and Western Europe* (Hampshire, Eng.: Palgrave/Macmillan, 2002), 128–62; Ronald J. Granieri, *The Ambivalent Alliance: Konrad Adenauer, the CDU/CSU, and the West, 1949–1966* (New York: Berghahn Books, 2003), 150–90; *FRUS, 1961–1963*, 13: 739–61; Hans Peter-Schwarz, *Konrad Adenauer, the Statesman, 1952–1967*, trans. by Geoffrey Penny (Providence, R.I.: Berghahn Books, 1997), 662–76; Jeffrey Glenn Giauque, *Grand Designs and Visions of Unity: The Atlantic Powers and the Reorganization of Western Europe, 1955–1963* (Chapel Hill: University of North Carolina Press, 2002), 158–237; Tony Judt, *Postwar* (New York: Penguin Press, 2005), 278–92.

99. "Summary Record of NSC Executive Committee Meeting," 25 January 1963, *FRUS, 1961–1963*, 13: 487–91.

100. McGeorge Bundy to director of Central Intelligence, 1 February 1963, NSAM 219, Records of the NSC, RG 273, NA.

101. For the quotations, see Memorandum for the Record, 18 January 1963, box 317, Memoranda and Meetings, NSF, JFKL; "Notes of January 12 Meeting with the President re Nassau Implementation," by John McNaughton, 14 January 1963, box 5, Records of the Deputy Assistant Secretary for

Political-Military Affairs, 1961–1963, MLR 3063A, RG 59, NA; also see "Notes on Remarks by President Kennedy before the NSC," by CIA reporter, 22 January 1963, box 314, NSF, JFKL; Trachtenberg, *A Constructed Peace*, 302–21.

102. Jeffrey Kitchen to Rusk, 11 January 1963, box 5, Deputy Assistant Secretary for Political-Military Affairs, MLR 3063A, RG 59; also see Memorandum, by Kitchen, 27 December 1962, box 4, *ibid.*; for McNamara's quotation, see Secretary of Defense Staff Meeting, 7 January 1963, box 23, Maxwell Taylor Papers, Records of the Joint Chiefs of Staff, RG 218, NA.

103. Harriman to Kennedy, 23 January 1963, Harriman Papers. I am indebted to Kai Bird for sharing this document with me. Frank Costigliola illuminates U.S. officials' worries about the evolution of German power in "Lyndon B. Johnson, Germany and the 'End of the Cold War' " in *Lyndon Johnson Confronts the World: American Foreign Policy, 1963–1968*, ed. by Warren I. Cohen and Nancy Bernkopf Tucker (New York: Cambridge University Press, 1994), 173–92.

104. For the decision to explore the possibility of an MLF, see *FRUS, 1961–1963*, 13: 487–511; for Kennedy's attitude toward discussions with the Soviets regarding Berlin and Germany, see Memorandum of Conversation, 15 February 1963, *FRUS, 1961–1963*, 15: 486–88; for overall policy toward Western Europe, see the important paper (untitled) written by David Bruce, 9 February 1963, box 314, NSF, JFKL; also Editorial Note, *FRUS, 1961–1963*, 188–89.

105. Meeting with the Joint Chiefs of Staff, 15 January 1963, PRP, MC.

106. Editorial Notes, *FRUS, 1961–1963*, 5: 596–97, 664; Fursenko and Naftali, *Khrushchev's Cold War*, 517.

107. "Test-Ban, Disarmament Talks Reopen Under GOP Fire," *Congressional Quarterly Weekly Report*, 15 February 1963, 176; "Geneva Talks Continue Amidst U.S. Political Rumbling," 19 April 1963, *ibid.*, 634; Erin Mahan, "Public Opinion and Détente During the Kennedy Administration," unpublished research paper.

108. Theodore C. Sorensen, *Kennedy* (New York: Bantam, 1965), 822–23; Arthur M. Schlesinger, Jr., *A Thousand Days: John F. Kennedy in the White House* (Greenwich, Conn.: Fawcett/Houghton Mifflin, 1965), 821–23.

109. "Commencement Address at American University," 10 June 1963, *PPP: Kennedy, 1963*, 459–64.

110. For Khrushchev's praise of the speech in his conversations with Harriman, Paul Henri-Spaak, and Indira Gandhi, see Harriman to Rusk, 27 July 1963, box 187 (Gromyko Talks–Harriman), USSR, NSF, JFKL; Bohlen to Rusk, 11 July 1963, box 187 (Khrushchev-Spaak), *ibid.*; Transcript of conversation between Khrushchev, Gandhi, and Kaul, [late July 1963], box 188 (Freeman and Gandhi/Kaul), *ibid.*

111. Editorial Note, *FRUS, 1961–1963*, 7: 656; Memorandum of Conversation, by Harriman, 29 April 1963, box 315, Meetings and Memoranda, NSF, JFKL.

112. Cousins, *Improbable Triumvirate*, 114–22; Memorandum of Conversation, 22 April 1963, box 188, NSF, JFKL.

113. Memorandum of Conversation, by Harriman, 26 April 1963, box 315, Meetings and Memoranda, NSF, JFKL; Glenn T. Seaborg, *Kennedy, Khrushchev, and the Test Ban* (Berkeley: University of California Press, 1981), 204–205.

114. "Highlights from the Secretary of State's Policy Planning Meeting," 26 March 1963, *FRUS, 1961–1963*, 5: 654–60, quotation on 656; NIE 11-4-63, "Soviet Military Capabilities and Policies, 1962–1967," 22 March 1963, *ibid.*, 8: 469–77, quotation on 471; also see NIE 11-63, "Main Trends in Soviet Foreign Policy," 22 May 1963, *ibid.*, 685–701.

115. For the quotation, see William Manchester, *One Brief Shining Moment: Remembering Kennedy* (Boston: Little, Brown and Company, 1983), 215; for Kennedy's confidence in U.S. strategic superiority, see, for example, the taped conversation with McNamara, Maxwell Taylor, and others, "Meeting on Defense Budget," 5 December 1962, PRP, MC.

116. For the inaugural address, 20 January 1961, see *PPP: Kennedy, 1961*, 1–3.

117. NIE 10-63, "Bloc Economic and Military Assistance Programs," 10 January 1963, box 1, NIEs, NSF, LBJL; Memoranda for the Record, by Robert Komer, 2, 8 May 1963, box 322, Meetings and Memoranda, NSF, JFKL.

118. Memorandum for the President, by Komer, 19 January 1963, box 314, *ibid.*; for Hughes's views, see Hughes to Rusk, 28 May 1963 and 12 July 1963, box 2, Records of the Undersecretary for Political Affairs, 1961–1963, MLR 3055A, RG 59, NA; also see Memorandum of Conversation between French and U.S. Officials, 10 June 1963, *ibid.*

119. "Highlights from the Secretary of State's Policy Planning Meeting," 26 March 1963, *FRUS, 1961–1963*, 5: 654–60; NIE 11-63, "Main Trends in Soviet Foreign Policy," 22 May 1963, *ibid.*, 685–701.

120. "Record of Meeting of the NSC," 22 January 1963, *ibid.*, 8: 462, including footnote 6; also see Kennedy to Harriman, 15 July 1963, *ibid.*, 7: 801; also see Kennedy Meeting with Vasili Kuznetsov, 9 January 1963, RADD 208, NSA; Burr and Richelson, "Whether to 'Strangle the Baby in the Cradle,' " 54–99.

121. " 'Peace' Groups, Active in 1962, Look Toward 1964," *Congressional Quarterly, Weekly Report* 20 (2 November 1962): 2101.

122. "Outlook for Peace," 4 January 1963, George H. Gallup, *The Gallup Poll: Public Opinion, 1935–1971* (New York: Random House, 1972), 3: 1797; "Outlook for Peace," 5 July 1963, *ibid.*, 1826; for background, also see Wittner, *Struggle Against the Bomb*, 370–414.

123. *FRUS, 1961–1963*, 7: 753–54, 783–84, 802, 821, 829–31.

124. NIE 11-63, "Main Trends in Soviet Foreign Policy," 22 May 1963, *ibid.*, 5: 685–701, esp. 697, 699.

125. "Highlights from the Secretary of State's Policy Planning Meeting," 26 March 1963, *ibid.*, 654–60.

126. *Ibid.*, 7: 728–863; *ibid.*, 5: 712–13; for Khrushchev's approach, see "Stenographic Notes of the Presidium of the CC of the CPSU," 25 April 1963, Malin Notes.

127. Harriman to Rusk, 23 July 1963, box 187 (Gromyko Talks–Harriman), USSR, NSF, JFKL; Rusk to Department of State, 10 August 1963, *FRUS, 1961–1963*, 5: 748.

128. Rusk to Department of State, 5 August 1963, *FRUS, 1961–1963*, 5: 733; Memorandum of Conversation between Orville L. Freeman and Khrushchev, 30 July 1963, box 188, USSR, NSF, JFKL; Harriman to Rusk, 26 July 1963, box 187, *ibid.*; Harriman to Department of State, 15, 22 and 23 July 1963, *FRUS, 1961–1963*, 7: 799–800, 824–26, 833; regarding trade, see the Memorandum of Conversation, 8 August 1963, *ibid.*, 5: 738–40.

129. Rusk to Department of State, 5 August 1963, *ibid.*, 5: 731; for Thompson's quotation, see Editorial Note, *ibid.*, 5: 750.

130. Memorandum of Conversation between Dobrynin and Kennedy, 26 August 1963, *ibid.*, 751–55; Memorandum, "Outlook for Future Discussions," by Harriman, 30 July 1963, box 480, Harriman Papers, LC.

131. "Statements Made by N. S. Khrushchev at the Session of the Presidium of the CC of the CPSU," 10 September 1963, Malin Notes; also see Minutes no. 107, 23 July 1963, Minutes no. 113, 4 September 1963, Minutes no. 114, 10 September 1963, *ibid.*; for quotation, see Khrushchev to Kennedy, 10 September 1963, *FRUS, 1961–1963*, 6: 306–307; also see Fursenko and Naftali, *Khrushchev's Cold War*, 510.

132. Dallek, *An Unfinished Life*, 628–29; Michael Beschloss, *Kennedy v. Khrushchev: The Crisis Years, 1960–1963* (London: Faber and Faber, 1991), 631–37; *FRUS, 1961–1963*, 7: 783, 802, 821–22.

133. For the wheat deal, see "Summary Record of the NSC Meeting," 1 October 1963, *FRUS, 1961–1963*, 5: 774–78; Memorandum of Conversation, 23 October, *ibid.*, 796*ff*; for criticism, see "President Approves Private Wheat Sales to Soviet Bloc," *Congressional Quarterly, Weekly Report* 21 (11 October 1963): 1760; "Communist Wheat Deal Provokes Mixed Reactions," *ibid.*, 21 (18 October 1963): 1804.

134. "Address Before the 18th General Assembly of the United Nations," 20 September 1963, *PPP: Kennedy, 1963*, 693–98, quotation on 694; for his previous view on winning the space race, see his taped conversation with James Webb, 21 November 1962, PRC, MC.

135. Schwarz, *Adenauer*, 692–93; Kennedy to Adenauer, 6 August 1963, *FRUS, 1961–1963*, 7: 870–71; also see Kennedy to de Gaulle, 25 July 1963, *ibid.*, 851–53.

136. Rusk to Department of State, 10 August 1963, *FRUS, 1961–1963*, 7: 875; Memorandum for the Record, 25 October 1963, *ibid.*, 15: 618; also see Rusk's talks with French Foreign Minister Couve de Murville, 7 October 1963, *ibid.*, 587–90. In cordial talks with Gromyko, Rusk also stressed that the United States was not prepared to acknowledge the division of Germany or formally accept the existing borders. Memorandum of Conversation, 2 October 1963, box 187, USSR, NSF, JFKL.

137. "Remarks at Dinner of the Protestant Council of the City of New York," 8 November 1963, *PPP: Kennedy, 1962*, 838–41.

138. For the quotation, see Komer to Bundy, 16 October 1963, box 322, Meetings and Memoranda, NSF, JFKL; Komer to Bundy, 15 October 1963, *ibid.*; Memorandum of Conversation between Gromyko and Rusk, 3 October 1963, box 187, USSR, *ibid.*; for Vietnam and Laos, see also Memorandum of Conversation between Khrushchev and Harriman, 26 April 1963, box 187, *ibid.*; Thompson to Rusk, 20 May 1963, box 185, *ibid.*; S. Khrushchev, *Superpower*, 695; Fursenko and Naftali, *Khrushchev's Cold War*, 542.

139. "Summary Record of NSC Meeting," 31 July 1963, box 314, Meetings and Memoranda, NSF, JFKL; SNIE 13-4-63, "Possibilities of Greater Militancy by the Chinese Communists," 31 July 1963, box 4, NIEs, NSF, LBJL.

140. Komer to Bundy, 16 October 1963, box 322, Meetings and Memoranda, NSF, JFKL.

141. For Nixon's criticism, see "President Approves Private Wheat Sales to Soviet Bloc," 1760; for Goldwater, see "Foreign Trade: Impasse on Wheat," *Time*, 11 October 1963, 30.

142. Komer to Bundy, 15 October 1963, box 322, Meetings and Memoranda, NSF, JFKL.

143. "Remarks in the Rudolph Wilde Platz," 26 June 1963, *PPP: Kennedy, 1963*, 524–25.

144. "Address at the University of Maine," 19 October 1963, *ibid.*, 795–96.

145. For the quotations, see *ibid.*, 796; "Address Before the 18th General Assembly of the United Nations," 20 September 1963, *ibid.*, 694.

146. Memorandum of Conversation between Dobrynin and Thompson, 21 November 1963, *FRUS, 1961–1963*, 5: 829–30; Dobrynin, *In Confidence*, 113–14; Andrei Gromyko, *Memoirs*, trans. by Harold Shukman (New York: Doubleday, 1989), 181–82.

147. Rostow to Rusk, 17 September 1963, *FRUS, 1961–1963*, 8: 507–10.

148. Thompson to Bohlen, 21 September 1963, box 72, France—General, NSF, JFKL; Memorandum of Conversation between Kennedy and George McGhee, 19 September 1963, *FRUS, 1961–1963*, 15: 578; Department of State to Embassy in Germany, 24 September 1963, *ibid.*, 581–82; for the quotation, see Memorandum of Conversation between Couve de Murville and Rusk, 7 October 1963, *ibid.*, 588.

149. These different possibilities are illuminated in "Highlights from Secretary of State's Policy Planning Meeting," 26 March 1963, *ibid.*, 5: 654–60.

150. S. Khrushchev, *Superpower*, 698; Talbott, *Khrushchev Remembers*, 500; also see Kohler to Department of State, 23 November 1963, *FRUS, 1961–1963*, 5: 831.

151. Sergei Khrushchev, *Khrushchev on Khrushchev: An Inside Account of the Man and His Era*, ed. and trans. by William Taubman (Boston: Little, Brown and Company, 1990), 50–51; S. Khrushchev, *Superpower*, 700; Schecter with Luchkov, *Khrushchev Remembers: Glasnost Tapes*, 181; Troyanovsky, "Making of Soviet Foreign Policy," 229–41.

152. Khrushchev to Johnson, 24 November 1963, *FRUS, 1961–1963*, 6: 311–13.

153. Jacqueline Kennedy to Khrushchev, 1 December 1963, *ibid.*, 314; also see Kohler to Department of State, 23 November 1963, *ibid.*, 5: 831.

154. Khrushchev to Johnson, 24 November 1963, *ibid.*, 6: 311–13; Thompson to Rusk, 24 November 1963, *ibid.*, 5: 832–33; Memorandum of Conversation, 26 November 1963, *ibid.*, 833–37.

155. Speech at Kalinin textile factory, 17 January 1964, FBIS, 20 January 1964, BB 22.

156. Minutes no. 122a, no. 126b, no. 128a, 10 November 1963, 23 December 1963, 9 January 1964, Malin Notes; Concluding Speech at CPSU Central Committee plenum, 13 December 1963, located in box 217, USSR, NSF, JFKL.

157. Speech at Kalinin textile factory, 17 January 1964, FBIS, 20 January 1964, BB 18; Concluding Speech at CPSU Central Committee plenum, 13 December 1963, located in box 217, USSR, NSF, JFKL.

158. Speech at Kalinin textile factory, 17 January 1964, FBIS, 20 January 1964, BB 21.

159. *Ibid.*

160. For the quotation, see oral message from Khrushchev, 15 May 1964, *FRUS, 1964–1968: The Soviet Union* (Washington, D.C.: Government Printing Office, 2001), 14: 71, footnote 3; for the letters, see Khrushchev Message to World Leaders, 31 December 1963, FBIS, 6 January 1964, BB 1–12; Khrushchev to Johnson, 11 February 1964, *FRUS, 1964–1968: Arms Control and Disarmament* (Washington, D.C.: Government Printing Office, 1997), 11: 31–34; Khrushchev to Johnson, 2 April 1964, *ibid.*, 14: 49–52; Khrushchev to Johnson, 17 and 20 April 1964, *ibid.*, 11: 47–50, 50–53; Khrushchev to Johnson, 5 June 1964, *ibid.*, 14: 85–94.

161. Khrushchev to Johnson, 2 April 1964, *FRUS, 1964–1968*, 14: 49–52, quotation on 49.

162. Khrushchev to Johnson, 5 June 1964, *ibid.*, 85–94, quotations on 86 and 89.

163. Blair to Department of State, 3 March 1964, box 1, Memos to the President, NSF, LBJL.

164. For Khrushchev's views on Germany, as described in the following paragraphs, see, for example, Khrushchev to Johnson, 5 June 1964, *FRUS, 1964–1968*, 14: 85–94; Speech at Soviet–German Democratic Republic Friendship Meeting, 12 June 1964, located in box 228, USSR, NSF, LBJL; references to Germany in Khrushchev's talks with Japanese parliamentary leaders, 15 September 1964, FBIS, 21 September 1964, BB 1–9; Khrushchev's address to graduates of military academies, 8 July 1964, FBIS, 9 July 1964, CC 1–9; see also *FRUS, 1964–1968: Germany and Berlin* (Washington, D.C.: Government Printing Office, 1999), 15: 8–18, 142–44, 191–94, 204–207, 210–12, 322–23, 335–39.

165. For Adzhubei's visit to the FRG, see Douglas Selvage, "The Warsaw Pact and Nuclear Non-Proliferation, 1963–1965," CWIHP Working Paper No. 32 (Washington, D.C.: Woodrow Wilson International Center, 2001), 9–12; for Adzhubei and Khrushchev, see S. Khrushchev, *Superpower*, 706–14; for Khrushchev's consideration of rapprochement and acceptance of the MLF, see Memorandum [from Soviet Government to Polish Government], October 1963, in Selvage, "Warsaw Pact and Nonproliferation," 20–21.

166. Address to military graduates, 8 July 1964, FBIS, 9 July 1964, CC 1–9, quotation on CC-3; also see Khrushchev's letter to world leaders, 31 December 1963, *ibid.*, 6 January 1964, BB 1–12.

167. Conflating quotations from different speeches: speech at Kalinin textile factory, 17 January 1964, FBIS, 20 January 1964, BB 22; Khrushchev speech at World Youth Forum, 19 September 1964, FBIS, 22 September 1964, BB 10–11; Khrushchev speech to CC Plenum, 13 December 1963, p. 31, in box 217, USSR, NSF, LBJL.

168. Khrushchev Speech, World Youth Forum, 19 September 1964, FBIS, 22 September 1964, esp. BB 11–12.

169. Khrushchev to Johnson, 5 June 1964, *FRUS, 1964–1968*, 14: 92–93.

170. "Stenographic Notes of the Session of the Presidium of the CC of the CPSU," 19 August 1964, Malin Notes.

171. Speech, 19 September 1964, FBIS, 22 September 1964, BB 9, 12; also see his speech to the CC of the CPSU, 13 December 1963, in box 217, USSR, NSF, LBJL; Speech at the CC of the CPSU,

14 February 1964, *ibid.*; Remarks regarding the economy, by Khrushchev, 22 Sept 1964, *Istochnik* 6 (2003): 183-89.

172. Memorandum, ND [October 1963], Selvage, "Warsaw Pact and Nonproliferation," 20-21; Excerpts from Discussion between Kuznetsov and the SED Politburo, 14 October 1963, *ibid.*, 30-35; Gomulka to Khrushchev, 8 October 1963, *ibid.*, 22-29; Memorandum of Discussion at the Session of the Political Consultative Committee of the Warsaw Pact Member States, ND [20 January 1965], *ibid.*, 36-39.

173. Conversation between Mao Zedong and the Head of the Cultural Group of the Laotian Patriotic Front Sangsiv, 4 September 1964, in *77 Conversations Between Chinese and Foreign Leaders on the Wars in Indochina, 1964-1977*, ed. by Odd Arne Westad et al. (Washington, D.C.: CWIHP Working Paper No. 22, 1998), 70; Record of Conversation between Romanian Prime Minister Ion Maurer and Zhou Enlai, 28 September 1964, document prepared and translated for the Conference "New Central and East European Evidence on the Cold War in Asia," 31 October-1 November 2003, deposited at the NSA.

174. Gomulka to Khrushchev, 8 October 1963, Selvage, "Warsaw Pact and Nonproliferation," 27-28.

175. Khrushchev speech to graduates of military academies, 8 July 1964, FBIS, 9 July 1964, CC 3; Khrushchev to Johnson, 5 August 1964, *FRUS, 1964-1968: Vietnam, 1964* (Washington, D.C.: Government Printing Office, 1992), 1: 636-38; Khrushchev comments, 28 August 1964, FBIS, 31 August 1964, BB 4; Dobrynin, *In Confidence*, 115-16.

176. Khrushchev's response to questions, 3 August 1964, FBIS, 4 August 1964, BB 13-14.

177. For a wonderful illustration of the disillusionment, see Romanian Record of Conversation between Maurer and Mao, 8 October 1964, document prepared and translated for the Conference "New Central and East European Evidence on the Cold War in Asia," 31 October-1 November 2003, deposited at the NSA.

178. Medvedev, *Khrushchev*, 226-27; Fedor Burlatsky, *Khrushchev and the First Russian Spring*, trans. by Daphne Skillen (London: Weidenfeld and Nicolson, 1991), 196-200; Doklad Prezidiuma Ts K KPSS na oktiabr'skom Plenume Ts K KPSS (variant) [Report of the Presidium of the CC of the CPSU at the October Plenum], 14 October 1964, esp. 1-7, RADD 3292, NSA.

179. Report of the Presidium, 14 October 1964, 7-24, RADD 3292, NSA.

180. *Ibid.*, 31-45.

181. *Ibid.*, 38-45.

182. Meeting of the CC CPSU, ND [14 October 1964], Malin's notes.

183. *Ibid.*; reflections by P. E. Shelest, "Reminiscences of a Participant About Difficult Times in the Country's History: About Khrushchev, Brezhnev, and Others," *Argumenty i fakty* 4 (14-20 January 1989): 5-6; S. Khrushchev, *Superpower*, 734-36; Fursenko and Naftali, *Khrushchev's Cold War*, 532-38.

184. Brezhnev speech in Red Square honoring crew of Voskhod, 19 October 1964, FBIS, 20 October 1964, CC 11; Memorandum of Conversation between Dobrynin and Johnson, 16 October 1964, *FRUS, 1964-1968*, 14: 127; Kohler to Rusk, 23 October 1964, *ibid.*, 152-56.

185. Regarding Brezhnev, see Georgi Arbatov, *The System: An Insider's Life in Soviet Politics* (New York: Random House, 1992), 171, 248; Georgi Arbatov, "My obankrotili America" ["We Bankrupted America"], *Argumenty i fakty* 8 (21 February 2001): 1061; Kosygin, "The Day of Deliverance," 7 May 1965, in A. S. Kosygin, *Selected Speeches and Writings* (Oxford, Eng.: Pergamon Press, 1981), 37; for background on Brezhnev, also see chap. 4, infra.

186. Kosygin reception speech for cosmonauts, 19 October 1964, FBIS, 20 October 1964, CC 14-15.

187. For the quotation, see Intelligence and Research Report, "The Fall of Khrushchev," 4 November 1964, box 54, Komer Files, NSF, LBJL; also see Kohler to Rusk, 17 October 1964, *FRUS,*

1964–1968, 14: 132–35; Memorandum, by the CIA, 22 October 1964, *ibid.*, 148–50; Briefing, by Thompson, 22 October 1964, *ibid.*, 144–48; John Huizenga, "Thoughts on the Meaning of the Moscow Events," 19 October 1964, box 219, USSR, NSF, LBJL; CIA, Intelligence Information Cable, "CPSU Document on Khrushchev's Ouster," 2 November 1964, *ibid.*

188. Memorandum for the Record, by Ray S. Cline, 16 October 1964, *FRUS, 1964–1968*, 14: 124–25.

189. Memorandum of Conversation between Johnson and Dobrynin, 16 October 1964, *ibid.*, 127–30; for the importance attached to preserving peace and avoiding nuclear holocaust, see Memorandum to the President, 5 December 1963, by Bundy, *FRUS, 1961–1963*, 8: 540–42; "Summary Record of the Meeting of the NSC," 5 December 1963, *ibid.*, 543–44.

190. In the paragraphs that follow regarding Johnson's upbringing and early career, see Robert Caro, *The Years of Lyndon Johnson*, 3 vols. (New York: Knopf, 1992); Robert Dallek, *Lone Star Rising: Lyndon Johnson and His Times, 1908–1960* (New York: Oxford University Press, 1991); Paul R. Conkin, *Big Daddy from the Pedernales: Lyndon Baines Johnson* (Boston: Twayne Publishers, 1986), 1–86; Randall B. Woods, *LBJ: Architect of American Ambition* (New York: The Free Press, 2006).

191. Quoted in Robert Dallek, *Flawed Giant: Lyndon Johnson and His Times* (New York: Oxford University Press, 1998), 6.

192. Schlesinger, *A Thousand Days*, 50–63.

193. Lyndon B. Johnson, *The Vantage Point: Perspectives of the Presidency, 1963–1969* (New York: Holt, Rinehart and Winston, 1971), 18–25; Dallek, *Flawed Giant*, 50–62; Woods, *LBJ*, 375–429.

194. Memorandum of Conversation between Johnson and Dobrynin, 17 April 1964, *FRUS, 1964–1968*, 14: 65; Dobrynin, *In Confidence*, 117–20.

195. Tapes of telephone conversation, (separate) conversations with McNamara, Bundy, and Rusk, 2 January 1964, PRP, MC; also see Michael R. Beschloss, *Taking Charge: The Johnson White House Tapes, 1963–1964* (New York: Simon and Schuster, 1997), 144–46.

196. Memorandum for the Record, by Bundy, 13 January 1964, box 1, Bundy Files, NSF, LBJL; Memorandum to the President, 13 January 1964, box 1, Memos to the President, *ibid.*; regarding trade, see Memorandum for the President, 14 April 1964, *ibid.*; "Summary Record of the NSC Meeting," 16 April 1964, box 2, NSC Meetings File, NSF, LBJL.

197. Johnson to Khrushchev, 17 April 1964, *FRUS, 1964–1968*, 14: 69–71; oral message from Johnson to Khrushchev, 1 May 1964, *ibid.*, 11: 53–56.

198. For the meeting with Dobrynin, see Memorandum of Conversation, 17 April 1964, *ibid.*, 14: 64–66; Dobrynin, *In Confidence*, 119; for Johnson's statement, see Beschloss, *Taking Charge*, 114.

199. "Annual Message to the Congress on the State of the Union," 8 January 1964, *Public Papers of the Presidents: Lyndon Baines Johnson, 1964* (Washington, D.C.: Government Printing Office, 1965), 112–115 (hereafter cited as *PPP: Johnson, year*, page).

200. For Johnson's quotations, see *ibid.*, 113; Johnson, *Vantage Point*, 157; also see Mary L. Dudziak, *Cold War Civil Rights: Race and the Image of American Democracy* (Princeton, N.J.: Princeton University Press, 2000), 203–37; Woods, *LBJ*, 415–66.

201. Beschloss, *Taking Charge*, 169.

202. "U.S. Government Planning for Internal Defense (BNSP Planning Task II E)" [March 1964], *FRUS, 1964–1968*, 10: 51.

203. Memorandum for the President, 13 May 1964, by Bundy, box 1, Memos to the President, NSF, LBJL; see also Department of State, *FRUS, 1964–1968: South and Central America; Mexico* (Washington, D.C.: Government Printing Office, 2004), 31: 45, 574–75.

204. Memorandum for the President, 29 March 1964, box 2, Bundy Files, NSF, LBJL; illustratively, see also Memorandum for the Record, by McCone, 3 April 1964, box 1, John McCone Papers, LBJL.

205. For the CIA report, see NIE 80/90-64, "Communist Potentialities in Latin America," 19 August 1964, *FRUS, 1964–1968*, 31: 65; for Johnson's query, see Memorandum for the Record, 3 February 1964, box 1, McCone Papers, LBJL; see also Telephone Conversation between Johnson and Thomas C. Mann, 11 June 1964, *FRUS, 1964–1968*, 31: 41–50.

206. Rabe, *The Most Dangerous Area in the World*, 79–99.

207. See, for example, Memorandum of Meeting with President Johnson, 19 December 1963, *FRUS, 1961–1963*, 11: 904–909; Memorandum for the Record, 7 April 1964, box 1, McCone Papers, LBJL; Johnson, *Vantage Point*, 24.

208. "British Guiana," no signature [Bundy], ND [February 1964?], box 1, Memos to the President, NSF, LBJL.

209. Memorandum for the Record, 25 November 1963, box 1, McCone Papers, LBJL; for Johnson's initial approach, see Kaiser, *American Tragedy*, 284–90; Jones, *Death of a Generation*, 444–47; Fredrik Logevall, *Choosing War: The Lost Chance for Peace and the Escalation of War in Vietnam* (Berkeley: University of California Press, 1999), 1–107; Woods, *LBJ*, 501–506.

210. NSAM no. 273, 26 November 1963, box 3, Records of the National Security Council, RG 273, NA.

211. Quoted in John Dumbrell, *President Lyndon Johnson and Soviet Communism* (Manchester, Eng.: Manchester University Press, 2004), 11.

212. Johnson to Bohlen, 24 March 1964, *FRUS, 1964–1968*, 1: 191–93; see also Memorandum for the Record, 4 March 1964, box 2, Chester V. Clifton Files, NSF, LBJL.

213. Memorandum for the Record, 4 March 1964, box 2, Clifton Files, NSF, LBJL; Memorandum of a Conversation between Johnson and JCS, 4 March 1964, *FRUS, 1964–1968*, 1: 129–30.

214. For the quotation, see Telephone Conversation between Johnson and Richard Russell, 27 May 1964, *FRUS, 1964–1968: Mainland Southeast Asia; Regional Affairs* (Washington, D.C.: Government Printing Office, 2000), 27: 127; also see Telephone Conversation between Johnson and Bundy, 27 May 1964, *ibid.*, 137; "Vietnam," *Gallup Poll* 3: 1882; Kaiser, *American Tragedy*, 391; Logevall, *Choosing War*, 135–39.

215. Memorandum for the President, by Bundy, 9 January 1964, box 1, Memos to the President, NSF, LBJL; also citations in preceding note.

216. Beschloss, *Taking Charge*, 401–403; for entire conversation, see the recording at PRP, MC; even more revealing is the conversation with Russell, 27 May 1964, *FRUS, 1964–1968*, 27: 125–34.

217. "Special Message to the Congress on U.S. Policy in Southeast Asia," 5 August 1964, *PPP: Johnson, 1964*, 930–32; for his concern with precedent, honor, and credibility, see, for example, the especially revealing taped phone conversation with Martin Luther King, Jr., 7 July 1964, PRP, MC. A much shorter and less illuminating version appears in Beschloss, *Reaching for Glory*, 387–89.

218. "Special Message to Congress," 4 May 1965, *PPP: Johnson, 1965*, 495.

219. Telephone Conversation between Johnson and Bundy, 27 May 1964, *FRUS, 1964–1968*, 27: 135.

220. Memorandum of a Meeting, 9 September 1964, *ibid.*, 1: 749–55.

221. *Ibid.*, 753–55.

222. Memorandum of Conversation, 16 October 1964, *ibid.*, 14: 128–29.

223. Message from the Soviet Government to President Johnson, 3 November 1964, *ibid.*, 165–69.

224. Memorandum of Conversation, 5 December 1964, *ibid.*, 11: 130–35; also Memorandum of Conversation, 9 December 1964, *ibid.*, 135–40; for the second quotation, see Memorandum of Conversation, 2 December 1964, box 19, Intelligence and Research, Lot 87 D 337, RG 59, NA; a shorter version appears in *FRUS, 1964–1968*, 14: 184–89.

225. Memorandum of Conversation, 7 January 1965, *FRUS, 1964–1968*, 11: 157; see also the many memos and materials written and assembled by the Committee on Nuclear Proliferation, Arms Control and Disarmament Agency, "Europe, NATO, Germany, and the MLF," 12 December 1964, box 1, Committee Files, Committee on Nuclear Proliferation, LBJL; also "Value and Feasibility of

a Nuclear Non-Proliferation Treaty," 10 December 1964, box 2, *ibid.*; Frank J. Gavin, "Blasts from the Past: Proliferation Lessons from the 1960s," *International Security* 29 (Winter 2004/5): 106; Costigliola, "Lyndon B. Johnson, Germany and the 'End of the Cold War,' " 173–210.

226. Memorandum of Conversation, 9 December 1964, *FRUS, 1964–1968*, 11: 140.

227. "Annual Message to the Congress on the State of the Union," 4 January 1965, *PPP: Johnson, 1965*, 3; also see, for example, Rusk to McGhee, 14 January 1965, *FRUS, 1964–1968*, 15: 207.

228. Johnson to the Soviet Government, 14 January 1965, *FRUS, 1964–1968*, 14, 210–12; Bundy to Johnson, 10 January 1965, box 2, Memos to the President, NSF, LBJL; Memorandum to the President, by Bundy, 2 February 1965, box 8, Head of State Correspondence, NSF, *ibid.*; for Thompson's opposition, see Spurgeon Keeny to Bundy, 16 December 1964, box 5, Spurgeon Keeny Memoranda, Name Files, NSF, *ibid.*; Thompson to Foster, 10 December 1964, *FRUS, 1964–1968*, 11: 141–45.

229. James A. Bill, *George Ball: Behind the Scenes in U.S. Foreign Policy* (New Haven, Conn.: Yale University Press, 1997), 158–62; McNamara, *In Retrospect*, 156–59.

230. For the quotations, see Paper Prepared by the NSC Working Group, "Courses of Action in Southeast Asia," 21 November 1964, *FRUS, 1964–1968*, 1: 918–19; for Bundy, see Bird, *Color of Truth*, 292–98; Bill Bundy to Rusk, McNamara, Ball, and McGeorge Bundy, 19 October 1964, xeroxed copy provided by Kai Bird. The CIA already had questioned the validity of the domino theory. See Harold P. Ford, *CIA and the Vietnam Policymakers: Three Episodes, 1962–1968* (Washington, D.C.: Central Intelligence Agency, 1998), 56; also see the CIA examination of whether the loss of South Vietnam and Laos would precipitate a "domino effect," 11 June 1964, Declassified Documents Reference System, Document Number CK3100234322. I am indebted to Sarah Tuke for locating this document.

231. McNamara, *In Retrospect*, 168; Bundy to Johnson, 27 January 1965, *FRUS, 1964–1968*, 2: 95–96.

232. "Annual Message to the Congress on the State of the Union," 4 January 1965, *PPP: Johnson, 1965*, 9.

233. Bundy to Johnson, 7 February 1965, *FRUS, 1964–1968*, 2: 180; "Summary Notes of NSC Meeting," 8 February 1965, *ibid.*, 191; McNamara, *In Retrospect*, 170; Kaiser, *American Tragedy*, 393–98; Logevall, *Choosing War*, 319–22.

234. Memorandum for the Record, 6 February 1965, *FRUS, 1964–1968*, 2: 159.

235. *Ibid.*, 160; Memorandum for the Record, 7 February 1965, *ibid.*, 171–72.

236. Beschloss, *Reaching for Glory*, 174.

237. *Ibid.*, 195; also see Johnson's conversation with Bundy, 18 February 1965, *ibid.*, 184; for Johnson's great admiration of McNamara, see Lady Bird Johnson's diary entry, 14 February 1965, *ibid.*, 178; Johnson, *Vantage Point*, 20.

238. The contingent nature of the decision making, as well as the conflicting positions of advisers, is nicely portrayed in Andrew Preston, *The War Council: McGeorge Bundy, the NSC, and Vietnam* (Cambridge, Mass.: Harvard University Press, 2006), 160–90; for Johnson's penchant to keep his options open, see Woods, *LBJ*, 499–500.

239. All the major books on Vietnam agree that decisive decisions were made between February and July 1965. For a convenient summary, see George C. Herring, *America's Longest War: The United States and Vietnam, 1950–1975*, 2nd ed. (New York: Knopf, 1986), 108–43.

240. Tape of Telephone Conversation with Martin Luther King, Jr., 7 July 1965, PRP, MC.

241. Beschloss, *Reaching for Glory*, 274, 181–82.

242. Komer to Bundy, 6 October 1964, box 6, Name File, Komer Memos, NSF, LBJL; Komer to Bundy, 9 October 1964, *ibid.*; for Bundy's high regard for Komer, see Bundy's Memorandum to the President, 22 March 1965, box 3, Memos to the President, NSF, LBJL. Bundy's other assistants, Chester Cooper and James C. Thomson, opposed the escalation, but their views did not prevail. See Preston, *War Council*, 191–207.

243. Komer to Rusk, 11 March 1964, DDRS, Document Number CK3100212412. I am indebted to Sarah Tuke for bringing this document to my attention.

244. Paper prepared by the members of the Bundy Mission, "A Policy of Sustained Reprisal," 7 February 1965, *FRUS, 1964–1968*, 2: 184–85.

245. "Special Message to the Congress on the State of the Nation's Defenses," 18 January 1965, *PPP: Johnson, 1965*, 63; for McNamara's statement, see "President's Meeting with Congressional Leaders," 22 January 1965, box 18, Bundy Files, LBJL.

246. See the Memorandum for President Kennedy, [23 August 1962], *FRUS, 1961–1963*, 8: 355–58.

247. Rusk testimony, 8 January 1965, *Executive Sessions of the Senate Foreign Relations Committee* (Washington, D.C.: Government Printing Office, 1990), 17: 106; for assessments of Soviet intentions and capabilities, see CIA, Office of National Estimates, "Trends in World Situations," by Walter Matthias, 9 June 1964, box 1, NIEs, NSF, LBJL; NIE 11-9-65, "Main Trends in Soviet Foreign Policy," 27 January 1965, *FRUS, 1964–1968*, 14: 215–27; NIE 11-4-65, "Main Trends in Soviet Military Policy," 14 April 1965, *ibid.*, 10: 231–32.

248. Thompson to Bundy, 1 February 1965, box 8, Heads of State Correspondence, NSF, LBJL; Raymond Garthoff, "The Aborted U.S.-U.S.S.R. Summit of 1965," *SHAFR Newsletter* 32 (June 2001): 1–3.

249. George C. Denney to Acting Secretary, 1 February 1965, box 219, USSR, NSF, LBJL; OCI No. 0341/65, Intelligence memorandum, 1 February 1965, *FRUS, 1964–1968*, 2: 120–21; United Kingdom Foreign Office Assessment, "Kosygin's Visit to Hanoi," box 219, USSR, NSF, LBJL; Ilya V. Gaiduk, *The Soviet Union and the Vietnam War* (Chicago, Ill.: Ivan R. Dee, 1996), 3–34.

250. Tyler to Ball, 8 February 1965, *FRUS, 1964–1968*, 2: 197–98; Kohler to Department of State, 11 February 1965, *ibid.*, 14: 240; Memorandum for the Record, by McCone, 10 February 1965, *ibid.*, 2: 220–25.

251. For the quotes, see McNamara, *In Retrospect*, 173; Rusk testimony, 8 January 1965, *Executive Sessions of the Senate Foreign Relations Committee*, 17: 99–100.

252. For the quotation, see "Statement before House Foreign Affairs Committee," 5 June 1961, box 11, Vice President Security File, LBJL; also see, for example, Telephone Conversation between Bundy and Johnson, 27 May 1964, *FRUS, 1964–1968*, 27: 135; Telephone Conversation with Martin Luther King, Jr., 7 July 1965, PRP, MC.

253. Memorandum of Phone Conversation between Ball and Johnson, 6 March 1965, box 1, Ball Papers, LBJL; Logevall, *Choosing War*, 206, 336–37, 348, 363; John W. Young, "Britain and LBJ's War," *Cold War History* 2 (April 2002): 67–69.

254. Telephone Conversation between Johnson and Russell, 27 May 1964, *FRUS, 1964–1968*, 27: 125.

255. For surveys and polls, see "The Deadly and Perplexing War," *Newsweek*, 18 January 1965, 34; "Vietnam," 16 May 1965, *Gallup Poll* 3: 1939–40; "Viet Nam: Chronology," *Congressional Quarterly*, 22 January 1965, 91.

256. Telephone Conversation between Johnson and Russell, 27 May 1964, *FRUS, 1964–1968*, 27: 133.

257. Vladislav Zubok, *A Failed Empire: The Soviet Union in the Cold War from Stalin to Gorbachev, 1945–1991* (Chapel Hill: University of North Carolina Press, forthcoming), chap. 7; Breslauer, *Khrushchev and Brezhnev as Leaders*, 137–78; for tensions in the Warsaw Pact after the Cuban missile crisis, see Mark Kramer, " 'Lessons' of the Cuban Missile Crisis for Warsaw Pact Nuclear Operations," Cold War International History Project *Bulletin* 8–9 (Winter 1996/1997): 348–54; Selvage, "The Warsaw Pact and Nuclear Non-Proliferation, 1963–1965."

258. For a superb analysis of Soviet thinking that was largely correct, see CIA, "Post-Khrushchev Soviet Policy and the Vietnam Crisis," 3 April 1965, box 220, USSR, NSF, LBJL.

259. For Brezhnev quotation, see his speech at Soviet-Czech Friendship Meeting, 3 December 1964, FBIS, 4 December, BB 4; also see Kosygin's report to the Supreme Soviet, 9 December 1964, *ibid.*,

NOTES TO PAGES 225-229

10 December 1964, CC 2–25; Kosygin speech at GOSPLAN session, 19 March 1965, *ibid.*, 28 March 1965, CC 1–9.

260. Meeting no. 179b, 2 December 1964, Malin Notes; Summary of Kosygin speech, 9 December 1964, FBIS, 9 December 1964, CC 2–4; Report to the Supreme Soviet, 9 December 1964, *ibid.*, 10 December 1964, CC 2–25; Brezhnev speech at Soviet-Czech Friendship Meeting, 3 December 1964, *ibid.*, 4 December 1964, BB 7–9; for the debate over economic reform, see Sergei Freidzon, *Patterns of Soviet Economic Decision-Making: An Insider's View of the 1965 Reform* (Falls Church, Va.: Delphic Associates, 1987); for Johnson's recognition of the parallel cuts and his awareness that his actions in Vietnam put them in jeopardy, see his phone conversation with Richard Russell, 26 July 1965, PRP, MC; for the importance of trade with the West, see Jeremi Suri, "The Promise and Failure of 'Developed Socialism': The Soviet 'Thaw' and the Crucible of the Prague Spring, 1964–1972," *Contemporary European History* 15 (2006): 138–43.

261. "Minutes of Discussion at Political Consultative Committee Meeting," 20 January 1965, in Vojtech Mastny and Malcolm Byrne, *A Cardboard Castle?: An Inside History of the Warsaw Pact, 1955–1991* (Budapest: Central European University Press, 2005), 180, 182; also see citations in note 257 above.

262. Brezhnev speech at Soviet-Czechoslovak Friendship Meeting, 3 December 1964, FBIS, 4 December 1964, BB 6.

263. Brezhnev speech at Warsaw rally, 8 April 1965, FBIS, 9 April 1965, FF 1.

264. "Minutes of Discussion at Political Consultative Committee Meeting," 20 January 1965, in Mastny and Byrne, *A Cardboard Castle?*, 184–85.

265. Kosygin to Johnson, 1 February 1965, *FRUS, 1964–1968*, 11: 186–88.

266. Excerpts of Kosygin speech in Hanoi, 8 February 1965, FBIS, 9 February 1965, BB 2; Gaiduk, *Soviet Union and the Vietnam War*, 15–34; Dobrynin, *In Confidence*, 136; CIA, "Post-Khrushchev Soviet Policy," 3 April 1965, box 220, USSR, NSF, LBJL.

267. All the quotes are from a translated Polish version of the Mao-Kosygin Summit, 11 February 1965, CWIHP Document Reader for the International Conference "Tracking the Dragon: National Intelligence Estimates on China During the Mao Era, 1948–1976" (Washington, D.C.: Woodrow Wilson International Center, 2004).

268. Kosygin television address, 26 February 1965, filed in box 220, USSR, NSF, LBJL.

269. Brezhnev speech at the 20th anniversary commemoration of the victory over fascism, 8 May 1965, FBIS, 10 May 1965, CC 21; Dobrynin, *In Confidence*, 115; also see Kosygin speech at a Mongolian Friendship Rally, 19 April 1965, FBIS, 20 April 1965, BB 9–10; Gaiduk, *Soviet Union and the Vietnam War*, 22–50.

270. Brezhnev speech at Warsaw rally, 8 April 1965, FBIS, 9 April 1965, FF 6.

271. Brezhnev speech, 8 May 1965, *ibid.*, 10 May 1965, CC 18.

272. *Ibid.*, CC 19.

273. Harriman to Johnson and Rusk, 15 and 21 July 1965, *FRUS, 1964–1968*, 14: 306–13; for additional elucidation, see Memorandum of Conversation, Harriman and FRG President Heinrich Luebke, 23 July 1965, box 546, Harriman Papers, LC.

274. Zubok, *A Failed Empire*, ch. 7.

275. Harriman to Johnson and Rusk, 21 July 1965, *FRUS, 1964–1968*, 14: 309–13.

276. Memorandum of Conversation, 12 March 1965, *ibid.*, 257.

277. Alan McPherson, "Misled by Himself: What the Johnson Tapes Reveal about the Dominican Intervention in 1965," *Latin American Research Review* 38: 2(2003): 137; see also Johnson, *Vantage Point*, 200–201.

278. See especially Rusk testimony, 8 January 1965, *Executive Sessions of the Senate Foreign Relations Committee*, 17: 100.

279. NIE 13-9-65, "Communist China's Foreign Policy," 5 May 1965, box 4, NIEs, NSF, LBJL.

280. Rusk testimony, 8 January 1965, *Executive Sessions of the Senate Foreign Relations Committee*, 17: 97-100, 106-108.

281. Memorandum for the President, by Bundy, 8 April 1965, box 3, Memos to the President, NSF, LBJL.

282. Brezhnev's phrase in speech on Lenin's birthday, 22 April 1965, FBIS, 23 April 1965, BB 1.

283. Kohler to Rusk, 5 April 1965, box 3, Memos to the President, NSF, LBJL; also see Harriman's reports on his talks with Kosygin, Harriman to Johnson and Rusk, 15 and 21 July 1965, *FRUS, 1964-1968*, 14: 306-13; Telephone Conference, Ball/Dewey, 16 March 1965, box 6, Ball Papers, LBJL; CIA, "Post-Khrushchev Soviet Policy," 3 April 1965, box 220, NSF, *ibid.*

284. CIA, Special Report, "The Soviet Union Since Khrushchev," 9 April 1965, *FRUS, 1964-1968*, 14: 284-85; also see George C. Denney, "Current Trends in Soviet Policy," 5 April 1965, box 54, Komer, NSF, LBJL; NIE 11-5-65, "Soviet Economic Problems and Prospects," 22 January 1965, NSA; Telephone Conference between Ball and Dewey, 16 March 1965, box 6, Ball Papers, LBJL.

285. NIE 11-9-65, "Main Trends in Soviet Foreign Policy," 27 January 1965, *FRUS, 1964-1968*, 14: 216; also see Walter Matthias, "Trends in the World Situation," 9 June 1964, box 1, NIEs, NSF, LBJL.

286. Rostow, "Some Reflections on National Security Policy," 5 March 1965, *FRUS, 1964-1968*, 10: 220-26; Douglas Cater to Johnson, 28 December 1964, box 13, Cater Files, LBJL.

287. Komer to Bundy, 9 October 1964, box 6, Name File, Komer Memos, LBJL.

288. For assessments of developments in Eastern Europe, see *FRUS, 1964-1968: Eastern Europe* (Washington, D.C.: Government Printing Office, 1996), 17: 1-55.

289. Hubert H. Humphrey, *The Education of a Public Man: My Life and Politics* (Garden City, N.Y.: Doubleday & Company, 1976), 320-24.

290. Fredrik Logevall, *The Origins of the Vietnam War* (Essex, Eng.: Longman, 2001), 77.

291. "The President's Inaugural Address," 20 January 1965, *PPP: Johnson*, 1965, 71-75.

292. Brezhnev speech, 8 April 1965, FBIS, 9 April 1965, FF 6. For reference to Lenin's greatness, see Brezhnev's speech on Lenin's birthday, 22 April 1965, *ibid.*, 23 April 1965, BB 1.

293. Brezhnev speech, 8 May 1965, *ibid.*, 10 May 1965, CC 18.

294. Brezhnev speech, 8 April 1965, *ibid.*, 9 April 1965, FF 8.

295. Firth and Noren, *Soviet Defense Spending*, 122; U.S. Arms Control and Disarmament Agency, *World Military Expenditures*, 56.

IV: The Erosion of Détente, 1975-80: Brezhnev and Carter

1. "A Star Studded Summit Spectacular," *Time* 106 (4 August 1975): 16-22.

2. William Tompson, *The Soviet Union Under Brezhnev* (London: Pearson, 2003), 47-49.

3. *Ibid.*, 15-34; Ian D. Thatcher, "Brezhnev as Leader," in *Brezhnev Reconsidered*, ed. by Edwin Bacon and Mark Sandle (Houndsmills, Eng.: Palgrave, 2002), 22-37; Vladislav Zubok, *A Failed Empire: The Soviet Union in the Cold War from Stalin to Gorbachev, 1945-1991* (Chapel Hill: University of North Carolina Press, forthcoming), chap. 7; George W. Breslauer, *Khrushchev and Brezhnev as Leaders: Building Authority in Soviet Politics* (London: George Allen & Unwin, 1982), 169-99; Anatoly Dobrynin, *In Confidence: Moscow's Ambassador to America's Six Cold War Presidents* (New York: Random House, 1995), 218-19, 228-31; Harry Gelman, *The Brezhnev Politburo and the Decline of Détente* (Ithaca, N.Y.: Cornell University Press, 1984).

4. Leonid Ilyich Brezhnev, *Memoirs*, trans. by Penny Dole (Oxford, Eng.: Pergamon Press, 1982), 4; Basil Dmytryshyn, "Brezhnev, Leonid Il'ich," *The Modern Encyclopedia of Russian and Soviet History*, ed. by Joseph L. Wieczynski, 47 (Gulf Breeze, Fla.: Academic International Press, 1988), 131-32.

5. Brezhnev, *Memoirs*, 18.

6. *Ibid.*, 6–21; also see Dmytryshyn, "Brezhnev," 131; for Brezhnev's early education, see the scornful memoir of Brezhnev's niece, Luba Brezhneva, *The World I Left Behind: Pieces of a Past* (New York: Random House, 1995), 13, 14, 18.

7. Brezhnev, *Memoirs*, 25–27; for his private misgivings, see L. Brezhneva, *World I Left Behind*, 26–31.

8. For the biographical data in the previous two paragraphs, see Brezhnev, *Memoirs*, 20–41; Dmytryshyn, "Brezhnev," 131–32; Academy of Sciences of the U.S.S.R., *Leonid I. Brezhnev: Pages from His Life* (New York: Simon and Schuster, 1978), 22–35.

9. Academy of Sciences of the U.S.S.R., *Brezhnev*, 49.

10. For the impact of the war on Brezhnev, see the comments of acquaintances in "SALT II and the Growth of Mistrust," Oral History Conference No. 2 of the Carter-Brezhnev Project (held at Musgrove Plantation, Ga., 6–9 May 1994), 13, 148–49 (transcript available at Thomas J. Watson, Jr., Institute for International Studies, Brown University, and at the National Security Archive (NSA), George Washington University, Washington, D.C.); Nobel Symposium 95, David A. Welch and Odd Arne Westad, eds., trans. by Svetlana Savranskaya, "The Intervention in Afghanistan and the Fall of Détente" (Oslo: The Norwegian Nobel Institute, 1995), 229; also see Helmut Schmidt, *Men and Powers: A Political Retrospective*, trans. by Ruth Hein (New York: Random House, 1989), 3–4, 46; Zubok, *Failed Empire*, chap. 7.

11. Memorandum of Conversation between W. Averell Harriman and Brezhnev, 4 June 1974, document collection, "SALT II and the Growth of Mistrust," NSA; also see comments by Viktor Sukhodrev (Brezhnev's interpreter and aide), "SALT II and the Growth of Mistrust," 16; Vladislav Zubok, "The Brezhnev Factor in Détente," in *Cold War and the Policy of Détente: Problems and Discussions* (Moscow: Institute of Universal History, Russian Academy of Sciences, 2003), 288.

12. For Brezhnev's career, see Dmytryshyn, "Brezhnev," 132–33; "Brezhnev, Leonid Il'ich," *Great Soviet Encyclopedia*, translation of the 3rd ed., vol. 4 (New York: Macmillan, 1974), 71–72; Zubok, *Failed Empire*, chap. 7.

13. For insights into the Soviet decision-making process, see comments by Viktor Starodubov, Sergei P. Tarasenko, Dobrynin, and Nikolay N. Detinov, "SALT II and the Growth of Mistrust," 149–60, 177–80, 187, 193, 231–42, 259, 293–96; Dobrynin, *In Confidence*, 193–94, 218–20, 404–405; Aleksandr' G. Savel'yev and Nikolay N. Detinov, *The Big Five: Arms Control Decision-Making in the Soviet Union*, trans. by Dmitriy Trenin, ed. by Gregory Varhall (Westport, Conn.: Praeger Publishers, 1995), 31–53; Zubok, *Failed Empire*, chap. 7; Tompson, *Soviet Union Under Brezhnev*, 26–34. I am also indebted to Mark Kramer for explaining the decision-making process.

14. Zubok, *Failed Empire*, chap. 7; for statistics on the Soviet arms buildup, see David Holloway, *The Soviet Union and the Arms Race* (New Haven, Conn.: Yale University Press, 1983), 58–60, 114, 122; for Chinese meddling in Eastern Europe, see Mark Kramer, "The Czechoslovak Crisis and the Brezhnev Doctrine," in *1968: The World Transformed*, ed. by Carole Fink, Philipp Gassert, and Detlef Junker (Cambridge, Eng: Cambridge University Press and the German Historical Institute, 1998), 119.

15. For Shelest's quotation, see Mark Kramer, "Ukraine and the Soviet-Czechoslovak Crisis of 1968 (Part I): New Evidence from the Diary of Petro Shelest," Cold War International History *Bulletin* 10 (March 1998): 235; also see Kramer, "The Czechoslovak Crisis and the Brezhnev Doctrine," 121–45.

16. For the enunciation of the Brezhnev Doctrine, see Kramer, "The Czechoslovak Crisis and the Brezhnev Doctrine," 168; for the thinking of Czechoslovak military leaders, see *ibid.*, 137–41; for Brezhnev's anxiety during the crisis, see Zubok, *Failed Empire*, chap. 7.

17. For the ramifications of the Czech crisis, see Kramer, "The Czechoslovak Crisis and the Brezhnev

Doctrine," 162–71; Jeremi Suri, "The Promise and Failure of 'Developed Socialism': The Soviet 'Thaw' and the Crucible of the Prague Spring, 1964–1972," *Contemporary European History* 5 (2006): 150–58; Tony Judt, *Postwar: A History of Europe Since 1945* (New York: Penguin, 2005), 446–47; Tompson, *Soviet Union Under Brezhnev*, 36–39.

18. Zubok, *Failed Empire*, chap. 7.

19. *Ibid.*

20. For the quotation, see Speech, by Brezhnev, 13 November 1968, http://www.cnn.com/SPECIALS/cold.war/episodes/14/documents/doctrine; for background, see Tompson, *Soviet Union Under Brezhnev*, 35–49; Matthew J. Ouimet, *The Rise and Fall of the Brezhnev Doctrine in Soviet Foreign Policy* (Chapel Hill: University of North Carolina Press, 2003), 36–37, 67–69; Georgi Arbatov, *The System: An Insider's Life in Soviet Politics* (New York: Random House, 1992), 127–89; Zubok, "The Brezhnev Factor in Détente," 287–88.

21. Vojtech Mastny and Malcolm Byrne, eds., *A Cardboard Castle?: An Inside History of the Warsaw Pact, 1955–1991* (Budapest: Central European University Press, 2005), 361; for background, see Schmidt, *Men and Powers*, 3–47; Zubok, "Brezhnev Factor," 294–96; Arbatov, *The System*, 171–72; William Hitchcock, *The Struggle for Europe: The Turbulent History of a Divided Continent, 1945 to the Present* (New York: Anchor Books, 2004), 293–99; Judt, *Postwar*, 496–503.

22. Willy Brandt, *My Life in Politics* (New York: Viking Penguin, 1992), 154–243; A. James McAdams, *Germany Divided: From the Wall to Reunification* (Princeton, N.J.: Princeton University Press, 1993), 79–105; Gottfried Niedhart, "Ostpolitik: The Role of the Federal Republic of Germany in the Process of Détente," in *1968: A World Transformed*, ed. by Fink, Gassert, and Junker, 173–92; M. E. Sarotte, *Dealing with the Devil: East Germany, Détente, and Ostpolitik, 1969–73* (Chapel Hill: University of North Carolina Press, 2001); Zubok, *Failed Empire*, chap. 7.

23. Zubok, *Failed Empire*, chap. 7; for Brezhnev's personality, also see Victor Israelyan, *Inside the Kremlin During the Yom Kippur War* (University Park: Pennsylvania State University Press, 1995), 25; Arbatov, *The System*, 124–25; for stability of cadres, see Geoffrey Hosking, *The First Socialist Society: A History of the Soviet Union from Within* (Cambridge, Mass.: Harvard University Press, 1996), 376–78; Tompson, *Soviet Union Under Brezhnev*, 22–34; for Brezhnev's ardor for peace and détente, also see Anatoli Cherniaev, "The Unknown Brezhnev," *Russian Politics and Law* 42 (May–June 2004): 34–66.

24. For defense expenditures, see Holloway, *Soviet Union and the Arms Race*, 114; for the motives of Brezhnev and other supporters of détente, see Tompson, *Soviet Union Under Brezhnev*, 30–34; Zubok, *Failed Empire*, chap. 7; Dobrynin, *In Confidence*, 209–10; Philip Hanson, *The Rise and Fall of the Soviet Economy: An Economic History of the USSR from 1945* (London: Longman, 2003), 108–12; comments by Detinov, "SALT II and the Growth of Mistrust," 147–48; Department of State [Office of Intelligence and Research], "The Politburo and Détente: Measuring the Consensus," 1 January 1976, Freedom of Information Act (FOIA).

25. For the quotation, see Report of the Central Committee (CC) of the Communist Party of the Soviet Union (CPSU) to the 24th Congress of the CPSU, 30 March 1971, in L. I. Brezhnev, *Selected Speeches and Writings on Foreign Affairs* (Oxford, Eng.: Pergamon Press, 1979), 5; also see Dobrynin, *In Confidence*, 216–19; Breslauer, *Khrushchev and Brezhnev*, 179–99.

26. For the quotation, see comment by Sukhodrev, "SALT II and the Growth of Mistrust," 15–16; also see Memorandum of Conversation between Brezhnev and Gerald Ford, 23 November 1974, 2:30 p.m., NSA.

27. Hitchcock, *Struggle for Europe*, 301; Judt, *Postwar*, 501–502.

28. Raymond L. Garthoff, *Détente and Confrontation: American-Soviet Relations from Nixon to Reagan*, rev. ed. (Washington, D.C.: Brookings Institution, 1994), 326–38.

29. For Brezhnev's comment, see Protocol of Central Committee of CPSU Secretariat Session, 20 November 1972, Record 10325, Yakovlev Papers, NSA; also see Garthoff, *Détente and Confrontation*, 57–73.

NOTES TO PAGES 243–251 511

3430. Report at a gala joint meeting of the CPSU Central Committee, the USSR Supreme Soviet, and the RSFSR Supreme Soviet, 21 December 1972, in Brezhnev, *Selected Speeches*, 9.

31. For the quotation, see Starodubov's comments, "SALT II and the Growth of Mistrust," 35; also see Detinov's comments, *ibid.*, 50–51.

32. For Brezhnev's commitment to détente, see Zubok, *Failed Empire*, chap. 7; for background, also see Garthoff, *Détente and Confrontation*, 360–525; Dobrynin, *In Confidence*, 191–359; Gelman, *The Brezhnev Politburo*.

33. Memorandum of Conversation between Brezhnev and Ford, 23 November 1974, 2:30 p.m., p. 6, NSA.

34. Memorandum of Conversation between Brezhnev and Ford, 23 November 1974, 6:30 p.m., p. 2, NSA.

35. *Ibid.*, p. 19; also see 2:30 conversation, p. 10.

36. Memorandum of Conversation between Brezhnev and Ford, 23 November 1974, 2:30 p.m., p. 5.

37. *Ibid.*, p. 7.

38. Memorandum of Conversation between Brezhnev and Ford, 23 November 1974, 6:30 p.m., p. 15.

39. *Ibid.*, p. 10.

40. Comments by Dobrynin, "SALT II and the Growth of Mistrust," 17; Arbatov, *The System*, 201–202.

41. Memorandum of Conversation between Brezhnev and Ford, 23 November 1974, 6:30 p.m., pp. 11*ff*, 19, NSA.

42. *Ibid.*, p. 20.

43. Memorandum of Conversation between Brezhnev and Ford, 24 November 1974, pp. 15–16, NSA.

44. Gerald Ford, *A Time to Heal: The Autobiography of Gerald R. Ford* (New York: Harper & Row, 1979), 218.

45. Memorandum of Conversation between Brezhnev and Ford, 24 November 1974, p. 20, NSA.

46. Ford, *Time to Heal*, 218–19.

47. Arbatov, *The System*, 191–92; albeit overstated, see Michael Dobbs, *Down with Big Brother: The Fall of the Soviet Empire* (New York: Alfred A. Knopf, 1997), 6–8; E. I. Chazov, *Zdorovie i vlast'* [Health and Power] (Moscow: Novosti, 1992), 74–91, 115–48.

48. Svetlana Savranskaya, "Unintended Consequences: The Emergence of Human Rights Movements in the USSR After the Signing of the Helsinki Final Act, and the Reaction of Soviet Authorities," unpublished paper; for background, see Daniel C. Thomas, *The Helsinki Effect: International Norms, Human Rights, and the Demise of Communism* (Princeton, N.J.: Princeton University Press, 2001); the quotations are from the brief description of the Helsinki Agreement in Hitchcock, *The Struggle for Europe*, 301.

49. Record of Conversation of Cde. L. I. Brezhnev with Leaders of Fraternal Parties of Socialist Countries in Budapest, 18 March 1975, R 1940, Volkogonov Collection, NSA (also accessible on the website of the National Security Archive); also see Savranskaya, "Unintended Consequences," 4–9. Brezhnev was exaggerating the influence of the expellee organizations whose influence had waned since the late 1960s. See Pertii Ahonen, *After the Expulsion: West Germany and Eastern Europe, 1945–1990* (New York: Oxford University Press, 2003).

50. Record of Conversation, 18 March 1975, R 1940, Volkogonov Collection, NSA; also see Memorandum of Conversation between Brezhnev and Ford, 24 November 1974, p. 20, NSA.

51. For the quotation, see Memorandum of Conversation between Gromyko and Kissinger, 11 July 1975, 1:10 p.m., NSA; also see Memoranda of Conversation between Gromyko and Kissinger, 19 May 1975, 10 July 1975, *ibid.*

52. Memoranda of Conversations between Ford and Brezhnev, 30 July 1975, 9:35 a.m. and 12:00 p.m., NSA.

53. Brezhnev, "In the Name of Peace, Security and Co-operation," 31 July 1975, in Brezhnev, *Follow-*

ing Lenin's Course: Speeches and Articles (1972–1975) (Moscow: Progress Publishers, 1975), 577–83.

54. *Ibid.*

55. Memorandum of Conversation between Brezhnev and Ford, 30 July 1975, 9:35 a.m., pp. 10–11, NSA.

56. Quotation on p. 3, Memorandum of Conversation between Brezhnev and Ford, 2 August 1975, NSA.

57. For defense expenditures, see U.S. Arms Control and Disarmament Agency, *World Military Expenditures and Arms Transfers, 1967–1976* (Washington, D.C.: Government Printing Office, 1977), 6, 62, 66; for the domestic and international context described in this and the subsequent paragraph, see especially Ford, *Time to Heal*, 306–307, 345–82; Garthoff, *Détente and Confrontation*, 489–620; Anne Hessing Cahn, *Killing Détente: The Right Attacks the CIA* (University Park: The Pennsylvania State University Press, 1998).

58. Garthoff, *Détente and Confrontation*, 604*ff.*

59. For the quotations, see "SALT II and the Growth of Mistrust," 148–49; A. A. Grechko, *The Armed Forces of the Soviet Union* (Moscow: Progress Publishers, 1977), 79.

60. L. I. Brezhnev, "Report of the CPSU Central Committee and the Immediate Tasks of the Party in Home and Foreign Policy," 24 February 1976, *Information Bulletin*—Special Issue No. 1, 1976 (Prague: Peace and Socialism Publishers, 1976), especially 20, 25–26.

61. For the dialogue between Gromyko and Kissinger, see Memorandum of Conversation between Gromyko and Kissinger, 23 January 1976, NSA.

62. See comments by Tarasenko, Dobrynin, and Kondrashev, "SALT II and the Growth of Mistrust," 293–301; comments by Karen Neressovich Brutents, in "US-Soviet Relations and Soviet Foreign Policy Toward the Middle East and Africa in the 1970s," transcript from a workshop at Lysebu, October 1–3, 1994 (Oslo: Norwegian Nobel Institute, 1995), 44–45, 35; for background, see Piero Gleijeses, *Conflicting Missions: Havana, Washington, and Africa, 1959–1976* (Chapel Hill: University of North Carolina Press, 2002); W. Martin James III, *A Political History of the Civil War in Angola, 1974–1990* (New Brunswick, N.J.: Transaction Publishers, 1992), 41–88; Odd Arne Westad, *The Global Cold War: Third World Interventions and the Making of Our Times* (New York: Cambridge University Press, 2006), 218–49; Garthoff, *Détente and Confrontation*, 556–94; Tompson, *Soviet Union Under Brezhnev*, 52–53.

63. Brezhnev, "Report of the CPSU Central Committee," 24 February 1976, p. 16.

64. *Ibid.*, 5.

65. Brezhnev address at luncheon for the delegation of the Democratic Republic of Vietnam, 28 October 1975, Foreign Broadcast Information Service (FBIS), 28 October 1975, L 3–5.

66. Brezhnev, "Report of the CPSU Central Committee," 24 February 1976, pp. 15–41, quotation on 34.

67. Alexei Yurchak, *Everything Was Forever, Until It Was No More: The Last Soviet Generation* (Princeton, N.J.: Princeton University Press, 2006), 8; also see the comments of the journalist Vladimir Konstantinov in Tompson, *Soviet Union Under Brezhnev*, 146, also 83–85; for the everyday transgressions of official ideology, see James R. Millar, "The Little Deal: Brezhnev's Contribution to Acquisitive Socialism," *Slavic Review* 4 (Winter 1985): 694–706.

68. Brezhnev, "Report of the CPSU," 24 February 1976, p. 103.

69. Brezhnev Speech on the 60th Anniversary of the October Socialist Revolution, 2 November 1977, FBIS, 2 November 1977, P 4.

70. Brezhnev, "Answers to Questions," 6 June 1977, FBIS, 6 June 1977, R 11.

71. For the quotations, see Brezhnev, "Report of the CPSU," 24 February 1976, 104; Brezhnev, "An-

swers to Questions," 6 June 1977, FBIS, 6 June 1977, R 11; also see Brezhnev Speech, 2 November 1977, FBIS, 2 November 1977, P 2–16.

72. Brezhnev Speech at the Plenary Meeting of the CC of the CPSU, 25 October 1976, in Leonid Brezhnev, *Peace, Détente and Soviet-American Relations: A Collection of Public Statements* (New York: Harcourt Brace Jovanovich, 1979), 134.

73. Quoted in Zubok, *Failed Empire*, chap. 7.

74. Hanson, *Rise and Fall of the Soviet Economy*, 5; Tompson, *Soviet Union Under Brezhnev*, 83–84; Mark Harrison, "Economic Growth and Slowdown," in *Brezhnev Reconsidered*, ed. by Edwin Bacon and Mark Sandle (Houndsmills, Eng.: Palgrave Macmillan, 2002), 44–52.

75. Hanson, *Rise and Fall of the Soviet Economy*, 143–54; Harrison, "Economic Growth and Slowdown," 38–67; Linda J. Cook, *The Soviet Social Contract and Why It Failed: Welfare Policy and Workers' Politics from Brezhnev to Yeltsin* (Cambridge, Mass.: Harvard University Press, 1993), 1–81.

76. "Leonid Brezhnev's Speech in Tula," 18 January 1977, FBIS, 18 January 1977, R 8.

77. *Ibid.*, R 3–13, for the quotation, see R 7; also see, for example, Brezhnev speech at the sixteenth congress of trade unions, 21 March 1977, FBIS, 21 March 1977, R 1–17; Brezhnev speech to the leaders of the academies of science of socialist countries, 17 February 1977, FBIS, D 1–4; for an excellent summary of economic performance and abortive reforms, see Tompson, *Soviet Union Under Brezhnev*, 64–86.

78. For Andropov's views, see Y. V. Andropov, "Leninism: The Science and Art of Revolution," 22 April 1976, in Y. V. Andropov, *Speeches and Writings* (Oxford, Eng.: Pergamon Press, 1983), 152–70; Martin Ebon, *The Andropov File: The Life and Ideas of Yuri V. Andropov, General Secretary of the Communist Party of the Soviet Union* (New York: McGraw-Hill, 1983), 213.

79. Memorandum of Conversation between Brezhnev and W. Averell Harriman, 20 September 1976, U.S.S.R., Vertical File (VF), Jimmy Carter Library (CL) (Atlanta, Ga.).

80. Message from Brezhnev, delivered to Harriman by Dobrynin, 21 November 1976, *ibid.*; also see Lawrence S. Eagleburger to Tony Lake, 2 December 1976, *ibid.*; Alex R. Seith to Harriman, 3 December, *ibid.*

81. "Leonid Brezhnev's Speech in Tula," 18 January 1977, FBIS, 18 January 1977, R 3–13.

82. For the quotations, see the dinner speech by Nikolai Podgorny, the president of the Presidium of the U.S.S.R., in honor of the visiting delegation from socialist Ethiopia, 4 May 1977, FBIS, H 1–4; also see Brezhnev, "Report of the CPSU," 24 February 1976, pp. 8–41; Brezhnev speech, 2 November 1977, FBIS, 2 November 1977, P 3; for analysis of Soviet policy, see Westad, *Global Cold War*, 207–87.

83. Brezhnev, "Report of the CPSU," 24 February 1976, p. 16.

84. *Ibid.*

85. For background on Carter, see Jimmy Carter, *An Hour Before Daylight: Memories of a Rural Boyhood* (New York: Simon and Schuster, 2001); Peter G. Bourne, *Jimmy Carter: A Comprehensive Biography from Plains to Postpresidency* (New York: Scribner, 1997); Betty Glad, *Jimmy Carter: In Search of the Great White House* (New York: W. W. Norton, 1980).

86. For the quotation, see "Interview with Jimmy Carter," 29 November 1982, Carter Presidency Project (Charlottesville, Va.: Miller Center Foundation, 2003), 69 (hereafter cited as MC Interview); for Carter's character, personality, and values, also see Jimmy Carter, *Keeping Faith: Memoirs of a President* (London: Collins, 1982), esp. 17–62; and the interviews in Don Richardson, ed., *Conversations with Carter* (Boulder, Colo.: Lynne Rienner Publishers, 1998).

87. See, for example, Sidney Kraus, ed., *The Great Debates: Carter vs. Ford, 1976* (Bloomington: Indiana University Press, 1979), 489–90.

88. MC Interview, 69.

89. *Ibid.*, 8.

90. Zbigniew Brzezinski, *Power and Principle: Memoirs of a National Security Adviser, 1977–1981* (New York: Farrar, Straus and Giroux, 1983), 22.

91. Cyrus Vance, *Hard Choices: Critical Years in America's Foreign Policy* (New York: Simon and Schuster, 1983), 31–33.

92. Carter, *Keeping Faith*, 143; Jimmy Carter, *Why Not the Best?* (Nashville, Tenn.: Broadman Press, 1975).

93. Brzezinski, *Power and Principle*, 3.

94. Vance, *Hard Choices*, 23, 502–20.

95. Brzezinski, *Power and Principle*, 63.

96. For Vance's thinking when he came to Washington, see Vance, *Hard Choices*, 17–25; for Carter's view of Vance, see Carter, *Keeping Faith*, 50–51; MC Interview, 38; for Brzezinski's view, see Brzezinski, *Power and Principle*, 36–44.

97. Hamilton Jordan, *Crisis: The Last Year of the Carter Presidency* (New York: G. P. Putnam's Sons, 1982), 46–47; Carter, *Keeping Faith*, 55–56; MC Interview, 38–39.

98. Inaugural address, 20 January 1977, *Public Papers of the Presidents: Jimmy Carter, 1977* (Washington, D.C.: Government Printing Office, 1977), 1–4 (hereafter cited as PPP: Carter, year, page).

99. Carter, *Keeping Faith*, 141; comments by Brzezinski and Vance, *SALT II and the Growth of Mistrust*, 202–203, 207–208.

100. Herman Van Der Wee, *Prosperity and Upheaval: The World Economy, 1945–1980* (Berkeley: University of California Press, 1983), 50, 77, 81–93, 472–512.

101. See, for example, Forrest D. Colburn, *The Vogue of Revolution in Poor Countries* (Princeton, N.J.: Princeton University Press, 1994); Crawford Young, *Ideology and Development in Africa* (New Haven, Conn.: Yale University Press, 1982), esp. 1–183; John Walton, *Reluctant Rebels: Comparative Studies of Revolution and Underdevelopment* (New York: Columbia University Press, 1984); Mark N. Katz, ed., *The USSR and Marxist Revolutions in the Third World* (Cambridge, Mass.: Woodrow Wilson International Center for Scholars and Cambridge University Press, 1990).

102. "Can Capitalism Survive?," *Time* 106 (14 July 1975): 52–63; for real wages, see the table in Van Der Wee, *Prosperity and Upheaval*, 237.

103. Brzezinski to Carter, 11 March 1977, box 41, Brzezinski Collection (BC), CL; also see Brzezinski to Carter, 9 April 1977, 2 December 1977, 9 February 1978, *ibid.*; Richard N. Gardner, *Mission Italy: On the Front Lines of the Cold War* (Lanham, Md.: Rowman & Littlefield, 2005), 19–20, 42–48.

104. Vance, *Hard Choices*, 23; Brzezinski to Carter, 1 April 1977, box 41, BC, CL.

105. Address at Commencement Exercises, 22 May 1977, PPP: Carter, 1977, 954–62, quotation on 957.

106. Brzezinski to Carter, 1 April 1977, box 41, BC, CL; Brzezinski comments in "SALT II and the Growth of Mistrust," 202–203.

107. Brzezinski to Carter, 1 April 1977, box 41, BC, CL; also see Brzezinski to Carter, 16 April 1977, *ibid.*

108. Carter, *Keeping Faith*, 155–56.

109. Carter to Brezhnev, 26 January 1977, USSR, VF, CL.

110. Brezhnev to Carter, 4 February 1977, *ibid.*

111. Carter to Brezhnev, 14 February 1977, box 17, Plains File, CL; also Dobrynin, *In Confidence*, 383–90; comments by Dobrynin, "Global Competition," 170–73.

112. Andrei Sakharov, *Memoirs*, trans. by Richard Lourie (New York: Alfred A. Knopf, 1990), 464–66, 687.

113. Comments by Kornienko, "US-Soviet Relations and Soviet Foreign Policy," 11–12; comments by Dobrynin, "SALT II and Growth of Mistrust," 6–8, 16–17, 58–61, 73–74, 96; comments by Dobrynin,

"Global Competition and the Deterioration of U.S.-Soviet Relations, 1977–80", the Third Oral History Conference of the Carter-Brezhnev Project (Fort Lauderdale, Fla., 23–26 March 1995), 171–72.

114. For the quotation, see "Vypiska iz protokola No. 56 zasedaniia Politburo TsK KPSS ot 19 maia 1977 goda: Ob ukazaniiakh sovposlam v sviazi s shumikhoy na Zapade po voprosu o pravakh cheloveka," ["An Extract from Protocol No. 56 of CC CPSU Politburo Meeting on 19 May 1977: Regarding Directions to Soviet Ambassadors in Connection to the Ballyhoo in the West about Human Rights"], R 136, box 9, Volkogonov Collection, NSA; comments by Shakhnazarov, "Global Competition," 170–75, 192–93; Dobrynin, *In Confidence*, 386–90.

115. Savranskaya, "Unintended Consequences," 21–26; Andropov's reports to the USSR Council of Ministers and to the Central Committee of the CPSU, 29 December 1975, 15 November 1976, 20 January 1977, READD-RADD Collection, NSA (also accessible on NSA website).

116. Instructions to Dobrynin for his conversation with Vance regarding "human rights," 18 February 1977, *ibid*.

117. Brezhnev's foreword to French collection of his speeches, 31 December 1976, FBIS, 3 January 1977, E 2.

118. Comments by Dobrynin, "SALT II and the Growth of Mistrust," 81.

119. Savranskaya, "Unintended Consequences," 21–30; for accounts of the dissidents, see Joshua Rubinstein, *Soviet Dissidents: Their Struggle for Human Rights* (Boston: Beacon Press, 1980); Paul Goldberg, *The Final Act: The Dramatic, Revealing Story of the Moscow Helsinki Watch Group* (New York: William Morrow, 1988).

120. "An Extract from Protocol No. 56 of CC CPSU Politburo Meeting," 19 May 1977, R 136, box 9, Volkogonov Collection, NSA; Instructions to Dobrynin for his conversation with Vance regarding "human rights," 18 February 1977, READD-RADD Collection, NSA.

121. Brezhnev report to CPSU Central Committee Plenum, 24 May 1977, FBIS, 25 May 1977, R 1–3; Brezhnev report to the CPSU Central Committee Plenum, 27 November 1978, FBIS, 30 November 1978, R 3–8; also see Andropov, "Leninism: the Science and Art of Revolution," 22 April 1976, in Andropov, *Speeches and Writings*, 159.

122. Brezhnev address to trade unions, 21 March 1977, FBIS, 21 March 1977, R 7; Andropov, "Faith in Communism as the Source of Inspiration for the Builders of a New World," 9 September 1977, in Andropov, *Speeches and Writings*, 171–89; fragment from Brezhnev's diary, 5 March 1977, box 9, Volkogonov Collection, NSA.

123. Dobrynin's comments, "Global Competition," 204–205.

124. Kondrashov comments, "SALT II and the Growth of Mistrust," 24, 97–100.

125. Memorandum of Conversation between Brezhnev and Ford, 30 July 1975, 9:35 a.m., pp. 12–13, NSA.

126. Dobrynin's comments, "Global Competition," 173; Dobrynin, *In Confidence*, 380–92; also see Dobrynin's comments, "SALT II and the Growth of Mistrust," 58–60, 66–67, 80–81.

127. Sukhodrev's comments, "SALT II and the Growth of Mistrust," 306, 63–64.

128. For Vance's views, see his comments, *ibid.*, 59–62; also see Vance, *Hard Choices*, 53–55.

129. Brzezinski, *Power and Principle*, 158–60.

130. For their acknowledgment that they had overreached, see *ibid.*, 162–64; comments by Brzezinski and Brown, "SALT II and the Growth of Mistrust," 100–102; Carter's comments in MC Interview; Vance, *Hard Choices*, 55.

131. Gromyko's press conference, 31 March 1977, FBIS, 1 April 1977, B 1–10; Vance, *Hard Choices*, 54; Sukhodrev's comments, "SALT II and the Growth of Mistrust," 140–41; Brezhnev to Carter, 4 April 1977, box 17, Plains File, CL.

132. Brzezinski, *Power and Principle*, 165; Brzezinski to Carter, 1 April 1977, box 41, BC, CL; Paul Warnke and Vance to Carter, 27 April 1977, Meetings, BC, CL; also see Brzezinski to Carter, 7 June 1977, *ibid*.

133. Carter to Brezhnev, 9 June 1977, box 17, Plains File, CL.

134. Much of this hostility emerged during the Senate debate over the nomination of Paul Warnke to head the U.S. negotiating team in the SALT talks. See "Warnke Is Carter Choice for Arms Control Agency," *Congressional Quarterly*, 5 February 1977, 242; "Foreign Relations Approval Expected of Warnke Despite Concerted Opposition Effort," *ibid.*, 12 February 1977, 255; "Debate Begins on Warnke Nomination," *ibid.*, 5 March 1977, 405; also see Senator Henry Jackson's letters to Brzezinski, 22 April 1977 and 27 April 1977, Henry Jackson Papers, University of Washington Libraries (Seattle, Wash.); Jackson to Carter, 22 August 1977, *ibid.* I am indebted to Josh Botts for sharing these documents with me.

135. Vance's comments, "SALT II and the Growth of Mistrust," 10–12, 267, 167; for the impact of domestic politics and the turbulence of international politics, also see comments by Les Gelb and Marshal Shulman, *ibid.*, 192, 212–15, 338–39; Dan Caldwell, "The Demise of Détente and US Domestic Politics," in Odd Arne Westad, ed., *The Fall of Détente: Soviet-American Relations During the Carter Years* (Oslo: Scandinavian University Press, 1997), 95–117.

136. Comment by Gelb, "SALT II and the Growth of Mistrust," 271.

137. *Ibid.*

138. Some of these qualities emerge clearly in the MC Interview; others will be discussed below.

139. Meeting of the Special Coordinating Committee, "Summary of Conclusions," 7 July 1977, Meetings, BC, CL.

140. Brzezinski to Carter, 24 June 1977, box 41, BC, CL; also see Brzezinski to Carter, 26 May 1977, 8 July 1977, *ibid.*; Central Intelligence Agency (CIA), "Prospects for Eastern Europe," 10 June 1977, box 1, End of Cold War Collection, NSA; CIA, "Soviet Economic Problems and Prospects," July 1977, *ibid.*

141. Chazov, *Health and Power*, 74–91, 115–48; Dobrynin, *In Confidence*, 397–98; L. Brezhneva, *World I Left Behind*, 362–64; V. M. Sukhodrev, *Iazyk moy—drug moy: ot Khrushcheva do Gorbacheva* [My Tongue—My Friend: From Khrushchev to Gorbachev] (Moscow AST: Olimp, 1999), 190–346; fragments from Brezhnev's diary, located in box 9, Volkogonov Collection, NSA; Vadim Alekseevich Pechenev, *Gorbachev: k vershinam vlasti* [Gorbachev: To the Heights of Power] (Moscow: Gospodin Narod/Fenomen Cheloveka, 1991), 35–39; Tompson, *Soviet Union Under Brezhnev*, 15–25.

142. For Dobrynin's quotation, see his comment, "SALT II and the Growth of Mistrust," 239; also see Dobrynin, *In Confidence*, 404–405; Arbatov, *The System*, 191–92, 198–202, 245–54; Tompson, *Soviet Union Under Brezhnev*, 17–34. These generalizations emerge from the observations of the Soviet participants during the oral history conferences on the Carter/Brezhnev years. See "SALT II and the Growth of Mistrust"; "Global Competition"; "Intervention in Afghanistan and the Fall of Détente"; "US-Soviet Relations and Soviet Foreign Policy."

143. Gleijeses, *Conflicting Missions*.

144. [East German] Minutes of the conversation between Comrade Erich Honecker and Comrade Fidel Castro, 3 April 1977, U.S.S.R., VF, CL.

145. Brezhnev speech in honor of Fidel Castro, 5 April 1977, FBIS, 6 April 1977, N 2–3.

146. Podgorny's speech in Mozambique (before he was ousted by Brezhnev), 31 March 1977, FBIS, 1 April 1977, H 2–6.

147. CPSU CC to SED [East German] CC, 13 May 1977, CWIHP *Bulletin* 8–9 (1996/1997), 62.

148. Dobrynin, *In Confidence*, 404–405; Gribkov's comment, "Global Competition," 59–61; also comments by Brutents, *ibid.*, 49–51; comments by V. V. Shlykov, department chief at the Main Intelligence Administration [GRU] of the General Staff, in Michael Ellman and Vladimir Kontorovich, eds., *The Destruction of the Soviet Economic System: An Insiders' History* (Armonk, N.Y.: M. E. Sharpe,

1998), 42; Dobrynin's comments, "SALT II and the Growth of Mistrust," 232–36; Westad, *Global Cold War*, 253–79; Zubok, *Failed Empire*, chapters 7 and 8.

149. For statistical data, see U.S. Arms Control and Disarmament Agency, *World Military Expenditures and Arms Transfers, 1967–1976* (Washington, D.C.: Government Printing Office, 1978), 9, 10, 149, 153; also see Orah Cooper and Carol Fogarty, "Soviet Economic and Military Aid to the Less Developed Countries, 1954–78," in *Soviet Economy in a Time of Change*, vol. 2, by Joint Economic Committee, Congress of the United States (Washington, D.C.: Government Printing Office, 1979), 648–62. Although Carter sought to reduce U.S. arms sales, Brzezinski was well aware of the embarrassing data. See, for example, Brzezinski to Carter, 26 May 1977, box 41, BC, CL; for Gromyko's remonstrations about U.S. double-standards, see Warren Christopher to Vance, 12 December 1977, box 27 (SCC 45), Meetings, BC, CL.

150. For the quotation, see Podgorny's speech in honor of Mohammad Daud, 12 April 1977, FBIS, 13 April 1977, J 4; for other affirmations of the need to spread détente, see, for example, Kosygin speech in honor of Hedi Nouira, 4 April 1977, *ibid.*, 5 April 1977, F 2; Gromyko's statement in India, 26 April 1977, *ibid.*, 29 April 1977, J 2–3; for Gromyko, also see Christopher to Vance, 12 December 1977, box 27 (SCC 45), Meetings, BC, CL; for Brezhnev's disinterest in the Horn of Africa, see Dobrynin's comments, "SALT II and the Growth of Mistrust," 230–39.

151. Presidential Review Memorandum/NSC-21, "The Horn of Africa," [ND], USSR, VF, CL.

152. Brzezinski to Carter, 8 July 1977, box 41, BC, CL.

153. Presidential Review Memorandum/NSC-21, "The Horn of Africa," [ND], USSR, VF, CL.

154. Brzezinski to Carter, [ND], box 1, Horn/Special, National Security Affairs (NSA) Staff, CL; Paul Henze to Brzezinski, 15 August 1977 and 9 December 1977, *ibid.*

155. Memorandum of Conversation between Vance and Huang Hua, 23 August 1977, China, VF, CL.

156. Policy Review Committee Meeting, 25 August 1977, box 34, Meetings, BC, CL; Henze to Brzezinski, 9 December 1977, box 1, Horn/Special, NSA Staff, CL.

157. See the documents in CWIHP *Bulletin* 8–9 (1996/1997): 73–83; Henze to Brzezinski, especially 17 August 1977 and 9 December 1977, box 1, Horn/Special, NSA Staff, CL.

158. [Soviet] Record of the Main Content of A. A. Gromyko's Conversation with U.S. President J. Carter, 23 September 1977, USSR, VF, CL; also see Memorandum of Conversation between Vance and Gromyko, 30 September 1977, 9:30 a.m., USSR, VF, CL; [U.S. Department of State briefing paper] "Africa," [ND], part of document collection for the conference "Global Competition." Bill Quandt, then Brzezinski's Middle East expert, calls the Soviet proposal "remarkably balanced." See William B. Quandt, *Peace Process: American Diplomacy and the Arab-Israeli Conflict Since 1967*, 3rd ed. (Washington, D.C.: Brookings Institution, 2005), 187; for Soviet desires to cooperate in the Middle East, see the comments of Kornienko and Brutents, "U.S.-Soviet Relations and Soviet Foreign Policy," 53–72.

159. Vance, *Hard Choices*, 59–61, 191–93. Many of the Gromyko-Vance conversations and the Gromyko-Carter exchanges in September 1977 are declassified and can be found in USSR, VF, CL.

160. Vance to Christopher, 1 October 1977, document collection for the conference "Global Competition."

161. Vance, *Hard Choices*, 59; for the discussions on 22 September, one in the morning and the other in the evening, see the Memorandum of Conversations between Vance and Gromyko, 22 September 1977, USSR, VF, CL; for information on the Backfire bomber, see Zaloga, *Kremlin's Nuclear Sword*, 173–75.

162. Carter, *Keeping Faith*, 221–22; Carter to Brezhnev, 4 November 1977, box 17, Plains File, CL; for background, also see Strobe Talbott, *Endgame: The Inside Story of SALT II* (New York: Harper Colophon Books, 1979), 88–132.

163. Quandt, *Peace Process*, 188–91; comments by Vance, "Global Competition," 96–101.

164. For Vance's quotation, see his comments, "Global Competition," 94; Quandt, *Peace Process*, 189–91.

165. Brezhnev to Carter, 16 December 1977, box 17, Plains File, CL; for Soviet feelings of exclusion, see, for example, the comments by Kornienko, Tarasenko, and Brutents, "U.S.-Soviet Relations and Soviet Foreign Policy," 53–72.

166. Carter to Brezhnev, 21 December 1977, box 17, Plains File, CL.

167. Brzezinski, *Power and Principle*, 113; also see Marshall Shulman's comment, "SALT II and the Growth of Mistrust," 285; for Soviet resentment, see the many comments in "Global Competition," 89–121; "US-Soviet Relations and Soviet Foreign Policy," 53–72.

168. For a description of the meeting, see CPSU CC to SED CC, 8 November 1977, CWIHP *Bulletin* 8–9 (1996/1997): 81–82.

169. For the figures, see Westad, *Global Cold War*, 276; also see Dobrynin, *In Confidence*, 405.

170. Christopher to Vance, 12 December 1977, box 27, Meetings, BC, CL; Dobrynin, *In Confidence*, 406.

171. Brezhnev to Carter, 12 January 1978, box 17, Plains File, CL.

172. Carter to Brezhnev, 25 January 1978, ibid.

173. Address Delivered Before a Joint Session of the Congress, 19 January 1978, *PPP: Carter, 1978*, 90–91*ff.*

174. *Ibid.*, 95, 97.

175. Schmidt to Carter, 22 December 1977, box 6, FRG (3), NSA, BC, CL.

176. Brzezinski to Carter, 9 February 1978, box 41, BC, CL; also see Brzezinski to Carter, 8 July 1977, *ibid.*

177. Brzezinski to Carter, 18 November 1977, *ibid.*; Hamilton Jordan and Frank Moore to Carter, 17 November 1977, box 37 (SALT 1977), Chief of Staff Papers, CL.

178. Carter to Valery Giscard d'Estaing, 27 January 1978, box 28, Meetings, BC, CL; Carter to Josip Broz Tito [draft], [ND], box 1, Horn/Special, NSA Staff, CL.

179. SCC Meeting on Horn of Africa, 2 March 1978, box 28, Meetings, BC, CL.

180. *Ibid.*

181. For Mondale's view, see *ibid.*; for views of Siad Barre, see Henze to Brzezinski, 10 and 16 March 1978, box 28, Meetings, BC, CL.

182. SCC Meeting on Horn of Africa, 2 March 1978, box 28, Meetings, BC, CL.

183. Brzezinski to Carter, 24 February 1978, box 41, BC, CL.

184. Brzezinski to Carter, 3 March 1978, box 28, Meetings, BC, CL; also see Dobrynin, *In Confidence*, 406.

185. Brzezinski to Carter, 3 March 1978, box 28, Meetings, BC, CL.

186. Carter, *Keeping Faith*, 171.

187. Brezhnev to Carter, 27 February 1978, box 17, Plains File, CL.

188. Memorandum of Conversation between Harriman and Dobrynin, 14 March 1978, USSR, VF, CL.

189. Dobrynin, *In Confidence*, 405–408; see the exchanges between Soviet and East German officials, CWIHP *Bulletin* 8–9 (1996–97): 84–90; Westad, *Global Cold War*, 280–81.

190. Conversation between Carlos Rafael Rodriguez and Thomas L. Hughes, 16 March 1978, box 10, Geographic File, China, BC, CL; for Cuban policy, see Piero Gleijeses, "Moscow's Proxy? Cuba and Africa," *Journal of Cold War Studies* 8 (Fall 2006): 98–146.

191. Comments by Vance and Shulman, in "SALT II and the Growth of Mistrust," 12, 246–47; comments by Shulman, in "Global Competition," 31–32.

192. Address at Wake Forest University, 17 March 1978, *PPP: Carter, 1978*, 529–35.

193. Remarks at the Palais des Congres, 4 January 1978, *ibid.*, 22.

194. *Ibid.*

195. Text of Remarks at a Meeting of the North Atlantic Council, 6 January 1978, *ibid.*, 36.

196. SCC Meeting on Horn of Africa, 2 March 1978, box 28, Meetings, BC, CL.

197. Brzezinski to Carter, 21 April 1978, box 41, BC, CL; Brzezinski to Carter, 4 February 1977, China, VF, CL; Michael Oksenberg to Brzezinski, 4 February 1977, *ibid.*

198. Carter, *Keeping Faith*, 186–93; Vance, *Hard Choices*, 45–46, 75–83. Memoranda of the conversations between Vance and Chinese officials in August 1977 may be found in China, VF, CL.

199. Carter, *Keeping Faith*, 194; Vance, *Hard Choices*, 116.

200. Carter to Brzezinski, 17 May 1978, document collection for "Global Competition"; for background, also see Brzezinski, *Power and Principle*, 202–209.

201. Brzezinski, *Power and Principle*, 213, 209.

202. Memorandum of Conversation between Brzezinski and Teng Hsiao P'ing [Deng Xiaoping], 21 May 1978 [dated 25 May 1978], China, VF, CL.

203. Memorandum of Conversation between Brzezinski and Hua Kuo-feng [Guofeng], 22 May 1978, *ibid.*

204. The toasts can be found in box 9, China, BC, CL.

205. Brzezinski, *Power and Principle*, 220–21.

206. Carter, *Keeping Faith*, 193–94.

207. Address at the Commencement Exercises, 7 June 1978, *PPP: Carter, 1978*, 1052–57, quotation on 1053.

208. President's News Conference, 26 June 1978, *ibid.*, 1180.

209. Memorandum of Conversation between Gromyko and Carter, 27 May 1978, USSR, VF, CL; Memorandum of Conversation between Gromyko and Vance, 31 May 1978, *ibid.*; [Soviet] Record of the Main Content of the Conversation between A. A. Gromyko and U.S. Secretary of State C. Vance, 31 May 1978, *ibid.*; Memorandum of Conversation between Vance and Gromyko, 12 and 13 July 1978, *ibid.*; [Soviet] Record of the Main Contents of A. A. Gromyko's Negotiations with the Secretary of State of the USA C. Vance, 12–13 July 1978, *ibid.* The quotations are on pp. 33 and 37 of the 27 May conversation.

210. For the Politburo discussion of Shcharansky, see Session of the Politburo of the CC CPSU, 22 June 1978, READD, NSA (accessible on the NSA website); for Shcharansky, also see Rubinstein, *Soviet Dissidents*, 245–48.

211. Statement on the Sentence Announced at the Soviet Dissident's Trial, 14 July 1978, *PPP: Carter, 1978*, 1281.

212. Comment by Dobrynin, "SALT II and the Growth of Mistrust," 210; for Soviet anger about the U.S. position on human rights and the U.S. employment of the China card, also see Report of the Meeting between SED General Secretary E. Honecker and L. I. Brezhnev in the Crimea, 25 July 1978, CWIHP *Bulletin* 8–9 (1997/97): 122–23.

213. Alexeyeva, *Soviet Dissent*; Rubinstein, *Soviet Dissidents*, 213–70.

214. Brzezinski to Carter, 9 December 1977, box 41, BC, CL.

215. [Soviet] Record of the Main Content of A. A. Gromyko's Conversation with US President J. Carter, 23 September 1978, USSR, VF, CL.

216. Patrick Tyler, *Six Presidents and China: A Great Wall: An Investigative History* (New York: A Century Foundation Book, 1999), 229–85; James Mann, *About Face: A History of America's Curious Relationship with China from Nixon to Clinton* (New York: Alfred A. Knopf, 1999), 81–102.

217. Brzezinski to Carter, 1 September 1978, box 41, BC, CL.

218. Brzezinski to Carter, 6 October 1978, *ibid.*; for Carter's comment, see his marginal notes on Brzezinski to Carter, 13 October 1978, *ibid.*; Brzezinski to Carter, 2 December 1978, 12 January 1979, box 42, *ibid.*; Tyler, *Six Presidents and China*, 259–75.

219. Brzezinski, *Power and Principle*, 232; Dobrynin's comments, "Global Competition," 131–32; Shulman's comment, *ibid.*, 150.

220. Brzezinski to Carter, 28 December 1978, box 42, BC, CL.
221. Brzezinski to Carter, [24 and 26 January 1979], box 9, China, BC, CL; for the aims of the talks with Deng, see the documents in box 9.
222. Address Delivered Before a Joint Session of the Congress, 23 January 1979, *PPP: Carter, 1979,* 103–109; Annual Message to the Congress, 25 January 1979, *ibid.,* 163.
223. Carter to Brezhnev, 14 December 1978, box 17, Plains File, CL.
224. Address, 23 January 1979, *PPP: Carter, 1979,* 107.
225. News Conference, 16 November 1978, *ibid., 1978,* 2045; News Conference, 26 January 1979, *ibid., 1979,* 170.
226. Harriman to Vance, 13 December 1978, USSR, VF, CL.
227. Speech by Brezhnev at the Political Consultative Committee Meeting [of the Warsaw Pact], 22 November 1978, in Mastny and Byrne, *A Cardboard Castle?,* 418–21.
228. *Ibid.,* 420.
229. Brezhnev interview with *Time,* 15 January 1979, FBIS, 16 January 1979, B 1.
230. For background, see Mohsen M. Milani, *The Making of Iran's Islamic Revolution: From Monarchy to Islamic Republic,* 2nd ed. (Boulder, Colo.: Westview, 1988); S. A. Arjomand, "Iran's Islamic Revolution in Comparative Perspective," *World Politics* 38 (April, 1986): 383–400; Westad, *Global Cold War,* 288–96.
231. James A. Bill, *The Eagle and the Lion: The Tragedy of American-Iranian Relations* (New Haven, Conn.: Yale University Press, 1988), 236.
232. Vance to U.S. embassies in the Middle East, 23 November 1978, document collection associated with the oral history conference "Intervention in Afghanistan and the Fall of Détente"; CIA, "Soviet Involvement in the Iranian Crisis," 12 February 1979, *ibid.;* Vance, *Hard Choices,* 326.
233. Brzezinski to Carter, 28 December 1978, box 42, BC, CL.
234. Brzezinski to Carter, 2 December 1978, *ibid.;* Brzezinski, *Power and Principle,* 372.
235. Brezhnev to Carter, 17 November 1978, box 17, Plains File, CL; for Soviet fears, also see comments by Brutents and Leonid Shebarshin, "Intervention in Afghanistan and the Fall of Détente," 28–29, 48–49.
236. Carter to Brezhnev, 21 November 1978, box 17, Plains File, CL.
237. Bill, *The Eagle and the Lion,* 261.
238. Toasts at a White House Dinner Honoring Governors, 27 February 1979, *PPP: Carter, 1979,* 359–60.
239. Question-and-Answer Session with Bill Moyers, 13 November 1978, *ibid.,* 2019; Remarks at Georgia Institute of Technology, 20 February 1979, *ibid.,* 301–302.
240. Toasts at White House Dinner, 27 February 1979, *ibid.,* 355–56.
241. Vasiliy Mitrokhin, "The KGB in Afghanistan," ed. Odd Arne Westad and Christian Ostermann, CWIHP Working Paper No. 40 (Washington, D.C.: Woodrow Wilson International Center, 2001), 21–23; Georgi Markovich Kornienko, *Kholodnaia voyna: svidetel'stvo ee uchastnika* [The Cold War: A Testimony of Its Participant] (Moscow: Mezhdunar otnosheniia, 1994), 188–89; comments by Brutents, Varennikov, and Dobrynin, "Intervention in Afghanistan and the Fall of Détente," 6–15; Odd Arne Westad, "The Road to Kabul: Soviet Policy on Afghanistan, 1978–1979," in Westad, *Fall of Détente,* 119.
242. Mitrokhin, "KGB in Afghanistan," 21–24; Westad, "Road to Kabul," 119–22; Puzanov to Ministry of Foreign Affairs, USSR, 31 May 1978, document collection associated with the conference "Intervention in Afghanistan and the Fall of Détente."
243. Theodore Eliot to Vance, 6 May 1978, document collection associated with the conference "Intervention in Afghanistan and the Fall of Détente."
244. Comments by Dobrynin, document collection associated with the conference "Intervention in

Afghanistan and the Fall of Détente," 14; Douglas J. MacEachin, *Predicting the Soviet Invasion of Afghanistan: The Intelligence Community's Record* (Washington, D.C.: Central Intelligence Agency, Center for the Study of Intelligence, 2002), 8–10; Westad, "Fall of Kabul," 121–22.

245. Eliot to Vance, 13 June 1978, document collection associated with the conference "Intervention in Afghanistan and the Fall of Détente."

246. Mitrokhin, "KGB in Afghanistan," 24–40; Westad, "Fall of Kabul," 120–24; Aleksandr Antonovich Lyakhovskiy, "Inside the Soviet Invasion of Afghanistan and the Seizure of Kabul, December 1979," CWIHP Working Paper No. 51 (Washington, D.C.: Woodrow Wilson International Center, 2007), 3–5.

247. Westad, *Global Cold War*, 304–305; CC CPSU to Honecker, 13 October 1978, CWIHP *Bulletin* 8–9 (1996/1997): 135.

248. Brezhnev Dinner Speech, 5 December 1978, FBIS, 6 December 1978, J 2.

249. Westad, *Global Cold War*, 305–306.

250. Brezhnev Dinner Speech, 5 December 1978, FBIS, 6 December 1978, J 2.

251. Westad, *Global Cold War*, 299–309; Steve Coll, *Ghost Wars: The Secret History of the CIA, Afghanistan, and Bin Laden, from the Soviet Invasion to September 10, 2001* (New York: The Penguin Press, 2004), 40–41.

252. Meeting of the Politburo of the CC of the CPSU, 17 March 1979, in Westad, *Fall of Détente*, 287–98.

253. Transcript of Telephone Conversation between Kosygin and Taraki, 17 or 18 March 1979, CWIHP *Bulletin* 8–9 (1996/1997): 145–46.

254. Meeting of the Politburo of the CC of the CPSU, 18 March 1979, in Westad, *Fall of Détente*, 298–303.

255. Meeting of the Politburo of the CC of the CPSU, 19 March 1979, *ibid.*, 303–10.

256. Record of Meeting of A. N. Kosygin, A. A. Gromyko, D. Ustinov, and B. N. Ponomarev with N. M. Taraki, 20 March 1979, CWIHP *Bulletin* 8–9 (1996/1997): 146–48.

257. For Brezhnev's comments, see his remarks to the Politburo, in Session of Politburo of CC CPSU, 22 March 1979, *ibid.*, 150–51.

258. Dobrynin, *In Confidence*, 418; Brezhnev's speech to the electorate of Moscow's Bauman district, 2 March 1979, FBIS, 5 March 1979, R 5.

259. Brezhnev to Carter, 19 March 1979, box 17, Plains File, CL.

260. Brezhnev to Carter, [late April], *ibid.*

261. Comments by Dobrynin, "SALT II and the Growth of Mistrust," 156–58.

262. For Detinov's quotation, see his comments, *ibid.*, 180; for further elucidation of Soviet thinking and decision making on arms control, see *ibid.*, 32–45, 87–88, 134–35, 144–82; Savel'yev and Detinov, *Big Five*, 15–53; for a cogent summary of the issues, see Powaski, *March to Armageddon*, 162–79.

263. Brezhnev speech in East Berlin, 6 October 1979, FBIS, 9 October 1979, F 3; Chazov, *Health and Power*, 89–91.

264. Dobrynin, *In Confidence*, 417–18.

265. Brzezinski to Carter, 30 March 1979, box 42, BC, CL.

266. Policy Review Committee Meeting, 14 May 1979, box 25 (PRC 106), Meetings, *ibid.*; Brzezinski to Carter, 14 May 1979, *ibid.*; also see Victor Utgoff and Jake Stewart to Brzezinski and Aaron, 10 May 1979, *ibid.*; Vance's handwritten notes, 3 April 1979, USSR, VF, CL. These fears were not imaginary, but they were exaggerated. The trend in the military balance between NATO and the Warsaw Pact, according to the International Institute for Strategic Studies, was sufficiently dangerous "to warrant urgent remedies." See International Institute for Strategic Studies, *The Military Balance, 1981–82* (New York: Facts on File, Inc., 1981), 123. But notwithstanding the trend, there was still a rough equivalence. See the figures in Holloway, *Soviet Union and the Arms Race*, 58–60. In retro-

spect, it is apparent that the numbers of Soviet ICBMs, intermediate-range ballistic missiles, and strategic bombers did not grow rapidly in the late 1970s, but the number of Soviet submarine-launched ballistic missiles did increase significantly, as did the total number of strategic warheads in the Soviet arsenal. The latter climbed from 3,423 in 1975 to 6,667 in 1980. Moreover, the accuracy of Soviet missiles grew enormously during this period, although the Soviet Union never got close to achieving the capability to launch a preemptive attack. See the tables and commentary in Zaloga, *Kremlin's Nuclear Sword*, 176–77, 241–48.

267. Brzezinski to Carter, 12 April 1979, box 42, BC, CL.

268. Patrick Caddell to Carter, 11 June 1979, box 33, Chief of Staff Papers, CL; see also Cambridge Survey Research to the Democratic Committee, 24 and 25 May 1979, *ibid.*; Caddell, "A Memorandum on Current Public Attitudes on SALT," [May 1979], box 37, *ibid*; Carter, *Keeping Faith*, 236–39.

269. Carter, *Keeping Faith*, 241; Vance, *Hard Choices*, 134–35; Talbott, *Endgame*, 94–202, 237–44, 256–59; Garthoff, *Détente and Confrontation*, 889–904.

270. Remarks and a Question-and-Answer Session, 30 March 1979, *PPP: Carter, 1979*, 564–66.

271. "Comprehensive Net Assessment, 1978," 30 March 1979, box 42, BC, CL.

272. Statement of Turner, 26 June 1979, Subcommittee on Priorities and Economy in Government, Joint Economic Committee of the Congress of the United States, *Allocation of Resources in the Soviet Union and China—1979* (Washington, D.C.: Government Printing Office, 1980), 2, 11, located in box 1, End of the Cold War Collection, NSA; also CIA, "Consumer Frustrations and the Soviet Regime," 23 August 1979, box 1, *ibid.*

273. For the interview with Moyers, see Question-and-Answer Session, 13 November 1978, *PPP: Carter, 1978*, 2017; Remarks at Jefferson-Jackson Dinner, 7 April 1979, *ibid., 1979*, 636–37; Remarks at the Annual Convention of the American Newspaper Publishers Association, 25 April 1979, *ibid.*, 693; Remarks at a State [Iowa] Democratic Party Convention, 4 May 1979, *ibid.*, 805.

274. Vance to Carter, 8 June 1979, document collection associated with the conference "Global Competition"; Notes from Conversation between Harriman and Dobrynin, 4 June 1979, USSR, VF, CL; Memorandum of Conversation between Harriman and Carter, 6 June 1979, *ibid.*; Carter, *Keeping Faith*, 241.

275. Carter, *Keeping Faith*, 240–41; Vance to Carter, 8 June 1979, document collection associated with the conference "Global Competition"; for transcripts of the conversations between Carter and Brezhnev, see Memorandum of Conversations, 16, 17, 18 June 1979, USSR, VF, CL.

276. In addition to the transcripts cited in the preceding note, see Carter, *Keeping Faith*, 242–65; Dobrynin, *In Confidence*, 422–27.

277. See esp. Memorandum of Conversation, 17 June 1979, 5:30 p.m. session, p. 6, USSR, VF, CL.

278. Memorandum of Conversation between Brown and Ustinov and Ogarkov, 17 June 1979, Meetings, BC, CL; see comments by Dobrynin, "SALT II and the Growth of Mistrust," 136–38; also Dobrynin, *In Confidence*, 426–27.

279. Memorandum of Conversation, 16 June 1979, 11:00 a.m., p. 7, USSR, VF, CL.

280. Carter, *Keeping Faith*, 245.

281. Memorandum of Conversation, 16 June 1979, 11:00 a.m., p. 5, USSR, VF, CL.

282. Dobrynin, *In Confidence*, 426; Chazov, *Health and Power*, 91.

283. Dobrynin, *In Confidence*, 421–22.

284. Carter, *Keeping Faith*, 261; Carter to Brezhnev, 18 June 1979, box 17, Plains File, CL.

285. Address Delivered Before a Joint Session of the Congress, 18 June 1979, *PPP: Carter, 1979*, 1087–92.

286. Minutes of the Presidential Review Committee, 11 June 1979, box 25, Meetings (PRC 111), BC, CL; also see Brzezinski to Carter, 13 June 1979, *ibid.*

287. Brzezinski to Carter, 23 June 1979, box 30 (SCC 170), *ibid.*

288. *Ibid.*

289. Robert A. Pastor to Brzezinski, 19 July 1979, box 30 (SCC 183), *ibid.*

290. Brown to Carter, 25 June 1979, *ibid.*

291. Pastor to Brzezinski, 19 July 1979, *ibid.*

292. Special Coordinating Committee Meeting, "Summary of Conclusions," 20 July 1979, box 30 (SCC 184), *ibid.*

293. Brzezinski to Carter, 20 July 1979, box 30 (SCC 183), *ibid.*

294. President's News Conference, 25 July 1979, *PPP: Carter, 1979*, 1307–308; Announcement of Emergency Assistance, 27 July 1979, *ibid.*; for a firsthand account of the fall of Somoza by the U.S. ambassador, see Lawrence Pezzullo and Ralph Pezzullo, *At the Fall of Somoza* (Pittsburgh, Penn.: University of Pittsburgh Press, 1993); for the assistance, see Alan McPherson, *Intimate Ties, Bitter Struggles: The United States and Latin America Since 1945* (Washington, D.C.: Potomac Books, 2006), 85.

295. Address to the Nation, 15 July 1979, *PPP: Carter, 1979*, 1235–41.

296. Brzezinski to Carter, 27 July 1979, box 42, BC, CL; Brzezinski to Carter, 1 August 1979, box 25, Meetings (PRC 120), *ibid.*

297. David D. Newsom, *The Soviet Brigade in Cuba: A Study in Public Diplomacy* (Bloomington: Indiana University Press, 1987), vii–xiii, 1–36; Vance, *Hard Choices*, 358–62.

298. Vance, *Hard Choices*, 358–64; Brzezinski, *Power and Principle*, 346–53; Carter, *Keeping Faith*, 262–64.

299. Brzezinski to Carter, 13 September 1979, box 42, BC, CL.

300. *Ibid.*; also see Brzezinski to Carter, 17 September 1979, box 10, Cuba, *ibid.*; Brzezinski to Carter, 18 September 1979, box 9, China, *ibid.*; Brzezinski to Carter, 21 September 1979, box 42, *ibid.*; Brzezinski, *Power and Principle*, 346–53.

301. Vance, *Hard Choices*, 360–64; also see Brezhnev to Carter, 27 September 1979, box 17, Plains File, CL; Meeting of the CC CPSU Politburo, 27 September 1979, USSR, VF, CL.

302. Carter's Speech to the Nation, 1 October 1979, in Newsom, *Soviet Brigade in Cuba*, 81–86; also see Carter's comments at his news conference, 9 October 1979, *PPP: Carter, 1979*, 1838.

303. For Carter's thoughts about meeting the Pope, see Remarks and a Question-and-Answer Session, 16 October 1979, *PPP: Carter, 1979*, 1940–41; for the quotation, see President's News Conference, 9 October 1979, *ibid.*, 1839; also see Judt, *Postwar*, 585–87.

304. Brzezinski, *Power and Principle*, 296–300, 463–67, quotation on p. 464; for other quotation, see Brzezinski to Carter, 13 September 1979, box 42, BC, CL; for developments in Poland and Eastern Europe, also see the discussion in "Global Competition," 237–50, 263–64; also see Bennett Kovrig, *Of Walls and Bridges: The United States and Eastern Europe* (New York: New York University Press, 1991), 121–30, 177–80.

305. CIA, "Consumer Frustrations and the Soviet Regime," 2 August 1979, iii–vi, box 1, End of the Cold War Collection, NSA.

306. For Carter's reiteration of the prevailing "malaise," see President's News Conference, 9 October 1979, *PPP: Carter, 1979*, 1842–43.

307. Caddell to Carter, 6 November 1979, box 33, Chief of Staff Papers, CL.

308. Jordan to Carter, [ND; early November 1979?], box 34, *ibid.*: Bill, *Eagle and the Lion*, 294–95.

309. For the quotations, see Remarks at the Convention of the American Federation of Labor and the Congress of Industrial Organizations, 15 November 1979, *PPP: Carter, 1979*, 2123; President's News Conference, 28 November 1979, *ibid.*, 2168, 2167.

310. Jordan, *Crisis*, 69–70, 55.

311. President's News Conference, 28 November 1979, *PPP: Carter, 1979*, 2168; Remarks and a Question-and-Answer Session, 13 December 1979, *ibid.*, 2240; for various options, see Brzezinski to Carter, 21 December 1979, box 42, BC, CL.

312. Brzezinski, *Power and Principle*, 484-85; Brzezinski to Carter, 14 and 21 December 1979, box 42, BC, CL.

313. See Carter's comment on Brzezinski to Carter, 21 December 1979, box 42, BC, CL.

314. On 6 December, Dobrynin and Brzezinski were still discussing plans for SALT III. See Dobrynin's comments, "Intervention in Afghanistan and the Fall of Détente," 156.

315. *USSR and the Third World* 9 (1 June-30 November 1979): 83.

316. Suslov speech, 18 September 1979, FBIS, 21 September 1979, R 8.

317. See, for example, Ustinov speech, 7 November 1979, FBIS, 7 November 1979, F 19; B. N. Ponomarev, "The 60th Anniversary of the Founding of the Communist International," in B. N. Ponomarev, *Selected Speeches and Writings* (Oxford, Eng.: Pergamon Press, 1981), 335-51.

318. *USSR and the Third World* 9 (1 June-30 November 1979): 57.

319. Gromyko, Andropov, Ustinov, and Ponomarev to CC CPSU, 12 April 1979, CWIHP *Bulletin* 3 (Fall 1993): 67-69.

320. See, for example, Record of Conversation between Puzanov and Taraki, 10 July 1979, *ibid.*, 8-9 (1996/1997): 153; Ponomarev to CC CPSU, 19-20 July 1979, *ibid.*; Conversation between Gorelov and Amin, 11 August 1979, *ibid.*, 153-54; Report from I. Pavlovski, 25 August 1979, *ibid.*, 154.

321. Gromyko, Ustinov, Andropov, and Ponomarev to CC CPSU, 28 June 1979, *ibid.*, 152.

322. Mitrokhin, "KGB in Afghanistan," 41-45; Westad, *Global Cold War*, 312-13.

323. Mitrokhin, "KGB in Afghanistan," 45-46.

324. Comments by Lyakhovski, "Intervention in Afghanistan and the Fall of Détente," 77-80; Westad, *Global Cold War*, 311-13; Mitrokhin, "KGB in Afghanistan," 45-53.

325. Transcript of Brezhnev-Honecker Summit, 4 October 1979, CWIHP *Bulletin* 8-9 (1996/1997): 156-57; Information from the CC CPSU to Honecker, 1 October 1979, *ibid.*, 156.

326. Gromyko, Andropov, Ustinov, and Ponomarev to CC CPSU, [29 October 1979], in Lyakhovski, "New Russian Evidence," 10-15; also in CWIHP *Bulletin* 8-9 (1996/1997): 157-58.

327. Quoted by Dobrynin, "Intervention in Afghanistan and the Fall of Détente," 90; also see Andropov to Brezhnev [early December 1979], CWIHP *Bulletin* 8-9 (1996-97): 159.

328. Lyakhovski, "New Russian Evidence," 23-25.

329. Comments by Varennikov, "Intervention in Afghanistan and the Fall of Détente," 73; also see Westad, *Global Cold War*, 320.

330. Comment by Dobrynin, *ibid.*, 95; also see Lyakhovski, "New Russian Evidence," 23-25; Westad, *Global Cold War*, 316-26.

331. Lyakhovski, "New Russian Evidence," 24-26; comments by Gribkov, "Global Competition," 291.

332. Lyakhovski, "New Russian Evidence," 22-23.

333. For the quotation, see comments by Brutents, "Intervention in Afghanistan and the Fall of Détente," 177; Lyakhovski, "New Russian Evidence," 28-40; also see Westad, *Global Cold War*, 320-21.

334. For the quotation, see Lyakhovski, "New Russian Evidence," 27-28; for Brezhnev's concern with U.S. modernization of its theater nuclear forces, see Brezhnev Speech in East Berlin, 6 October 1979, FBIS, 9 October 1979, F 1-5; Brezhnev Answers Questions, 5 November 1979, *ibid.*, 6 November 1979, AA 1; Ustinov Speech, 7 November 1979, *ibid.*, P 18-20; Ponomarev, "In the Interests of Détente, in the Interests of the Peoples of the World," 18 November 1979, *ibid.*, 20 November 1979, G 3; Gromyko Statement and Press Conference, 23 November 1979, *ibid.*, 26 November 1979, G 1-7; Dobrynin, *In Confidence*, 429-33.

335. Gromyko Statement and Press Conference, 23 November 1979, FBIS, 26 November 1979, G 4;

Dobrynin, *In Confidence*, 437; comment by Dobrynin, "Intervention in Afghanistan and the Fall of Détente," 54-55.

336. For the quotation, see comment by Shebarshin, "Intervention in Afghanistan and the Fall of Détente," 42-43; also see Westad, *Global Cold War*, 323-36.

337. Brezhnev Speech to CPSU Central Committee Plenum, 27 November 1979, FBIS, 29 November 1979, R 1-13, quotations on R 4, 9, 10, 12.

338. Lyakhovski, "New Russian Evidence," 22.

339. Ponomarev, "In the Interests of Détente, in the Interests of the Peoples of the World," 18 November 1979, FBIS, 20 November 1979, G 3.

340. [East German] Stenographic Minutes of Meeting between Honecker and Brezhnev, 4 October 1979, "The September 11 Sourcebooks," NSA.

341. Jordan, *Crisis*, 99.

342. Carter to Brezhnev, 28 December 1979, box 17, Plains File, CL.

343. Brezhnev to Carter, 29 December 1979, *ibid.*

344. For Carter's actions, see, *PPP: Carter, 1980*, 11, 12, 23-24, 87-88, 106; NSC Meeting on Afghanistan, January 1980, in Westad, *Fall of Détente*, 332-51.

345. Remarks at a White House briefing for religious leaders, 10 January 1980, *PPP: Carter, 1980*, 49.

346. Remarks at a White House briefing for members of Congress, 8 January 1980, *ibid.*, 40; Remarks and a question-and-answer session, 15 January 1980, *ibid.*, 87; Address, 23 January 1980, *ibid.*, 196.

347. Interview on *Meet the Press*, 20 January 1980, *ibid.*, 108; Address delivered before a joint session of Congress, 23 January 1980, *ibid.*, 197.

348. Address delivered before a joint session of Congress, 23 January 1980, *ibid.*, 194-200, quotation on 197.

349. *Ibid.*, 194.

350. Fritz Ermath to Brzezinski, 2 January 1980, document collection associated with the conference "Intervention in Afghanistan and the Fall of Détente."

351. Dobrynin, *In Confidence*, 446-47; Dobrynin's comments, "Intervention in Afghanistan and the Fall of Détente," 22-23.

352. Dobrynin comment, "Intervention in Afghanistan and the Fall of Détente," 219.

V: The End of the Cold War, 1985-90: Gorbachev, Reagan, and Bush

1. George P. Shultz, *Turmoil and Triumph: My Years as Secretary of State* (New York: Charles Scribner's Sons, 1993), 531-32.

2. Kiron K. Skinner, Annelise Anderson, and Martin Anderson, eds., *Reagan in His Own Hand* (New York: Simon and Schuster, 2001), 10-12.

3. "President's News Conference," 29 January 1981, *Public Papers of the Presidents: Ronald Reagan* (Washington, D.C.: Government Printing Office, 1982), 57 (hereinafter cited as *PPP: Reagan, year, page*).

4. Skinner, Anderson, and Anderson, *Reagan in His Own Hand*, 15.

5. "Remarks at the Annual Convention of the National Association of Evangelicals," 8 March 1983, *PPP: Reagan, 1983*, 743.

6. "Address at Commencement Exercises," *ibid., 1981*, 434.

7. "Address to Members of British Parliament," 8 June 1982, *ibid., 1982*, 743.

8. *Ibid.*, 745.

9. *Ibid.*, 746-47.

10. Skinner, Anderson, and Anderson, *Reagan in His Own Hand*, 4.

11. Ronald Reagan, *An American Life* (New York: Simon and Schuster, 1990), 28, 22, 27; also see Lou

Cannon, *President Reagan: The Role of a Lifetime* (New York: Public Affairs, 2000); Edmund Morris, *Dutch: A Memoir of Ronald Reagan* (New York: Random House, 1999); Richard Reeves, *President Reagan: The Triumph of Imagination* (New York: Simon and Schuster, 2005); John P. Diggins, *Ronald Reagan: Fate, Freedom, and the Making of History* (New York: W. W. Norton and Company, 2007).

12. Skinner, Anderson, and Anderson, *Reagan in His Own Hand*, xiii; Nancy Reagan with William Novak, *My Turn: The Memoirs of Nancy Reagan* (New York: Random House, 1989), 104, 108.

13. Reagan, *An American Life*, 19–34.

14. *Ibid.*, 31.

15. N. Reagan, *My Turn*, 106; Cannon, *President Reagan*, 172–95; Morris, *Dutch*, 61.

16. Reagan, *An American Life*, 22.

17. N. Reagan, *My Turn*, 107.

18. Reagan, *An American Life*, 20–21.

19. Michael K. Deaver, *A Different Drummer: My Thirty Years with Ronald Reagan* (New York: HarperCollins, 2001), 68; also see Paul Kengor, *God and Ronald Reagan* (New York: Harper-Collins, 2004).

20. Reagan, *An American Life*, 44–61; Morris, *Dutch*, 64–75.

21. Reagan, *An American Life*, 66; also see Reagan to Ron Cochran, 12 May 1980, in *Reagan: A Life in Letters*, ed. by Kiron K. Skinner, Annelise Anderson, and Martin Anderson (New York: The Free Press, 2003), 27–31.

22. Reagan, *An American Life*, 75–104.

23. *Ibid.*, 114–15; Cannon, *President Reagan*, 242–44.

24. Kengor, *God and Ronald Reagan*, 94–96.

25. Reagan, *An American Life*, 126–36; Paul Lettow, *Ronald Reagan and His Quest to Abolish Nuclear Weapons* (New York: Random House, 2005), 10–18.

26. Reagan, *An American Life*, 129–30, 137–43; N. Reagan, *My Turn*, 124–31.

27. Reagan, *An American Life*, 141–43.

28. *Ibid.*, 219. "Morning in America" was the theme of the 1984 campaign, but it also captures the essence of Reagan's run for the presidency in 1980. See James T. Patterson, *Restless Giant: The United States from Watergate to Bush v. Gore* (New York: Oxford University Press, 2005), 145–51.

29. "Inaugural Address," 20 January 1981, *PPP: Reagan, 1981*, 3.

30. David A. Stockman, *The Triumph of Politics: How the Reagan Revolution Failed* (New York: Harper and Row, 1986), 108–109; Ronald E. Powaski, *Return to Armageddon: The United States and the Nuclear Arms Race, 1981–1999* (New York: Oxford University Press, 2000), 15; John M. Collins, *U.S.-Soviet Military Balance, 1980–1985* (New York: Pergamon-Brassey's International Defense Publishers, 1985), 19–22; Christopher Simpson, *National Security Directives of the Reagan and Bush Administrations: The Declassified History of U.S. Political & Military Policy, 1981–1991* (Boulder, Colo.: Westview Press, 1995), 46–49.

31. "Address on the State of the Union," 26 January 1982, *PPP: Reagan, 1982*, 78; "Interview with Walter Cronkite," 3 March 1981, *ibid., 1981*, 195; "President's News Conference," 19 January 1982, *ibid., 1982*, 43; also see "Interview with Skip Weber," 9 February 1982, *ibid.*, 151; Reagan to John Matzger, 11 May 1982, in Skinner, Anderson, and Anderson, *A Life in Letters*, 405; Reagan to Irving S. Schloss, 28 June 1982, *ibid.*, 406–407.

32. CIA, Directorate of Intelligence, "Soviet Society in the 1980s: Problems and Prospects," December 1982, box 1, End of Cold War Collection, National Security Archive (NSA); CIA, Directorate of Intelligence, "Soviet Elite Concerns About Popular Discontent and Official Corruption," December 1982, *ibid.*; Robert M. Gates, *From the Shadows: The Ultimate Insider's Story of Five Presidents and How They Won the Cold War* (New York: Simon and Schuster, 1996), 194–97.

33. Skinner, Anderson, and Anderson, *Reagan in His Own Hand*, 147; "Interview with the Editorial Board of the *New York Post*," 23 March 1982, PPP: *Reagan, 1982*, 368; Reagan to Mrs. Jay Harris, 26 April 1982, in Skinner, Anderson, and Anderson, *A Life in Letters*, 402–403.

34. Reagan, *An American Life*, 267; Lettow, *Reagan and Nuclear Weapons*, 35.

35. Reagan, *An American Life*, 268; for signs of dialogue, also see Anatoly Dobrynin, *In Confidence: Moscow's Ambassador to America's Six Cold War Presidents* (New York: Random House, 1995), 490–93.

36. Reagan, *An American Life*, 269.

37. *Ibid.*, 270–71; also see Skinner, Anderson, and Anderson, *A Life in Letters*, 737–41.

38. Reagan, *An American Life*, 272–73. His real reason for lifting the grain embargo was because "no other free world nations would join us and we were therefore hurting our own farmers." Reagan to Franciszek Lachowicz, 9 December 1982, in Skinner, Anderson, and Anderson, *A Life in Letters*, 377–78.

39. Martin Anderson, *Revolution: The Reagan Legacy* (Stanford, Calif.: Hoover Institution Press, 1990), 289–90; Stockman, *Triumph of Politics*, 76; Richard Pipes, *Vixi: Memoirs of a Non-Belonger* (New Haven, Conn.: Yale University Press, 2003), 166; Alexander M. Haig, Jr., *Caveat: Realism, Reagan, and Foreign Policy* (New York: Macmillan Publishing Company, 1984), 77.

40. Pipes, *Vixi*, 153; Robert C. McFarlane and Zophia Smardz, *Special Trust* (New York: Cadell and Davies, 1994), 171–83; Haig, *Caveat*, 80–86, 311–15.

41. National Security Decision Directive (NSDD) 32, "U.S. National Security Strategy," 20 May 1982, NSDD 32, Executive Secretariat, Ronald Reagan Presidential Library (RRPL).

42. *Ibid.*

43. Lettow, *Reagan and Nuclear Weapons*, 61–70.

44. For dismissal of Haig and appointment of Shultz, see Haig, *Caveat*, 311–15; Reagan, *An American Life*, 255–56, 360–62; Shultz, *Turmoil and Triumph*, 3–15.

45. Shultz, *Turmoil and Triumph*, 12, 10 (for quotations), also 162–67, 268–70, 309–22.

46. *Ibid.*, 119.

47. NSDD 75, "U.S. Relations with the USSR," 17 January 1983, in Simpson, *National Security Directives*, 255–63; also see materials regarding NSDD 75, in box 91644, William Clark Papers, RRPL.

48. Clark to Reagan, 16 December 1982, NSDD 75, Executive Secretariat, RRPL.

49. "Response to NSSD 11-82: U.S. Relations with the USSR," pp. 13–14, 6 December 1982, *ibid.*; Lettow, *Reagan and Nuclear Weapons*, 75–79.

50. Shultz to Reagan, 19 January 1983, box 1, End of Cold War Collection, NSA.

51. "Remarks at the Annual Convention of the National Association of Evangelicals," 8 March 1983, PPP: *Reagan, 1983*, 359–64; Reagan to John O. Koehler, 9 July 1981, in Skinner, Anderson, and Anderson, *A Life in Letters*, 375; Reagan to Suzanne Massie, 15 February 1984, *ibid.*, 379; also see Dobrynin, *In Confidence*, 517–20; Shultz, *Turmoil and Triumph*, 159–71.

52. Shultz, *Turmoil and Triumph*, 267–71; Clark to Shultz, 26 May 1983, box 91644, Clark Papers, RRPL.

53. Lettow, *Reagan and Nuclear Weapons*, 81–121, with quotations from Reagan's speech on 111–12; John L. Gaddis, *Strategies of Containment: A Critical Appraisal of American National Security During the Cold War*, revised and expanded ed. (New York: Oxford University Press, 2005), 356–59.

54. Lettow, *Reagan and Nuclear Weapons*, 117–21.

55. Jack F. Matlock, Jr., *Autopsy of an Empire: The American Ambassador's Account of the Collapse of the Soviet Union* (New York: Random House, 1995), 77; Lettow, *Reagan and Nuclear Weapons*, 124–26; for an overall critique of Reagan and Star Wars, see Frances Fitzgerald, *Way Out There in the Blue: Reagan, Star Wars and the End of the Cold War* (New York: Simon and Schuster, 2000).

56. "President's News Conference," 11 November 1982, PPP: *Reagan, 1982*, 1450.

57. "Radio Address," 8 January 1983, *ibid., 1983*, 23–25.

58. Reagan to Yuri Andropov, 11 July 1983, Executive Secretariat, National Security Council (NSC), Head of State, USSR, box 38–39, RRPL; Reagan, *An American Life*, 576–82.

59. Andropov to Reagan, 27 August 1983, Executive Secretariat, NSC, Head of State, USSR, box 38–39; Shultz to Reagan, 29 August 1983, *ibid.*

60. Reagan, *An American Life*, 584.

61. Shultz, *Turmoil and Triumph*, 365.

62. See, for example, "Address Before a Joint Session of the Tennessee State Legislature," 15 March 1982, *PPP: Reagan, 1982*, 296–99.

63. Don Oberdorfer, *The Turn: From the Cold War to a New Era* (New York: Poseidon Press, 1991), 65–66; Ben B. Fischer, *A Cold War Conundrum: The 1983 Soviet War Scare* (Washington, D.C.: Center for the Study of Intelligence, 1997), 24.

64. Comments by Douglas MacEachin, in Nina Tannenwald, ed., "Understanding the End of the Cold War, 1980–1987: An Oral History Conference, 7–10 May 1998" (Brown University, Watson Institute for International Affairs, Provisional Transcript, 1999, available at NSA), 262, 242–43; Fischer, *Cold War Conundrum*, 6–12.

65. Reagan, *An American Life*, 449–51; Shultz, *Turmoil and Triumph*, 323–45; McFarlane, *Special Trust*, 257–67; Cannon, *President Reagan*, 339–401.

66. NIE 11-18-85, "Domestic Stresses on the Soviet System," November 1985, p. 5, box 1, End of Cold War Collection, NSA.

67. Gates, *From the Shadows*, 245; Cannon, *President Reagan*, 306–307.

68. Department of State, "Resistance Movements," [mid-November 1985], "1985 Geneva Summit," box 2, *ibid.*; also see Gates, *From the Shadows*, 346–56; Odd Arne Westad, "Reagan's Anti-Revolutionary Offensive in the Third World," in *The Last Decade of the Cold War: From Conflict Escalation to Conflict Transformation*, ed. by Olav Njolstad (London: Frank Cass, 2004), 241–61.

69. For Romanov's statement, see Raymond L. Garthoff, *The Great Transition: American-Soviet Relations and the End of the Cold War* (Washington, D.C.: Brookings Institution, 1994), 135–36; Arthur Hartman to Lawrence Eagleburger and Richard Burt, 19 October 1983, box 90888, Jack Matlock Papers, RRPL; for reflections on how the Soviets saw themselves, see comments by Anatoly Chernyaev, in Tannenwald, "Understanding the End of the Cold War," 251–52.

70. Comments by Oleg Grinevsky, in Tannenwald, "Understanding the End of the Cold War," 15–16.

71. Svetlana Savranskaya, "The Emergence of Human Rights Movements in the USSR After the Signing of the Helsinki Final Act, and the Reaction of Soviet Authorities," unpublished paper.

72. "Statement by Marshal Ustinov at the Warsaw Pact Meeting of the Committee of Ministers of Defense," 5–7 December 1983, in Vojtech Mastny and Malcolm Byrne, eds., *A Cardboard Castle? An Inside History of the Warsaw Pact, 1955–1991* (Budapest: Central European University Press, 2005), 490–93; comments by Vladimir Slipchenko, in Tannenwald, "Understanding the End of the Cold War," 264.

73. Fischer, *Cold War Conundrum*, 12–16; Oberdorfer, *The Turn*, 66.

74. Comments by Douglas MacEachin, in Tannenwald, "Understanding the End of the Cold War," 26.

75. Garthoff, *Great Transition*, 134–41; Fischer, *Cold War Conundrum*, 25.

76. Reagan, *An American Life*, 588–89; Reagan to Brent Scowcroft, [ND], box 23, Matlock Papers, RRPL.

77. Reagan, *An American Life*, 588, 589, 595.

78. For quotations, see Reagan, *An American Life*, 585–86; for fuller development, see Beth A. Fischer, *The Reagan Reversal: Foreign Policy and the End of the Cold War* (Columbia: University of Missouri Press, 1997).

79. McFarlane, *Special Trust*, 188–89, 193–94, 200–205, 217–18, 254–56, 294–96; for the antinuclear

movement and the reaction of the Reagan administration, see Lawrence S. Wittner, *Toward Nuclear Abolition: A History of the World Nuclear Disarmament Movement, 1971–Present*, vol. 3 (Stanford, Calif.: Stanford University Press, 2003), esp. 252–68.

80. "Address to the Nation and Other Countries," 16 January 1984, *PPP: Reagan, 1984*, 40–44; also Interview with Lou Cannon, David Hoffman, and Juan Williams, 16 January 1984, *ibid.*, 62.

81. Reagan, *An American Life*, 592; Howard Baker to Reagan, 17 February 1984, box 2, Matlock Papers, RRPL.

82. Reagan to Konstantin Chernenko, 11 February 1984, Executive Secretariat, NSC, Head of State, USSR, boxes 38–39, RRPL.

83. Reagan to Chernenko, 6 March 1984, *ibid.*

84. Reagan to Chernenko, 16 April 1984, *ibid.*

85. McFarlane to Matlock, 28 January 1984, box 90888, Matlock Papers, RRPL.

86. McFarlane, *Special Trust*, 308–309; Jack Matlock, Jr., *Reagan and Gorbachev: How the Cold War Ended* (New York: Random House, 2004), 132–34.

87. Shultz, *Turmoil and Triumph*, 490. The attitudes of CIA director William Casey are described in Bob Woodward, *Veil: The Secret Wars of the CIA, 1981–87* (New York: Simon and Schuster, 1987), esp. 125–26, 135–36, 162–63, 293–95.

88. McFarlane, *Special Trust*, 286–87; for the acrimony, also see "Interview with James Baker," 15–16 June 2004, Presidential Oral History Program, Miller Center, University of Virginia (hereafter cited as Baker Interview, MC).

89. Shultz, *Turmoil and Triumph*, 497–98.

90. Reagan, *An American Life*, 605–606.

91. *Ibid.*, 590, 587.

92. Harry S. Truman, *Memoirs: 1945, Year of Decisions* (New York: Signet, 1955), 72; Reagan to Alan Brown, 22 January 1985, in Skinner, Anderson, and Anderson, *A Life in Letters*, 413; Reagan to Marmaduke Bayne, 12 September 1983, *ibid.*, 410.

93. Anderson, *Revolution*, 288; also see Deaver, *A Different Drummer*, 86, 169; McFarlane, *Special Trust*, 21–22, 269.

94. Stockman, *Triumph of Politics*, 74; Shultz, *Turmoil and Triumph*, 131.

95. Pipes, *Vixi*, 167; Dobrynin, *In Confidence*, 605–12; Helmut Schmidt, trans. by Ruth Hein, *Men and Powers: A Political Retrospective* (New York: Random House, 1989), 241–46; Eduard Shevardnadze, *The Future Belongs to Freedom* (New York: The Free Press, 1991), 81–90.

96. N. Reagan, *My Turn*, 114; Shultz, *Turmoil and Triumph*, 145; Anderson, *Revolution*, 285; Deaver, *A Different Drummer*, 71; Schmidt, *Men and Powers*, 241–56; Dobrynin, *In Confidence*, 605–12; Baker Interview, 41–42, MC.

97. "Address on the State of the Union," 25 January 1984, *PPP: Reagan, 1984*, 87–94.

98. For Reagan's contempt for political pandering, see N. Reagan, *My Turn*, 111; Deaver, *A Different Drummer*, 26–27; Cannon, *President Reagan*, 390.

99. "Inaugural Address," 21 January 1985, *PPP: Reagan, 1985*, 55–58; for the election, Patterson, *Restless Giant*, 188–92; Gil Troy, *Morning in America: How Ronald Reagan Invented the 1980s* (Princeton, N.J.: Princeton University Press, 2005).

100. Chernenko to Reagan, 19 March 1984, 7 May 1984, 6 June 1984, 7 July 1984, 26 July 1984, 8 November 1984, 20 December 1984, Executive Secretariat, NSC, Head of State, box 38–39, RRPL.

101. Reagan, *An American Life*, 604–605; Shultz, *Turmoil and Triumph*, 471, 484.

102. Dobrynin, *In Confidence*, 605–12.

103. Nicholas Platt to McFarlane and Donald P. Gregg, 11 March 1985, Executive Secretariat, NSC, Head of State, USSR, box 39, RRPL.

104. Shultz, *Turmoil and Triumph*, 531–32.

105. Quoted in Anatoly S. Chernyaev, *My Six Years with Gorbachev*, trans. and ed. by Robert D. English and Elizabeth Tucker (University Park: Pennsylvania State University Press, 2000), 20; also see comments by Alexander A. Bessmertnykh, in William C. Wohlforth, *Witnesses to the End of the Cold War* (Baltimore, Md.: Johns Hopkins University Press, 1996), 106–107, 184.

106. Shultz, *Turmoil and Triumph*, 532. British prime minister Margaret Thatcher also had a positive impression of Gorbachev when they met in December 1984. She communicated her views to Reagan. Memorandum of conversation between Thatcher and Reagan, 28 December 1984, website of Margaret Thatcher Foundation, http://www.margaretthatcher.org/archive/.

107. Mikhail Gorbachev, *Memoirs* (New York: Doubleday, 1995), 22–28, quotation on 23; for baptism, see Archie Brown, *The Gorbachev Factor* (Oxford, Eng.: Oxford University Press, 1997), 27.

108. Gorbachev, *Memoirs*, 28.

109. *Ibid.*, 31.

110. *Ibid.*, 32.

111. *Ibid.*, 33–34; for impact of the war, also see Raisa Gorbachev, *I Hope*, trans. by David Floyd (New York: HarperCollins, 1991), 12, 97.

112. Gorbachev, *Memoirs*, 38–39.

113. Mikhail Gorbachev and Zdenek Mlynar, *Conversations with Gorbachev on Perestroika, the Prague Spring, and the Crossroads of Socialism*, trans. by George Shriver (New York: Columbia University Press, 2002), 17–18.

114. *Ibid.*, 18, 149–50; Mikhail Gorbachev, *On My Country and the World*, trans. by George Shriver (New York: Columbia University Press, 2000), 28–29.

115. Gorbachev and Mlynar, *Conversations*, 15, 150.

116. Gorbachev, *Memoirs*, 38–42; Brown, *Gorbachev Factor*, 28.

117. Gorbachev, *Memoirs*, 43–46; graduates of the Moscow School of Law often staffed the punitive agencies of the state.

118. Gorbachev and Mlynar, *Conversations*, 21, 23; Gorbachev, *Memoirs*, 48.

119. R. Gorbachev, *I Hope*, 47–52, 70–72; Brown, *Gorbachev Factor*, 32–34; for very negative views of Raisa Gorbachev, see Valery Boldin, *Ten Years That Shook the World: The Gorbachev Era as Witnessed by His Chief of Staff*, trans. by Evelyn Rossiter (New York: Basic Books, 1994), esp. 83–91; N. Reagan, *My Turn*, 336–64.

120. Gorbachev, *Memoirs*, 77; Gorbachev and Mlynar, *Conversations*, 47–48, 30–31; also see R. Gorbachev, *I Hope*, 107–19.

121. Gorbachev, *Memoirs*, 102–103; R. Gorbachev, *I Hope*, 116; Matthew Evangelista, *Unarmed Forces: The Trans-National Movement to End the Cold War* (Ithaca, N.Y.: Cornell University Press, 1999), 260–63; Paul Hollander, *Political Will and Personal Belief: The Decline and Fall of Soviet Communism* (New Haven, Conn.: Yale University Press, 1999), 102.

122. Gorbachev and Mlynar, *Conversations*, 150–51; Gorbachev, *On My Country*, 27–28, 50, 53.

123. Gorbachev and Mlynar, *Conversations*, 49; Brown, *Gorbachev Factor*, 46.

124. Gorbachev, *Memoirs*, 56–107; Brown, *Gorbachev Factor*, 36–52; Martin McCauley, *Gorbachev* (London: Longman, 1998), 21–39; R. Gorbachev, *I Hope*, 113; Hollander, *Political Will and Personal Belief*, 103.

125. Brown, *Gorbachev Factor*, 58–60; for the influence of ideas and experts, see Sarah E. Mendelson, *Changing Course: Ideas, Politics, and the Soviet Withdrawal from Afghanistan* (Princeton, N.J.: Princeton University Press, 1998), 78–91; Jeffrey T. Checkel, *Ideas and International Political Change: Soviet/Russian Behavior and the End of the Cold War* (New Haven, Conn.: Yale University Press, 1997), 77–90; Robert D. English, *Russia and the West: Gorbachev, Intellectuals and the End of the Cold War* (New York: Columbia University Press, 2000).

126. Gorbachev, *Memoirs*, 136 (for quotation), also see 109–21, 134–36; R. Gorbachev, *I Hope*, 120–24.

127. Gorbachev and Mlynar, *Conversations*, 49–50.

128. English, *Russia and the West*, 184 (for quotation), also 180–86; Brown, *Gorbachev Factor*, 89–105.

129. Gorbachev, *Memoirs*, 140, 146; Gorbachev and Mlynar, *Conversations*, 51.

130. Gorbachev, *Memoirs*, 153.

131. Andropov plenum speech, 15 June 1983, Foreign Broadcast Information System (FBIS), 16 June 1983, R5, R7.

132. *Ibid.*, R8.

133. *Ibid.*, R9–R10.

134. *Ibid.*, R11–R12.

135. Gorbachev, *Memoirs*, 154–68, quotation on 167–68; Gorbachev, *On My Country*, 65–66, 171–80.

136. Chernyaev, *Six Years with Gorbachev*, 19–20. Gorbachev's election was very close, and he had to maneuver adroitly to win. See Mark Kramer, "The Reform of the Soviet System and the Demise of the Soviet State," *Slavic Review* 63 (Fall 2004): 511.

137. Brown, *Gorbachev Factor*, 121–29.

138. Gorbachev speech, 10 December 1984, FBIS, 28 March 1985, R1–R4; Gorbachev and Mlynar, *Conversations*, 199–200; "Conference of the Secretaries of the CC CPSU," 15 March 1985, Volkogonov Collection, NSA.

139. For emphasis on social justice, see the Political Report of the CPSU Central Committee, presented by Gorbachev to the 27th CPSU Party Congress, 25 February 1986, FBIS, 28 March 1986, especially O19*ff*, O37.

140. Gorbachev, *On My Country*, 180; Gorbachev, *Memoirs*, 167.

141. Gorbachev Speech at Ministry of Foreign Affairs, 28 May 1986, REEAD 3486, Chernyaev Collection, NSA; comments by Nikolai Detinov, in Tannenwald, "Understanding the End of the Cold War," 151–52.

142. For the quotation, see comments by Chernyaev in Tannenwald, "Understanding the End of the Cold War," 139; also comments by Georgi Shakhnazarov, *ibid.*, 69; also his comments in Wohlforth, *Witnesses*, 37.

143. Comments by Chernyaev in William C. Wohlforth, *Cold War Endgame* (University Park: Pennsylvania State University Press, 2003), 21; Gorbachev Speech at Ministry of Foreign Affairs, 28 May 1986, REEAD 3486, Anatoly S. Chernyaev Collection, NSA; also see Wohlforth, *Witnesses*, 5.

144. Gorbachev, *On My Country*, 66; Chernyaev, *Six Years with Gorbachev*, 55.

145. See, for example, Gorbachev's Speech in Smolensk, 27 June 1984, FBIS, 29 June 1984, R9; Gorbachev's comments at meeting between Erich Honecker and Chernenko, 17 August 1984, Mastny and Byrne, *A Cardboard Castle?*, 497–98.

146. Chernyaev's Notes from the Politburo Session, 16 October 1986, REEAD 2953, NSA; also Chernyaev's Notes from the Politburo Session, 22 September 1986, REEAD 2956, *ibid.*; also see, for example, Gorbachev Speech at Ministry of Foreign Affairs, 28 May 1986, REEAD 3486, Chernyaev Collection, *ibid.*; Transcript of Conversation between Gorbachev and François Mitterrand, 7 July 1986, REEAD 3366, *ibid.*

147. "Conference at the CC CPSU on preparation for the XXVII Congress of the CPSU," 28 November 1985, NSA; also see Anders Aslund, *Gorbachev's Struggle for Economic Reform* (Ithaca, N.Y.: Cornell University Press, 1989), 15–16; Noel E. Firth and James H. Noren, *Soviet Defense Spending: A History of CIA Estimates, 1950–1990* (College Station: Texas A & M Press, 1998), 98–110; Stephen Kotkin, *Armageddon Averted: The Soviet Collapse, 1970–2000* (Oxford, Eng.: Oxford University Press, 2001), 61.

148. Gorbachev Speech at Ministry of Foreign Affairs, 28 May 1986, p. 7, REEAD 3486, Chernyaev Collection, NSA.

149. Gorbachev Speech, 4 November 1987, FBIS, 4 November 1987, 23.

150. "Conference of Secretaries of the CC CPSU," 15 March 1985, Volkogonov Collection, NSA; Political Report of the CPSU Central Committee, presented by Gorbachev to the 27th CPSU Party Congress, 25 February 1986, FBIS, 28 March 1986, O32.

151. Comments by Chernyaev, in Tannenwald, "Understanding the End of the Cold War," 78–79; Chernyaev's Notes from the Politburo Session, 4 October 1986, READD 2954, NSA; Gorbachev Speech at Ministry of Foreign Affairs, 28 May 1986, p. 4, REEAD 3486, Chernyaev Collection, *ibid.*; comments by Bessmertnykh in Wohlforth, *Witnesses*, 33.

152. Comments by Chernyaev, in Tannenwald, "Understanding the End of the Cold War," 78–80; comments by Sergei Tarasenko, in *ibid.*, 75.

153. Gorbachev to Reagan, 24 March 1985, Executive Secretariat, NSC, Head of State, USSR, box 39, RRPL.

154. Comments by Chernyaev, in Tannenwald, "Understanding the End of the Cold War," 78.

155. Gorbachev, *On My Country*, 181; Reagan to Gorbachev, 4 April 1985, Executive Secretariat, NSC, Head of State, USSR, box 39, RRPL.

156. For Gorbachev's "New Thinking," see *On My Country*, 171–90; Gorbachev, *Memoirs*, 237–40, 401–62; for the fullest rendition, see Mikhail Gorbachev, *Perestroika: New Thinking for Our Country and the World* (New York: Harper and Row, 1987); for background, see esp. Evangelista, *Unarmed Forces*; English, *Russia and the Idea of the West*; Checkel, *Ideas and International Political Change*.

157. See Gorbachev's first conversation with Babrak Karmal, the communist leader of Afghanistan, 14 March 1985, "Zolotoi Fond," NSA; Comments by Chernyaev and Detinov, in Tannenwald, "Understanding the End of the Cold War," 95–97, 275–77; also see analysis below, pp. 403–14.

158. Gorbachev Speech, 26 April 1985, in Mastny and Byrne, *A Cardboard Castle?*, 509.

159. Evangelista, *Unarmed Forces*, 264–65.

160. Gorbachev, *Memoirs*, 166.

161. Comments by Anatoli Gromyko, "Moscow Cold War Conference" (oral history conference organized by Richard Ned Lebow and Richard K. Herrmann of the Mershon Center of Ohio State University, 1999; transcript available at NSA).

162. Shevardnadze, *Future Belongs to Freedom*, 23–39.

163. *Ibid.*, 13–14.

164. *Ibid.*, 19, 14, 34–35, 37; Hollander, *Political Will and Personal Belief*, 117–25.

165. Shevardnadze, *Future Belongs to Freedom*, 38–39.

166. *Ibid.*, 48, 81; also see Pavel Palazchenko, *Gorbachev and Shevardnadze: The Memoir of a Soviet Interpreter* (University Park: Pennsylvania State University Press, 1997), 33–35; comments by Tarasenko, in Tannenwald, "Understanding the End of the Cold War," 190–91.

167. Shevardnadze address, 31 July 1985, FBIS, 31 July 1985, CC1–6.

168. Gorbachev's address and interview on French television, 30 September 1985, FBIS, 2 October 1985, G1–11, quotations on G5 and G11.

169. Gorbachev Speech at the Political Consultative Meeting of the Warsaw Pact, 22 October 1985, website of the Parallel History Project, http://www.isn.ethz.ch/php/documents/2/851022.htm; for increased spending on strategic defense during 1985–87, see Firth and Noren, *Soviet Defense Spending*, 107.

170. Gorbachev to Reagan, 12 October 1985, Executive Secretariat, NSC, Head of State, USSR, box 39; Reagan, *An American Life*, 622; Shultz to Reagan, 7 November 1985, End of Cold War Collection, NSA.

171. Reagan, *An American Life*, 634.

172. Shultz to Reagan, 7 November 1985, End of Cold War Collection, NSA.

173. Department of State, Intelligence and Research, "USSR: A Society in Trouble," 25 July 1985, box 1,

End of Cold War Collection, NSA; CIA, "Gorbachev's Approach to Societal Malaise: A Managed Revitalization," 24 July 1985, box 1, *ibid.*; CIA, "Gorbachev's Economic Agenda: Promises, Potentials, and Pitfalls," September 1985, *ibid.*; Gates, *From the Shadows*, 342–44.

174. See Reagan's comments to Shevardnadze on 27 September 1985, "Draft U.S. Themes on the Shevardnadze Visit and Soviet Counter-Proposal," box 92129, Matlock Papers, RRPL; for the importance of trust, see Reagan's opening remarks to Gorbachev when they met at Geneva. Memorandum of Conversation, 19 November 1985, 10:20–11:20 a.m., box 2, End of Cold War Collection, NSA; Shultz to Reagan, 7 November 1985, *ibid.*

175. Reagan, *An American Life*, 628.

176. *Ibid.*; for disparate views in the administration, see Ofira Seliktar, *Politics, Paradigms, and Intelligence Failures: Why So Few Predicted the Collapse of the Soviet Union* (New York: M. E. Sharpe, 2004), 136–38; Shultz, *Turmoil and Triumph*, 578–80; Gates, *From the Shadows*, 341–43, 199–213; Kenneth Adelman to McFarlane, 3 July 1985, box 90706, Donald Fortier Papers, RRPL. Caspar Weinberger's attitudes are reflected in Caspar W. Weinberger with Gretchen Roberts, *In the Arena: A Memoir of the Twentieth Century* (Washington, D.C.: Regnery Publishing, 2001), 269–86.

177. Shultz to Reagan, 7 November 1985, End of Cold War Collection, NSA; Reagan, *An American Life*, 631–32.

178. Reagan, *An American Life*, 637.

179. *Ibid.*, 11–12; N. Reagan, *My Turn*, 340.

180. Memorandum of Conversation, 19 November 1985, 10:20–11:20 a.m., box 2, End of Cold War Collection, NSA.

181. *Ibid.*

182. Memorandum of Conversation, 19 November 1985, 11:27 a.m.–12:15 p.m., box 2, End of Cold War Collection, NSA.

183. *Ibid.*; Memorandum of Conversation, 19 November 1985, 2:30–3:40 p.m., *ibid.*; Memorandum of Conversation, 3:40–4:45 p.m., *ibid.*; Memorandum of Conversation, 20 November 1985, 11:30 a.m.– 12:40 p.m., *ibid.*; Memorandum of Conversation, 20 November 1985, 2:45–3:30 p.m., *ibid.*

184. Memorandum of Conversation (between Shultz, Shevardnadze, and their assistants), 19 November 1985, 3:35–4:30 p.m., box 92137, Matlock Papers, RRPL.

185. Memorandum of Conversation, 19 November 1985, 3:40–4:45 p.m., box 2, End of Cold War Collection, NSA. According to Jack Matlock, President Reagan never grasped that "SDI could be used offensively." See comments by Matlock in Tannenwald, "Understanding the End of the Cold War," 183–84.

186. Gorbachev, *Memoirs*, 405; comments by Chernyaev, in Tannenwald, "Understanding the End of the Cold War," 115.

187. N. Reagan, *My Turn*, 342.

188. Reagan, *An American Life*, 639.

189. Memorandum of Conversation, 19 November 1985, 8:00–10:30 p.m., box 2, End of Cold War Collection, NSA.

190. Memorandum of Conversation, 20 November 1985, 8:00–10:30 p.m., *ibid.*

191. Deaver, *A Different Drummer*, 118; also see Reagan to Alan Brown, 10 December 1985, in Skinner, Anderson, and Anderson, *A Life in Letters*, 415.

192. Reagan to George Murphy, 19 December 1985, in Skinner, Anderson, and Anderson, *A Life in Letters*, 415–16.

193. Reagan to Gorbachev, 28 November 1985, Executive Secretariat, NSC, Head of State, USSR, box 39, RRPL.

194. Gorbachev to Reagan, 24 December 1985, Executive Secretariat, NSC, Heads of State, USSR, Box 40, RRPL; for the intense competition in the third world, see Gates, *From the Shadows*, 346–56; Westad, "Reagan's Anti-Revolutionary Offensive," 241–61.

195. For Afghanistan, see below, pp. 403–14.

196. For human rights, see the Meeting of the Politburo, 25 September 1986, document package associated with the conference "Understanding the End of the Cold War," Brown University, May 1998; Max M. Kampelman, *Entering New Worlds: The Memoirs of a Private Man in Public Life* (New York: HarperCollins, 1991), 374.

197. For shifting personnel, see Brown, *Gorbachev Factor*, 89–129; for changes in the foreign ministry, see Carolyn McGiffert Ekedahl and Melvin A. Goodman, *The Wars of Eduard Shevardnadze*, 2nd ed., revised and updated (Washington, D.C.: Brassey's, 2001), 73–88. For attitudes toward Gorbachev during these early years, 1985–88, the transcripts of two oral history conferences are illuminating—for many of his supporters, see "Understanding the End of the Cold War"; for many of his opponents, see "Moscow Cold War Conference."

198. Comments by Detinov and Grinevsky, "Understanding the End of the Cold War," 112–13, 120–23.

199. Chernyaev, *Six Years with Gorbachev*, 45–46; for a typical U.S. "expert" reaction, see Paul H. Nitze, *From Hiroshima to Glasnost: At the Center of Decision—A Memoir*, with Ann M. Smith and Steven L. Rearden (New York: Grove Weidenfeld, 1989), 421.

200. Comments by Edward Rowny, in Tannenwald, "Understanding the End of the Cold War," 132–33; also see Nitze, *From Hiroshima to Glasnost*, 422; Max Kampelman, another influential member of the administration, recounted the same meeting. See "Bombs Away," *New York Times*, 26 April 2006.

201. Political Report of the CPSU Central Committee, 25 February 1986, FBIS, 28 March 1986, O 8.

202. Ibid., O 9, O 24; for assessments of his economic ideas, see, for example, Brown, *Gorbachev Factor*, 130–54; Aslund, *Gorbachev's Struggle for Economic Reform*; Philip Hanson, *The Rise and Fall of the Soviet Economy: An Economic History of the USSR from 1945* (London: Pearson Education, 2003), 177–92.

203. Political Report of the CPSU Central Committee, 25 February 1986, FBIS, 28 March 1986, O 33, O 29.

204. Chernyaev, *Six Years with Gorbachev*, 54 (for quotation), also 50–60.

205. Ibid., 57.

206. Chernyaev's Notes from the Politburo Sessions, 24 March 1986, 15 April 1986, REEAD 2966 and 2963, NSA; also see Gorbachev to Reagan, 2 April 1986, Executive Secretariat, NSC, Heads of State USSR, box 40, RRPL.

207. Gorbachev Speech, 31 July 1986, FBIS, 12 August 1986, R4–17, quotations on R4, R13.

208. David Reynolds, *One World Indivisible: A Global History Since 1945* (New York: Norton, 2000), 534.

209. Gorbachev Address, 14 May 1986, FBIS, 15 May 1985, L1–4, quotations on L3, L4; also see Gorbachev's Speech at the Foreign Ministry, 28 May 1986, REEAD 3486, Chernyaev Collection, NSA.

210. Comment by Chernyaev, in Tannenwald, "Understanding the End of the Cold War," 195; also see Wohlforth, *Witnesses*, 5, 166–68.

211. Comment by Chernyaev, in Tannenwald, "Understanding the End of the Cold War," 155.

212. Resolution of the Politburo of the CC of the CPSU, 4 September 1986, REEAD, Chernyaev Collection, NSA (also published in *Istochnik* 2 [1995]); Chernyaev's Notes from the Politburo Session, 22 September 1986, REEAD 2956, NSA.

213. Gorbachev to Reagan, 15 September 1986, Executive Secretariat, NSC, Heads of State, USSR, box 40; for Gorbachev's thinking, also see Chernyaev's Notes from the Politburo Session, 4 October 1986, REEAD 2954, NSA.

214. Reagan, *An American Life*, 668–74.

215. Shultz to Reagan, 2 October 1986, box 2, End of Cold War Collection, NSA.

216. Comments by Rowny and Matlock, in Tannenwald, "Understanding the End of the Cold War," 143–48; Nitze, *From Hiroshima to Glasnost*, 424–25; Shultz, *Turmoil and Triumph*, 718–27.

217. Reagan, *An American Life*, 675.

218. Memorandum of Conversation, 11 October 1986, 10:40 a.m.–12:30 p.m., quotations on pp. 2–3, 4, box 2, End of Cold War Collection, NSA; citations are from the American transcript, but there is also a translated version of the Russian minutes. See Brown Conference Documents, NSA.

219. *Ibid.*

220. *Ibid.*, p. 10.

221. Memorandum of Conversation, 11 October 1986, 3:30–5:40 p.m., box 2, End of Cold War Collection, NSA; Memorandum of Conversation, 12 October 1986, 10:00 a.m.–1:35 p.m., *ibid.*

222. Memorandum of Conversation, 12 October 1986; 3:25–6:00 p.m., box 3, *ibid.*, quotations on pp. 3, 4.

223. *Ibid.*, quotation on p. 9.

224. *Ibid.*, 10–15.

225. N. Reagan, *My Turn*, 345.

226. Comments by Chernyaev, in Tannenwald, "Understanding the End of the Cold War," 199.

227. Comments by Matlock and John Whitehead, in *ibid.*, 175–77, 184–85; for a good retrospective account of the conference, see Shultz, *Turmoil and Triumph*, 751–80.

228. For the quotations, see Meeting of the Politburo of the CC CPSU, 14 October 1986, box 9, Volkogonov Collection, NSA; Chernyaev's Notes from the Politburo Session, 1 December 1986, 23 and 26 February 1987, REEAD 2949 and 2944, NSA; also see Chernyaev's Notes of Conversation with Gorbachev, 17 November 1986, REEAD 2948, *ibid.*

229. Chernyaev's Notes from the Conference with Heads of Departments of the Central Committee, 12 December 1986, REEAD 2946, *ibid.*; for the growing impetus toward political reform, see Brown, *Gorbachev Factor*, 155–72; George W. Breslauer, *Gorbachev and Yeltsin as Leaders* (Cambridge, Eng.: Cambridge University Press, 2002), 41–78.

230. Comments by Detinov and Grinevsky, in Tannenwald, "Understanding the End of the Cold War," 37–45; Mendelson, *Changing Course*, 70; comment by M. A. Gareev and V. V. Shlykov in Michael Ellman and Vladimir Kontorovich, *The Destruction of the Soviet Economic System: An Insiders' History* (New York: M. E. Sharpe, 1998), 56–57.

231. Chernyaev's Notes from the Politburo Session, 1 December 1986, REEAD 2949, NSA; for Gorbachev's attitudes toward his military establishment, see Roger R. Reese, *Red Commanders: A Social History of the Soviet Army Officer Corps, 1918–1991* (Lawrence: University Press of Kansas, 2005), 238–45.

232. William E. Odom, *The Collapse of the Soviet Military* (New Haven, Conn.: Yale University Press, 1998), 104–17; Ekedahl and Goodman, *Wars of Shevardnadze*, 83–85.

233. Comments by Chernyaev, in Tannenwald, "Understanding the End of the Cold War," 43–44.

234. Gorbachev Speech, 28 May 1987, in Mastny and Byrne, *A Cardboard Castle?*, 563.

235. Chernyaev's Notes from the Politburo Session, 8 May 1987, Brown University Conference Documents, NSA; also see comments by Chernyaev in Tannenwald, "Understanding the End of the Cold War," 33, 223.

236. Comments by Detinov in Tannenwald, "Understanding the End of the Cold War," 204–207, 286–89; Mastny and Byrne, *A Cardboard Castle?*, 551–71; Odom, *Collapse of the Soviet Military*, 126–35; Stephan Kux, *New Soviet Thinking on Nuclear Deterrence* (Geneva: Program for Strategic and International Security Studies), Occasional Paper No. 3, 1990, 30–45.

237. Chernyaev's Notes from the Politburo Session, 23 and 26 February 1987, READD 2944, NSA.

238. Shultz, *Turmoil and Triumph*, 863–86, quotation on 881; Reagan, *An American Life*, 684–87.

239. Reagan to Gorbachev, 10 April 1987, Executive Secretariat, NSC, Heads of State, USSR, box 41, RRPL.

240. Record of a Conversation between Gorbachev and Shultz, 14 April 1987, REEAD 3337, Chernyaev Collection, NSA.

241. Gorbachev, *Memoirs*, 444; Shultz, *Turmoil and Triumph*, 886–900.

242. Shultz, *Turmoil and Triumph*, 896.

243. Memorandum, by Gates, 24 November 1987, box 3, End of the Cold War Collection, NSA; also see CIA, "Gorbachev and the Military: Managing National Security Policy," October 1987, *ibid.*; Shultz, *Turmoil and Triumph*, 899–924, 988–89; Gates, *From the Shadows*, 420–26.

244. Conversation between Gorbachev and Shultz, 23 October 1987, REEAD 2942, Chernyaev Collection, NSA; Shultz, *Turmoil and Triumph*, 995–1002.

245. Gorbachev to Reagan, ND [October 1987], Executive Secretariat, NSC, Heads of State, USSR, box 41, RRPL.

246. Shultz to Reagan, 30 October 1987, *ibid.*

247. Shultz, *Turmoil and Triumph*, 1003.

248. Gorbachev, *Memoirs*, 448–50.

249. Oberdorfer, *The Turn*, 264–65.

250. Memorandum of Conversation, 9 December 1987, 10:55 a.m.–12:35 p.m., box 3, End of the Cold War Collection, NSA; for the quotation, see Gorbachev, *Memoirs*, 447.

251. For the quotation, see Memorandum of Conversation, 8 December 1987, 2:30–3:15 p.m., p. 10, box 3, End of Cold War Collection, NSA; also see Memorandum of Conversation, 9 December 1987, 10:55 a.m.–12:35 p.m., *ibid.*

252. "Address to the Nation," 10 December 1987, *PPP: Reagan, 1987*, 1501; Reagan, *An American Life*, 698–701; Comments by Chernyaev in Wohlforth, *Witnesses*, 49.

253. "Address to the Nation," 10 December 1987, *PPP: Reagan, 1987*, 1501.

254. "Toasts at the State Dinner," 8 December 1987, *ibid.*, 1487.

255. "Written Responses to Questions Submitted by the Soviet Newspaper *Izvestiya*," *ibid.*, 1441; "Remarks at the Welcoming Ceremony," 8 December 1987, *ibid.*, 1452.

256. Reagan, *An American Life*, 683.

257. "Address to the Nation," 10 December 1987, *ibid.*, 1504; also see "Remarks at a Luncheon at the Heritage Foundation," 30 November 1987, *ibid.*, 1389–94; "Remarks and a Question-and-Answer Session with Area High School Seniors," 1 December 1987, *ibid.*, 1398–1405.

258. Gorbachev Speech, 15 December 1987, FBIS, 15 December 1987, 14–16.

259. Chernyaev's Notes from the Politburo Session, 17 December 1987, REEAD 2940, NSA.

260. *Ibid.*

261. Gorbachev Speech at News Conference, 10 December 1987, FBIS, 15 December 1987, 16–21, quotations on 19 and 21.

262. For the quotation, see Mendelson, *Changing Course*, 117; also see Gorbachev, *Memoirs*, 171.

263. Record of a Conversation between Gorbachev and B. Karmal, 14 March 1985, "Zolotoi fond," NSA.

264. Anatoly Chernyaev, "The Afghanistan Problem," *Russian Politics and Law* 42 (September–October 2004): 30.

265. Westad, *Global Cold War*, 348–53; Steve Coll, *Ghost Wars: The Secret History of the CIA, Afghanistan, and Bin Laden, from the Soviet Invasion to September 10, 2001* (New York: Penguin Press, 2004), 21–70.

266. Chernyaev, "The Afghanistan Problem," 29–31; Mendelson, *Changing Course*, 115–16; Elizabeth Kridl Valkenier, "New Soviet Thinking About the Third World," *World Policy Journal* 4 (Fall 1987): 651–74; Francis Fukuyama, *Moscow's Post-Brezhnev Reassessment of the Third World* (Santa Monica, Calif.: Rand Publication R-3337-USDP, 1986); George W. Breslauer, "Ideology and Learning in Soviet Third World Policy," *World Politics* 39 (April 1987): 429–48; Checkel, *Ideas and International Political Change*, 79–99.

267. Chernyaev, "Afghanistan Problem," 32–33; Chernyaev, *Six Years with Gorbachev*, 42.

268. Memorandum of Conversation, 19 November 1985, 2:30–3:40 p.m., p. 3, box 2, End of Cold War Collection, NSA.

269. *Ibid.*

270. *Ibid.*, p. 6.

271. Quoted in Westad, *Global Cold War*, 354.

272. Shultz, *Turmoil and Triumph*, 525–26, 692; Gates, *From the Shadows*, 251–52, 348–50; NSDD 166, "Expanded U.S. Aid to Afghan Guerillas," [April 1985?], in Simpson, *National Security Directives*, 446–47; Coll, *Ghost Wars*, 88–106; for the $300 million figure (and $470 million in 1986), see Peter Schweizer, *Reagan's War: The Epic Story of His Forty-Year Struggle and Final Triumph Over Communism* (New York: Anchor Books, 2002), 234–35; also see Woodward, *The Veil*, 316–18, 372–73, 384–86; Paul Kengor, *The Crusader: Ronald Reagan and the Fall of Communism* (New York: Reagan, 2006), 230–37; James M. Scott, *Deciding to Intervene: The Reagan Doctrine and American Foreign Policy* (Durham, N.C.: Duke University Press, 1996), especially 14–27, 43–57.

273. Chernyaev, "Afghanistan Problem," 34–35; Record of a Conversation of Gorbachev with Giulio Andreotti, 27 February 1987, Cold War International History Project (CWIHP) *Bulletin* 14/15 (Winter 2003–Spring 2004): 147; Notes from the Politburo Meeting, 23 February 1987, *ibid.*, 146.

274. For background on Najibullah, see the GRU (military intelligence) dossier, CWIHP Archival Materials, Woodrow Wilson International Center (WWIC); Westad, *Global Cold War*, 375.

275. Chernyaev, "Afghanistan Problem," 35–37.

276. Notes from the Politburo Meetings, 21–22 May 1987, CWIHP *Bulletin* 14/15 (Winter 2003–Spring 2004), 148–49; Chernyaev, "Afghanistan Problem," 40–41.

277. Westad, *Global Cold War*, 367–69; Fred Halliday, "Soviet foreign policymaking and the Afghanistan war: from 'second Mongolia' to bleeding wound,' " *Review of International Studies* 25 (October 1999): 683–86.

278. Notes from the Politburo Meetings, 21–22 May 1987, CWIHP *Bulletin* 14/15 (Winter 2003–Spring 2004): 149.

279. Record of a Conversation of Gorbachev with Comrade Najib[ullah], 20 July 1987, *ibid.*

280. Record of a Conversation of Gorbachev with Najibullah, 3 November 1987, *ibid.*, 162.

281. *Ibid.*, 163–66.

282. Shultz, *Turmoil and Triumph*, 987; Comments by Shultz, in Wohlforth, *Witnesses*, 145–46.

283. Record of a Conversation of Gorbachev with Comrade Najibullah, 3 November 1987, CWIHP *Bulletin* 14/15 (Winter 2003–Spring 2004): 165.

284. Gorbachev Speech, 4 November 1987, FBIS, 4 November 1987, 22–24; Checkel, *Ideas and International Political Change*, 77–105.

285. Matlock to Shultz, 3 November 1987, box 3, End of Cold War Collection, NSA; for the Soviet effort to arrange a peaceful settlement in southwest Africa, see Anatoly Adamishin, *Beloe solntse Angoly* [The White Sun of Angola] (Moscow: Vagrius, 2001), esp. 23, 58–60, 65, 63, 88, 93. I am indebted to Allen Lynch for his translation; also see Chester A. Crocker, *High Noon in Southern Africa: Making Peace in a Rough Neighborhood* (New York: W. W. Norton and Company, 1992), 348–49, 409ff.

286. Record of a Conversation of Gorbachev and Daniel Ortega, 4 November 1987, REEAD 3346, Chernyaev Collection, NSA; for a more conciliatory approach to Sandinistas, see Scott, *Deciding to Intervene*, 184–85.

287. See Gorbachev Speech on the 70th Anniversary of the Bolshevik Revolution, 2 November 1987, FBIS, 3 November 1987, 38–60.

288. Memorandum of Conversation, 9 December 1987, 10:55 a.m.–12:35 p.m., pp. 15ff, box 3, End of Cold War Collection, NSA.

289. Record of Conversation of Gorbachev with Shultz, 22 February 1988, CWIHP *Bulletin* 14/15 (Winter 2003–Spring 2004): 171.

290. *Ibid.*, 172.

291. *Ibid.*, 173.

292. Chernyaev, "Afghanistan Problem," 41–42.

293. Record of Conversation of Gorbachev with Najibullah, 7 April 1988, CWIHP *Bulletin* 14/15 (Winter 2003–Spring 2004): 174–81; for Soviet goals, also see Record of Conversation of Gorbachev with Alessandro Natta, 29 March 1988, *ibid.*, 173.

294. Oberdorfer, *The Turn*, 280–81.

295. Coll, *Ghost Wars*, 170–86.

296. Shultz, *Turmoil and Triumph*, 1003.

297. Record of a Conversation of Gorbachev with Najibullah, 13 June 1988, CWIHP *Bulletin* 14/15 (Winter 2003–Spring 2004): 185.

298. *Ibid.*, 181–86, quotation on 186; for internecine strife among the Mujahedin, see Coll, *Ghost Wars*, 176–86.

299. *Ibid.*, quotations on 182 and 186.

300. Chernyaev, "Afghanistan Problem," 45.

301. *Ibid.*, 46–48.

302. *Ibid.*, 48.

303. Record of a Conversation of Gorbachev with Najibullah, 23 August 1990, CWIHP *Bulletin* 14/15 (Winter 2003–Spring 2004): 188–89; James A. Baker, III, with Thomas M. Defrank, *The Politics of Diplomacy: Revolution, War and Peace, 1989–1992* (New York: G. P. Putnam's Sons, 1995), 74.

304. Meeting of the Politburo of the CC CPSU, 27–28 December 1988, REEAD 2922, NSA.

305. Gorbachev's Meeting with Representatives of the French Public, 29 September 1987, FBIS, 30 September 1987, 35.

306. Combining quotations from the session of the Politburo of the CC CPSU, 15 October 1987, REEAD 10012[?] pp. 140–41, NSA; also see Gorbachev's Speech, 2 November 1987, FBIS, 3 November 1987, 45 for the quotation.

307. Gorbachev Speech, 2 November 1987, *ibid.*, 3 November 1987, quotations on 61 and 49.

308. Session of the Politburo of the CC CPSU, 15 October 1987, REEAD 10012[?], pp. 166–67, NSA.

309. Gorbachev Speech, 2 November 1987, FBIS, 3 November 1987, 54.

310. Shevardnadze Speech, 27 June 1987, FBIS, 27 October 1987, 52; Gorbachev Speech, 18 February 1988, *ibid.*, 19 February 1988, 58.

311. Gorbachev Speech, 2 November 1987, *ibid.*, 3 November 1987, 55–57; Gorbachev Speech, 4 November 1987, *ibid.*, 4 November 1987, 22–24; also see Odom, *Collapse of the Soviet Military*, 88–117; Checkel, *Ideas and International Political Change*, 77–105.

312. Gorbachev Speech, 4 November 1987, FBIS, 4 November 1987, 22–24; also see Gorbachev Speech, 18 February 1988, *ibid.*, 19 February 1988, esp. 57–58; also see Janice Gross Stein, "Political Learning by Doing: Gorbachev as Uncommitted Thinker and Motivated Learner," *International Organization* 48 (Spring 1994): 156–83.

313. Gorbachev Speech, 2 November 1987, *FBIS*, 3 November 1987, 57.

314. Gorbachev Speech, 4 November 1987, *ibid.*, 4 November 1987, 23.

315. For Gorbachev's sense of security, see comments by Chernyaev in Wohlforth, *Witnesses*, 5, 37; also in Wohlforth, *Cold War Endgame*, 21; for Shevardnadze, see Shevardnadze Speech, 23 October 1989, FBIS, 24 October 1989, 45; Shevardnadze, *Future Belongs to Freedom*, 54–55.

316. Akhromeyev Speech, 6 May 1988, FBIS, 10 May 1988, 75.

317. Gorbachev Speech, 18 February 1988, *ibid.*, 19 February 1988, 57–58.

318. Gorbachev Speech, 4 November 1987, *ibid.*, 4 November 1987, 23.

319. Memorandum of Conversation, 29 May 1988, box 3, End of Cold War Collection, NSA.

320. *Ibid.*

321. Kengor, *God and Ronald Reagan*, 298–320.

322. Memorandum of Conversation, 29 May 1988, box 3, End of Cold War Collection, NSA.

323. Memorandum of Conversation, 1 June 1988, 10:05–11:20 a.m., box 3, End of Cold War Collection, NSA.

324. Chernyaev, *Six Years with Gorbachev*, 160*ff;* Chernyaev's Notes from the Politburo Meeting, 20 June 1988, REEAD 2939, NSA; for background on political reform, see, for example, Brown, *Gorbachev Factor*, 166–86.

325. Chernyaev's Notes from the Politburo Meeting, 20 June 1988, REEAD 2939, NSA; Gorbachev Speech at the Political Consultative Committee of the WP, 15 July 1988, in Mastny and Byrne, *A Cardboard Castle?*, 611.

326. Shevardnadze Speech, 27 September 1988, FBIS, 28 September 1988, 2–10, quotation on 6; Gorbachev Speech, 7 December 1988, *ibid.*, 8 December 1988, 11–19.

327. Gorbachev Speech, 7 December 1988, *ibid.*, 8 December 1988, 17–18.

328. For a discussion of the speech and the reaction, see Gorbachev, *Memoirs*, 459–62; for Gorbachev's intentions, see Chernyaev's Notes from the Politburo Session, 31 October 1988, REEAD 2924, NSA; for some additional reaction, see Oberdorfer, *The Turn*, 318–19.

329. Reagan, *An American Life*, 720; for an assessment of Reagan's evolving perception of the Soviet threat, see Barbara Farnham, "Reagan and the Gorbachev Revolution: Perceiving the End of Threat," *Political Science Quarterly* 116 (Summer 2001): 225–52.

330. For Gorbachev's appreciation of Reagan, see Chernyaev's comments in Tannenwald, "Understanding the End of the Cold War," 221; Gorbachev, "A President Who Listened," *New York Times*, 7 June 2004; N. Reagan, *My Turn*, 355–56.

331. Gorbachev Speech, 31 December 1988, FBIS, 3 January 1989, 41–42.

332. Meeting of the Politburo, 27–28 December 1988, REEAD, 2922, NSA.

333. "Inaugural Address," 20 January 1989, *Public Papers of the Presidents: George H. W. Bush, 1989* (Washington, D.C.: Government Printing Office, 1990), 1 (hereafter cited as *PPP: Bush, year, page*).

334. "Address Before a Joint Session of Congress," 9 February 1989, *ibid.*, 79; also see "President's News Conference," 27 January 1989, *ibid.*, 23; George Bush and Brent Scowcroft, *A World Transformed* (New York: Vintage Books, 1998), 8–11.

335. Bush and Scowcroft, *World Transformed*, 13; Gates, *From the Shadows*, 449–61.

336. Baker, *Politics of Diplomacy*, 69, 70, 83.

337. "Remarks at the Swearing-in Ceremony," 21 March 1989, *PPP: Bush, 1989*, 277.

338. Matlock to Baker and Scowcroft, 3 February 1989, box 3, End of Cold War Collection, NSA.

339. Matlock to Baker and Scowcroft, 13 February 1989 and 22 February 1989, *ibid.*

340. Matlock to Baker and Scowcroft, 22 February 1989, *ibid.*

341. Baker, *Politics of Diplomacy*, 68.

342. Bush and Scowcroft, *World Transformed*, 41.

343. "Remarks at the Texas A & M University Commencement Ceremony," 12 May 1989, *PPP: Bush, 1989*, 540–43, quotation on 541.

344. "Remarks at the United States Coast Guard Academy Commencement Ceremony," 24 May 1989, *ibid.*, 601; "Remarks at Texas A & M," 12 May 1989, *ibid.*, 541.

345. National Security Directive 23, "United States Relations with the Soviet Union," 22 September 1989, Document Collection for Oral History Conference, "End of the Cold War in Europe, 1989: 'New Thinking' and New Evidence" (Musgrove, Ga., 1998), CWIHP Archival Materials.

346. "President's News Conference," 30 May 1989, *PPP: Bush, 1989*, 638; Baker, *Politics of Diplomacy*, 71–72, 156; Bush and Scowcroft, *World Transformed*, 40–45, 59, 81.

347. Bush and Scowcroft, *World Transformed*, 44; Baker, *Politics of Diplomacy*, 93–94.

348. "Remarks Concerning a Conventional Arms Control Initiative," 29 May 1989, *PPP: Bush, 1989*, 618; Baker, *Politics of Diplomacy*, 94; Bush and Scowcroft, *World Transformed*, 73; Oberdorfer, *The Turn*, 349–51.

349. Bush and Scowcroft, *World Transformed*, 83.

350. Quoted in Bennett Kovrig, *Of Walls and Bridges: The United States and Eastern Europe* (New York: New York University Press, 1991), 153; also see Gorbachev Speech, 6 July 1989, FBIS, 7 July 1989, 29–34.

351. For Honecker quotation, see Memorandum of Conversation between Gustav Husak and Erich Honecker, 3 May 1989, "Briefing Book" associated with Oral History Conference "The Democratic Revolution in Czechoslovakia: Its Precondition, Course, and Immediate Repercussions, 1987–89," CWIHP Archival Materials.

352. "Interview with Members of the White House Press Corps," 13 July 1989, *PPP: Bush, 1989*, 951–53; "Interview with Hungarian Journalists," 6 July 1989, *ibid.*, 914; "President's News Conference," 6 July 1989, *ibid.*, 899, 900; "The President's News Conference in Paris," 16 July 1989, *ibid.*, 973.

353. "Remarks to the Polish National Assembly," 10 July 1989, *ibid.*, 920–24, quotations on 920, 923.

354. Record of Gorbachev's Concluding Conversation with Mitterrand, 6 July 1989, Oral History Conference "End of the Cold War in Europe," CWIHP Archival Materials; also see Record of Conversation between Gorbachev and Helmut Kohl, 12 June 1989, *ibid.*

355. Gorbachev Speech, 7–8 July 1989, in Mastny and Byrne, *A Cardboard Castle?*, 644–46.

356. Speeches by Ceausescu, Honecker, and Gorbachev, 7–8 July 1989, *ibid.*, 650, 646, 652.

357. Recollections of Heinz Kessler, *ibid.*, 653.

358. Record of Conversation between Gorbachev and Kohl, 12 June 1989, Oral History Conference "End of the Cold War in Europe," CWIHP Archival Materials; Jacques Levesque, *The Enigma of 1989: The USSR and the Liberation of Eastern Europe* (Berkeley: University of California Press, 1997), 125, 153; for background, based on the most recent accessible sources, see Svetlana Savranskaya, "The Logic of 1989: Soviet Withdrawal from Eastern Europe," unpublished paper.

359. Levesque, *Enigma of 1989*, 155–56; for appraisals stressing Gorbachev's ambivalence, see Hannes Adomeit, *Imperial Overstretch: Germany in Soviet Policy from Stalin to Gorbachev* (Baden-Baden: Nomos, 1998), 401–17; Charles S. Maier, *Dissolution: The Crisis of Communism and the End of East Germany* (Princeton, N.J.: Princeton University Press, 1997), 155–56.

360. Record of conversation between Gorbachev and Egon Krenz, 1 November 1989, REEAD 2885, NSA; for the quotation, see Maier, *Dissolution*, 223; also see Levesque, *Enigma of 1989*, 156; Adomeit, *Imperial Overstretch*, 425–29.

361. Record of Conversation between Kohl and Lech Walesa, 9 November 1989, Briefing Book associated with Oral History Conference "Poland 1986–1989: The End of the System," CWIHP Archival Materials.

362. Meeting of the Politburo, 9 November 1989, Oral History Conference "End of the Cold War in Europe," CWIHP Archival Materials; see also Chernyaev, *Six Years with Gorbachev*, 226–32.

363. Memorandum of Telephone Conversation, 10 November 1989, box 3, End of Cold War Collection, NSA.

364. Excerpt from the Diary of Chernyaev, 10 November 1989, Oral History Conference "End of the Cold War in Europe," CWIHP Archival Materials.

365. Gorbachev Speech, 18 January 1989, FBIS, 19 January 1989, 8; Comments by Chernyaev in Wohlforth, *Witnesses*, 5, 37; Chernyaev, *Six Years with Gorbachev*, 45–46; Comments by Chernyaev in Wohlforth, *Cold War Endgame*, 21; Shevardnadze Speech, 23 October, FBIS, 24 October 1989, 44–45; Shakhnazarov, "Comments on the Report of V. G. Kulikov," 25 May 1988, Oral History Conference "End of the Cold War in Europe," CWIHP Archival Materials.

366. For the quotation and for analysis, see Andrew O. Bennett, "Trust Busting Out All Over: The Soviet Side of German Unification," in Wohlforth, *Cold War Endgame*, 199*ff*; also Garthoff, *Great Transition*, 605; Yazov Speech, 9 May 1988, FBIS, 10 May 1988, 69–72.

367. International Department of the CC CPSU to Yakovlev, February 1989, Oral History Conference "End of the Cold War in Europe," CWIHP Archival Materials.

368. Conflating quotations from Bogomolev Institute (Marina Sylvanskaya) to Yakovlev, February 1989, *ibid.*, and from an assessment by Alexei Izyumov and Andrei Kortunov, in Kennety A. Oye, "Explaining the End of the Cold War: Morphological and Behavioral Adaptations to the Nuclear Peace?" in *International Relations Theory and the End of the Cold War*, ed. by Richard Ned Lebow and Thomas Risse-Kappen (New York: Columbia University Press, 1995), 76.

369. This view comports with Levesque, *Enigma of 1989*; Savranskaya, "Logic of 1989."

370. Chernyaev, *Six Years with Gorbachev*, 224–32; Brown, *Gorbachev Factor*, 252–69. Anger with Gorbachev over his failure to use force at home was especially evident in the criticisms leveled against him by his detractors at the oral history conference held in Moscow in 1999. See "Moscow Cold War Conference."

371. Gorbachev Speech, 15 November 1989, FBIS, 16 November 1989, 64–75.

372. Memorandum of Conversation between Gorbachev and Krenz, 1 November 1989, REEAD 2885, NSA; Record of Conversation between Gorbachev and Mauno Koivisto, 25 October 1989, REEAD 2886, *ibid.*

373. Najibullah to Gorbachev, 5 November 1989, CWIHP Archival Materials.

374. Record of Telephone Conversation between Gorbachev and Kohl, 11 November 1989, Oral History Conference "End of the Cold War in Europe," CWIHP Archival Materials.

375. Record of Telephone Conversation between Gorbachev and Mitterrand, 14 November 1989, *ibid.*

376. Shevardnadze Speech, 17 November 1989, FBIS, 20 November 1989, 46.

377. Gorbachev, *Memoirs*, 517.

378. Shevardnadze's Speech, 23 October 1989, FBIS, 24 October 1989, esp. 45; Shevardnadze Speech, 17 November 1989, *ibid.*, esp. 44–46.

379. Baker, *Politics of Diplomacy*, 149.

380. Philip Zelikow and Condoleezza Rice, *Germany Unified and Europe Transformed* (Cambridge, Mass.: Harvard University Press, 1995), 120.

381. Margaret Thatcher, *The Downing Street Years* (New York: HarperCollins, 1993), 794–98; Bush and Scowcroft, *World Transformed*, 193; Record of Telephone Conversation between Gorbachev and Mitterrand, 14 November 1989, Oral History Conference "End of the Cold War in Europe," CWIHP Archival Materials; David S. Bell, *François Mitterrand: A Political Biography* (Cambridge, Eng.: Polity Press, 2005), 138–39; Frédéric Bozo, "Mitterrand's France, the End of the Cold War, and German Unification: A Reappraisal," *Cold War History* (forthcoming, January 2008).

382. Bush and Scowcroft, *World Transformed*, 182–95, quotation on 187; for memoranda of the phone calls, see box 3, End of Cold War Collection, NSA.

383. Bush and Scowcroft, *World Transformed*, 182–203, quotation on 195; Baker, *Politics of Diplomacy*, 158–68.

384. Bush and Scowcroft, *World Transformed*, 186; Baker, *Politics of Diplomacy*, 23–32.

385. Bush and Scowcroft, *World Transformed*, 154–55; Baker, *Politics of Diplomacy*, 169–71.

386. Bush and Scowcroft, *World Transformed*, 160–64, quotation on 162.

387. *Ibid.*, 164–72, quotations on 164, 167; also see Gorbachev, *Memoirs*, 510–15.

388. Baker to NATO capitals, 6 December 1989, box 3, End of Cold War Collection, NSA; comments by Baker, Scowcroft, and Chernyaev, in Wohlforth, *Cold War Endgame*, 45–48; Bush and Scowcroft, *World Transformed*, 173; Gorbachev, *Memoirs*, 510–15; Chernyaev, *Six Years with Gorbachev*, 233–34; Palazchenko, *Gorbachev and Shevardnadze*, 154–58.

389. Chernyaev, *Six Years with Gorbachev*, 242-66; Boldin, *Ten Years*, 175-300; Brown, *Gorbachev Factor*, 155-211; McCauley, *Gorbachev*, 92-232.

390. Record of Conversation between Gorbachev and Genscher, 5 December 1989, REEAD 2876, NSA.

391. Gorbachev, *Memoirs*, 528; for the momentum among the East German people toward unity, see Konrad H. Jarausch, *The Rush to German Unity* (New York: Oxford University Press, 1994), 75-134.

392. Baker, *Politics of Diplomacy*, 204, 237; Shevardnadze, *Future Belongs to Freedom*, 132, 144.

393. Excerpts from Chernyaev's Journal, 28 January 1990, Oral History Conference "End of the Cold War in Europe," CWIHP Archival Materials; Anatolii Cherniaev [*sic*], "The Unification of Germany," *Russian Social Science Review* 40 (May–June 1999): 60; Chernyaev, *Six Years with Gorbachev*, 271-72; Adomeit, *Imperial Overstretch*, 478-80; Bozo, "Mitterrand's France and the End of the Cold War."

394. Shevardnadze Speech, 15 February 1990, FBIS, 21 February 1990, 913, quotation on 10.

395. Gorbachev, *Memoirs*, 529; for the absence of a plan, see the comments of Aleksandr Bessmertnykh, in Wohlforth, *Cold War Endgame*, 68.

396. Quoted in Adomeit, *Imperial Overstretch*, 490-91; also see Palazchenko, *Gorbachev and Shevardnadze*, 158-83.

397. Baker, *Politics of Diplomacy*, 208, 250-52; Palazchenko, *Gorbachev and Shevardnadze*, 184-87.

398. Palazchenko, *Gorbachev and Shevardnadze*, 187.

399. Baker, *Politics of Diplomacy*, 252.

400. Bush and Scowcroft, *World Transformed*, 279-89, quotation on 280; Palazchenko, *Gorbachev and Shevardnadze*, 184-94; Chernyaev, *Six Years with Gorbachev*, 272-75; Gorbachev, *Memoirs*, 536-42.

401. Bush and Scowcroft, *World Transformed*, 281.

402. *Ibid.*, 282-83; Chernyaev, *Six Years with Gorbachev*, 273.

403. Bush and Scowcroft, *World Transformed*, 283.

404. Shevardnadze Speech, 18 April 1990, FBIS, 26 April 1990, 5-11, quotation on 10.

405. Gorbachev, *Memoirs*, 533; Bush and Scowcroft, *World Transformed*, 281-82; Baker, *Politics of Diplomacy*, 234-39; conversation between Kohl and Gorbachev, 15 July 1990, REEAD 2669, NSA.

406. Gorbachev, *Memoirs*, 533, also 516-22; for an extremely important meeting between Gorbachev and Kohl on 10 February 1990, see Horst Teltschik, *329 Tage Innenansichten der Einigung* (Berlin: Siedler, 1991), 140; Helmut Kohl, with Kai Diekmann and Ralf Georg Reuth, *Ich wollte Deutschlands Einheit* (Berlin: Propylaen, 1996), 273; Adomeit, *Imperial Overstretch*, 554-55; for the evolution of the Kohl-Gorbachev relationship, also see Chernyaev, *Six Years with Gorbachev*, 198-200, 223; also illuminating is the conversation between Kohl and Gorbachev, 14 June 1989, REEAD 2902, NSA.

407. Mark Kramer, "The Collapse of East European Communism and the Repercussions Within the Soviet Union," *Journal of Cold War Studies* 7 (Winter 2005): 27-39.

408. Conversation between Gorbachev and Kohl, 15 July 1990, REEAD 2669, NSA; for slightly different summation of meeting, see Gorbachev, *Memoirs*, 534.

409. Conversation between Gorbachev and Kohl, 15 July 1990, REEAD 2669, NSA.

410. Shevardnadze Speech, 18 April 1990, FBIS, 26 April 1990, 5-11, quotation on 11.

411. Conversation between Gorbachev and Kohl, 15 July 1990, REEAD 2669, NSA; Gorbachev, *Memoirs*, 534; Kohl, *Ich wollte Deutschlands Einheit*, 418-40; Teltschik, *319 Tage*, 321-41; Angela E. Stent, *Russia and Germany Reborn: Unification, the Soviet Collapse, and the New Europe* (Princeton, N.J.: Princeton University Press, 1999), 134-50; Adomeit, *Imperial Overstretch*, 524-28, 539-55.

412. Bush and Scowcroft, *World Transformed*, 299.

413. Yakovlev, "About Reagan," 12 March 1985, REEAD 10867, Yakovlev Collection, NSA.

414. Shevardnadze, *Future Belongs to Freedom*, 81-86; Gorbachev, "A President Who Listened," *New York Times*, 7 June 2004.

415. N. Reagan, *My Turn*, 355-56.

416. Bush and Scowcroft, *World Transformed*, 164–65; comments by Chernyaev in Wohlforth, *Cold War Endgame*, 48–49; Palazchenko, *Gorbachev and Shevardnadze*, 194.

417. This is apparent throughout Baker's memoir, *Politics of Diplomacy*.

Conclusion

1. Acheson testimony, 8 March 1945, U.S. Senate Committee on Banking and Currency, *Bretton Woods Agreements*, 1:35.

2. For a recent interpretation that also stresses Stalin's preoccupation with security, see Tony Judt, *Postwar: A History of Europe Since 1945* (New York: Penguin Press, 2005), 117–21.

3. "Can Capitalism Survive?," *Time* 106 (14 July 1975): 52–63.

4. Fred Halliday, *The Making of the Second Cold War* (London: Verso, 1983), 104–33, quotation on 116; for the rise of neoconservatism, see Gary Dorrien, *The Neoconservative Mind: Politics, Culture, and the War of Ideology* (Philadelphia, Pa.: Temple University Press, 1993); Murray Friedman, *The Neoconservative Revolution: Jewish Intellectuals and the Shaping of Public Policy* (New York: Cambridge University Press, 2005).

5. Samuel P. Huntington, *The Third Wave: Democratization in the Late Twentieth Century* (Norman: University of Oklahoma Press, 1991), 21.

6. L. I. Brezhnev, *Report of the CPSU Central Committee and the Immediate Tasks of the Party in Home and Foreign Policy*, Information Bulletin—Special Issue No. 1 (Toronto: Progress Books, 1976), 5, 103.

7. Philip Hanson, *The Rise and Fall of the Soviet Economy: An Economic History of the USSR from 1945* (London: Pearson Education Limited, 2003), 5, 241–53.

8. Forrest D. Colburn, *The Vogue of Revolution in Poor Countries* (Princeton, N.J.: Princeton University Press, 1994), 89, 14.

9. Atul Kohli, "Politics of Economic Liberalization in India," *World Development* 17, no. 3 (1989): 307.

10. James C. Scott, *Seeing Like a State: How Certain Schemes to Improve the Human Condition Have Failed* (New Haven, Conn.: Yale University Press, 1998), 7.

11. Michael Scott Christofferson, *French Intellectuals Against the Left: The Antitotalitarian Moment of the 1970s* (New York: Berghahn Books, 2004); Colburn, *Vogue of Revolution*.

12. Michael Dobbs, *Down with Big Brother: The Fall of the Soviet Empire* (New York: Alfred A. Knopf, 1997), 92–93; Judt, *Postwar*, 586–87.

13. For the quotation, see Mark Kramer, "Soviet Deliberations During the Polish Crisis, 1980–1981," Cold War International History Project, Special Working Paper No. 1 (Washington, D.C.: Woodrow Wilson International Center, 1999), 25–26; Judt, *Postwar*, 585–86*ff.*

14. Martin Malia, "The Archives of Evil: Soviet Studies after the Soviet Union," *New Republic* 231 (November 29 and December 6, 2004): 36; also Vojtech Mastny, *The Cold War and Soviet Insecurity: The Stalin Years* (New York: Oxford University Press, 1996), 9.

15. Linda J. Cook, *The Soviet Social Contract and Why It Failed: Welfare Policy and Workers' Politics from Brezhnev to Yeltsin* (Cambridge, Mass.: Harvard University Press, 1993), 19–20.

16. Y. V. Andropov, *Speeches and Writings* (Oxford, Eng.: Pergamon Press, 1983), 207.

17. For aspirations to catch up, see Hanson, *Rise and Fall of the Soviet Economy*, 71–72.

18. "The Statements Made by Khrushchev at the Session of the Presidium of the CC," 10 September 1963, Malin Notes.

19. Stephen Kotkin, *Armageddon Averted: The Soviet Collapse, 1970–2000* (Oxford, Eng.: Oxford University Press, 2001), 44.

20. Hanson, *Rise and Fall of the Soviet Economy*, 244–45.

21. For views of Soviet citizens about their living conditions, see Irene A. Boutenko and Kirill E.

Razlogov, *Recent Social Trends in Russia, 1960–1995* (Montreal: McGill-Queen's University Press, 1997), 330; for figures on consumption, see *ibid.*, 235; and esp. Gertrude E. Schroeder, "Soviet Living Standards in Comparative Perspective," in *Quality of Life in the Soviet Union,* ed. by Horst Herlemann (Boulder, Colo.: Westview Press, 1987), 16; for workers' expectations and disillusionment, see Cook, *Social Contract,* 19–93; for background, also see Alex Inkeles and Raymond A. Bauer, *The Soviet Citizen: Daily Life in a Totalitarian Society* (Cambridge, Mass.: Harvard University Press, 1961), 377–98.

22. He also wanted to harness the military sector for civilian production. See Bruce Parrott, "Soviet National Security Under Gorbachev," *Problems of Communism* 37 (November–December 1988): 1–36; also see Clifford G. Gaddy, *The Price of the Past: Russia's Struggle with the Legacy of a Militarized Economy* (Washington, D.C.: Brookings Institution Press, 1996), 47–48.

23. Quoted in Gaddy, *Price of the Past,* 49.

24. Jonathan Harris, *Subverting the System: Gorbachev's Reform of the Party's Apparat, 1986–1991* (Lanham, Md.: Rowman and Littlefield, 2004); John W. Parker, *Kremlin in Transition: Gorbachev, 1985–1989,* vol. 2 (Boston: Unwin Hyman, 1991).

25. For the discussion of political prisoners, see Meeting of the Politburo of CPSU, 25 September 1986, National Security Archive (NSA). After Reagan raised the human rights issue at Reykjavik, Gorbachev insisted to his colleagues that they work out a conception of human rights and allow the dissidents—"the trash"—who posed no security threats to leave. See Chernyaev's Notes from the Politburo Session, 13 November 1986, REEAD 2951, NSA. For Gorbachev's exchange with Reagan on human rights at the Washington summit, see Gorbachev's account in Chernyaev's Notes from the Politburo Session, 17 December 1987, REEAD 2940, *ibid.* Amnesty International worked in behalf of 530 individuals of conscience inside the U.S.S.R. in 1986 but said the real total might be much higher. See *Amnesty International Report 1987* (London: Amnesty International Publications, 1987), 320. In its report in 1989, Amnesty International thought there were still 140 prisoners of conscience, most of them would-be emigrants, and that 374 had been freed since 1987. See *Amnesty International Report 1989* (New York: Amnesty International USA, 1989), 237.

26. For Reagan's quotation, see "Farewell Address to the Nation," 11 January 1989, *Reagan: PPP, 1988,* 1720; for Shultz, see George Shultz, "National Success and International Change in a Time of Change," p. 3, 4 December 1987, *Current Policy* No. 1029, Bureau of Public Affairs, U.S. Department of State; Shultz, "The Winning Hand: American Leadership and the Global Economy," 28 April 1988, *Current Policy* No. 1070, *ibid.*; Shultz, "The Ecology of International Change," 28 October 1988, *Current Policy* No. 1120, *ibid.*; George P. Shultz, *Turmoil and Triumph: My Years as Secretary of State* (New York: Charles Scribner's Sons, 1993), 586–87, 712–16, 887–93. Many scholars agree that command economies based on national planning lacked the capacity to innovate and compete. See, for example, Hanson, *Rise and Fall of the Soviet Economy,* 240–55; Charles Maier, *Dissolution: The Crisis of Communism and the End of East Germany* (Princeton, N.J.: Princeton University Press, 1997), 59–107; Daniel Chirot, "What Happened in Eastern Europe in 1989," in *The Revolutions of 1989: Rewriting Histories,* ed. by Vladimir Tismaneau (London: Routledge, 1999), 20–26.

27. "Address to the Nation and Other Countries," 16 January 1984, *PPP: Reagan, 1984,* 44.

28. *Ibid.*, 42.

29. Paul Lettow, *Ronald Reagan and His Quest to Abolish Nuclear Weapons* (New York: Random House, 2005).

30. "Remarks Following the Soviet–United States Summit Meeting, 2 June 1988," *PPP: Reagan, 1988,* 715.

31. "Farewell Address to the Nation," 11 January 1989, *Reagan: PPP, 1988,* 1721.

BIBLIOGRAPHY

United States Archival Materials

MANUSCRIPT COLLECTIONS AND ORAL HISTORIES

Kenneth Adelman Interview, Ronald Reagan Oral History Project, Miller Center of Public Affairs, University of Virginia, Charlottesville, Va.

James Baker Interview, Reagan Oral History Project, Miller Center

James F. Byrnes Papers, Clemson University Library, Clemson, S.C.

Jimmy Carter Interview, Carter Presidency Project, Miller Center

Joseph Davies Diary, Library of Congress, Washington, D.C.

John Foster Dulles Papers, Seely G. Mudd Library, Princeton University, Princeton, N.J.

James V. Forrestal Papers, Mudd Library

W. Averell Harriman Papers, Library of Congress

Emmet John Hughes Diary, Mudd Library

George F. Kennan Papers, Mudd Library

William Leahy Diary, Library of Congress

George Shultz Interview, Reagan Oral History Project, Miller Center

Henry L. Stimson Diary, Sterling Library, Yale University, New Haven, Conn.

NATIONAL ARCHIVES OF THE UNITED STATES

Record Group 56, Records of the Treasury Department

Declassified Documents from Secretary Dillon's and Fowler's Classified Files, MLR No. 198G

Office Files of Secretaries and Undersecretaries, 1932–1965, Files of Henry Fowler, 1961–1964, MLR No. 198F

Record Group 59, General Records of the Department of State

Papers of Charles E. Bohlen, Lot 74 D 379

Records of the Bureau of Intelligence and Research, Subject Files, 1945–1960, Lot 58 D 776

Records of the Bureau of Intelligence and Research, Lot 78 D 394

Records of the Bureau of Intelligence and Research, Lot 87 D 337

Records of the Bureau of Intelligence and Research, Office of the Director, 1949–1959, Lot 60 D 403

Records of the Bureau of Intelligence and Research, Office of the Director, 1950–1959, Lot 58 D 528

Records of the Bureau of Intelligence and Research, Office of the Director, 1949–1955, Lot 59 D 27

Records of the Deputy Assistant Secretary for Political-Military Affairs, Subject Files, 1961–1963, MLR 3063A

Records of the Policy Planning Staff, 1947–1953, Lot 64 D 563

Records of the Policy Planning Staff, 1962, Lot 69 D 121

Records of the Policy Planning Staff/National Security Council, Lot 66 D 95

Records Relating to the State Department Participation in the Operations Coordinating Board (OCB) and the NSC, 1947–1953, Lot 66 D 148

Records of State/JCS Meetings, 1959–1963, MLR 1604

Records of the Under Secretary for Political Affairs, 1961–1963, MLR 3055A

Records of the Under Secretary for Political Affairs, Subject Files, 1961–1963, HM 1993

Record Group 107, Records of the Office of the Secretary of War, Robert P. Patterson Papers

Record Group 165, Records of the War Department General and Special Staffs, Records of American-British Conversations

Record Group 218, Records of the Joint Chiefs of Staff

Geographic Files

William Leahy Papers

Arthur Radford Papers

Maxwell Taylor Papers

Record Group 273, Records of the National Security Council

Record Group 319, Records of the Army Plans and Operations Division

Record Group 330, Records of the Office of the Secretary of Defense

NATIONAL SECURITY ARCHIVE, GEORGE WASHINGTON UNIVERSITY, WASHINGTON, D.C.

End of the Cold War Collection

PRESIDENTIAL LIBRARIES

Harry S. Truman Library

Clark M. Clifford Oral History

Matthew J. Connelly Papers

President's Secretary's File

Dwight David Eisenhower Library

Ann Whitman File, Cabinet Series

Ann Whitman File, Diary Series

Ann Whitman File, Dulles-Herter Series

Ann Whitman File, International Series

Ann Whitman File, Legislative Meetings Series

Ann Whitman File, NSC Series

Papers of John Foster Dulles, Telephone Conversation Series
Papers of John Foster Dulles, White House Memo Series
Papers of C. D. Jackson, 1931–1967
Records of C. D. Jackson, 1953–1954
White House Memo Series, General Foreign Policy Subseries
White House Office, NSC Staff: Papers, 1948–1961
   Psychological Strategy Board, Central Files
White House Office, Office of Special Assistant for National Security Affairs
   Administrative Subseries
   Briefing Notes Subseries
   Policy Paper Subseries
   Status of Projects Subseries
   Subject Subseries
John F. Kennedy Library
  National Security Files
   McGeorge Bundy Correspondence
   France-General
   Meetings and Memoranda
   Staff Memos
   Standing Groups Meetings
   United Kingdom
   U.S.S.R.
  Papers of Theodore Sorensen
Lyndon Baines Johnson Library
  Cabinet Papers
  National Security Files
   Agency Files
   McGeorge Bundy Files
   Douglas Cater Files
   C. V. Clifton Files
   Committee Files, Committee on Nuclear Proliferation
   Country Files—USSR
   Head of State Files
   Intelligence File
   Spurgeon Keeny Files
   Robert Komer Files
   Meetings
   Memos to the President
   National Intelligence Estimates
   Special Head of State
  Papers of George Ball
  Papers of John McCone
  Papers of Bromley K. Smith
  Vice President Security File
Jimmy Carter Library
  Zbigniew Brzezinski Collection
  Chief of Staff Papers
  National Security Affairs Staff, Horn/Special

Plains File
James Schlesinger Oral History
Vertical Files
   China
   U.S.S.R.
White House Central Files, Countries
Ronald Reagan Library
   Coordinating Office: NSC Records
   Executive Secretariat, National Security Council: Country
   Executive Secretariat, National Security Council: Head of State
   Executive Secretariat, National Security Council: Meetings
   Executive Secretariat, National Security Council: System Files
   Executive Secretariat, National Security Decision Directives
   Papers of William Clark
   Papers of Donald Fortier
   Papers of John Lenczowski
   Papers of Richard Linhard
   Papers of Jack Matlock
   Papers of Colin Powell
   Presidential Briefing Papers

PRESIDENTIAL TAPES
John F. Kennedy, Presidential Recordings Project, Miller Center
Lyndon Baines Johnson, Presidential Recordings Project, Miller Center

U.S. DEPARTMENT OF STATE, FREEDOM OF INFORMATION ACT ELECTRONIC READING ROOM
http://foia.state.gov/SearchColls/CollsSearch.asp.

RUSSIAN, EAST EUROPEAN, CHINESE, AND VIETNAMESE ARCHIVAL MATERIALS
Cold War International History Project, Woodrow Wilson International Center, Washington, D.C.
   Document Collections and Oral Histories
      "Conversations with Stalin," a Cold War International History Project Document Reader, prepared
      for the conference "Stalin and the Cold War, 1945–1953," organized by the Cold War Interna-
      tional History Project, the Council of European Studies and the International Security Studies
      Program at Yale University, 23–26 September 1999
      "The Democratic Revolution in Czechoslovakia: Its Precondition, Course, and Immediate Reper-
      cussions, 1987–1989," an International Conference, Prague, 14–16 October 1999, organized by
      the National Security Archive, the Czechoslovak Documentation Centre, and the (Czech) Insti-
      tute of Contemporary History
      "Documents from the 'Other Side' ": A Document Reader Compiled for the International Confer-
      ence "Tracking the Dragon: National Intelligence Estimates on China During the Mao Era,
      1948–1976," organized by the National Intelligence Council and the Woodrow Wilson Interna-
      tional Center for Scholars, 18 October 2004
      "The End of the Cold War in Europe, 1989: 'New Thinking' and New Evidence," a Critical Oral
      History Conference, organized by the National Security Archive, 1–3 May 1998
      "Poland: 1986–1989: The End of the System," Miedzeszyn–Warsaw, Poland, 20–24 October 1999,
      organized by the Institute of Political Studies of the Polish Academy of Sciences and the National
      Security Archive

"Political Transition in Hungary, 1989–1990," International Conference, June 12, 1999, Budapest, organized by the National Security Archive, Cold War History Research Center (Budapest), Hungarian Academy of Sciences, and the Cold War International History Project

"Toward an International History of the War in Afghanistan, 1979–1989," organized by the Cold War International History Project, 29–30 April 2002

LAMONT LIBRARY, HARVARD UNIVERSITY

Rossiiskii gosudarstvennyi arkhiv noveishei istorii (RGANI), "Plenumy Tsentral'nogo Komiteta Kommunisticheskoi partii Sovetskogo Soiuza, 1941–1990," fond 2, opis' 1 [Russian State Archives of Contemporary History, "Plenums of the Central Committee of the Communist Party of the Soviet Union, 1941–1990,"] collection 2, catalog 1, Microforms, Film A1059

Rossiskii gosudarstvennyi arkhiv noveishei istorii (RGANI), "Obshchii otdel Tsk KPSS, 1953–1966 gody," fond 5, opis' 30 [Russian State Archive of Contemporary History, "The General Department of the Central Committee of the CPSU, 1953–1966,"] collection 5, catalog 30, Microforms, Film A1046

Rossiskii gosudarstvennyi arkhiv noveishei istorii (RGANI), Otdel TsK KPSS po sviaziam s inostrannymi Kompartiiami (Mezhdunarodnyi otdel TsK KPSS), 1953–1957 gody," fond 5, opis' 28, [Russian State Archive of Contemporary History, "Department of the Central Committee of the CPSU for Relations with Foreign Communist Parties (International Department of the Central Committee of the CPSU), 1953–1957," collection 5, catalog 28], Microforms, Film A1050

MILLER CENTER, UNIVERSITY OF VIRGINIA

Translation of Vladimir Malin's notes of the Presidium Meetings, in A. A. Fursenko (et al.), ed., Prezidium TsK KPSS, 1954–1964: Chernovye protokol'nye zapisi zasedanii, stenogrammy, postanovleniia [The Presidium of the CC of the CPSU, 1954–1964: Draft Records of Session Proceedings, Stenographic Transcripts, Resolutions], vol. 1 (Moscow: ROSSPEN, 2003). Accessible on the Internet at http://millercenter.virginia.edu/scripps/digitalarchive/kremlin

NATIONAL SECURITY ARCHIVE, GEORGE WASHINGTON UNIVERSITY, WASHINGTON, D.C.

Analtoli Chernyaev Collection

Russian Archives Documents Database

Russian and East European Archives Database

The September 11 Sourcebooks

Dmitri Volkogonov Collection

Aleksandr Yakovlev Collection

Zoltoi fond

Oral History and Conference Documents Collections

"Global Competition and the Deterioration of U.S.-Soviet Relations, 1977–1980," a Conference of Russian and U.S. Policymakers and Scholars, Fort Lauderdale, Fla., 23–26 March 1995, sponsored by the Carter-Brezhnev Project, Thomas J. Watson Institute, Brown University, Providence, Rhode Island

"Intervention in Afghanistan and the Fall of Détente." Ed. David A. Welch and Odd Arne Westad. Trans. Svetlana Savranskaya. Nobel Symposium, Oslo, 17–20 September 1995, organized by the Norwegian Nobel Institute

"Moscow End of Cold War Conference: U.S.-Soviet Military and Security Relationships at the End of the Cold War, 1988–91," organized by the Mershon Center, Ohio State University, 15–17 October 1999

"New Central and East European Evidence on the Cold War in Asia," Budapest, 31 October–1 November 2003, organized by the National Security Archive and the Cold War History Research Center (Budapest)

"SALT II and the Growth of Mistrust," a Conference of Russian and U.S. Policymakers and Scholars, Musgrove Plantation, 6–9 May 1994, St. Simons Island, sponsored by the Carter-Brezhnev Project, Watson Institute, Brown University

"Understanding the End of the Cold War, 1980–1987," an oral history conference. Ed. Nina Tannenwald. Watson Institute, Brown University, May 7–10, 1998

NORWEGIAN NOBEL INSTITUTE
Oral history, "U.S.-Soviet Relations and Soviet Foreign Policy Toward the Middle East and Africa in the 1970s"

PARALLEL HISTORY PROJECT
http://www.isn.ethz.ch/php/documents

Published U.S. Government Documents

CONGRESS
Joint Economic Committee of the Congress of the United States. *Soviet Economy in a Time of Change.* Vol. 2, 1979.
———. Subcommittee on Priorities and Economy in Government. *Allocation of Resources in the Soviet Union and China—1979.* 96th Cong., 1st sess., 1980.

SENATE
Appendix to the Congressional Record. Vol. 93.
Committee on Banking and Currency, *Bretton Woods Agreements Act.* 79th Cong., 1st sess., 1945.
———. *Anglo-American Financial Agreement.* 79th Cong., 2nd sess., 1946.
Committee on Foreign Relations. *Executive Sessions of the Senate Foreign Relations Committee, Together with Joint Sessions with the Senate Armed Services Committee (Historical Series), 17* (Washington, D.C.: Government Printing Office, 1990).

EXECUTIVE BRANCH
Cabinet
Department of State. *Bulletin.*
———. *Current Policy* (Bureau of Public Affairs).
———. *Foreign Relations of the United States, 1947.* Vols. 2, 3, 5, 1972.
———. *Foreign Relations of the United States, 1948.* Vols. 2, 3, 5, 1973, 1974, 1975–76.
———. *Foreign Relations of the United States, 1952–54.* Vols. 2, 5, 7, 8, 12, 14, 1984, 1983, 1986, 1988, 1984, 1985.
———. *Foreign Relations of the United States, 1961–1963.* Vols. 5–8, 11, 13, 15, 1998, 1996, 1995, 1996, 1997, 1994, 1994.
———. *Foreign Relations of the United States, 1964–1968.* Vols. 1, 2, 10, 11, 13, 14, 15, 17, 21, 27, 31, 1992, 1996, 2002, 1997, 1995, 2001, 1999, 1996, 2000, 2000, 2004.
———. *Foreign Relations of the United States. Conference of Berlin (Potsdam), 1945.* 2 vols., 1960.
Nelson, Anna Kasten, ed. *Policy Planning Staff Papers.* Vols. 1–3. New York: Garland, 1983.
U.S. Arms Control and Disarmament Agency. *World Military Expenditures and Arms Trade, 1963–1973.* Washington D.C.: Government Printing Office, 1975.

————. *World Military Expenditures and Arms Transfers, 1967–1976.* Washington Government Printing Office, D.C.: 1978.

Central Intelligence Agency

Foreign Broadcasting Information System

Steury, Donald P., ed. *Intentions and Capabilities: Estimates on Soviet Strategic Forces, 1950–1983.* Washington, D.C.: Central Intelligence Agency, 1996.

White House

Bush, George H. W. *Public Papers of the Presidents: 1989.* Washington, D.C.: GPO, 1990.

Carter, Jimmy. *Public Papers of the Presidents: 1977, 1978, 1979, 1980.* Washington, D.C.: GPO, 1977, 1978, 1979, 1980–81.

Eisenhower, Dwight D. *Public Papers of the Presidents: 1953.* Washington, D.C.: GPO, 1960.

Johnson, Lyndon Baines. *Public Papers of the Presidents: 1964, 1965.* Washington, D.C.: GPO, 1965, 1966.

Kennedy, John F. *Public Papers of the Presidents: 1961, 1962, 1963.* Washington, D.C.: GPO, 1962, 1963, 1964.

Reagan, Ronald. *Public Papers of the Presidents: 1981, 1982, 1983, 1984, 1985, 1987, 1988.* Washington, D.C.: GPO, 1982, 1983, 1984, 1987, 1988, 1989, 1990.

Truman, Harry S. *Public Papers of the President: 1945, 1947, 1949, 1952–53.* Washington, D.C.: GPO, 1961, 1963, 1964, 1966.

Magazines and Periodicals

Argumenty i fakty
Cold War International History Bulletin
Congressional Quarterly Weekly Report
Current Digest of the Soviet Press
Current History
Istochnik
New Republic
Newsweek
The New York Times
Pravda
Time
U.S. News & World Report
U.S.S.R. and the Third World
Vital Speeches of the Day

Other Cited Sources: Primary and Secondary

Abrams, Bradley. *The Struggle for the Soul of the Nation: Czech Culture and the Rise of Communism.* Lanham, Md.: Rowman and Littlefield, 2004.

Academy of Sciences of the USSR. *Leonid I. Brezhnev: Pages from His Life.* New York: Simon and Schuster, 1978.

Acheson, Dean. *Present at the Creation: My Years at the State Department.* New York: Norton, 1969.

Adams, Michael C. *The Best War Ever: America and World War II.* Baltimore, Md.: Johns Hopkins University Press, 1994.

Adomeit, Hannes. *Imperial Overstretch: Germany in Soviet Policy from Stalin to Gorbachev.* Baden-Baden: Nomos, 1998.

Ahonen, Pertti. *After the Expulsion: West Germany and Eastern Europe, 1945–1990.* New York: Oxford University Press, 2003.

Aldrich, Richard J. *The Hidden Hand: Britain, America, and Cold War Secret Intelligence.* Woodstock, New York: Overlook Press, 2001.

Alexeyeva, Ludmilla. *Soviet Dissent: Contemporary Movements for National, Religious, and Human Rights.* Trans. Carol Pearce and John Glad. Middletown, Conn.: Wesleyan University Press, 1985.

Alliluyeva, Svetlana. *20 Letters to a Friend.* Trans. Priscilla Johnson McMillan. New York: Harper and Row, 1967.

———. *Only One Year.* London: Hutchinson, 1969.

Ambrose, Stephen E. *Eisenhower.* Vols. 1–2. New York: Simon and Schuster, 1983 and 1984.

Amnesty International. *Amnesty International Report 1987.* London: Amnesty International Publications, 1987.

———. *Amnesty International Report 1989.* New York: Amnesty International USA, 1989.

Anderson, Martin. *Revolution: The Reagan Legacy.* Stanford, Calif.: Hoover Institution Press, 1990.

Andropov, Y. V. *Speeches and Writings.* Oxford, Eng.: Pergamon Press, 1983.

Applebaum, Anne. *Gulag: A History of the Soviet Camps.* London: Allen Lane, 2003.

Arbatov, Georgi. *The System: An Insider's Life in Soviet Politics.* New York: Random House, 1992.

Arjomand, S. A. "Iran's Islamic Revolution in Comparative Perspective," *World Politics* 38 (April 1986): 383–414.

Aslund, Anders. *Gorbachev's Struggle for Economic Reform.* Ithaca, N.Y.: Cornell University Press, 1989.

Baker, James A. III, with Thomas M. Defrank. *The Politics of Diplomacy: Revolution, War and Peace, 1989–1992.* New York: G. P. Putnam's Sons, 1995.

Bekes, Csaba. "Soviet Plans to Establish the Cominform in Early 1946: New Evidence from the Hungarian Archives," *CWIHP Bulletin* 10 (March 1998): 135–37.

Bell, David S. *François Mitterrand: A Political Biography.* Cambridge, Eng.: Polity Press, 2005.

Bell, Jonathan. *The Liberal State on Trial: The Cold War and American Politics in the Truman Years.* New York: Columbia University Press, 2004.

Bennett, Andrew O. "Trust Busting Out All Over: The Soviet Side of German Unification." In *Cold War Endgame: Oral History, Analysis, Debates.* Ed. William C. Wohlforth, 175–204. University Park: Pennsylvania State University Press, 2003.

Beria, Sergo. *My Father: Inside Stalin's Kremlin.* Ed. Françoise Thom. Trans. Brian Pearce. London: Gerald Duckworth and Co., 2001.

Beschloss, Michael. *Kennedy v. Khrushchev: The Crisis Years, 1960–1963.* London: Faber and Faber, 1991.

———. *Taking Charge: The Johnson White House Tapes, 1963–1964.* New York: Simon and Schuster, 1997.

———. *Reaching for Glory: Lyndon Johnson's Secret White House Tapes, 1964–1965.* New York: Simon and Schuster, 2001.

Bill, James A. *The Eagle and the Lion: The Tragedy of American-Iranian Relations.* New Haven, Conn.: Yale University Press, 1988.

———. *George Ball: Behind the Scenes in U.S. Foreign Policy.* New Haven, Conn.: Yale University Press, 1997.

Bird, Kai. *Color of Truth: McGeorge Bundy and William Bundy, Brothers in Arms: A Biography.* New York: Simon and Schuster, 1998.

Blight, James G., and David A. Welch. *On the Brink: Americans and Soviets Reexamine the Cuban Missile Crisis.* New York: Noonday Press, 1990.

Bohning, Don. *The Castro Obsession: U.S. Covert Operations, 1959–1965.* Washington, D.C.: Potomac Books, 2005.

Boldin, Valery. *Ten Years That Shook the World: The Gorbachev Era as Witnessed by His Chief of Staff.* Trans. Evelyn Rossiter. New York: Basic Books, 1994.

Borhi, Lazlo. "Rollback, Liberation, Containment, or Inaction? U.S. Policy and Eastern Europe in the 1950s." *Journal of Cold War Studies* 1 (Summer 1999): 67–110.

Bourne, Peter G. *Jimmy Carter: A Comprehensive Biography from Plains to Postpresidency.* New York: Scribner, 1997.

Boutenko, Irene A., and Kirill E. Razlogov. *Recent Social Trends in Russia, 1960–1995.* Montreal: McGill-Queen's University Press, 1997.

Boyle, Peter G., ed. *The Churchill-Eisenhower Correspondence, 1953–1955.* Chapel Hill: University of North Carolina Press, 1990.

Bozo, Frédéric. "Mitterrand's France, the End of the Cold War, and German Unification: A Reappraisal." *Cold War History* (forthcoming, January 2008).

Brackman, Roman. *The Secret File of Joseph Stalin: A Hidden Life.* London: Frank Cass, 2001.

Brandenberger, David. *National Bolshevism: Stalinist Mass Culture and the Formation of Modern Russian National Identity, 1931–1956.* Cambridge, Mass.: Harvard University Press, 2002.

Brandt, Willie. *My Life in Politics.* New York: Viking Penguin, 1992.

Breslauer, George W. *Khrushchev and Brezhnev as Leaders: Building Authority in Soviet Politics.* London: George Allen and Unwin, 1982.

———. "Ideology and Learning in Soviet Third World Policy." *World Politics* 39 (April 1987): 429–48.

———. *Gorbachev and Yeltsin as Leaders.* Cambridge, Eng.: Cambridge University Press, 2002.

Brezhnev, L. I. *Following Lenin's Course: Speeches and Articles (1972–1975).* Moscow: Progress Publishers, 1975.

———. *Report of the CPSU Central Committee and the Immediate Tasks of the Party in Home and Foreign Policy, Information Bulletin—Special Issue No. 1.* Toronto: Progress Books, 1976.

———. *Peace, Détente and Soviet-American Relations: A Collection of Public Statements.* New York: Harcourt Brace Jovanovich, 1979.

———. *Selected Speeches and Writings on Foreign Affairs.* Oxford, Eng.: Pergamon Press, 1979.

———. *Memoirs.* Trans. Penny Dole. Oxford, Eng.: Pergamon Press, 1982.

Brezhneva, Luba. *The World I Left Behind: Pieces of a Past.* New York: Random House, 1995.

Broadwater, Jeff. *Eisenhower and the Anti-Communist Crusade.* Chapel Hill: University of North Carolina Press, 1992.

Brooks, Jeffrey. *Thank You, Comrade Stalin: Soviet Public Culture from Revolution to Cold War.* Princeton, N.J.: Princeton University Press, 2000.

———. "Stalin's Ghost: Cold War Culture and U.S.-Soviet Relations." In *After Stalin's Death: The Cold War as International History.* Ed. Klaus Larres and Kenneth Osgood, 1–35. Harvard Cold War Series, Lanham, Md.: Rowman and Littlefield, 2005.

Brown, Archie. *The Gorbachev Factor.* Oxford, Eng.: Oxford University Press, 1997.

Brugioni, Dino A. *Eyeball to Eyeball: The Inside Story of the Cuban Missile Crisis.* New York: Random House, 1991.

Brzezinski, Zbigniew. *Power and Principle: Memoirs of a National Security Adviser, 1977–1981.* New York: Farrar, Straus and Giroux, 1983.

Bundy, McGeorge. *Danger and Survival: Choices About the Bomb in the First Fifty Years.* New York: Random House, 1998.

Burds, Jeffrey. "The Early Cold War in Soviet West Ukraine, 1944–1948." *The Carl Beck Papers in Russian and East European Studies,* No. 1505. Pittsburgh, Pa.: University of Pittsburgh Press, 2001.

———. "The Soviet War Against 'Fifth Columnists': The Case of Chechnya, 1942–4." *Journal of Contemporary History* 42(2): 267–314.

Burk, Robert F. *Dwight D. Eisenhower: Hero and Politician.* Boston: Twayne Publishers, 1986.

Burlatsky, Fedor. *Khrushchev and the First Russian Spring.* Trans. by Daphne Skillen. London: Weidenfeld and Nicolson, 1991.

Burr, William, and Jeffrey T. Richelson. "Whether to 'Strangle the Baby in the Cradle': The United States and the Chinese Nuclear Program, 1960–1964." *International Security* 25 (Winter 2000): 54–99.

Bush, George, and Brent A. Scowcroft. *A World Transformed.* New York: Vintage Books, 1998.

Cahn, Anne Hessing. *Killing Détente: The Right Attacks the CIA.* University Park: Pennsylvania State University Press, 1998.

Caldwell, Dan. "The Demise of Détente and US Domestic Politics." In *The Fall of Détente: Soviet-American Relations During the Carter Years.* Ed. Odd Arne Westad, 95–117. Oslo: Scandinavian University Press, 1997.

Cannon, Lou. *President Reagan: The Role of a Lifetime.* New York: Public Affairs, 2000.

Caro, Robert. *The Years of Lyndon Johnson.* Vols. 1–3. New York: Knopf, 1992.

Carter, Jimmy. *Why Not the Best?* Nashville, Tenn.: Broadman Press, 1975.

———. *Keeping Faith: Memoirs of a President.* London: Collins, 1982.

———. *An Hour Before Daylight: Memories of a Rural Boyhood.* New York: Simon and Schuster, 2001.

Central Committee of the CPSU (B), *History of the Communist Party of the Soviet Union (Bolshevik): Short Course.* New York: International Publishers, 1939.

Chang, Jung, and Jon Halliday. *Mao: The Unknown Story.* New York: Knopf, 2005.

Chazov, E. I. *Zdorovie i vlast'* [Health and Power]. Moscow: Novosti, 1992.

Checkel, Jeffrey T. *Ideas and International Political Change: Soviet/Russian Behavior and the End of the Cold War.* New Haven, Conn.: Yale University Press, 1997.

Chen, Jian. *China's Road to the Korean War: The Making of the Sino-American Confrontation.* New York: Columbia University Press, 1994.

Chernus, Ira. *Eisenhower's Atoms for Peace.* College Station: Texas A & M University Press, 2002.

———. "Operation Candor: Fear, Faith, and Flexibility." *Diplomatic History* 29 (November 2005): 779–809.

Chernyaev, Anatoly. "The Unification of Germany." *Russian Social Science Review* 40 (May–June 1999): 50–65.

———. *My Six Years with Gorbachev.* Trans. and ed. by Robert D. English and Elizabeth Tucker. University Park: Pennsylvania State University Press, 2000.

———. "The Unknown Brezhnev." *Russian Politics and Law* 42 (May–June 2004): 34–66.

———. "The Afghanistan Problem." *Russian Politics and Law* 42 (September–October 2004): 29–49.

Christensen, Thomas J. *Useful Adversaries: Grand Strategy, Domestic Mobilization, and Sino-American Conflict, 1947–1958.* Princeton, N.J.: Princeton University Press, 1996.

Christofferson, Michael Scott. *French Intellectuals Against the Left: The Antitotalitarian Moment of the 1970s.* New York: Berghahn Books, 2004.

Clay, Lucius D. *The Papers of General Lucius D. Clay: Germany, 1945–1949.* Vols. 1–2. Ed. Jean Edward Smith. Bloomington: Indiana University Press, 1974.

Clayton, Will. *Selected Papers of Will Clayton.* Ed. Frederick J. Dobney. Baltimore, Md.: Johns Hopkins University Press, 1971.

Colburn, Forrest D. *The Vogue of Revolution in Poor Countries.* Princeton, N.J.: Princeton University Press, 1994.

Coll, Steve. *Ghost Wars: The Secret History of the CIA, Afghanistan, and Bin Laden, from the Soviet Invasion to September 10, 2001.* New York: Penguin, 2004.

Collins, John M. *U.S.-Soviet Military Balance, 1980–1985.* New York: Pergamon-Brassey's International Defense Publishers, 1985.

Conkin, Paul R. *Big Daddy from the Pedernales: Lyndon Baines Johnson.* Boston: Twayne Publishers, 1986.

Conquest, Robert. *Stalin: Breaker of Nations.* New York: Penguin, 1991.

Cook, Linda J. *The Soviet Social Contract and Why It Failed: Welfare Policy and Workers' Politics from Brezhnev to Yeltsin.* Cambridge, Mass.: Harvard University Press, 1993.

Costigliola, Frank. "Lyndon B. Johnson, Germany and the 'End of the Cold War.' " In *Lyndon Johnson Confronts the World: American Foreign Policy, 1963–1968.* Ed. Warren I. Cohen and Nancy Bernkopf Tucker, 173–192. New York: Cambridge University Press, 1994.

Cousins, Norman. *The Improbable Triumvirate: John F. Kennedy, Pope John, Nikita Khrushchev.* New York: Norton, 1972.

Crocker, Chester A. *High Noon in Southern Africa: Making Peace in a Rough Neighborhood.* New York: Norton, 1992.

Cullather, Nick. *Secret History: The CIA's Classified Account of Its Operations in Guatemala, 1952–1954.* Stanford, Calif.: Stanford University Press, 1999.

Dallek, Robert. *Lone Star Rising: Lyndon Johnson and His Times, 1908–1960.* New York: Oxford University Press, 1991.

———. *Flawed Giant: Lyndon Johnson and His Times.* New York: Oxford University Press, 1998.

———. *An Unfinished Life: John F. Kennedy, 1917–1963.* Boston: Little, Brown and Company, 2003.

Dean, Robert D. *Imperial Manhood: Gender and the Making of Cold War Foreign Policy.* Amherst: University of Massachusetts Press, 2000.

Deaver, Michael K. *A Different Drummer: My Thirty Years with Ronald Reagan.* New York: Harper-Collins, 2001.

Diggins, John P. *Ronald Reagan: Fate, Freedom, and the Making of History.* New York: Norton, 2007.

Dimitrov, Georgi. *The Diary of Georgi Dimitrov.* Ed. Ivo Banac. New Haven, Conn.: Yale University Press, 2003.

Dimitrov, Vesselin. "Revolutions Released: Stalin, the Bulgarian Communist Party, and the Establishment of the Cominform." In *The Soviet Union and Europe in the Cold War, 1943–1953.* Eds. Francesca Gori and Silvio Pons. New York: Macmillan, 1996.

———. *Stalin's Cold War: Soviet Foreign Policy, Democracy, and Communism in Bulgaria, 1941–1948.* Hampshire, UK: Palgrave Macmillan, 2007.

Divine, Robert A. *Blowing on the Wind: The Nuclear Test Ban Debate, 1954–1960.* New York: Oxford University Press, 1978.

Dobbs, Michael Down. *Down with Big Brother: The Fall of the Soviet Empire.* New York: Knopf, 1997.

Dobrynin, Anatoly. *In Confidence: Moscow's Ambassador to America's Six Cold War Presidents.* New York: Random House, 1995.

Dorrien, Gary. *The Neoconservative Mind: Politics, Culture, and the War of Ideology.* Philadelphia, Pa.: Temple University Press, 1993.

Dudziak, Mary L. *Cold War Civil Rights: Race and the Image of American Democracy.* Princeton, N.J.: Princeton University Press, 2000.

Dumbrell, John. *President Lyndon Johnson and Soviet Communism.* Manchester, Eng.: Manchester University Press, 2004.

Duskin, J. Eric. *Stalinist Reconstruction and the Confirmation of a New Elite, 1945–1953.* Houndsmills, Eng.: Palgrave, 2001.

Ebon, Martin. *The Andropov File: The Life and Ideas of Yuri V. Andropov, General Secretary of the Communist Party of the Soviet Union.* New York: McGraw-Hill, 1983.

Ehrenburg, Ilya. *The War, 1941–1945.* London: McGibbon and Kee, 1964.

Eisenhower, Dwight. *The Eisenhower Diaries.* Ed. Robert Ferrell. New York: Norton, 1981.

———. *Ike's Letters to a Friend, 1941–1958.* Ed. Robert Griffith. Lawrence: University Press of Kansas, 1984.

———. *The Papers of Dwight David Eisenhower: NATO and the Campaign of 1952.* Ed. Louis Galambos. Baltimore, Md.: Johns Hopkins University Press, 1989.

———. *The Papers of Dwight David Eisenhower: The Middle Way.* Ed. Louis Galambos. Baltimore: Johns Hopkins University Press, 1996.

Ekedahl, Carolyn McGiffert, and Melvin A. Goodman. *The Wars of Eduard Shevardnadze*. 2nd ed. Washington, D.C.: Brassey's, 2001.

Ellman, Michael, and Vladimir Kontorovich, eds. *The Destruction of the Soviet Economic System: An Insiders' History*. Armonk, N.Y.: M. E. Sharpe, 1998.

Engerman, David C. "The Romance of Economic Development and New Histories of the Cold War." *Diplomatic History* 28 (January 2004): 23–54.

English, Robert D. *Russia and the West: Gorbachev, Intellectuals and the End of the Cold War*. New York: Columbia University Press, 2000.

Etzold, Thomas H., and John L. Gaddis, eds. *Containment: Documents on American Policy and Strategy*. New York: Columbia University Press, 1978.

Evangelista, Matthew. *Unarmed Forces: The Trans-National Movement to End the Cold War*. Ithaca, N.Y.: Cornell University Press, 1999.

Fair, John D. "The Intellectual JFK: Lessons in Statesmanship from British History." *Diplomatic History* 30 (January 2006): 119–42.

Farnham, Barbara. "Reagan and the Gorbachev Revolution: Perceiving the End of Threat." *Political Science Quarterly* 116 (Summer 2001): 225–52.

Ferrell, Robert. *Truman and Pendergast*. Columbia: University of Missouri Press, 1999.

Filtzer, Donald. *Soviet Workers and Late Stalinism: Labour and the Restoration of the Stalinist System After World War II*. Cambridge, Eng.: Cambridge University Press, 2002.

Firth, Noel E., and James H. Noren. *Soviet Defense Spending: A History of CIA Estimates, 1950–1990*. College Station: Texas A & M Press, 1998.

Fischer, Ben B. *A Cold War Conundrum: The 1983 Soviet War Scare*. Washington, D.C.: Center for the Study of Intelligence, 1997.

Fischer, Beth A. *The Reagan Reversal: Foreign Policy and the End of the Cold War*. Columbia: University of Missouri Press, 1997.

Fitzgerald, Frances. *Way Out There in the Blue: Reagan, Star Wars, and the End of the Cold War*. New York: Simon and Schuster, 2000.

Foliot, Denise, ed. *Documents on International Affairs, 1953*. London: Oxford University Press, 1956.

———. *Documents on International Affairs, 1954*. London: Oxford University Press, 1957.

Ford, Gerald. *A Time to Heal: The Autobiography of Gerald R. Ford*. New York: Harper and Row, 1979.

Ford, Harold P. *CIA and the Vietnam Policymakers: Three Episodes, 1962–1968*. Washington, D.C.: Central Intelligence Agency, 1998.

Forrestal, James. *The Forrestal Diaries*. Ed. Walter Millis. New York: Viking, 1951.

Frankel, Max. *High Noon in the Cold War: Kennedy, Khrushchev, and the Cuban Missile Crisis*. New York: Ballantine Books, 2004.

Freeland, Richard M. *The Truman Doctrine and the Origins of McCarthyism: Foreign Policy, Domestic Politics, and Internal Security, 1946–48*. New York: New York University Press, 1985.

Freidzon, Sergei. *Patterns of Soviet Economic Decision-Making: An Inside View of the 1965 Reform*. Falls Church, Va.: Delphic Associates, 1987.

Friedman, Murray. *The Neoconservative Revolution: Jewish Intellectuals and the Shaping of Public Policy*. New York: Cambridge University Press, 2005.

Fukuyama, Francis. *Moscow's Post-Brezhnev Reassessment of the Third World*. Santa Monica, Calif.: Rand Publication R-3337-USDP, 1986.

Fursenko, Aleksandr, and Timothy Naftali. *"One Hell of a Gamble": The Secret History of the Cuban Missile Crisis*. New York: Norton, 1997.

———. *Khrushchev's Cold War: The Inside Story of an American Adversary*. New York: Norton, 2006.

Gaddis, John L. *The United States and the Origins of the Cold War, 1941–47*. New York: Columbia University Press, 1972.

————. *Strategies of Containment: A Critical Appraisal of American National Security Policy During the Cold War*, rev. ed. New York: Oxford University Press, 2005.

Gaddy, Clifford G. *The Price of the Past: Russia's Struggle with the Legacy of a Militarized Economy*. Washington, D.C.: Brookings Institution Press, 1996.

Gaiduk, Ilya V. *The Soviet Union and the Vietnam War*. Chicago, Ill.: Ivan R. Dee, 1996.

————. *Confronting Vietnam: Soviet Policy Toward the Indochina Conflict, 1954–1963*. Stanford, Calif.: Stanford University Press, 2003.

Gallup, George H. *The Gallup Poll: Public Opinion, 1935–1971*. 3 vols. New York: Random House, 1972.

Gardner, Richard N. *Mission Italy: On the Front Lines of the Cold War*. Lanham, Md.: Rowman and Littlefield, 2005.

Garternschlager, Uwe. "Living and Surviving in Occupied Minsk." In *The People's War: Responses to World War II in the Soviet Union*. Eds. Robert W. Thurston and Bernd Bonwetsch, 13–28. Urbana: University of Illinois Press, 2000.

Garthoff, Raymond. *Détente and Confrontation: American-Soviet Relations from Nixon to Reagan*, rev. ed. Washington, D.C.: Brookings Institution Press, 1994.

————. *The Great Transition: American-Soviet Relations and the End of the Cold War*. Washington, D.C.: Brookings Institution Press, 1994.

————. "The Aborted U.S.-U.S.S.R. Summit of 1965." *The SHAFR Newsletter* 32 (June 2001): 1–3.

Gasiorowski, Mark, and Malcolm Byrne, eds. *Mohammad Mosaddeq and the 1953 Coup in Iran*. Syracuse, N.Y.: Syracuse University Press, 2004.

Gates, Robert M. *From the Shadows: The Ultimate Insider's Story of Five Presidents and How They Won the Cold War*. New York: Simon and Schuster, 1996.

Gavin, Frank J. "Blasts from the Past: Proliferation Lessons from the 1960s." *International Security* 29 (Winter 2004–2005): 100–135.

Gelman, Harry. *The Brezhnev Politburo and the Decline of Détente*. Ithaca, N.Y.: Cornell University Press, 1984.

Getty, J. Arch, and Oleg V. Naumov. *The Road to Terror: Stalin and the Self-Destruction of the Bolsheviks, 1932–39*. New Haven, Conn.: Yale University Press, 1999.

Giauque, Jeffrey Glen. *Grand Designs and Visions of Unity: The Atlantic Powers and the Reorganization of Western Europe, 1955–1963*. Chapel Hill, N.C.: The University of North Carolina Press, 2002.

Gibianskii, Leonid. "Stalin's Policy in Eastern Europe, the Cominform, and the First Split in the Soviet Bloc," 17–22, paper prepared for the conference "Stalin and the Cold War." Yale University, 1999.

Glad, Betty. *Jimmy Carter: In Search of the Great White House*. New York: Norton, 1980.

Gleijeses, Piero. *Conflicting Missions: Havana, Washington, and Africa, 1959–1976*. Chapel Hill: University of North Carolina Press, 2002.

————. "Moscow's Proxy: Cuba and Africa, 1975–1988." *Journal of Cold War Studies* 8 (Fall 2006): 98–146.

Goncharov, S. N., John W. Lewis, and Xue Litai. *Uncertain Partners: Stalin, Mao, and the Korean War*. Stanford, Calif.: Stanford University Press, 1993.

Gooding, John. *Socialism in Russia: Lenin and His Legacy, 1890–1991*. Houndsmills, Eng.: Palgrave, 2002.

Gorbachev, Mikhail. *Perestroika: New Thinking for Our Country and the World*. New York: Harper and Row, 1987.

————. *Memoirs*. New York: Doubleday, 1995.

————. *On My Country and the World*. Trans. George Shriver. New York: Columbia University Press, 2000.

Gorbachev, Mikhail, and Zdenek Mlynar. *Conversations with Gorbachev on Perestroika, the Prague Spring, and the Crossroads of Socialism*. Trans. George Shriver. New York: Columbia University Press, 2002.

Gorbachev, Raisa. *I Hope*. Trans. David Floyd. New York: HarperCollins, 1991.

Gori, Francesca, and Silvio Pons, eds. *The Soviet Union and Europe in the Cold War*. New York: St. Martin's Press, 1996.

Gorlizki, Yoram, and Oleg Khlevniuk. *Cold Peace: Stalin and the Soviet Ruling Circle, 1945–1953*. New York: Oxford University Press, 2004.

Gorodetsky, Gabriel. *Grand Delusion*. New Haven, Conn.: Yale University Press, 1999.

Granieri, Ronald J. *The Ambivalent Alliance: Konrad Adenauer, the CDU/CSU, and the West, 1949–1966*. New York: Berghahn Books, 2003.

Great Soviet Encyclopedia. Translation of the 3rd ed. New York: Macmillan, 1974.

Grechko, A. A. *The Armed Forces of the Soviet Union*. Moscow: Progress Publishers, 1977.

Greenstein, Fred I. *The Hidden-Hand Presidency: Eisenhower as Leader*. New York: Basic Books, 1982.

Griffith, Robert S. *The Politics of Fear: Joseph R. McCarthy and the Senate*. Lexington: University of Kentucky Press, 1970.

Griffith, Robert W. F. "Dwight D. Eisenhower and the Corporate Commonwealth." *American Historical Review* 87 (February 1982): 87–122.

Gromyko, Andrei. *Memoirs*. Trans. Harold Shukman. New York: Doubleday, 1989.

Gross, Jan. *Revolution from Abroad: The Soviet Conquest of Poland's Western Ukraine and Western Belorussia*. Princeton, N.J.: Princeton University Press, 1988.

Grossman, Vasily. *A Writer at War: Vasily Grossman with the Red Army, 1941–1945*. Ed. Antony Beevor and Luba Vinogradova. New York: Pantheon Books, 2005.

Guhin, Michael A. *John Foster Dulles: A Statesman and His Times*. New York: Columbia University Press, 1972.

Hahn, Werner G. *Postwar Soviet Politics: The Fall of Zhdanov and the Defeat of Moderation*. Ithaca, N.Y.: Cornell University Press, 1982.

Haig, Alexander M., Jr. *Caveat: Realism, Reagan, and Foreign Policy*. New York: Macmillan, 1984.

Halliday, Fred. *The Making of the Second Cold War*. London: Verson, 1983.

———. "Soviet foreign policymaking and the Afghanistan war: from 'second Mongolia' to 'bleeding wound.' " *Review of International Studies* 25 (October 1999): 683–86.

Hamby, Alonzo. *Man of the People: A Life of Harry S. Truman*. New York: Oxford University Press, 1995.

Hamilton, Nigel. *JFK: Reckless Youth*. New York: Random House, 1992.

Hanhimaki, Jussi, and Odd Arne Westad, eds. *The Cold War: A History in Documents and Eyewitness Accounts*. Oxford: Oxford University Press, 2003.

Hanson, Philip. *The Rise and Fall of the Soviet Economy: An Economic History of the USSR from 1945*. London: Longman, 2003.

Hara, Teruyuki, and Kimitaka Matsuzato, eds. *Empire and Society: New Approaches to Russian History*. Sapporo, Japan: Slavic Research Center, Hokkaido University, 1997.

Harriman, W. Averell, and Elie Abel. *Special Envoy to Churchill and Stalin, 1941–1946*. New York: Random House, 1975.

Harris, Jonathan. *Subverting the System: Gorbachev's Reform of the Party's Apparat, 1986–1991*. Lanham, Md.: Rowman and Littlefield, 2004.

Harrison, Hope M. *Driving the Soviets Up the Wall: Soviet-East German Relations, 1953–1961*. Princeton, N.J.: Princeton University Press, 2003.

Hasegawa, Tsuyoshi. *Racing the Enemy: Stalin, Truman, and the Surrender of Japan*. Cambridge, Mass.: Harvard University Press, 2005.

Haslam, Jonathan. "The Making of Foreign Policy Under Stalin." In *Empire and Society: New Approaches to Russian History*. Ed. Teruyuki Hara and Kimitaka Matsuzato, 167–79. Sapporo, Japan: Slavic Research Center, Hokkaido University, 1997.

————. "The Cold War as History." *Annual Review of Political Science* 6 (2003): 77–98.

Herf, Jeffrey. "Amnesty and Amnesia." *The New Republic* 231 (10 March 2003): 33–35.

Herken, Gregg. *The Winning Weapon: The Atomic Bomb in the Cold War.* New York: Knopf, 1980.

Herlemann, Horst, ed. *Quality of Life in the Soviet Union.* Boulder, Colo.: Westview Press, 1987.

Herring, George C. *America's Longest War: The United States and Vietnam, 1950–1975,* 2nd ed. New York: Knopf, 1986.

Hershberg, James G. "More on Bobby and the Cuban Missile Crisis." Cold War International History Program *Bulletin* 8–9 (Winter 1996/97): 274, 344–47.

————. "New Evidence on the Cuban Missile Crisis: More Documents from the Russian Archives." Cold War International History Program *Bulletin* 8–9 (Winter 1996/97): 270–343.

Hilty, James W. *Robert Kennedy: Brother Protector.* Philadelphia, Pa.: Temple University Press, 1997.

Hitchcock, William. *France Restored: Cold War Diplomacy and the Quest for Leadership in Europe, 1944–54.* Chapel Hill: University of North Carolina Press, 1998.

————. *The Struggle for Europe: The Turbulent History of a Divided Continent, 1945 to the Present.* New York: Anchor Books, 2004.

Hollander, Paul. *Political Will and Personal Belief: The Decline and Fall of Soviet Communism.* New Haven, Conn.: Yale University Press, 1999.

Holloway, David. *The Soviet Union and the Arms Race.* New Haven, Conn.: Yale University Press, 1983.

————. *Stalin and the Bomb.* New Haven, Conn.: Yale University Press, 1994.

Hoopes, Townsend. *The Devil and John Foster Dulles.* Boston: Little, Brown, and Company, 1973.

Hopf, Ted. *Social Construction of International Politics: Identities and Foreign Policies, Moscow, 1955 and 1999.* Ithaca, N.Y.: Cornell University Press, 2002.

Hosking, Geoffrey. *The First Socialist Society: A History of the Soviet Union from Within.* Cambridge, Mass.: Harvard University Press, 1985.

Hughes, Emmet John. *The Ordeal of Power: A Political Memoir of the Eisenhower Years.* New York: Atheneum, 1975.

Humphrey, Hubert H. *The Education of a Public Man: My Life and Politics.* Garden City, N.Y.: Doubleday, 1976.

Huntington, Samuel P. *The Third Wave: Democratization in the Late Twentieth Century.* Norman: University of Oklahoma Press, 1991.

Iatrides, John O. "Revolution or Self-Defense? Communist Goals, Strategy, and Tactics in the Greek Civil War." *Journal of Cold War Studies* 7 (Summer 2005): 3–33.

Immerman, Richard H. *John Foster Dulles: Piety, Pragmatism, and Power in U.S. Foreign Policy.* Wilmington, Del.: Scholarly Resources, 1999.

————, ed. *John Foster Dulles and the Diplomacy of the Cold War.* Princeton, N.J.: Princeton University Press, 1990.

India, Government of India Planning Commission. *Second Five-Year Plan.* New Delhi, 1956.

Inkeles, Alex, and Raymond A. Bauer. *The Soviet Citizen: Daily Life in a Totalitarian Society.* Cambridge, Mass.: Harvard University Press, 1961.

International Institute for Strategic Studies. *The Military Balance, 1981–82.* New York: Facts on File, 1981.

Jacobs, Meg. *Pocketbook Politics: Economic Citizenship in Twentieth-Century America.* Princeton, N.J.: Princeton University Press, 2005.

James, W. Martin III. *A Political History of the Civil War in Angola, 1974–1990.* New Brunswick, N.J.: Transaction Publishers, 1992.

Jarausch, Konrad H. *The Rush to German Unity.* New York: Oxford University Press, 1994.

Johnson, Lyndon Baines. *The Vantage Point: Perspectives on the Presidency, 1963–1969.* New York: Holt, Rinehart and Winston, 1971.

Jones, Howard. *Death of a Generation: How the Assassinations of Diem and JFK Prolonged the Vietnam War.* New York: Oxford University Press, 2003.

Jordan, Hamilton. *Crisis: The Last Year of the Carter Presidency.* New York: G. P. Putnam's Sons, 1982.

Judt, Tony. *Postwar: A History of Europe Since 1945.* New York: Penguin, 2005.

Kaiser, David. *American Tragedy: Kennedy, Johnson, and the Origins of the Vietnam War.* Cambridge, Mass.: Harvard University Press, 2000.

Kampelman, Max M. *Entering New Worlds: The Memoirs of a Private Man in Public Life.* New York: HarperCollins, 1991.

Katz, Mark N., ed. *The USSR and Marxist Revolutions in the Third World.* Cambridge, Eng.: Woodrow Wilson International Center for Scholars and Cambridge University Press, 1990.

Kengor, Paul. *God and Ronald Reagan.* New York: HarperCollins, 2004.

———. *The Crusader: Ronald Reagan and The Fall of Communism.* New York: Regan, 2006.

Kennan, George F. *Memoirs, 1925–1950.* New York: Bantam, 1967.

Kennedy, David M. *Freedom from Fear: The American People in Depression and War, 1929–1945.* New York: Oxford University Press, 1999.

Kennedy, Paul. *The Rise and Fall of the Great Powers: Economic Change and Military Conflict from 1500 to 2000.* New York: Random House, 1987.

Kennedy, Robert F. *Robert F. Kennedy: In His Own Words.* Eds. Edwin O. Guthman and Jeffrey Shulman. New York: Bantam Books, 1988.

Khlevniuk, Oleg. *In Stalin's Shadow: The Career of "Sergo" Ordzhonikidze.* Ed. Donald J. Raleigh, with the assistance of Kathy S. Transchel. Trans. David J. Nordlander. Armonk, N.Y.: M. E. Sharpe, 1995.

———. "The Reasons for the 'Great Terror': The Foreign-Political Aspect." In *Russia in the Age of Wars, 1914–1945.* Eds. Silvio Pons and Andrea Romano. Milan, Italy: Fondazione Giangiacomo Feltrinelli, 2000.

Khrushchev, Nikita S. *Khrushchev Remembers.* Ed. and trans. Strobe Talbott. Boston: Little, Brown and Company, 1970.

———. *Khrushchev Remembers: The Glasnost Tapes.* Ed. and trans. Jerrold L. Schecter with Vyacheslav V. Luchkov. Boston: Little, Brown and Company, 1990.

Khrushchev, Sergei N. *Nikita Khrushchev and the Creation of a Superpower.* Trans. Shirley Benson. University Park: Pennsylvania State University Press, 2000.

Knight, Amy. *Beria: Stalin's First Lieutenant.* Princeton, N.J.: Princeton University Press, 1993.

Kohl, Helmut, with Kai Diekmann and Ralf Georg Reuth. *Ich wollte Deutschlands Einheit.* Berlin: Propylaen, 1996.

Kohli, Atul. "Politics of Economic Liberalization in India." *World Development* 17 (March 1989): 305–28.

Kornienko, Georgiy Markovich. *Kholodnaia voyna: svidetel'stvo ee uchastnika* [The Cold War: A Testimony of Its Participant]. Moscow: Mezhdunar otnosheniia, 1994.

Kosygin, A. N. *Selected Speeches and Writings.* Oxford: Pergamon Press, 1981.

Kotkin, Stephen. *Armageddon Averted: The Soviet Collapse, 1970–2000.* Oxford, Eng.: Oxford University Press, 2001.

———. "A Conspiracy So Immense: Terror and Tea Leaves in the Kremlin," *The New Republic* 234 (13 February 2006): 28–34.

Kovrig, Bennett. *Of Walls and Bridges: The United States and Eastern Europe.* New York: New York University Press, 1991.

Kramer, Mark. "Lessons of the Cuban Missile Crisis for Warsaw Pact Nuclear Operations." Cold War International History Project *Bulletin* 8–9 (Winter 1996/1997): 348–54.

———. "The Czechoslovak Crisis and the Brezhnev Doctrine." In *1968: The World Transformed.* Ed. Carole Fink, Philipp Gassert, and Detlef Junker. Cambridge, Eng.: Cambridge University Press, 1998.

————. "The Early Post-Stalin Succession Struggle and Upheavals in East-Central Europe: Internal-External Linkages in Soviet Policy Making (Part 1)." *Journal of Cold War Studies* 1 (Winter 1999): 3–55.

————. "The Early Post-Stalin Succession Struggle and Upheavals in East-Central Europe: Internal-External Linkages in Soviet Policy Making (Part 2)." *Journal of Cold War Studies* 1 (Spring 1999): 3–38.

————. "The Soviet Union and the Founding of the German Democratic Republic: 50 Years Later—A Review Article," *Europe-Asia* 51 (September 1999): 1093–106.

————. "The Early Post-Stalin Succession Struggle and Upheavals in East-Central Europe: Internal-External Linkages in Soviet Policy Making (Part 3)." *Journal of Cold War Studies* 1 (Fall 1999): 3–66.

————. "Soviet Deliberations During the Polish Crisis, 1980–1981," Cold War International History Project, Special Working Paper No. 1. Washington, D.C.: Woodrow Wilson International Center, 1999.

————. "The Reform of the Soviet System and the Demise of the Soviet State." *Slavic Studies* 63 (Fall 2004): 505–12.

————. "The Collapse of East European Communism and the Repercussions within the Soviet Union (Part 3)." *Journal of Cold War Studies* 7 (Winter 2005): 3–96.

Kraus, Sidney, ed. *The Great Debates: Carter vs. Ford, 1976.* Bloomington: Indiana University Press, 1979.

Krebs, Ronald R. *Dueling Visions: U.S. Strategy toward Eastern Europe Under Eisenhower.* College Station: Texas A & M University Press, 2001.

Krylova, Anna. " 'Healers of Wounded Souls': The Crisis of Private Life in Soviet Literature, 1944–1946." *The Journal of Modern History* 73 (June 2001): 307–331.

Kuromiya, Hiroaki. *Freedom and Terror in the Donbas: A Ukrainian-Russian Borderland, 1870s–1990s.* New York: Cambridge University Press, 1998.

————. *Stalin.* Harlow, Eng.: Pearson, 2005.

Kux, Stephan. *New Soviet Thinking on Nuclear Deterrence.* Geneva: Program for Strategic and International Security Studies. Occasional Paper Number 3 (1990): 30–45.

Larres, Klaus. "Eisenhower and the First Forty Days After Stalin's Death: The Incompatibility of Détente and Political Warfare." *Diplomacy and Statecraft* 6 (July 1995): 431–69.

————. *Churchill's Cold War: The Politics of Personal Diplomacy.* New Haven, Conn.: Yale University Press, 2002.

Larson, Deborah Welch. *Origins of Containment: A Psychological Explanation.* Princeton, N.J.: Princeton University Press, 1985.

Lawrence, Mark Atwood. *Assuming the Burden: Europe and the American Commitment to War in Vietnam.* Berkeley: University of California Press, 2005.

Lebow, Richard Ned, and Thomas Risse-Kappen, eds. *International Relations Theory and the End of the Cold War.* New York: Columbia University Press, 1995.

Leffler, Melvyn P. *A Preponderance of Power: National Security, the Truman Administration, and the Cold War.* Stanford, Calif.: Stanford University Press, 1993.

Leighton, Richard M. *Strategy, Money, and the New Look, 1953–1956: History of the Office of the Secretary of Defense.* Washington, D.C.: Government Printing Office, 2001.

Lettow, Paul. *Ronald Reagan and His Quest to Abolish Nuclear Weapons.* New York: Random House, 2005.

Levesque, Jacques. *The Enigma of 1989: The USSR and the Liberation of Eastern Europe.* Berkeley: University of California Press, 1997.

Lewin, Moshe. *The Soviet Century.* Ed. Gregory Elliott. London: Verso, 2005.

Logevall, Fredrik. *Choosing War: The Lost Chance for Peace and the Escalation of War in Vietnam.* Berkeley: University of California Press, 1999.

_____. *The Origins of the Vietnam War*. Essex, Eng.: Longman, 2001.

Loth, Wilfried. *Stalin's Unwanted Child: The Soviet Union, the German Question, and the Founding of the GDR*. New York: St. Martin's Press, 1998.

Lukacs, John. *June 1941: Hitler and Stalin*. New Haven, Conn.: Yale University Press, 2006.

Lundestad, Geir. "Empire by Invitation? The United States and Western Europe, 1945–1952." *Journal of Peace Research* 23 (September 1986): 263–77.

Lyakhovski, Aleksandr. "New Russian Evidence on the Crisis and War in Afghanistan." Cold War International History Project Working Paper No. 51. Washington, D.C.: Woodrow Wilson International Center, 2007.

McAdams, A. James. *Germany Divided: From the Wall to Reunification*. Princeton, N.J.: Princeton University Press, 1993.

McCauley, Martin. *Gorbachev*. London: Longman, 1998.

McCullough, David. *Truman*. New York: Simon and Schuster, 1992.

MacEachin, Douglas J. *Predicting the Soviet Invasion of Afghanistan: The Intelligence Community's Record*. Washington, D.C.: Central Intelligence Agency, Center for the Study of Intelligence, 2002.

McFarlane, Robert C., and Zophia Smardz. *Special Trust*. New York: Cadell and Davies, 1994.

McMahon, Robert J. *The Limits of Empire: The United States and Southeast Asia Since World War II*. New York: Columbia University Press, 1999.

McNamara, Robert S., with Brian VanDeMark. *In Retrospect: The Tragedy and Lessons of Vietnam*. New York: Times Books, 1995.

McPherson, Alan. "Misled by Himself: What the Johnson Tapes Reveal about the Dominican Intervention in 1965." *Latin American Research Review* 38 (June 2003): 127–46.

_____. *Intimate Ties, Bitter Struggle: The United States and Latin America Since 1945*. Washington, D.C.: Potomac Books, 2006.

Mahan, Erin. *Kennedy, De Gaulle, and Western Europe*. Hampshire: Palgrave/Macmillan, 2002.

_____. "Public Opinion and Détente During the Kennedy Administration." Unpublished research paper.

Maier, Charles. *Dissolution: The Crisis of Communism and the End of East Germany*. Princeton, N.J.: Princeton University Press, 1997.

Malia, Martin. "The Archives of Evil: Soviet Studies after the Soviet Union," *The New Republic* 231 (November 29 and December 6, 2004): 34–41.

Manchester, William. *One Brief Shining Moment: Remembering Kennedy*. Boston: Little, Brown and Company, 1983.

Mann, James. *About Face: A History of America's Curious Relationship with China from Nixon to Clinton*. New York: Knopf, 1999.

Mark, Eduard. "American Policy Toward Eastern Europe and the Origins of the Cold War, 1941–46: An Alternative Interpretation." *The Journal of American History* 68 (September 1981): 313–36.

_____. "The War Scare of 1946 and Its Consequences." *Diplomatic History* 21 (Summer 1997): 383–415.

_____. "Revolution by Degrees: Stalin's National Front Strategy for Europe, 1941–47." Cold War International History Project Working Paper No. 31. Washington, D.C.: Woodrow Wilson International Center, 2001.

Mastny, Vojtech. *The Cold War and Soviet Insecurity: The Stalin Years*. New York: Oxford University Press, 1996.

Mastny, Vojtech, and Malcolm Byrne, eds. *A Cardboard Castle?: An Inside History of the Warsaw Pact, 1955–1991*. Budapest: Central European University Press, 2005.

Matlock, Jack, Jr. *Autopsy of an Empire: The American Ambassador's Account of the Collapse of the Soviet Union*. New York: Random House, 1995.

————. *Reagan and Gorbachev: How the Cold War Ended*. New York: Random House, 2004.

May, Ernest R., ed. *American Cold War Strategy: Interpreting NSC 68*. Boston: Bedford Books, 1993.

Mearsheimer, John. *The Tragedy of Great Power Politics*. New York: Norton, 2001.

Medvedev, Roy. *On Stalin and Stalinism*. Trans. Ellen de Kadt. Oxford, Eng.: Oxford University Press, 1979.

————. *Khrushchev: A Biography*. Trans. Brian Pearce. Garden City, N.Y.: Anchor Books, 1984.

Medvedev, Roy A., and Zhores A. Medvedev. *The Unknown Stalin*. London: I. B. Tauris, 2002.

Megargee, Geoffrey P. *War of Annihilation: Combat and Genocide on the Eastern Front, 1941*. Lanham, Md.: Rowman and Littlefield, 2006.

Mendelson, Sarah E. *Changing Course: Ideas, Politics, and the Soviet Withdrawal from Afghanistan*. Princeton, N.J.: Princeton University Press, 1998.

Merridale, Catherine. *Night of Stone: Death and Memory in Twentieth-Century Russia*. New York: Vintage, 2001.

————. *Ivan's War: Life and Death in the Red Army, 1939–1945*. New York: Metropolitan Books, 2006.

Messer, Robert L. *The End of an Alliance: James F. Byrnes, Roosevelt, Truman, and the Origins of the Cold War*. Chapel Hill: University of North Carolina Press, 1982.

Milani, Mohsen M. *The Making of Iran's Islamic Revolution: From Monarchy to Islamic Republic*, 2nd ed. Boulder, Colo.: Westview, 1994.

Millar, James R. "The Little Deal: Brezhnev's Contribution to Acquisitive Socialism." *Slavic Review* 4 (Winter 1985): 694–706.

Miner, Steven Merritt. *Stalin's Holy War: Religion, Nationalism, and Alliance Politics, 1941–1945*. Chapel Hill: University of North Carolina Press, 2003.

Miscamble, Wilson D., C.S.C. *From Roosevelt to Truman: Potsdam, Hiroshima, and the Cold War*. New York: Cambridge University Press, 2007.

Mitrokhin, Vasili. "The KGB in Afghanistan." Cold War International History Program Working Paper No. 40. Introduced and Edited by Christian F. Ostermann and Odd Arne Westad. Washington, D.C.: Woodrow Wilson International Center, 2002.

Mitrovich, Gregory. *Undermining the Kremlin: America's Strategy to Subvert the Soviet Bloc*. Ithaca, N.Y.: Cornell University Press, 2000.

Montefiore, Simon Sebag. *Stalin: The Court of the Red Tsar*. London: Weidenfeld and Nicolson, 2003.

Morris, Edmund. *Dutch: A Memoir of Ronald Reagan*. New York: Random House, 1999.

Mukhina, Irina. "New Revelations from the Former Soviet Archives: The Kremlin, the Warsaw Uprising, and the Coming of the Cold War." *Cold War History* 6 (August 2006): 397–411.

Murashko, Galina P., and Albina F. Noskova. "Stalin and the National-Territorial Controversies in Eastern Europe, 1945–1947 (Part 1)." *Cold War History* 1 (April 2001): 161–72.

Murphy, David E. *What Stalin Knew: The Enigma of Barbarossa*. New Haven, Conn.: Yale University Press, 2005.

Naimark, Norman M. "The Soviets and the Christian Democrats: The Challenge of a 'Bourgeois' Party in Eastern Germany, 1945–1949." *East European Politics and Society* 9 (Fall 1995): 369–92.

————. *The Russians in Germany*. Cambridge, Mass.: Harvard University Press, 1996.

————. "Cold War Studies and New Archival Materials on Stalin." *The Russian Review* 61 (January 2002): 1–15.

————. "Stalin and Europe in the Postwar Period, 1945–1953: Issues and Problems. *Journal of Modern European History* 2 (2004): 28–56.

————, and Leonid Gibianskii, eds. *The Establishment of Communist Regimes in Eastern Europe, 1944–1949*. Boulder, Colo.: Westview Press, 1997.

Newsom, David D. *The Soviet Brigade in Cuba: A Study in Public Diplomacy*. Bloomington: Indiana University Press, 1987.

Niedhart, Gottfried. "Ostpolitik: The Role of the Federal Republic of Germany in the Process of Détente." In *1968: The World Transformed*. Ed. Carole Fink, Philipp Gassert, and Detlef Junker. Cambridge, Eng.: Cambridge University Press, 1998.

Nitze, Paul H., with Ann M. Smith and Steven L. Rearden. *From Hiroshima to Glasnost: At the Center of
Decision—A Memoir*. New York: Grove Weidenfeld, 1989.

Njolstad, Olav, ed. *The Last Decade of the Cold War: From Conflict Escalation to Conflict Transformation*.
London: Frank Cass, 2004.

Noonan, Norma C. "Malenkov." *The Modern Encyclopedia of Russian and Soviet History* (Gulf Breeze,
Fla.: Academic International Press, 1989), vol. 50 (Supplement).

Oberdorfer, Don. *The Turn: From the Cold War to a New Era*. New York: Poseidon Press, 1991.

O'Brien, Michael. *John F. Kennedy: A Biography*. New York: Thomas Dunne/St. Martin's Press, 2005.

Odom, William E. *The Collapse of the Soviet Military*. New Haven, Conn.: Yale University Press, 1998.

Offner, Arnold. *Another Such Victory: President Truman and the Cold War*. Stanford, Calif.: Stanford University Press, 2002.

Osgood, Kenneth A. "Form Before Substance: Eisenhower's Commitment to Psychological Warfare and
Negotiations with the Enemy." *Diplomatic History* 24 (Summer 2000): 405–33.

———. *Total Cold War: Eisenhower's Secret Propaganda Battle at Home and Abroad*. Lawrence: University Press of Kansas, 2006.

———, and Klaus Larres, eds. *The Cold War After Stalin's Death*. Lawrence: University Press of Kansas,
2006.

Oshinsky, David M. *A Conspiracy So Immense: The World of Joe McCarthy*. New York: The Free Press,
1983.

Ostermann, Christian F., ed. *Uprising in East Germany, 1953*. Budapest and New York: Central European University Press and the National Security Archive, 2001.

Ouimet, Matthew J. *The Rise and Fall of the Brezhnev Doctrine in Soviet Foreign Policy*. Chapel Hill: University of North Carolina Press, 2003.

Overy, Richard J. *Why the Allies Won*. London: Jonathan Cape, 1995.

———. *Russia's War*. London: Penguin, 1997.

Oye, Kenneth A. "Explaining the End of the Cold War: Morphological and Behavioral Adaptations to
the Nuclear Peace?" In *International Relations Theory and the End of the Cold War*. Ed. Richard Ned
Lebow and Thomas Risse-Kappen. New York: Columbia University Press, 1995.

Pach, Chester J., Jr., and Elmo Richardson. *The Presidency of Dwight D. Eisenhower*. Lawrence: University Press of Kansas, 1991.

Palazchenko, Pavel. *Gorbachev and Shevardnadze: The Memoir of a Soviet Interpreter*. University Park:
Pennsylvania State University Press, 1997.

Parker, John W. *Kremlin in Transition: Gorbachev, 1985–1989*, Vol. 2. Boston: Unwin Hyman, 1991.

Parrott, Bruce. "Soviet National Security Under Gorbachev." *Problems of Communism* 37 (November–
December 1988): 1–36.

Patterson, James T. *Restless Giant: The United States from Watergate to Bush v. Gore*. New York: Oxford
University Press, 2005.

Pechatnov, V. O. "The Big Three After World War II: New Documents on Soviet Thinking About Postwar Relations with the United States and Great Britain." Cold War International History Project
Working Paper No. 13. Washington, D.C.: Woodrow Wilson International Center, 1995.

———. " 'The Allies Are Pressing on You to Break Your Will . . .': Foreign Policy Correspondence Be-
tween Stalin and Molotov and Other Politburo Members, September 1945–December 1946." Cold
War International History Project Working Paper No. 26. Trans. Vladislav M. Zubok. Washington,
D.C.: Woodrow Wilson International Center, 1999.

———. "Averell Harriman's Mission to Moscow." *The Harriman Review* 14 (July 2003): 1–47.

Pechenev, Vadim Alekseevich. *Gorbachev: k vershinam vlasti* [Gorbachev: To the Heights of Power]. Moscow: Gospodin Narod/Fenomen Cheloveka, 1991.

Pezzullo, Lawrence, and Ralph Pezzullo. *At the Fall of Somoza*. Pittsburgh, Pa.: University of Pittsburgh Press, 1993.

Pickett, William B. *Dwight David Eisenhower and American Power*. Wheeling, Ill.: Harlan Davidson, 1995.

Pipes, Richard. *Vixi: Memoirs of a Non-Belonger*. New Haven, Conn.: Yale University Press, 2003.

Pleshakov, Constantine. *Stalin's Folly: The Tragic First Days of World War II on the Eastern Front*. Boston: Houghton Mifflin, 2005.

Pollock, Ethan. "Conversations with Stalin on Questions of Political Economy." Cold War International History Project Working Paper No. 33. Washington D.C.: Woodrow Wilson International Center, 2001.

Ponomarev, B. N. *Selected Speeches and Writings*. Oxford: Pergamon Press, 1981.

Pons, Silvio. "In the Aftermath of the Age of Wars: The Impact of World War II on Soviet Security Policy." In *Russia in the Age of Wars, 1914–1945*. Ed. Silvio Pons and Andrea Romano, 277–307. Milan, Italy: Fondazione Giangiacomo Feltrinelli, 2000.

———. "Stalin, Togliatti, and the Origins of the Cold War in Europe." *Journal of Cold War Studies* 3 (Spring 2001): 3–27.

———. *Stalin and the Inevitable War, 1936–1941*. London: Frank Cass, 2002.

———, and Andrea Romano, eds. *Russia in the Age of Wars, 1914–1945*. Milan, Italy: Fondazione Giangiacomo Feltrinelli, 2000.

Porter, Gareth. *Perils of Dominance: Imbalance of Power and the Road to War in Vietnam*. Berkeley: University of California Press, 2005.

Powaski, Ronald E. *Return to Armageddon: The United States and the Nuclear Arms Race, 1981–1999*. New York: Oxford University Press, 2000.

Powers, Richard Gid. *Not Without Honor: The History of American Anti-Communism*. New York: The Free Press, 1995.

Preston, Andrew. *The War Council: McGeorge Bundy, the NSC, and Vietnam*. Cambridge, Mass.: Harvard University Press, 2006.

Pruessen, Ronald W. *John Foster Dulles: The Road to Power*. New York: The Free Press, 1982.

Quandt, William B. *Peace Process: American Diplomacy and the Arab-Israeli Conflict Since 1967*, 3rd ed. Washington, D.C.: Brookings Institution Press, 2005.

Rabe, Stephen G. *Eisenhower and Latin America: The Foreign Policy of Anti-Communism*. Chapel Hill: University of North Carolina Press, 1988.

———. *The Most Dangerous Area in the World: John F. Kennedy Confronts Communist Revolution in Latin America*. Chapel Hill: University of North Carolina Press, 1999.

Ragsdale, Hugh. "Comparative Historiography of the Social History of Revolutions: English, French, and Russian." *The Journal of the Historical Society* 3 (Summer–Fall 2003): 323–71.

Reagan, Nancy, with William Novak. *My Turn: The Memoirs of Nancy Reagan*. New York: Random House, 1989.

Reagan, Ronald. *An American Life*. New York: Simon and Schuster, 1990.

———. *Reagan in His Own Hand*. Ed. Kiron K. Skinner, Annelise Anderson, and Martin Anderson. New York: Simon and Schuster, 2001.

———. *Reagan: A Life in Letters*. Ed. Kiron K. Skinner, Annelise Anderson, and Martin Anderson. New York: Simon and Schuster, 2003.

Reed, Thomas C. *At the Abyss: An Insider's History of the Cold War*. New York: Ballantine Books, 2004.

Reese, Roger R. *Red Commanders: A Social History of the Soviet Army Officer Corps, 1918–1991*. Lawrence: University Press of Kansas, 2005.

Reeves, Richard. *President Kennedy: Profile of Power*. New York: Simon and Schuster, 1993.

———. *President Reagan: The Triumph of Imagination.* New York: Simon and Schuster, 2005.

Resis, Albert, ed. *Molotov Remembers: Inside Kremlin Politics: Conversations with Felix Chuev.* Chicago, Ill.: Ivan R. Dee, 1993.

Richardson, Don, ed. *Conversations with Carter.* Boulder, Colo.: Lynne Rienner Publishers, 1998.

Richardson, Rosamond. *Stalin's Shadow: Inside the Family of One of the World's Greatest Tyrants.* New York: St. Martin's Press, 1993.

Rieber, Alfred J. "Stalin, Man of the Borderlands." *American Historical Review* 106 (December 2001): 1651–91.

Roberts, Geoffrey. "Moscow and the Marshall Plan: Politics, Ideology, and the Onset of the Cold War." *Europe-Asia* 46 (1994): 1371–85.

———. "Ideology, Calculation, and Improvisation: Spheres of Influence and Soviet Foreign Policy, 1939–1945." *Review of International Studies* 25 (October 1999): 655–73.

———. "The Fascist War Threat and Soviet Politics in the 1930s." In *Russia in the Age of Wars, 1914–1945.* Ed. Silvio Pons and Andrea Romano. Milan, Italy: Fondazione Giangiacomo Feltrinelli, 2000.

———. "Sexing Up the Cold War: New Evidence on the Molotov-Truman Talks of April 1945." *Cold War History* 4 (April 2004): 105–25.

———. *Stalin: His Times and Ours.* Cork, Ireland: Irish Association for Russian and East European Studies, 2006.

———. *Stalin's Wars: From World War to Cold War, 1939–1953.* New Haven, Conn.: Yale University Press, 2007.

Romano, Andrea. "Permanent War Scare: Mobilisation, Militarisation and Peasant War." In *Russia in the Age of Wars, 1914–1945.* Ed. Silvio Pons and Andrea Romano. Milan, Italy: Fondazione Giangiacomo Feltrinelli, 2000.

Rostow, W. W. *Europe After Stalin: Eisenhower's Three Decisions of March 11, 1953.* Austin: University of Texas Press, 1982.

Rubenstein, Joshua. *Soviet Dissidents: Their Struggle for Human Rights.* Boston: Beacon Press, 1980.

Rzheshevsky, Oleg A., ed. *War and Diplomacy: The Making of the Grand Alliance: Documents from Stalin's Archives.* Amsterdam: Harwood Academic Publishers, 1996.

Sakharov, Andrei. *Memoirs.* Trans. Richard Lourie. New York: Knopf, 1990.

Samuelson, Lennart. "Wartime Perspectives and Economic Planning: Tukhachevsky and the Military-Industrial Complex, 1925–1937." In *Russia in the Age of Wars, 1914–1945.* Ed. Silvio Pons and Andrea Romano. Milan, Italy: Fondazione Giangiacomo Feltrinelli, 2000.

Sarotte, M. E. *Dealing with the Devil: East Germany, Détente, and Ostpolitik, 1969–1973.* Chapel Hill: University of North Carolina Press, 2001.

Savel'yev, Aleksandr' G., and Nikolay N. Detinov. *The Big Five: Arms Control Decision-Making in the Soviet Union.* Ed. Gregory Varhall. Trans. Dmitriy Trenin. Westport, Conn.: Praeger Publishers, 1995.

Savranskaya, Svetlana. "The Logic of 1989: Soviet Withdrawal from Eastern Europe." Unpublished paper.

———. "Unintended Consequences: The Emergence of Human Rights Movements in the USSR after the Signing of the Helsinki Final Act, and the Reaction of Soviet Authorities." Unpublished paper.

Schaller, Michael. *Altered States: The United States and Japan Since the Occupation.* New York: Oxford University Press, 1997.

Schlesinger, Arthur M., Jr. *A Thousand Days: John F. Kennedy in the White House.* Greenwich, Conn.: Fawcett/Houghton Mifflin, 1965.

———. *Robert Kennedy and His Times.* Boston: Houghton Mifflin, 1978.

Schmidt, Helmut. *Men and Power: A Political Retrospective*. Trans. Ruth Hein. New York: Random House, 1989.

Schroeder, Gertrude E. "Soviet Living Standards in Comparative Perspective." In *Quality of Life in the Soviet Union*. Ed. Horst Herlemann. Boulder, Colo.: Westview Press, 1987.

Schwarz, Hans-Peter. *Konrad Adenauer: A German Politician and Statesman in a Period of War, Revolution and Reconstruction. Vol. 2: The Statesman, 1952–1967*. Trans. Geoffrey Penny. Providence, R.I.: Berghahn Books, 1997.

Schweizer, Peter. *Reagan's War: The Epic Story of His Forty-Year Struggle and Final Triumph Over Communism*. New York: Anchor Books, 2002.

Scott, James C. *Seeing Like a State: How Certain Schemes to Improve the Human Condition Have Failed*. New Haven, Conn.: Yale University Press, 1998.

Scott, James M. *Deciding to Intervene: The Reagan Doctrine and American Foriegn Policy*. Durham, N.C.: Duke University Press, 1996.

Seaborg, Glenn T. *Kennedy, Khrushchev, and the Test Ban*. Berkeley: University of California Press, 1981.

Seliktar, Ofira. *Politics, Paradigms, and Intelligence Failures: Why So Few Predicted the Collapse of the Soviet Union*. New York: M. E. Sharpe, 2004.

Selvage, Douglas. "The Warsaw Pact and Nuclear Non-Proliferation, 1963–1965." Cold War International History Project Working Paper No. 32. Washington, D.C.: Woodrow Wilson International Center, 2001.

Service, Robert. *A History of Twentieth-Century Russia*. London: Penguin, 1997.

————. *Stalin: A Biography*. Cambridge, Mass.: Harvard University Press, 2005.

Shamberg, Vladimir. "Stalin's Last Inner Circle." *The Harriman Review* 10 (Spring 1997): 29–41.

Shapoval, Iurii. "The Ukrainian Years." In *Nikita Khrushchev*. Ed. William Taubman, Sergei Khrushchev, and Abbott Gleason, 8–43. New Haven, Conn.: Yale University Press, 2000.

Sheng, Michael J. *Battling Western Imperialism: Mao, Stalin, and the United States*. Princeton, N.J.: Princeton University Press, 1997.

Shevardnadze, Eduard. *The Future Belongs to Freedom*. New York: The Free Press, 1991.

Shultz, George P. *Turmoil and Triumph: My Years as Secretary of State*. New York: Scribner, 1993.

Sibley, Katherine A. S. *Red Spies in America: Stolen Secrets and the Dawn of the Cold War*. Lawrence: University Press of Kansas, 2004.

Simpson, Christopher, ed. *National Security Directives of the Reagan and Bush Administrations: The Declassified History of U.S. Political and Military Policy, 1981–1991*. Boulder, Colo.: Westview Press, 1995.

Small, Melvin. *Democracy and Diplomacy: The Impact of Domestic Politics on U.S. Foreign Policy, 1789–1994*. Baltimore, Md.: Johns Hopkins University Press, 1996.

Snead, David L. *The Gaither Committee, Eisenhower, and the Cold War*. Columbus: Ohio State University Press, 1999.

Sorensen, Theodore C. *Kennedy*. New York: Bantam, 1965.

Spalding, Elizabeth Edwards. *The First Cold Warrior: Harry Truman, Containment, and the Remaking of Liberal Internationalism*. Lexington: University Press of Kentucky, 2006.

Stalin, Joseph. *For Peaceful Coexistence: Postwar Interviews*. New York: International Publishers, 1951.

————. *The Essential Stalin: Major Theoretical Writings, 1905–1952*. Ed. Bruce Franklin. New York: Anchor Books, 1972.

Stein, Janice Gross. "Political Learning by Doing: Gorbachev as Uncommitted Thinker and Motivated Learner." *International Organization* 48 (Spring 1994): 156–83.

Stent, Angela E. *Russia and Germany Reborn: Unification, the Soviet Collapse, and the New Europe*. Princeton, N.J.: Princeton University Press, 1999.

Stern, Sheldon M. *The Week the World Stood Still: Inside the Secret Cuban Missile Crisis.* Stanford, Calif.: Stanford University Press, 2005.

Stickle, D. M., ed. *The Beria Affair: The Secret Transcripts of the Meetings Signaling the End of Stalinism.* New York: Nova Science Publishers, 1992.

Stockman, David A. *The Triumph of Politics: How the Reagan Revolution Failed.* New York: Harper and Row, 1986.

Stueck, William W. *The Korean War: An International History.* Princeton, N.J.: Princeton University Press, 1995.

Sudaplatov, Pavel, and Anatoli Sudaplatov, with Jerrold L. and Leona P. Schecter. *Special Tasks: The Memoirs of an Unwanted Witness—A Soviet Spymaster.* Boston: Little, Brown and Company, 1994.

Sukhodrev, V. M. *Iazyk moy—drug moy: ot Khrushcheva do Gorbacheva* [My Tongue—My Friend: From Khrushchev to Gorbachev]. Moskva: AST: Olimp, 1999.

Suri, Jeremy. "The Promise and Failure of 'Developed Socialism': The Soviet 'Thaw' and the Crucible of the Prague Spring." *Contemporary European History* 15 (2006): 133–58.

Swain, Geoff. *Between Stalin and Hitler: Class War and Race War on the Dvina, 1940–1946.* London: RoutledgeCurzon, 2004.

Talbott, Strobe. *Endgame: The Inside Story of SALT II.* New York: Harper Colophon Books, 1979.

Taubman, William, ed. *Khrushchev on Khrushchev: An Inside Account of the Man and His Era.* Boston: Little, Brown and Company, 1990.

Taubman, William, Sergei Khrushchev, and Abbott Gleason, eds. *Nikita Khrushchev.* Trans. David Gehrenbeck, Eileen Kane, and Alla Bashenko. New Haven, Conn.: Yale University Press, 2000.

———. *Khrushchev: The Man and His Era.* London: The Free Press, 2003.

Taylor, A.J.P. "The European Revolution." *The Listener* 34 (22 November 1945): 576.

Teltschik, Horst. *329 Tage Innenansichten der Einigung.* Berlin: Siedler, 1991.

Thatcher, Ian D. "Brezhnev as Leader." In *Brezhnev Reconsidered.* Ed. Edwin Bacon and Mark Sandle, 22–37. Houndsmills, Eng.: Palgrave, 2002.

Thatcher, Margaret. *The Downing Street Years.* New York: HarperCollins, 1993.

Thomas, Daniel C. *The Helsinki Effect: International Norms, Human Rights, and the Demise of Capital-ism.* Princeton, N.J.: Princeton University Press, 2001.

Thurston, Robert W., and Bernd Bonwetsch. *The People's War: Responses to World War II in the Soviet Union.* Urbana: University of Illinois Press, 2000.

Tismaneau, Vladimir, ed. *The Revolutions of 1989: Rewriting Histories.* London: Routledge, 1999.

Tompson, William. *The Soviet Union Under Brezhnev.* London: Pearson, 2003.

Toulouse, Mark G. *The Transformation of John Foster Dulles: From Prophet of Realism to Priest of Nationalism.* Macon, Ga.: Mercer University Press, 1985.

Trachtenberg, Marc. *A Constructed Peace: The Making of the European Settlement, 1945–1963.* Prince-ton, N.J.: Princeton University Press, 1999.

Troy, Gil. *Morning in America: How Ronald Reagan Invented the 1980s.* Princeton, N.J.: Princeton Uni-versity Press, 2005.

Troyanovsky, Oleg. "The Making of Soviet Foreign Policy." In *Nikita Khrushchev.* Ed. William Taubman, Sergei Khrushchev, and Abbott Gleason, 209–241. New Haven, Conn.: Yale University Press, 2000.

Truman, Harry S. *Memoirs: 1945: Year of Decisions.* New York: Signet, 1955.

———. *Memoirs: Years of Trial and Hope, 1946–1952.* New York: Signet, 1956.

———. *Truman Speaks.* New York: Columbia University Press, 1960.

———. *Off the Record: The Private Papers of Harry S. Truman.* Ed. Robert H. Ferrell. New York: Harper and Row, 1980.

———. *Dear Bess: The Letters From Harry to Bess Truman, 1910–1959.* Ed. Robert H. Ferrell. New York: Norton, 1983.

Truman, Margaret, ed. *Letters from Father: The Truman Family's Personal Correspondence*. South Yarmouth, Mass.: John Curley and Associates, 1981.

Tudda, Chris. *The Truth Is Our Weapon: The Rhetorical Diplomacy of Dwight D. Eisenhower and John Foster Dulles*. Baton Rouge: Louisiana State University Press, 2006.

Tyler, Patrick. *Six Presidents and China: A Great Wall: An Investigative History*. New York: A Century Foundation Book, 1999.

Ulam, Adam B. *Stalin: The Man and His Era*. New York: Viking, 1973.

Uldricks, Teddy J. "The Icebreaker Controversy: Did Stalin Plan to Attack Hitler?" *Slavic Review* 58 (Fall 1999): 626–43.

Valkenier, Elizabeth Kridl. "New Soviet Thinking About the Third World." *World Policy Journal* 4 (Fall 1987): 651–74.

Vance, Cyrus. *Hard Choices: Critical Years in America's Foreign Policy*. New York: Simon and Schuster, 1983.

Van Meter, Robert H. "Secretary of State Marshall, General Clay, and the Moscow Council of Foreign Ministers of 1947: A Response to Philip Zelikow." *Diplomacy and Statecraft* 16 (2005): 139–67.

Van Ree, Erik. *The Political Thought of Joseph Stalin: A Study in Twentieth-Century Revolutionary Patriotism*. London: RoutledgeCurzon, 2002.

Volkogonov, Dmitri. *Stalin: Triumph and Tragedy*. New York: Grove Weidenfeld, 1988.

Volkov, Vladimir K. "The German Question as Stalin Saw It." Draft paper for the conference "Stalin and the Cold War, 1945–1953." New Haven, Conn.: Yale University, 1999.

Wallace, Henry A. *The Price of Vision: The Diary of Henry A. Wallace, 1942–1946*. Ed. John M. Blum. Boston: Houghton Mifflin, 1973.

Walton, John. *Reluctant Rebels: Comparative Studies of Revolution and Underdevelopment*. New York: Columbia University Press, 1984.

Watson, Robert J. *History of the Joint Chiefs of Staff: The Joint Chiefs of Staff and National Policy, 1953–1954*. Washington, D.C.: Government Printing Office, 1986.

Weinberger, Caspar W., with Gretchen Roberts. *In the Arena: A Memoir of the 20th Century*. Washington, D.C.: Regnery Publishing, 2001.

Weinstein, Allen, and Alexander Vassiliev. *The Haunted Wood: Soviet Espionage in America—the Stalin Era*. New York: Modern Library, 1999.

Westad, Odd Arne, ed. *Cold War and Revolution: Soviet-American Rivalry and the Origins of the Chinese Civil War, 1944–1946*. New York: Columbia University Press, 1993.

———, ed. *The Fall of Détente: Soviet-American Relations During the Carter Years*. Oslo: Scandinavian University Press, 1997.

———. *Brothers in Arms: The Rise and Fall of the Sino-Soviet Alliance, 1945–1963*. Washington, D.C.: Woodrow Wilson International Center, 1998.

———. "Reagan's Anti-Revolutionary Offensive in the Third World." In *The Last Decade of the Cold War: From Conflict Escalation to Conflict Transformation*. Ed. Olav Njolstad. London: Frank Cass, 2004.

———. *The Global Cold War: Third World Interventions and the Making of Our Times*. Cambridge, Eng.: Cambridge University Press, 2005.

———, Jian Chen, Stein Tonnesson, Nguyen Vu Tung, and James G. Hershberg, eds. "77 Conversations Between Chinese and Foreign Leaders on the Wars in Indochina, 1964–1977." Cold War International History Project Working Paper No. 22. Washington, D.C.: Woodrow Wilson International Center, 1998.

———, Sven Holsmark, and Ivers B. Neumann, eds. *The Soviet Union in Eastern Europe, 1945–1989*. New York: St. Martin's Press, 1994.

Westoby, Adam. *Communism Since World War II*. New York: St. Martin's Press, 1981.

Wieczynski, Joseph, ed. *The Modern Encyclopedia of Russian and Soviet History*. Gulf Breeze, Fla.: Academic International Press, 1988.

Wittner, Lawrence S. *Resisting the Bomb: A History of the World Nuclear Disarmament Movement, 1954–1970*, Vol. 2. Stanford, Calif.: Stanford University Press, 1997.

————. *Toward Nuclear Abolition: A History of the World Nuclear Disarmament Movement, 1971–Present*, Vol. 3. Stanford, Calif.: Stanford University Press, 2003.

Wohlforth, William C., ed. *Witnesses to the End of the Cold War*. Baltimore, Md.: Johns Hopkins University Press, 1996.

————, ed. *Cold War Endgame: Oral History, Analysis, Debates*. University Park: Pennsylvania State University Press, 2003.

Woods, Randall B. *LBJ: Architect of American Ambition*. New York: The Free Press, 2006.

————, and Howard Jones. *Dawning of the Cold War: The United States' Quest for Order*. Athens: University of Georgia Press, 1991.

Woodward, Bob. *Veil: The Secret Wars of the CIA, 1981–87*. New York: Simon and Schuster, 1987.

Young, Crawford. *Ideology and Development in Africa*. New Haven, Conn.: Yale University Press, 1982.

Young, John W. "Britain and LBJ's War." *Cold War History* 2 (April 2002): 63–93.

Yurchak, Alexei. *Everything Was Forever, Until It Was No More: The Last Soviet Generation*. Princeton, N.J.: Princeton University Press, 2006.

Zaloga, Steven J. *The Kremlin's Nuclear Sword: The Rise and Fall of Russia's Strategic Nuclear Forces, 1945–2000*. Washington, D.C.: Smithsonian Institution Press, 2002.

Zelikow, Philip, and Ernest R. May, eds. *John F. Kennedy: The Presidential Recordings: The Great Crises*. Vols. 1–3. New York: Norton, 2001.

————, and Condoleezza Rice. *Germany Unified and Europe Transformed*. Cambridge, Mass.: Harvard University Press, 1995.

Zhang, Shuguang, and Jian Chen. *Chinese Communist Policy and the Cold War in Asia: New Documentary Evidence, 1944–1950*. Chicago, Ill.: Imprint Publications, 1996.

Zubkova, Elena. *Russia After the War: Hopes, Illusions, and Disappointments, 1945–1957*. Ed. and trans. Hugh Ragsdale. New York: M. E. Sharpe, 1998.

Zubok, Vladislav. "New Evidence on the Cuban Missile Crisis." *Cold War International History Program Bulletin* 5 (Spring 1995): 59, 89–109, 159.

————. "The Brezhnev Factor in Détente." In *Kholodnaia voina i politika razriadki: diskussionnye problemy* [Cold War and the Policy of Détente: Problems and Discussions]. Ed. Nataliia Ivanovna and Aleksandr Oganovich. Moskva: Rossiiskaia akademiia nauk, In-t vseobshchei istorii [Institute of Universal History, Russian Academy of Sciences], 2003.

————. *A Failed Empire: The Soviet Union in the Cold War from Stalin to Gorbachev*. Chapel Hill: University of North Carolina Press, forthcoming.

————. "Limits of Empire: Stalin and the Lean Year of 1946." Unpublished paper.

————, and Constantine Pleshakov. *Inside the Kremlin's Cold War: From Stalin to Khrushchev*. Cambridge, Mass.: Harvard University Press, 1996.

INDEX